CHINA MOON

COOKBOOK

CHINA MOON

COOKBOOK

BY BARBARA TROPP

Assisted by Arminda Asprer Schreil
Dessert and Bread Recipes by Amy Ho

Illustrations by Sandra Bruce

WORKMAN PUBLISHING • NEW YORK

Library of Congress Cataloging-in-Publication Data

Tropp, Barbara.
  China moon cookbook / by Barbara Tropp.
     p.   cm.
  Includes index.
  ISBN 1-56305-315-2 : —ISBN 0-89480-754-4
(pbk.)
  1. Cookery, Chinese.   2. Cookery, American.
I. Title.
TX724.5.C5T684   1992
641.5951—dc20   92-50283
                                              CIP

Cover and book design: Lisa Hollander
Cover photographs by John Vaughan

Workman books are available at special discounts
when purchased in bulk for premiums and sales
promotions as well as for fund-raising or
educational use. Special editions or book excerpts
can also be created to specification. For details,
contact the Special Sales Director at the address
below.

Workman Publishing Company, Inc.
708 Broadway
New York, NY 10003

Manufactured in the United States of America
First printing October 1992
10 9 8 7 6 5 4

CATALOGUE-LOVERS ALERT!

We're busy putting together a fabulous mail-order source book for top-quality Chinese cooking ingredients and tools. To be included on our mailing list, send your name and address to China Moon Catalogue, c/o China Moon Cafe, 639 Post Street, San Francisco, CA 94109.

*To the China Moon Staff
for their loyalty and excellence
and to B.R.
who fills my heart with joy*

■ ■ ■

ACKNOWLEDGMENTS

The chef gets all the glory, but it is the staff—the cooks, dishwashers, waiters, prep people, hosts, and managers—who give a restaurant its renown. To the fine staff who have given a slice of their lives to China Moon Cafe, my first thanks go to you.

I owe a particular debt to my lineage of sous-chefs. These are the senior cooks who do daily battle against the forces of restaurant mayhem—receiving produce, overseeing the kitchen staff, tasting their way through everything, and somehow doing it all with streaks of brilliance in spite of plumbing backups and people freakouts—the untimely chaos

that is the essence of restaurant life. Barbara Haimes, our opening sous-chef, set our standards and devised many of our favorite dishes. She trained me to run a restaurant, and a better teacher and friend could not be had. Rachel Gardner, Camille Convy, Mindy Schreil, André Fecteau, Katy Ross, Nance Tourigny, and Betsy Davidson have each followed in her path, enriching our cooking and my knowledge both. To these special cooks, my special thanks.

For me, writing a cookbook is a good deal easier than running a restaurant. However, I could not have done it these past three years without extraordinary help.

Mindy Schreil, our finest sous-chef as well as my twin palate and right hand in teaching, tested the recipes through two pregnancies and gave birth without missing a beat. André Fecteau, our most gifted natural cook, took over when Mindy was too big to fit behind the stoves. Barbie Debarros, our effervescent floor manager, and Mr. Luong, our impeccable senior scrubber, kept the business going gracefully while their boss was going bonkers. Amy Ho, China Moon's superlative pastry chef since Day One, committed to paper many of her recipes for desserts and doughs. Such is my delight in what Amy brings to China Moon Cafe and its cookbook that I can't imagine either of them without her.

Writing a book can be a joy or a horror. Thanks to Workman Publishing, it was a joy. Suzanne Rafer, my editor, is the best. Every cookbook author should be so lucky. Lisa Hollander, the designer, and Lori Malkin, her assistant, made the book fun and beautiful. Andrea Glickson got it all off to a sweet, cool start, figuring out how to dish up ginger ice cream to a thousand starving booksellers at their annual convention. Peter Workman heads a wonderful family, and I'm lucky to be in the wings.

Life is hard when you're a single parent and your child is a restaurant. Fortunately, I have great friends. If not for them, cheering loudly on the sidelines, I would have long ago fled the Moon and gone home to polish my toenails. Among the best friends one could have are Ellen Brown, Denise Fiedler, Rosemary Manell, Margaret Fox, Maggie Mah, Suzy Davidson, Barbara Kafka, Susan Herrmann Loomis, and Jan Weimer. Hooray for my buddies!

My last and sweetest thanks to Bart, my new husband. (I never had an old one; it just took many years to find him.) Life without your love would be like food without flavor. Je t'adore.

Barbara Tropp

崔宝蘭

C O N T E N T S

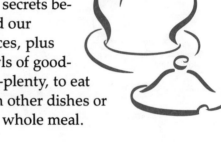

FIRST THOUGHTS

///

This book is a private cooking school. Its curriculum is the world of traditional Chinese flavors combined with exclusively fresh ingredients, a corner of the good-cooking universe I call California-Chinese cuisine. This is a world where cans and bottles are banished in favor of fresh foods, and the tyranny of MSG and cornstarch holds no sway. It is the world of a traditional, albeit slightly eccentric Chinese home cook, who shops a daily market with intelligence and passion, and who would sooner use a fresh American ingredient than a canned one from China.

This book is also the culinary record of a small restaurant called China Moon Cafe, which I opened in 1986 in downtown San Francisco, in a 1930s art deco coffee shop. The setting was small and my goal was equally modest: I wanted to introduce fresh Chinese home-style cooking to a city that adored good food. My eyes on fire with missionary zeal, waving fresh water chestnuts in each fist, I found myself with a roaring restaurant beast and no cage in which to put it. China Moon consumed me, and somehow in the process, I became a professional chef.

What I am, at heart, however, is a cooking teacher. My subject is Chinese cooking, but my passions are the alchemy of food and flavor, and the way we nurture ourselves. The food I cook is colorful, light, and wildly flavorful, and while traditionally Chinese at the root, it is contemporary at the branches.

Here, then, are the recipes. Though China Moon in origin, they've all been tested in a home kitchen to ensure that they will work for a home cook. I've included every ingredient and every single worthwhile technique. You may need some gutsiness in the face of the seemingly exotic in addition to a good market to speed you on your way, but everything else is here—including the confidence of a teacher who says, "Just cook it. You'll love it!"

REALITY CHECK

///

This is an odd moment in American history to be writing such a cookbook. The Fear of Food is upon us with a vengeance. If we're not eating in order to lose weight, we're eating in hopes of fending off fatal disease. Supermarket real estate is clogged with aisles of frozen dinners, and hardly anyone seems to have the time to cook, never mind to dine.

So along comes this cookbook with its multiple layers of details for making fine food from scratch. There's nary a word about microwaves and hardly a mention of freezing. Calories and carbohydrates are mentioned only once (right here), whereas salt, sugar, oil, fish, poultry, or red meat are cited on nearly every page. As if this weren't enough, I presume that there are people out there who are happy to forage at the market, and people in front of their stoves who have the energy to cook.

Am I crazy? I hope not!

This is the way I cook for myself, and this is the food I love. It speaks of a Chinese world that fed my soul and my body when I was first becoming a healthy grown-up. The Chinese diet insists that *no* food is fearful except if it isn't fresh. *No* meal is to be feared as long as it is in balance. Deep-fried foods are healthy in partnership with steamed and poached foods. Beef is fine when joined with greater amounts of vegetables and rice. Soy sauce in combination with sugar and wine not only tastes good on the tongue, but contributes to bodily well-being when gracing a

freshly steamed fish served with a mound of plain rice. The Chinese people are vastly healthy and wholly unneurotic about eating. I think it's a lesson for our day.

I also write this book in the shadow of fast-food restaurants because I believe that cooking at home is vital. Sure, it takes time to cook, but it takes time to live! What other activity in the sphere of human pleasure makes our dwellings aromatic and brings friends and family to our table? If we value these aspects of our lives, then we cook. If we savor the food we prepare and the environment in which it is presented, then we dine.

My first book, *The Modern Art of Chinese Cooking,* was dedicated to real Chinese cooking, a realm apart from the glop and goo and cans and bottles of Chinese-American restaurant cooking. This book is dedicated to real *eating.* Not what happens in the sterility of a fast-food outlet, or what comes antiseptically out of a microwave to be eaten in front of the TV, but what occurs when you've fired your stove with effort, filled your home with the perfume of great ingredients, and enriched yourself with a meal that knits together the people you love.

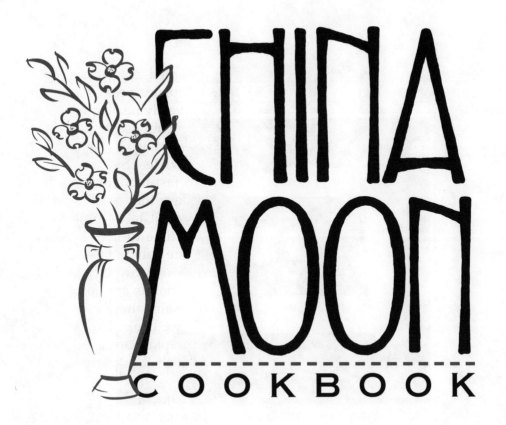

CHINA MOON
COOKBOOK

VERSATILE VINAIGRETTES • FRAGRANT INFUSED CHILI OILS

FRAGRANT INFUSED CHILI OILS • VERSATILE VINAIGRETTES

THE CHINA MOON PANTRY

CONTENTS

Our bulging pantry shelf replete with its house-infused oils, vinegars, and homemade spices is the centerpiece of the China Moon kitchen. Similarly, this chapter—and particularly the first dozen recipes—is the heart of the *China Moon Cookbook*.

Like painters with a finely honed palate of colors, we rely on these seasonings to give savor to our food. You can't cook a spectacular dish without a terrific-tasting oil; neither can you make a dish sing without a lively, full-flavored spice! That's the first message I teach to every cook in our kitchen. The levels of flavor we strive for begin with these pantry basics.

The good news is that it is both easy and quick to make a full array of China Moon seasonings in your own kitchen. A short day devoted to shopping and simple cooking will give you a proud shelf of home-toasted spices, freshly infused oils, and a jar boasting pickled ginger. That in turn will launch dozens of our recipes and months of great eating! Sure, you can buy a bottle of commercial chili oil, but why bother? It takes only minutes to make your own, and the flavor will knock you over. Why settle for what's standard when you can make something truly great?

■ ■ ■

WHAT TO
MAKE FIRST?

Before you turn an-other page, resolve to make these four items: Roasted Szechwan Pepper-Salt; China Moon Pickled Ginger; China Moon Hot Chili Oil or China Moon Chili-Orange Oil; and Five-Flavor Oil. All total, that will come to about $15 worth of ingredients and 2 to 3 hours of shopping and cooking.

These four items are the gateway to our recipes. As you work through the book and are inspired with confidence by the great food you are making, you can launch into all of the others. But these four are the basic must-do's and must-have's.

They are also my personal survival kit! A couple of years ago when I made plans over Valentine's Day to vacation on a Hawaiian island in a cottage with a kitchen, I brought along little packages of the above plus a small bottle of mushroom soy sauce. With some dried pasta and locally available fish and veggies, I sustained my boyfriend and myself for a week of fabulous eating. The boyfriend married me a year later, surely a question of the right seasonings.

ROASTED SZECHWAN PEPPER-SALT

MAKES ½ CUP

What salt and pepper are to a Western cook, roasted Szechwan pepper-salt is to a Chinese cook. It is one of those cases where one and one equals far more than two, such is the flavor dimension achieved when salt and Szechwan peppercorns are roasted and ground together. A little bit goes a long way, and for that little bit, there is no substitute. For people watching salt, as well as for any would-be-better Chinese cook, a jar of roasted pepper-salt is a fabulous kitchen gift.

The only salt, in my opinion, that gives the requisite flavor is *kosher* salt. And the only brand, again in my opinion, that has the mild and clean flavor of "real" kosher salt is *Diamond* kosher salt. Table salt makes a hideous blend, even when you halve the amount. Sea salt is better, but the flavor balance is wrong.

The Szechwan peppercorns (see glossary) used here should be picked and picked through with care. Use the most fragrant ones you can find, and sift through to discard twigs and thorns.

Once made, Szechwan pepper-salt should be stored in an airtight container away from light and heat. If you are keeping it in a glass jar that was used for another purpose, pull away the original cardboard lid liner to remove any contaminants. As long as the mixture remains wonderfully fragrant, it is a worthy addition to most any dish.

¼ cup Szechwan peppercorns, any thorns or twigs removed

½ cup kosher salt

1. Combine the peppercorns and salt in a heavy skillet and toast over moderate heat, stirring, until the salt turns off-white, about 5 minutes. Adjust the heat so the peppercorns do not burn, but expect them to smoke.

2. Remove the hot mixture to a food processor and process for 1 full minute to obtain a fine powder. Alternatively, grind the mixture in a spice grinder. Sieve to remove the peppercorn husks. Store the mixture in a clean dry bottle, sealed airtight.

MENU SUGGESTIONS: Roasted Szechwan pepper-salt is an all-purpose seasoning salt. It is good for marinating meats and poultry, and it is a fabulous final seasoning for soups and salads. A bit tossed into just-made popcorn or sprinkled on a grilled burger is terrific.

CHINA MOON TEN-SPICE

MAKES ¾ CUP

The classic Chinese seasoning known as five-spice powder is probably the stuff of antiquity. Blessed with the mystic cosmological designation of five—a scheme the Chinese used over and over in their culture to designate propitiously harmonious aspects of a complete whole—it is comprised of flavors that gather in a sultry union. Orange, cassia (cinnamon), anise, Szechwan peppercorn, and clove are the usual congregants in the mix, a mélange that was probably designed to preserve or mask as well as to flavor foods.

Unfortunately, there is little cosmic or culinary harmony to most commercial blends of five-spice. Cheaply and poorly made for the most part, they usually contribute little but a strident cinnamony taste.

Enter the do-it-yourself blend! Complex though it might seem if you have never before roasted and ground your own spices, it is actually very easy. In addition to perfuming your home evocatively for several hours, no more than 15 minutes of simple work will endow your cupboard with a novel, versatile spice.

So why ten-spice instead of five? I can't say, except to suggest that the result is doubly good.

WHY BOTHER MAKING IT WHEN YOU CAN BUY IT?

The answer to this question is to have fun; to make something that tastes fabulous; and to save money in the process. How many things in life can make these three promises in combination?

Making your own hot chili oil is a great example. For about 20 years I have been trying commercially infused Chinese chili oils as each new brand has emerged, and most are junk—pressed from cheap oils with poor-grade aromatics while someone was sleeping on the job and not watching the oil thermometer. There is no range of flavor, just a sharp, cutting jab to the tastebuds and nothing to linger but the taste of burnt or rancid oil. You go to the store, you purchase the bottle, and that's what you wind up with: a lot of oil, a lot of bucks, and no flavor except searing hot. This is a gyp, made all the worse if you've bought a fancy bottle at a fancy price.

Instead imagine this scenario: You jot down the brand names of the corn and sesame oils I give you along with the tips on the properly flavorful varieties of black beans and dried red chili flakes. You go to the market, have some fun scouting for the ingredients, then come home and get to play junior scientist with a deep-fry thermometer and a small potful of bubbling oil. Cool it, taste it, and there's an explosion of flavor on your palate. All of this for a slim several dollars.

A similar tale could be devised for pickled ginger, which sits on most Chinese grocery shelves in a bath of red food dye and harshly acidic vinegar. Or for commercially blended five-spice powder with scents that only an exterminator could love. Or a mustard sauce that tastes like poison.

No, if you're going to cook well, you need great blended ingredients, and these (at least in the Chinese realm) are most easily made at home. Out there in the market, you can buy something, but quality is rarely what's for sale.

WHOLE SPICES:

2 tablespoons fennel seeds
10 star anise, broken into points
2 tablespoons Szechwan peppercorns
1 tablespoon coriander seeds
¾ teaspoon whole cloves
¾ teaspoon cumin seeds
1½ teaspoons black peppercorns

GROUND SPICES:

½ teaspoon ground cinnamon
¼ teaspoon ground ginger
½ teaspoon turmeric

1. Toast the whole spices together in a small dry skillet over low heat, stirring and adjusting the heat so that the spices toast without burning. Stir until the spices are fully fragrant and the fennel seeds and lighter-colored spices are lightly browned, about 5 minutes. Stir in the ground spices.

2. Using a spice grinder or a clean coffee grinder, grind the mixture finely. Store in a tightly covered jar.

MENU SUGGESTIONS: We use this seasoning in many of our marinades and sauces. It is equally useful, however, in mayonnaises, chopped meat mixtures, sautéed vegetables, and pastas.

CHINA MOON CURRY POWDER

MAKES ABOUT 1 CUP

ommercially made curry powder is like a cake mix—it might be an admirable product in a pinch, but it rarely affords a cook the opportunity to shade a recipe according to his or her tastes. When we couldn't find a curry powder that suited our China Moon taste, we experimented and came up with our own. Fragrant and spicy, it blends well with the vegetable and fruit flavors in our curried dishes.

If you do not have a spice grinder, you can use a coffee grinder as long as you clean it well.

Store the curry powder, like any dry spice, in an airtight container away from light and heat. As long as it is fully fragrant, it is usable.

WHOLE SPICES:
2 tablespoons coriander seeds
1 tablespoon cardamom seeds
1 tablespoon cumin seeds
1 tablespoon yellow mustard
*   seeds*
2 teaspoons fenugreek seeds
1 teaspoon whole cloves
½ cinnamon stick (1½ inches
*   long)*
½ teaspoon black peppercorns

GROUND SPICES:
¾ teaspoon cayenne pepper
1 tablespoon ground ginger
2 tablespoons plus 1 teaspoon
*   turmeric*

1. Toast the whole spices together in a small dry skillet over low heat, stirring and adjusting the heat so that the spices toast without scorching. Stir until the spices are fully fragrant and the fennel seeds and lighter-colored spices are lightly browned, 4 to 5 minutes. Stir in the ground spices.

2. Using a spice grinder or a clean coffee grinder, grind the mixture finely. Store in a tightly covered jar.

CHINA MOON PICKLED GINGER

SMALL BATCH MAKES ¾ CUP GINGER AND 2 CUPS JUICE; LARGE BATCH MAKES 1⅓ QUARTS GINGER AND 2½ QUARTS JUICE.

This is a terrific item to have on hand, both for the zippy slices of ginger and the sweet and tart juice. Even if you were never to cook a specifically Chi-

PEELING GINGER

I confess to never peeling ginger in the days before China Moon. In the privacy of my own home kitchen, I shook my fist at Chinese tradition (and at my Jewish forbears who washed even the bottom of their pots three times) and said, "Why bother?" It wasn't dirty, the skin of properly rock-hard ginger is paper-thin and innocuous, and I hadn't died yet from eating it. I was a rebel and proud of it.

Life at China Moon humbled me. My Chinese-Vietnamese prep staff was adamant that the ginger be peeled. Amy, our Chinese-

American pastry chef, was horrified that we'd use "dirty ginger." (She is my grandmother incarnate.) The sous-chef muttered in my ear that we could use the ginger peel for seasoning stock and the task of peeling it would keep the dishwashers busy. What was a girl to do, pitted against the force of tradition and the vision of unemployed dishwashers?

So we accumulate buckets of the stuff every day, and it goes to enhance the stock and keeps everyone happy. If peeling ginger thrills you, use it in this way. Or, make a ginger tea—cover the peel with boiling water, steep and strain the liquid, and add a drizzle of honey to taste.

In the comfort of my home, I still never peel ginger—except for ginger threads, when the look of a uniformly golden julienne is important. For this, I use a very sharp Chinese cleaver with a very thin blade. My dishwashers, on the other hand, pare the ginger with a vegetable peeler.

Choose your weapon and choose to peel or not to peel. When I am president, I'll have a town meeting on the subject.

nese dish, you would find the juice a great addition to salad dressings and the minced pickled ginger a novel refreshment in a meat patty. If you are a Chinese- or Asian-inclined cook, you will quickly find that you cannot do without this condiment.

Pickled ginger, like any pickled product, begins with impeccably fresh produce. Look for hands of ginger that have a thin skin stretched taut over the tuber, with no soft or moldy spots. If it is the season for young, fiberless ginger and you can find some in stellar shape—its translucent yellow-gold skin is as perishable as it is delicate and deteriorates rapidly—by all means use it. If not, the typical fibrous ginger is just fine as long as you slice it to paper thinness against the grain. A super-sharp thin-bladed chef's knife or Chinese cleaver will help you on your way, as will the nifty plastic-housed Japanese mandoline called the Benriner.

For best flavor, let the pickled ginger sit for at least a day before using. It will keep for months in the refrigerator, although the juice is likely to become cloudy, which is not important to taste but is a slight aesthetic loss.

If you are making a large batch and have to divide it among several jars, be sure the ginger in each jar is covered with liquid.

SMALL BATCH:
½ pound peeled fresh ginger, sliced crosswise against the grain into paper-thin coins
1⅓ cups unseasoned Japanese rice vinegar
3 tablespoons cider vinegar
2 tablespoons distilled white vinegar
½ cup plus 1 tablespoon sugar
1 tablespoon plus 1 teaspoon kosher salt

LARGE BATCH:
3 pounds peeled fresh ginger, sliced crosswise against the grain into paper-thin coins
2 quarts unseasoned Japanese rice vinegar
1 cup cider vinegar
1 cup distilled white vinegar
3 cups sugar
½ cup kosher salt

1. Cover the ginger with boiling water. Let stand for 2 minutes, then drain in a colander. Put the ginger in a large, impeccably clean glass jar or plastic container.

2. Combine the remaining ingredients in a non-aluminum pot. Stir over moderate heat just until the sugar and salt dissolve. Pour over the ginger.

3. Let cool completely, then cover and refrigerate for at least 24 hours before using.

MENU SUGGESTIONS: Paper-thin slices of pickled ginger make a great addition to plates of grilled meat, fish, or poultry. Minced or julienned, they appear in many of our dishes and cold sauces. The juice is something we use in hot and cold sauces, springroll dips, and salad dressings.

CHINA MOON HOT CHILI OIL

MAKES ABOUT 3 CUPS

The day I made my own hot chili oil, I swear I grew a foot as a cook! Not at all difficult and eminently satisfying, I recommend this recipe to any aspiring cook. Like grinding and brewing your own coffee after a lackluster life of instant, the sheer flavor and freshness of this chili oil will knock your socks off.

As with everything we cook with chili at China Moon Cafe, our chili oil aims for flavor as well as heat. This is an oil with taste, not merely fire.

The oil is only as good as the sum of its parts. Use a good-quality corn or peanut oil, a rich-smelling Japanese sesame oil, and red chili flakes that are bitingly fragrant. Once made, store this kitchen treasure in an impeccably clean glass jar or plastic container and keep it in a cool (though not refrigerated) place.

PICKY ABOUT SIZE

Cooks new to our kitchen usually go berserk with the specificity with which we cut things. A dice isn't just a dice; it's a "neat, tiny dice." A coin isn't a coin; it's a "scant ¼-inch coin" or a "1/16-inch coin." Cooks in their first days at China Moon must feel like they're in cutting kindergarten. There they are, armed with their sharp knives and the occasional diploma from a prestigious cooking school, and the short boss lady is eyeing the width and length of their julienne! "Does it really make such a difference?" they ask politely.

In classic Chinese cooking, it does. In the relatively high heat of stir-frying, for one, the difference between the harder carrot that is cut precisely 1/16 inch thin and the softer eggplant that is cut a scant ¼ inch thick means the two ingredients will cook to doneness at about the same time. Or, with a potent ingredient like fresh ginger, a thread-like julienne will steam through perfectly in the few minutes it takes to cook the fish beneath it, *whereas a thick, irregular julienne would taste raw.*

At least in part because of the requirements of these faster cooking methods, Chinese will judge a dish foremost on the finesse of the cutting. It is the very first thing marked by the traditional Chinese eye, way before the traditional tongue makes a comment on the flavor. Chinese writers on cooking will always note the color, size, and shape of a dish's components, and dwell on them happily and long-windedly, in advance of any discussion of the taste.

I confess there might be an element of Virgo madness in the culture. Certainly, there is one in our kitchen! My only defense is one of my favorite quotes from the whole of Chinese history. It comes from a character in an official history of first-century China: "When my mother cuts the meat, the chunks are invariably in perfect squares, and when she chops the scallions, they are always in nuggets exactly 1 inch long." What can I say? History centuries-old supports me in my obsessions!

⅔ cup shockingly pungent dried red chili flakes
⅓ cup Chinese fermented black beans (do not rinse them), coarsely chopped
4 large cloves garlic, lightly smashed and peeled
2 tablespoons minced fresh ginger
2½ cups corn or peanut oil
⅓ cup Japanese sesame oil

1. Combine all of the ingredients in a heavy, non-aluminum 2- to 2½-quart saucepan. Rest a deep-fry thermometer on the rim of the pot. Over moderately low heat, bring the mixture to a bubbly 225° to 250°F, stirring occasionally. Let simmer for 15 minutes, checking to ensure the temperature does not rise. Remove from the heat and let stand until cool or overnight.

2. Scrape the oil and solids into an impeccably clean glass or plastic container. Store at cool room temperature.

MENU SUGGESTIONS: Use the oil wherever you want to light a spark. The "goop" that settles to the bottom is a wonderful spicy addition to sauces, noodles, fillings, and marinades.

CAYENNE PEPPER OIL

MAKES 3 CUPS

A whoppingly spicy-hot oil, this is the perfect seasoning to use when you are wanting 1,000-watt chili power with only a few drops of oil. It was suggested by a recipe in one of my all-time favorite cooking-as-culture books, *Chinese Gastronomy* by the erstwhile ladies Lin.

Be strict about observing the oil temperature, and do not add the cayenne if the oil is hotter than 250°F, or it will burn to a hideous mess.

Like any dry spice, the cayenne should smell "alive" if the results are to be good. The kind we buy from our spice merchant comes in three grades of ferocity. We buy the hottest. Why fool around?

3 cups corn or peanut oil   *¾ cup cayenne pepper*

1. Pour the oil into a heavy, non-aluminum 1½- to 2-quart saucepan. Bring to 225°F on a deep-fry thermometer over moderately low heat. Remove the pan from the heat, stir in the cayenne powder, and let cool to room temperature undisturbed, or overnight if you like.

2. Strain the oil slowly and patiently through one or more large paper coffee filters into an impeccably clean glass jar. Store at cool room temperature.

China Moon Chili-Lemon Oil

MAKES ABOUT 2 CUPS

A lemon-zesty oil with many uses in basting or steaming fish and poultry as well as in cold dishes. Keep at cool room temperature in a clean jar.

1½ cups corn or peanut oil
2 tablespoons Japanese sesame oil
¼ cup shockingly pungent dried red chili flakes
1 tablespoon Szechwan brown peppercorns
1 large clove garlic, lightly smashed and peeled

2 tablespoons finely julienned fresh ginger
⅓ cup green and white scallion rings
2 plump stalks fresh lemongrass, pounded, then cut crosswise into finger lengths
Finely minced zest of 3 to 4 well-scrubbed lemons

come to room temperature before using.

Refrigerated or not, many infused oils and vinegars will grow cloudy. This has no effect on the taste. As always, trust your own good tongue and nose; if something looks or smells fishy, throw it out.

The above is also applicable to your home-toasted spice mixtures. In addition, don't store them above the stove, where they will be bathed by heat and humidity; you will be condemning them to a dispirited, tasteless death.

1. Combine all the ingredients except for the lemon zest in a heavy, non-aluminum 1½-quart saucepan. Bring to 225°F on a deep-fry thermometer over moderately low heat and let bubble for 15 minutes.

2. Remove the pan from the heat and let stand for 5 minutes, then stir in the lemon zest and let stand overnight or until cool.

3. Remove and discard the lemongrass. Scrape the oil and seasonings into an impeccably clean container.

FIVE-FLAVOR OIL

MAKES 1 ¾ CUPS

Perhaps the most versatile of our seasoned oils, this is a light infusion speaking equally of different flavors. The oil may cloud, but the flavor will not be impaired.

1⅓ cups corn or peanut oil
½ cup Japanese sesame oil
3 large scallions, cut into thick green and white rings
10 quarter-size thin coins fresh ginger, smashed

1½ teaspoons shockingly pungent dried red chili flakes
2 teaspoons Szechwan peppercorns

1. Combine all of the ingredients in a heavy, non-aluminum 1- to 1½-quart saucepan. Rest a deep-fry thermometer on the rim of the pot. Over moderately low heat, bring the mixture to a bubbly 225°F, stirring occasionally. Let simmer for 15 minutes, checking to ensure the temperature does not rise. Remove from the heat and let stand until cool or overnight.

2. Strain the oil without pressing the solids; then, discard the solids. Store the oil in an impeccably clean glass jar at cool room temperature.

MENU SUGGESTIONS: This is a wonderful oil for dressing noodles and salads. Its lemony tang makes it a great partner for fish.

INGREDIENTS FOR INFUSIONS

My simple rule in making infused oils and vinegars is to begin with products that have great flavor and aroma. Oils are a bit of a separate question in that, flavor aside, they require additional considerations of heating quality and viscosity. *Mazola corn oil* is my first choice; *Planter's peanut oil* is my second. Both these oils can be heated to a high temperature without burning and both have a light consistency and a neutral taste on the tongue. I avoid using cold-pressed oils for infusions; often they taste too strongly of corn or peanut.

For the accent oil, I choose *Kadoya sesame oil*. The toasting and pressing of this particular brand of sesame oil is done with such consistent care that I have never had a burnt-tasting or rancid bottle in all my years of cooking. If your market does not have Kadoya brand, taste the other candidates with a critical tongue and nose.

Marukan unseasoned rice vinegar (with the green label) and *Heinz distilled white vinegar* and *Heinz apple cider vinegar* are my vinegars of choice in making infusions. Mitsukan unseasoned rice vinegar is another good brand. These are not the least expensive, but in my experience they are the most tasty, with a broad range of flavor in addition to the acidic bite.

In the realm of dry and fresh aromatics used for infusing, you must also choose with care:

Dried red chili flakes should be red (indicating sweetness and fire), not brown or purple-black. They should be so pungent that you rear back when you smell them. The bag should contain no more than 25 percent seeds.

Szechwan peppercorns should smell profoundly good and herbal. The bag should contain few if any black seeds. Twigs and tiny leaves are part of the bundle, along with a good-size thorn every so often (that should be picked out).

Chinese fermented black beans should be moist and pliable to the touch. They should taste good, with a nice range of flavor in the aftertaste. My favorite brand is *Pearl River Bridge*, in a round yellow box. Don't use beans that are hard and shriveled. Likewise, don't wash them before use; you want the salt they carry as a contribution to the infusion.

Garlic, ginger, and lemongrass should be rock-hard fresh, with no hint of mold to the eye or the nose.

Scallions should be straight-standing and perky, ideally wearing their white beards as a sign of freshness. They should feel dry or pleasantly moist from the grocer's water pistol, not slimy.

Orange and lemon zest should be washed well in warm water with an abrasive scrubber and then rinsed squeaky-clean, even if the fruit came from your backyard tree.

Last, but not least, *Diamond kosher salt* is the only kind I use unless a recipe specifies otherwise. It comes in a big red and gold box and is a feature of most good restaurant kitchens. No other brand, in my experience, is so consistently mild and clean-tasting. Buy a box from a neighborhood restaurant if you can't convince your grocer to order it.

For ingredients not covered here specifically—also, in the happy instance that making our infusions starts you creating your own—trust your own good nose and tongue: If you don't like the smell or the taste of something, then don't use it.

CHINA MOON CHILI-ORANGE OIL

MAKES ABOUT 2½ CUPS

I adore citrus flavors and love the combination of chili and orange, so making this oil was inevitable. It is a fabulous ingredient and a mainstay of my kitchen cupboard.

Choose oranges with unblemished skins that have been kept as free as possible of waxes and dyes, then wash them carefully with a light liquid detergent, warm water, and an abrasive sponge. The effort may seem kooky, but it makes a difference. So too will a sharp vegetable peeler that will pare off the flavorful skin (zest) and not the bitter white pith.

3 large oranges with unblemished skins
½ cup shockingly pungent dried red chili flakes

3 tablespoons Chinese black beans (do not rinse them), coarsely chopped
1 to 2 large cloves garlic, lightly smashed and peeled
2 cups corn or peanut oil
¼ cup Japanese sesame oil

1. Wash the oranges as described above. Peel away the thin layer of orange zest (leaving behind the white pith) and finely mince it.

2. Combine the minced zest with all of the remaining ingredients in a heavy, non-aluminum 2- to 2½-quart saucepan. Bring to 225° to 250°F on a deep-fry thermometer over moderately low heat, stirring occasionally, and let bubble for 15 minutes. Remove from the heat and let stand until cool or overnight.

3. Scrape the oil and seasonings (we call these the "goop") into a glass or plastic container, cover, and store at cool room temperature.

MENU SUGGESTIONS: Be creative with the "goop" made from the seasonings as well as the oil. A spoonful stirred into noodles or meat loaf is a tasty revelation.

TOOLS FOR INFUSING OILS AND VINEGARS

The single most important tool for infusing oils successfully is *a deep-fry thermometer*. I use the kind with a friendly, round face about 2 inches wide that sits atop a long spoke outfitted with a kettle clamp. I never use the clamp; I simply rest the face on the rim of the pot and let the spoke dangle into the oil. Don't think it's a problem if the spoke touches the bottom of the pot; the temperature will still be true.

The great thing about this arrangement is you can read the oil temperature from across the room. Never one to do one thing while I could be doing two, I love the freedom to chop or read while the oil is coming to a bubble.

If you think you can do without a thermometer, you are taking a calculated risk. Even a 25-degree variance in the temperature of the oil will turn an infusion from wondrous to bitter. Figure it's like being outside in hopes of a tan; the extra degrees take you quickly from seeming beauty to burnt.

Next and almost equal in importance to the deep-fry thermometer is *a heavy pot of sufficient depth*. The chosen pot must be two or three times the depth of the oil plus the aromatics you are going to infuse. For example, if you are setting about an infusion that involves 2 cups of oil and 1 cup of aromatics, you will need a pot that holds 6 cups or 1½ quarts at the minimum.

This space allows the oil to bubble up (literally) as it cooks, a fascinating eyeful if you have a big enough pot, but a dangerous experiment if you don't. When in doubt, always choose a bigger pot. A heavy pot is mandated on account of its heating and holding qualities. It will heat slowly and steadily, just the kind of environment an infusion loves if it is to be full-flavored. It will also hold the heat even after the infusion has cooked, leaching an extra nuance of taste and perfume from the aromatics.

A *non-aluminum pot* is also essential for infusing vinegars, lest you wind up with an unforgettably metallic-tasting brew. It is not a problem if the pot is made with aluminum on the outside or has aluminum sandwiched in between the inner and outer surfaces, so long as the inside of the pot itself is not bare aluminum.

Likewise, *non-aluminum tools* are required. That Chinese mesh spoon that looks so lyric hanging on the wall and can accomplish so many wonders in Chinese cooking can undo your treasured efforts to make pickled ginger, for example, if it is made from uncoated aluminum. Such tools are rare, but it is best to play it safe: Stir your infusions with wooden chopsticks or wooden spoons, and use stainless steel sieves if needed. Likewise, chop ingredients only with a stainless steel knife or with one made from a nonreactive carbon alloy.

MA-LA OIL

MAKES ABOUT 2½ CUPS

Whereas many Chinese cooks will combine peanut and toasted sesame oils in a pan and then bring them to heat with a bit of ginger, chili, and Szechwan peppercorn before stir-frying a dish, I have long practiced the northern Chinese method of infusing oil with these flavors, and using it then as a seasoning as opposed to a cooking oil. In northern China with its colder climates, such oils are kept easily. In my Western kitchen, not only do they keep but they lend a dimension of flavor to a dish that otherwise cannot be had.

Ma-La, or "numbing and spicy," is a classic central Chinese configuration of tastes that combines Szechwan peppercorns and chilis. This oil combines them both, as well as ginger, scallion, and toasted sesame.

Like all infused oils, this one should be stored in an impeccably clean glass jar or plastic container at cool room temperature. The oil may turn cloudy, but its flavor will not be affected. If mold develops from a contaminated utensil or it smells off owing to age or heat, toss it out and make a fresh batch.

1 cup corn or peanut oil
1 cup Japanese sesame oil
½ cup thinly sliced green and white scallion rings
15 quarter-size coins fresh ginger, smashed

2 tablespoons Szechwan peppercorns
2 tablespoons shockingly pungent dried red chili flakes
2 teaspoons kosher salt

1. Combine all of the ingredients in a heavy, non-aluminum 1½-quart saucepan. Rest a deep-fry thermometer on the rim of the pot. Over moderately low heat, bring the mixture to a bubbly 225°F, stirring occasionally. Let simmer for 15 minutes, checking to ensure the temperature does not rise. Remove from the heat and let stand until cool or overnight.

2. Strain the oil without pressing on the solids; then, discard the solids. Store the oil in an impeccably clean glass jar at cool room temperature.

MENU SUGGESTIONS: Because of the large proportion of sesame oil, this is a rich oil. A little bit goes a long way. A spoonful added to a salad dressing or brushed on the plate on which a fish will steam or on the skin of a just-smoked or roasted bird gives an inimitable touch of lushness. If you are a bread baker, brush a bit on your next loaf; if you are tossing pasta, drizzle a bit on the noodles just before serving.

SZECHWAN PEPPERCORN OIL

MAKES 2 CUPS

Redolent of the herbal qualities of Szechwan pepper, this is an intriguingly flavored spicy oil. The oil may cloud on account of the ginger, but that will not impair its taste.

6 tablespoons Szechwan
  peppercorns
2 cups corn or peanut oil
2 tablespoons shockingly
  pungent dried red chili flakes

2½ tablespoons finely minced
  fresh ginger
2 tablespoons thinly sliced green
  and white scallion rings

1. Heat a large heavy skillet over moderate heat until hot enough to evaporate a bead of water on contact. Add the Szechwan peppercorns and stir until toasted and fragrant, 2 to 3 minutes. Adjust the heat so the peppercorns brown without scorching.

2. Combine the peppercorns and all of the remaining ingredients in a heavy, non-aluminum 1- to 1½-quart saucepan. Heat over moderately low heat, stirring occasionally, until a deep-fry thermometer registers a bubbly 225°F. Let simmer for 15 minutes, then remove the pot from the heat. Let stand until cool or overnight.

CHOOSING DRY SPICES

It may seem a contradiction in terms to call a dry spice "fresh," but there is a great difference between a dry spice that is dead on the tongue and one that is fresh and lively. It is most discernible in the bouquet. Dried red chili flakes, for example, should be so pungent that a good whiff makes you rear back and sneeze. Szechwan peppercorns should exude a strong, camphor-like perfume. Even the hard, more secretive black peppercorn, if it is lively in flavor, will send out a burst of fragrance once crushed. Much like wine, it is the quality and nuance of a spice's fragrance—its "nose"—that holds the key to its flavor range.

I always prefer to buy spices in stores where I can sniff them, and in places where turnover is brisk and there is somebody feverishly devoted to the quality of the goods. Specialty spice emporiums that buy their spices at the source have knowledge to offer in addition to fine things to sell. If there's not one locally, write to the fabulous Penzey's Spice House, P.O. Box 1633, Milwaukee, WI 53201. Natural food stores where you can open the bin and sniff for yourself are another option. The nose knows all in choosing spices; if a spice smells moldy or musty or burnt, then don't buy it.

If you are forced to buy spices in antiseptic tiny cans or sealed bottles from a supermarket shelf, check carefully among brands to gauge the best. A company that touts "Salt Free!" on its bottle of ground cinnamon is probably not to be trusted. Ditto for a company that puts chic packaging first.

Buy the best spices you can, even if they're costly. Remember that the sum of the final mixture, if you're making our ten-spice or curry powders, is only as great as the quality of its parts.

3. Strain the oil through a fine-mesh sieve and discard the solids. Store the oil in an impeccably clean glass jar at cool room temperature.

MENU SUGGESTIONS: This oil is particularly good for salads. Its herbal quality also makes it a nice partner to poultry or beef dishes.

SERRANO-LEMONGRASS VINEGAR

MAKES ABOUT 3 CUPS

A dressed-up rice vinegar lively with the tastes of serrano chili and lemongrass. Shop for Marukan rice vinegar with the green label (unseasoned), which is easily found, or the harder to find but equally good Mitsukan.

Those who avoid chili can simply omit it here.

3 cups unseasoned Japanese rice vinegar
½ cup quarter-size thin coins fresh ginger, smashed

1 fat or 2 thinner stalks fresh lemongrass, pounded, then cut crosswise into finger lengths
6 green and/or red serrano chilis, tipped and halved

1. Combine all of the ingredients in a non-aluminum pot, then bring to a simmer over moderate heat. Remove the pot from the heat and let stand until cool.

2. Store the mixture in an impeccably clean glass jar. If you wish, you may strain out the solids before storing, but do not press down on them while doing so. Another alternative is to leave only the chilis in the jar for color. The vinegar may cloud, but its flavor will not be affected.

MOONSPEAK

Moonspeak is the zany combination of Chinese, Yiddish, English, and pidgin that permeates our kitchen communication. Some of it has to do with my own fascination with language and the love of a verbal tickle. But a lot of it is the necessary oral shorthand that guides any frantic business that relies on humans and their words. Here, then, is a guide to Moonspeak in semi-random order:

MOONS: Wedges of things that have the shape of a half- or crescent moon. Applies to onions, leeks, water chestnuts, and whole pastry turnovers or cookies.

COINS: Rounds or oblong slices of otherwise round things. Applies to carrots, zucchini, Chinese eggplant, water chestnuts, and so on.

RINGS: Highly specific to green and white scallion rings, used ubiquitously as an aromatic and as a garnish.

DIAGS: Highly specific to diagonally cut rings of scallions that are used frequently as a garnish.

THREADS: Shared turf between scallions and ginger. Green and white scallion julienne (called "silk threads"

in Chinese, hence the abbreviation) are used often as a garnish. Ginger threads are either strewn raw, typically on top of a fish to be steamed, or are deep-fried and used as a garnish or in salads.

SQUARES AND STRIPS: Applies to vegetable cuts for stir-frying. To cut an onion into "squares," you halve it through the root end, cut each half lengthwise into 2 or 3 wedges, then cut the wedges crosswise into rounded squares. To cut a bell pepper into squares, lop off the top and bottom, slit the pepper lengthwise, then open the pepper and remove the seeds and ribs. The denuded flesh can then be cut into neat squares approximately ¾ inch in size.

BUTTS: Highly specific, in our non-sexist kitchen, to the bottom ends of bell peppers. These are cut along their natural crevices into thirds or fourths, and used primarily in sandpots.

BATONS: A thick julienne. Used in our kitchen to apply exclusively to carrots. Instituted as menu lingo by the owner (a failed junior high majorette), upon discovering that you could sell a lot more carrot sticks if you called

them by their French name.

BIND: A verb. Refers to the last step in the stir-fry dance, whereby one adds a mixture of cornstarch and cold stock or water to the simmering sauce, binding it to the main ingredients.

BINDER: The mixture that makes this happen. The wok cooks keep binder on the stovetop in plastic squeeze bottles (the kind that houses mustard and ketchup).

SQUEEZE BOTTLES: See *binder* above. These containers are also used by the cooks to hold and apply (or *ziggle,* see below) all of our vinaigrettes and cold sauces.

SCHLEP: Yiddish. Refers specifically to the steep staircase that separates our large downstairs prep kitchen from the tiny upstairs finishing kitchen, and the need to carry all the food upstairs twice daily. Schlep, in English, means "to haul, moaning and groaning, things that if otherwise trained would move on their own."

ZIGGLE: As a noun, refers to a back and forth dashing (wiggle) of sauce on top of a dish. Can also be used as a verb, to ziggle, implying the act itself of ziggling.

CHINA MOON HOUSE MUSTARD SAUCE

MAKES ABOUT 1 CUP

An invariable disappointment to those who expect the standard Chinese restaurant mustard sauce— an acrid blend of dry mustard and water—this is a silky sauce lush with the flavors of dark sesame oil and Dijon mustard. It will keep forever in the refrigerator.

½ cup unflavored Dijon
   mustard
¼ cup Japanese sesame oil

3 tablespoons unseasoned
   Japanese rice vinegar
¼ teaspoon sugar
Pinch of fine sea salt

Whisk all of the ingredients together until well blended. Store, refrigerated, in an impeccably clean glass jar. If the sauce separates, simply whisk it to emulsify.

MENU SUGGESTIONS: We use this sauce with many of our cold beef, lamb, and chicken dishes. It is also very nice spread on a piece of steamed fish and goes wonderfully with foods that come straight off the grill. Ham-and-cheese-sandwich lovers would like it.

SWEET MUSTARD SAUCE

MAKES ABOUT 1½ CUPS

A variation on a much-loved theme, this is a lighter, tart and sweet version of our house mustard sauce. Like the original, it keeps indefinitely refrigerated, needing nothing more than a brisk whisking if it separates.

¼ cup plus 2 teaspoons
    unflavored Dijon mustard
½ cup rice bran oil or corn or
    peanut oil
⅓ cup Five-Flavor Oil (page 13)

1 teaspoon fine sea salt
3 tablespoons sugar
½ cup juice from
    China Moon
    Pickled Ginger
    (page 8)

Whisk together all of the ingredients until well blended. Store, refrigerated, in an impeccably clean glass jar. Should the sauce separate, whisk to emulsify.

MENU SUGGESTIONS: I adore this sauce with our pork and lamb sausages (pages 323 and 282). It also has a great fan club among the won-ton and springroll dunkers in our kitchen. Our brined loins of pork (page 310 and page 313) and Wok-Seared Beef Tenderloin (page 253) would also partner it well, even if between two slices of rye.

SPICY HOISIN SAUCE

MAKES ABOUT 2 CUPS

The fruity taste of hoisin sauce and the sharp-earthy flavor of garlic wed perfectly in this sauce. It is rich and spicy, and a real kitchen favorite.

Minus the garlic, the sauce can be refrigerated indefinitely. We always keep the garlic-less mixture on hand, then add the garlic only as needed.

12 large cloves garlic, peeled
1 teaspoon kosher salt
¼ cup "goop" from China
    Moon Hot Chili Oil
    (page 10)
2 tablespoons China Moon Hot
    Chili Oil
2 tablespoons Japanese sesame
    oil

¼ cup soy sauce
¼ cup plus 1 teaspoon
    unseasoned Japanese rice
    vinegar
½ cup hoisin sauce
½ teaspoon sugar
2 tablespoons warm water

POUND AWAY

Pounding garlic to a paste (as opposed to mincing it) gives it an inimitable mellowness. The salt speeds the process; it also adds flavor.

In a mortar with a pestle, pound the garlic cloves with the salt to a fine paste. Combine with all of the remaining ingredients until well blended.

MENU SUGGESTIONS: We love this sauce as a dressing for boiled dumplings and won-tons. It is also delicious spooned on top of pork, lamb, or chicken. Our staff will eat it with most everything—raw vegetables, cold springrolls, on top of simple steamed rice—and so, I suspect, will you.

MINTED CUCUMBER SAUCE

MAKES ABOUT 3 CUPS

Falling somewhere between a vinaigrette and a sauce, this is a mélange of cool, clean flavors in a light dressing that is particularly good with fish and cold vegetables. The cucumber you use must taste fresh and sweet. If you are forced to buy commercial cucumbers with their thick, waxy skin, peel and seed them before incorporating into the recipe.

1 large Japanese or English
    cucumber, seeded and cut
    into chunks
5 large fresh mint leaves
Zest of ½ scrubbed lemon,
    finely minced
1 small red Fresno or yellow
    wax chili, seeded and cut
    into chunks (optional)
Juice of ½ lemon
¼ teaspoon finely minced garlic

½ teaspoon finely minced fresh
    ginger
½ teaspoon freshly ground black
    pepper
½ teaspoon sugar
½ teaspoon fine sea salt
¼ cup unseasoned Japanese rice
    vinegar
2 tablespoons distilled white
    vinegar
1 cup rice bran, corn, or peanut
    oil

Place the cucumber, mint, lemon zest, and chili (if you'd like a spicy vinaigrette) in a food processor and process until nearly smooth, pausing to scrape down the sides of the bowl

SEA SALT

It is in just this type of recipe, where the flavors are mild and there is a bit of lemon, that we tend to use sea salt instead of kosher salt. The more pronounced flavor of sea salt is good here, and it is a perfect mate to the lemon. If you have only kosher salt in your house, use twice as much to equal the sea salt's degree of saltiness.

with a rubber spatula. Add the rest of the ingredients except the oil and process briefly to combine. With the machine running, slowly drizzle in the oil and process until the vinaigrette is emulsified. The sauce may be refrigerated for several hours. Store in an impeccably clean bowl with a piece of plastic wrap pressed directly on the surface. Bring to room temperature and stir well before serving.

MENU SUGGESTIONS: We especially like this sauce with Gold Coin Salmon Cakes (page 188) and Wok-Seared Tuna (page 198). It would also be good with many of our steamed fish and chicken dishes.

FRESH GINGER VINAIGRETTE

MAKES ABOUT ⅔ CUP

Zippy and light, this is a versatile vinaigrette, bright with the flavors of fresh ginger and duskily sweet with the taste of balsamic vinegar. It is the China Moon house vinaigrette.

If you are using sea salt, use only half as much. No good flavor will come from table salt, at least not to my tongue.

2 tablespoons ginger juice
   (squeezed from finely minced
   fresh ginger)
2 tablespoons plus 1 teaspoon
   balsamic vinegar

½ cup rice bran, corn, or
   peanut oil
1 teaspoon kosher salt

Whisk together all of the ingredients in a mixing bowl until emulsified. Store, refrigerated, in an impeccably clean glass jar. Bring to room temperature and shake well before using.

FRESH GINGER JUICE

As a general rule, start out with 3 tablespoons of finely minced fresh ginger for every 1 tablespoon of juice you wish to extract. The yield will differ, depending upon the juiciness of the ginger and/or the fineness of the mince.

We mince our ginger in a food processor by the cupful to a near purée and then squeeze it by hand. The pulp simply gets thrown away.

One sexy girlfriend prefers to squeeze ginger through a nylon stocking. Interesting and maybe even a bit kinky!

Some of my favorite food photos are from the now out-of-print Time-Life **Foods of the World** *series. It was a brave new world of ethnic cookery when they were published in the 1960s and 70s, and it is sad to see them gone.*

I learned to cook out of the Chinese volume, an extraordinary combination of superlative photographs, lively prose, and tell-it-all traditional recipes. One photograph in particular stands out in my mind. It was of several women workers in a mung bean noodle "plant"—an outdoor scene of bamboo drying poles layered with silken noodles. Somehow, the half-seen faces of these peasant women shadowed by bamboo hats and flowered bandanas, and the wide swathe of drying noodles held me spellbound.

Another photo, from the Japanese book in the series, held me equally captive. It showed a persimmon tree in a snowfall, with an icy contrast of white snow, orange fruit, and black branch. These are food photos to remember: They taught me about ingredients, put them in a setting, and fueled an intrigue that will be, I suspect, lifelong.

ORANGE VINAIGRETTE

MAKES ¾ CUP

When we are putting a salad of baby greens alongside smoked poultry or brined pork, we will often use this orange-infused vinaigrette. The combination of mustard, orange zest, and balsamic vinegar is very appealing.

Vinaigrettes made with fruit zests and/or fruit juices are best made just before using so their flavors are lively and clear.

½ cup rice bran, corn, or peanut oil
¾ teaspoon Dijon mustard
¾ teaspoon finely grated zest from a well-scrubbed orange
1 tablespoon freshly squeezed orange juice
1 tablespoon balsamic vinegar

1 tablespoon sherry vinegar
½ teaspoon soy sauce
¼ teaspoon kosher salt
Pinch of Roasted Szechwan Pepper-Salt (page 5)
⅛ teaspoon freshly ground black pepper

Shortly before using, whisk together all of the ingredients until emulsified. Leftovers can be refrigerated, but first strain out the zest, which can grow bitter. Bring to room temperature before using and shake well to recombine.

A QUARTET OF SPRINGROLL DIPPING SAUCES

This is a rousing foursome of dipping sauces most typically used with our springrolls, but in fact lavished by the staff upon most anything edible. Each sauce has its own character—the spicy green chili, the light and tart pickled ginger, the nutty peanut-lime, and the lushly sweet honey ten-spice—that makes it better or less suited to any particular springroll. For the most part, we mix and match and choose whichever sauce we're inspired to make.

This is a delicious departure from the traditional. When I first started China Moon, I outfitted each table with cruets of soy, vinegar, and chili oil and waited for my Western patrons to combine them in a personalized puddle on their serving dish, as is the habit in China. No such thing happened. So while the cruets accumulated dust, we came up with the dipping sauces and spared our customers the work of blending their own. The result is absolutely untraditional and perfectly delicious.

GREEN CHILI DIPPING SAUCE

MAKES ABOUT 1½ CUPS

5 Anaheim chilis, seeded and
    cut into ½-inch rounds
2 yellow wax chilis, tipped and
    cut into ½-inch rounds
2 large cloves garlic
¾ cup juice from China Moon
    Pickled Ginger (page 8)
2 tablespoons distilled white
    vinegar
2 tablespoons corn or peanut oil
1½ packed cups fresh coriander
    leaves and stems
Fine sea salt or kosher salt, if
    needed

Thinly sliced Fresno chili rings,
    for garnish

1. Process the chilis and garlic in a food processor until nearly smooth. With the machine running, add the ginger

TOOLS FOR GRINDING YOUR OWN SPICES

Once you are hooked on the idea of grinding your own spices, the obvious question of tools arises.

*A **mortar and pestle** is one possibility. Lyric, aerobic, and inexpensive, it is the fountain pen of the kitchen, something that imbues a cook with a feeling of artistry. For grinding small amounts of tiny spices, like the Szechwan peppercorns in Roasted Szechwan Pepper-Salt, it is a good tool.*

*A **spice grinder** is more versatile, making up in speed and efficiency what it lacks in poetic appeal. It can easily handle the pods of star anise in China Moon Ten-Spice and will happily whirl to smithereens the stick cinnamon in China Moon Curry Powder. A spice grinder should be sturdy so don't fall for a svelte model before asking a knowledgeable kitchenware salesperson if its muscle equals its chic. Remember, also, with a spice grinder, to fill it only half full; the spices need to whirl around freely to achieve an even grind. When cleaning, use only a faintly damp cloth, then follow with a very careful dry wipe. Store the grinder with its top off and exposed to the air, lest last* week's pepper-salt perfumes this month's ten-spice.

A **coffee grinder** can be called into service as an occasional spice grinder. Wipe and air it as above before and after it has done its duty. Pay special attention to the initial cleaning on account of the coffee bean oils. If you are about to become a homemade spice maven, you will want a separate spice grinder, but for the let-me-try-it-and-see cook, this staves off an additional purchase.

Lastly, a **food processor** outfitted with a very sharp steel knife will work wonders with smaller spices like Szechwan peppercorns. I don't like it for grinding bulkier spices (like star anise or cinnamon) because they can catch on the blade and lift it off the stem. However, if this is all you've got, you can first bash the larger spices with a mallet to make them behave better in the workbowl.

A **blender** is sometimes posed as an alternative spice grinder, but it has never worked well for me. I confess I have never lived with one and identify it mostly with the ghastly wheat germ milkshakes my mother would whip up to stony silence in her Adelle Davis years. Yet, if you love your blender, by all means try it for our recipes.

juice and vinegar, then add the oil in a thin stream and process until emulsified. If using the sauce at once, add the coriander and process until smooth. If working in advance, leave out the coriander; mince and add it just before serving. Taste and season with salt if needed.

2. When serving, garnish the sauce bowls with thin rings of fresh red chilis for color and heat.

3. Store, refrigerated, in a clean container. The sauce will lose its bright color, but will be tasty for 1 to 2 days.

MENU SUGGESTIONS: In addition to springrolls, these sauces have been hits as dips for fried won-ton, grilled and wok-seared fish and poultry, and our house-cured beef, lamb, and pork. For dieters faced with an eternity of cold poached chicken breast, a dip dish of one of these sauces is a lifesaver.

TEN-SPICE HONEY DIP

MAKES 1 CUP

Leftovers of this dip are great for basting meat, fish, or poultry.

½ cup honey
¼ cup plus 1 tablespoon soy sauce
¼ cup juice from China Moon Pickled Ginger (page 8)

¼ teaspoon China Moon Ten-Spice (page 6)

Combine all of the ingredients in a small non-aluminum saucepan. Heat, stirring, over low heat until the honey dissolves, 3 to 4 minutes. Store, refrigerated, in a clean container. Warm over low heat to a liquid consistency before using.

PEANUT-LIME DIPPING SAUCE

MAKES 1 ¾ CUPS

½ cup unseasoned peanut
   butter, preferably homemade
   (page 32)
⅓ cup unsweetened coconut
   milk
1 teaspoon finely minced fresh
   ginger
3 tablespoons packed brown
   sugar
¼ cup soy sauce
½ teaspoon kosher salt

2 tablespoons freshly squeezed
   lime juice
2 tablespoons unseasoned
   Japanese rice vinegar
1½ tablespoons Ma-La Oil
   (page 17)
½ teaspoon Cayenne Pepper Oil
   (page 11)
1 tablespoon "goop" from
   China Moon Hot Chili Oil
   (page 10)

    Blend together all of the ingredients until thoroughly emulsified and smooth, either in a food processor or by hand. Taste and adjust the seasoning if needed with an extra dash of soy sauce or sugar to obtain a full, rich, spicy flavor. Store, refrigerated, in an impeccably clean container. Bring to room temperature and shake well before using.

PICKLED GINGER DIPPING SAUCE

MAKES 1 ½ CUPS

1 cup juice from China Moon
   Pickled Ginger (page 8)
¼ cup plus 2 tablespoons
   unseasoned Japanese rice
   vinegar
2 tablespoons sugar

1 tablespoon soy sauce
Thinly sliced green and white
   scallion rings, for garnish
Thinly sliced Fresno chili rings,
   for garnish

   1. Heat the pickled ginger juice, rice vinegar, and sugar in a small non-aluminum saucepan over low heat, stirring,

GARNISHES
**(an admittedly cranky
admonition)**

   I am a strong believer in the simple, edible garnish that has a close flavor kinship to the dish. In my world, dyed daikon flamingos, writhing carrot dragons, and blinking Christmas lights in the empty eye sockets of a stir-fried lobster—all garnishes of the Hong Kong sort—are out. So, too, are radish flowers, tomato rosettes, and vegetable pellets sculpted to look like suppositories. I find all of this loathsome.

   In my own rather minimalist style, the fanciest I get is an occasional scallion brush. Otherwise, a leggy piece of coriander or a flourish of scallion rings are all that our already colorful dishes require. Or, if the dish is green, a confetti of finely diced red bell pepper will do the job.

   The issue is a visible one, but it needs to make

sense on your tongue. A garnish is primarily designed to tickle the eye, but it also should meld seamlessly with the other flavors on the plate or contrast with them in a meaningful way.

Garnishing the rims of plates—a current feature of trendy restaurants in the 90s—is something I find very peculiar. I spill and splatter my own food quite nicely, thank you, and don't want the kitchen to do it for me.

Ditto the rage for a whole chive aloft each appetizer or a cage of spun sugar looming above a dessert. It is admittedly wonderful to give a little height to a dish: One can arrange cold shrimp, for example, in a lively tumble with just a touch or two. But the unrelated vertical garnish is often absurd, a bit of Dr. Seuss on the plate.

I sound cranky, and perhaps I am! Restaurant cooks frequently spend too much time decorating their food, and too little time paying attention to its taste. This, I think, is sad.

until the sugar dissolves. Add the soy sauce and let cool to room temperature.

2. When serving, garnish the sauce bowls with thin rings of scallions and fresh red chilis for color and heat.

3. Store, refrigerated, in a clean glass jar. Shake well before using.

FRIED GINGER THREADS

MAKES 1 CUP

This is a startling ingredient—a hair-fine sliver of deep-fried fresh ginger that tingles the palate and gives zest to a dish. We use pinches of them to garnish most anything that needs a jolt of spice.

Your knife must be sharp and your julienne very fine or the ginger threads will look klutzy. The frying oil will taste terrifically of ginger. Keep it for dressing noodles and salads, basting fish and meats, sautéeing vegetables, and so on.

My friend Anne Rosenzweig, who runs Arcadia, the wonderful New York City restaurant, calls this "frizzled ginger." It loses its frizzle if kept for more than several days, so fry only what you need.

2½ to 3 ounces fresh ginger in long rectangular pieces

2 to 4 cups corn or peanut oil for deep-frying

1. Peel the ginger and trim it into 1 or more easily managed rectangular blocks.

2. With a sharp knife, slice the ginger lengthwise into thin, nearly translucent slices. Stack or fan the slices, then cut them lengthwise into a fine julienne. You should have about ½ cup. (The julienne should fall from your fingers in separate threads; if it sticks and wads, you've cut it too fine or with too much pressure. If the edges are raggedy, your blade is dull.)

3. In a wok or deep, heavy skillet, add oil to a depth of 1½ inches, and balance a deep-fry thermometer on the rim of the pot. Heat the oil to 375°F; a thread of ginger will bubble on contact. Adjust the heat so the temperature doesn't rise.

4. Fry the ginger in 2 batches until golden, about 10 seconds per batch. Scoop swiftly from the oil with a Chinese mesh spoon, then set aside on a paper towel–lined plate to drain and crisp. Don't fry it too brown or it will taste bitter.

5. Use within a day or two. Store at room temperature in a paper towel–lined bowl sealed with plastic wrap.

INFUSED GLASS NOODLES

MAKES 1½ CUPS

This is a great addition to soups and saucy casseroles, where you want the slithery glass noodles to contribute taste as well as texture. Simmered in stock after softening in water, these glass noodles are a cut above the everyday.

You can simmer the noodles in whatever stock you like. If you have a fancy stock nested in the freezer and need to dress up a simple spinach stir-fry, now is the time to use it.

Infused glass noodles are perishable and should be refrigerated until you're ready to use them. Use them within 2 to 3 days of simmering, or they may sour.

1 small package PRC glass   *2 cups China Moon Infusion*
* noodles (1.75 to 2 ounces)*   *(page 72) or any tasty stock*

1. Remove the noodles from the package, but don't remove the strings binding the skein. These will hold the skein together and make cutting the noodles easier. Count the number of strings so you will know how many to cut off and won't wind up eating them.

2. Put the noodles in a heatproof bowl. Cover with simmering water. Let stand until translucent, 5 to 10 minutes, then drain. Flush with cold water; drain again.

A ROSE IS A ROSE

"Glass noodles" is the fanciful English name for what in Chinese are called "starch threads." Made from mung bean starch, these thin, dry noodles turn translucent and glassy once soaked.

Look for glass noodles (aka mung bean threads, cellophane noodles, Chinese vermicelli) in small cellophane bags. A superior variety is made in the PRC (People's Republic of China) and bagged with a jaunty red or argyle ribbon. Avoid Taiwanese brands, which are not as silken and delicate as their communist cousins. Unless you run a restaurant, buy the diminutive 1.75- to 2-ounce packages. These are sold individually or in nifty webbed bags containing eight or so skeins.

The one sure thing about glass noodles is that you never know with a new brand whether they need to be soaked in hot tap water, barely simmered water, or dramatically boiling water. The only sure way is to make a test.

Begin with hot tap water and patiently work your way up through the other degrees of heat. A mere 5 minutes will give the results. If the noodles have turned silky and transparent, you've achieved what you've set out to do. If they remain wiry and opaque, try the next water temperature on the ascending scale.

Every once in a while, some jack-rabbit cook will cover an as yet untested brand with simmering or boiling water, and they'll turn instantly into a weird, jellyfish-like mass. They are great objects of kitchen curiosity—the cooks, waiters, and janitors will take turns poking them as they lie ignominiously in the trash can. So unless you're looking for a fun-house thrill for your kids, take the sure route and begin with the hot tap water test.

3. Cut the softened noodles into 2-inch lengths. Snip and discard the strings. If the noodles have a pronounced smell, flush them once again with cool water and drain.

4. In a small, heavy saucepan, bring the stock to a steaming near-simmer over moderate heat. Add the noodles, stir to combine, and bring the mixture to a weak simmer. Adjust the heat to maintain a weak simmer and cook the noodles, stirring occasionally, until the stock is mostly absorbed, about 10 minutes.

5. Transfer the noodles to a shallow dish. Use immediately or let cool, stirring occasionally to release the heat. Once cool, seal and refrigerate until ready to use.

CRISPY RICE STICKS

MAKES 1 ½ CUPS, ENOUGH TO DRESS 4 TO 6 SALADS OR
STIR-FRIES

One of the great thrills of Chinese cooking is to toss a handful of dry rice noodles into hot oil and watch them puff up in a nest. It's a swift bit of kitchen magic: The opaque, wire-like strands loop and bloom within seconds into a snowy tangle. One can get easily carried away, producing buckets of the stuff.

A small wad of noodles and a modest amount of oil will yield enough noodles to enliven a stir-fry or salad dramatically. Try it when your spirits are low and/or your lettuce leaves need a lift.

Rice sticks are best used within a day of frying, while they're crisp and fresh. The frying oil is easily strained and recycled for another use.

Use only fresh, pristine oil for frying rice sticks. If the oil has been filtered from other frying, the sticks won't fry properly and will be gray instead of snowy.

½ ounce dry rice sticks

2 to 4 cups corn or peanut oil, for deep-frying

1. Carefully pull apart the rice sticks so that you have a very thin web. If fried in too thick a layer, the outer sticks will puff while the inner ones stay wire-like.

2. In a wok or deep, heavy skillet, add oil to a depth of 2 inches. Balance a deep-fry thermometer on the rim of the pan. Bring the oil to 375°F, hot enough to puff a single rice stick on contact. Adjust the heat so the temperature doesn't climb.

3. Toss half of the noodles into the oil. They should puff and turn snowy white on contact. Turn the nest over with chopsticks or tongs, wait a second or two for them to puff, then transfer them immediately to a paper towel–lined baking sheet. Repeat with the remaining rice sticks.

4. Just before using, gently press on the nest to break it into bits.

BUYING RICE STICKS

The best rice sticks for frying are sold in rectangular cellophane packages about 7 inches long and 4 inches wide, 4 rectangular wads to a package. The sticks themselves are 1/16 inch thin, opaque, and slightly wavy. Look for rice sticks that are loosely packed and relatively straight; the denser, coiled wads are impossible to pull apart.

We use a PRC brand of rice sticks called Sailing Boat, bound in 1-pound packages with a lyric pink ribbon.

HOMEMADE PEANUT BUTTER

If you have a food processor, it's a quick and easy step to producing your own peanut butter. One can buy delicious peanuts in a natural food store, and for a fraction of the cost make a product that doesn't have any salt, sugar, or lesser quality oil. If the control issue doesn't turn you on, the taste will.

Homemade peanut butter stores indefinitely in the refrigerator. We always keep it on hand—for marinades, sauces, cookies, and staff sandwiches.

For every 1 cup of peanut butter, you'll need 2 cups of raw peanuts. They can be skinless or still wearing their jackets. We use skinless peanuts. However, the skins give a rich taste with a hint of a pleasantly bitter edge, which some people really like.

Two versions are given below. They're equally tasty. The nuts can be ground hot or cold; it doesn't matter. Do

PEANUTTIER BUTTER

If you want your peanut butter to taste extra peanutty, here is the place to use cold-pressed peanut oil. I find this kind of oil too strong for general cooking (where I want the food to taste like itself, not peanuts), but in a peanut-centered preparation like this one, it's perfect.

take care not to overcook the nuts. If they're too dark, they can taste burnt. Go for golden, as opposed to brown.

ROASTED PEANUT BUTTER

MAKES 1 CUP

2 cups raw peanuts   ¼ cup peanut or corn oil

1. Preheat the oven to 350°F. Move a rack to the middle position.

2. Spread the peanuts in a thin layer on a heavyweight jelly roll pan. Roast until golden, 20 to 25 minutes. Midway through roasting, shuffle the nuts and rotate the pan to ensure even coloring.

3. Combine the nuts and the oil in a food processor. Blend to the desired texture, either chunky or smooth.

FRIED PEANUT BUTTER

MAKES 1 CUP

2 cups raw peanuts   2 to 4 cups peanut or corn oil, for deep-frying

1. In a wok or deep, heavy skillet, add the oil to a depth of 1½ to 2 inches. Balance a deep-fry thermometer on the rim of the pan.

2. Bring the oil to 350°F. Adjust the heat so the temperature doesn't rise.

3. Fry the peanuts in 2 or 3 batches, stirring until golden, 30 to 40 seconds. Remove the nuts to an unlined plate. (You want them oily to aid in the grinding.)

4. Combine the peanuts and 2 tablespoons of the frying oil in a food processor. Blend to a chunky or fine texture, as desired.

FRESH ROASTED AND FRIED NUTS

ROASTED (OR TOASTED) NUTS: Like Chinese cooks everywhere, I love using freshly roasted nuts in stir-fries, salads, and springroll fillings. Aside from their own intrinsic good taste, they are a great texture foil to soft foods like chicken nuggets and glass noodles. They also dress up a dish wonderfully, as anyone who has ever gilded last night's leftovers with a flourish of toasted pine nuts knows well. Here are the how-to's of nut roasting:

▲ Buy raw, unseasoned nuts to begin with, ideally from bins in a natural food store where you can nibble on one to check the flavor. If nibbles are illegal, sniff the goods—rancid nuts smell soapy and unappealing. Don't fall for the little cellophane packs of nuts sold in supermarkets. They're almost always mediocre.

▲ Preheat the oven to 350°F and move a rack to the middle position. A preheated oven will cook more evenly, a special concern with oil-rich nuts that will turn golden in minutes. Roasting in the middle of the oven avoids the temperature extremes of the top and bottom thirds.

▲ Use a jelly-roll pan (a baking sheet with sides) and spread the nuts in a thin, even layer to within an inch of the edge. The sides of the pan generate excess heat, and nuts placed close to them will darken too quickly. Ideally, use a heavy-weight pan that will hold the heat and distribute it evenly.

▲ When the nuts are just beginning to color, pull the pan from the oven and shuffle the nuts around before returning them to the oven. This ensures even cooking. Move quickly. Or close the oven door if you're a slow shuffler.

▲ Finally, remove the nuts from the oven when they are a shade *lighter* than desired and let them cool on the pan. They will continue to darken a bit from their own internal heat as they cool.

▲ Small or sliced or slivered nuts—like pine nuts or slivered almonds—will turn golden in 5 to 10 minutes. Larger nuts like peanuts or cashews will take 20 to 25 minutes to turn gold. If you're using nuts pulled straight from the refrigerator (the ideal place to store raw nuts), expect them to take 2 to 3 minutes longer.

▲ Watch roasting nuts like a hawk! It's a sure thing that the minute you take to sprint to the john is the minute during which they'll burn.

▲ Nuts are tastiest freshly roasted. Toast only as much as you need at any one time.

FRIED NUTS: The Chinese tradition (from a country oil-rich but fuel-poor) is to fry nuts for cooking rather than roasting them. If you're comfortable with deep-frying, raw nuts cooked in this manner have an inimitable texture and sheen. Here are the kitchen how-to's of nut-frying:

▲ Use plump, raw, skinless nuts of the best quality. Not only do they taste best, they also color best in frying.

▲ Use fresh corn or peanut oil that has not been used before, as opposed to oil that has been filtered from other frying. Pristine oil will give the most even, attractive color, whereas the particles in recycled oil can too quickly turn the nuts brown.

▲ Fry only as many nuts as you need at one time. Fried nuts do not hold their crispness or flavor well. They get soggy and taste stale.

▲ Fill your frying vessel with oil to a depth of at least 1½ inches and give the nuts plenty of room to float. A round-bottomed wok, because of its shape, is most economical of all. If you're frying more than a cup of nuts in a standard-size home wok or large skillet, fry in two or three batches for best results and maximum control.

▲ Preheat the oil to 350°F and adjust the heat so the temperature doesn't rise. Balance a deep-fry thermometer on the side of the pan so you can check the temperature both before and during the frying.

▲ Stir the nuts gently while they fry to ensure even coloring. A Chinese mesh spoon or a pair of long wooden cooking chopsticks both do the job well.

▲ Expect the nuts to fry quickly, and watch them like a hawk! A single cup of room-temperature peanuts will fry to doneness in about 35 seconds. That's fast!

▲ Remove the nuts promptly from the oil when they are a shade or two *lighter* than desired. They will continue to color from their own internal

heat after draining. To remove the nuts, you can scoop them out in a single sweep with the aid of a heatproof strainer or a Chinese mesh spoon. Or you can set a heatproof strainer over a heatproof bowl and carefully pour the nuts and oil into the strainer.

▲ To cool, crisp, and drain properly, immediately spread the fried nuts in a single layer on a large platter or jelly roll pan lined with a triple thickness of paper towels.

▲ Recycle the nut-frying oil. It is perfect for everyday stir-frying, for deep-frying other foods, for making cold dishes, and making your own peanut butter (page 32). Let the oil cool, strain it through several layers of dry cheesecloth, then store it at cool room temperature or in the refrigerator.

OVEN-DRIED PLUM TOMATOES

MAKES ABOUT 25 PIECES

ood cooks get ideas from other good cooks, and this recipe is no exception. I first had these plush-yet-intense tomatoes in a dish prepared by San Francisco chef Donna Nicoletti, and they have since become a China Moon staple. For giving color and a winning jolt of fresh tomato flavor to a stir-fry, I know of nothing better.

Shop for firm, red Roma tomatoes (also called Italian plum tomatoes) that have a good tomato smell. Count on about 4 hours to dry them to the correct consistency. Once "dried" (wrinkled a bit on the outside but bursting with concentrated juice within), they can be kept in the refrigerator for several days.

Don't pass this recipe by if you're not a fan of sun-dried tomatoes. This is a tomato of a wonderfully different sort!

¾ pound sweet-smelling, firm,
   medium to large Italian plum
   tomatoes

1. Preheat the oven to 250°F. Move a rack to the middle position.

2. Slice off the stem end of the tomatoes, discarding as little of the flesh as possible. Quarter each tomato lengthwise. Cut fat tomatoes into sixths. Put the tomatoes, cut side up and ½ inch apart, on 1 large or 2 small cooling racks. Put the rack(s) on a baking sheet to catch any drips.

3. Put the tomatoes in the oven for 2 hours. Turn the baking sheet front to back midway through the process to ensure even drying.

4. Turn off the heat and let the tomatoes dry in the oven until a bit wrinkled but still very pliable and moist, 1½ to 2 hours longer. If you have any doubt, take them out sooner

BAGUETTES

We use dense and sweet (as opposed to sourdough) baguettes that are 2 feet long and leave them in an open bag at room temperature overnight to dry a bit before slicing; otherwise, the bread is too soft and fresh and sops up the oil.

Don't buy a squishy supermarket bread for croutons, even if it calls itself a baguette. You'll need a firm bread with body.

THE SERRATED BREAD KNIFE

A serrated bread knife is a must-have for crouton-lovers; don't buy a wimpy one. What you want is a straight blade a full 8 to 10 inches long, with a handle you can wrap your mitt around.

rather than later. You want them to "pop" in your mouth with a moist tomato flavor.

5. If not using immediately, let cool to room temperature on the rack(s). The tomatoes can be refrigerated for 2 to 3 days, lined up in a single layer on a plate and sealed with plastic wrap. Let come to room temperature before using.

GARLIC CROUTONS

MAKES ABOUT 90 CROUTONS

When I was a kid, a crouton was a little square of seasoned toast that my mother would buy in a bag and toss in salads when company came. As a grown-up, I discovered European-style croutons—thin slices of sturdy bread, brushed with a bit of oil and lightly toasted en route to becoming a landing pad for a smear or strip of something savory.

We use croutons of this second sort, sliced from thin baguettes, both with Strange-Flavor Eggplant (page 62) and as an extra-crunchy note in our House Salad (page 442). I also consume vast amounts of them as shovels for cold springroll filling—one of my favorite midday snacks.

A dense baguette coupled with a good oil makes for a great crouton. Croutons are most flavorful on the day they are toasted; after 2 or 3 days, they taste stale.

1 day-old baguette (about 2 feet long, weighing ½ pound)
Scant ¼ cup corn or peanut oil
1 large clove garlic, smashed

1. With a serrated knife, cut the baguette crosswise into ¼-inch-thick rounds. If you're working a day in advance, leave them in a covered bowl at room temperature; in spite of the cover, they'll firm up. Or, if you're wanting to bake them in several hours, spread them on a rack to dry a little.

2. Combine the oil and garlic. Let stand 30 to 45 minutes to infuse the oil, then discard the garlic.

3. Preheat the oven to 350°F. Move a rack to the middle position.

4. Arrange the bread rounds side by side on a baking sheet. Brush the tops lightly with the infused oil. Bake until light gold, 8 to 10 minutes, turning the baking sheet midway for even coloring.

5. Let the croutons cool on the baking sheet. For best flavor, use shortly after toasting. Store leftovers in an airtight container at room temperature and use within 1 to 2 days.

GINGER-LEMON ICED TEA

MAKES 1 GALLON

It was a hellishly hot day in Los Angeles when I stopped into CITY restaurant to visit my friends who own it, the wonderful and eccentric chefs Mary Sue Milliken and Susan Feniger. Everything about them and their restaurant is unique and appealing, including the iced tea they served to revive me.

We recreated the recipe the next week at China Moon, and it's a house favorite that has a steady, addicted following. It is spicy and herbal in the most compelling way, with a last-minute hit of sweetness that comes as a big surprise. Lots of verbiage for a glass of iced tea? Try it and see.

3 medium lemons
1 gallon cold water
4 ounces peeled fresh ginger,
   sliced paper thin

¾ cup honey
Mint sprigs, for garnish

1. Scrub the lemons thoroughly under warm running water with a light liquid soap and an abrasive scrubber until squeaky clean. Slice in half crosswise.

OTHER CHINESE-STYLE ICED TEAS

On a daily basis at China Moon, we also offer jasmine iced tea and peach iced tea, the first being a green and the latter being a black tea blend. One of our waiters, Chinese-Vietnamese performance artist Paul Kwan, also makes a blend of baby chrysanthemums, lichee, black, and peach teas that is delicious hot as well as iced. On a traditional note, we'll also make an iced tea with baby chrysanthemums, at least in partial homage to some of my favorite southern Chinese poets who cooled themselves off in centuries past with this brew.

All of our iced-tea making follows the same rules: Start with a stainless steel pot and highly fragrant ("fresh") tea leaves, about ⅓ cup per gallon of cold water.

Bring the cold water (ideally purified) to a rolling boil, then turn off the heat (moving the pot to a cold burner if your stove is electric), add the tea, and cover the pot. Let the mixture steep undisturbed for a full half hour. Strain through an impeccably clean sieve into an impeccably clean glass container.

The resulting tea will be strong and clear. Iced, it should be just right in strength. Stirring a bit of honey into the just-strained hot tea can be intriguing, especially if you experiment with herbal honeys such as lavender and thyme, but we generally prefer ours unsweetened for the sake of the tea flavor itself.

2. Add the water and ginger slices to a heavy non-aluminum pot. Holding each lemon half over the pot, extract as much juice and pulp as possible by vigorously twisting with a fork. Drop the pulped lemon halves into the pot. Bring to a boil over moderate heat, then immediately remove from the heat, cover, and let steep undisturbed for 30 minutes.

3. Strain the tea through a fine-mesh strainer, and while it is still hot, stir in the honey. Let cool to room temperature, then chill in the refrigerator.

4. Serve over ice and garnish with mint sprigs, or top with boiling water for a hot drink.

ZESTY BABY BEANS • CRUNCHY PICKLES •

FAVORITE FINGER FOODS

HUNAN EGGPLANT CAVIAR

FAVORITE FINGER FOODS

HUNAN EGGPLANT CAVIAR

NUTS, PICKLES AND NIBBLES

• CRUNCHY PICKLES • ZESTY BABY BEANS •

CONTENTS

Nuts and pickles are the cheerful accessories of the world of good eating, at least as defined by me! As a kid, I was enraptured by them: bowls of peanuts that staved off kiddie hungers at my grandparents, fat dill pickles that we fished out of the wooden deli barrel, the olives and celery stalks that came iced to the table at our local diner. More than any memories of main-course foods, I savor the remembrance of these pre-liminary nibbles.

I was thus happily programmed for the customs at Chinese tables when I encountered them in my 20s. A northern Chinese meal in a Peking mode (as translated to the Taipei tables where I had my culinary upbringing) meant a trio of tiny nibbles to begin—typically a plate of lightly oiled cold wheat noodles wearing a dash of minced scallion, a saucer of boiled peanuts splashed with a little soy, and a counterpoint dish of pickled Napa cabbage with a pleasant jolt of chili. These were the appetite-arousers, the nibbles that the French call "throat-ticklers" and the Chinese call "mouth-openers."

What the Pekinese loved, the Hunanese elevated to an art form. Their meals would begin with no fewer than four to six of these so-called "little dishes." James and Lucy Lo, who became adopted family and kitchen mentors when I returned to Princeton from Taiwan, weighted their refriger-ator with these little gems. There were apricots stewed with purple basil, tiny cubes of tofu steeped in anise-flavored soy, silken cucumber slivers spotted with garlic, crispy nori dipped in sugar. It was a blissful playground for a begin-ning cook.

In the China Moon kitchen, these savory opening salvos are the happiest part of my work. I love making them almost as

Everyone remembers the agony of going to someone's home—never mind, someone's restaurant!—and waiting endlessly to be fed. The stomach gurgles and the eyes roll. One feels deprived of more than just food.

This chapter is filled with helpmates to get you through the opening crunch of early dinner guests or friends who arrive with starvation written on their faces! A little bowl of nuts or pickles already put out within reach are great appetite-appeasers. In the Chinese fashion, they are also appetite-arousers.

Beginning tastes at a Chinese meal always include salty, sweet, and piquant. These are flavors that enliven the tongue. Intriguing textures are also important. Hence, a spread of spicy eggplant on crispy, garlic-tinged croutons—our opening "hello" to our hungry dinner guests—while not authentically Chinese, is nonetheless in a very traditional mode. The flavors of chili and garlic tantalize the palate and pique the appetite for what lies ahead.

much as I love eating them! We usually have at least half a dozen pickled vegetables on any week's menu. Not merely garnishes, they are integral parts of the sensory experience of a dish. A baked bun stuffed with chicken and oyster sauce, for example, would be too rich without a bit of spicy pickled cabbage to nibble alongside. Similarly, thin slivers of wok-seared beef require the complementary tastes and colors of pickled carrots and gingered red cabbage to show off their flavor. In the world of Chinese cooking, this is the necessary yin and yang—those counterpoints of taste, color, and texture that make a meal sing.

■ ■ ■

SPICY ORANGE PECANS

MAKES 2 CUPS

A variation on a Hunanese sweetmeat that was a favorite recipe in my first cookbook, this has become an equally popular predinner treat at China Moon. The combination of rich pecans, fresh orange zest, and sugar zapped with a bit of salt is wonderful.

Soaking and drying the nuts alters them intriguingly. The soaking purges the bitter oils and brings out a striking richness. The drying leaves the nuts chewy. This step may be done as much as a week ahead of time. You can also caramelize the nuts in advance, but I like to do it just as the guests arrive. The warm pecans mate perfectly with a glass of cool Champagne or white wine.

If you are not a fan of spicy foods but have made it this far into the introduction anyway, simply use corn or peanut oil in place of the seasoned chili oil. The pecans will be delicious!

2 cups plump, perfect pecan
   halves
1 orange
¾ teaspoon kosher
   salt

2 tablespoons plus ½ teaspoon
   sugar
Several twists freshly ground
   black or white pepper
2 teaspoons China Moon Chili-
   Orange Oil (page 15)

1. Place the nuts in a large bowl and cover with boiling water. Let stand 30 minutes, then drain. Flush with cold water, then drain again. To blot off excess moisture, roll the nuts in a colored kitchen towel or in a thick wad of paper towels. (The nuts will stain a white towel.)

2. Preheat the oven to 300°F. Move a rack to the middle position.

3. Spread the nuts on a baking sheet and dry in the oven for 30 minutes. Turn the tray and stir the nuts, moving the ones on the outside to the center. Return the nuts to the oven and reduce the temperature to 250°F. Check every 10 minutes and remove the nuts when they are 95 percent dry. Break one open; it should have a kernel of moistness at the core. If you are not proceeding immediately to caramelize them, let the nuts cool entirely, then seal airtight against moisture.

4. While the nuts dry, wash the orange in warm water with an abrasive scrubber and a dash of liquid soap. When squeaky clean, rinse thoroughly and wipe dry.

5. Combine the salt, sugar, and pepper in a small bowl. Using the small flat holes or small S-shaped figures on a grater, lightly grate the orange peel directly onto the sugar mixture. Do not grate any of the bitter white pith. Stir the mixture to incorporate the orange. If you are working in advance, seal the sugar airtight until you caramelize the pecans.

6. To finish the pecans, heat a wok or medium-size heavy skillet over high heat until a bead of water evaporates on contact. Add the oil, swirl to glaze the pan, then reduce the heat to moderate. Add the nuts and toss (or stir) to glaze. When the nuts are very hot to the touch, sprinkle them evenly with a teaspoon of the sugar mixture and toss to coat. Continue tossing until the sugar melts, then sprinkle on a second teaspoon of the sugar mixture and toss again. Adjust the heat so the sugar melts quickly without scorching. Continue in this fashion, sprinkling the sugar and tossing the nuts, until the sugar is used up and the nuts are wearing a clear shell of caramel. The whole process will take about 4 minutes.

FLIP TIP

Flipping the nuts in the pan while caramelizing them is a trick I learned in the restaurant. It prevents the sugar mixture from caramelizing onto a spoon. If you are a new or hesitant flipper, practice with a damp sponge. It's really very easy and lots of fun. Or, if flipping is beyond you, simply stir the nuts with wooden chopsticks. There's less surface area for the sugar to adhere to on chopsticks than on a spoon.

7. Serve the nuts warm or at room temperature. Resist handling them hot from the pan because the sugar will burn your fingers.

BARTON'S PEPPERED PECANS

MAKES 1 CUP

This is one of those nutty munchies, like nuts tossed with cayenne pepper, that keeps your tongue racing to eat more fired by the mistaken idea that it will cool it down! This recipe from Barton Levenson, one of the most unique cooks I know, is for pepper lovers only.

As in any pepper-centered dish, take heed to the peppercorns you choose. They come in different varieties and flavors, just like coffee. A mix of Malabar, Tellicherry, and Lampong black peppercorns is a China Moon house favorite. (If you do not have a local dealer for fine pepper, write to ours: Freed, Teller, & Freed at 1326 Polk Street, San Francisco, CA 94109; phone (415) 673-0922. They also blend our teas and coffee.)

¼ cup sugar
1 tablespoon kosher salt

2 tablespoons coarsely ground
    black pepper
1 cup pecans

1. Combine the sugar, salt, and pepper.
2. Heat a very heavy skillet, preferably cast iron, over high heat until hot enough to evaporate a bead of water on contact. Add the pecans and toss for 1 minute to bring the nut oil to the surface.
3. Sprinkle the nuts with half of the spice mixture and shake the pan vigorously until the sugar melts, about 1 minute. Add the remaining mixture and continue shaking the pan until the sugar melts again and coats the pecans.
4. Immediately turn the nuts out onto a baking sheet. When they are cool enough to handle, separate the nuts with

PLUMP PECANS

Pecans need to be plump to be tasty. They should also smell rich and good. A shriveled pecan or one that smells soapy is not worth using here. Shop for top-quality pecans in a natural foods store or specialty nut shop; supermarket pecans are rarely very good. Also shop for perfectly shaped nuts. The Chinese liken them to butterflies, which are a symbol of good fortune.

your fingers. Let cool completely before storing in a tightly sealed, impeccably clean glass jar.

MENU SUGGESTIONS: Something lemony would follow well on the heels of these pecans, for example Stir-Fried Shrimp with Fennel and Noodles (page 214).

CHINESE CRACKERJACKS

MAKES 2 CUPS

A great snack, this has everything but a prize. The textures are terrific, and the flavors are a tongue-provoking blend. The recipe comes from Barton Levenson, an unsung hero among Berkeley's women chefs and a real Svengali of flavors.

A spice grinder is a must, unless you have a mortar and pestle and a lot of muscle. Or, you might use your coffee grinder, but only after cleaning it thoroughly.

½ cup sugar
1 tablespoon kosher salt
1 tablespoon freshly ground
　black pepper
¼ teaspoon freshly ground
　cinnamon
1½ whole star anise, broken
　into 12 points

6 whole cloves
2 teaspoons Szechwan
　peppercorns
1½ teaspoons whole Java
　peppercorns (optional)
2 cups mixed hazelnuts and
　peanuts, toasted and skinned

1. Blend the sugar, salt, ground pepper, and cinnamon in a small bowl.

2. Finely grind the anise, cloves, and the peppercorns in a spice grinder. Strain through a fine-mesh sieve to eliminate the husks, then combine with the sugar mixture.

3. Heat a large heavy skillet, preferably cast iron, or a wok over high heat until hot enough to evaporate a bead of water on contact. Add the nuts and toss until the nuts are hot to the touch and the nut oil has come to the surface, about 1 minute; reduce the heat if needed to prevent scorching.

4. Sprinkle the nuts with half the seasoning mixture, then shake the pan vigorously until the sugar melts and turns a dark caramelized brown, about 1 minute. Add the remaining seasoning mixture and continue shaking the pan until the sugar melts again and coats the nuts. (Do not use a spatula or spoon for this process because the sugar will caramelize onto it instead of the nuts.)

5. Immediately turn the nuts onto a foil-lined baking sheet. Use your fingers to separate the nuts when cool enough to handle, then let them cool completely. Store in a tightly sealed, impeccably clean glass jar.

SWEET AND TANGY RED ONION PICKLE

MAKES ABOUT 3 CUPS

This recipe was inspired by Judy Rogers, now the chef at San Francisco's Zuni Cafe. Spiced with Szechwan peppercorns, rice vinegar, and garlic (instead of the more Western pickling seasonings Judy uses), these crunchy and spicy pink onion rings are a visual knockout.

I look for onions that are smallish and very round, with a thin dry skin. These yield rings that slice cleanly and are pleasantly thick, but are still small and thin enough to be twisted into attractive piles. Onion pickle lasts for a week or more if kept in the refrigerator.

1 pound small or medium-size firm red onions, round or torpedo shape (not flat)
¾ cup plus 1 tablespoon unseasoned Japanese rice vinegar
6 to 7 tablespoons sugar

Scant ¼ teaspoon dried red chili flakes
¼ teaspoon Szechwan peppercorns
3 large cloves garlic, lightly smashed and peeled

COOK'S QUERY

///

Well-behaved red onions turn fabulously hot pink in the steaming pickling liquids, while not so well-behaved batches turn anemically white. If anyone can tell me how to know one from the other when buying them, I will reward them with a dinner at China Moon!

1. Remove the ends of the onions, peel, then cut into even rings ⅜ inch thick. Carefully separate the outer rings, removing the white membrane if loose. Central clusters may be left intact for a nice mouthful.

2. Combine the remaining ingredients in a non-aluminum, heavy 2½- to 3-quart saucepan. Bring to a simmer over moderate heat, stirring to dissolve the sugar, then simmer 3 minutes to infuse. Taste and adjust with a dash more sugar or chili if desired.

3. Add the onions, reduce the heat to low, and toss with chopsticks or the handle ends of wooden spoons until the onions turn pink and soften and the liquid simmers, 3 to 4 minutes. Scrape the mixture into a shallow bowl. Refrigerate, uncovered, until cool, stirring occasionally. When cool, seal airtight. The onions will keep for 1 to 2 weeks if refrigerated.

4. Serve chilled or as a garnish, twisted into figure-eights. Remove the garlic and peppercorns and garnish with a bit of the juice.

MENU SUGGESTIONS: As part of a cold pickle plate, try teaming the onions with Barton's Peppered Pecans (page 45) and Ma-La Cucumber Fans (below). On their own, they have a particular affinity with orange-zested dishes, such as Chili-Orange Cold Noodles (page 396).

MA-LA CUCUMBER FANS

SERVES 6 TO 8 AS A NIBBLE

M a means numbing, as in Szechwan peppercorns; "la" means spicy, as in hot peppers. The combination is a classic one in central Chinese cooking, where these crispy cucumber pickles claim their origin.

Slender, seedless Japanese cucumbers are ideal for their sweet taste and solid texture. Kirby pickling cucumbers or slender hydroponic or English cucumbers (scooped of their seeds if large) are good second choices.

1 pound firm Japanese or Kirby
   cucumbers
2 teaspoons kosher salt

AROMATICS:
1½ teaspoons finely julienned
   fresh ginger
1 tablespoon finely minced
   garlic
Scant ½ teaspoon dried red chili
   flakes
½ teaspoon Szechwan
   peppercorns

SAUCE:
1 teaspoon soy sauce
2 tablespoons unseasoned
   Japanese rice vinegar
3 tablespoons sugar

1 scant tablespoon corn or
   peanut oil
Several drops of Japanese
   sesame oil

VEGETABLE FANS

One of the great tricks of a Chinese kitchen is to use simple wooden chopsticks to cut a vegetable into a fan shape. Simply set the chopsticks in a V-shape on a cutting board and pin the vegetable (cucumber segment, carrot, zucchini, etc.) inside the point of the V. With a thin-bladed paring knife or cleaver, cut the vegetable crosswise at close intervals. The chopsticks prevent the knife from cutting all the way through the vegetable, leaving the cook with a pretty fan.

1. Remove the ends from the cucumbers and cut into 2-inch lengths. Grasping a segment at a time, cut the cucumber crosswise at ⅛-inch intervals into a fan (see Vegetable Fans, this page).

2. Toss the cucumber fans with the salt and set aside for 30 minutes. (They will soften and a pool of liquid will appear in the bottom of the bowl.) Drain, rinse with cool water, then squeeze the cukes gently to remove excess water.

3. Combine the aromatics in a small dish. Combine the sauce ingredients in a small bowl.

4. Heat a wok or medium-size heavy skillet over moderate heat until hot enough to slowly sizzle a bead of water. Add the corn and sesame oils, swirl to glaze the bottom, and reduce the heat to low. When the oil is hot enough to sizzle a bit of minced garlic, add the aromatics. Stir until fully fragrant, about 10 seconds, adjusting the heat so the mixture foams without browning. (Judge with your nose whether to add another pinch of chili; the smell should be zesty enough to make you rear back.)

5. Add the cucumbers, toss to combine, then add the sauce. Toss gently to blend and dissolve the sugar. Taste and adjust with more sugar if required to bring out the fullness of the chili. Stir until the liquid steams, then remove from the heat.

6. Layer the cucumbers, fan side down, in a shallow bowl, and scrape the liquids on top. For best flavor, let cool, then seal and refrigerate overnight. Serve slightly chilled.

MENU SUGGESTIONS: These fans are a pretty addition to

most any cold plate featuring noodles or cured or smoked meats. They are also nice when fanned and mounded in a small bowl at the beginning of a meal.

LONI'S CUCUMBER PICKLES WITH CHINESE BLACK BEANS

SERVES 8 TO 10

L oni Kuhn is one of the great people in San Francisco's cooking world. Warm, generous, and a naturally fine cook, she has gifted me for years with jars of pickles and preserves. Last year's Christmas bounty included the cousin to this crisp and zesty cucumber pickle accented with the dusky flavor of fermented black beans. Very easy to make and requiring no canning skills, it's a short-cut pickle that has become a China Moon favorite.

Like most all of our pickles, this one is best made a day ahead of serving to give the flavors a chance to develop. Once made, it will hold well in the refrigerator for a week or so.

If you do not have access to fresh water chestnuts, jicama makes a good substitute. I never use canned water chestnuts, but if you are enamored of them, first slice, then blanch them in unsalted water for 10 to 15 seconds to rid them of any tinny taste.

The way to get the best flavor from Chinese dried black mushrooms is to soak them overnight in cool water. Warm to hot water may be used if you are pressed for time.

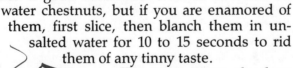

½ cup dried black Chinese
  mushrooms
1½ pounds English cucumbers,
  cut lengthwise in half,
  seeded, then cut crosswise
  into ½-inch moons
1 tablespoon kosher salt

AROMATICS:
1½ teaspoons finely minced
  garlic
1 tablespoon finely minced fresh
  ginger
¾ teaspoon dried red chili flakes

SAUCE:
2 tablespoons packed brown
  sugar
2½ tablespoons balsamic
  vinegar
1 tablespoon soy sauce

2 tablespoons corn or peanut oil
1 tablespoon Japanese sesame oil
1½ teaspoons Szechwan
  peppercorns
6 to 8 fresh water chestnuts, cut
  into thin half-moons
2 teaspoons Chinese black beans
  (do not rinse them)
1 small Fresno chili, cut into
  thin rings

SZECHWAN PEPPERCORNS

Some people, and I'm one of them, like the texture and flavor of whole Szechwan peppercorns in this dish. If you're more of a purist, fish them out once the oil has infused.

1. Cover the mushrooms with cool water. Soak until supple, about 1 hour. Or, for best flavor, soak overnight. Drain, rinse with cool water to dislodge any grit, then squeeze gently to remove excess water. Snip off the stems and cut the caps into quarters or sixths.

2. While the mushrooms soak, toss the cucumbers with the salt. Let stand 1 hour, then drain. Rinse with cool water; drain again.

3. Combine the aromatics in a small dish.

4. Combine the sauce ingredients in a bowl, leaving the spoon in the bowl.

5. Heat a wok or large heavy skillet over moderate heat until a bead of water evaporates on contact. Add the corn oil and sesame oil, and swirl to glaze the pan. Add the Szechwan peppercorns and let infuse for 30 seconds, adjusting the heat so they bubble without blackening. Add the aromatics and stir gently until fully fragrant, about 20 seconds. Add the water chestnuts, mushrooms, black beans, and chili rings, and toss to combine. Add the cucumbers and toss until hot, about 30 seconds. Stir the sauce and add it to the pan. Raise the heat and bring the mixture to a simmer, stirring.

6. Scrape the mixture into a shallow non-aluminum dish and let cool, stirring occasionally to redistribute the sauce. For best flavor, seal and refrigerate overnight before serving. Serve slightly chilled.

MENU SUGGESTIONS: Something about the combination of black beans and balsamic vinegar makes this pickle a good match for red meat. Try it alongside any pork or beef stir-fry, or on an antipasto plate with any of our cured meats.

PEKING SPICY CABBAGE PICKLE

MAKES 3 CUPS

This is our version of a northern Chinese classic, a cold and crisp pickle of lightly sweet and sour Napa cabbage. It is a distant cousin to Korean *kim-chee*, although that is like comparing a fresh-faced young girl to a feisty old crone. This pickle will be tasty just after making, great one day later, and will increase and hold in flavor for up to a week if refrigerated.

1 small Napa cabbage (1½
   pounds)
1 tablespoon kosher salt

AROMATICS:
1 tablespoon plus 1 teaspoon
   finely minced fresh ginger
½ teaspoon dried red chili flakes
½ teaspoon Szechwan
   peppercorns

2 tablespoons corn or peanut oil
Several drops Japanese sesame
   oil

SAUCE:
1 tablespoon soy sauce
1 tablespoon cider vinegar
4 to 6 tablespoons sugar

1. Cut across the base of the cabbage so that the outer circle of 4 to 6 leaves falls free. Continue until you reach the heart. Stack the leaves and cut them crosswise into strips ¾ inch wide. Cut the base pieces into thin wedges as you would a pie. Put the cabbage in a large bowl, add the salt, and toss well. Let sit for 6 hours at room temperature, or overnight, covered, in the refrigerator. Toss occasionally to redistribute the salt.

2. Drain the cabbage and rinse briefly with cold water.

Gently press the cabbage between your palms, shaking off any excess liquid.

3. Combine the aromatics in a small dish.

4. Combine the sauce ingredients in a bowl, leaving the spoon in the bowl.

5. Heat a wok or large heavy skillet over high heat until hot. Add the oils, reduce the heat to moderate, and swirl to coat the pan. When the oils are hot enough to gently sizzle a pepper flake, add the aromatics to the pan. Stir gently until fragrant, about 15 seconds, adjusting the heat so they foam without browning. Add the cabbage to the pan and toss to combine and heat the cabbage through. Stir the sauce ingredients and add them to the pan. Toss until the cabbage is well coated and the liquid thoroughly hot, about 1 minute. (The sugar will pull the juices from the cabbage and the liquid will continue to increase somewhat, even as the cabbage cools.) Remove the pan from the heat. Taste the liquid for desired sweetness and hotness and add a dash more chili or sugar if needed.

6. Remove the mixture to a glass or non-aluminum bowl to cool, gently pressing the cabbage under the liquid. For fullest flavor, cool to room temperature, stirring occasionally, then refrigerate. Serve slightly chilled or at room temperature. Store in the refrigerator, sealed airtight.

MENU SUGGESTIONS: Cabbage pickle is excellent with a wide variety of meat, poultry, and vegetable dishes. If you are looking to team pickles together, this one contrasts wonderfully with the color and flavor of Orange-Pickled Carrot Coins (page 58).

GINGER-PICKLED DAIKON

MAKES ABOUT 2½ CUPS

Daikon is the Japanese name, best known in American markets, for what the Chinese call *bai-law-baw*— a long white tuber that has the crispness and slight sharpness of a radish. Peeled with a vegetable peeler and

---

SALT FOR PICKLING

While I go on and on about the merits of kosher salt in my style of cooking in general, in pickling it is an imperative. Only kosher salt has the light, clean, mild flavor that imparts a good taste to the final pickles. Were you to use table salt, they'd taste acrid. With sea salt, they'd taste too salty.

This is particularly true when salting the vegetable is the first step in pickling. It is an interesting phenomenon: The salt simultaneously leaches the water from the vegetable cells, leaving them open to soak up the other flavors, and at the same time stiffens the cell walls to yield a crunchy pickle. Done with kosher salt, it is magic. Done with either table or sea salt, the flavor is ghastly.

sliced crosswise into thin rounds, it is a great vehicle for stir-frying or quick pickling.

This easy-to-do pickle blends the flavor of daikon with ginger and lemon. It is a pretty addition to a plate; the white discs of daikon turn translucent in pickling and the slices can be pinched into a ribbony mound.

Daikon pickle is best made a half or full day ahead. It keeps nicely refrigerated for up to a week.

1 pound daikon, cut into paper-thin slices
10 paper-thin coins fresh ginger
2 small green serrano chilis, cut into paper-thin rings
2 small red Fresno chilis, cut into paper-thin rings
1 cup unseasoned Japanese rice vinegar

¼ cup plus 2 tablespoons cider vinegar
2 tablespoons distilled white vinegar
¼ cup plus 1 tablespoon sugar
½ teaspoon kosher salt
1 tablespoon very finely julienned lemon zest

1. Cover the daikon with boiling water. Let steep for 1½ minutes, stirring to separate the slices. Drain and immediately plunge the daikon into icy water to stop the cooking; drain well.

2. Combine the remaining ingredients in a non-aluminum pot and bring the mixture to a boil over moderate heat, stirring occasionally. Once the mixture boils, add the daikon and remove from the heat. Let the mixture cool to room temperature, uncovered.

3. Store in the refrigerator, in a clean container, sealed airtight. Serve cold or at room temperature, pinched into a pretty mound, garnished with a ring or two of the red and green pickled chilis.

MENU SUGGESTIONS: Fish and pork dishes are fine complements to the pickled daikon. A flatbread stuffed with brined pork (page 310 and 313) or most any of our salmon or steamed fish dishes come immediately to mind.

VINEGARS FOR PICKLING

There are big flavor differences among brands of vinegars, so it is important to choose what tastes best for pickling. When the major component of a dish is vinegar, what you put in is what you get!

I am a big fan of Heinz vinegars, both the white and apple cider varieties. We do lip-puckering taste tests every once in a while, and the Heinz vinegars always come out ahead of the cheaper brands.

For rice vinegar, I use Marukan unseasoned rice vinegar (the green label) or

Mitsukan as a second choice.
Chinese brands are too
harsh, at least to my tongue.

Experiment a bit. Tast-
ing vinegars may not be quite
as much fun as tasting wine,
but it is very interesting,
nonetheless, and it is a real
challenge to one's palate.

As in all tasting, I look
for discernible and well-
balanced beginning, middle,
and end flavors. A good
product will give you all
three—real flavor dimension,
instead of mere zap.

LEMON-PICKLED LOTUS ROUNDS

MAKES ABOUT 3 CUPS

Fresh lotus root is the stuff of Chinese mythology and modern kitchen dreams! Crunchy, sweet, and possessing the beautiful look of a wheel spoked with dewdrops, it is revered by Chinese Buddhists for its purity of flavor and color in spite of birth in a muddy bog. In American Chinatowns you will see it piled in vegetable bins looking like muscular links of thick sausage. A smooth outer skin and a pure white inner flesh mark the freshest roots. The canned stuff is garbage, to be spurned at all costs.

Lotus pickle is hardy and will keep for up to two weeks. Give it two to three days to come to fullest flavor.

1 to 1¼ pounds fresh, rock-hard
   lotus root, peeled and cut
   into paper-thin rounds
3 cups unseasoned Japanese rice
   vinegar
½ cup sugar
½ teaspoon dried red chili flakes
½ teaspoon kosher salt

⅛ teaspoon freshly ground black
   pepper
1 tablespoon finely julienned
   lemon zest
1 tablespoon finely julienned
   fresh ginger

1. To keep their color, drop the lotus root slices as they are cut into a large non-aluminum bowl filled with water and 1 tablespoon vinegar.

2. Bring a generous amount of water to a boil in a non-aluminum pot, then drain the slices, add them to the boiling water, and blanch until pleasantly crunchy, 8 to 10 minutes, stirring occasionally. Drain promptly and flush with cold water until thoroughly cooled. Drain and set aside. (At this point, the blanched lotus root may be covered with cold water and refrigerated overnight. Drain thoroughly before proceeding.)

3. Combine the remaining ingredients in a non-aluminum saucepan and bring to a simmer over moderate heat, stirring to dissolve the sugar. Simmer 1 minute, remove the pan from the heat, cover, and let stand for 5 minutes.

4. Put the drained lotus root in a non-aluminum bowl or in an impeccably clean, broad-mouthed glass jar. Stir the hot brine and pour it over the lotus root. Let stand until cool, stirring occasionally.

5. For best flavor, seal airtight and refrigerate for 1 to 2 days. Serve cool or at room temperature, pinching the lotus root into a pretty mound accented by the julienned lemon and ginger.

MENU SUGGESTIONS: The lemon flavor of this pickle makes it a happy accompaniment to pork and seafood. If you are partnering pickles, pair these with Turmeric Tomatoes (page 59) or Orange-Pickled Carrot Coins (page 58).

PICKLED RED CHERRY PEPPERS

MAKES ABOUT 4 CUPS

Red cherry peppers are a small sweet pepper about the size and shape of a fat child's thumb. They are wonderful when pickled and make a pretty addition to a plate. Red bell pepper squares could also be pickled in this fashion, and if you are a glutton for fire, you could try small spicy peppers as well.

Best made a day or two ahead to give the flavors a chance to penetrate, this pickle will hold for up to two weeks refrigerated.

1 pound firm, unblemished red
   cherry peppers, stems intact
1½ cups unseasoned Japanese
   rice vinegar
⅔ cup sugar
½ teaspoon cracked black
   peppercorns

3 large cloves garlic, slivered
1 small thin stalk fresh
   lemongrass, cut into finger
   lengths and smashed
2 small green or red serrano
   chilis, cut into paper-thin
   rings (optional)

NON-ALUMINUM REQUIRED!

It is imperative when working with highly acidic ingredients like vinegar that you do not use aluminum-coated pots or implements. There may be a heat-conducting filling of aluminum in between a different metal sandwich, but the direct contact of aluminum and acid is off limits, as it will give you a bitter taste and a black pot. Even with modest amounts of acidic ingredients like ginger and lemongrass, I steadfastly avoid cooking on or with something surfaced with aluminum.

This fact was brought home to me in one of my more dramatic early cooking escapades, when I cooked up a Moroccan stew called "Al

Harumbah" in one of my Grandma Millie's stockpots. I was to take it to an international folk dance pot-luck supper (hence the culinary excursion to the Middle East) and had worked on it for hours. The tomatoes in "Al," as I later came to call the mess, were so foul when cooked in aluminum that I can taste them still, almost 20 years later. Folk dancers' stomachs are notoriously strong, but "Al" would have felled an ox.

1. Rinse the peppers under cold running water and drain.

2. Combine the peppers, vinegar, sugar, peppercorns, garlic, lemongrass, and chili rings in a non-aluminum heavy saucepan. Bring to a simmer over moderate heat, stirring to dissolve the sugar. Remove the pan from the heat, cover, and let stand for 10 to 15 minutes.

3. Transfer the mixture to a bowl and refrigerate, uncovered, until cool. Then, for best flavor, seal airtight and refrigerate a day or more before serving. Serve whole, garnished with a sliver of the pickled garlic or a ring or two of chili.

MENU SUGGESTIONS: These are a great garnish for cold noodle dishes if you're looking for a Chinese mate, or they would be equally happy teamed with a burger or a plate of cold cuts.

GINGER-PICKLED RADISH ROUNDS

MAKES 1 ¾ CUPS

If a bunch of perfect radishes doesn't inspire you to eat them in the raw and you have China Moon Pickled Ginger juice on hand, here is a quick way to a pretty, pickled vegetable. They are ready in an hour, no cooking necessary, and are a great way to garnish a dish of cold noodles or that slice of last night's meat loaf.

Buy the largest, fattest radishes you can find.

2 bunches fat red radishes (1 pound with leafy tops)

About 2 cups juice from China Moon Pickled Ginger (page 8)

1. Rinse and trim the radishes, cutting as much of the top away as needed for the radish interior to be perfectly white.

2. Slice the radishes very thinly into rounds; they should be nearly paper-thin (see Tool Note, this page).

3. Put the radishes in a bowl and cover with the pickled ginger juice. Let stand 1 hour to pickle. Sealed and refrigerated, they may be stored overnight.

4. To serve, drain off the juice. Pinch a tablespoon of the radish rounds between your fingers to form a pretty hill.

MENU SUGGESTIONS: The radishy bite is a perfect complement to Dragon Noodles (page 391), Paris Noodles (page 395), and Peppered Loin of Lamb (page 274).

ORANGE-PICKLED CARROT COINS

MAKES ABOUT 2½ CUPS

Hardly a less threatening vegetable exists for pickling, and hardly a prettier pickle can be made. The orange of the carrots turns a vibrant hue in pickling, and the chili-zested coins can be pinched easily into a mound to give a plate a little dimension. With the flavors of ginger and fresh orange zest in addition, this is new life for an overly familiar vegetable.

For best flavor, make the carrot pickle a day or two in advance. It keeps nicely refrigerated for up to two weeks.

1 pound carrots, trimmed, peeled, and cut slightly on the diagonal into $1/16$-inch-thick coins

2 teaspoons finely julienned fresh ginger

1 red or green serrano chili or 1 small yellow wax chili, sliced into paper-thin rings, or ½ to ¾ teaspoon dried red chili flakes

¾ cup unseasoned Japanese rice vinegar

½ cup cider vinegar

⅓ cup sugar

2½ teaspoons kosher salt

1 small well-scrubbed orange

1. Pour enough boiling water over the carrots to amply cover them. Let stand for 1 minute, stirring to separate the slices. Drain and immediately plunge the carrots into icy water to chill, then drain again.

2. Combine the ginger, chili, vinegars, sugar, and salt in a non-aluminum saucepan and bring to a simmer over moderate heat, stirring to dissolve the salt and sugar. Add the carrots, stirring and pushing the slices down into the brine. Remove from the heat.

3. Lightly grate the zest from the orange into the pan, using the small flat holes of a four-sided grater, and stir to combine. Taste and add a bit more zest if you like, taking care not to grate any of the bitter white pith.

4. Transfer the pickle to a storage container and let stand, uncovered, at room temperature until cool.

5. For fullest flavor, seal and refrigerate overnight. Serve cool or at room temperature, pinching the carrot coins into a jaunty-looking mound topped with several strands of the pickled ginger and a ring or two of pickled chili.

MENU SUGGESTIONS: For its contrast of taste and crunch, this is the perfect pickle to pair with steamed or baked buns. It is equally at home next to a good corned beef sandwich.

TURMERIC TOMATOES

SERVES 8 TO 10

The owners of Los Angeles's CITY restaurant, Mary Sue Milliken and Susan Feniger, are two of my favorite cooks and people, and this recipe hails from their kitchen. Originally slanted in a very Indian direction (Susan being a devotee of that continent and its cuisine), I took it in a China Moon direction with the addition of pickled ginger, black beans, and a bit of house-infused oil.

For fullest flavor, make this pickle at least a half day in advance. The firmness of the tomatoes will dictate the shelf life of the pickle; firm ones will hold for 5 to 6 days. Of course, in choosing, go first for taste. A sweeter, softer tomato is far better than a firmer one lacking in flavor.

2 pounds cherry tomatoes,
    halved through the stem end
    if large
6 fat scallions, cut into
    1-inch nuggets, white
    parts cut lengthwise in
    half

VINEGAR MIXTURE:
½ cup sugar
3 tablespoons salt
¼ cup cider vinegar
¼ cup unseasoned Japanese rice
    vinegar
¼ cup juice from China Moon
    Pickled Ginger (page 8)
½ cup Serrano-Lemongrass
    Vinegar (page 19)
12 to 15 nickel-size coins fresh
    ginger, sliced paper-thin
    against the grain

OIL MIXTURE:
½ cup plus 2 tablespoons Five-
    Flavor Oil (page 13)
1 tablespoon Cayenne Pepper
    Oil (page 11)
1 tablespoon whole Chinese
    black beans (do not rinse
    them)
5 large cloves garlic, peeled and
    halved lengthwise
1 teaspoon kosher salt
1 teaspoon turmeric
¼ teaspoon Roasted Szechwan
    Pepper-Salt (page 5)

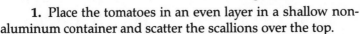

1. Place the tomatoes in an even layer in a shallow non-aluminum container and scatter the scallions over the top.

2. Combine the vinegar mixture in a non-aluminum saucepan. Bring to a gentle simmer over moderate heat, stirring to dissolve the sugar and salt. Remove the pan from the heat and let sit for 15 minutes.

3. Combine the oils, black beans, garlic, and kosher salt in a small heavy saucepan over moderate heat. Bring the mixture to 200°F on a deep-fry thermometer. Remove from the heat and let sit 5 minutes. Add a pinch of turmeric. The oil should be cool enough so it foams gently. Wait a minute more before adding the rest, if need be. Add the pepper-salt.

4. Immediately pour the warm oil mixture into the vinegar mixture and stir to blend. Pour this mixture over the tomatoes and, using a large rubber spatula, gently toss together. Let stand at room temperature. Taste and adjust with a dash more pepper-salt and/or serrano vinegar if necessary.

5. For best flavor, seal and refrigerate 6 to 8 hours or overnight. Serve at room temperature, spooning a bit of the juices over the tomatoes along with some black bean, scallion, and pickled garlic for color and taste.

MENU SUGGESTIONS: We love to serve these pickled tomatoes with fish and shellfish. See what they do to even a dieter's dinner of poached fresh shrimp!

GINGER-PICKLED RED CABBAGE SLAW

MAKES ABOUT 4 CUPS

*S*omewhere between a pickle and a vegetable, this is a stunning, day-glo pink tangle of finely shredded red cabbage. It is also a no-cook dish. The acid in the ginger juice is what "cooks" the slaw.

For best flavor, make this slaw a full day or two in advance. The cabbage will retain its taste and texture for a week or more.

*1 pound head of red cabbage or
half a 2-pound head
1 cup juice from China Moon
Pickled Ginger (page 8)
1 tablespoon finely minced
China Moon Pickled Ginger*

*2 tablespoons plus 1 teaspoon
sugar
1¼ teaspoons coarse kosher salt
Toasted black sesame seeds and/
or thinly cut green and white
scallion rings, for garnish*

1. Discard any limp leaves from the outside of the cabbage. Cut the cabbage into wedge-like fourths and remove the core. Using a mandoline or a Benriner, shred each wedge crosswise into long fine strands.

2. Combine the pickled ginger juice, minced pickled ginger, sugar, and salt in a large, non-aluminum bowl. Add the cabbage and toss well to mix. Set aside for 10 to 20 minutes; toss again.

3. Transfer the mixture to a square or rectangular, non-aluminum container. Press the cabbage lightly to flatten and expose as much of it as possible to the juice. Seal and refrigerate for at least 24 hours. The cabbage keeps nicely for up to a week. Toss several times during the first day and occasionally thereafter to redistribute the juices. As the cabbage "cooks" in the acids, it will turn hot pink.

4. Serve chilled in small mounds as an accompaniment. Garnish with a dusting of the sesame seeds and/or a sprinkling of the scallions.

MENU SUGGESTIONS: We feature this slaw regularly on our antipasto plates. It is especially good with smoked quail, chicken, and duck (pages 160, 155, and 166) and a salad of baby greens. Orange-Pickled Carrot Coins (page 58), if you're up for another pickle, are a sensational color contrast. For an element of tang and surprise, serve the gingered slaw alongside potato salad, or spread it thinly in the top storey of a Western club sandwich.

STRANGE-FLAVOR EGGPLANT

MAKES 2 CUPS

This is an "eggplant caviar" if you will, a spicy-sweet-tart purée of eggplant that beguiles even those who think they hate eggplant. One of the first dishes I ever made, it has become a China Moon hallmark. Served in tiny bowls ringed by crispy garlic croutons, it is the *amuse-gueule* (throat-tickler) we send to all our guests.

Unlike traditional Chinese eggplant dishes, which are steamed or fried, this one is baked. It makes it easy and texturally interesting. I use Western eggplant purposely here for its slightly bitter edge! The sweeter Chinese and Japanese varieties taste wimpy in this dish.

The eggplant is most flavorful when made in ad-

COSMIC CHAOS

In the Chinese language, homonyms written with different characters abound, and the meanings of words can shift and sometimes nearly reverse themselves on the roller-coaster ride through the centuries.

"Strange-flavor" is a great example of a puzzle to chew on: Why would a culture name a dish so oddly? (Some of our reviewers have cited this as a culinary turn-off.) It turns out that in some of the more golden eras of Chinese history, the character for "strange" meant a positive-sounding "elusive" or "ineffable," as in a wonderful combination of flavors that can't be pulled apart. Maybe if I renamed the dish "Elusive Eggplant" the critics would be pleased.

"Fish-Flavor" is another amusing Chinese menu puzzle. The modern characters for these words do, indeed, translate as "fish flavor," inspiring writers on Chinese cooking to propose that the spicy flavors of these mostly pork and chicken

■■

dishes imitate the seasonings used for fish. What? Enter the weighty dictionary of Chinese homonyms. It turns out that these same sounds in ancient Chinese apply to two entirely different characters, which are the old names for Hunan and Szechwan. Suddenly, the spicy dimensions of a mystery sauce make sense: The real meaning is "Szechwan-Hunan" flavor, nothing fishy about it!

"Cosmic chaos" is my favorite pun of all. This is the meaning of won-ton as it appears in the first line of every ancient Chinese cosmology. ("In the beginning, the universe was a won-ton (chaos) inside a thin shell, before the earth separated into the dark and the heaven into the light . . .") Perhaps Confucius slurping his soup at dinner named the dumplings after the theory! Only much later did the phrase reinvent itself in two other modern characters meaning "swallowing clouds." A prettier lyric image, but not the richly ironic one of antiquity.

vance and it can be kept in the refrigerator for up to a week. The croutons are sublime when eaten freshly baked and merely excellent done a day in advance and stored at room temperature with an airtight seal.

1 to 1¼ pounds large Western eggplant

AROMATICS:
1 tablespoon finely minced garlic
1 tablespoon finely minced fresh ginger
¼ cup thinly sliced green and white scallion rings
¼ to ½ teaspoon dried red chili flakes

SAUCE:
3 tablespoons soy sauce
3 tablespoons packed brown sugar
1 teaspoon unseasoned Japanese rice vinegar
1 tablespoon hot water

2 tablespoons corn or peanut oil
½ teaspoon Japanese sesame oil
Garlic Croutons (page 37)
Thinly sliced green and white scallion rings, for garnish

1. Preheat the oven to 475°F. Move the rack to the middle position.

2. Prick the eggplant well in several places with a fork or the tip of a sharp knife and remove the leaves. Bake on a baking sheet, turning once, until fork-tender, 20 to 40 minutes, depending on the size. Remove the eggplant and slit it lengthwise to speed the cooling.

3. While still warm, remove the tough stem end and the peel, scraping off and retrieving any pulp. Cube the pulp, then process the pulp and any thick baking juices in a food processor or blender until nearly smooth. (Eggplant differs enormously in water content. Some will leach nothing when baked, others leach a tasteless water, while some ooze a tasty liquor. It is only the latter that should be used.)

4. Combine the aromatics in a small dish. Combine the sauce ingredients in a small bowl, stirring to dissolve the sugar.

5. Heat a wok or large heavy skillet over high heat until hot enough to evaporate a bead of water on contact. Add the 2 tablespoons corn oil, swirl to glaze the pan, then reduce the heat to moderately high. When hot enough to foam a scallion ring, add the aromatics and stir-fry until fragrant, about 15 seconds, adjusting the heat so they sizzle without scorching. Add the sauce ingredients and stir until simmering. Then add the eggplant, stir well to blend, and heat through. Remove from the heat, then taste and adjust with a dash more chili flakes, brown sugar, or vinegar, if needed to achieve a zesty flavor. Stir in the sesame oil.

6. Allow to cool, stirring occasionally. The flavor is fullest if the eggplant is refrigerated overnight, sealed airtight. Serve at room temperature, spooned onto the croutons and garnished with a sprinkling of scallion.

MENU SUGGESTIONS: A perfect munchie at most any time of the day or evening, this is also a good foil to the flavors of most all of our cold noodles and cold poultry or meat dishes. It would also be wonderfully at home at a Western barbecue.

SZECHWAN-STYLE BABY STRING BEANS WITH MINCED DRIED SHRIMP

SERVES 5 TO 6 AS A NIBBLE, 3 TO 4 AS AN ACCOMPANIMENT TO A COLD SUPPER

O ver the last 10 years, my cooking has evolved in a distinctly lighter direction, this recipe being a foremost example. A take-off on the very delicious, traditional Szechwanese dish of deep-fried string beans with minced pork (see my first cookbook, *The Modern Art of Chinese Cooking*, for the recipe), this is a meatless cold bean salad using the classic condiments. We offer it in little dishes when our customers are first seated and their appetites are keenest, and the crunch of the baby beans makes a big impression.

You may omit the dried shrimp if health or diet demands it, but for the true Szechwanese taste its funky flavor is *de rigueur*.

The "goop" that dresses the beans may be made well in advance. For best color and flavor, blanch and dress the beans just before serving them.

ABOUT STRANGE-FLAVOR

A classic name for a series of Chinese dishes that typically employ a mixture of vinegar, sugar, and chili (and—if you are sitting in central China—also a dollop of peanut butter or sesame paste), this is strange as in "wonderful," "unique," or "ineffable." Weird-flavor eggplant it is not!

A thesis could be written on the evolution of the meaning of the word "gwai" or "strange" in not only Chinese cooking but also in Chinese art and literary criticism. And if I ever break away from the stove, it is something I'd love to do!

PRESERVED CABBAGE

As with many classically inspired Szechwanese recipes, this one features a variety of preserved and dried condiments. Szechwan, while rich in land and water, was mountain-bound, meaning its cooks learned early on how to preserve foodstuffs and exploit their concentrated tastes in cooking.

Preserved cabbage is a salt-cured, leafy Napa-style cabbage that is traditionally sold in brown pottery crocks and sealed with paper lids. The lids are now being made in plastic and the crocks are too, a victory for the FDA but a sadness to those who love things the way they were.

Preserved cabbage does not require rinsing. One need only chop it to expose more of the surface for seasoning. Eaten from the jar or thrown judiciously into a variety of dishes, it is deliciously tangy stuff. Once opened, it should be sealed airtight. Refrigeration is unnecessary; this food was designed to be immortal.

I once opened a jar of preserved cabbage that had crystallized and turned jet black. This intriguing oddity aside, every crock I have opened has been brown, supple, and very pungent.

AROMATICS:
1 tablespoon dried shrimp
1 tablespoon finely minced fresh ginger
1 tablespoon finely minced garlic
¼ cup thinly sliced green and white scallion rings
2 packed tablespoons preserved Chinese cabbage, finely chopped

SAUCE:
¼ cup China Moon Infusion (page 72), Vegetable Infusion (page 82), or unsalted chicken or vegetable stock
2 tablespoons balsamic vinegar
1¼ teaspoons kosher salt
1 tablespoon sugar

3 to 4 tablespoons corn or peanut oil
1 to 1¼ pounds tender green beans, tipped
Thinly sliced green and white scallion rings, for garnish

1. Place the shrimp in a small bowl, cover with warm water, and let stand until slightly softened, 10 to 15 minutes. Drain, discarding any overt bits of shell. Finely chop the shrimp.

2. Combine the minced shrimp with the remaining aromatics in a small dish.

3. Combine the sauce ingredients in a small bowl. Stir to blend, leaving the spoon in the bowl.

4. Heat a wok or small, heavy skillet over high heat until a bead of water evaporates on contact. Add 3 tablespoons of the oil, swirl to glaze the pan, and reduce the heat to moderately low. When the oil is hot enough to foam a scallion ring, add the aromatics. Stir gently until fully cooked and fragrant, about 2 minutes, adjusting the heat so the aromatics foam lazily without browning. Drizzle a bit more oil down the side of the pan, if the mixture seems dry or if needed to prevent sticking.

5. Stir the sauce and add it to the pan. Bring to a simmer, stirring. Simmer until reduced by half, about 1½ minutes. Scrape the sauce into a bowl and let cool to room temperature. Once cool, the sauce may be sealed and refrigerated for up to a week. Let come to room temperature before using.

6. Shortly before serving, blanch the beans in a generous amount of boiling unsalted walter until tender-crisp, 30 seconds to 3 minutes depending on their size. Do not under-blanch the beans; they must be cooked through to be tasty. Drain the beans and immerse them in ice water to chill. Drain thoroughly.

7. To serve, toss the beans with the sauce until thoroughly mixed. Mound the beans prettily on plates of contrasting color, with a sprinkle of scallion on top.

MENU SUGGESTIONS: For a duo of preliminary nibbles, the beans pair excellently with Spicy Orange Pecans (page 43). As a condiment, they are a wonderful partner to many of our cold noodle, meat, and poultry dishes.

MANDARIN BREADTWISTS

MAKES 18 BREADTWISTS

We offer these soft, baked breadtwists to our guests as beginning nibbles. They are also wonderful alongside soup or sandpots, where a bit of fragrant bread is welcome. I doubt there is any traceable precedent for them in Chinese cookbooks. However, I'd wager that some northern Chinese bread maker made something similar at one time, and that they're not merely a product of my lone, bread-loving imagination.

FOR THE SPONGE:
1 tablespoon active dry yeast
1 tablespoon sugar
¼ cup warm (110°F) water
¼ cup plus 2 tablespoons all-purpose flour

3¼ to 3½ cups all-purpose flour
½ cup thinly cut green and white scallion rings
2 teaspoons Roasted Szechwan Pepper-Salt (page 5)

2 tablespoons Ma-La Oil (page 17)
1 tablespoon Chili-Lemon Oil (page 12)
1 cup cold water
1 large egg whisked with 1 large egg yolk, for the egg wash
1 tablespoon white sesame seeds combined with 1 tablespoon black sesame seeds, for garnish

BABY VEGETABLES

Baby vegetables are only worth using if they taste good. If the baby beans in your market are tough or tasteless, choose the best-tasting beans available and cut them into pinky-lengths. Being small without character is not an advantage in either the world of vegetables or people. I am allowed my prejudice on this issue; I am barely 5 feet tall!

1. Make the sponge: In a medium-size bowl, combine the yeast, sugar, and warm water. Stir to dissolve the yeast. Add the flour for the sponge and stir to blend. Seal airtight with plastic wrap and set aside in a warm (70° to 85°F) spot until the mixture begins to rise, 5 to 10 minutes.

2. To complete the dough: Combine 3¼ cups flour, the scallion rings, and pepper-salt in the bowl of an electric mixer fitted with the flat paddle. Stir the oils and water into the sponge, then scrape the sponge into the mixer bowl. Blend on low speed until the dough comes together in a soft mass, 3 to 4 minutes. If the dough is too wet and sticks badly to the paddle, sprinkle in a bit more flour to make it behave. The dough, when properly mixed, will be a bit ragged, not smooth.

3. Remove the dough to a lightly floured board. Add to it any unincorporated bits from the bowl, then knead gently to blend, 8 to 10 times. Don't get aerobic or the dough will become elastic. Pat the dough into a brick, cover with plastic wrap, and let it rest for 10 minutes.

4. Lightly roll the dough into a rectangle 18 inches long, about 6 inches wide, and 1 inch thick. Cover the dough with plastic wrap and let it rest for another 10 minutes.

5. Line 2 baking sheets with baking parchment. Placing a ruler on the long side to guide you, cut the dough crosswise into 18 strips each 1 inch wide. With your palms, roll the first strip into a thin rope 20 inches long. Fold the rope in half to double it, then twist 3 or 4 times to form a breadtwist. Put the breadtwist aside on the prepared baking sheet. Repeat with the remaining dough strips, placing the finished breadtwists 1½ inches apart.

6. Brush the tops and exposed sides of the breadtwists with the egg wash. Sprinkle the tops lightly with the sesame seeds. Put the baking sheets aside in a warm (70° to 85°F) spot until the breadtwists rise to half again their size, 30 to 45 minutes.

7. While the breadtwists are rising, preheat the oven to 400°. Move the racks to divide the oven into even thirds.

8. Bake the breadtwists until lightly golden, 10 to 15 minutes. Midway through baking, rotate the trays front to back and between the racks to ensure even coloring.

9. Serve the breadtwists freshly baked. Or allow to cool to room temperature, then seal and refrigerate overnight. Let come to room temperature before reheating. Reheat in a 350°F oven until hot but not crispy or dry, 4 to 5 minutes.

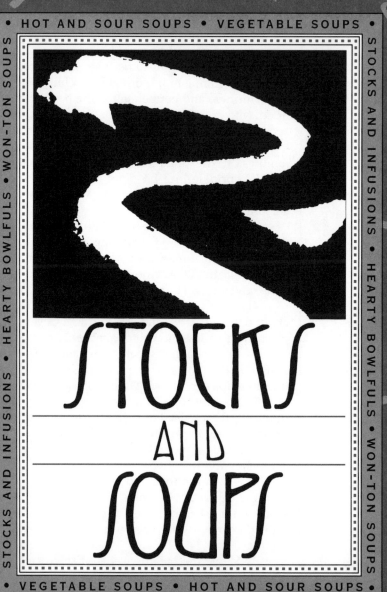

STOCKS
AND
SOUPS

• HOT AND SOUR SOUPS • VEGETABLE SOUPS •
STOCKS AND INFUSIONS
HEARTY BOWLFULS • WON-TON SOUPS
• VEGETABLE SOUPS • HOT AND SOUR SOUPS •
WON-TON SOUPS • HEARTY BOWLFULS
STOCKS AND INFUSIONS

CONTENTS

*S*oups are ancient Chinese stuff. Long before Confucius made pronouncements on liking his meat cut just so and Mencius rhapsodized on the merits of bear's paw, early Chinese man and woman were making soup. One needs only to peer into a museum case of Chinese antiquities to see the soup tureens of old—fabulously decorated cauldrons of bronze with sturdy legs designed to sit in the fire and transmit heat to the brew.

For the most part, these early soups were hearty porridges and soup-like stews. It took centuries of easier living to turn people's appetites to something lighter. By then, Chinese enjoyed a thin soup served almost as a beverage alongside the other courses in a meal. And it is in this form that Chinese continued to sip their soup into modern times—not poised at the beginning of a meal as a separate course, but as a warm punctuation mark to wash the other foods down. In fact, today in most Chinese homes, soups are served last. The idea is to give comfort to the belly while it does its work of digesting the meal.

I confess that these thin, brothy soups of daily Chinese life rarely excite me. It is always pleasurable to sip a hot liquid, but I tend by nature to like soup as a one-bowl meal, and love a full-bodied stock afloat with diverse things. Soups can be thicker or thinner to hold my interest, but the flavors must be full and lively.

This chapter combines a bit of Chinese tradition with a bit of my own tradition. There are takeoffs on some very authentic soups and spin-offs into personal eccentricity. Soup-lovers, I hope, will be delighted.

■ ■ ■

CHINA MOON CHICKEN STOCK (AKA SINGLE STOCK)

MAKES 12 CUPS

*The stock created from the China Moon Chicken Stock recipe has one important variation in our kitchen and that is a doubly rich and tasty version we call "double stock." Made by using half chicken stock and half cold water poured over fresh chicken bones—then skimming, seasoning, and simmering—this second cooking yields the more complex stock we use in most all of our preparations. Each time a recipe here calls for "chicken stock," what we use at China Moon is the extra-flavorful **double** stock.*

For a home cook this means one more step, but the results well justify the time. It is a consommé to the world of cans, a Brooklyn cheer in the face of fast food! And for those who love the alchemy of the kitchen, it is both a simple and intriguing process.

Making stocks in a restaurant kitchen is a near-religious experience. The pots are towering, the vapors waft steamily around their rims, and submerged in the depths is a holy mix of bones and aromatics decreed by the chef on the first day of the restaurant's creation. There are strict rules for their skimming and straining, and novice cooks are often judged on their care in tending them.

The reason for all the sanctity is well taken! A stock is a primary building block, and the sauces and soups put forth in a restaurant are only as good as the stocks from which they began (see Stock Shock, page 79).

In the case of chicken and stock and China Moon Cafe, I was thwarted from the start by a double tribal allegiance. While the ghost of my Jewish Grandma Millie spoke in one ear of the need for onion, carrot, celery, and neck bones—adding that one also needed a few chicken feet thrown in for extra lushness—the ghost of Po-fu, my mentor in Taiwan, spoke with Confucian righteousness of the need for whole chickens cooked with ginger, scallions, and Szechwan peppercorns. What was a filial Jewish-Chinese girl to do but listen to them both? Hence the East-West aromatics in our chicken stock.

In China Moon, we let the stocks simmer overnight. In a home kitchen, a chicken stock will be ready to strain in 3 to 4 hours. Fortunately, homemade chicken stock keeps well. It may be refrigerated for up to 3 days and frozen for about 2 weeks or more.

4 pounds fresh chicken bones
20 cups (5 quarts) cold water
4 quarter-size coins fresh ginger, smashed
2 fat scallions, cut into 1-inch nuggets
2 ribs celery, chopped
1 carrot, peeled and roughly chopped
1 yellow onion, thinly sliced
1 teaspoon black peppercorns
1 teaspoon white peppercorns
1 teaspoon Szechwan peppercorns

1. Rinse the chicken bones under cool running water to dislodge any blood. Put the bones in a non-aluminum, heavy 8-quart stockpot. Add the cold water and set the pot over high heat. Bring the liquid to a near boil. Reduce the heat to maintain a steady simmer and cook for 5 to 10 minutes, until a thick foam rises to the surface.

2. Use a large shallow spoon to skim off and discard the scum. Continue skimming until the surface is mostly clear. Add the ginger, scallions, celery, carrot, onion, and all of the peppercorns, and reduce the heat to maintain a weak simmer. Simmer the stock undisturbed until the liquids are reduced by about half, 3 to 4 hours. Do not stir the stock while simmering and do not let it boil.

3. Strain the finished stock through several layers of wet cheesecloth. Spoon off the fat that rises to the surface. Refrigerate, uncovered, until the remaining fat congeals. Discard the fat, seal the stock, and refrigerate or freeze for later use.

CHINA MOON INFUSION

MAKES 8 CUPS

In the course of looking for ever more flavor in our cooking, we latched onto the habit of infusing our double stocks by simmering them a further time with another layer of aromatics. At first, it was a bit cuckoo and we'd conjure a different infusion for every dish: Roasted duck bones went into an infusion for a hot and sour soup with shredded duck; basil stems and roasted garlic went into an infusion for a garlicky beef and basil stir-fry sauce; pounded ginger and lemongrass were added to infuse a base for a lemony ginger chicken. Pretty soon the stovetop was chockablock with pots and we were awash in infusions!

The fascinating experiment came to a happy end with this recipe for a single infusion that satisfied most all of our dishes. Tinged with the flavors of roasted

TO MAKE DOUBLE STOCK

Add 10 cups cold homemade unsalted chicken stock to the China Moon Chicken Stock recipe *in place of* 10 cups of the water. Or, if you want an even richer result, replace the water entirely with stock. Do not use canned chicken stock. The salt and seasonings in a canned stock can enlarge horrifically in re-cooking— the edible version of a fun-house mirror.

Double stock, like single stock, can be stored in the refrigerator for 2 to 3 days and freezes nicely.

garlic, fresh lemongrass, fresh ginger, and serrano chili, it is also perfumed with the sweetness of onion. There is nothing to replace it in our kitchen, and it is a key element in our cooking.

I have taught infusions to home cooks and the response is overwhelming. I thought it would be too much, this third step in stock-making; but we apparently need some special sustenance and this bowlful provides it.

Infusion is very simple to make, even for a novice. Even without the lemongrass and serrano chili—things that might be hard to get in your neighborhood—the infusion will be delicious. Once strained and cooled, it can be refrigerated or frozen.

CHICKEN STOCK

Two things are imperative to a good chicken stock: That the bones be fresh and the stock be skimmed. The bones should have no smell, and any bloody bits clinging to them should be rinsed off with cold water. If you stockpile bones in your freezer for a future stock, be sure they are fresh at the start, though the tastiest stock will result only from never-frozen fresh bones.

To rid the stock of impurities, cover the bones generously with cold water, then bring slowly to a near boil. Once the surface is skimmed, only then add the aromatics and the vegetables. Push them down into the liquid so they are doused from the start and cook well into the stock.

3 large, rock-hard heads garlic
2 tablespoons corn or peanut oil
1 small onion, thinly sliced
1 small green serrano chili, tipped and cut lengthwise in half
8 quarter-size coins fresh ginger, smashed

12 cups China Moon Double Stock (facing page) or unsalted chicken stock
1 stalk fresh lemongrass, pounded well, then chopped into finger lengths
Kosher salt
Roasted Szechwan Pepper-Salt (page 5)

1. Preheat the oven to 375°F. Move a rack to the middle position.

2. Roast the garlic on a baking sheet until tender, 30 to 40 minutes. A bit of black ooze may bubble from the top; don't worry. Smash the heads to break up the cloves.

3. Add the oil to the bottom of a non-aluminum, heavy 4-quart stockpot and swirl to glaze the bottom of the pot. Heat over low heat until a slice of onion sizzles gently upon contact with the oil. Add the onion slices, chili, ginger, and roasted garlic, stirring to combine. Cover the pot and, keeping the heat very low, sweat the vegetables until the onion turns translucent and the mixture is soupy, 10 to 15 minutes. Stir occasionally to prevent the vegetables from sticking to the bottom of the pot. This sweating step is crucial to the success of the flavors, so don't rush it.

4. Add the chicken stock, raise the heat to moderate, and bring the mixture to a near boil. Adjust the heat to maintain a steady simmer and simmer for 1 hour. Add the lemongrass during the last 15 minutes.

5. Remove the pot from the heat. Let the infusion steep, uncovered and undisturbed, for 1 hour.

6. Strain the infusion through a fine-mesh sieve lined with several layers of dampened cheesecloth. Spoon off any excess oil lingering on the surface.

7. If using immediately, season the infusion with enough kosher salt to bring out the garlic flavor, then end with roasted pepper-salt to taste. For future use, refrigerate the infusion for up to a week or freeze for up to a month. If storing freshly made infusion (like any stock), allow it first to cool, uncovered, in the refrigerator or at cool room temperature before sealing for storage.

DUCK INFUSION WITH SZECHWAN PEPPERCORNS

MAKES 10 CUPS

Dating from the heyday of our infusion experiments, this is a wonderful broth that is deeply colored with the flavors of roasted duck, garlic, and herbal Szechwan peppercorns. It is such a delicious stock that it may be served with nothing more than some softened glass noodles and a sprinkling of scallions, though you can of course embellish it with shreds of duck and vegetables.

If you have never enriched a stock with roasted bones and sweated vegetables, this process will be fascinating. It is also very easy—the kind of thing that can provide a morning's or evening's intrigue while you move about the house attending to other chores.

Once made and left to cool, this infusion can be refrigerated for up to a week or frozen for a month.

While we use fresh duck carcasses and bones, you might also use the leftover bones from a roasted duck. Toss them over heat as called for anyway; the additional roasting will bring out their savor.

VEGETABLE SAUNA

"Sweating vegetables" in a little oil over low heat in a covered pot is, in effect, a vegetable sauna. All of the flavors of the vegetables emerge slowly in a juicy tangle, in a much more intense manner than if you simply added them just-cut to the stock. Like roasting garlic, it is a way to enlarge the natural flavors very dramatically.

1 large, rock-hard head garlic
1 tablespoon corn or peanut oil
3 pounds fresh duck carcasses
and bones
1 medium yellow onion, thinly
sliced
2 carrots, peeled and chopped
1 small green serrano chili,
tipped and cut lengthwise in
half
2 whole scallions, cut into 1-
inch nuggets

16 cups cold China Moon
Double Stock (page 72) or
unsalted chicken stock
½ teaspoon black peppercorns
1 teaspoon Szechwan
peppercorns
1 stalk lemongrass, pounded
well, then chopped into
finger lengths
Kosher salt
Roasted Szechwan Pepper-Salt
(page 5), to taste

1. Preheat the oven to 375°F.

2. Roast the garlic until tender, 30 minutes. A bit of black ooze may bubble from the top; don't worry. Smash the head to break up the cloves.

3. Heat a wok or large heavy skillet over high heat until hot. Add the corn oil and swirl to glaze the pan. When the oil is nearly smoking, add the duck bones in a single layer (this can be done in batches, if necessary). Brown quickly on all sides, turning the bones once or twice. Reduce the heat to moderate and add the onion, carrots, chili, and scallions. Stir the vegetables until the edges start to curl and brown. Adjust the heat so the vegetables color nicely without scorching.

4. Transfer the duck bones and vegetables to a non-aluminum, heavy, 6- to 8-quart stockpot. Add the chicken stock and peppercorns, and bring the liquids to a boil over moderate heat. Immediately reduce the heat to maintain a steady simmer. Simmer the infusion for 1 hour. During the last 15 minutes, add the lemongrass.

5. Strain the infusion through a fine-mesh sieve lined with several layers of dampened cheesecloth. Spoon off any lingering fat.

6. If using immediately, season with enough kosher salt to bring out the garlic flavor, then end with roasted pepper-salt to taste. For future use, refrigerate the infusion for up to a week or freeze for up to a month. If storing freshly made infusion, allow it first to cool, uncovered, in the refrigerator or at cool room temperature before sealing for storage.

MENU SUGGESTIONS: This infusion can be seasoned with kosher salt and Roasted Szechwan Pepper-Salt (page 5) and used as a sauce for fettuccine tossed with duck and greens.

BROWNING BONES AND VEGGIES

A pair of 24-inch woks are our restaurant kitchen mainstay, hence we brown the duck bones and veggies in a wok. You could, of course, brown them as well and more conventionally in a roasting pan on the middle rack of a preheated 400°F oven. The smoke and the fun are confined, but that may suit you better.

MAKING YOUR OWN STOCK

Given our wildly busy modern lives, making one's own stock is not a problem—it's a solution! What cheaper, better, and healthier way to take a brief respite from the wacko affairs of the world and nurture one's self in the privacy of a pot?

Stock-making is a simple process that perfumes the house and enriches a dish far beyond the powers of a can. Cooks that make their own stock once never look back.

Try it. Just once. You'll be hooked.

INFUSION RULES AND TOOLS: Taking simple stock as a basic infusion, the primary rule is to start with the best ingredients. Water is a basic. We use filtered water to make our stocks in the restaurant, and I use filtered water for stock-making at home. As well, the chickens, ducks, vegetables, and spices that go into the pot should be fresh and of the best quality.

A large, heavy pot is your best friend for soup infusions. Bringing the liquids to a boil and then holding the heat at a steady slow simmer, or allowing vegetables to sweat and give up their tasty juices in a covered pot—these

being the essence of stock-making—are most easily achieved if the pot is heavy.

A large, fine-mesh strainer and a wide swath of cotton cheesecloth are handy tools for separating the liquid from the solids. I like to pass the completed infusion through the strainer first, and then let the solids sit in the strainer to drip their juices into the stock. Then I discard the solids, clean the strainer, and line it with a double layer of wet cheesecloth. I pass the stock through the strainer a second time and let the cheesecloth catch the debris. The result is not a clear stock (rarely a Chinese goal), but one with a minimum of solids to cloud it.

STORING STOCKS AND INFUSIONS: I find that most stocks and infusions, with the exception of those that use fish or shellfish, store quite nicely. As a general rule, a freshly made stock or infusion will hold in the refrigerator for about 3 days and can be frozen for about 2 weeks without a noticeable loss of flavor.

A stock or infusion made with fish bones or shrimp shells is more perishable. I hold these for only a day or so

in the refrigerator and do not freeze them.

On the other hand, an infusion made with roasted garlic has great staying power. One more kudo for the world of garlic cookery!

Properly cooling stocks and infusions before storing them in the refrigerator or freezer is a key to their healthfulness. The best route to safety is to strain and defat a stock very shortly after making it and then to refrigerate it until cool in an uncovered container. Taking the fat off the surface of the stock is crucial; it otherwise forms a seal and retains the heat. Chilling the stock uncovered is equally important; unless a stock cools quickly it can sour. If you are working with a thick soup or a tired refrigerator, you might choose to cool the stock rapidly by planting the container in a sink filled with ice and stirring the mixture until it chills.

If you worry that you have held a stock in the refrigerator for too long, smell it. Your nose will tell you if it has soured. Whatever the labor that went into it, throw a stock out if your nose tells you it's funny. It's not worth the risk, no matter what.

PEPPERY DUCK SOUP WITH ROAST DUCK AND SPRING PEAS

SERVES 4 TO 6 IN LARGE BOWLS, 8 TO 9 IN SMALL BOWLS

A duck soup can be very rich, but this one is sum-
mery light. Spiked with basil and fresh peas, it is
an unusually refreshing soup that is very memorable. If fresh peas are unavailable, I would omit them.
Half the fun of using peas, in my opinion, is the pleasure
to be had in the shelling. Fresh peas should taste strikingly sweet. If starchy, they're past their prime.

Preparations are best begun a day ahead, so the
duck grows tasty with marinating. All of the remaining
ingredients may also be prepared in advance, and then
the soup can be put together quickly.

*DUCK MARINADE
AND DUCK:*
1 tablespoon soy sauce
1½ teaspoons Chinese rice wine
  or dry sherry
2 teaspoons Ma-La Oil
  (page 17)
⅛ teaspoon finely minced fresh
  ginger
2 teaspoons chopped fresh
  coriander leaves and stems
¾ pound fresh duck breasts,
  skinned and filleted

½ cup fresh peas
1 tablespoon corn or peanut oil
10 cups Duck Infusion with
  Szechwan Peppercorns
  (page 74)
Kosher salt

*Roasted Szechwan Pepper-Salt
  (page 5)
Infused Glass Noodles (page 30)
¾ cup packed finely slivered
  Napa cabbage
1 inner rib celery, cut into thin
  commas
6 fresh water chestnuts, cut
  into thin half-moons
½ cup finely shredded carrot
2 tablespoons purple or green
  basil, julienned
2 tablespoons finely chopped
  Chinese or Western chives
¼ cup thinly cut green and
  white scallion rings
  Coriander sprigs, for
  garnish

1. Combine the marinade ingredients through the chopped coriander in a small bowl. Scrape over the duck breasts, massaging well into the surface. Seal airtight and marinate at room temperature for 1 to 2 hours or overnight in the refrigerator, turning once or twice for even marination. Bring to room temperature before proceeding.

2. In a small saucepan filled with rapidly boiling un-salted water, blanch the peas until tender-crisp, about 30 seconds. Immediately immerse in icy water to chill; drain.

3. Heat a wok or large heavy skillet over moderately high heat until hot. Add the oil, swirl to glaze the pan, and heat until nearly smoking. Add the duck breasts in a single layer and brown on both sides, turning once or twice, 2 to 3 minutes. Remove from the pan to a rack and let cool to room temperature. Slice the breasts into thin slivers, cutting cross-wise against the grain. The duck should be very rare inside. The hot soup will finish cooking it.

4. In a non-aluminum heavy pot, heat the duck infusion slowly over moderate heat. Season to taste with enough kosher salt to bring out the flavors of the garlic and duck bones. Then finish with a flourish of pepper-salt. The infusion should be well-seasoned to embrace the addition of the unsea-soned vegetables.

5. Portion the duck ribbons, glass noodles, cabbage, celery, water chestnuts, peas, carrot, basil, chives, and scal-lions among heated soup bowls. Ladle the steaming infusion into the bowls, top each bowl with a coriander sprig, and serve the soup immediately.

MENU SUGGESTIONS: This is a light meal-in-a-bowl that, if you wish, needs nothing but a fresh pear to follow. You could embellish the soup, on the other hand, with spring-rolls, Pan-Fried Scallion-Chive Bread (page 382), Many Mushroom Buns (page 374), or simply a toasty baguette.

In a Western setting, you could fol-low it nicely with fettuccine dressed lightly with olive oil and fresh herbs.

CHINA MOON FISH FUMET

MAKES 12 CUPS

This is a Chinese interpretation of a fish stock, known in French as a *fumet*, which I find very delicious. The flavors are light and are refreshed by the ginger and given a bit of sweetness by the wine.

The fish bones must be impeccably odor-free and fresh. They can seem a bit grisly if you've not worked with them before, but never fear. The result is so tasty that it's worth dealing with a skeleton.

Fish fumet is fragile. It holds its flavor only 1 to 2 days if refrigerated and is virtually destroyed if frozen.

STOCK SHOCK

After the San Francisco earthquake of 1989, I learned anew how important were our stocks. The restaurant was largely damage-free, but we were closed for almost five days without power, and then had to clean out our walk-in refrigerator and start totally from scratch. The first day of business, we could use only single stock in our cooking, and the sauces and soups were consequently simple and thin. Only after three days of cooking, enriching the stock each day in the process whereby we create "double stock" and infusion, did our food taste properly lush and complex.

1½ pounds fresh fish bones
   from white, non-oily fish
2 tablespoons corn or peanut oil
2 small yellow onions, thinly
   sliced
2 ribs celery, cut into nuggets
8 quarter-size coins fresh ginger,
   smashed
1 small green serrano chili,
   tipped and cut lengthwise in
   half

12 cups cold water
1 cup plum wine
1 cup Chinese rice wine or dry
   sherry
1½ cups dry white wine
Kosher salt
Roasted Szechwan Pepper-Salt
   (page 5)

1. Under cool running water, rinse the fish bones to dislodge any blood and bloody bits. Use a heavy, thick-bladed cleaver to chop the bones into 6-inch pieces.

2. Add the oil to a non-aluminum, heavy 4-quart stockpot and swirl to glaze the bottom of pot. Heat the oil over low heat until hot enough to sizzle an onion slice upon contact. Add the onions, celery, ginger, and chili, and toss well to mix. Cover the pot and sweat the vegetables until the onions turn translucent and the vegetables are soupy and fragrant, 10 to 15 minutes. (This sweating step is crucial for the depth of flavor of the fumet, so don't rush it.) Stir in the fish bones, replace the cover, and sweat for another 5 minutes.

3. Pour in the cold water along with the plum, rice, and white wines. Bring the liquids to a near boil, then reduce the heat to maintain a steady simmer. Cook, uncovered, for 5 minutes, until a grayish foam rises to the surface. Use a large shallow spoon to skim off and discard the scum. Continue skimming until the fumet is clear.

4. Simmer the fumet undisturbed for 30 minutes. Do not stir it or let the liquid boil.

5. Strain the fumet through a fine-mesh sieve lined with dampened cheesecloth.

6. If you are using immediately, season the fumet with enough kosher salt to bring out the flavors of the vegetables and wine, then end with a flourish of pepper-salt. Or allow to cool uncovered, at room temperature or in the refrigerator, then seal and refrigerate for 1 to 2 days. Season just before using.

MENU SUGGESTIONS: For an interesting accompaniment to most any fish dish, you might try cooking rice or dressing pasta with the fumet, seasoning it first with kosher salt and then Roasted Szechwan Pepper-Salt (page 5). Simpler still, season the fumet to your liking and add slices of poached fish or shellfish and whatever vegetables appeal, adding some thinly sliced chives and Fried Ginger Threads (page 29) as a garnish.

PLUM WINE FUMET WITH FISH BALLS AND GLASS NOODLES

SERVES 6 TO 8 IN LARGE BOWLS,
10 TO 12 IN SMALL BOWLS

A very delicate soup, this has a special refinement. There is nothing showy or spicy about it, just the light and refreshing flavors of fish and ginger and the pleasant crunch of fresh water chestnuts.

For a note on fish paste, see page 360. If the fish paste or the time to make the fish balls is unavailable, you might substitute fresh scallops or prawns (velveted and poached as on page 218), or slivers of any impeccably fresh non-oily fish.

Fish balls, once made, may be held in the refrigerator for 1 to 2 days.

FISH BALLS:
1 pound fish paste
3 tablespoons thinly sliced green
    and white scallion rings
1½ tablespoons slivered fresh
    coriander leaves and stems
¾ teaspoon fresh ginger juice
    (squeezed from finely minced
    fresh ginger)
½ teaspoon kosher salt
1 tablespoon Chinese rice wine
    or dry sherry
4 fresh water chestnuts, cut
    into tiny dice
¼ teaspoon Chinese chili sauce
3 to 4 twists freshly ground
    black pepper

China Moon Fish Fumet
    (page 79)
Kosher salt
Roasted Szechwan Pepper-Salt
    (page 5)

Infused Glass Noodles (page 30)
⅓ cup finely shredded carrot
1 packed cup finely slivered
    Napa cabbage
¼ cup finely chopped Chinese
    or Western chives
½ cup thinly sliced green and
    white scallion rings
Coriander sprigs (figure 1 per
    bowl), for garnish

WINE AS AN INGREDIENT

There are plum wines and plum wines, ranging from cough-syrup sweet to sweetly refined. If you have a choice of brand, go with the label with the least English. We use a Chinese plum wine in a clear squarish bottle that is made in Taiwan and has a gold metal cap topped with a red-stamped plum flower.

With both the plum wine and the rice wine or sherry, first taste what you're using. If you don't like the taste, don't use it!

1. To make the fish balls, combine all of the ingredients through the black pepper in a food processor and process until well blended. Press plastic wrap directly on top of the mixture and chill until firm, several hours or overnight.

2. Fill a wide, deep pot or skillet two-thirds full of water. Bring to a steaming near simmer, then adjust the heat to maintain the temperature. Using a spoon dipped periodically into ice water and with a bit of ice water spread on your palm, form a scant tablespoon of paste into a ball. Slide each ball onto a lightly oiled plate, then slide 6 to 8 balls at a time into the simmering water. Poach for 1 minute after they rise to the surface, 3 to 4 minutes in all. Remove the fish balls and set aside in a single layer to cool. Once cooled, the fish balls may be sealed and refrigerated for 1 to 2 days. Bring to room temperature before adding to the soup.

3. In a non-aluminum pot, bring the fish fumet to a near simmer over moderate heat, then season with enough kosher salt to bring out the flavor of the fumet. Finish with enough pepper-salt to leave a tingle on your lips.

4. Portion the glass noodles, carrot, cabbage, chives, and scallions among the bowls. Depending on the size of the servings, add 4 to 8 fish balls per bowl, nudging them alongside or under the vegetables. Ladle the hot fumet into the bowls and place a sprig of coriander on top. Serve immediately.

MENU SUGGESTIONS: A simple meal would star this soup in tandem with a basket of heated Mandarin Breadtwists (page 66). Or, for a heartier dinner, try this soup followed by something equally clean-tasting, perhaps the Ma-La Steamed Poussin with Roasted Szechwan Pepper-Salt (page 153).

VEGETABLE INFUSION

MAKES 12 CUPS

This is a wonderfully light vegetable stock that has great flavor and a lovely sweetness. For those who wish a non-meat alternative to our other stocks and infusions, it is a gem.

The infusion is a bit delicate and is best used within two days. Lengthy freezing will dull its flavors.

4 large, rock-hard heads garlic
5 to 6 large dried Chinese black
  mushrooms
2 teaspoons corn or peanut oil
2 yellow onions, thinly sliced
4 carrots, thinly sliced
10 quarter-size coins fresh
  ginger, smashed
6 to 8 fat scallions, cut into 1-
  inch nuggets and smashed

2 to 3 small green serrano
  chilis, halved lengthwise and
  smashed
1 tablespoon fragrant black
  peppercorns
1½ tablespoons Szechwan
  peppercorns
12 cups cold water
1 fat stalk fresh lemongrass, cut
  into 2-inch nuggets and
  smashed

SEASONING STOCKS AND INFUSIONS

It is a general rule of good cooking everywhere to season the stock or soup only just before you serve it. The same rule applies to our Chinese-style stocks and all of our soup infusions.

Why? Basically, it is to allow for flexibility and to avoid a concentration of salt. Let's say you refrigerate the stock or infusion, and then don't watch carefully when reheating it and discover it has boiled partly away. If you had seasoned it in advance, your dinner could be ruined. But as it is, you can simply taste the soup (it may be yummy for the reduction, or it may require a bit of water to make it palatable) and then blithely proceed to season it as you wish.

The China Moon style of seasoning stocks and infusions bound for the soup bowl is a 2-part process: The first step is to add kosher salt to the hot mixture until the flavors of the meats and vegetables come to the fore. The liquid should not taste salty! One is simply adding kosher salt to push the other tastes forward. Only then, as a final flourish, add Roasted Szechwan Pepper-Salt (page 5) to taste. This is a salty, *piquant seasoner and a little goes a long way. Were you to have added it in the beginning, you would have added too much. Like lip gloss after the lipstick, it's a last step only, designed to add a little shine.*

More soup seasoning advice: Do the tasting when the liquid is hot, but not yet simmering. If it is too hot, you won't be able to really taste the flavors, and you may burn your tongue besides. Also, taste with a spoon, ideally the porcelain Chinese type with a deep bowl. Cooks who taste with their fingers or a wooden spoon are often tasting what was last on them. Using a deep, clean spoon means that you can swirl the liquid over your tongue and really taste the full flavor range.

Stocks or infusions that are part of sauces should never be seasoned. They are simply one part in a sauce of many components, and whatever seasoning is done, is done to the whole.

1. Preheat the oven to 350°F. Move a rack to the middle position.

2. Roast the garlic heads on a baking sheet, root side down, until very soft, 30 to 40 minutes. Don't worry if a bit of brown bubbles volcano-like from the top. Let the garlic cool until you can touch it, then smash the heads lightly to expose the pulp. It will ooze a bit over the knife or mallet; no matter, just scrape the pulp back onto the cloves.

3. While the garlic is roasting, cover the mushrooms with 1 cup cold water. Weight the caps down with a saucer and let them soak until soft, about 30 minutes. Cut the caps with the stems intact into thick slices. Strain and reserve the soaking liquid.

4. Heat a heavy, non-aluminum stockpot over high heat until hot enough to evaporate a bead of water upon contact. Add the oil, swirl to glaze the bottom of the pan, then reduce the heat to low. Add the garlic, mushrooms, onions, carrots, ginger, scallions, and chilis. Stir to gloss the vegetables with the oil. Cover the pot tightly and let the vegetables sweat until they are very soft and soupy, about 20 minutes. Don't rush the process; the longer they sweat, the better the stock will taste. Lift the lid occasionally to stir the vegetables and ensure against scorching, tilting the lid at an angle so the condensation slides into the pot.

5. Add the peppercorns, water, and reserved mushroom-soaking liquid. Stir to blend, then bring the mixture to a lively simmer over moderate heat. Adjust the heat to maintain a weak simmer and cook, uncovered, for 45 minutes. Add the lemongrass and simmer 15 minutes more.

6. Strain the stock through a large, fine-mesh strainer and let the solids drip their juices into the stock. Discard the solids. For a clearer stock, clean the strainer, line it with a double layer of wet cheesecloth, and strain the liquid again.

MENU SUGGESTIONS: Vegetarians might season this stock to taste with mushroom soy sauce, kosher salt, and Roasted Szechwan Pepper-Salt (page 5) and garnish it with scallion rings and chives. It would be a fine partner to our Vegetarian Springrolls (page 349) or Buddha Buns (page 372), or the soup could be further embellished with glass noodles and Fried Ginger Threads (page 29) and a generous helping of wild mushrooms sliced paper-thin.

WILD SOUP!

SERVES 4 TO 5 IN LARGE BOWLS, 6 TO 8 IN SMALL BOWLS

This is a light soup made distinctive by the flavors of wild rice and wild mushrooms. It is a pretty mix of browns and greens, studded with glimmers of white. If the suggested ingredients are not available, feel free to improvise. It's hard to get too wild with such a simple soup.

½ cup wild rice
Roasted Szechwan Pepper-Salt
    (page 5)
4 cups water or unseasoned
    stock
8 cups China Moon Infusion
    (page 72)
Kosher salt

SOUP TRIMMINGS:
1 small or ½ medium bulb
    fennel, halved lengthwise,
    cored, and sliced crosswise
    paper-thin

2 small inner ribs celery, sliced
    on the diagonal into paper-
    thin commas
5 to 6 fresh shiitake mushroom
    caps, sliced paper-thin
½ cup finely shredded carrot
¼ cup thinly sliced green and
    white scallion rings
1 tablespoon chopped Chinese
    chives
Enoki mushrooms and chive
    blossoms for garnish, if
    available

WILD RICE

Wild rice is, to me, a fascinating ingredient, a bit of primitive nature to put into our bowls. Like most wild things, its flavor differs enormously depending on locale. I favor Mendocino wild rice, grown by the wild food folks on California's northern coast (call (707) 544-WILD). Its flavor is exceptionally light and clean, and the grain plumps nicely.

Depending on mood and recipe, I cook wild rice in water, vegetable or chicken stock, or China Moon Infusion. Choose whatever suits you here.

1. Rinse the wild rice under cool water; drain.

2. Combine the rice, ½ teaspoon pepper-salt, and 4 cups water or unseasoned stock in a saucepan. Bring to a simmer over moderate heat and cook, uncovered, until the rice grains are tender and only half are split, 30 to 40 minutes.

3. Heat the infusion over moderate heat in a non-aluminum pot. Season the infusion with enough kosher salt to bring out the flavor of the garlic and then enough pepper-salt to tingle your tongue. Don't be shy; the trimmings are largely unseasoned and mild.

4. Divide the wild rice, fennel, and celery among heated soup bowls. Ladle the steaming infusion into the bowls and top each with the shiitake slices, shredded carrot, scallion rings, chives, enoki mushrooms, and chive blossoms. Serve immediately.

MENU SUGGESTIONS: If you would like to make a one-dish meal of the soup, simply add cubes or slivers of cooked chicken, beef, or pork. Otherwise, the soup is a wonderful partner to any of our steamed or baked buns, as well as a fine prelude to a simple Western dinner of grilled or roasted meats or poultry.

CLAMS

I adore tiny fresh clams, particularly the so-called Manila clams. Whatever type you favor, be sure their "lips" are tightly sealed and their shells unbroken. If they are yawning in the bin, touch them to see if they quickly clam up. If not, pass them by.

Fresh clams are best stored no more than a day or two in the refrigerator, in a shallow dish with a damp cloth on top to allow them to breathe.

The tiny farmed clams sold in most of our markets hold little sand if any. They don't require soaking with baking soda or a new nail or any such exotic treatment. Simply scrub them for several minutes in a basin of cold water with a stiff brush. Any sand will fall to the bottom of the bowl.

CHINESE-STYLE SUMMER CLAM CHOWDER

SERVES 6 IN LARGE BOWLS, 10 IN SMALL BOWLS

This is a light and spritely soup featuring summer vegetables and chopped clams. It is easily put together and easier still to eat. The fried potatoes add a happy bit of savor, but simple boiled potatoes will taste fine and cut work and calories if you care.

½ cup unsalted chicken stock or water
½ cup Chinese rice wine or dry sherry
1½ pounds small, tightly sealed clams, scrubbed clean and rinsed
1 ear corn, cut into niblets
6 ounces small red potatoes, scrubbed clean and cut into large dice
1 to 2 teaspoons corn or peanut oil
Roasted Szechwan Pepper-Salt (page 5)

1 tablespoon finely chopped fresh coriander leaves and stems (optional but tasty)
8 cups China Moon Infusion (page 72)
Kosher salt
2 ripe plum tomatoes, peeled, seeded, and cut into tiny dice
¼ cup chopped Chinese chives
¼ cup thinly sliced green and white scallion rings
Fried Ginger Threads (page 29), for garnish

1. In a non-aluminum, shallow pan large enough to fit the clams snugly in a single layer, combine the chicken stock or water and rice wine. Bring to a simmer over moderately high heat and immediately add the clams. Cover tightly and bring to a boil, turning the heat to high and shaking the pan vigorously just until the clams open, 60 to 90 seconds. Drain the clams retaining the liquid. Discard any unopened clams (or any that don't easily pry open), then chop the meat coarsely. Strain the liquid to eliminate any sand and reserve ½ cup.

2. In a small saucepan filled with boiling unsalted water, blanch the corn kernels 3 to 5 seconds to set their color. Set aside.

3. Blanch the potato cubes until tender, 2 to 3 minutes. Drain well.

4. Heat a heavy skillet or wok over moderately high heat until hot. Add enough of the oil to thinly glaze the bottom of the pan and heat until nearly smoking. Add the potato cubes, stir gently once or twice, and brown all sides, about 2 minutes. Drain on a paper towel–lined plate. Season to taste with pepper-salt and finely chopped coriander, if desired.

5. To serve, bring the infusion to a near simmer over moderate heat. Add the reserved clam cooking liquid and season to taste with enough kosher salt to bring out the flavors (little to none, depending on the clam liquid) and then enough pepper-salt to tingle your tongue. Portion the chopped clams, potatoes, corn, and tomatoes among heated bowls. Top with the steaming infusion and garnish with the chives, scallions, and ginger threads and more chopped coriander, if desired.

MENU SUGGESTIONS: For light summertime eating, a loaf of hot garlic bread or a basket of hot Mandarin Breadtwists (page 66) is all that is required. For a more substantial meal, I would choose Many Mushroom Buns (page 374).

EGGROLL-CARTWHEEL SOUP

SERVES 3 TO 4 IN LARGE BOWLS, 6 TO 7 IN SMALL BOWLS

CHINESE VOCABULARY NOTE

This very same egg crêpe, rolled with a mild pork forcemeat and steamed (then often deep-fried for added texture), is, in fact, the real Cantonese eggroll. Another beast entirely is the thin springroll of northern and central China (recipes begin page 333).

Both delicious and fun to make, this soup is a takeoff on a recipe of Irene Kuo's in her wonderful book, *The Key to Chinese Cooking*. Done in China Moon style, as opposed to classic Chinese style, this is a more complex-flavored bowlful garnished with a sprinkling of market vegetables. In summer, you might also add fresh corn and/or diced tomato to the bowl. Or in winter, when fresh peas are only a memory, you might instead use blanched spinach.

The cartwheels are easily made 1 to 2 days in advance. Slicing them into pinwheels and putting together the soup is an easy, last-minute business.

PORK FILLING:
1 tablespoon soy sauce
¼ teaspoon kosher salt
1 teaspoon Chinese rice wine or dry sherry
¼ teaspoon freshly ground black pepper
Ma-La Oil (page 17), Five Flavor Oil (page 13), or ½ teaspoon Japanese sesame oil
1 egg, beaten
1 tablespoon chopped Chinese chives
2 tablespoons thinly sliced green and white scallion rings
½ teaspoon finely minced fresh ginger
2 teaspoons cornstarch dissolved in 1½ teaspoons cold stock or water
10 ounces coarsely ground pork butt

EGG CREPES:
2 whole eggs
4 egg yolks
1 tablespoon chopped Chinese chives

SOUP AND TRIMMINGS:
1 cup fresh peas
8 cups China Moon Infusion (page 72)
Kosher salt
Roasted Szechwan Pepper-Salt (page 5)
4 to 6 fresh shiitake mushroom caps, sliced paper-thin
⅓ cup finely shredded carrots
¼ cup finely chopped Chinese chives
½ cup thinly sliced green and white scallion rings

1. Combine the filling ingredients through the cornstarch mixture in a large mixing bowl. Add the pork and stir briskly in one direction until well blended. If working in advance, press a piece of plastic wrap directly on the pork and refrigerate for several hours or overnight. Bring to room temperature before making the crêpes.

2. To make the egg crêpes, whisk the eggs, yolks, and chives in a mixing bowl. Heat a 12-inch nonstick skillet over moderate heat until hot enough to evaporate a bead of water. Add ⅓ cup of the egg mixture and quickly rotate the skillet to cover the bottom with a thin film of egg. Adjust the heat so the egg congeals quickly but doesn't brown, 30 to 45 seconds. Loosen the crêpe with a spatula and slide it gently onto a clean, dry surface. Repeat the process with the remaining egg mixture. You will get 3 crêpes and you need only 2; take the worst-looking one and eat it as a prize.

3. To make the cartwheels, gently spread half of the pork mixture evenly over each of the 2 cool crêpes, leaving a ⅛-inch hem at the edge. Carefully roll each crêpe into a log, not too tight or it will split when steamed. Put the logs, with an inch between them, on a heatproof plate at least 1 inch smaller in diameter than your steamer.

4. Bring ample water for steaming to a gushing boil. Put the plate in place, cover the steamer, and steam the eggrolls for 15 minutes. Turn off the heat and let the eggrolls rest undisturbed for 5 minutes more. Carefully remove the plate from the steamer and let the eggrolls stand for at least 10 minutes before slicing.

5. For immediate use, gently slice the eggrolls on a slight diagonal into ¼-inch pinwheels. (The ends make great nibbles.) Or, if working in advance, let the eggrolls come to room temperature; then, seal and refrigerate them for up to 3 days. Slice when chilled for cleanest cutting, but let the slices come to room temperature before adding to the soup.

6. To finish the soup, blanch the peas until tender-crisp, about 30 seconds. Drain, chill in ice water, then drain again.

7. Bring the infusion to a steaming near simmer in a non-aluminum pot. Add enough kosher salt to bring out the garlic flavor, then enough pepper-salt to tingle your tongue.

8. Portion the pinwheels, peas, mushrooms, carrots, chives, and scallions among heated soup bowls. Ladle the hot infusion on top and serve at once.

NOT A QUIET COOK

Some cooks excel at subtle flavors and soft nuance. I'm not one of them. I've tried now and then to do simple dishes with just one or two flavors woven quietly into the fabric, but I'm not good at it. Alas.

China Moon food is, at its best, gutsy and bold. There is a loud stereo of flavor emanating from our dishes—not the equivalent of a rock concert, thank you, but more like the gallop of Vivaldi's "Four Seasons" with its big crescendos of tonality followed by moments of quiet resonance.

Thank goodness for the quiet moments! Between the bursts of ginger and chili, everyone needs a rest.

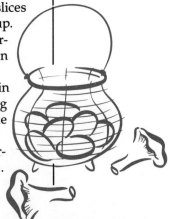

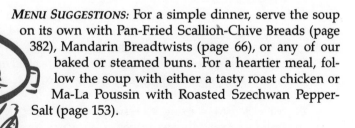

MENU SUGGESTIONS: For a simple dinner, serve the soup on its own with Pan-Fried Scallion-Chive Breads (page 382), Mandarin Breadtwists (page 66), or any of our baked or steamed buns. For a heartier meal, follow the soup with either a tasty roast chicken or Ma-La Poussin with Roasted Szechwan Pepper-Salt (page 153).

CHICKEN AND COCONUT SOUP WITH CRISPY ALMONDS

SERVES 3 TO 4 IN LARGE BOWLS, 6 TO 7 IN SMALL BOWLS

This is our takeoff on a classic Thai soup, done here with an appealing lightness. With its combination of velvety chicken cubes, crispy ginger threads, and sliced almonds, virtually no one can resist it.

Several steps are involved in making the soup, but it is a meal-in-a-bowl and well worth the effort.

VELVET MARINADE:
1 large egg white
1 tablespoon Chinese rice wine or dry sherry
1 tablespoon cornstarch
1 teaspoon kosher salt

½ pound fresh chicken breast, skinned, boned, and cut into ½-inch cubes
8 cups China Moon Infusion (page 72)

8 ounces unsweetened coconut milk
Kosher salt
Roasted Szechwan Pepper-Salt (page 5)
2 inner ribs celery, cut crosswise on the diagonal into paper-thin commas
¼ cup toasted, sliced almonds
2 to 3 tablespoons Fried Ginger Threads (page 29)
Whole coriander leaves, for garnish

1. In a bowl, whisk together the ingredients for the velvet marinade until thickened. Add the chicken and toss well to coat each cube. Seal airtight and marinate in the refrigerator for 2 to 3 hours or overnight. Allow the chicken to come to room temperature before cooking and re-toss to loosen the cubes.

2. Just prior to serving the soup, partially cook the chicken. Bring a small saucepan filled with water to a gentle simmer over moderate heat. Add the chicken cubes, stir with chopsticks, and cook until the outside turns 90 percent white, 30 to 40 seconds. Drain the chicken and set aside. The chicken will be rare inside but will finish cooking in the soup.

3. In a non-aluminum, heavy pot, heat the infusion over moderate heat; do not let it boil. Add the coconut milk, whisking it into the broth and breaking up any lumps. Season the infusion to taste with enough kosher salt to bring out the flavors of the infusion and then a dash or more of pepper-salt to tingle the tongue.

4. Portion the chicken cubes and celery among heated soup bowls. Ladle the steaming infusion into the bowls and top each with some of the toasted almonds, fried ginger, and several whole coriander leaves. Serve immediately.

MENU SUGGESTIONS: I enjoy this soup best in the company of a hot loaf of good bread, cut thinly and roasted or grilled with a light film of olive oil. If you wish it as an opener to a meal, one of our steamed salmon or baked fish dishes would follow well.

COCONUT MILK

Coconut milk differs greatly from brand to brand; we use Chaokah, which is unsweetened. The thick solids and thin liquid often separate in the can. Whisk them together before adding to the soup.

SIMPLE SOUP OF CHICKEN, WATER CHESTNUTS, AND FRIED GINGER

SERVES 2 TO 3 IN LARGE BOWLS, 4 TO 6 IN SMALL BOWLS

My staff always laughs at me for floating a dozen ingredients in any bowl of soup, so this very pleasant soup with only *nine* components came to be called "simple soup." No reason, however, to hold back! Some fresh kernels of corn and a bit of fresh tomato dice—now that I look at it—would be simply lovely in this soup.

This is an easy soup to prepare. Once the chicken is marinated it can be finished in minutes.

GINGER

///

The easiest ginger to use for Fried Ginger Threads is mature Hawaiian ginger with its long finger-like extensions. So-called "baby ginger" with its translucent skin and rosy and pale green shoots—the same beast pulled from the ground several months earlier—has the advantage of being fiber-free but is usually too moist to fry successfully. Fijian ginger, which is round and knobby, will not give you an appropriately long and pretty julienne, though the taste and frying will be fine.

VELVET MARINADE:
1 large egg white
1 tablespoon Chinese rice wine
   or dry sherry
1 teaspoon kosher salt
1 tablespoon cornstarch

¾ pound fresh chicken breast,
   skinned, boned, and cut into
   ½-inch cubes
8 cups China Moon Infusion
   (page 72)
Kosher salt
Roasted Szechwan Pepper-Salt
   (page 5)

SOUP TRIMMINGS:
1 packed cup finely slivered
   Napa cabbage
6 large fresh water chestnuts,
   cut into thin half-moons
⅓ cup finely shredded carrot
½ cup thinly sliced green and
   white scallion rings
¼ cup finely chopped Chinese
   chives
⅓ cup toasted, sliced almonds
¼ to ⅓ cup Fried Ginger
   Threads (page 29)

1. In a bowl, whisk together the ingredients for the velvet marinade until thickened. Add the chicken and toss well to coat each cube. Seal airtight and marinate in the refrigerator for 2 to 3 hours or overnight. Allow the chicken to come to room temperature before cooking and re-toss to loosen the cubes.

2. Just prior to serving the soup, partially cook the chicken: Bring a small saucepan filled with water to a gentle simmer over moderate heat. Add the chicken cubes, stir with chopsticks, and cook until the outside is 90 percent white, 30 to 40 seconds. Drain the chicken and set aside. The chicken will be rare inside but will finish cooking in the soup.

3. In a non-aluminum, heavy pot, heat the infusion over moderate heat to a gentle simmer. Season with enough kosher salt to bring out the garlic flavor, then with a dash or more of pepper-salt to excite the tongue.

4. Portion among heated soup bowls the chicken, cabbage, water chestnuts, and carrots. Ladle the steaming infusion into the bowls and top each with some of the scallions, chives, almonds, and a small mound of fried ginger.

MENU SUGGESTIONS: A light soup such as this invites the company of springrolls or buns. A long baguette toasted in the oven or a basket of hot Mandarin Breadtwists (page 66) would be another delicious alternative.

SUMMER MEATBALL SOUP WITH GLASS NOODLES

SERVES 4 TO 6 IN LARGE BOWLS, 8 TO 10 IN SMALL BOWLS

My favorite way of making this light and colorful soup is with pork meatballs and a mixture of red and Golden Jubilee tomatoes. Then it really seems a celebration! However, beef meatballs are also delicious, and if you're hungry for this soup in winter, simply substitute a scattering of cold-weather vegetables.

The meatballs may be poached a day or more in advance. Putting the soup together takes little time.

BASIL STEMS

When you make China Moon Infusion (page 72) for this soup, add the basil stems to the pot for the final 15 minutes of steeping. The flavor is superb.

MEATBALL MIXTURE:
2 tablespoons finely minced green and white scallion
1 tablespoon plus 1 teaspoon finely minced fresh ginger
1 tablespoon plus 1 teaspoon finely minced garlic
2 tablespoons finely chopped Chinese chives, or 2 teaspoons finely minced Thai or opal basil
2 tablespoons soy sauce
2 tablespoons Chinese rice wine or dry sherry
1 teaspoon kosher salt
Freshly ground black pepper
1 egg, beaten
¼ cup unsalted cold chicken stock
1 pound finely ground pork butt or beef round

8 cups China Moon Infusion (page 72)
Kosher salt
Roasted Szechwan Pepper-Salt (page 5)

SOUP TRIMMINGS:
Infused Glass Noodles (page 30)
1 pound baby spinach
½ cup finely shredded carrot
¾ cup seeded, diced tomatoes
Thinly sliced green and white scallion rings, chopped Chinese chives, and Thai or opal basil julienne, for garnish

1. To make the meatballs, combine all of the ingredients through the chicken stock in a large mixing bowl. Add the meat and, using your hand, blend briskly in one direction until thoroughly blended. Press plastic wrap directly on top of the mixture and chill. (The chilling binds the seasonings to the meat and makes the meatballs easier to roll.)

2. Fill a wide pot with water and bring to a gentle simmer. To shape the meatballs, wet your palms and a tea-spoon measure with ice water and roll rounded teaspoons of the mixture to form tiny meatballs, ½ to ¾ inch in diameter. Put the meatballs on a lightly oiled plate. When 8 or so are made, slide them into the shimmering water. Poach for 1 to 2 minutes after they have come to the surface. They should be cooked through. Remove the meatballs to a plate to cool. Repeat the process until all the meatballs are cooked.

If working in advance, let the meatballs come to room temperature, then seal and refrigerate for 2 to 3 days. Bring to room temperature before using.

3. Bring the infusion to a gentle simmer in a non-aluminum pot over moderate heat. Taste and season first with enough kosher salt to bring out the flavor of the garlic and then a dash or more of pepper-salt to please your tongue.

4. To serve, divide the noodles among warmed bowls. Portion the meatballs, spinach, carrot, and tomatoes among the bowls. Ladle the infusion on top. Then garnish with scallion rings, chives, and a chiffonnade of basil.

MENU SUGGESTIONS: This is a fine one-bowl meal in the warm months, needing only a Pan-Fried Scallion-Chive Bread (page 382) or a bundle of hot Mandarin Breadtwists (page 66) to complete it. In the colder months, or when you are wanting a heartier dinner, follow with a simple dish of fettuccine dressed with oil and fresh herbs.

CHINA MOON PORK WON-TON IN ROASTED GARLIC BROTH

FILLING MAKES ABOUT 40 WON-TON
SOUP SERVES 4 IN LARGE BOWLS,
6 TO 8 IN SMALL BOWLS

This is our version of won-ton soup, an admittedly zippy bowlful that is a full league away from the mild Cantonese classic. It is an unabashed best-seller, and a soup of which I never tire.

Making won-ton is a labor of love. Or at least it is a labor. Were I doing this soup at home, I would wrap the won-ton in the morning and serve the soup in the evening as a one-bowl meal to reward me for my fuss.

Won-ton are heavenly freshly made. Once poached, they may be refrigerated for 2 to 3 days but they lose their savor. To freeze these won-ton is to commit a crime, at least in my obsessive kitchen.

VOCABULARY NOTE

Given China Moon's location in California, I've always called our Infusion "Roasted Garlic Broth" on our menu, lassoing in all those folks who, like me, believe in garlic's curative powers.

WON-TON:
¼ cup thinly sliced green and white scallion rings
1 tablespoon plus 1 teaspoon finely chopped Chinese chives
1 tablespoon finely minced fresh ginger
1 tablespoon finely minced garlic
2 tablespoons soy sauce
2 teaspoons Chinese rice wine or dry sherry
½ teaspoon kosher salt
¼ teaspoon freshly ground black pepper
½ teaspoon Cayenne Pepper Oil (page 11)
1 tablespoon China Moon Infusion (page 72)

1 pound coarsely ground fresh pork butt
About 40 thinnest possible 3-inch-square won-ton skins
2 egg yolks, beaten (optional)

8 cups China Moon Infusion
Kosher salt
Roasted Szechwan Pepper-Salt (page 5)

SOUP TRIMMINGS:
½ pound spinach leaves
½ cup finely shredded carrot
¼ cup finely chopped Chinese chives
¼ cup thinly sliced green and white scallion rings

1. To make the won-ton filling, combine the ingredients through the tablespoon of infusion in a large bowl. Add the pork and stir well in one direction until thoroughly blended. If working in advance, press plastic wrap directly on top of the filling and refrigerate several hours or overnight.

2. To shape the won-ton: Set a wrapper before you in a diamond position and put 1 teaspoon of the filling just above the center. With a small pastry brush or your finger, moisten the exposed edges of the wrapper with the egg yolks, or you can use water instead. Then bring the bottom of the wrapper up over the filling, press gently to expel any air, and seal the wrapper itself neatly in a triangle. Next, bring the 2 side points up over the filling, overlap the points, and seal with a bit of egg yolk or water by pinching the ends firmly together. As they are made, stand the won-ton with a bit of room between them on a baking sheet lined with parchment, waxed paper, or a thin dusting of flour, and cover with a light towel.

At this point, the won-ton may be sealed with plastic wrap and refrigerated for several hours or overnight. Poach them directly from the refrigerator so the wrappers don't get sticky.

If you are bent on freezing won-ton, place them on their

baking sheet in the freezer, then seal airtight once firm. Poach (see next step) only partially defrosted, adding up to several minutes to the simmering time until they are cooked through.

3. To poach the won-ton, fill a large wok or pot half-full with water and bring it to a simmer. Drop the won-ton into the water and stir gently to separate them. Poach for a full 2 minutes after the won-ton float to the surface, adjusting the heat so the water never boils. The wrappers will be translucent and the filling should be cooked through; slice open a won-ton to check. Remove the won-ton with a large mesh spoon and hold them briefly aloft to drain. Spread them apart on 2 or more baking sheets so they don't stick together. If the pot is too small to comfortably hold all of the won-ton, poach them in 2 batches.

Sheer heaven is to eat the won-ton freshly poached. If you are working in advance, however, let them come to room temperature, then seal and refrigerate in their spread-apart form for up to 3 days. Bring to room temperature before rewarming.

4. To make the soup, heat the infusion to a simmer in a non-aluminum pot large enough to hold the won-ton as well. Season with enough kosher salt to bring out the garlic and then with a pinch or more of pepper-salt to tingle your tongue.

5. Slide the won-ton into the pot, stir gently, then allow the soup to regain a steaming near simmer, by which time the won-ton will have heated through.

6. Meanwhile, blanch the spinach 5 seconds to wilt it. Plunge it under cold water to chill, then press the leaves between your palms to remove the excess water.

7. Fluff the spinach leaves to loosen and portion among heated soup bowls. Remove the won-ton and divide them among the bowls. Ladle the infusion on top, garnish with big pinches of carrot, chives, and scallion, and serve at once.

MENU SUGGESTIONS: If someone else would make them for me, a plate of Pan-Fried Scallion-Chive Bread (page 382) or a big bundle of hot Mandarin Breadtwists (page 66) would be a wonderful addition to the soup, as would most any great loaf of hot, crusty bread.

WRAPPING WON-TON

Witness lunchtime or off-hours at most any Chinese-American restaurant and you will see waiters hunched around a table, folding won-ton as fast as the eye can see (and usually flipping them over their shoulders into a big bowl). If you are not gifted with the right gene pool or delicate fingers made for edible ori-gami, the only surefire tech-nique is practice. That aside, lightly moistening the wrap-pers evenly around the edges is the only advice I can offer.

DUCK WON-TON IN PEPPERY DUCK INFUSION

FILLING MAKES ABOUT 40 WON-TON
SOUP SERVES 4 IN LARGE BOWLS, 6 TO 8 IN SMALL BOWLS

This is a wonderful thing to do with the fresh duck meat left behind when you make duck infusion. It is a delicious twist on the ever-popular won-ton and makes for a light but earthy soup.

Like all won-ton, these may be made and poached a day in advance. However, they are truly spectacular when very fresh so, if possible, make them on the same day that you are planning on serving the soup.

WON-TON:
3 tablespoons thinly sliced green and white scallion rings
2 tablespoons finely chopped Chinese chives
2 teaspoons finely minced fresh ginger
2 teaspoons Five-Flavor Oil (page 13)
½ teaspoon Cayenne Pepper Oil (page 11)
1 teaspoon Chinese rice wine or dry sherry
1 tablespoon Duck Infusion with Szechwan Peppercorns (page 74)
2 tablespoons soy sauce
2 teaspoons mushroom soy sauce
Pinch of sugar

½ teaspoon Roasted Szechwan Pepper-Salt (page 5)
1 pound skinless raw duck meat, cubed
1 small rib celery, finely diced
3 tablespoons finely diced carrot
About 40 thinnest possible 3-inch-square won-ton skins

8 cups Duck Infusion with Szechwan Peppercorns
Kosher salt
Roasted Szechwan Pepper-Salt

SOUP TRIMMINGS:
½ pound spinach leaves
½ cup finely shredded carrot
¼ cup finely chopped Chinese chives
¼ cup thinly sliced green and white scallion rings
Fried Ginger Threads (page 29)

1. To make the won-ton filling, combine all the ingredients through the pepper-salt in a bowl. Scrape the mixture into a food processor, add the duck, and process to blend; do not quite purée the duck, but leave a bit of texture. Stir in the celery and carrot by hand. If working in advance, press plastic wrap directly on the surface of the mixture and refrigerate for up to a day. The mixture will solidify, making the won-ton a bit easier to wrap.

2. Fill, shape, and poach the won-ton following steps 2 and 3, pages 95 and 96.

3. Prepare and finish the soup following steps 4 through 7, page 96, garnishing with big pinches of carrot, chives, scallions, and fried ginger.

MENU SUGGESTIONS: Though it might seem a bit redundant, if I were to partner the soup with anything other than a glass of dry white wine, it would be a steamer of Steamed Buns Stuffed with Chicken and Oyster Sauce (page 369) or a platter of Vegetarian Springrolls (page 349).

BEEF AND CHIVE WON-TON IN ROASTED GARLIC BROTH

FILLING MAKES ABOUT 40 WON-TON
SOUP SERVES 4 IN LARGE BOWLS, 6 TO 8 IN SMALL BOWLS

Another twist on classic pork won-ton, these are filled with minced beef and enlivened by the addition of chopped chives and a dash of chili sauce. In the winter, we add to the bowl the garnishes listed below, but in the summer they are equally wonderful with fresh corn kernels and diced tomato and maybe a fine julienne of fresh basil.

The won-ton may be filled and poached a day or two in advance. Leftovers are tasty deep-fried, especially with a dab of Sweet Mustard Sauce (page 21).

CONSPIRACY OF FLAVORS

The ideal China Moon dish is one that has a medley of flavors that can't be pulled apart. This looks like poppycock on paper, but it makes sense on the palate. Some cuisines offer bits and bites of flavor that sit quietly on the plate and parade neatly across the tongue. (Think of a classic cream soup, followed by a savory roasted meat, and then a sweet sorbet.) China Moon cuisine is, instead, a cacophony of flavor—a vibrant weave of contrasts that is very Chinese at the core. There is a conspiracy of aromatics at work in each dish, a joining of garlic, ginger, scallion, and chili that's a kaleidoscope of taste.

For those into fashion, this is no svelte Calvin Klein. It's a big Missoni sweater that's a rainbow of complex color.

WON-TON:

¼ cup thinly sliced green and white scallion rings
3 tablespoons finely chopped Chinese chives or fresh coriander leaves and stems
1 tablespoon finely minced fresh ginger
1 tablespoon finely minced garlic
½ cup tiny carrot cubes
2 tablespoons soy sauce
1 tablespoon Chinese rice wine or dry sherry
¼ teaspoon Roasted Szechwan Pepper-Salt (page 5)
1½ tablespoons Ma-La Oil (page 17) or Five-Flavor Oil (page 13)
½ teaspoon Chinese chili sauce
1 pound coarsely ground beef top round

About 40 thinnest possible 3-inch-square won-ton skins
2 egg yolks, beaten (optional)

8 cups China Moon Infusion (page 72)
Kosher salt
Roasted Szechwan Pepper-Salt

SOUP TRIMMINGS:

½ pound spinach leaves
½ cup finely shredded carrot
½ cup finely chopped Chinese chives
¼ cup thinly sliced green and white scallion rings

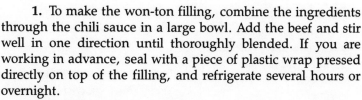

1. To make the won-ton filling, combine the ingredients through the chili sauce in a large bowl. Add the beef and stir well in one direction until thoroughly blended. If you are working in advance, seal with a piece of plastic wrap pressed directly on top of the filling, and refrigerate several hours or overnight.

2. Fill, shape, and poach the won-ton, following steps 2 and 3, pages 95 and 96.

3. Prepare and finish the soup, following steps 4 through 7, page 96.

Menu Suggestions: In the winter, the soup would be delicious with Mandarin Breadtwists (page 66), Many Mushroom Buns (page 374), or thick, toasty slices of garlic bread. In summer, grilled corn and a summer salad would be wonderful, as would some simply cooked fish from the grill.

WHITEFISH WON-TON IN CHINA MOON FISH FUMET

FILLING MAKES 40 WON-TON
SOUP SERVES 4 IN LARGE BOWLS, 6 TO 8 IN SMALL BOWLS

The fish purée that is the base of these delicate won-ton is easily bought in a Chinatown fish market, or you may make your own by grinding impeccably fresh fish in a food processor. Moist fish with a high oil content, such as sablefish (black cod) and salmon, work well. Use an additional egg white to bind the fish together if its own fats are not sufficient to form a gelatinous purée.

The won-ton may be filled and poached a day or two in advance of serving. Leftovers are yummy deep-fried with most any of our dipping sauces.

WON-TON:
2 cups finely diced Napa cabbage
Kosher salt
⅓ cup finely shredded carrot
1 tablespoon finely minced fresh ginger
2 tablespoons thinly sliced green and white scallion rings
2 tablespoons finely chopped Chinese chives
2 tablespoons finely chopped coriander
1½ teaspoons Chinese rice wine or dry sherry
1 tablespoon China Moon Hot Chili Oil (page 10)
¼ teaspoon freshly ground black pepper
1 medium egg white, lightly beaten
1 pound fish paste

6 fresh water chestnuts, finely diced
About 40 thinnest possible 3-inch-square won-ton skins

8 cups China Moon Fish Fumet (page 79)
Kosher salt
Roasted Szechwan Pepper-Salt (page 5)

SOUP TRIMMINGS:
1 cup finely slivered Napa or celery cabbage
½ cup finely shredded carrot
¼ cup finely chopped Chinese chives
¼ cup thinly sliced green and white scallion rings
Sprigs of fresh coriander (optional) and Fried Ginger Threads (page 29), for garnish

ICE BUCKET CAPER

During my second year in Taiwan, I lived in the blissful indulgence of a household run by an imperious Chinese gourmand. This old gentleman had the fortunate weekly habit of playing mah-jongg with his cronies, leaving his two wives, the servant girl, and me to get "takeout" from our favorite Moslem restaurant around

*the block. No sooner did the
tiles start clicking in the
closed room of men friends,
than I would be dispatched
by the female battalion to pick
up an order of four dozen
lamb potstickers and a triple
order of the hot and sour
soup of the day. Moslems
eschew pork, so the soup
might have beef, chicken, or
lamb, according to the whims
of the cook and the stinginess
of the owner.*

*On each of these run-
and-fetch excursions, my
companion was a rather
grand insulated ice bucket. It
had been a presentational gift
to the old man from one of
his Shanghai banking bud-
dies and, symbolizing the
grandeur and longevity of the
culture, it was modeled on
the outside to resemble an
ancient Chinese bronze ritual
vessel. It amused me greatly
to know that the real bronze
object had once held soup,
much as it relieved me that of
all the vessels for transport-
ing soup while juggling
dumplings, none can beat an
insulated plastic ice bucket.*

*I consider this a unique
bit of insider knowledge on
the subject of Chinese picnics
and potlucks, herewith of-
fered to the cooking world at
large.*

1. To make the won-ton filling, toss the diced cabbage with ½ teaspoon kosher salt and let stand for 30 minutes. Drain, then squeeze the cabbage to extract any excess water. Combine the cabbage with the remaining ingredients through the egg white. Scrape the mixture into a food processor, add the fish paste, and process to combine. Stir in the water chestnuts by hand to retain their crunch. Poach a dab of the purée in unsalted water and taste. Adjust with additional salt, pepper, and/or chili oil if needed.

2. If working in advance, press plastic wrap directly on the surface of the purée and refrigerate over a bowl of ice for up to a day. The purée will firm up after several hours chilling and be easier to handle, so you may wish to refrigerate it even if you plan to wrap the won-ton almost immediately.

3. Fill, shape, and poach the won-ton following steps 2 and 3, pages 95 and 96. Do not freeze these won-ton; the fish paste loses its texture and moistness.

4. To make the soup: Heat the infusion to a simmer in a non-aluminum pot large enough to hold the won-ton as well. Season with enough kosher salt to bring out the flavor of the fumet, then with a pinch or more of pepper-salt to tingle your tongue. Slide the won-ton into the pot, stir gently, then allow the soup to regain a steaming near simmer, by which time the won-ton will have heated through.

5. Portion the slivered cabbage among heated bowls. Remove the won-ton and divide among the bowls. Ladle the infusion on top. Garnish with big pinches of the remaining trimmings and a sprig of coriander and serve immediately.

MENU SUGGESTIONS: For a simple supper, the soup pairs wonderfully with springrolls, Mandarin Breadtwists (page 66), or baked or steamed buns. A long baguette, split and toasted in the oven with a brushing of oil and topped with paper-thin slices of cured ham or aged Parmesan cheese, is another personal, Marco-Polo favorite.

HOT AND SOUR SOUP WITH CHICKEN RIBBONS AND SUMMER VEGETABLES

SERVES 3 TO 4 IN LARGE BOWLS, 6 TO 7 IN SMALL BOWLS

Classic hot and sour soup, a creation of northern Chinese cooks, is designed to warm your toes in winter. This lighter, unorthodox version is keyed to summer and all its glories. The preparations may be done up to a full day ahead.

Hot and sour soup is a great one-bowl meal. It doubles easily for a crowd, and if you've made too much, survives reheating nicely. Both my first cookbook and this one were written on the fuel of hot and sour soup reheated over the course of many days! For the mother of all hot and sour soups, see Mongolian-Style Hot and Sour Soup in *The Modern Art of Chinese Cooking*. Ten years later, I have not been able to improve upon it.

Preparations may be done up to a full day ahead. The final cooking and combining is done in minutes.

VELVET MARINADE:
1 large egg white
1 tablespoon Chinese rice wine
*   or dry sherry*
1 tablespoon cornstarch
1 teaspoon kosher salt

½ to ¾ pound fresh skinless
*   chicken breast, cut crosswise*
*   against the grain into thin*
*   slivers*
3 tablespoons cornstarch
8 cups China Moon Infusion
*   (page 72) or China Moon*
*   Double Stock (page 72)*
1 cup fresh corn kernels
⅓ cup fresh peas

¼ cup plus 3 tablespoons soy
*   sauce or 3 tablespoons*
*   mushroom soy sauce*
Kosher salt
Freshly ground black pepper
Serrano-Lemongrass Vinegar
*   (page 19) or unseasoned*
*   Japanese rice vinegar*

SOUP TRIMMINGS:
½ cup seeded and diced
*   tomatoes*
3 tablespoons julienned purple
*   or green basil*
⅓ cup thinly sliced green and
*   white scallion rings*
¼ cup finely chopped Chinese
*   chives*

HOW TO TASTE

At China Moon, I school our cooks in the beginning, middle, and end tastes of a sauce or a dish. The idea is that the tongue is most excited when it experiences a vibrant range of flavor in a single lick. In this way, the palate senses one thing when it first tastes, another a second or so later, and yet another when the dab of stuff has just slid down the throat. To be the flavorful China Moon ideal, a dish (or a complex component of that dish, such as a dipping sauce) should have this three-tiered range of flavor.

This isn't as esoteric as it sounds. Wine tasters, for one, know this sort of thing well. It's really as simple as differentiating monotone from stereo. So, if you're wanting monotone in food, you're reading the wrong book!

1. In a bowl, combine the velvet marinade ingredients and whisk until thickened. Add the chicken and stir to coat each slice well. Seal airtight and marinate in the refrigerator for 2 to 4 hours or overnight. Bring to room temperature before cooking, and re-toss to loosen the slivers.

2. About 20 minutes before serving the soup, dissolve the cornstarch in ½ cup of the cold infusion, leaving the spoon in the bowl. Bring the remaining infusion to a steaming near simmer over low heat in a large, non-aluminum pot.

3. While the soup heats, separately blanch the corn, peas, and chicken in a large saucepan of simmering water. Blanch the corn only 3 to 5 seconds to set its color, then set aside. Blanch the peas until tender-crisp, about 30 seconds depending on size, then chill in ice water, drain, and set aside. Adjust the water to a steaming near simmer, then add the chicken. Stir gently to separate the slivers, then drain when the outside turns 90 percent white. Spread on a plate to cool. The chicken should be a bit rare; it will cook to doneness in the soup.

4. Once the soup reaches a near simmer, add the soy sauce, stir, and taste. Add enough kosher salt to bring out the flavor of the stock and then enough pepper to zing your lips. The amount needed will vary depending on the stock used. Last, add the vinegar in a thin stream, tasting until the flavor is pleasantly sour. You may need as much as ⅓ cup. When the flavors are strong and balanced, bring the soup to a simmer, stir the cornstarch mixture to recombine, then add it to the pot, stirring. Once the soup turns glossy, in 2 to 3 minutes, turn off the heat.

5. Portion among heated soup bowls the chicken, corn, peas, tomatoes, basil, scallions, and chives. Ladle the steaming seasoned soup into the bowls and serve immediately.

MENU SUGGESTIONS: Thick wedges of hot bread are my favorite mate to a hot and sour soup. If you are in the mood for more work than heating a loaf from the local bakery, try Mandarin Breadtwists (page 66) or the savory Pan-Fried Scallion-Chive Bread (page 382). If you wished a soup to open a dinner, this one would be a great introduction to a meal of grilled fish.

HOT AND SOUR SOUP WITH SLIVERED PORK AND WINTER VEGETABLES

SERVES 3 TO 4 IN LARGE BOWLS, 6 TO 7 IN SMALL BOWLS

Embellished with the flavors of fresh fennel and leeks, this is a delicious soup that is good at any time of year.

For a Moslem-style soup, substitute the traditional pork with beef or lamb or chicken. Moslems, like Jews, have dietary prohibitions against pork.

The soup preparations may be done up to a day in advance. The final cooking takes little time.

MARINADE:
1 tablespoon soy sauce
1½ teaspoons Chinese rice wine or dry sherry
2 teaspoons China Moon Hot Chili Oil (page 10) or China Moon Chili-Orange Oil (page 15)
½ teaspoon finely minced fresh ginger
2 teaspoons finely chopped fresh coriander
½ teaspoon cornstarch

½ to ¾ pound pork loin, cut crosswise against the grain into thin slivers
1 ounce dried tree ears (about ½ cup)
3 tablespoons cornstarch
8 cups China Moon Infusion (page 72) or China Moon Double Stock (page 72)

1 small leek, white part only, cut lengthwise, then crosswise into paper-thin half-moons
¼ cup plus 3 tablespoons soy sauce or 3 tablespoons mushroom soy sauce
Kosher salt
Freshly ground black pepper
Serrano-Lemongrass Vinegar (page 19) or unseasoned Japanese rice vinegar

SOUP TRIMMINGS:
1 small leek, white part only, halved lengthwise, then cut crosswise into thin half-moons
1 small carrot, shredded
½ small bulb fennel, halved lengthwise and cored, then cut crosswise into paper-thin arcs
1 small rib celery, cut crosswise on a diagonal into thin commas

excellent liquids, one should always drink directly with one's lips. Otherwise, there is a tragic loss of bouquet as well as flavor.

Even Chinese soup spoons make grand sense. Miniature ladles, they are made of cool porcelain. One never burns one's lips. Assuming there is something solid like a won-ton afloat in the bowl, they can easily be scooped up.

As for slurping, if done demurely, it is permissible in even the most exalted of settings. Pursed lips and little swooshing sounds are the ideal in genteel company. However, in the privacy of the family table or a casual restaurant, anything goes. More noise equals more pleasure at the traditional Chinese table, which begins to explain why Chinese eating is so joyful and Chinese eaters are so unneurotic.

1. Combine the marinade ingredients in a bowl and stir until well blended. Add the pork and toss well. Seal airtight and marinate in the refrigerator for 2 to 4 hours or overnight. Bring to room temperature before using, and re-toss to loosen the slivers.

2. Soak the tree ears in 3 cups cold water for 20 to 30 minutes. When supple, drain and rinse under cool running water to dislodge any grit. Tear into nickel-size pieces, discarding any tough or woody bits.

3. About 20 minutes before serving the soup, dissolve the cornstarch in ½ cup of the cold infusion and leave the spoon in the bowl. Over low heat, bring the remaining stock to a steaming near simmer in a large non-aluminum pot.

4. While the soup heats, separately blanch the leek and pork in a large saucepan of simmering water. Lower the leek pieces into the water in a strainer for 5 seconds to wilt, then refresh under cold water and set aside to drain. Adjust the heat so the water barely simmers, then slide in the pork and stir gently to separate the slivers. When the meat is 90 percent cooked, 20 to 45 seconds depending on thickness, remove it and spread on a plate to cool. Don't worry if it is a tad underdone; it will cook to completion in the soup.

5. Once the soup reaches a near simmer, add the soy sauce, stir, and taste. Add enough kosher salt to bring out the flavor of the stock and then enough pepper to zing your lips. The amount needed will vary depending on the stock used. Last, add the vinegar in a thin stream, tasting until the flavor is pleasantly sour. You may need as much as ⅓ cup. When the flavors are strong and balanced, bring the soup to a simmer, stir the cornstarch mixture to recombine, then add it to the pot, stirring. Once the soup turns glossy, in 2 to 3 minutes, turn off the heat.

6. Portion among heated soup bowls the tree ears, pork ribbons, leek, carrot, fennel, and celery. Ladle the seasoned soup into the bowls and serve immediately.

MENU SUGGESTIONS: A good Chinese companion to this soup would be Pan-Fried Scallion-Chive Bread (page 382) or Many Mushroom Buns (page 374). A Western replacement would be a buttered hot baguette, a crusty loaf of garlic bread, or our East-West Mandarin Breadtwists (page 66).

HOT AND SOUR SOUP WITH DUCK RIBBONS AND WILD MUSHROOMS

SERVES 4 TO 5 IN LARGE BOWLS, 6 TO 8 IN SMALL BOWLS

Redolent of the smoky tones of duck and fresh shiitake mushrooms, this is a rather splendid soup, fit for impressing someone special if not only yourself. Haul out the Queen Victoria china and toast with a fine red wine—none of which is traditional, but neither is this soup.

The preparations may be done a day in advance. Then you can heat it up in minutes and eat it like a queen.

MARINADE:
1 tablespoon soy sauce
1½ teaspoons Chinese rice wine or dry sherry
2 teaspoons Ma-La Oil (page 17) or China Moon Chili-Orange Oil (page 15)
½ teaspoon finely minced fresh ginger
½ teaspoon finely minced garlic
1 tablespoon finely chopped fresh coriander leaves and stems
½ teaspoon cornstarch

½ to ¾ pound fresh skinless duck breasts, cut crosswise against the grain into thin ribbons
¼ cup dried tree ears
20 dried lily buds
3 tablespoons cornstarch

8 to 10 cups Duck Infusion with Szechwan Peppercorns (page 74)
⅓ cup soy sauce or 2½ tablespoons mushroom soy sauce
Kosher salt
Freshly ground black pepper
Serrano-Lemongrass Vinegar (page 19) or unseasoned Japanese rice vinegar
¼ to ½ teaspoon Five-Flavor Oil (page 13), Ma-La Oil, or ¼ to ½ teaspoon Japanese sesame oil
4 to 5 fresh shiitake mushroom caps, sliced paper-thin
¼ cup thinly sliced green and white scallion rings
½ cup finely shredded carrots
3 tablespoons finely chopped Chinese or Western chives

DUCK HUNT

At the restaurant, I favor Maple Leaf ducks, which come to us fresh from the Midwest and have a mild, sweet flavor. Beware of ducks that taste like old socks and the very rich Moscovy wild ducks that taste like liver. Neither is stellar in won-ton.

LILY BUDS

*These oddly fragrant,
long buds (the dried,
brown flower of the unopened
tiger lily) are a classic fixture
in hot and sour soups. They
are sold in plastic pouches,
and are perhaps best when
they are a lighter color and a
bit supple in the bag. To use,
soak in cool water until limp,
about 15 minutes, then cut
off the hard end where the
flower once joined the stem.
An overnight soak will give
a lighter, cleaner flavor. To
use, tie into a knot, shred
lengthwise or cut crosswise
in half; all three methods are
traditional.*

*I confess to an aversion
to lily buds. I was once
stranded in a village in Taiwan's central mountains on
account of a rope bridge that
blew away in a storm. Lilies
were the village's major crop,
and I ate and smelled nothing
but lily buds (and rice) for
the two days it took to recon-
struct the bridge. To brave
crossing the bridge on the
way back, I had only to think
of one more meal of lilies!*

1. Combine the marinade ingredients; toss well with the duck. Seal airtight and marinate in the refrigerator for 2 to 4 hours or overnight. Bring to room temperature before cooking and re-toss to loosen the ribbons.

2. Soak the tree ears in 3 cups cold water until supple, about 30 minutes. Rinse under cool running water to dislodge any grit. Tear into nickel-size pieces, discarding any tough or woody bits.

3. Soak the lily buds in cold water to cover until soft, about 20 minutes. Drain; snip off the tough woody tips. Cut each bud crosswise in half.

4. About 20 minutes before serving the soup, dissolve the 3 tablespoons cornstarch in ½ cup of the cold infusion and leave the spoon in the bowl. Over low heat, bring the remaining infusion to a steaming near simmer in a large, non-aluminum pot.

5. While the soup heats, blanch the duck in a saucepan of water brought to a steaming near simmer. Slide the duck into the pot and swish gently to separate the slivers. Drain the duck when it is only 80 percent gray on the outside, as little as 10 seconds, and spread on a plate to cool. The duck should be very undercooked. It will poach to appropriate rareness in the soup.

6. Once the soup reaches a near simmer, add the soy sauce, stir, and taste. Add enough kosher salt to bring out the flavor of the stock and then enough pepper to zing your lips. Last, add the vinegar in a thin stream, tasting until the flavor is pleasantly sour. You may need as much as ⅓ cup. When the flavors are strong and balanced, bring the soup to a simmer, stir the cornstarch mixture to recombine, then add it to the pot, stirring. Once the soup turns glossy, in 2 to 3 minutes, turn off the heat. Stir in the oil.

7. Portion among heated soup bowls the duck, lily buds, tree ears, shiitake slices, scallions, carrots, and chives. Ladle the steaming seasoned infusion into the bowls and serve immediately.

MENU SUGGESTIONS: To continue in a regal, unorthodox way, you could follow this soup with a lightly bitter salad and pasta with truffles. If your mood is more Chinese and home-spun, a savory Pan-Fried Scallion Bread (page 382) or a hot bundle of Mandarin Breadtwists (page 66) would be nice.

SWEET MAMA SQUASH SOUP

SERVES 6 TO 8

The name of this soup is as beguiling as its taste. The brainchild of André Fecteau, one of China Moon's more colorful sous-chefs (for a sideline, he manages a rock group), it is a fabulously smooth and velvety soup with a vibrant gold-orange hue. Very un-Chinese in its basic ingredient, this is nonetheless a soup that goes wonderfully well with many of our foods.

Sweet Mama is a variety of winter squash that tastes to my tongue like a cross between butternut and pumpkin. Most any sweet, nutty squash may be used in its stead. Perfection and Delicata are other suitably delicious, poetic varieties.

Baking the squash may be done in advance. The whole soup stores and reheats beautifully.

3 pounds hard-skinned yellow squash, such as Sweet Mama, Perfection, or Delicata
1 tablespoon corn or peanut oil
1 small yellow onion, thinly sliced
1 tablespoon finely minced fresh ginger
1½ teaspoons finely minced garlic
1 thumbnail-size piece cassia or cinnamon bark
1 whole star anise, broken into 8 points

10 cups China Moon Double Stock (page 72) or Vegetable Infusion (page 82)
Sugar
Kosher salt
Freshly ground pepper

GARNISHES:
Fried Ginger Threads (page 29)
¼ cup toasted sliced almonds
Whole coriander leaves

1. Preheat the oven to 400°F.

2. Cut the squash in half, discard the seeds, and place cut side down on a foil-lined baking sheet. Bake in the oven until very soft and oozing, 50 to 60 minutes for a large squash.

Let cool. Discard the peel (scraping well to reserve any flesh), then cut the squash into chunks.

3. In a large, heavy, non-aluminum stockpot, heat the oil over moderate heat until hot enough to sizzle an onion slice slowly. Add the onion, ginger, garlic, cassia, and star anise, tossing well to combine. Cover the pot, lower the heat to prevent scorching, and sweat the onion until very soft and juicy, about 15 minutes. This sweating is crucial; don't rush it, or the soup will lack depth.

4. Add the squash and stock, stir to mix, and bring slowly to a near boil over moderate heat, stirring occasionally. Turn off the heat, cover the pot, and let the soup stand for 30 minutes for the flavors to marry. If serving immediately, discard the cassia and anise, then purée the soup in batches in a blender or food processor.

If working in advance, the purée may be left, uncovered, at room temperature or in the refrigerator to cool, then sealed and refrigerated for several days before serving. Be careful when cooling the purée—its thickness traps the heat. To cool it swiftly (to avoid souring), you may wish to divide it into 2 or 3 containers and nest them uncovered in an ice bath, stirring occasionally to release the steam.

5. To serve the soup, bring it slowly to a near simmer over moderate heat, whisking occasionally to prevent scorching. Turn off the heat, taste, and adjust as required first with sugar, then with kosher salt, and finally, with enthusiastic twists of pepper. Don't be hesitant; the soup invites generous seasoning and the squash may require several tablespoons of sugar if it lacked sweetness at the start.

Serve in heated bowls of contrasting color, garnished with a hill of the fried ginger, a sprinkling of the almonds, and a scattering of coriander leaves.

MENU SUGGESTIONS: Our steamed and baked buns (pages 363 to 376) are delicious with this soup. Its flavors also suggest pairing with many pork or poultry dishes. For Thanksgiving or Christmas, its taste and color cannot be beat!

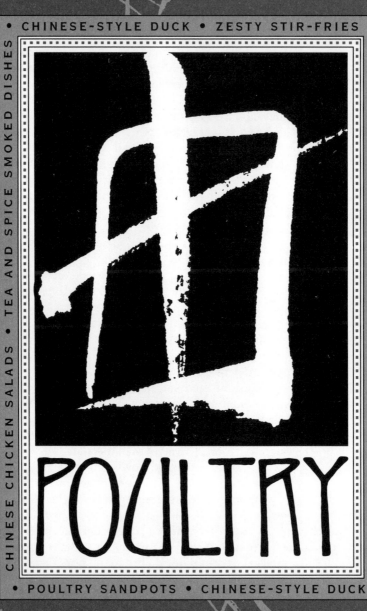

• CHINESE-STYLE DUCK • ZESTY STIR-FRIES •

POULTRY SANDPOTS • TEA AND SPICE SMOKED DISHES

CHINESE CHICKEN SALADS • TEA AND SPICE SMOKED DISHES

POULTRY

• POULTRY SANDPOTS • CHINESE-STYLE DUCK •

CONTENTS

Ask any restaurant chef for a surefire, hot-selling dish, and the answer will surely come back "Chicken with Blahbedy-Blah," no matter what the Blahbedy-Blah. If I put a dish on the China Moon menu tomorrow called "Stir-Fried Black Chicken with Tienstin Gnarly Potatoes, Thousand-Year-Old Brussels Sprouts, and Ugly Fruit," I can almost guarantee that it will sell like wildfire.

Given the popularity of the bird—and why not, with its light color and clean, sweet taste?—it rests upon any chef to cook it well and imaginatively. And in this the Chinese tradition is a rich helpmate. Probably more than in any other cuisine, the chicken and its cousins—duck, squab, quail, and rabbit—undergo fabulous trans-formations in texture and taste. Classic Chinese chefs over the centuries have developed a great bagful of tricks: They plucked chickens hot from the steamer and threw them down deep wells, gelling the juices and firming the skin; buried the birds in clay and lotus leaves to bake them to a particular succulence; and blew a bamboo pipe down a slit in a duck's neck to separate the skin from the flesh so as to drain the fat away in roasting.

In the China Moon kitchen, I confess we tend to favor the home-style as opposed to the showy. I once dreamed of icy backyard wells and fiery vertical ovens, but none were to be had in our 1930's coffee shop. I tried draping whole ducks and chickens to dry from the ceiling, but they just drove everyone wild. Drama notwithstanding, our poultry dishes are delicious. They run a varied gamut from crunchy cold salads to tea-smoked birds to deep-fried nuggets, all easily prepared at home. They are inevitably among our most popular dishes, and justifiably so!

■ ■ ■

GINGER-SPIKED CHOPPED LIVER WITH GARLIC CROUTONS

SERVES 10 TO 12 AS AN APPETIZER

This is a Chinese tilt on a Jewish classic, which is amusing as well as delicious. For those intrigued by cross-cultural history, there were in fact communities of Jews living in China as early as the T'ang dynasty. Sprung from Jewish traders traveling the Silk Route into China from Central Asia, the Chinese Jews created gorgeous Torahs emblazoned with Chinese-featured Queen Esthers, opened kosher butcher shops, and perhaps even ate chopped liver. Their story is documented by the erstwhile Bishop William White in his long out-of-print tome, *The Jews in China*, which I find an altogether fascinating volume.

Meanwhile, this is a simple recipe and a delightfully light variation on a theme.

AROMATICS:
2 tablespoons finely minced fresh ginger
2 teaspoons finely minced garlic
¼ cup thinly sliced green and white scallion rings

3 tablespoons rendered chicken fat or corn or peanut oil
1 pound fresh chicken livers, fatty veins removed
2 tablespoons plum wine
½ small yellow onion, finely diced
1 tablespoon Chinese rice wine or dry sherry

2 tablespoons thinly sliced green and white scallion rings
½ teaspoon kosher salt
¼ teaspoon freshly ground black pepper
1 teaspoon ginger juice (squeezed from very finely minced fresh ginger)
Pinch of Roasted Szechwan Pepper-Salt (page 5)
Garlic Croutons (page 37)
Thinly sliced green and white scallion rings and/or finely chopped Chinese or Western chives, for garnish

1. Combine the aromatics in a small bowl.
2. Heat a wok or heavy skillet over moderate heat until

GRANDMA AND ME

My Grandma Millie used to serve her chopped liver stone-cold on top of saltines. ("God forbid, bacteria should come!") Her granddaughter (God help her) likes the still-warm liver spread on still-warm croutons.

hot enough to evaporate a bead of water on contact. Add 2 tablespoons of the chicken fat and swirl to glaze the pan. Add the aromatics and stir until fully fragrant, 2 to 3 minutes. Adjust the heat so the aromatics foam gently without browning. Add the chicken livers and toss gently until the livers are firm but still quite rosy at the center, 6 to 7 minutes. Add the plum wine and simmer to reduce the liquids, stirring to loosen the flavorful bits from the bottom of the pan. When the liquids are almost gone, scrape the contents of the pan onto a plate. Clean the pan.

3. Set the pan over moderate heat until hot. Add the remaining 1 tablespoon chicken fat. When hot enough to foam a bit of onion, add the onions and stir-fry briskly until translucent and golden brown at the edges, 2 to 3 minutes. Sprinkle the wine around the edge of the pan and simmer until the liquid is all but cooked away, stirring gently. Stir in the scallions at the last minute, then remove the pan from the heat.

4. In a food processor, combine the chicken liver mixture with the kosher salt, black pepper, ginger juice, and pepper-salt. Process until nearly smooth.

5. Transfer the mixture to a mixing bowl. Fold in the onion and scallion rings. Taste and adjust the seasonings, if needed, with a dash more salt and/or pepper-salt. If you are working in advance, press plastic wrap directly on top of the chopped liver and refrigerate. It will keep nicely for several days.

6. Serve the chopped liver at room temperature spread on croutons, garnished with a sprinkling of scallion and/or chives.

MENU SUGGESTIONS: In a somewhat Jewish mode, I would follow the chopped liver with *knaidlach* (Whitefish Won-Ton in China Moon Fish Fumet, page 100) and lokshen kugel (Pot-Browned Noodle Pillow, page 395) topped with one of our stir-fried chicken dishes. If you are thinking of using the chopped liver at a Jewish festival meal, also think of making our Chinese-Style Pickled Salmon (page 186).

THE IMPORTANCE OF FRESHNESS

I don't have a television, so it came to me belatedly that a network program had blown the lid off some shady practices in the chicken industry and that people were now scared of eating chicken. The news arrived via a frantic call from a food magazine test kitchen, where my directions for no-poach chicken (page 116) had caused an editorial hulabaloo. The magazine's solution was to boil the required chicken breast for 35 minutes, which certainly killed everything, including any taste.

Industry standards being what they may, it is imperative to buy chicken that looks and smells fresh, to know the signs that indicate freshness, and to know also the questions to ask a butcher if you are new to a shop. We all have eyes and noses and brains to apply to the matter of getting our foodstuffs. Our job is to use them, not to quiver in a corner and be afraid of our food!

The good news about food scares is they get the industry people to shape up a little, and they alert us to a potential problem. I think we should shriek and holler to get fresher poultry instead of boiling it to bits. And we should get out there and fight the demons instead of swallowing bad food. Every grocer should hear from every cook who thinks that poultry should be better and fresher!

COLD CHICKEN SALAD WITH TOASTED COCONUT, PEANUTS, AND CRISPY RICE STICKS

SERVES 2 AS A MAIN COURSE, 4 TO 5 AS PART OF A MULTICOURSE MEAL

This dish has all the buzzwords of a successful menu item: "cold chicken salad," "toasted," "peanuts," and "crispy." It fairly insists that you order (or make) it!

Its popularity is well justified. It is a refreshing cold dish with great texture and great taste. The vinaigrette features pickled ginger, which is sure to arouse most anyone's appetite.

NO-POACH CHICKEN:
1½ to 2 pounds whole fresh chicken breasts, bone in and skin on, at room temperature
2 quarter-size slices fresh ginger, smashed
1 whole fat scallion, cut into 1-inch nuggets, smashed
⅛ teaspoon Szechwan peppercorns

VINAIGRETTE:
3 tablespoons juice from China Moon Pickled Ginger (page 8)
1 tablespoon distilled white vinegar
¼ teaspoon kosher salt
¼ teaspoon dried red chili flakes
¼ cup plus 2 tablespoons rice bran, corn, or peanut oil

SALAD:
2 tablespoons sesame seeds
3 tablespoons sweetened coconut flakes
⅓ cup fried or roasted peanuts (page 34)
1 cup thickly julienned Japanese or English cucumber
Scant teaspoon paper-thin rings red Fresno and/or green serrano chili
1½ tablespoons finely julienned China Moon Pickled Ginger
3 cups Crispy Rice Sticks (page 31)
Coriander sprigs, for garnish

1. Rinse the chicken breasts with cold water, dislodging any bloody bits near the bone. Choose a heavy pot with a close-fitting lid that will hold the chicken snugly with enough water to cover it by 2 inches. Do not add the chicken at this time. Partially fill the pot with cold water, add the ginger, scallion, and peppercorns, then bring the water to a rolling boil over high heat.

2. Submerge the chicken in the liquid, cover the pot tightly, and turn off the heat. If your stove is electric, carefully move the covered pot to a cool burner. Let the chicken sit, tightly covered and undisturbed, for 2 hours. If you like, it may be left longer in the liquid for convenience, although it will not cook further.

3. Drain the chicken and discard the liquid. (It absorbs very little flavor from the chicken, which is part of the beauty of the method.) Remove the skin and discard it. Use a small sharp knife to free the breast meat from the center bone, then use your fingers to pull the meat from the bone in one piece. Carefully pull the fillet from the underside of each breast half. Trim away and discard any fat, veins, membrane, or bits of bone from the breasts. Strip the fillets of their glove-like membrane; extract the white tendon from the center of each fillet. Cut the meat crosswise against the grain into long diagonal ribbons ¼ inch thick. At this point, or before it has been trimmed and cut, the chicken may be sealed and refrigerated overnight; bring to room temperature before using. Or, in order to preserve the plush texture of the meat, the chicken may be left covered at a cool room temperature for several hours.

4. To make the vinaigrette, whisk together the pickled ginger juice, vinegar, salt, and chili flakes, and let stand 5 minutes to infuse. Add the oil in a thin stream, whisking to emulsify.

5. Toast the sesame seeds and the coconut separately in a dry, heavy skillet over moderate heat, stirring frequently until light gold, several minutes each.

6. Shortly before serving, toss together the chicken, peanuts, sesame seeds, coconut, cucumber, chili rings, and pickled ginger. Whisk the vinaigrette to reblend, then add it to the mixture and toss to combine. Add half the rice sticks and toss just to mix.

7. Mound the salad on individual plates or a large platter of contrasting color. Crown and rim with the reserved rice sticks, then add sprigs of fresh coriander to garnish.

NO-POACH CHICKEN

I know of no better way to cook a chicken breast for salads than "no-poaching." A modification on a classic Chinese technique, it involves nothing more than submerging a whole chicken breast with its skin and bone intact in lightly seasoned water that has been brought to a boil. The heat is then turned off, a lid clamped on the pot, and the meat left to cook through passively for 2 hours. It's a no-brainer in the words of my husband, and a technique that amazes every cook in our kitchen. The result is a chicken breast that is tender, perfectly cooked, and unsurpassed for moistness.

Three things are important to the success of no-poach chicken:

First, the chicken must be impeccably fresh. That is, it should have no smell, leach no blood, and the raw meat should cling tenaciously to the skin and bone.

Second, the breast must be at room temperature when it is submerged in the boiling water.

Third, the pot should be a heavy one with a close-fitting lid to hold in the heat.

With all three in line, no-poaching is flawless. If you're lacking in any one, poach the chicken in the government safety-approved, far less flavorful manner, i.e., by actively poaching in simmering water for upwards of 40 minutes.

MENU SUGGESTIONS: This is a fine one-dish meal for the warm months, bedded on a nest of baby lettuces dressed with our Fresh Ginger Vinaigrette (page 24) or an extra batch of the chicken salad vinaigrette. For a cold buffet, you might pair it with Cold Tomato Noodles (page 394) and Cold Poached Salmon Tiles with Ginger–Black Bean Vinaigrette (page 183). To follow it with something simple, try a grilled meaty fish.

COLD CHICKEN SALAD WITH MUSTARD AND PINE NUTS

SERVES 2 TO 3 AS A MAIN COURSE, 4 TO 5 AS PART OF A MULTICOURSE MEAL

Cold chicken and mustard are wonderful in combination, particularly in this salad. Fresh coriander, crunchy celery, and toasted pine nuts add their various accents to a dish that is good in any season.

If you love a bit of heat, a judicious sprinkling of fresh chili rings will taste great. Most of the time we use green and red serranos because they are tiny and firm and can be easily sliced into paper-thin rounds. You might use red Fresnos or yellow wax chilis, but be sure to slice them paper-thin (a firm chili and a very sharp, thin-bladed knife are the secrets) so that they zing rather than zap the tongue.

You will, by the way, wind up with more sauce than you need. It keeps beautifully in the refrigerator and is a fine sandwich spread.

MUSTARD SAUCE:
1 cup Dijon mustard
½ cup Japanese sesame oil
3 tablespoons unseasoned
    Japanese rice vinegar
Dash of fine sea salt, or to taste
1½ teaspoons sugar
¼ cup plus 2 tablespoons juice
    from China Moon Pickled
    Ginger (page 8)

MUSTARD
VINAIGRETTE:
½ cup rice bran, corn, or
    peanut oil
1 teaspoon Ma-La Oil (page
    17), Five-Flavor Oil (page
    13), or Japanese sesame oil
1 tablespoon Serrano-
    Lemongrass Vinegar (page
    19) or unseasoned Japanese
    rice vinegar

1 teaspoon Mustard Sauce (see
    left)
Dash of fine sea salt, or to taste

6 cups assorted small lettuce
    leaves
No-poach chicken (page 115,
    and page 116, steps 1
    through 3)
2 inner ribs celery, thinly sliced
    on the diagonal
1 to 2 small serrano chilis, cut
    into paper-thin rings
1 to 2 tablespoons coarsely
    chopped coriander leaves and
    stems
1 small red bell pepper,
    julienned
1 small yellow bell pepper,
    julienned
⅓ cup toasted pine nuts
Coriander leaves, for garnish

1. To make the mustard sauce, whisk together all of the sauce ingredients until emulsified.

2. To make the vinaigrette, whisk together all of the vinaigrette ingredients through the sea salt until emulsified.

3. Toss the lettuces with a light dressing of the vinaigrette and arrange them around the rim of individual plates or on a serving platter of contrasting color. Place the greens strategically, vein side down and prettiest edges showing out.

4. In a large bowl, toss the chicken, celery, and serrano rings with a light coating of the mustard sauce. Taste to be sure you've used a nice amount and add an extra dollop if needed. Sprinkle the chopped coriander, half the bell peppers, and half the pine nuts into the bowl and toss to blend. Place the mixture on top of the greens.

5. Toss the remaining bell peppers with a light dressing of the vinaigrette and scatter them over the chicken. Garnish with a flurry of coriander leaves and the remaining pine nuts and serve.

MENU SUGGESTIONS: This is a one-dish meal along with a bowl of Turmeric Tomatoes (page 59), if you're eating light. As

STORING
FRESH POULTRY

I do three things as soon as I get home with fresh poultry: I rinse it with cold water, I put it in a draining device, and I refrigerate it. Rinsing poultry might seem a bit absurd ("Do we rinse hamburger?" queried one cook), but the fact of the matter is that standing blood decays meat, so if I can rinse it off, I do. For that same reason, I fashion some way for the bird or birdy parts to drip freely while in the cooler. In our large restaurant walk-in refrigerator that means keeping the birds in shallow perforated pans nested in even bigger pans to catch the juice. At home, I usually just wrap poultry in a clean tea towel (one that has no scent from a laundry product that could transfer to the bird) and then pop the bundle into a plastic bag before refrigerating it. The towel soaks up the blood and keeps the uncooked poultry fresh for a day or two longer than if it hadn't been wrapped.

If I am storing a whole bird—even a tiny one like a quail—I add one more step to the routine: I flush the cavity with cold water, pull out any loose blood vessels and membranes, and gouge out the kidneys that nestle alongside the backbone just above the tail. When the cavity is perfectly clean, I stuff it with a ball of paper towel to soak up any blood.

If all this seems pretty kooky, the only proof is in the poultry! Birds and poultry parts cleaned and refrigerated in this manner stay sweet-smelling and fresh-tasting for many days longer than those that come home in a package and are never given a fresh wrapping.

an appetizer, follow it with a simple steamed or baked fish embellished with ginger and scallion. As part of a cold buffet, most any of the cold noodles dishes and/or Cold Poached Salmon Tiles with Ginger–Black Bean Vinaigrette (page 183) would go nicely.

TEA-SMOKED CHICKEN SALAD WITH RADICCHIO, MINT, AND WILD MUSHROOMS

SERVES 3 TO 4 AS A MAIN COURSE,
6 TO 8 AS PART OF A MULTICOURSE MEAL

This recipe was the creation of one of our early sous-chefs, Camille Convy, and I think it is a great example of East-Westism. It is also delicious (not always the case when East and West meet), absolutely beautiful, and very easy to do in spite of a plethora of ingredients. If you have someone to impress, this very upscale chicken salad is an ideal candidate.

All the preparations may be done a day in advance. Toss the salad together at the last minute.

2 *whole boneless fresh chicken*
   breasts with skin on, split in
   half (4 pieces)
½ *teaspoon Roasted Szechwan*
   Pepper-Salt (page 5)
2 *to 3 tablespoons corn or*
   peanut oil, for searing

SMOKING MIXTURE:
¼ *cup fragrant dry black tea*
   leaves, such as lichee black or
   rose black
¼ *cup packed brown sugar*
¼ *cup raw rice*
1 *tablespoon Szechwan*
   peppercorns
Several pieces cassia or
   cinnamon bark, crumbled
Several finger-lengths of fresh
   orange zest, coarsely chopped

VINAIGRETTE:
½ *cup juice from China Moon*
   Pickled Ginger (page 8)
2½ *teaspoons distilled white*
   vinegar

½ *teaspoon soy sauce*
½ *teaspoon Roasted Szechwan*
   Pepper-Salt
1 *teaspoon rice bran, corn, or*
   peanut oil

2½ *cups thinly sliced (¼ inch)*
   radicchio ribbons
2½ *cups thinly sliced (¼ inch)*
   spinach leaves
¼ *cup lightly packed purple or*
   green basil leaves (cut in half
   if large)
¼ *cup lightly packed fresh mint*
   leaves (cut in half if large)
¼ *cup sliced (½ inch) Chinese*
   or Western chives
2 *tablespoons thinly sliced green*
   and white scallion rings
½ *cup finely slivered fresh*
   shiitake caps and/or trimmed
   and slivered chanterelles
Enoki mushrooms, spongy bases
   removed, for garnish

SMOKING TIP

Dry or overly smoked chicken will ruin this dish, so take care to cook the breasts only halfway in searing and only 99 percent of the way in smoking. If you have under-done it, the breasts can be finished off by baking in a 350°F oven. Check every minute or so with your finger to gauge firmness and/or thrust the tip of a sharp knife into the thickest part of the breast for a peek. If you've overdone it, don't fret; ante up the vinaigrette to give the chicken some extra moistness and record the time change for your next attempt.

1. Remove the fillet, membranes, and cartilage from the underside of the chicken breasts. Trim the skin where it overhangs the meat. Reserve the fillets for another use. Sprin-kle the top and bottom of each breast with ⅛ teaspoon of the pepper-salt.

2. In a large heavy skillet, heat the oil over moderately high heat until nearly smoking. Sear the breasts on both sides just until golden, about 15 seconds, then remove them; the breasts will be raw in the middle.

3. Line a 14- to 16-inch wok or heavy pot and lid with heavy-duty aluminum foil, leaving hems of at least 3 inches. Combine all of the smoking mixture ingredients. Spread the smoking mixture in a ½-inch-thick layer in the bottom of the wok. Arrange the breasts, skin side up and not touching, on a rack that fits into the wok and stands 1½ to 2 inches above the bottom. Set the rack in place over the mixture and turn the heat as high as possible. Wait for the mixture to send up several thick plumes of smoke, 5 to 10 minutes, depending, on your stove. Cover the wok, crimp the foil hems shut, and smoke the chicken for 3 minutes. Turn off the heat (if the stove is electric, carefully move the pot to a cool burner) and let the wok rest undisturbed for 2 minutes. Remove the lid and discard the foil. The chicken should be cooked through but still juicy (see Smoking Tip, facing page). Let the breasts cool to room temperature. Remove and discard the skin. Cut the meat across the grain into thin ribbons.

4. In a bowl, whisk together all of the vinaigrette ingredients through the oil until emulsified. All the above, including the vegetable cutting, may be done a full day in advance. Seal and refrigerate the ingredients; bring to room temperature before using.

5. Just before serving, gently toss the chicken and all of the remaining ingredients in a large bowl to combine. Whisk the dressing again, then toss with the salad mixture. Mound the salad loosely on individual plates or a platter whose color will show off the red radicchio and deep greens. Scatter or cluster the enoki on top, to garnish.

MENU SUGGESTIONS: For a lunch or a simple dinner, I might follow this salad with a hot or cold noodle dish. To begin a ritzy dinner, choose something a bit more elegant like one of the steamed salmon dishes (pages 190 and 192) or Baked Snapper with Red Curry Sauce (page 199).

PLUM WINE CHICKEN SALAD WITH SWEET MUSTARD SAUCE

SERVES 2 TO 3 AS A MAIN COURSE, 4 TO 5 AS PART OF A MULTICOURSE MEAL

This is my favorite, and perhaps the most untraditional, of all our chicken salads. The sweet mustard sauce and the pairing of cold chicken slivers with crunchy almonds would win loud Chinese applause, but the greens are frankly, and deliciously, California-born.

Preparations can be done up to a day in advance. Last-minute tossing is imperative but a cinch.

CHICKEN AND
MARINADE:

2 whole boneless fresh chicken
   breasts with skin on, split in
   half (4 pieces)
½ cup soy sauce
3 tablespoons plum wine
1 tablespoon Chinese rice wine
   or dry sherry
1½ tablespoons China Moon
   Chili-Orange Oil (page 15)
1½ teaspoons sugar
1 fat scallion, cut into 1-inch
   nuggets and smashed
3 quarter-size coins fresh ginger,
   smashed
1 tablespoon finely slivered
   coriander leaves and stems

1 tablespoon plus 1 teaspoon
   corn or peanut oil, for
   searing

SWEET MUSTARD
SAUCE:

¼ cup juice from China Moon
   Pickled Ginger (page 8)

3 tablespoons Dijon mustard
1 tablespoon sugar
1 tablespoon Five-Flavor Oil
   (page 13)
½ cup rice bran, corn, or
   peanut oil
¼ to ½ teaspoon fine sea salt

SALAD:

2 inner ribs celery, thinly sliced
   on the diagonal
6 cups mixed baby lettuces
3 cups baby spinach
½ cup Ginger-Pickled Red
   Cabbage Slaw (page 61)
3 tablespoons purple basil
   julienne
¼ cup thinly sliced green and
   white scallion rings
½ cup toasted, sliced almonds

1. Remove the fillet, membranes, and cartilage from the underside of the chicken breasts. Trim the skin where it overhangs the meat.

2. Combine all of the marinade ingredients in a bowl big enough to hold the chicken. Let stand for 15 minutes to infuse. Add the chicken and marinate for 1 hour at cool room temperature, turning the chicken once or twice midway.

3. Preheat the oven to 375°F. Move a rack to the upper third of the oven.

4. Drain the chicken and discard the marinade. Don't worry about any bits of green that cling to the meat.

THE
VEGETARIAN LIFE
OF A
MEAT MALLET

Chinese cooks and China Moon cooks smash a lot of vegetables: coins of ginger, nuggets of scallions and lemongrass, fresh chili peppers, and heads of roasted garlic on a regular basis, and lots of other things on an occasional basis. Aside from being a fair amount of fun, the smashing accomplishes an important task. It releases the vegetable juices from the peel, skin and/or fibers, leaving them ready to infuse in liquids or oils.

In the world of the Chinese home kitchen, much of this kind of smashing is done with the smooth end of a cleaver handle.

In our larger, smash-filled restaurant kitchen, we've discovered a meat mallet is a great alternative. Offering more heft and surface for smashing, the flat side does a terrific, speedy job. Only with lemongrass, which is like pounding rocks, do we use the toothy, irregular sides.

So, if you've had a meat mallet collecting dust in the kitchen in the wake of that chic recipe for paillards, here's to its second, vegetarian life!

5. Heat a large heavy skillet over high heat until a bead of water evaporates on contact. Add 1 tablespoon of the oil and swirl to glaze the pan. Reduce the heat to moderately high. Add the chicken breasts, skin side down, in a single layer and sear until deeply golden, 1 to 1½ minutes. Turn the breasts and sear the other side, 30 to 60 seconds more. Drizzle a bit more oil down the side of the pan, if needed to prevent sticking. Remove the breasts and place skin side up on a rack set over a baking sheet.

6. Bake the breasts until just cooked through, 5 to 10 minutes depending on the thickness of the breast and the intensity of the sear. Slice open a breast in the thickest part to check for doneness; it should be very moist at the core. The breasts will continue to cook a bit while cooling. Remove the chicken and let it cool on the rack. If working in advance, the chicken can be sealed and refrigerated overnight. Let come to room temperature before using.

7. To make the mustard sauce, whisk all of the sauce ingredients except the sea salt in a bowl. Add the salt to taste, beginning with ¼ teaspoon. The flavor of the mustard will dictate the amount of salt required. Seal and refrigerate until ready to use, overnight if you like. Re-whisk to blend before using.

8. Slice the chicken on a slight diagonal into thin ribbons, cutting crosswise against the grain. If you are adverse to chicken skin, remove it. Otherwise, leave it on as the Chinese do; it is tasty and adds texture.

9. Just before serving, toss the chicken and celery with half of the mustard sauce. In a separate bowl, combine the baby lettuces and spinach, and toss with the remaining mustard sauce. Sprinkle the slaw, basil, scallion rings, and half of the almonds over the greens and toss to combine. Add the chicken mixture to the greens and gently toss to blend.

10. Mound the salad on individual plates of a color that shows off the greens. Add a flurry of the remaining almonds to decorate each plate.

MENU SUGGESTIONS: You might pair this light main course salad with something hot and lush like Many Mushroom Buns (page 374) or Vegetarian Springrolls (page 349). Or if the weather is warm and you don't want to turn on the oven, it would be terrific as part of a cold buffet alongside a platter of Dragon Noodles (page 391) and a bowl of Loni's Cucumber Pickles with Chinese Black Beans (page 50).

FREEZING FRESH POULTRY

I am devoting a separate section to say that I never do it! I don't buy frozen chicken and I don't freeze chicken after purchase. There is nothing philosophical about it. I simply experimented years ago while writing my first cookbook and discovered that even a night in the freezer strikingly lessened the taste and texture of good chicken. I have since found the same appreciable loss with duck and quail that are frozen. That's why all of these recipes begin with the word "fresh."

SESAME-WALNUT CHICKEN WITH PINEAPPLE DIPPING SAUCE

SERVES 8 TO 10 AS PART OF A MULTICOURSE MEAL,
18 TO 20 AS AN HORS D'OEUVRE

I am not a big pineapple fan—ghastly visions of sweet and sour horrors come to mind—but I am wild for this sauce! It would be tasty with grilled pork or fish, but it is devastatingly good with these crispy chicken slices.

This is a "big deal dish." There is nothing especially hard about it, but it is rich and plush enough for only special occasions or a truly decadent mood. You'll think I made a mistake in giving the yield for this dish, but I didn't! No single pound of chicken has ever served so many.

CHICKEN AND VELVET MARINADE:

1 pound skinless, boneless fresh chicken breasts (2 pounds with skin and bone)
1 large egg white
1 tablespoon Chinese rice wine or dry sherry
1 teaspoon kosher salt
1½ tablespoons cornstarch

SESAME-WALNUT COATING:

3 cups finely chopped walnuts
2½ cups white sesame seeds
½ cup black sesame seeds

PINEAPPLE SAUCE:

1 can (28 ounces) pineapple chunks, in their own juice, drained, ½ cup juice reserved

1 small red Fresno chili
½ small green serrano chili
2 tablespoons coarsely chopped China Moon Pickled Ginger (page 8)
⅓ cup packed coriander leaves and stems
1 tablespoon juice from China Moon Pickled Ginger
1 tablespoon sugar or honey
¾ teaspoon fine sea salt
1 tablespoon Five-Flavor Oil (page 13)
¼ teaspoon China Moon Hot Chili Oil (page 10)
½ teaspoon Serrano-Lemongrass Vinegar (page 19)

4 to 6 cups corn or peanut oil, for deep-frying
Roasted Szechwan Pepper-Salt (page 5), to taste

THE WHEAT GERM CAPER

I was stunned when I gave up vegetarianism in Taiwan to discover the astoundingly sweet taste of Taiwan's chickens. I would write of this flavor to even my parents, who thought I was a nut anyway for becoming a vegetarian.

I uncovered the reason for the poultry's superb flavor when I visited a Taiwanese chicken farm. The chickens were fed on a rich diet of corn and wheat germ! (I was hooked on making crunchy granola in the big family wok, and one of my teachers had directed me to the farm in search of this last missing ingredient.)

Years later, I revisited the issue of East not meeting West in the chicken department when I flew from San Francisco to Tokyo. The first leg of the flight was catered by an American firm. The menu featured chicken à la something, and the chicken itself was tasteless. The second leg of the flight was cooked by a Japanese firm. In exactly the same preparation, the chicken, probably wheat-germ fed, was strikingly sweet.

So perhaps if we fed our chickens wheat germ, we could buy better tasting chickens.

1. Remove the fillet, membranes, and cartilage from the underside of the chicken breasts. Holding your knife at a 30-degree angle to the board, cut the chicken into diagonal strips about ¼ inch thick and 1 inch wide. Cut the longer strips in half. Use the broad side of the cleaver or knife to gently smack and flatten any slices that are thicker at one end.

2. In a bowl, briskly whisk together all of the marinade ingredients until smooth and thick. Add the chicken and toss well to coat and separate each slice. Seal airtight and refrigerate for several hours or overnight. Let come to room temperature before coating and re-toss to separate the slices.

3. To coat the chicken, combine the walnuts and white and black sesame seeds. Spread a thin layer of this mixture over the bottom of a large baking dish or plate. Arrange the chicken slices almost next to one another on top of the coating mixture. Sprinkle a thin, even layer on top of the chicken and press down with dry fingers to help the mixture adhere. Transfer the slices in a single layer to a parchment- or waxed paper–lined tray or plate. Repeat with the remaining coating mixture until all of the chicken slices have been coated. Put sheets of parchment or waxed paper between the layers of coated slices. Seal airtight and refrigerate the slices for 1 to 24 hours before frying.

4. To make the sauce, combine all of the ingredients in a food processor and whirl until smooth. Taste; add a bit more sugar or honey, if needed. If you are working in advance, buzz the coriander in only shortly before serving to preserve its color and taste. The sauce can be refrigerated overnight, if desired; press a piece of plastic wrap directly on the surface.

5. About 20 minutes before serving, fill a wok or deep heavy skillet with oil to a depth of 3 inches and rest a deep-fry thermometer on the rim. Heat the oil to the light-haze stage, 350°F, when a single slice of the chicken bubbles to the surface within 2 to 3 seconds. Adjust the heat so the temperature does not climb. Fry 10 to 15 slices of the chicken at a time, slipping them into the oil one by one in close succession. Adjust the heat as required to maintain a steady 350°F temperature. When the slices are cooked through, about 1 minute, the walnuts will be only lightly golden and the slices will float visibly high on the surface of the oil. With a large Chinese mesh spoon, promptly remove the cooked slices and transfer them to a baking sheet lined with a triple thickness of paper towels to drain. Don't fry the chicken to a deep gold or you will overcook it. Between batches, put the tray in a low oven to keep the chicken warm. Dredge the oil of loose nuts and reheat the oil to 350°F.

6. Once all of the slices are fried, sprinkle them lightly with pepper-salt. Station a large dip dish of sauce in the center of a dramatic platter and rim it with layers of the chicken.

OIL NOTE: Oil used for frying nut-coated foods is usually too full of debris for re-use. Wait until it cools and then discard it. Or, if it seems worthwhile, filter it through a fine-mesh strainer and several layers of cheesecloth, then bottle and refrigerate it for stir-frying.

MENU SUGGESTIONS: A crispy, cold salad of baby greens, including some peppery-bitter lettuces like baby mustard or watercress, would be a fine refreshment for the chicken. Dress it with our Fresh Ginger Vinaigrette (page 24).

STRANGE-FLAVOR CHICKEN NUGGETS (AKA "MCMANDARINS")

SERVES 2 AS A MAIN COURSE, 4 AS PART OF A MULTICOURSE MEAL

If you ever wish to bring the wrath of culinary corporate America down on your head, post a dish called McSomething on your menu! No sooner had I placed this combo of deep-fried chicken nuggets and a zingy Chinese strange-flavor sauce on our menu with the amusing (I thought) title of "McMandarins" than I received a letter from McDonald's trademark lawyers citing infringement. One of those guys (or gals) must have eaten my nuggets and thought them competitively delicious, thought I, and I brazenly kept the name as it was. *Another* letter came. I then hired the same firm to trademark the China Moon name and never heard another peep about "McMandarins." It's amazing what a good plate of fried chicken can do.

SPOTTING A FRESH BIRD

Buying poultry is easy in an ethnic market. Unless the Feds have made an inroad, the birds are usually sold with their heads and feet intact. One looks the bird straight in the beady eye for brightness and looks at the toes for good color and moistness, then knows if all is fresh and well. When I first moved to San Francisco almost 15 years ago, birds sold thusly wore a little tag around the ankle. "Kosher for Buddhist Religion," it read, which I thought was a great cross-cultural gag.

So, what are we to do if the chicken lobby has lopped off the heads and feet of our poultry in order to sell us older birds? Or if we're not buying a whole beast but just the breast? Here are some tips en route to fresh poultry.

Certainly go out of your way to find a shop that sells poultry exclusively. Ethnic poultry markets in large cities are a great resource. These shops are common in big American Chinatowns, where it is not unusual to see a dozen poultry parts displayed in a front window and whole birds of several varieties swinging by their necks in the rear.

If such a store is not to be found, scout out a market

that puts a high priority on fresh poultry. Lots of shaved ice, gleaming counters, and knowledgeable, friendly poultry patter from the butcher are signs of a good place. Trust those who don't have freezers and who butcher the birds themselves.

If even this is far-fetched in your neighborhood, look for the sure signs of fresh poultry in the supermarket cooler: Be it a duck, chicken, quail, squab, or rabbit, the skin should have a good gleam and a taut, moist look. As the piece of poultry ages— just like us human birds—the skin is the first thing to go; skin hung too long on a dead bird will look dry and wrinkled. Likewise, whatever meat is visible should look moist and plump. A whole bird or any pre-cut piece of it should not be sitting in blood. If it is, it has been sitting too long or without proper drainage. The kidneys, if you can look inside the bird to either side of the backbone, should be red or rosy. Like the gills of a fish, they turn to gray or brown the longer the beast is dead. Finally—and foremost!— fresh poultry has no odor. If it stinks, don't buy it, no matter what your plans for dinner.

For do-ahead bribers, the chicken can be marinated and the sauce ingredients assembled a night in advance. Do the frying and sauce-making just before serving.

VELVET MARINADE AND CHICKEN:

1 large egg white
1 tablespoon Chinese rice wine or dry sherry
1 teaspoon kosher salt
1 tablespoon cornstarch
1 pound skinless, boneless fresh chicken breasts (2 pounds with skin and bone), cut into 1-inch cubes

AROMATICS:

1 tablespoon finely minced fresh ginger
1 tablespoon finely minced garlic
2 tablespoons thinly sliced green and white scallion rings
1½ teaspoons dried red chili flakes

SAUCE:

1½ cups China Moon Double Stock (page 72) or unsalted chicken stock
2 tablespoons plus ½ teaspoon sugar
1 tablespoon cider vinegar
2 tablespoons balsamic vinegar
¼ cup soy sauce

½ cup water chestnut starch
3 to 4 cups corn or peanut oil
1 tablespoon cornstarch dissolved in 2 tablespoons cold chicken stock or water
Red and yellow bell pepper julienne, for garnish
Green and white scallion julienne, for garnish

1. Briskly whisk together all of the marinade ingredients through the cornstarch until smooth and thick. Toss well with the chicken. Seal airtight and refrigerate for 3 to 24 hours to set the marinade and infuse the chicken with its flavor. Let the chicken come to room temperature before frying.

2. Combine the aromatics in a small dish.

3. In a small bowl, combine the sauce ingredients, leaving a spoon in the bowl. Both the aromatics and the sauce may be sealed and refrigerated until cooking.

4. Just before frying, spread the water chestnut starch in a large bowl or plate. In small batches, add the chicken cubes and toss well to coat. Shake lightly in a colander to remove any excess starch.

5. Proceed immediately to fry the chicken: Fill a wok or deep heavy skillet with oil to a depth of 2 inches and rest a deep-fry thermometer on the rim. Heat the oil to the medium-haze stage, 375°F. Carefully slide the chicken into the oil and fry, using tongs or chopsticks to separate the cubes, until fully

cooked but only lightly golden, about 1½ minutes. Quickly scoop the cubes from the oil with a Chinese mesh spoon and drain on several sheets of paper towels. Do not fry the chicken to a deeper gold or it will be overcooked.

6. About 25 minutes before serving, finish the sauce: Heat a small heavy saucepan over high heat until hot enough to evaporate a bead of water on contact. Add 2 teaspoons oil, swirl to glaze the bottom, then reduce the heat to moderate. Add the aromatics and stir gently until fully fragrant, about 1 minute, adjusting the heat so they foam without browning. Stir the sauce mixture, add it to the pan, and turn the heat to high. Bring the liquids to a simmer, stirring. Stir the cornstarch mixture to recombine, add to the pan, and stir until the sauce turns glossy, 10 to 20 seconds. Turn off the heat and cover the pan.

7. Promptly transfer the chicken to heated plates and drizzle the sauce evenly on top. Garnish with a scattering of the bell pepper julienne and scallion threads. Serve at once.

OIL NOTE: Let the oil cool, strain it through a fine-mesh sieve and several layers of cheesecloth, then bottle and refrigerate for stir-frying.

MENU SUGGESTIONS: For lunch, I'd pair the chicken with a light green salad. For dinner, a stir-fry of seasonal greens and steamed or stir-fried rice would complete the plate.

GRILLED CHINESE CHICKEN WINGS WITH ORANGE ZEST AND GARLIC

SERVES 3 TO 4 AS A LIGHT MAIN COURSE, 5 TO 6 AS AN HORS D'OEUVRE

This is a dish I designed years before China Moon opened, when we had a lease on a very spiffy restaurant site adjacent to the San Francisco Opera

SAVE THE WORLD! LEARN TO COOK!

I cherish a wacky notion that our American world would be a lot saner if we all had the time and knowledge to cook. If every one of our kids had a cooking class in school, if harried workers had a cooking holiday instead of sick days, and if politicians had to make a meal for their constituents and serve it to them once a month, our world might spin a bit better.

We'd grow more aware of our resources. We'd prize the land that brought us real cherries and great-tasting meat. We'd never pollute our oceans if we caught and cooked our own fish.

If I were president, I'd call for a full week's work halt so everyone could stay at home and cook. Friends would gather and eat, kids would curl up in contented balls, and the sound of happy burping would resound throughout the world.

House that was to have a wine bar and a grill. In my dreams, I still serve these chicken wings to throngs of glamorous opera-goers, who glitter with jewels and toast Pavarotti with Champagne.

This is a simple dish to do, for four if not a hundred. The chicken wings are good hot or cold, cooked on the grill or in the broiler. Marinate them for as long as you can; they get better and better.

MARINADE:
Grated zest of 2 large scrubbed oranges
1½ tablespoons finely minced garlic
1½ tablespoons finely minced fresh ginger
2 hefty scallions, cut into 1-inch nuggets, smashed
¼ cup soy sauce

¼ cup plus 2 tablespoons Ma-La Oil (page 17) or Five-Flavor Oil (page 13)
2 tablespoons China Moon Chili-Orange Oil (page 15)
1 teaspoon Roasted Szechwan Pepper-Salt (page 5)

3 pounds (about 15) fresh plump chicken wings
Coriander sprigs, for garnish

1. Whisk together all of the marinade ingredients to combine. Add the chicken wings to the marinade and toss well to coat. Set aside at cool room temperature for several hours or refrigerate for up to 2 days. Toss occasionally to redistribute the marinade. The longer the marination, the better the flavor. Let come to room temperature before grilling.

2. Drain the wings and reserve the excess marinade. Grill the wings, skin side down, over moderately hot coals (just beginning to wear a jacket of white ash) until scored by the grill rack, about 6 minutes. Baste the wings with the reserved marinade as they grill. Turn over and grill and baste the second side until the juices run clear when the tip of a knife is poked into the thickest part of the wing.

3. Pile the wings on a large festive platter, garnish with the coriander sprigs, and serve.

MENU SUGGESTIONS: The chicken wings would be perfect with a salad of baby greens tossed with Fresh Ginger Vinaigrette (page 24). Steamed corn sprinkled with Roasted Szechwan Pepper-Salt (page 5) would be another ideal partner.

STIR-FRIED SPICY CHICKEN WITH ORANGE ZEST AND CRISPY CASHEWS

SERVES 2 TO 3 AS A MAIN COURSE,
4 TO 5 AS PART OF A MULTICOURSE MEAL

The flavors of chili, orange, and hoisin are wonderful together, the heat and zest of the first two providing relief from the sweetness of the third. Add to the dish the combination of plush chicken cubes and crispy cashews, and you have an entrée that is a sure crowd-pleaser. This is the sort of thing I can serve to both spice-lovers and meat-and-potatoes parental types—a rare achievement for any single dish.

VELVET MARINADE AND CHICKEN:
1 large egg white
1 tablespoon Chinese rice wine
   or dry sherry
1 teaspoon kosher salt
1 tablespoon cornstarch
1 pound skinless, boneless fresh
   chicken breasts (2 pounds
   with skin and bone), cut into
   1-inch cubes

AROMATICS:
1 tablespoon finely minced fresh
   ginger
1 tablespoon finely minced
   garlic
2 tablespoons thinly sliced green
   and white scallion rings
½ teaspoon finely minced red
   Fresno chilis, or ¼ to ½
   teaspoon dried red chili flakes
Grated zest of 1 scrubbed small
   orange

SAUCE:
1½ cups China Moon Infusion
   (page 72), China Moon
   Double Stock (page 72), or
   unsalted chicken stock
2 tablespoons hoisin sauce
2 teaspoons Chinese rice wine
   or dry sherry
2 teaspoons soy sauce
2 tablespoons freshly squeezed,
   strained orange juice
1 tablespoon balsamic
   vinegar
1 tablespoon cider vinegar

1 cup finger-lengths Chinese broccoli or broccoli rape, or 1 carrot, diagonally cut into plain or rippled coins

8 to 10 ears fresh baby corn, halved lengthwise if large, or ½ cup fresh corn kernels

2 to 3 tablespoons corn or peanut oil, for stir-frying

1 small yellow onion, cut into ¾-inch squares

1 red bell pepper, cut into ¾-inch squares

2 cups Napa cabbage or ruby chard squares (1 inch)

1 teaspoon paper-thin red Fresno chili rings

1 teaspoon paper-thin yellow wax chili rings

1 tablespoon cornstarch dissolved in 1½ tablespoons cold chicken stock or water

⅓ cup fried or roasted cashews (page 34), for garnish

COLORFUL CHILIS

The combination of fresh red and yellow chilis adds great color and flavor to the dish. If they aren't easily available, however, simply up the dried red chili flakes in the aromatics to ½ to ¾ teaspoon.

1. In a bowl, briskly whisk together the marinade ingredients through the cornstarch until smooth and thick. Add the chicken and toss well. Cover and marinate in the refrigerator for 3 to 24 hours. Let come to room temperature and re-toss before cooking.

2. Combine the aromatics in a small dish; cover until ready to use.

3. Combine all of the sauce ingredients in a bowl. Stir to blend, leaving the spoon in the bowl.

4. Blanch the broccoli or carrot in simmering water to cover to seal the color and cook the outside, 15 to 30 seconds. Plunge the vegetable into ice water to chill, then drain. Blanch the baby corn, if using, in boiling water for 1 minute, or blanch the corn kernels, if using, for 5 seconds. Chill in ice water and drain. All the above, including the vegetable cutting, may be done a full day ahead. Seal and refrigerate the ingredients; bring to room temperature before cooking.

5. About 15 minutes before serving, bring 4 cups of water to a steaming near simmer. Add the chicken, stir to separate the cubes, and cook until the outside turns 90 percent white, 40 to 50 seconds. Drain and set aside. The chicken will be cooked on the outside and a bit raw in the center.

6. Heat a wok or large heavy skillet over high heat until hot enough to evaporate a bead of water on contact. Add 2 tablespoons of the oil and swirl to glaze the pan. When the oil is hot enough to sizzle a scallion ring on contact, reduce the heat to moderate and add the aromatics. Stir gently until fully fragrant, 20 to 30 seconds, adjusting the heat so they foam without browning. Add the onion and bell pepper, and toss briskly until softened, 2 to 3 minutes. Add the carrots and baby corn, if using, and toss until hot, about 1 minute. Add the cabbage, broccoli, and fresh chilis, and toss until the cabbage is wilted, about 1 minute. As you stir-fry, adjust the heat to maintain a merry sizzle and drizzle a bit more oil down the side of the pan, if needed to prevent sticking.

7. Stir the sauce and add it to the pan. Raise the heat to high, cover the pan, and bring the sauce to a simmer. Stir the cornstarch mixture, add it to the pan, and stir the sauce until it turns glossy, 10 to 20 seconds. Add the chicken cubes and corn kernels, if using, and toss gently until the chicken is cooked through, about 30 seconds. Serve on a heated platter or individual plates of contrasting color. Garnish with fried cashews.

MENU SUGGESTIONS: This is a one-dish meal, needing only a bowl of rice, a plate of simple pasta, or a Pot-Browned Noodle Pillow (page 401) to complete it.

STIR-FRIED HOISIN CHICKEN CUBES WITH LEMON ZEST

SERVES 3 TO 4 AS A MAIN COURSE, 5 TO 6 AS PART OF A MULTICOURSE MEAL

For lovers of flavor contrast, this is an eminently appealing dish—sweet by virtue of the hoisin sauce and sparkly with the (literal) zest of lemon.

VELVET MARINADE AND CHICKEN:
1 large egg white
1 tablespoon Chinese rice wine or dry sherry
1 teaspoon kosher salt
1 tablespoon cornstarch
1 pound skinless, boneless chicken breasts (2 pounds with skin and bone), cut into 1-inch cubes

AROMATICS:
1 tablespoon finely minced fresh ginger
1½ tablespoons finely minced garlic
Grated zest of 1 scrubbed plump lemon
½ to ¾ teaspoon dried red chili flakes

WOK-HEY

Wok-hey! is my threatened name for a fast-food Chinese restaurant. It is also the Cantonese phrase for "wok spirit"—as in "wok energy."

If you stand outside our streetside kitchen window at China Moon, wok-hey is the cauldron of smoke in front of the stir-fry cook. It begins with a heat so intense that a necklace of oil drizzled around the inner rim of the wok slides to the bottom in a trail of smoke, scenting and flavoring the food being stir-fried.

Wok-hey is hard though not impossible to achieve at home. It implies a willingness to fill your kitchen with a bit of smoke and suffer the thrill of potentially burning the food. Most new stir-fry cooks incinerate the food on the path to learning proper wok-hey. This is the stage known in our kitchen as "Old Cigar"—descriptive of the taste and smell of the scorched food. Once mastered, wok-hey is a light smokiness that leaves only a pleasant, faint char at the edges of the food and layers the sauce with a dusky note. With a bit of char, you've achieved a bit of wok-hey, and hey, that's not bad!

SAUCE:

1⅓ cups China Moon Infusion (page 72), China Moon Double Stock (page 72), or unsalted chicken stock
3 tablespoons hoisin sauce
1½ tablespoons freshly squeezed lemon juice
1 tablespoon Chinese rice wine or dry sherry
1 tablespoon soy sauce
1 tablespoon Serrano-Lemongrass Vinegar (page 19) or unseasoned rice vinegar
¼ teaspoon kosher salt

3 ounces baby yellow and/or green zucchini, halved lengthwise if large, or 1 small zucchini, cut into ¼-inch coins

2 to 3 tablespoons corn or peanut oil, for stir-frying
1 small yellow onion, cut into ½-inch half-moons
1 red bell pepper, cut into ½-inch squares
1 small Chinese or Japanese eggplant, cut diagonally into ¼-inch coins
2 large scallions, cut into 1-inch nuggets
2 cups Napa cabbage squares (1 inch)
1 tablespoon cornstarch dissolved in 1½ tablespoons cold chicken stock or water
Finely julienned zest of 1 scrubbed small lemon
2 tablespoons purple or green basil julienne
Thinly sliced green and white scallion rings, for garnish

1. In a bowl, briskly whisk together the marinade ingredients through the cornstarch until smooth and thick. Add the chicken and toss well. Cover and marinate in the refrigerator for 3 to 24 hours. Let come to room temperature and re-toss before cooking.

2. Combine the aromatics in a small dish; cover until ready to use.

3. Combine all of the sauce ingredients in a small bowl. Stir to blend, leaving the spoon in the bowl.

4. Blanch the zucchini in boiling water to cover to cook part-way, 30 seconds for baby zucchini, 5 seconds for coins. Plunge into ice water to chill; drain. All the above, as well as cutting the vegetables, may be done a full day ahead. Seal and refrigerate the ingredients; bring to room temperature before cooking.

5. About 15 minutes before serving, bring 4 cups of water to a steaming near simmer. Add the chicken, stir gently to separate the cubes, and cook until the outside turns 90 percent white, 40 to 50 seconds. Drain immediately and set

aside. The chicken will be cooked on the outside but a bit raw in the middle.

6. Heat a wok or large heavy skillet over high heat until hot enough to evaporate a bead of water on contact. Add 2 tablespoons of the oil and swirl to glaze the pan. When the oil is hot enough to sizzle a pinch of the aromatics, reduce the heat to moderate and add the aromatics. Stir gently until fully fragrant, 20 to 30 seconds, adjusting the heat so they foam without browning. Add the onion and bell pepper and stir-fry briskly until softened, 2 minutes. Add the eggplant and toss gently for 1½ minutes. Adjust the heat to maintain a merry sizzle and drizzle a bit more oil down the side of the pan, if needed to prevent sticking. Add the zucchini and scallions, and toss for 2 minutes. Add the cabbage and toss for 1 minute.

7. Stir the sauce and add it to the pan. Raise the heat to high, cover the pan, and bring the sauce to a simmer. Stir the cornstarch mixture to recombine and add it to the pan. Stir the sauce until it turns glossy, 10 to 20 seconds. Add the chicken, the lemon zest, and half the basil, and toss gently to cook the chicken through, about 30 seconds. Serve immediately on a heated platter or individual plates of contrasting color. Garnish with the scallion rings and the remaining basil julienne.

MENU SUGGESTIONS: Steamed rice, simply dressed pasta, or a Pot-Browned Noodle Pillow (page 401) would be good catch-alls for the lush sauce. In summer, add a salad of watercress or garden-ripe tomatoes.

STIR-FRIED CHICKEN IN HOT BEAN SAUCE

SERVES 3 TO 4 AS A MAIN COURSE, 6 TO 7 AS PART OF A MULTICOURSE MEAL

T he kitchen staff loves this dish! No matter how weary our palates get tasting and adjusting all the dozens of things that go by in the course of a

HOLD THE SOAP

There is only one moment in your wok's long life when you can reasonably attack it with soap.

This is the moment after purchase. You and your new wok are home, and the chore is to dunk it in a sink full of hot soapsuds and scrub its belly, butt, and little ears to rid it of the manufacturer's protective coat of oil. Naked to the world, it then needs a careful drying and the application of a patina.

A wok patina is that sheen of slick (not sticky) blackness that is worn on the inside of every wok that is well cared for. If your wok has one, the food doesn't stick to it and you use a third to half the oil you would otherwise use for stir-frying. A proper patina also means your wok will never rust.

To patina a wok, put the newly washed wok with its clean, gray metal face on top of your strongest burner. Set the heat to maximum. (If you have a gas stove, remove the burner grid and balance the wok directly on the burner so as to bring the wok closer to the flame.) When the wok is so hot that a bead of water placed near the rim evaporates instantly—a stage that can take a good 5 minutes to reach—wipe a lint-free cloth moistened with pristine corn or peanut oil evenly all around the interior of the wok. The hot metal will soak up the oil, begin turning black, and smoke. Turn off the heat and let the wok cool for 2 minutes. Then, wipe off any excess oil with a dry cloth. Reheat the wok and repeat the process 5 or 6 times. The goal is a lightly blue-black surface from the center of the wok clear up to the rim.

If you have a grungy, dusty, or unsmooth wok that was not well cared for in the past, scrub it clean down to the metal with soap and an abrasive scrubber. Then, apply a new patina following the steps outlined above.

Once you have applied the initial patina, never again scrub your wok with soap! Use only hot water and the mildest of scrubbers. Soap will remove the protective patina.

After each of its first several uses, wash the wok well with hot water alone, and then repeat the heating and oiling steps once or twice. The patina will gradually build and blacken. You may have nightmares of your Western grandmother accusing you of dirty pots, but your Chinese granny will smile down on you and promise you an extra rice bowl in heaven.

working day, the pleasures of chicken, peanuts, and chili are a sure lure to wakefulness. Lunch or dinner, winter or summer, this is one of my personal favorites.

The slicing, mincing, and marinating can all be done ahead. The stir-frying, to be perfect, should be done at the last minute.

VELVET MARINADE AND CHICKEN:
1 large egg white
1 tablespoon Chinese rice wine or dry sherry
1 teaspoon kosher salt
1 tablespoon cornstarch
1 pound skinless, boneless fresh chicken breasts (about 2 pounds with bone and skin), cut across the grain into ribbons about 2 inches long and ¼ inch wide

AROMATICS:
1 tablespoon finely minced garlic
1 tablespoon finely minced fresh ginger
2 tablespoons thinly sliced green and white scallion rings

SAUCE:
½ cup China Moon Infusion (page 72), China Moon Double Stock (page 72), or unsalted chicken stock
1 tablespoon hot bean sauce
1 tablespoon Chinese rice wine or dry sherry

1 tablespoon unseasoned Japanese rice vinegar
¼ to ½ teaspoon sugar
2 tablespoons soy sauce

½ cup 2-inch lengths Chinese longbeans or flavorful green or yellow beans
1 small carrot, cut diagonally into rippled or plain coins ⅛ inch thick
2½ to 3 tablespoons corn or peanut oil, for stir-frying
1 small yellow onion, cut into ¼-inch half-moons
1 small red bell pepper, cut into ¼-inch strips
1 tender inner rib celery, cut diagonally into thin commas
1 to 1½ teaspoons paper-thin rings of red Fresno and/or yellow wax chilis
1 cup Napa cabbage ribbons (1½ inches wide)
1 tablespoon cornstarch dissolved in 1½ tablespoons cold chicken stock or water
½ cup fried or roasted peanuts (page 34), for garnish

1. In a bowl, briskly whisk together the marinade ingredients through the cornstarch until smooth and thick. Add the chicken and toss well. Seal airtight and marinate in the refrigerator for 3 to 24 hours.

2. Combine the aromatics in a small bowl; cover until ready to use.

3. Combine all of the sauce ingredients through the soy sauce in a small bowl. Stir to blend, leaving the spoon in the bowl.

4. Blanch the beans in simmering water to cover until tender-crisp, about 1 minute. Chill the beans in ice water; drain. Blanch the carrot coins 15 seconds. Refresh in ice water; drain. All the above, including the vegetable cutting, may be done a full day ahead. Seal and refrigerate the ingredients; bring to room temperature before cooking.

5. About 15 minutes before serving, bring 4 cups of water to a steaming near simmer. Add the chicken, stir gently to separate the shreds, and poach until 90 percent white, 40 to 50 seconds. Drain promptly and set aside. The chicken will be cooked on the outside but a bit raw in the middle.

6. Heat a wok or large heavy skillet over high heat until hot enough to evaporate a bead of water on contact. Add 2 tablespoons of the oil and swirl to glaze the pan. When the oil is hot enough to foam a scallion ring, reduce the heat to moderate. Add the aromatics and stir gently until fully fragrant, 15 to 20 seconds, adjusting the heat so they foam without browning. Add the onion and toss briskly until somewhat softened, about 2 minutes. Add the bell pepper and toss until the pepper strips are curly looking at the edges, 2 to 3 minutes more. Adjust the heat to maintain a merry sizzle and drizzle a bit more oil down the side of the pan, if needed to prevent sticking. Don't worry if the vegetables brown a bit; they will be flavorful.

7. Add the carrot coins, celery, and chili rings, and toss for 1 minute. Add the cabbage ribbons and toss until the cabbage is slightly wilted, 1 to 2 minutes longer. Toss in the beans.

8. Stir the sauce and add it to the pan. Raise the heat to high, cover the pan, and bring the sauce to a simmer. Stir the cornstarch mixture to recombine it and add it to the pan. Stir until the sauce turns glossy, 10 to 20 seconds. Add the chicken and toss gently to cook through, about 30 seconds.

THE ORGANIC QUESTION

Organics can be an emotional tug of war for a cook. Visions of happy chickens pecking corn to Beethoven make us all want to stand up and cheer, and we certainly want our poultry to taste good and to be good for us, but whether all organic poultry is better in this regard than all commercial poultry is a difficult question.

My counsel is to make a test, lining up the different organic and commercial poultry available in your area. Chicken breasts are an easy target for such a test. You can buy one of every brand, poach them in exactly the same way, and line them up for a comparative sampling. Mission accomplished (may the best breast win!), you can shred them all into a big salad for your friends. We regularly do such tastings at China Moon, and it is easy and fun to do at home.

The nose knows and the tongue knows, and if they don't know, neither do you! Don't make your food choices merely philosophical; after all, you have to eat what you think.

9. Serve at once on a heated platter or individual plates of contrasting color, garnished with a flurry of peanuts.

MENU SUGGESTIONS: I love this dish with noodles, rice, or a Pot-Browned Noodle Pillow (page 401). For a side-dish adornment, a green salad or fresh corn would be great. As a contrasting appetizer, try one of our non-poultry springrolls or a cold dish of salmon tiles (page 183).

STIR-FRIED HOT AND SOUR CHICKEN WITH BLACK BEANS AND BASIL

SERVES 2 TO 3 AS A MAIN COURSE, 4 TO 5 AS PART OF A MULTICOURSE MEAL

One of the pleasures of cooking in a restaurant with its assorted cooks and the pressure to always create new dishes—or new twists on old ones—is the frequent discovery of "new" ingredients. Fresh basil was never part of my kitchen until one of my sous-chefs suggested its flavor might go well with Chinese black beans. Indeed it does, and nowhere with greater success than in this otherwise very traditional, country-style Chinese dish.

This is a great one-dish supper. The preparation is easy and can be done up to a night ahead, leaving only the simple cooking for the last minute.

*VELVET MARINADE
AND CHICKEN:*
1 large egg white
1 tablespoon Chinese rice wine
   or dry sherry
1 teaspoon kosher salt
1 tablespoon cornstarch
1 pound skinless, boneless fresh
   chicken breasts (2 pounds
   with skin and bone), cut into
   1-inch cubes

AROMATICS:
1 tablespoon finely minced fresh
   ginger
1½ tablespoons finely minced
   garlic
1½ teaspoons coarsely chopped
   Chinese black beans (do not
   rinse them)
1½ teaspoons dried red chili
   flakes

SAUCE:
1⅓ cups China Moon Infusion
   (page 72), China Moon
   Double Stock (page 72), or
   unsalted chicken stock
1½ teaspoons sugar
2 teaspoons juice from China
   Moon Pickled Ginger
   (page 8)
½ teaspoon kosher salt

6 to 8 ounces baby squash,
   halved lengthwise if large, or
   small zucchini, cut into
   ¼-inch coins
8 to 12 ears fresh baby corn,
   halved lengthwise if large, or
   ½ cup fresh corn kernels
2½ to 3 tablespoons corn or
   peanut oil, for stir-frying
1 small yellow onion, cut into
   ¾-inch squares
1 red bell pepper, cut into
   ¾-inch squares
1 small carrot, cut diagonally
   into rippled or plain coins
   ⅛ inch thick
1 cup domestic white or brown
   (crimini) mushrooms, halved
   or quartered if large
2 fat scallions, cut into 1-inch
   nuggets
2 cups Napa cabbage squares
   (1 inch)
1 tablespoon cornstarch
   dissolved in 1½ tablespoons
   cold chicken stock or water
¼ to ⅓ cup coarsely chopped
   purple or green basil (leaves
   left whole if small)
2 teaspoons chopped Chinese
   black beans, for garnish
Diagonally cut green and white
   scallion rings, for garnish

BASIL NOTE

*Always judge the
amount of basil to use
in a stir-fry by first nibbling
on a leaf. From plant to plant
and from one variety to the
next, the taste can be dramatically different. As a general
rule, green basil is sharper
and stronger in flavor than
the duskier-tasting purple
varieties, but beyond that, I
commit myself to tasting.*

1. In a bowl, briskly whisk together the marinade ingredients through the cornstarch until smooth and thick. Add the
chicken and toss well. Cover and marinate in the refrigerator
for 3 to 24 hours. Let come to room temperature and re-toss
before cooking.

2. Combine the aromatics in a small dish; cover until
ready to use.

3. Combine all of the sauce ingredients in a small bowl.
Stir to blend, leaving the spoon in the bowl.

4. In a large saucepan of simmering water, blanch the

baby squash, if using, to cook part-way, for 30 seconds, or blanch the zucchini coins, if using, for 5 seconds to seal the color and cook the outside. Plunge the vegetable into ice water to chill; drain. Return the water to a simmer and blanch the baby corn, if using, for 1 minute, or blanch the kernels, if using, for 3 seconds. Refresh in ice water and drain. All of the above, as well as the vegetable cutting, may be done a full day ahead. Seal and refrigerate the ingredients; bring to room temperature before cooking.

5. About 15 minutes before serving, bring 4 cups of water to a steaming near simmer. Add the chicken, stir gently to separate the cubes, and cook until the outside turns 90 percent white, 40 to 50 seconds. Drain immediately and set aside. The chicken will be cooked on the outside but a bit raw in the middle.

6. Heat a wok or large heavy skillet over high heat until hot enough to evaporate a bead of water on contact. Add 2 tablespoons of the oil and swirl to glaze the pan. When the oil is hot enough to sizzle a bit of minced ginger, reduce the heat to moderate. Add the aromatics and stir gently until fully fragrant, about 30 seconds, adjusting the heat so they foam without browning. Add the onion and toss for 2 minutes. Add the bell pepper and carrot, and toss briskly until half-cooked, 2 to 3 minutes more. Adjust the heat to maintain a merry sizzle and drizzle a bit more oil down the side of the pan, if needed to prevent the vegetables from sticking.

7. Add the mushrooms and scallions, and toss briskly until the mushrooms are seared, about 2 minutes. Add the squash and baby corn, if using, and toss until hot, 1 minute. Add the cabbage and toss until slightly wilted, 2 minutes.

8. Stir the sauce and add it to the pan. Raise the heat to high, cover the pan, and bring the sauce to a simmer. Stir the cornstarch mixture to recombine, add it to the pan, and stir until the sauce turns glossy, 10 to 20 seconds. Add the chicken cubes, corn kernels, if using, and basil; toss gently until the chicken is cooked through, about 30 seconds.

9. Serve at once on a heated platter or individual plates of contrasting color. Garnish with a sprinkling of the chopped black beans and scallion rings.

MENU SUGGESTIONS: If you are a noodle-lover, this dish is wonderful on top of a Pot-Browned Noodle Pillow (page 401). Otherwise, it is happily partnered by rice or some thick wedges of hot garlic bread.

FRESH CHICKEN TALE 1

Years ago I lived with a Chinese family on the rural outskirts of Taipei, and the bus on which I rode was always jammed with peasants traveling to and from their fields. I sat down next to a cheery ancient lady, who stared at me brightly and gave me a big, mostly toothless, beetle-nut-red grin. Then she nipped my ankle. Or rather, her chicken did. It turned out that she was taking a pack of her birds to the city market, and one especially lively chicken head had poked through the bundle under her seat. There was a cackle: whether from the chicken or the lady I do not know.

STIR-FRIED CURRIED CHICKEN SLIVERS WITH ONIONS, TOMATOES, AND EGGPLANT

SERVES 2 TO 3 AS A MAIN COURSE, 4 TO 6 AS PART OF A MULTICOURSE MEAL

This is a great dish in the summertime, when most of the ingredients can be pulled from the garden. It is more a Chinese than an Indian style of curry, seasoned with the sweet tastes of the vegetables and the tartness of the vinegars and sherry.

The preparations may all be done a day or so ahead. The final cooking takes only minutes.

VELVET MARINADE AND CHICKEN:
1 large egg white
1 tablespoon Chinese rice wine or dry sherry
1 teaspoon kosher salt
1 tablespoon cornstarch
1 pound skinless, boneless fresh chicken breasts (2 pounds with skin and bone), cut across the grain into ribbons about 2 inches long and ¼ inch thick

AROMATICS:
1 tablespoon finely minced fresh ginger
1 tablespoon finely minced garlic
2 tablespoons thinly sliced green and white scallion rings
¼ to ½ teaspoon dried red chili flakes (optional)

SAUCE:
1½ cups China Moon Infusion (page 72), China Moon Double Stock (page 72), or unsalted chicken stock
2 teaspoons balsamic vinegar
2 teaspoons unseasoned Japanese rice vinegar
2 teaspoons Chinese rice wine or dry sherry
2½ teaspoons soy sauce
1 teaspoon sugar
½ teaspoon Chinese chili sauce
½ teaspoon China Moon Ten-Spice (page 6)
½ teaspoon China Moon Curry Powder (page 7)

WOK TEARJERKERS

From the annals of wok misery, there are several categories worth publishing. Offenders will thus be notified and potentially rehabilitated, and the responsible citizenry shall beware.

▲ *Rusty woks:* These woks are scrubbed clean of their protective manufacturer's grease and then scrubbed clean again after use, leaving them naked to the elements. A wok needs a protective patina (see page 134). Attack it repeatedly with soap, and you are committing a crime.

▲ *Dusty, tacky woks:* These woks were left with excess oil on their faces. Either the villainy was done in the initial patina process (whereby the Person-In-Charge didn't wipe off the excess oil after heating the metal) or the wok was cleaned in cold water rather than hot, which would have shed it of excess grease. The cure for this wok is to be scrubbed clean down to the metal with soapsuds and a stiff abrasive pad; then a new patina should be applied.

▲**Woks that are black in the center and tacky, dusty, or rusty at the top:** These poor woks are being perverted for stir-frying on a stovetop that doesn't generate sufficient heat, hence the uneven face. These woks need a bath, a re-oiling, and a new life in deep-frying, steaming, or smoking. The offending adult addicted to stir-frying needs to get him/herself a large, heavy skillet.

2 to 2½ tablespoons corn or peanut oil
1 small yellow onion, cut into ¼-inch half-moons
1 small yellow bell pepper, cut into ¼-inch strips
1 small red bell pepper, cut into ¼-inch strips
1 small Chinese or Japanese eggplant, cut into ¼-inch half-moons
1 small carrot, cut into rippled or plain coins ⅛ inch thick
1 small green or yellow zucchini, cut into ¼-inch coins

8 pieces Oven-Dried Plum Tomatoes (page 36), or 1 to 2 firm red tomatoes, cut into wedges, or ½ cup halved cherry tomatoes
2 tablespoons purple or green basil julienne
1 tablespoon cornstarch dissolved in 1½ tablespoons cold chicken stock or water
Coriander sprigs, for garnish

1. In a bowl, briskly whisk together the marinade ingredients through the cornstarch until smooth and thick. Add the chicken and toss well. Seal airtight and marinate in the refrigerator for 3 to 24 hours. Let come to room temperature and re-toss before cooking.

2. Combine the aromatics in a small bowl. Seal airtight until needed.

3. Combine all of the sauce ingredients in a bowl. Stir to blend, leaving the spoon in the bowl. All the above, and the vegetable cutting as well, may be done up to a day ahead. Seal and refrigerate the ingredients; bring to room temperature before cooking.

4. Just before stir-frying, bring 4 cups of water to a steaming near simmer. Add the chicken, stir gently to separate the shreds, and poach until the chicken is 90 percent white, 40 to 50 seconds. Drain promptly and set aside. The chicken will be cooked on the outside but a bit raw in the middle.

5. Heat a wok or deep heavy skillet over high heat until hot enough to evaporate a bead of water on contact. Add 1½ tablespoons of the oil and swirl to glaze the pan. When the oil is hot enough to sizzle a scallion ring, reduce the heat to moderate. Add the aromatics and stir gently until fully fragrant, about 30 seconds. Adjust the heat so the aromatics foam without browning. Add the onion and toss briskly until the edges start to wilt, about 1 minute. Add the yellow and red bell peppers and toss until curly looking at the tips, about 2 minutes more. Adjust the heat to maintain a merry sizzle and don't worry if the onions brown; they will be flavorful.

6. Add the eggplant and toss until hot, about 1 minute. Drizzle a bit more oil down the side of the pan if needed to prevent sticking. Add the carrots, toss for 1½ minutes, then add the zucchini and toss 1 minute more.

7. Stir the sauce and add it to the pan. Raise the heat to high, cover, and bring the sauce to a simmer. Add the tomatoes and half the basil, and toss gently to blend. Stir the cornstarch mixture to recombine it and add it to the pan. Stir the sauce until glossy, 10 to 20 seconds. Add the chicken slivers and toss gently to cook through, about 15 seconds.

8. Serve immediately on a heated platter or individual plates of contrasting color. Garnish with the remaining basil and some leggy sprigs of fresh coriander.

MENU SUGGESTIONS: We love to ladle this dish over rice or wedges of Pot-Browned Noodle Pillow (page 401). It could also be paired with lightly oiled fettuccine, maybe tossed with a sprinkling of fresh herbs. If you are serving it in summer, ears of fresh corn would be a wonderful accompaniment.

SWEET, SOUR, AND SPICY CHICKEN NUGGETS

SERVES 2 TO 3 AS A MAIN COURSE, 4 TO 6 AS PART OF A MULTICOURSE MEAL

I am not a great fan of sweet and sour dishes *or* pineapple, but I like this spicy variation, the invention of one of our early sous-chefs. The "sour" is made interesting by a mixture of fresh lemon and orange juices and plum wine, and the "sweet" is offset by the addition of fresh ginger and chilis. I recommend it to the Trader Vics of the 90s!

Frying the chicken adds a wonderful lushness.

FRY,
THEN STIR-FRY

In a classic Chinese dish such as this one, where you are preceding the stir-frying by frying, it's a big relief to have a separate pan for each step. That way you can avoid handling the hot oil and instead deal with it easily once it is cool. On a Western stovetop, I always choose to do my frying in a wok (its shape conserves oil) and my stir-frying in a large skillet.

However, if you are oil-shy, you can instead poach the chicken in water as described in any of the preceding several recipes.

VELVET MARINADE AND CHICKEN:
1 large egg white
1 tablespoon Chinese rice wine or dry sherry
1 teaspoon kosher salt
1 tablespoon cornstarch
1 pound skinless, boneless fresh chicken breasts (2 pounds with skin and bone), cut into 1-inch cubes

AROMATICS:
1½ tablespoons finely minced fresh ginger
1½ tablespoons finely minced garlic
1 to 2 small red Fresno chilis, cut crosswise into paper-thin rings
2 tablespoons thinly cut green and white scallion rings

SAUCE:
2 cups China Moon Double Stock (page 72) or unsalted chicken stock
¼ cup cider vinegar
¼ cup sugar
1 tablespoon freshly squeezed orange juice
¼ cup unsweetened pineapple juice
1 tablespoon freshly squeezed lemon juice
2 tablespoons plum wine
1 tablespoon distilled white vinegar
1 tablespoon kosher salt
2 tablespoons soy sauce

3 cups corn or peanut oil
½ cup water chestnut starch
1 yellow onion, cut into 1-inch squares
1 red bell pepper, cut into 1-inch squares
1 yellow bell pepper, cut into 1-inch squares
4 fat scallions, cut into 1-inch nuggets
1¼ cups pineapple chunks
1 tablespoon cornstarch dissolved in 1½ tablespoons cold chicken stock or water
Diagonally sliced green and white scallion rings, for garnish

1. In a bowl, briskly whisk together the marinade ingredients through the cornstarch until smooth and thick. Add the chicken and toss well. Seal airtight and marinate for 3 to 24 hours, refrigerated. Let come to room temperature and re-toss before cooking.

2. Combine the aromatics in a small bowl; cover until ready to use.

3. Combine the sauce ingredients through the soy sauce in a bowl. Stir to blend, leaving the spoon in the bowl. All of the above, including the vegetable cutting, may be done a day in advance. Seal and refrigerate the ingredients; bring to room temperature before cooking.

4. About 30 minutes before serving, add oil to a depth of 2 inches in a wok or deep heavy skillet; rest a deep-fry thermometer on the rim. Heat the oil to the medium-haze stage, 375°F, until hot enough to foam a pinch of water chestnut starch. Adjust the heat so the temperature does not climb. Station a large bowl with the water chestnut starch, a large Chinese mesh spoon or a fry basket, and a tray lined with a triple thickness of paper towels alongside your stove-top.

5. Drain the chicken of excess marinade. Toss a third of the chicken cubes with the water chestnut starch to coat them well. Put them in the mesh spoon or basket and shake off any excess. Carefully slide the chicken cubes into the hot oil, swish gently to separate, and fry until the cubes float high on the oil and the chicken is 90 percent cooked but still pale, about 2 minutes. Quickly scoop the cubes from the oil and drain on the waiting paper towels. Repeat with the remaining chicken, allowing the oil to return to 375°F between each batch. Do not overcook the chicken in the oil. It will continue to cook from its own heat as it drains and will finish cooking in the sauce.

6. Carefully drain all but 2½ tablespoons of the oil into a heatproof container or glaze a second wok or skillet with 2½ tablespoons of the oil. Set over moderately high heat until the oil is hot enough to sizzle a bit of ginger on contact. Add the aromatics and stir gently until fully fragrant, 20 to 30 seconds, adjusting the heat so they foam without browning. Add the onion and toss briskly until softened, about 2 minutes. Add the red and yellow bell peppers and toss until the peppers are curled at the edges, about 2 minutes more. Adjust the heat to maintain a merry sizzle and drizzle a bit more oil down the side of the pan, if needed to prevent sticking. Add the scallions and toss for 1 minute.

7. Stir the sauce and add it to the pan. Turn the heat to high, cover the pan, and bring the sauce to a simmer. Add the pineapple chunks. Stir the cornstarch mixture to recombine it and add it to the pan. Stir until the sauce turns glossy, 10 to 20 seconds. Add the chicken and toss gently to cook through, about 30 seconds.

FRESH CHICKEN TALE 2

In the sparsely populated and very beautiful central mountains of Taiwan, on the same bus where I'd gotten nipped by the chicken six months earlier, I met a Chinese character named Fred. Fred was the head of a mountain climbing club. The club took me and a few of my American student friends along on a climbing trip, and we promptly got lost. It was a cold night-and-a-half in a rain forest before we were rescued by a keenly amused group of aborigines. My ankle (the one that had been pecked) had been twisted in the process of climbing, so I was ceremonially carried on the back of one of our Rambo-type rescuers and plopped down as a trophy on the doorstep of the tribal chief. In celebration of our rescue, the chief's wife killed a fresh chicken in our honor. The whole tribe clustered in the doorway to watch me, while I watched her—her face was beautifully tattooed—slitting the throat of a squealing chicken and stripping it of its feathers. The fact that I fainted was taken as a sign of our ordeal.

8. Serve on a heated platter or individual plates of contrasting color. Garnish with a sprinkling of the scallion rings.

OIL NOTE: Once the frying-oil has cooled, strain it through a fine-mesh strainer lined with a triple thickness of cheesecloth. Bottle, refrigerate, and re-use for stir-frying and frying.

MENU SUGGESTIONS: Tradition and the palate both call out for simple steamed rice to accompany this dish. A salad of baby greens dressed lightly with Fresh Ginger Vinaigrette (page 24) could precede or follow it as a refreshment. Be sure to include some peppery lettuces like mizuna, baby mustard, or watercress to balance the sweetness of the sauce.

STIR-FRIED CHICKEN RIBBONS AND SHANGHAI NOODLES IN SPICY BEAN SAUCE

SERVES 4 TO 6 AS A MAIN COURSE

This is a wonderful dish for late summer or fall, when basil and tomatoes are still around and the turn in the weather is suggesting a bit of spice. The combination of flavors is terrific, and there is nothing to derail even a very new cook.

Shanghai noodles are pudgy egg noodles with a chewy texture; many Chinatown noodle factories package them in one-pound bags. If they are not readily available, any similar egg noodle of Chinese or Italian heritage can be substituted with success.

All of the preparations can be done hours or a day in advance. The final cooking takes only a few minutes.

VELVET MARINADE
AND CHICKEN:
1 large egg white
1 tablespoon Chinese rice wine
    or dry sherry
1 teaspoon kosher salt
1 tablespoon cornstarch
1 pound skinless, boneless fresh
    chicken breasts (2 pounds
    with skin and bone), cut
    across the grain into ribbons
    about 2 inches long and ¼
    inch thick

AROMATICS:
1 tablespoon chopped Chinese
    black beans (do not rinse
    them)
⅓ cup Chinese rice wine or dry
    sherry
1 tablespoon finely minced
    garlic
2 tablespoons thinly sliced green
    and white scallion rings
½ teaspoon dried red chili flakes

SAUCE:
1⅔ cups China Moon Infusion
    (page 72), China Moon
    Double Stock (page 72), or
    unsalted chicken stock
1 tablespoon soy sauce
2 teaspoons mushroom soy
    sauce

1 teaspoon Chinese chili sauce
1 tablespoon cider vinegar
1½ teaspoons sugar

½ pound fresh Shanghai
    noodles (see page 399)
2 teaspoons Ma-La Oil (page
    17), Five-Flavor Oil (page
    13), or Japanese sesame oil
1 small carrot, julienned
½ cup yellow wax beans (2-inch
    lengths)
2 to 3 tablespoons corn or
    peanut oil, for stir-frying
1 small red onion, cut into ½-
    inch squares
4 domestic white or brown
    (crimini) mushrooms,
    quartered
2 fat scallions, cut into 1-inch
    nuggets
6 to 8 pieces Oven-Dried Plum
    Tomatoes (page 36)
1 tablespoon cornstarch
    dissolved in 1½ tablespoons
    cold chicken stock or water
2 tablespoons purple basil
    julienne

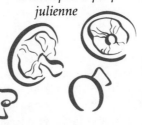
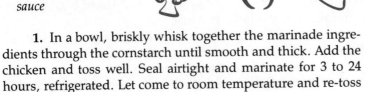

1. In a bowl, briskly whisk together the marinade ingredients through the cornstarch until smooth and thick. Add the chicken and toss well. Seal airtight and marinate for 3 to 24 hours, refrigerated. Let come to room temperature and re-toss before cooking.

2. Soak the chopped Chinese black beans in the rice wine for 10 minutes. Drain, reserving the wine. In a bowl, combine the black beans with all of the other aromatic ingredients. Cover and set aside.

FRESH CHICKEN
TALE 3

///

A more recent, albeit less colorful, chicken memory is from a few years ago in the China Moon kitchen, when one of our purveyors delivered several dozen freshly killed organic chickens, heads and feet left on, for an experiment. The experiment was delayed for several days and so was all traffic in the walk-in refrigerator. The birds were in such an extreme state of rigor mortis that they were totally stiff and couldn't be stored in any typical, anonymous way. Someone stuck them in odd postures on every shelf in the walk-in— dangling by a stiff toe or wing, or belly up on top of a stock bucket with a tomato stuck on its beak. I double up with laughter remembering them there, like some wacko scene from a movie called "Chicken Nightmares."

3. In a small bowl, combine all of the sauce ingredients through the sugar. Stir in the reserved wine from soaking the black beans. Set aside, leaving the spoon in the bowl.

4. Fluff the noodles in a colander to separate and untangle the strands. Bring a generous amount of water to a rolling boil. Add the noodles, swish gently with chopsticks, and cook until the noodles are al dente, about 3 minutes. Drain promptly, plunge briefly into ice water to chill, then drain thoroughly. Toss the noodles with the infused oil. Cover and set aside.

5. In a small saucepan filled with rapidly boiling water, blanch the carrot julienne until tender-crisp, about 30 seconds. Immediately plunge the carrots into ice water to chill; drain. Blanch the wax beans until tender-crisp, 30 to 60 seconds. Immerse in ice water to chill, then drain thoroughly. All the above, including the cutting of the vegetables, may be done up to a day ahead. Seal and refrigerate the ingredients; bring to room temperature before cooking.

6. About 15 minutes before serving, bring 4 cups of water to a steaming near simmer. Add the chicken, stir gently to separate the ribbons, and poach until the outside is 90 percent white, 40 to 50 seconds. Drain promptly and set aside. The chicken will be cooked on the outside but a bit raw in the middle.

7. Heat a wok or heavy skillet over high heat until hot enough to evaporate a bead of water on contact. Add 2 tablespoons of the oil and swirl to glaze the pan. When the oil is hot enough to sizzle a scallion ring, reduce the heat to moderate. Add the aromatics and stir gently until fully fragrant, 20 to 30 seconds. Adjust the heat so the aromatics foam without browning. Add the red onion and toss briskly until softened, about 2 minutes. Add the mushrooms and toss for 1½ minutes. Add the scallions and noodles, and toss for 3 minutes more. Adjust the heat to maintain a merry sizzle and drizzle a bit more oil down the side of the pan, if needed to prevent sticking. Don't worry if the vegetables or noodles brown a bit; they will be flavorful. Add the blanched beans, carrots, and oven-dried tomatoes, and toss to combine.

8. Stir the sauce and add it to the pan. Raise the heat to high, cover the pan, and bring the sauce to a simmer. Stir the cornstarch mixture to recombine and add it to the pan. Stir until the sauce turns glossy, 10 to 20 seconds. Add the chicken and half of the basil julienne. Toss gently to cook the chicken through, about 30 seconds.

9. Serve on a heated platter or individual plates. Garnish with a sprinkling of the remaining basil julienne.

MENU SUGGESTIONS: This is a fine one-dish supper. A bowl of Turmeric Tomatoes (page 59) or a pre-dinner munchie of Strange-Flavor Eggplant with garlic croutons (page 62) could be added, if you like.

HOT AND SOUR CHICKEN SANDPOT

SERVES 3 TO 4 AS A MAIN COURSE, 6 TO 8 AS PART OF A MULTICOURSE MEAL

This is a terrific choice for a fall dinner, when there's a chill in the air and the soul needs warming. Or if your soul is chilly and it's winter, simply substitute a handful of red chard for the bell peppers.

*VELVET MARINADE
AND CHICKEN:*
1 large egg white
1 tablespoon Chinese rice wine
   or dry sherry
1 teaspoon kosher salt
1 tablespoon cornstarch
1 pound skinless, boneless fresh
   chicken breasts (2 pounds
   with skin and bone), cut into
   1-inch cubes

AROMATICS:
1 tablespoon finely minced fresh
   ginger
1 tablespoon finely minced
   garlic
2 teaspoons coarsely chopped
   Chinese black beans (do not
   rinse them)

2 tablespoons thinly sliced green
   and white scallion rings
¾ to 1 teaspoon dried red chili
   flakes

SAUCE:
1 cup China Moon Infusion
   (page 72), China Moon
   Double Stock (page 72), or
   unsalted chicken stock
2 tablespoons plus 2 teaspoons
   mushroom soy sauce
1 tablespoon plus 2 teaspoons
   Serrano-Lemongrass Vinegar
   (page 19) or distilled white
   vinegar
1½ teaspoons sugar
1 teaspoon Chinese rice wine or
   dry sherry
¼ teaspoon kosher salt

MUSHROOM SOY SAUCE

*Mushroom soy sauce—
infused with dried
black (shiitake) mushrooms—
is the flavorful star of the
black soy sauce family, lend-
ing great savor to a dish such
as this. There is no substitute, but if you are hankering
for the sandpot and are without the special soy, use 3½
tablespoons of a good-tasting
regular soy sauce (the greater
amount being needed because
black soys are stronger) and
maybe add a handful of sliced
wild mushrooms to the pot.*

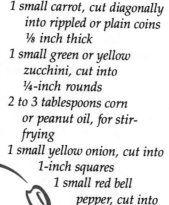

1 small carrot, cut diagonally into rippled or plain coins ⅛ inch thick

1 small green or yellow zucchini, cut into ¼-inch rounds

2 to 3 tablespoons corn or peanut oil, for stir-frying

1 small yellow onion, cut into 1-inch squares

1 small red bell pepper, cut into 1-inch squares

1 small yellow bell pepper, cut into 1-inch squares

¾ cup domestic white or brown (crimini) mushrooms, halved, or quartered if large

1 leek, white part only, halved lengthwise, then cut crosswise into ⅛-inch half-moons

1½ cups Napa cabbage squares (1 inch)

Scant ½ teaspoon minced Chinese black beans, for garnish

Diagonally cut green and white scallion rings, for garnish

1. In a bowl, briskly whisk together the marinade ingredients through the cornstarch until smooth and thick. Add the chicken and toss well. Cover and marinate for 3 to 24 hours, refrigerated. Let come to room temperature and re-toss before cooking.

2. Combine the aromatics through the red chili flakes in a small bowl; cover until ready to use.

3. Combine all of the sauce ingredients in a bowl. Stir to blend, leaving the spoon in the bowl.

4. Blanch the carrot in a generous amount of boiling water until half-cooked, 20 to 30 seconds. Immerse the carrots in ice water to chill. Drain and set aside. Return the water to a boil, blanch the zucchini for 5 seconds; then, chill and drain.

5. Heat a wok or large heavy skillet over high heat until hot enough to evaporate a bead of water on contact. Add 2 tablespoons of the oil and swirl to glaze the pan. When the oil is hot enough to foam a bit of scallion on contact, reduce the heat to moderate. Add the aromatics and stir gently until fully fragrant, 15 to 20 seconds, adjusting the heat so they foam without browning. Add the onion and toss until a bit softened, 2 minutes. Add the red and yellow bell peppers and toss for 2 minutes. Add the mushrooms and leek, and toss for 2 minutes more. Adjust the heat to maintain a merry sizzle and drizzle a bit more oil down the side of the pan, if needed to prevent sticking. Don't worry if the vegetables brown a bit; they will be flavorful. Add the Napa cabbage and toss until the cabbage is slightly wilted, about 1 minute. Add the carrots and zucchini, and toss to combine.

6. Spread the vegetables on a large platter to cool. All the above may be done up to a day in advance. Seal and refrigerate the ingredients; bring to room temperature before the final cooking.

7. About 20 minutes before serving, bring 4 cups of water to a steaming near simmer. Add the chicken, stir gently to separate the cubes, and cook until the outside is 90 percent white, 40 to 50 seconds. Drain immediately and set aside. The chicken will be cooked on the outside but a bit raw in the center.

8. Arrange the vegetables in the bottom of a 2- to 3-quart Chinese sandpot or other heavy casserole. Stir the sauce and add it to the pot. Cover and bring to a simmer. Cook the vegetables until hot and tender-crisp, 3 to 4 minutes. Turn off the heat, fold the chicken into the pot, then replace the cover and let the casserole stand undisturbed for 1 minute to cook the chicken through. Serve promptly, garnished with a light sprinkling of minced black beans and a flurry of scallion rings.

MENU SUGGESTIONS: I love potatoes with this dish—boiled little potatoes, Wok-Seared New Potatoes (page 424), Crispy Potatoes (page 425), or mashed big potatoes! As a refreshment, you could follow the sandpot with a salad of baby greens dressed with Orange Vinaigrette (page 25).

SANDPOT CASSEROLE OF CURRIED CHICKEN NUGGETS

SERVES 3 TO 4 AS A MAIN COURSE, 6 TO 8 AS PART OF A MULTICOURSE MEAL

This is a lightly spiced, curried casserole that is as simple as it is appealing. Its beauty resides in the freshness of the poultry and vegetables and the quality of the curry powder. Bitter curry powders will

SANDPOTS

Stewing is probably the earliest form of Chinese cookery. Many of the priceless Chinese bronze vessels we see in museums today once upon a time held savory stews of dog, goat, or bear—nuggets of ancient yumminess that turned tender with long cooking.

I don't know much about the evolution of the pots of antiquity to the Chinese sandpots of today, but a stew is a stew—and what a stew needs is a squat pot that retains the heat and conducts it slowly. For this purpose, nothing beats a sandpot for ease and price.

Chinese sandpots come in several shapes and designs. The most versatile is a squat pot with a "sandy" unglazed white exterior and a smooth glazed chocolate brown interior. It comes with a slightly domed or squared-off lid, with a knob on top or two tiny ears holding a wire handle. Klutzy types will appreciate the sort of sandpot with a wire brace around the bottom; these are typically favored by restaurants in order to keep them from breaking. From-stove-to-table types will want the pristine, wireless style and will strive to treat it gently.

The size of the sandpot casserole needed depends on how many people you customarily serve. The recipes in this book are geared mostly for 4 to 6 servings, and this is best accommodated in a sandpot that will hold 2 to 3 quarts of food. Smaller sandpots (we use them in the restaurant) are delightful for individual servings and can cheerily be used as long as you have enough burners to hold them.

Of course, one doesn't need a sandpot at all. Any heavy metal casserole will do. However, if culture is what you're serving, choosing and using a sandpot is lots of fun.

wreck the dish, and I heartily endorse either making your own or doing a bit of market research to uncover a desirable brand.

The preparations can all be done in advance. As with most one-dish casserole meals, there is an hour or so of slicing and mixing to slog through, but at the end all that is required is a mere 15 minutes for cooking.

VELVET MARINADE AND CHICKEN:
1 large egg white
1 tablespoon Chinese rice wine or dry sherry
1 teaspoon kosher salt
1 tablespoon cornstarch
1 pound skinless, boneless fresh chicken breasts (2 pounds with skin and bone), cut into 1-inch cubes

AROMATICS:
1 tablespoon finely minced fresh ginger
1½ tablespoons finely minced garlic
2 tablespoons thinly sliced green and white scallion rings
1 teaspoon China Moon Curry Powder (page 7)

SAUCE:
1 cup China Moon Infusion (page 72), China Moon Double Stock (page 72), or unsalted chicken stock
2 tablespoons unseasoned Japanese rice vinegar

½ teaspoon China Moon Ten-Spice (page 6)
1 teaspoon China Moon Curry Powder
½ cup unsweetened coconut milk
1 tablespoon packed brown sugar
½ to 1 teaspoon Chinese chili sauce

1 small carrot, cut diagonally into rippled or plain coins ⅛ inch thick
2 to 3 tablespoons corn or peanut oil, for stir-frying
1 small yellow onion, cut into 1-inch squares
1 small red bell pepper, cut into 1-inch squares
2 inner ribs celery, cut diagonally into commas ⅛ inch thick
2 fat scallions, cut into 1-inch nuggets
1½ cups Napa cabbage squares (1 inch)
Toasted sliced almonds, for garnish
Coriander sprigs, for garnish

1. In a bowl, briskly whisk together the marinade ingredients through the cornstarch until smooth and thick. Add the chicken and toss well. Cover and marinate in the refrigerator for 3 to 24 hours. Let come to room temperature and re-toss before cooking.

2. Combine the aromatics in a small dish; cover until ready to use.

3. Combine the sauce ingredients through the chili sauce in a bowl. Stir to blend, leaving the spoon in the bowl.

4. In a small saucepan filled with boiling water, blanch the carrots until half-cooked, 20 to 30 seconds. Immerse the carrots in ice water to chill, then drain.

5. Heat a wok or large heavy skillet over high heat until hot enough to evaporate a bead of water on contact. Add 2 tablespoons of the oil and swirl to glaze the pan. When the oil is hot enough to foam a scallion ring on contact, reduce the heat to moderate. Add the aromatics and stir gently until fully fragrant, 20 to 30 seconds, adjusting the heat so they foam without browning. Add the onion and toss briskly until it is a bit soft, about 2 minutes. Add the bell peppers and toss until they curl at the edges, 2 minutes more. Adjust the heat to maintain a merry sizzle and drizzle a bit more oil down the side of the pan, if needed to prevent sticking. Don't worry if the vegetables brown a bit. Add the celery and scallions, and toss for 1 minute. Add the cabbage and toss until wilted, about 1 minute more. Add the carrots and toss to combine.

6. Spread the vegetables on a large platter to cool. All the above can be done up to a day in advance. Seal and refrigerate the ingredients; bring to room temperature before using.

7. About 20 minutes before serving, bring 4 cups of water to a steaming near simmer. Add the chicken, stir gently to separate the cubes, and cook until the outside turns 90 percent white, 40 to 50 seconds. Drain immediately and set aside. The chicken will be cooked on the outside but a bit raw in the middle.

8. Arrange the vegetables in the bottom of a 2- or 3-quart Chinese sandpot or other heavy casserole. Stir the sauce to recombine and add it to the pot. Cover and bring to a simmer. Cook until the vegetables are tender-crisp, 3 to 4 minutes. Turn off the heat, fold the chicken into the pot, cover, and let stand undisturbed to cook the chicken through, 1 minute. Serve at once, garnished with a flurry of toasted almonds and some celebratory sprigs of fresh coriander.

MENU SUGGESTIONS: Wok-Seared New Potatoes (page 424), steamed rice, or the ever-appetizing loaf of hot garlic bread are my personal favorites to accompany the sandpot and soak up the sauce. For summer eating, corn in most any form would be another great addition.

MA-LA STEAMED POUSSIN WITH ROASTED SZECHWAN PEPPER-SALT

SERVES 4 AS A MAIN COURSE, 6 TO 8 AS PART OF A MULTICOURSE MEAL

Here is a perfectly steamed dish of poultry drizzled with a freshly infused oil. It is an exceedingly simple and lovely way to cook a baby chicken—or, for that matter, a larger chicken or capon, as long as the cooking time is extended accordingly. It is also just the type of thing to plan when your taste buds are feeling abused from too much this or that, or when the person coming to dinner has a simple refinement. The taste is what the redoubtable M.F.K. Fisher calls "mysteriously fragile." Poetry aside, it's a good way to cook a bird.

The poussin can be marinated a full night ahead. The final cooking is a mere 10-minute affair.

The drizzling oil is a mini version of our Ma-La Oil (page 17). Freshly made, it is a wonderfully aromatic dressing for the chicken.

2 very fresh poussin (trimmed weight 10 to 12 ounces each)
2 teaspoons Roasted Szechwan Pepper-Salt (page 5)
½ tablespoon fine fresh ginger julienne
2 tablespoons fine green and white scallion julienne

DRIZZLING OIL:
3½ tablespoons Japanese sesame oil
3½ tablespoons corn or peanut oil

1½ tablespoons thinly sliced green and white scallion rings
1½ teaspoons finely minced fresh ginger
½ teaspoon Szechwan peppercorns
1 teaspoon dried red chili flakes
1 teaspoon kosher salt

Coriander sprigs or scallion brushes, for garnish

1. Remove and discard the tail and the skinny wingtips of the birds. Clean the cavities well of kidneys, blood, loose membranes, and fat sacs, then flush with cold water. Pat dry inside and out.

2. Sprinkle ¼ teaspoon of the pepper-salt in the cavity of each poussin. Sprinkle and then massage ¾ teaspoon of the pepper-salt on the outside of each bird. Let the poussin marinate for 4 to 6 hours at room temperature or refrigerate overnight. Let come to room temperature before steaming.

3. With a sharp Chinese cleaver or chef's knife, cut each poussin lengthwise in half, cutting along the breast and backbones. Discard the backbone. Lay each half, skin side up, on your cutting board; then, cut the leg, thigh, and wing at the joint and cut the breast piece crosswise into three. Reassemble the pieces in their original shape, then transfer each pair of chopped halves to a shallow heatproof plate at least 1 inch smaller in diameter than your steamer. Sprinkle the ginger and half of the scallion julienne evenly over the birds. At this point, the poussin may be sealed and refrigerated up to 8 hours for convenience. Bring fully to room temperature before steaming.

4. About 20 minutes before serving, bring ample water for steaming to a gushing boil. Put the birds in the steamer and cover the steamer tightly. Steam the poussin until the juices run clear at the thigh bone when you pierce it with a knife, 8 to 9 minutes. (If you are steaming the birds in 2 layers, one on top of the other, expect to steam the top layer an additional 1 to 2 minutes.)

5. While the birds steam, combine the sesame and vegetable oil in a heavy 1-quart saucepan. Heat over moderate heat until hot enough to foam a scallion ring, 250°F on a deep-fry thermometer. Let sizzle for 5 seconds, then remove the pan from the heat. Promptly add the scallion rings, minced ginger, peppercorns, chili flakes, and salt, and stir gently to mix. The oil will foam up an inch or two. Cover the pot once the foaming subsides to keep the oil warm.

6. As soon as the birds are done, tilt the plate to decant the steaming liquids and slip the poultry onto heated plates of contrasting color. Scatter the remaining scallion threads over the birds.

7. Drizzle the warm oil evenly on top of each serving, complete with the colorful bits of the aromatic "goop." Serve immediately, garnished with the sprigs of green. Put an empty bowl for the bones on the table, encouraging your guests to nibble them clean.

TWO BIRDS, TWO TRAYS

To steam two poussin simultaneously, you probably will need two 12- to 14-inch steamer trays. Rather than pile them in a double tier for steaming—the recommended option when steaming dumplings, other small items, or foods that can happily steam in a lazy haze for long periods of time—I suggest you steam them in single tiers over two pots of water. It uses twice the space on your stovetop, but you gain more than twice the degree of ease and control, as well as a good rush of steam unimpeded over each layer. Liken it to bathing twins in a small basin—the pile-up is double but not very efficient.

MENU SUGGESTIONS: The poussin mates beautifully with a stir-fry of seasonal vegetables and simply cooked rice or pasta. If your steamers allow it, you might try steaming each poussin as an entire meal in a bowl. Putting cooked noodles or rice in the bottom, barely sautéed and lightly seasoned vegetables on top of that, and then layer the poussin on top. The chicken juices will seep into the bottom layers; it will be a delicious tangle.

If you are wanting a non-Chinese way out, a simple green salad and a hot loaf of good bread would not be an affront to the bird.

TEA AND SPICE SMOKED POUSSIN

SERVES 4 AS A MAIN COURSE, 6 TO 8 AS PART OF A MULTICOURSE MEAL

When I appeared on a television program (see Note) pulling a plump, golden chicken from a foil-lined smoker, it seemed as if every viewer remembered it as a must-have dish. At least that's the only way I can account for the dozens of requests we get for this recipe most every month! Because a full-size bird is difficult to portion in the restaurant, we serve poussin—baby chickens—instead. At home as well they make a pretty presentation.

If you like to work in advance, you can marinate and even steam the poussin ahead. Or, if you've come home with the birds in hand and are hungering to eat them, the whole process can be telescoped to under an hour; sprinkle the marinade ingredients on the birds and move straightaway to steaming them.

NOTE

The show I appeared on with the chicken was part of a PBS series called "Great Chefs of San Francisco," which continues to be shown. It took a whole tube of hot pink lipstick, two hours of filming, and four fat chickens to make me and the bird presentable.

2 fresh poussin (trimmed
    weight 10 to 12 ounces each)
2½ teaspoons Roasted
    Szechwan Pepper-Salt
    (page 5)
1 whole scallion, cut into 1-inch
    nuggets
4 quarter-size coins fresh ginger,
    smashed
1 scrubbed large orange

SMOKING MIXTURE:
¼ cup fragrant dry black tea
    leaves, such as lichee black or
    rose black
¼ cup packed brown sugar

¼ cup raw rice
1 tablespoon Szechwan
    peppercorns
Several pieces cassia or
    cinnamon bark, crumbled
Several finger-lengths of fresh
    orange zest, coarsely chopped

1 teaspoon China Moon Chili-
    Orange Oil (page 15), Ma-La
    Oil (page 17), Five-Flavor
    Oil (page 13), or Japanese
    sesame oil
Coriander sprigs or scallion
    brushes, for garnish

THE ORDER OF THINGS

The three ordered steps in this recipe—marinating, steaming, and smoking—reflect classic Chinese technique. You can turn tradition on its head, however, and smoke the bird second and steam it third. You can also smoke the bird second and then finish it in the oven. Either way, the end result is delicious as long as you take care not to overcook the poussin.

1. Remove and discard the tail and skinny wingtips of the birds. Clean the cavities well of kidneys, blood, loose membranes, and fat sacs, then flush with cold water. Pat dry inside and out.

2. Sprinkle ¼ teaspoon of the pepper-salt in the cavity of each poussin. Divide the scallion and ginger between the cavities. Evenly sprinkle 1 teaspoon of the pepper-salt on the outside of each bird. Massage the outside to work the spices into the skin. Grate orange zest lightly over each poussin. Put the birds, breast side up, on 1 or 2 shallow plates at least 1 inch smaller in diameter than your steamer. If you are steaming the birds side by side, leave at least 1 inch between them. Seal and marinate for several hours at room temperature or in the refrigerator overnight. Let come to room temperature before steaming.

3. Bring ample water for steaming to a rolling boil over high heat. Put the birds in place and cover the steamer. Steam the birds until only about 80 percent done, 8 to 9 minutes. Add an extra minute for larger poussin.

4. Using a chopstick or wooden spoon placed in the cavity, gently tilt the birds to decant any cooking juices. Carefully transfer the birds to a cooling rack, breast side up. At this point, you can either smoke the birds directly or leave them to cool and then cover and refrigerate overnight. Let come to room temperature before smoking.

5. Line a 14- to 16-inch wok or heavy pot and lid with heavy-duty aluminum foil, leaving hems of at least 3 inches.

Combine the smoking mixture ingredients through the orange zest. Spread the smoking mixture in a ¼-inch-thick layer in the bottom of the pot. Arrange the poussin, breast side up, not touching, on a rack that fits into the pot and stands 1½ to 2 inches above the bottom. Set the rack in place over the mixture and raise the heat as high as possible. Wait for the mixture to send up several thick plumes of smoke in different parts of the pot, 5 to 10 minutes, depending on your stove.

6. Cover the pot tightly, crimp the foil hems shut, and smoke the poussin for 8 minutes. Turn off the heat (if the stove is electric, carefully move the pot to a cool burner) and let the poussin rest, undisturbed, for 3 to 4 minutes. Remove the lid part-way and peek quickly inside, blowing the smoke aside to clear your view. The poussin should be a rich golden brown on the breast side. If they are pale and undersmoked, follow the rescue advice beginning on page 166.

7. Tilt the birds to decant any liquid from the cavities. Carefully transfer them, breast side up, to a cooling rack or plate. Immediately brush the infused oil lightly over the outside.

8. Serve the poussin fresh from the smoker, tepid, or at room temperature. The birds are most easily cut when they've cooled for at least 10 minutes: Sever the legs and wings at the joint. Cut the bird lengthwise in half through the breast and along one side of the backbone. Cut the backbone free along the other side and discard. Finally, chop each breast crosswise into 3 or 4 pieces.

9. Arrange the pieces attractively on a plate of contrasting color, adding a green flourish with the coriander or scallion. Traditional Chinese recipes invariably read "Reassemble [the pieces] in a chicken shape," but any pretty mound will do.

MENU SUGGESTIONS: Served cold, the smoked poussin goes beautifully with any of our lightly sauced cold noodle dishes and Szechwan-Style Baby String Beans (page 64). Hot, I like it best with either stir-fried seasonal vegetables and fried rice or a warm salad of greens and new potatoes.

MASTER SAUCE POUSSIN

SERVES 4 AS A MAIN COURSE,
6 TO 8 AS PART OF A MULTICOURSE MEAL

Master sauce dishes are among the most approachable in the Chinese culinary lexicon, the coq au vin of the would-be-Chinese-cook's world.

Baby chickens—poussin, in French, and now commonly called so in gastronomic English—are ideal when cooked whole in a master sauce. The flavors and colors of soy, rice wine, cassia bark, and orange zest penetrate the skin and accentuate the sweet goodness of the flesh.

The poussin can be served hot and freshly pulled from the sauce or left to chill and enrich in the sauce as detailed below. Either way, it is a simply done dish, requiring only a few ingredients and no culinary bravery.

In addition to larger breasts that can be stewed successfully in master sauce, the succulent liquid is also a great vehicle for flavoring heartier vegetables like mushrooms, carrots, and potatoes, as well as hard-cooked eggs (the latter a traditional Chinese snack). Simmered briefly in the sauce, the vegetables become quite rich and potent, and offer a very nice contrast to an otherwise mild dish of rice or pasta.

2 fresh poussin (trimmed
    weight 10 to 12 ounces
    each)

MASTER SAUCE:
2½ cups China Moon Double
    Stock (page 72) or unsalted
    chicken stock
2 cups soy sauce
⅓ cup Chinese rice wine, plum
    wine, or dry sherry
6 quarter-size coins fresh ginger,
    smashed
4 fat scallions, cut into 1-inch
    nuggets and smashed

1½ star anise, broken into their
    12 individual points
2 ounces Chinese golden rock
    sugar, smashed into bits (⅓
    cup after smashing)
1 tablespoon crumbled cassia or
    cinnamon bark
Thinly pared zest (no white
    pith) of ½ scrubbed orange
½ teaspoon Szechwan
    peppercorns

Coriander sprigs or scallion
    brushes, for garnish

LEFTOVER
MASTER SAUCE

///

In traditional northern Chinese homes, master sauces were added to and kept simmering literally over several generations, much like a mother yeast starter in other parts of the world. Enriched by the first stewing, the sauce becomes the base of the next dish—whether it be another chicken, a dinner of chicken or duck legs, or perhaps a pork butt or loin of beef. The method for renewal is simply to heat the original sauce (which may be frozen) and then taste and "adjust up" with more of whatever ingredient the tongue desires in roughly equal proportion to the original recipe. Sauce renewals inevitably involve adding more stock or water to cut the richness (and saltiness) gained from the initial simmering. Do not be surprised if all that is required for the first rerun is the simple addition of stock or water; if your aromatics were very fresh, their potency from the first use will last through the second.

BIRDS AND
BUBBLES

One of the finest cooks in the world—and surely one of the most charming men on the planet—is the French chef, Jacques Pépin. Shortly after China Moon opened, Jacques was in San Francisco filming a week or so of his TV series and he became an after-midnight habitué in our large prep kitchen downstairs. He'd perch on a stool night after night, a glass of Champagne in hand, and entertain me and my first sous-chef, Barbara Haimes, until 2 or 3 A.M. while we stirred great batches of poussin in woks full of master sauce. While the birds got sauced, he somehow stayed sober. I considered it a blessing on our chickens that we'd had his benediction!

1. Chop off and discard the tail and skinny wingtips of the birds. Clean the cavities well of kidneys, blood, loose membranes, and fat sacs, then flush with cold water. Pat dry inside and out.

2. In a wok or heavy, non-aluminum pot large enough to hold the chickens snugly, bring all of the sauce ingredients through the peppercorns to a simmer over moderate heat, stirring to dissolve the sugar.

3. Add the poussin and ladle the liquid over the top while the sauce returns to a simmer. The repeated shower of hot liquid will sear and color the birds. Cover the pot and simmer the poussin for 15 minutes. Turn and baste the birds midway through cooking. (If you are cooking a single large chicken, extend the simmering time to 40 minutes.)

4. Carefully remove the birds to a large plate, breast side up. The skin will be very fragile; take care not to tear it. Tilt the birds over the pot to drain the cavities of sauce. Strain the sauce, discarding the solids.

5. To serve the birds freshly stewed, let them stand 10 minutes before cutting so the juices do not run freely. With a sharp, thin-bladed cleaver or chef's knife, cut off the wings and legs at the joints. Cut through the breastbone and along both sides of the backbone; discard the backbone. Put each half, bone side down, on the board and cut it crosswise into pieces. Whack with a conviction you may not feel so the knife cuts cleanly through the bone. Rearrange the birds in more or less their original shape on heated plates of contrasting color. Spoon a bit of the hot sauce on top and garnish with a fresh flag of coriander sprigs or scallion brushes.

6. Or, for fuller flavor, refrigerate the birds covered in the sauce for 1 to 2 days and serve them cold or at room temperature. First refrigerate the sauce, uncovered, until it is just cool enough to handle (and no longer hot enough to further cook the chickens). Return the birds, breast side down, to the casserole or a container of similar size. Pour the sauce over the birds, cover, and refrigerate. The juices will gel upon cooling. To serve, use your fingers to gently clean the birds of clinging sauce, then chop the birds as described. Arrange the pieces on plates or a platter of contrasting color. Spoon a bit of the jellied sauce on top and garnish with the coriander or scallion.

7. Refrigerate or freeze the excess master sauce for further use.

MENU SUGGESTIONS: Cold, the poussin is perfect alongside a simple salad or as part of a "Peking antipasto" platter with one of our cold noodle dishes. If you are serving the poussin hot, it is most delicious alongside rice and a simply sautéed green vegetable or a colorful vegetable mélange.

TEA AND SPICE SMOKED QUAIL

SERVES 4 AS A MAIN COURSE, 6 TO 8 AS PART OF A MULTICOURSE MEAL

These little birds smoke and cook through in one step; they are both easy and delicious. Unlike many restaurant preparations involving quail, here the bones are left in and the eating is done with the fingers. It's fun and informal, and the juices retained by cooking the bird on the bone more than compensate for any inelegance when you go at it with your hands.

8 fresh whole quail

MARINADE:
5 teaspoons Roasted Szechwan Pepper-Salt (page 5)
8 quarter-size coins fresh ginger, smashed and cut in half
8 scallion nuggets, 1 inch long, smashed
1 scrubbed small orange

SMOKING MIXTURE:
¼ cup fragrant dry black tea leaves, such as lichee black or rose black
¼ cup packed brown sugar
¼ cup raw rice

1 tablespoon Szechwan peppercorns
Several pieces cassia or cinnamon bark, crumbled
Several finely pared strips of fresh orange zest, coarsely chopped
2 tablespoons China Moon Chili-Orange Oil (page 15), Ma-La Oil (page 17), Five-Flavor Oil (page 13), or Japanese sesame oil, for brushing the quail

Coriander sprigs or scallion brushes, for garnish

SEASONING REASONING

Rubbing poultry with seasoned salt and stuffing its cavity with ginger and scallion serve a two-fold purpose in the traditional, refrigerator-less world of Chinese cooking. One, the seasonings flavor and perfume the bird. Two, they preserve it. It is still important that you start with a very fresh bird, but one should not be afraid to marinate it this way at a cool room temperature.

1. With a thin-bladed cleaver or chef's knife, cut off and discard the neck of the quail. Cut off any long pieces of neck skin, leaving a little turtleneck of skin to shield the breast during smoking. Cut off the feet just below the knees. Discard the kidneys and any bloody bits or loose membranes. Flush the birds well with cold water. Pat dry inside and out.

2. Sprinkle ⅛ teaspoon of the pepper-salt in the inside of each quail. Sprinkle the outside of each bird with ½ teaspoon of the pepper-salt and rub the seasoning into the skin. Put the quail in "lotus position" by folding their wings behind them; this plumps the breast. Stuff the cavity of each bird with a piece of ginger and scallion. Complete the lotus posture by crossing the legs over one another and anchoring the knees in the cavity; this makes each bird an attractive package that looks especially nice when cut. Arrange the quail, breast side up, with ½ inch between them on a large plate. Grate a light sprinkling of orange zest evenly on top. Seal and marinate 3 to 4 hours at room temperature or refrigerate overnight. Let come fully to room temperature before smoking.

3. Line a 14- to 16-inch wok or heavy pot and lid with heavy-duty aluminum foil, leaving hems of at least 3 inches. Combine the tea, sugar, rice, peppercorns, bark, and zest. Arrange the quails, breast side up with at least ½ inch between them, on a rack that fits into the pot and stands 1½ to 2 inches above the bottom. Spread the smoking mixture in a ¼-inch-thick layer in the bottom of the pot. Set the rack in place over the mixture. Turn the heat as high as possible and wait for the mixture to send up several thick plumes of smoke, 5 to 10 minutes depending on your stove. Cover the pot, crimp the foil hems shut, and smoke the quail for 8 minutes. Turn off the heat (if the stove is electric, carefully move the pot to a cool burner) and let the quail rest, undisturbed, for 5 minutes. Remove the lid and discard the foil. The birds should be a lovely gold. If they are pale, turn to page 166 for rescue advice. Test for doneness by piercing the thickest portion of the breast with the tip of a paring knife. If the juices do not run clear, pop the quail into the upper third of a 400°F oven to finish cooking to the desired doneness, 2 to 4 minutes or more. Brush the birds with the infused oil.

4. Serve the quail freshly smoked or at room temperature. If serving hot from the smoker, let the birds rest for 5 minutes before cutting. Otherwise, let the quail come to room temperature and seal and refrigerate uncut. Bring to room temperature before serving. To serve: Cut the quail in half lengthwise through the breast and backbone. Remove the

SMOKING RACK TIP

To get the most quail onto the smoking rack at one time, arrange them head to tail in concentric rings starting near the outside of the rack. The configuration suggests an aerial view of an Esther Williams fantasy—a very amusing notion when one is smoking a bunch of quail.

scallion and ginger from the cavities. Arrange the quail on individual plates or a platter, piling them at an angle for height. Garnish with coriander sprigs or scallion brushes.

MENU SUGGESTIONS: We like to feature the quail as part of a China Moon antipasto plate, along with Chili-Orange Cold Noodles (page 396), a salad of baby greens dressed with Orange Vinaigrette (page 25), and a hill of Ginger-Pickled Red Cabbage Slaw (page 61).

BUNNY STEW

SERVES 4 TO 5 AS A MAIN COURSE,
6 TO 8 AS PART OF A MULTICOURSE MEAL

Our first Easter at the restaurant, I had the misguided notion to put a rabbit sandpot with this name on the menu. I found it vastly amusing—not to mention delicious—but that weekend's guests roundly ignored it in favor of less symbolic fare. Oh, well. The irony continued years later when the creator of the dish, one of our very talented cooks, left her husband to take up with a man who raised rabbits.

For fullest flavor, the rabbit should be marinated overnight. The remaining preparations, including the cooking, take less than an hour.

1 whole fresh rabbit (2 to 2½ pounds), cut into small serving pieces

MARINADE:
2 tablespoons Chinese rice wine, plum wine, or dry sherry
3 tablespoons hoisin sauce
1 teaspoon soy sauce

2 tablespoons Ma-La Oil (page 17), Five-Flavor Oil (page 13), or Japanese sesame oil
1 teaspoon Chinese chili sauce
1½ tablespoons finely minced garlic
3 tablespoons thinly sliced green and white scallion rings
1 tablespoon finely minced fresh ginger

THE RABBIT QUERY

When my husband, who is funny and brilliant, was reviewing this chapter, the question came up as to why a rabbit was included in the poultry chapter. I sluffed it off with a comment about traditional order in cookbooks, but then I thought, "Why, indeed?" Bunnies lack wings, beaks, stiletto toes, and other such appendages, so why be-fowl them? Any answers to this puzzle will be respectfully received. We have addressed it to several friends, a courtly stuffed rabbit among them, and no one has a good response.

AROMATICS:

1½ tablespoons finely minced fresh ginger

1½ tablespoons finely minced garlic

3 tablespoons thinly sliced green and white scallion rings

SAUCE:

1 cup China Moon Infusion (page 72), China Moon Double Stock (page 72), or unsalted chicken stock

2 tablespoons Chinese rice wine, plum wine, or dry sherry

1 tablespoon hoisin sauce

1 tablespoon soy sauce

4 to 5 tablespoons corn or peanut oil, for searing and stir-frying

1 small carrot, diced

1 small yellow onion, diced

2 ribs celery, diced

1 small stalk fresh lemongrass, smashed

Diagonally cut green and white scallion rings, for garnish

1. If you are cutting up the rabbit yourself, use a large, heavy, sharp knife and chop forcefully with a conviction you may be lacking. First cut the forelegs from the trunk. Then sever the hind legs at the hip and knee. Cut the body lengthwise, separating the rib cage from the saddle into 3 pieces. Chop off and discard the bony hem of the rib pieces. Cut the loin and rib sections crosswise into 3 pieces. Reserve the heart and liver, if you like, for another use.

2. In a bowl, combine all of the marinade ingredients through the ginger. Add the rabbit and toss well. Cover and marinate for several hours at room temperature; or, for best flavor, refrigerate overnight. Let come to room temperature before searing.

3. Combine the aromatics in a small dish; cover until ready to use.

4. Combine all of the sauce ingredients through the soy sauce in a bowl. Stir to blend, leaving the spoon in the bowl.

5. Heat a wok or large heavy skillet until hot enough to evaporate a bead of water on contact. Add 1½ tablespoons of the oil and swirl to coat the pan. When the oil is nearly smoking, add the rabbit pieces 4 or 5 at a time, without crowding, and brown until evenly deep gold, about 2 minutes on each side. The rabbit will still be raw in the middle. Remove the seared rabbit to a plate lined with a triple thickness of paper towels. Wipe the pan clean, add more oil, and sear the remaining pieces. All the above, including the vegetable cutting, may be done a full day ahead. Seal and refrigerate the

ingredients; let come to room temperature before cooking.

6. About 30 minutes before serving, heat a wok or large heavy casserole over high heat until hot enough to evaporate a bead of water on contact. Add 1½ tablespoons of the oil and swirl to glaze the pan. When the oil is hot enough to sizzle a scallion ring on contact, turn the heat down to moderate. Add the aromatics and stir gently until fully fragrant, 20 to 30 seconds, adjusting the heat so they foam without browning. Add the carrot dice and toss for 1 minute. Add the onion and celery, and toss for 2 minutes more. Adjust the heat to maintain a merry sizzle and drizzle a bit more oil down the side of the pan, if needed to prevent sticking. Add the rabbit leg pieces and toss to combine. Stir the sauce and add it to the pan. Add the lemongrass, burying it under the liquid and the rabbit. Bring the sauce to a weak simmer.

7. Adjust the heat to prevent boiling, cover the pot, and gently simmer the stew for 5 minutes. Add the loin and rib pieces, stir to combine, then replace the cover and simmer for 10 minutes more. Check the thickest piece of rabbit to see that it is cooked through. Discard the lemongrass.

8. Serve the stew promptly in individual heated bowls of contrasting color. Garnish with the scallion rings.

MENU SUGGESTIONS: Some Stir-Fried Zucchini Ribbons (page 437) or seasonal greens would be nice with this dish, as would steamed or stir-fried rice. You might choose the lusher Shanghai Rice (page 418) if you're feeling dressy or Easter-festive. Or, if you're feeling lazy, accompany the stew with some hot crusty bread.

WOK-SEARED DUCK BREASTS

SERVES 4 AS A LIGHT MAIN COURSE, 6 AS PART OF A MULTICOURSE MEAL

This is a straightforward and very simple way to cook a duck breast. It is the first step to a salad, stir-fry, soup, or casserole that features intriguingly seasoned slices of rare or medium-rare duck meat.

For a dish involving further cooking—such as a sandpot or soup—you'll want to leave the breasts blood-rare as they come from the searing pan in order to give them room to cook further. For eating at room temperature, as in a salad or an antipasto, complete the cooking in the oven so the breast is medium-rare when sliced.

This is also a wonderful way to cook goose or squab breasts. (Squab breasts are so small, you'll want to cut the marination time to 15 minutes.) I cooked goose breasts this way for one Christmas feast, and the guests are still raving.

2 whole, boneless fresh duck
    breasts with skin on, cut in
    half (4 pieces)

MARINADE:
¼ cup soy sauce
2 tablespoons mushroom soy
    sauce
¼ cup Chinese rice wine or dry
    sherry
1 tablespoon China Moon Chili-
    Orange Oil (page 15)

1 tablespoon sugar
1 whole scallion, cut into 1-inch
    nuggets and smashed
4 quarter-size coins fresh ginger,
    smashed
1 tablespoon finely slivered
    coriander leaves and stems

2 to 4 teaspoons corn or peanut
    oil, for searing

POULTRY SKIN

The skin that ideally is left on the breast shields and bastes the meat during marination and cooking and gives it a wonderful plushness in hot dishes. If your butcher or conscience has removed the skin, cut the marination time in half, be especially attentive in the cooking, and expect the meat to be a bit drier in the end.

1. Neatly trim the borders of the duck breasts, removing the fillets, excess fat, and cartilage; reserve the fillets for another use.

2. In a bowl, mix together the marinade ingredients through the coriander. Add the duck breasts and turn to coat thoroughly. Set aside to marinate at room temperature for 1 hour. Drain the marinade and discard the solids.

3. Preheat the oven to 400°F. Move a rack to the upper-third.

4. Heat a large, heavy skillet over high heat until hot enough to evaporate a bead of water on contact. Add 2 teaspoons of the oil and swirl to glaze the bottom. When the oil is nearly smoking, add the duck breasts, skin side down, in a single layer and cook until the skin browns, about 2 minutes. Turn and brown the second side, 1 minute more. The duck should be golden brown on the outside and still raw inside. If the skillet is not large enough to hold all of the breast pieces at once, clean it well before searing the next batch. Drain the breasts, skin side down, on paper towels.

5. Place the breasts, skin side up, on a baking sheet and roast in the oven until medium-rare, 3 to 4 minutes. Test for doneness by inserting a knife point at the thickest portion.

6. Serve the breasts sliced thinly across the grain into rosy ribbons. They are delicious eaten immediately, tepid, or at room temperature.

MENU SUGGESTIONS: Ribbons of duck breast left blood-rare after searing are delicious folded into the sandpots on page 172 and 176 as replacements for the duck confit or duck legs. Simply bring the sandpots to a near boil, remove the pot from the heat, fold the ribbons into the sauce, and replace the lid for a minute or two to allow the meat to cook through.

Slivers of the partly cooked meat are wonderful in any of our hot and sour soups, again folded into the hot liquid just before serving.

When roasted to medium-rare, the breasts are delicious simply tossed with salad greens and any of our vinaigrettes, or added to a Paris Salad (page 444).

TEA AND SPICE SMOKED DUCK BREAST

SERVES 4 AS A LIGHT MAIN COURSE, 6 AS PART OF A MULTICOURSE MEAL

This is an easy route to elegance. Through a simple process of marinating, searing, and smoking in a foil-lined pot, one gets exotically flavored duck meat to add to a salad or sandpot.

The process can be shortened to an hour or stretched out over a day and a half. The ideal is in between: Allow the meat several hours or overnight for

SMOKING TIPS

Reading through any of the smoked dish recipes will put you well on the path to a wonderful smoked supper, but here are a few extra signposts to help you on your way:

▲ *Spread the smoke mixture over no more than a 6- to 7-inch area. If you spread it too thin, it will expire too quickly.*

▲ *Have the food to be smoked at room temperature (or warm from the steamer, if freshly cooked). It shouldn't be cold or the coloring and flavoring won't be even.*

▲ *Take care not to place the item(s) to be smoked too close to the edge of the pot or the lid. The heat generated by the pot and the foil will* over-smoke anything too close to them. For your best shot at even cooking, station the food in the center of the vessel, with at least 2 inches free all around.

▲ If you're smoking several small items, such as quail, leave at least a scant inch between them. Smoke, like steam, needs room to circulate.

▲ Remember that the less inside the smoker, the quicker it will smoke. If it took 10 minutes to smoke 10 quail, it will probably take only 5 or 6 minutes to smoke a half-batch.

▲ Wait until you see thick plumes of smoke in several areas of the pot before clamping on the lid. This can take upwards of 10 to 12 minutes on some stoves. Be patient. The sugar can take a long time to combust.

▲ If you're a first-time Chinese smoker or are working on a new stove, count on the possibility that the food will still be very pale after the time specified in the recipe. When you're ready to take a peek, uncrimp the foil with care not to rip it. If the food is under-smoked, spoon a wide hem of brown or white sugar around the periphery of the burnt smoke mixture, raise the heat to high and wait for the sugar to smoke. Replace the lid, recrimp the foil, and try again.

the flavors of the marinade to penetrate, then sear and smoke it just before serving.

2 whole, boneless duck breasts with skin on, cut in half (4 pieces)
1 teaspoon Roasted Szechwan Pepper-Salt (page 5)
1 tablespoon plus 1 teaspoon thinly sliced green and white scallion rings
1 teaspoon finely minced fresh ginger
1 scrubbed small orange

2 to 4 teaspoons corn or peanut oil, for searing

SMOKING MIXTURE:
¼ cup fragrant dry black tea leaves, such as lichee black or rose black
¼ cup packed brown sugar
¼ cup raw rice
1 tablespoon Szechwan peppercorns
Several pieces cassia or cinnamon bark, crumbled
Several thinly pared strips of fresh orange zest, coarsely chopped

1. Cut each whole duck breast into 2 halves, keeping the skin intact. Remove and discard the membranes and cartilage from the duck breasts; remove the fillets and reserve for another use. Trim the skin neatly at the borders of the breasts.

2. Evenly sprinkle both sides of each breast piece with ¼ teaspoon of the pepper-salt, 1 teaspoon of the scallion rings, and ¼ teaspoon of the ginger. Lay the breasts, skin side up, in a single layer on a plate. Grate a light sprinkle of the orange zest evenly on top. Seal airtight and marinate at cool room temperature for 2 to 4 hours or refrigerate overnight. Let come to room temperature before searing.

3. Heat a large heavy skillet over high heat until hot enough to evaporate a bead of water on contact. Add 2 teaspoons of the oil, swirl to glaze the pan, and heat until nearly smoking. Add the duck, skin side down, in a single layer and sear it on only the skin side until golden, less than 1 minute. The breast will be 80 percent raw. (If the pan isn't big enough to hold all 4 pieces, sear in 2 batches, cleaning the pan midway and adding additional oil.)

4. Line a 14- to 16-inch wok or heavy pot and its lid with heavy-duty aluminum foil, leaving hems of at least 3 inches. Combine all of the smoking ingredients and spread in a ¼-inch-thick layer in the bottom of the wok. Arrange the breasts, skin side up without touching, on a rack that fits into the pot and stands 1½ to 2 inches above the bottom. Set the rack in place over the smoking mixture and raise the heat as high as possible. Wait for the mixture to send up several thick plumes of smoke from different parts of the wok, 5 to 10 minutes, depending on your stove.

5. Cover the pot tightly, crimp the foil hems shut, and smoke the duck breasts for 4 minutes. Turn off the heat (if the stove is electric, carefully move the pot to a cool burner) and let the pot rest undisturbed for 3 to 4 minutes. Lift the lid, remove the duck, and discard the foil. Cut into the thickest part of one breast to test for doneness; the duck should be rare to medium-rare. If raw, roast the duck to the desired doneness skin side up on a baking sheet in the upper third of a 400°F oven.

6. The duck is delicious hot, tepid, or at room temperature. To serve, thinly slice the breasts against the grain.

MENU SUGGESTIONS: Slices of the seared, lightly smoked, very rare duck breasts can be substituted in all of our duck sandpots and many, if not all of the chicken sandpots. Add the slices just before serving, when the sauce is at a near boil; the duck meat can be cooked through simply by folding it into the hot sauce off the heat and replacing the lid for a moment or two.

Cooked to doneness, ribbons of smoked duck breast are wonderful tossed into salads or featured on an antipasto plate alongside Chili-Orange Cold Noodles (page 396) or Dragon Noodles (page 391) and Ginger-Pickled Red Cabbage Slaw (page 61) or Orange-Pickled Carrot Coins (page 58).

HOISIN ROAST DUCK BREAST

SERVES 4 AS A LIGHT MAIN COURSE,
6 AS PART OF A MULTICOURSE MEAL

This is a very easy way to inspire duck breasts with the flavors of hoisin sauce and ten-spice and cook them without any exotic tools or techniques. It is well within the reach of even a hesitant cook, yet the taste is complex enough to intrigue a professional.

For fullest flavor, the breasts should sit overnight in the marinade to allow it to penetrate. The final searing and cooking takes only 15 minutes.

2 whole skinless, boneless fresh duck breasts, cut in half (4 pieces)

MARINADE:
½ cup hoisin sauce
2 tablespoons soy sauce
¾ to 1 teaspoon China Moon Ten-Spice (page 6)
2 teaspoons Ma-La Oil (page 17), Five-Flavor Oil (page 13), or Japanese sesame oil

2 teaspoons China Moon Hot Chili Oil (page 10)
1 tablespoon Chinese rice wine or dry sherry
5 quarter-size coins fresh ginger, smashed
2 whole scallions, cut into 1-inch nuggets and smashed

1 to 2 tablespoons corn or peanut oil, for searing

1. Remove and discard any excess fat or cartilage from the duck breasts. Reserve the fillets for another use.

2. In a bowl, combine the marinade ingredients through the scallions. Add the duck breasts, turn to coat both sides, then rub well to facilitate penetration. Seal and marinate for 2 to 4 hours at cool room temperature or refrigerate overnight. Let come to room temperature before cooking.

3. Preheat the oven to 375°F and move an oven rack to the middle position.

4. Remove the duck from the marinade. Reserve the marinade; discard the ginger and scallions.

5. Heat a large heavy skillet over high heat until hot enough to evaporate a bead of water on contact. Reduce the heat to moderate, add 1 tablespoon of the oil, and swirl to coat the pan. When hot enough to sizzle the duck on contact, add the duck breasts in a single layer and cook until the duck turns a rich golden brown on one side, about 1½ minutes. Turn and brown the second side, about 1 minute more. The duck should be seared on the outside and very rare within. Remove to drain on paper towels. (If you have to sear the duck in 2 batches, clean the pan midway and add more oil.)

6. Arrange the breasts, in a single layer without touching, on a baking sheet. Brush the tops generously with the marinade and roast until a knife pierced in the thickest portion shows the duck to be medium-rare, about 5 minutes.

7. Serve the duck hot, tepid, or at room temperature, sliced crosswise against the grain into thin rosy ribbons. To give a pretty width to the slices, hold your knife at a sharp angle to the board.

MENU SUGGESTIONS: The flavor of the meat is so beguiling that I like to slice it fresh from the oven and serve it alongside something very simple like stir-fried Chinese broccoli and Wok-Seared New Potatoes (page 424). Or, you might do a variation on the same theme by presenting it with sautéed vegetables and good mashed potatoes or by tossing it into a simply cooked pasta or risotto.

The sliced, room temperature duck is excellent tossed into a green salad with Orange Vinaigrette (page 25) or Fresh Ginger Vinaigrette (page 24) and slices of pear, apple, or crispy persimmon.

CHINESE-STYLE DUCK CONFIT

MAKES ABOUT 3½ CUPS SHREDDED CONFIT

In the first year of the restaurant, when creativity and chaos often came together like Siamese twins, a talented French-trained American chef named Rachel Gardner briefly worked at China Moon and introduced me to confit-making, the process of cooking and preserving duck in its own fat, a grand tradition in France. Someday when the restaurant is behind me and I've retired to the peace of a scholar's nook, I'd love to explore the likelihood that the process originated in China. In the meantime, however, here is a dish to be savored on account of its deliciousness, with any spurious claims to authenticity aside!

RENDERING DUCK FAT

Finding a quart and a half of duck fat seems a daunting task for a new cook. Never fear! A trip to a Chinatown poultry market or a call to any fresh poultry shop should net you the desired fat sacs, plucked from beneath the tails of a dozen obliging ducks. (If that fails, call the chef of your nearest friendly fresh-food restaurant and ask for a source for fresh duck fat.)

Rendering the fat sacs is easy. The Western way is to put them in a heavy casserole with an equal amount of water and simmer the mixture, uncovered, until the water evaporates, the fat melts, and the tissue turns to cracklings. The fat this yields is a deep gold; take care not to burn it. The Chinese method is to steam the fat in a bowl over high heat, pausing every half hour or so to drain the rendered fat. This is a slower, less dramatic process, with no danger of scorching. The fat it produces is a pale gold with a lack of roasted flavor.

2 to 3 teaspoons Roasted
   Szechwan Pepper-Salt
   (page 5)
2 pounds (about 4) fresh, fat
   duck legs with thighs
   attached
6 to 7 cups freshly rendered
   duck fat (see Rendering Duck
   Fat, facing page)

CONFIT SEASONINGS:
1 small head garlic, smashed
Finely pared zest of ½ scrubbed
   orange
1½ star anise, broken into its
   12 points
8 quarter-size coins fresh ginger,
   smashed
¼ teaspoon whole coriander or
   fennel seeds, crushed
   (optional)
4 scallions, cut into 1-inch
   nuggets and smashed

1. Sprinkle the pepper-salt evenly over the duck legs, massaging it well into the skin. Seal airtight and marinate for several hours at cool room temperature or refrigerate overnight. Let come to room temperature before cooking.

2. Heat a wok or large heavy casserole over moderate heat until hot enough to evaporate a bead of water on contact. Add 2 tablespoons of the duck fat and swirl to glaze the bottom. When the duck fat is hot enough to sizzle a duck leg, add the duck legs in a single layer and brown on both sides. Adjust the heat so the skin browns without scorching and drizzle in a bit more fat if it is needed. Remove the pot from the heat and carefully drain off any burnt fat.

3. Return the pot and the seared duck legs to moderate heat. Add the duck fat and the confit seasonings. Nudge the legs from the bottom while the mixture comes to a gentle simmer, then adjust the heat so the fat doesn't boil. Simmer uncovered until the duck is very tender at its thickest part and almost falling from the bone, about 40 minutes.

4. Use tongs to carefully transfer the legs to a shallow, heatproof container. Let the fat cool until tepid, about 30 minutes, then carefully strain it over the duck legs. Discard the solids (excepting any ducky nuggets, which are spoils for the cook). Arrange the duck so it is totally submerged. Carefully transfer the container, still uncovered, to the refrigerator. Once the fat congeals, the container may be sealed.

5. Store the confit for 1 day to 2 weeks before using. Its flavor (surprisingly) will not change.

6. To serve, warm the container over low heat or in a slow oven until the fat turns liquid, then remove the legs. Strip the legs of skin, then pull the meat from the bone in chunky shreds. Discard the skin, bones, and any cartilage. The meat is most savory just plucked from the warm fat. It may, however, be refrigerated after shredding. Let come to room temperature before using; or, rewarm in a low oven for an extra bit of savor. Taste the newly picked shreds; depending on use, you may wish to accent them with a sprinkle more of pepper-salt.

7. The seasoned duck fat may be frozen indefinitely. Strain through several layers of dry cheesecloth to trap excess pepper-salt, then seal and freeze for your next batch of confit. On the second go-around, you don't need to season the duck fat, but you will need to add about 2 more cups of freshly rendered duck fat to the pot in order to cover the same amount of duck legs.

MENU SUGGESTIONS: Served at room temperature, the confit is excellent tossed in a green salad dressed with Orange Vinaigrette (page 25). It makes a fine embellishment for Paris Salad (page 444) and is also wonderful on an antipasto plate served with a tangle of baby greens, Wok-Seared New Potatoes (page 424), and a hill of Ginger-Pickled Red Cabbage Slaw (page 61). For inclusion in a hot dish, see Duck Confit Sandpot (recipe follows) and Stir-Fried Duck Confit and Broad Noodles in Spicy Orange Sauce (page 174).

DUCK CONFIT SANDPOT

SERVES 3 TO 4 AS A MAIN COURSE,
5 TO 6 AS PART OF A MULTICOURSE MEAL

This is a cozy, mushroomy sandpot that is especially nice in the fall when you're wanting to counter the sudden chill. It's simple to put together, and given the requisite confit is sitting in the refrigerator and ready to use, it can be prepared and on the table within an hour. The assortment of mushrooms may include any domestic or wild varieties, such as crimini, Italian field, and/or chanterelles.

NO SHOCKS, PLEASE!

Sandpots are delicate tools. They'll crack if you drop them. They'll also crack if you transfer them from a cold environment to a hot one.

If you stow your sandpot in the refrigerator (holding leftovers) or in some cold corner, allow it to warm nearly to room temperature before consigning it to the stove.

Always heat a sandpot carefully over low heat to begin, especially if you think it is any cooler than room temperature.

HOLD THE SEASONING!

As far as I'm concerned, a sandpot requires no special seasoning before use. I've read here and there about the need to soak and heat them, but I've never done it.

With the half-dozen sandpots I've used at home and the hundreds we've bought for China Moon, the only thing I ever do is rinse them of packing dust. That's all! Then they're happily on their way to long, productive lives.

AROMATICS:

1 tablespoon finely minced
  garlic
1½ tablespoons finely minced
  fresh ginger
1½ tablespoons thinly sliced
  green and white scallion
  rings
¼ teaspoon dried red chili flakes
½ teaspoon finely minced
  orange zest

SAUCE:

2 cups Duck Infusion with
  Szechwan Peppercorns (page
  74), China Moon Infusion
  (page 72), China Moon
  Double Stock (page 72), or
  unsalted duck or chicken
  stock
2 tablespoons mushroom soy
  sauce
2 tablespoons balsamic vinegar
1 tablespoon sugar

10 to 12 baby carrots, split
  lengthwise if fat, or 1 carrot,
  thickly julienned

1 to 2 tablespoons corn or
  peanut oil, for stir-frying
1 small red onion, cut into ½-
  inch moons
1 large red bell pepper, cut into
  1-inch squares
1 leek, white part only, split
  lengthwise, then cut
  crosswise into ¼-inch-thick
  half-moons
3 ounces (1 rounded cup)
  shiitake mushrooms,
  quartered
3 ounces (1 rounded cup) oyster
  mushrooms, separated into
  smaller clusters
10 to 12 fresh morel
  mushrooms, quartered
  lengthwise
2½ cups Napa cabbage squares
  (1 inch)
Chunky shreds of Chinese-Style
  Duck Confit (page 170)
Diagonally sliced green and
  white scallion rings, for
  garnish

1. Combine the aromatics in a small bowl. Cover until ready to use. Combine all of the sauce ingredients in a bowl. Stir to blend, leaving the spoon in the bowl.

2. Blanch the carrots in boiling water to cover until half-cooked, 10 to 30 seconds. Immediately plunge into ice water to chill; drain.

3. Heat a wok or large heavy skillet over high heat until hot enough to evaporate a bead of water on contact. Add 1 tablespoon of the oil and swirl to glaze the pan. When the oil is hot enough to sizzle a single scallion ring, reduce the heat to moderate. Add the aromatics and stir gently until fully fragrant, 20 to 30 seconds. Adjust the heat so that the aromatics foam without browning. Add the onion and bell peppers, and toss until slightly softened, 2 to 3 minutes. Add the leek and toss gently for 2 minutes more. Adjust the heat to maintain a merry sizzle and drizzle a bit more oil down the side of the pan, if needed to prevent sticking. Add all of the mushrooms and toss to heat through, 2 to 3 minutes. Add the cabbage and toss until slightly wilted, about 1 minute. Spread the vegetables on a large platter to cool.

The above may be done a day ahead. Seal and refrigerate the ingredients; bring to room temperature before use.

4. About 15 minutes before serving, layer the vegetables over the bottom of a 2- to 3-quart Chinese sandpot or other heavy casserole. Add the duck and the carrots. Stir the sauce and add it to the pot. Cover, bring to a simmer over moderate heat, and simmer gently for 8 to 10 minutes. Garnish with the scallions and serve immediately.

MENU SUGGESTIONS: Steamed or stir-fried rice or pasta with fresh herbs and light oil are perfect partners for the sandpot. Roasted or boiled potatoes would also be wonderful, as would Wok-Seared New Potatoes (page 424), Mandarin Breadtwists (page 66), or a Broad Noodle Pillow (page 403).

STIR-FRIED DUCK CONFIT AND BROAD NOODLES IN SPICY ORANGE SAUCE

SERVES 4 AS A MAIN COURSE

Once we mastered the quick and easy route to making duck leg confit, I began featuring the chunky duck shreds in a number of stir-frys—nowhere, with greater success than in this dish of egg noodles and winter vegetables in a fresh orange sauce.

AROMATICS:
2 tablespoons finely minced
    fresh ginger
¼ cup thinly sliced green and
    white scallion rings

2 teaspoons finely minced
    orange zest
¾ teaspoon China Moon Chili-
    Orange Oil (page 15)
1½ teaspoons "goop" from
    Chili-Orange Oil

SAUCE:

2 cups Duck Infusion with
  Szechwan Peppercorns (page
  74), China Moon Infusion
  (page 72), or unsalted duck
  or chicken stock
3 tablespoons soy sauce
¼ cup freshly squeezed orange
  juice
1 tablespoon plus 1 teaspoon
  sugar
2 tablespoons unseasoned
  Japanese rice vinegar
2 teaspoons distilled white
  vinegar
1 teaspoon Chinese chili sauce
¼ teaspoon kosher salt

1 small carrot, thickly julienned
½ pound fresh fettuccine
  noodles
1½ teaspoons China Moon
  Chili-Orange Oil
3 to 4 tablespoons corn or
  peanut oil, for stir-frying
½ red onion, cut into ¼-inch
  wedges

½ red bell pepper, cut into ¼-
  inch strips, or ¼ pound
  yellow wax beans, tipped and
  cut into finger-lengths
½ small bulb fennel, cored and
  cut crosswise into arcs ¹/₁₆
  inch thin
2 inner ribs celery, cut
  diagonally into commas ⅛
  inch thick
3 ounces Chinese celery cabbage
  or baby bok choy, leaves left
  whole and stems cut into ½-
  inch pieces (2 cups)
2 ounces fresh Chinese mustard
  stems, cut crosswise into ¼-
  inch slices, optional (⅓ cup)
4 fresh water chestnuts, cut
  into coins
Chunky shreds of Chinese-Style
  Duck Confit (page 170)
1 tablespoon cornstarch
  dissolved in 1½ tablespoons
  cold stock or water
Diagonally sliced green and
  white scallion rings, for
  garnish

1. Combine the aromatics in a small dish; cover until ready to use.

2. Combine all of the sauce ingredients in a bowl. Stir to blend, leaving the spoon in the bowl.

3. Blanch the carrots in boiling water to cover for 15 seconds. Refresh in ice water to chill, then drain. Blanch the yellow wax beans for 1 minute. Plunge into ice water; drain.

4. Fluff the noodles in a colander to separate and untangle the strands. Bring a generous amount of water to a rolling boil. Add the noodles, swish gently with chopsticks, and cook until the noodles are al dente, about 2 minutes. Plunge into ice water to chill, then drain well. Toss the noodles with the chili-orange oil. All the above, including cutting the vegetables, may be done a day ahead. Seal and refrigerate the ingredients; bring to room temperature before stir-frying.

5. About 15 minutes before serving, heat a wok or large heavy skillet over high heat until hot enough to sizzle a bead of water on contact. Add 2 tablespoons of the corn oil and swirl to glaze the pan. Reduce the heat to moderate. When the oil is hot enough to sizzle a scallion ring, add the aromatics and stir gently until fully fragrant, 20 to 30 seconds. Adjust the heat so the aromatics foam without browning. Add the red onion and toss briskly until softened, about 1½ minutes. Add the red bell pepper and fennel, and toss for 2 minutes. Add the celery and toss for 1 minute more. Adjust the heat to maintain a merry sizzle and drizzle a bit more oil down the side of the pan, if needed to prevent sticking. Add the Chinese cabbage, Chinese mustard, and noodles. Toss gently to mix for 1 minute. Add the carrots, wax beans, water chestnuts, and duck, and toss to combine.

6. Stir the sauce and add it to the pan. Raise the heat to high, cover the pan, and bring the sauce to a simmer. Stir the cornstarch mixture to recombine and add it to the pan. Stir the sauce until it turns glossy, 10 to 20 seconds. Serve immediately on heated plates or on a platter of contrasting color. Garnish with the scallions.

Menu Suggestions: This is a satisfying one-dish meal. If you wish a first course, Eggroll-Cartwheel Soup (page 87) or China Moon Infusion (page 72) enriched with shredded vegetables are good choices.

Sandpot Casserole of Seared Duck Legs and Wild Mushrooms

SERVES 2 TO 3 AS A MAIN COURSE, 4 TO 6 AS PART OF A MULTICOURSE MEAL

This is an excellent winter dish, dusky with the flavors of duck and wild mushrooms and enhanced by the richness of wine and star anise. It is a country-style dish that needs simmering for an hour or more and features duck that cooks juicily on the bone. If you wish to refine it, you can replace the duck legs with confit (page 170) or seared ribbons of duck breasts from any of the recipes on pages 164 to 169, but I have a fondness for it presented in this way that has much to do with the aromas that mingle headily in the kitchen and the nibbling that lasts long at tableside.

AROMATICS:

2 teaspoons finely minced garlic
1½ tablespoons finely minced
    fresh ginger
3 tablespoons thinly sliced green
    and white scallion rings
½ teaspoon dried red chili flakes
Finely minced zest of ½ small
    scrubbed orange

SAUCE:

2 cups Duck Infusion with
    Szechwan Peppercorns (page
    74), China Moon Infusion
    (page 72), China Moon
    Double Stock (page 72), or
    unsalted duck or chicken
    stock
½ cup Chinese rice wine or dry
    sherry
2½ tablespoons mushroom soy
    sauce
2½ tablespoons soy sauce
2 teaspoons packed brown sugar
Pinch of China Moon Ten-Spice
    (page 6)

2 pounds (about 4) fresh
    duck legs with thighs
    attached
3 to 4 tablespoons corn or
    peanut oil, for searing and
    stir-frying
1 small onion, cut into ¼-inch
    moons

1 small carrot, diagonally cut
    into thin rippled or plain
    coins ⅛ inch thick
1 small leek, white part only,
    slit lengthwise and cut
    crosswise into ¼-inch half-
    moons
2 fat whole scallions, cut into 1-
    inch nuggets
3 cups assorted fresh wild
    mushrooms, such as
    shiitake, oyster, Italian field,
    and/or chanterelles,
    quartered, or cut into thick
    strips if large
1 rounded cup Napa cabbage
    squares (1 inch)
1 rounded cup red chard ribbons
    1 inch wide
¼ teaspoon Roasted Szechwan
    Pepper-Salt (page 5)
Enoki mushrooms, spongy bases
    removed, for garnish
Diagonally sliced green and
    white scallion rings, for
    garnish

1. Combine the aromatics in a small dish; cover until ready to use.

2. Combine all of the sauce ingredients in a bowl. Stir to blend, leaving the spoon in the bowl.

3. Trim any excess fat from the duck legs near the thigh. Sever the legs at the joints; chop each thigh crosswise through the bone into 2 pieces. (For chopping through raw bones, use a thick-edged meat cleaver, not a thin-bladed vegetable cleaver, or you may nick the blade.)

4. Heat a wok or large heavy skillet over moderately high heat until hot enough to evaporate a bead of water on contact. Add 1 tablespoon of the oil and swirl to glaze the bottom. When the oil is hot enough to sizzle a duck piece, add the duck pieces in a single layer and brown well and evenly on both sides, keeping the heat as high as possible without burning the fat. Drain off the excess fat as it accumulates. Remove the browned duck pieces to paper towels to drain.

5. Heat a wok or large heavy skillet over high heat until hot enough to sizzle a bead of water on contact. Add 1½ tablespoons of the oil and swirl to glaze the pan. When the oil is hot enough to sizzle a scallion ring, reduce the heat to moderate and add the aromatics. Stir gently until fully fragrant, 20 to 30 seconds, adjusting the heat so they foam without browning. Add the onion and toss until slightly softened, about 2 minutes. Add the carrot and leek, and toss for 2 minutes more. Add the scallion nuggets and mushrooms, and toss until hot, about 2 minutes. Don't worry if the vegetables brown a bit; they will be flavorful. Adjust the heat to maintain a merry sizzle and drizzle a bit more oil down the side of the pan, if needed to prevent sticking. Add the cabbage and chard, and toss until slightly wilted. Spread the vegetables on a large platter to cool. Sprinkle with pepper-salt to taste.

6. Arrange the duck pieces in a 2- to 3-quart Chinese sandpot or large, heavy casserole. Stir the sauce and add it to the pot. Bring to a gentle simmer over moderate heat, cover closely, and simmer the duck until the thickest part is very tender when pierced with a knife, about 45 minutes. Add the vegetables to the pot, toss gently to combine, then replace the cover and heat the mixture through.

7. Ladle into warm bowls of contrasting color. Garnish with a scattering of enoki and a sprinkling of scallion. Place an empty bowl on the table to hold the bones and encourage your guests to use their fingers and enjoy every savory bit.

MENU SUGGESTIONS: The casserole is most delicious served with a Broad Noodle Pillow (page 403), but rice, pasta, potatoes, or a crusty loaf of good bread heated in the oven would not shame it.

FISH

AND

SHELLFISH

PAN-SEARED TUNA • CLEAR-STEAMED FISH

SPICY CALAMARI • SHELLFISH CASSEROLES • PAN-SEARED TUNA

CLEAR-STEAMED FISH • SPICY CALAMARI

CHILLED FISH SALADS • PRAWN AND SCALLOP STIR-FRIES

C O N T E N T S

For all the beauties and merits of Chinese cuisine, in no one area does it excel more than in the preparation of fish and shellfish. It has largely, I think, to do with three things: the traditional Chinese insistence on freshness, the technical tilt of the cuisine towards steaming and high-heat frying, and the native Chinese intrigue with all edible creatures and their parts without prejudice.

Freshness of fish and shellfish is an imperative in the traditional Chinese kitchen, perhaps equalled only in Japan. The Chinese word for shellfish translates literally as "sea freshness," which says it all. Traditional cooks bought their fish just-caught in the early morning markets. By midday, when the fish was merely puffing instead of jumping, the price was slashed in half. By the end of the market day, when not a wiggle was left and the fish was obviously dead, it cost merely a fraction of the midday price. Such was the premium put on freshness that in the case of fish, fresh meant *alive*.

Steaming is the perfect technique for cooking a very fresh fish. If the flesh is fine and sweet, the clear steam sears it without imparting any flavor of its own, leaving only the "sea freshness" on the tongue. For less pure fish and palates, stir-frying is unparalleled. The heat of the wok is so great that the fish cooks instantly, with not a moment or a drop of moisture lost. Better than high-heat grilling, the wok imparts no flavor of its own, leaving the fish tasting "new and clean," a Chinese phrase used particularly to glorify the taste of perfectly cooked fish.

Enjoyment of all sea and lake creatures helped the Chinese to cultivate a vast variety for their table. Untrammeled by prejudices against heads, tails, skin, or bones (lamentable

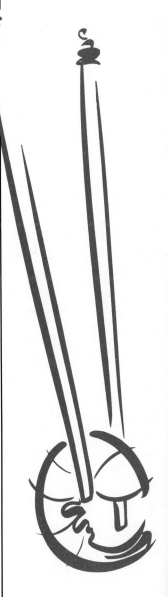

Western phobias based in equal parts upon imperfect cutlery, stiff manners, and the psychology of not wanting to eat anything that is identifiably an animal, and hence part of our clan), Chinese eaters are cheerfully free to enjoy crispy-skinned whole fried fish, velvety fish cheeks, and the sweet meat at the fish tail and near the neck, not to mention the pleasure of picking every edible tidbit from bone to mouth with chopsticks. Chinese cooks are likewise free to stir-fry shrimp in their shells and steam a whole fish in its jacket of skin—unsurpassed ways of sealing in flavor and juices—with every expectation that their public will adore eating them presented thus.

While this chapter strays in several inauthentic directions (mostly in search of the freshest fish and shellfish in our American fish markets), the China Moon approach to fish cookery is very Chinese: Start with only the freshest product, cook it swiftly and well, and present it with the respect due its excellence.

...

POACHING FISH

There is, as far as I know, no better way to poach fish than this: Rather than dunking the fish into the hot liquid to cook—as is typical—the fish is arranged in a heatproof dish and the hot liquid is poured on top. As soon as a knife tip shows the fish to be cooked on the outside but still rosy at the core (the perfect way to eat salmon, in my opinion), the liquid is poured off and the fish is rushed to the refrigerator to cool. It's foolproof.

COLD POACHED SALMON TILES WITH GINGER–BLACK BEAN VINAIGRETTE

SERVES 3 TO 4 AS A MAIN COURSE,
6 TO 8 AS PART OF A MULTICOURSE MEAL

This is one of the most popular dishes we serve in the restaurant, and justifiably so! The combination of cool, perfectly poached fresh salmon, crunchy watercress sprigs, and tangy herbal vinaigrette is a knockout.

If taste weren't enough, another beauty of this dish is that everything short of the final assembly can be done in advance.

Whereas most markets display salmon cut cross-wise into steaks, see if you can instead purchase a small side of salmon.

COURT BOUILLON AND SALMON:

2 cups dry white wine

1½ teaspoons black peppercorns

1 teaspoon Szechwan peppercorns

1 serrano chili, tipped and halved lengthwise

5 quarter-size coins fresh ginger, smashed

2 to 3 whole scallions, trimmed, cut into finger-lengths, and smashed

1 thin stalk fresh lemongrass, chopped into rings

1½ to 2 pounds impeccably fresh, skinned and boned side(s) of salmon, cut into 1-inch squares

GINGER–BLACK BEAN VINAIGRETTE:

2 serrano chilis, tipped and halved

1½ teaspoons finely minced garlic

1 tablespoon finely minced fresh ginger

½ cup China Moon Pickled Ginger (page 8)

1½ teaspoons "goop" from China Moon Hot Chili Oil (page 10)

⅔ cup packed coriander leaves and stems

3 tablespoons juice from China Moon Pickled Ginger

2 tablespoons distilled white vinegar

2½ teaspoons sugar

¾ teaspoon fine sea salt

¾ cup corn or peanut oil

½ small red onion, sliced paper-thin

2 to 3 bunches tender watercress, separated into sprigs, any thick stems removed

1 tablespoon finely minced Chinese black beans (do not rinse them)

1. Bring the court bouillon ingredients through the lemongrass to a boil in a large non-aluminum pot.

2. Arrange the salmon tiles in a single layer with space between them in one or more non-aluminum pans or heat-proof baking dishes. If you have larger and smaller tiles, separate them into 2 dishes so you can time the cooking

FRESHNESS
IS KEY

All fish, in my opinion, should be superbly fresh for use in our recipes, as well as others. Although you probably know this, I feel it never hurts to be reminded.

correctly. Pour the court bouillon on top to cover, then tightly cover the pan(s). Check after 1½ minutes; when the tile looks two-thirds cooked through when pierced with a small knife, drain the court bouillon at once and rush the fish, uncovered, into the refrigerator to cool. Perfectly cooked, it will still be rosy at the core after chilling.

The salmon may be poached up to a day in advance. Seal airtight once cool and serve at room temperature for best flavor. The court bouillon can be strained and refrigerated or frozen for use a second time.

3. To make the vinaigrette, combine the chilis, garlic, ginger, pickled ginger, "goop," and coriander in a food processor. Blend until smooth. Scrape down the sides of the bowl with a rubber spatula. With the machine running, slowly add the ginger juice, vinegar, sugar, and salt. Slowly add the corn oil and process until emulsified. Once made, the vinaigrette may be sealed and refrigerated for up to 8 hours. If you wish to make it a day ahead, leave out the coriander (which turns grayish) and buzz it in at the last minute.

4. Just before serving, toss the red onion in several tablespoons of the vinaigrette and let sit for several minutes to marinate. Toss the watercress separately in 1 to 2 tablespoons more vinaigrette; do not overdress. Make a pretty bed of the onion and about two-thirds of the watercress, then arrange the salmon tiles on top. Spoon about 1 teaspoon of the vinaigrette onto each tile, then garnish sparingly with the chopped Chinese black beans. Place the remaining watercress sprigs jauntily amidst the tiles to make the plate look lively.

MENU SUGGESTIONS: For a perfect lunch, I'd nominate salmon tiles with any of our buns or cold noodles and/or most any of our soups, especially one of the hot and sour variety. As the first course in a dinner or more formal luncheon, the salmon might best be followed by something a bit pristine, like the Ma-La Steamed Poussin with Roasted Szechwan Pepper-Salt (page 153).

CHINESE-STYLE PICKLED SALMON

SERVES 6 TO 8 AS PART OF A MULTICOURSE MEAL

Every year at Passover time, a small group of San Francisco's Jewish restaurateurs and chefs gather for a Seder dinner. It's always a splendid potluck feast of traditional Jewish fare, and it is often celebrated in one of the restaurants.

Late one Seder night, I returned stuffed and sleepy to China Moon to discover that we'd not been busy and there was a whole, beautifully fresh salmon left over. With the taste of my friend Joyce Goldstein's pickled salmon still on my lips, I concocted this pseudo-Chinese version with ginger and Szechwan peppercorns.

Grandma Millie, forgive me, I love it! To be truly delicious, the salmon must sit overnight in the brine, after which it will keep beautifully for up to 4 days.

PICKLING BRINE:
1 cup unseasoned Japanese rice vinegar
1 cup cider vinegar
1 cup distilled white vinegar
½ cup sugar
2 tablespoons plus 2 teaspoons kosher salt
¼ cup very fine fresh ginger julienne
2 to 3 small red Fresno chilis, cut into paper-thin rings

1 to 2 serrano chilis, cut into paper-thin rings
1 tablespoon Szechwan peppercorns

2 pounds impeccably fresh, boned and skinned side(s) of salmon, cut diagonally into ¼-inch-thick slices
½ yellow onion, cut into ¹⁄₁₆-inch half-moons

1. In a non-aluminum medium-size pot, bring all of the brine ingredients through the peppercorns to a steaming near simmer, stirring to dissolve the sugar. Remove from the heat and let cool. Add 3 cups of cold water to the mixture.

2. Arrange the salmon slices in a shallow dish or non-aluminum pan big enough so that the slices can be spread out to allow the brine to flow all around them. Scatter the onion on

CHOOSING FRESH FISH

The best way to choose a fresh fish is to pick up its cheek and check out the gill, which in a newly caught fish is literally blood-red, that is, engorged with blood. As the fish sits after death, its gill turns first rosy then paler pink, then brown and finally gray. A pink gill is acceptable, but a brown gill is definitely not, at least according to my own standards of freshness.

I make it a rule, then, to buy whole fish in a market where they are sold with their heads on, precisely so I can see the gill. Chinese markets usually have towels pinned on the wall for this reason, so that discerning gill-inspectors can wipe their fingers clean after prying open the cheek.

Many people say you should judge a fresh fish by looking it in the eye. It's true that a bright, black, and glassy eye adorns a lot of freshly caught fish. But I've seen many a spectacular, red-gilled fish with a cloudy eye. Cataracts, myopia, death trauma? I don't know the answer, so I still look at the gill first.

Many cooks also run their fingers along the body of the fish to check for firmness. This is not necessarily a sign of freshness, although it is an indication of the character of the particular fish. For example, a perfectly fresh whole salmon can feel soft if it is caught during spawning season. It will have a soft texture when cooked, but the flavor will be excellent.

If you are not blessed with a market where you can inspect the whole fish in this way, you need to look very discerningly at the pre-cut fillet or fish steak. Here are some good general rules for judging freshness: The flesh should look plump and moist, not sunken or dry (indicating that it's been sitting too long and has lost a lot of juice). Likewise, the pan it's sitting in should not hold a puddle of water. A pool of liquid means either soaked or frozen fish or a piece of fish that has been sitting too long. The skin, if it's still on, should hug the flesh tightly. Fish, like people, get saggy skinned when they're old. Finally, fish should not smell fishy! If you can smell it, don't buy it.

top of the fish. Stir the brine to recombine and pour over the fish so that the fish is submerged. For best flavor, refrigerate for at least 24 hours before serving.

MENU SUGGESTIONS: For a little nibble before dinner, I would serve a few slices of the salmon with a tangle of onions and ginger threads and maybe a sprig of watercress or daikon sprouts as a peppery complement. For a larger plate, the salmon is perfectly offset by Ginger-Pickled Red Cabbage Slaw (page 61), Dragon Noodles (page 391), and a salad of baby greens dressed with our Fresh Ginger Vinaigrette (page 24).

CHINESE-STYLE CURED SALMON

SERVES 12 TO 15 AS AN APPETIZER, 20 TO 24 AS AN HORS D'OEUVRE

This is the China Moon answer to gravlax, a fillet of lightly cured salmon hinting of ginger, coriander, and Szechwan peppercorn. I love it far better than the usual dill-inspired version, particularly when it is mated with our Sweet Mustard Sauce.

Cured salmon is surprisingly easy to make. Forget the many recipes that call for wrapping and turning the fish in inscrutably esoteric ways! A piece of plastic film and a few days' patience is all that is required.

3 to 3½ pounds impeccably fresh side(s) of salmon with skin left on, bones removed with tweezers or needle-nose pliers

2½ tablespoons sugar

2½ tablespoons Roasted Szechwan Pepper-Salt (page 5)

Several twists of black and white pepper

¼ cup very fine fresh ginger julienne

½ cup coarsely chopped coriander leaves and stems

1. Place the salmon fillet, skin side down, on a rimmed baking sheet or large, flat platter. (If the baking sheet is aluminum, line it with plastic wrap before placing the fish on it.) Combine the sugar, pepper-salt, and ground pepper, and sprinkle evenly over the fillet. Scatter the ginger julienne and coriander evenly on top. Cover with plastic wrap. Place another baking sheet over the salmon. Weigh it down with a 3- to 5-pound weight. Refrigerate for at least 24 hours or, for fuller flavor, up to 3 days. Every 8 to 10 hours, drain off any liquid that collects in the bottom of the pan.

2. To serve, discard the ginger and coriander. Slice the gravlax very thinly on the diagonal with a long and thin-bladed sharp knife.

MENU SUGGESTIONS: Along with the Sweet Mustard Sauce (page 21), I adore serving this fish with Mandarin Breadtwists (page 66) or hot wedges of Pan-Fried Scallion-Chive Bread (page 382) and mounds of brightly colored Orange-Pickled Carrot Coins (page 58), and/or Ginger-Pickled Red Cabbage Slaw (page 61).

GOLD COIN SALMON CAKES

SERVES 2 TO 3 AS A MAIN COURSE, 4 TO 5 AS PART OF A MULTICOURSE MEAL

Money imagery abounds in Chinese cooking, where any round, deep-fried or pan-fried patty is automatically saluted as a "gold coin."

Here, then, is edible treasure: a delectable fresh salmon patty that is to my adult tongue what my mother's canned salmon croquettes were to my childhood palate. Fresh from the skillet, they are equally delicious with the Minted Cucumber Sauce (page 23) we use in the dining room or the homemade mayo we whip up for staff lunches.

The salmon cakes will fry best and with the least oil if made and refrigerated in advance. The cooking takes only minutes.

1 pound fresh salmon, cut into chunks

2 ounces (about 2 thick slices) day-old white bread, crumbled into large chunks

1 large egg, beaten

1 tablespoon finely minced fresh ginger

2 teaspoons finely minced garlic

¼ cup finely chopped coriander leaves and stems

¼ cup thinly sliced green and white scallion rings

2 teaspoons Chinese chili sauce

½ teaspoon kosher salt

¼ teaspoon Roasted Szechwan Pepper-Salt (page 5)

2 teaspoons soy sauce

1 tablespoon Serrano-Lemongrass Vinegar (page 19) or unseasoned Japanese rice vinegar

1 tablespoon juice from China Moon Pickled Ginger (page 8)

Corn or peanut oil, for pan-frying

Minted Cucumber Sauce (page 23)

GARNISHES:

¼ cup diagonally sliced green and white scallion rings

¼ cup finely diced red bell pepper

4 to 8 coriander sprigs

1. Place the salmon pieces in a food processor. Pulse into pea-size bits, then scrape the salmon into a mixing bowl. Place the bread chunks in the food processor and process until the bread resembles coarse meal. Add the bread crumbs to the salmon in the mixing bowl. Add the egg and stir in one direction to mix. Add the seasonings through the pickled ginger juice and stir in one direction until well blended. Press plastic wrap directly on top of the mixture; refrigerate until chilled, overnight if you wish.

2. To shape the cakes, ready a ⅓-cup measure and a small bowl of ice water. Dip the measure in the ice water and shake the excess water from the cup. Pack the salmon mixture into the cup, using your fingers or the back of a spoon dipped in the water to even the mixture. Turn out onto a parchment- or waxed paper–lined baking sheet. If the cakes lose their shape somewhat, use your fingers to press them together. Repeat until all of the cakes are formed.

3. To pan-fry the cakes: Heat a large heavy skillet over moderate heat until hot enough to evaporate a bead of water. Add the oil to a depth of ¼ inch and heat until a bit of the salmon mixture sizzles immediately upon contact. Add the

STICK TIP

Dipping the cup or hand that shapes the patties into ice water helps to prevent sticking. It's a trick known to every grandmother around the world who's ever shaped a meat loaf.

salmon cakes, an inch or so apart, and pan-fry until golden brown and crusty, about 3 minutes, adjusting the heat so they sizzle without scorching. Carefully turn the cakes over with a spatula to cook and brown the other side, about 2 minutes more. The cakes are done when they are opaque all the way through. Transfer the cakes to a paper towel–lined plate to drain. Keep warm in a slow oven, if necessary, while the remaining cakes are pan-fried.

4. Serve immediately on a heated platter or individual plates of contrasting color, with a band of Minted Cucumber Sauce across the top of each cake and a scattering of scallion rings, red bell pepper dice, and coriander sprigs for garnish.

MENU SUGGESTIONS: For a simple dinner, the salmon cakes can be served with a green salad dressed with Fresh Ginger Vinaigrette (page 24) or an easy do-ahead dish like Wok-Seared Spinach Relish (page 438). Great mashed potatoes and gently sautéed greens—the inevitable partners to the salmon croquettes of my youth—would also be rather fine.

CLEAR-STEAMED SALMON WITH GINGER–BLACK BEAN VINAIGRETTE

SERVES 3 TO 4 AS A MAIN COURSE

This is heaven times two, a perfectly steamed fish fillet topped with the addictive Ginger–Black Bean Vinaigrette. For the vegetable bed, you could easily use paper-thin rounds of daikon in place of the spinach and onion.

I cooked this dish for my husband-to-be on our first weekend date, when I spirited him away to a cottage on an apple farm to celebrate his birthday. The promised hot plate in the cottage turned out to be in the bathroom, so I steamed the fish *en toilette*, as it were. Simple proof of a surefire dish.

STEAMING FISH

Steaming four portions of fish is relatively care-free given a 14-inch steamer, a 12- to 13-inch heatproof insert, and a finger or two to nudge the fish into close association. Otherwise, using or improvising two steamers side by side on the stove would be my choice. You can steam two layers of fish one on top of the other, but the upper bunk generally rains down on the lower one, and it is hard to gauge the precise moment of doneness.

The Chinese fashion is to serve fish (and poultry) with its skin and center bone intact, conserving the juices and the flavor of the beast. I extend this to steamed salmon steaks and allow guests to unzip their fish by themselves. You can be prudish and remove it for them, but why bother?

MARINADE:

¾ cup Chinese rice wine or dry sherry

¾ cup dry white wine

¼ cup soy sauce

1 tablespoon China Moon Hot Chili Oil (page 10)

1½ tablespoons coarsely chopped Chinese black beans (do not rinse them)

2 tablespoons finely chopped coriander leaves and stems

2 tablespoons Five-Flavor Oil (page 13), Ma-La Oil (page 17), or Japanese sesame oil

3 quarter-size coins fresh ginger, smashed

1 large clove garlic, smashed

½ teaspoon sugar

1½ to 2 pounds impeccably fresh, skinless, boneless salmon fillets, cut into 6- to 8-ounce portions, or 4 salmon steaks, skin left on for steaming, bones removed with tweezers or needle-nose pliers

1 bunch fresh spinach, stems removed

1 teaspoon Five-Flavor Oil, Ma-La Oil, or Japanese sesame oil, for the steaming plate

1 small red onion, sliced paper-thin

Ginger–Black Bean Vinaigrette (page 183)

2 teaspoons minced Chinese black beans

Finely diced red bell pepper, for garnish

1. Combine the marinade ingredients through the sugar in a bowl. Let stand for 5 to 10 minutes to infuse. Arrange the salmon in 1 layer in a shallow baking dish and scrape the marinade on top. Marinate for 20 minutes. If the marinade doesn't cover the fish completely, turn it midway through marination. Drain the fish. Allow some beans and bits of coriander to cling to each portion. Reserve ¼ cup of the marinade.

2. Blanch the spinach in boiling water for 5 seconds to wilt it. Drain and plunge into ice water to chill, then drain and squeeze to remove excess water. These preparations may be done up to a night in advance. Seal and refrigerate the fish, the marinade, and the spinach. Bring to room temperature before using and drain the spinach of any water.

3. About 15 minutes before serving, bring ample water for steaming to a boil. Choose a shallow heatproof plate (or 2) that is at least 1 inch deep and an inch or so smaller in diameter than your steamer. Brush the bottom and sides of the plate with a thin film of five-flavor oil and spread the spinach over the bottom to make a bed. Scatter the onion evenly over the spinach. Place the fish on top.

4. Drizzle each fillet with 1 tablespoon of the reserved marinade. Steam, tightly covered, over the highest heat until a

knife tip inserted in the thickest portion shows it to be medium-rare, 10 to 12 minutes for a 1-inch-thick fillet.

5. Promptly transfer the fish to heated plates to serve, using a spatula to lift the vegetable bed onto the plates along with the fish. Drizzle on a bit of the steaming juices, then top with a broad band of the vinaigrette and a sprinkling of the minced black beans and bell dice.

MENU SUGGESTIONS: Steamed or stir-fried rice is the ideal accompaniment to the fish. If you're trying to land a husband, add a platter of steamed corn or Gold Coin Corn Cakes (page 439).

CLEAR-STEAMED SALMON WITH FRESH CORIANDER PESTO

SERVES 3 TO 4 AS A MAIN COURSE

Another variation on our ever-popular steamed salmon entrée, this version features a slather of lush, fresh coriander pesto. The green of the pesto and the rose of the fish are perfect mates, and the combination is as delectable as it is pretty.

Salmon, of course, is the quintessential West Coast fish, fullest in flavor and color when it is caught wild. If fresh salmon is unavailable, choose a white-fleshed, sweet-tasting, impeccably fresh fish like bass or halibut, and cut the marinating and cooking times to account for thinner fish.

*Marinade ingredients (page
   191)*
*1½ to 2 pounds impeccably
   fresh, skinless, boneless
   salmon fillets, cut into 6- to
   8-ounce portions*

TOASTING PINE NUTS AND WALNUTS

To toast pine nuts or walnuts for pesto, preheat the oven to 350°F. Spread out the nuts on a baking sheet and toast, stirring occasionally, until the nuts are fully fragrant, 8 minutes for pine nuts and 15 minutes for walnuts. The nuts needn't be golden. You can also toast the nuts in a small heavy skillet over moderately low heat; they will cook in half the time.

CORIANDER PESTO:

2½ cups packed raw spinach leaves

1 cup packed coriander leaves and stems

¼ cup pine nuts or walnuts, toasted

1½ teaspoons finely minced garlic

2½ teaspoons freshly squeezed, strained lemon juice

¾ to 1 teaspoon kosher salt

¼ cup corn or peanut oil

1 to 1½ teaspoons China Moon Hot Chili Oil (page 10)

1 teaspoon Five-Flavor Oil (page 13), Ma-La Oil (page 17), or Japanese sesame oil, for brushing the steaming plate

¼ pound daikon, cut into paper-thin rounds, or 1 small red onion, cut into paper-thin rings

2 tablespoons very fine fresh ginger julienne

¼ cup finely diced red bell pepper, for garnish

1. Combine the marinade ingredients in a bowl. Let stand 5 to 10 minutes to infuse. Arrange the salmon in one layer in a shallow baking dish and scrape the marinade on top. Marinate for 20 minutes. If the marinade doesn't cover the fish completely, turn it midway through marination. Drain and discard the marinade. Allow some beans and bits of coriander to cling to each portion.

2. To make the pesto, blanch the spinach in a generous amount of boiling water until wilted, about 5 seconds. Refresh in ice water, then drain and squeeze dry.

3. Combine the spinach, coriander, toasted nuts, and garlic in a food processor and process to a paste. With the machine running, add the lemon juice and salt. Combine the oils and add in a thin stream until emulsified. If very thick, blend in a bit of warm water to obtain a rich, pourable consistency. Taste and adjust the seasoning, if needed, with more salt, lemon juice, and/or chili oil. The taste should be lively. The color is greenest when the pesto is made shortly before serving, but the flavors hold well overnight. If working in advance, seal with a piece of plastic wrap pressed directly on the surface and bring to room temperature before using.

4. About 15 minutes before serving, bring ample water for steaming to a boil. Choose a shallow heatproof plate (or 2) that is at least 1 inch deep and an inch or so smaller in diameter than your steamer. Brush the bottom and sides of the plate with a thin film of five-flavor oil and arrange the daikon or onion in overlapping rings to make a bed for the fish. Place the fish in a single layer on top and scatter ginger julienne evenly over all.

5. Steam, tightly covered, over the highest heat until a knife tip inserted in the thickest portion of the fish shows it to be medium-rare (or in the case of a white fish, until it is no longer translucent), 10 to 12 minutes for a 1-inch-thick fillet.

6. Promptly transfer the fish to heated plates of contrasting color. Discard any steaming juices or sip them later as soup. Top the fish with a broad band of pesto, then garnish with a sprinkling of red bell pepper dice.

MENU SUGGESTIONS: Steamed corn or Stir-Fried Zucchini Ribbons (page 437) are perfect alongside the fish, as is a portion of simply cooked rice or pasta garnished with toasted pine nuts and a flourish of scallion rings.

PAN-FRIED COHO SALMON WITH PLUM WINE

SERVES 4 AS A MAIN COURSE

Coho salmon is a small, often farmed salmon with finely textured pink meat and a delicate flavor. The individual butterflied fish makes a very pretty presentation, and the nuances given the dish by wine, lime, and ginger are memorable. If Coho salmon are not available, try substituting any small and delicate, very fresh fish, such as East Coast flounder or local trout.

This dish is simply done in under a half hour.

SAUCE:
1 cup China Moon Fish Fumet
   (page 79) or China Moon
   Infusion (page 72)
1 tablespoon soy sauce
½ teaspoon sugar

1 tablespoon good-tasting plum
   wine
½ teaspoon Serrano-
   Lemongrass Vinegar (page
   19) or unseasoned Japanese
   rice vinegar

PLUM WINE

Like most Chinese and Japanese bottled condiments, plum wine varies hugely from brand to brand. It can taste variously like cough syrup or an elixir for the gods. We use a made-in-Taiwan garden-variety that comes in a square clear bottle with a red plum flower stamped on its metal cap. If you cannot find it or one that tastes truly fine on your tongue, opt for a very good sweet sherry. The flavor will be different, but the results will be good.

NO DECAPITATED FISH

In Chinese culture, a fish without a head is like a body without a brain. The uncooked fish head tells the prospective buyer that its eye is clear, its gill is red, and hence it is fresh. The cooked fish head—placed facing the guest of honor—is the home of the sweet cheeks and prized lips sung about in every traditional treatise on Chinese cooking. Only a boor and a simpleton would whack off the head of a fish, or so think the Chinese.

4 fresh Coho salmon (8 to 10 ounces each), heads off if custom dictates
1 teaspoon Roasted Szechwan Pepper-Salt (page 5)
½ cup water chestnut starch
½ cup corn or peanut oil, for pan-frying

¼ cup very fine red bell pepper julienne
4 thin lime wedges
¼ cup green and white scallion julienne
¼ cup Fried Ginger Threads (page 29)

1. Combine all of the sauce ingredients through the vinegar in a small bowl, leaving the spoon in the bowl.

2. Just before pan-frying, sprinkle both sides of each fish evenly with ¼ teaspoon of the pepper-salt. Then immediately coat both sides well in the water chestnut starch, lightly shaking off the excess.

3. Heat a large heavy skillet over moderately high heat until hot enough to evaporate a bead of water on contact. Add the oil and swirl to glaze the pan. When hot enough to foam a bit of water chestnut starch, add the fish, flesh side down, and cook until lightly golden, about 2 minutes. (A 10-inch skillet will hold 2 fish.) Carefully turn and cook the skin side for 1 minute longer. Transfer the fish to a heated plate or platter and keep warm in a low oven while frying the remaining fish and making the sauce.

4. Wipe the skillet clean with paper towels. Stir the sauce to recombine and add to the pan. Bring to a near boil over moderate heat, then remove the pan from the heat and add the red bell pepper julienne. Transfer the fish to heated serving plates of contrasting color. Squeeze a lime wedge over each fish, then pour a portion of the sauce on top. Garnish with a sprinkling of scallion julienne and a scattering of Fried Ginger Threads and serve at once.

MENU SUGGESTIONS: In a Chinese mood, I would pair the fish with our Dinner Fried Rice (page 416) and a simply cooked green. If Marco Polo were my inspiration, I might instead choose risotto with a bit of shellfish or wild mushrooms.

PAN-SEARED TUNA WITH ROASTED RED BELL PEPPER SAUCE

SERVES 2 TO 3 AS A MAIN COURSE, 5 TO 6 AS PART OF A MULTICOURSE MEAL

This is one of the great dinnertime hits at China Moon. It is one of the first things that comes to mind when red bell peppers are at their sweet best, so beguiling and gorgeous is the sauce! Because our upstairs finishing kitchen is so tiny and our two stir-fry woks are always jammed, we cook the tuna to order in large Western skillets. A bit less sexy, perhaps, but the flavor is grand.

MARINADE AND TUNA:

½ cup soy sauce

1 tablespoon ginger juice (squeezed from finely minced fresh ginger)

¼ cup Chinese rice wine or dry sherry

1 teaspoon sugar

2 teaspoons Ma-La Oil (page 17), Five-Flavor Oil (page 13), or Japanese sesame oil

2 scallions, cut into 1-inch nuggets and smashed

1 pound fresh tuna fillets (ahi or yellowfin are best), cut ½ inch thick and then into 2½- to 3-inch triangular steaks

SAUCE:

3 medium red bell peppers, roasted (page 197), stemmed, peeled, and coarsely chopped

3 slices sun-dried tomato, soaked briefly in boiling water until softened, drained (if oil-packed, simply drain)

1½ teaspoons finely minced garlic

½ cup unseasoned Japanese rice vinegar

2 tablespoons cider vinegar

1 tablespoon sugar

1 teaspoon fine sea salt

¼ cup Five-Flavor Oil

1½ tablespoons China Moon Hot Chili Oil (page 10)

2 tablespoons "goop" from China Moon Hot Chili Oil

1 cup packed coriander leaves and stems, chopped

Corn or peanut oil, for searing

Chinese chives, cut into ½-inch lengths, for garnish

JUST TOMATOES

My favorite sun-dried tomatoes are called Just Tomatoes. Made by a California company and sold in small cellophane pouches with a couple of smiling tomatoes on the label, they contain no seasoning nor oil, just a bit of concentrated flavor to give oomph to the sauce.

ROASTING PEPPERS

I heartily dislike the gassy taste of peppers blackened over a gas flame, so I always choose to roast them in the oven if a wood-fired grill is unavailable.

Preheat the oven to 500°F. Place the peppers on a baking sheet and roast in the top third of the oven, turning frequently until they blacken and blister, 15 to 20 minutes for medium peppers. Put them directly in a bowl, seal airtight with plastic wrap, and let steam for 30 minutes. Discard the skin, stem, and seeds, using your fingers and an occasional swat with a paring knife to pull away all the blackened bits. Dip your fingers in water as you work, and retain any juices that the peppers release. Don't peel the peppers underwater, as is often done. It may be neater, but the flavor rinses away with the char.

1. Combine the marinade ingredients through the scallions and let stand for 5 to 10 minutes to infuse. Put the fish in a shallow dish large enough to hold it snugly. Scrape the marinade over the tuna and marinate for 15 minutes. Turn the fish once or twice for even marination. Drain and discard the marinade. At this point, the tuna may be sealed and refrigerated overnight if you like.

2. To make the sauce, combine the roasted bell peppers and sun-dried tomatoes in a food processor. Process until nearly smooth. Add the garlic and pulse to blend. Combine the vinegars with the sugar and sea salt and add to the red pepper mixture. With the machine running, combine the oils and "goop," and add slowly, running the machine until the sauce emulsifies, 1 to 2 minutes. Stop the machine, add the chopped coriander, and pulse until the coriander is finely minced. (If preparing in advance, add the coriander just before serving.) Taste and adjust with a bit more salt, sugar, and/or vinegar, if needed, depending on the flavor and sweetness of the peppers. Don't be shy. Fiddle with it until you get a taste you like.

At this point, the sauce may be refrigerated for several hours or overnight. Press a piece of plastic wrap directly on the surface to preserve the color. Bring the sauce to room temperature before using.

3. Heat a heavy skillet over high heat until hot enough to sizzle a bead of water on contact. Add 1 tablespoon corn oil and swirl to glaze the pan. When smoking, add the tuna steaks in a single layer. Do not crowd them; use 2 skillets or cook the fish in 2 batches, if need be. Pan-fry until nicely brown, 30 to 60 seconds. Turn and cook until the tuna is seared outside but still rare within, another 30 seconds or so. The timing will depend on the heat of your stove and your pan. Aim to undercook the fish, and you will not overcook it.

4. Transfer the fish to heated serving plates of contrasting color, overlapping the triangles to give them a bit of height. Serve immediately, topped with a wide ribbon of the sauce and a sprinkling of the chives.

MENU SUGGESTIONS: The red sauce calls out for a deep green vegetable to partner the fish. Wok-Seared Spinach Relish (page 438), Stir-Fried Zucchini Ribbons (page 437), or a simple stir-fried or parboiled dish of Chinese broccoli or rape would be my choice. Some rice or fettuccine would complete the plate perfectly.

WOK-SEARED TUNA

SERVES 2 TO 3 AS A MAIN COURSE,
5 TO 6 AS PART OF A MULTICOURSE MEAL

This is one of those dishes that by virtue of name and deliciousness seems to run out the door of the restaurant. More than a dish, it is a method of marinating and cooking tuna for inclusion in a composed salad, or alongside lightly dressed greens, colorful pickled vegetables, or a heap of cold noodles.

Marinating and cooking the fish takes only minutes, making this a great choice for dinner at the end of a busy day.

MARINADE:
⅔ cup soy sauce
¼ cup Chinese rice wine or dry sherry
1½ tablespoons Ma-La Oil (page 17), Five-Flavor Oil (page 13), or Japanese sesame oil
2 teaspoons sugar
2 quarter-size coins fresh ginger, smashed

3 scallions, cut into 1-inch nuggets and smashed

1 pound fresh tuna (ahi or yellowfin are best), cut ½ inch thick, then into 2½- to 3-inch triangular steaks
1 to 2 tablespoons corn or peanut oil, for searing

1. Combine all of the marinade ingredients in a small bowl and let stand for 5 to 10 minutes to infuse. Put the tuna in a shallow dish large enough to hold it snugly. Scrape the marinade on top and marinate for 15 minutes, turning the fish once or twice. Drain the tuna. (At this point it may be sealed and refrigerated overnight.) Discard the marinade.

2. Heat a wok or heavy skillet over high heat until hot enough to evaporate a bead of water on contact. Add 1 tablespoon of the corn oil, swirl to glaze the pan, and heat until nearly smoking. Add the tuna pieces, making sure not to crowd the pan (which will lower the heat and inhibit a good sear). If all of the pieces do not fit, clean the pan and repeat the process. Sear briefly until the tuna is browned and a bit charred at the edge, 30 to 60 seconds. Turn to brown the other side, another 15 to 30 seconds. For best flavor, the tuna should

WOK VS. SKILLET

The smoky contours of our giant red-hot restaurant wok make it an ideal vessel for cooking the tuna. However, at home, where the sides of a wok rarely get very hot perched atop a flat Western stove, your better choice might be to sear the fish in a heavy skillet. Cast iron, left to heat over high heat for 4 to 5 minutes, would be ideal, but most any heavy pan will do.

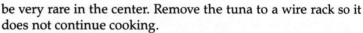

be very rare in the center. Remove the tuna to a wire rack so it does not continue cooking.

3. Serve hot or at room temperature as part of a salad plate, overlapping the triangles of fish for a bit of height. The tuna may be seared and refrigerated overnight, but its real flavor beauty is freshly seared. If you have refrigerated it, moisten the fish with a dab of Fresh Ginger Vinaigrette to give it a little gloss.

MENU SUGGESTIONS: For lunch or a light dinner, the tuna pairs perfectly with a mix of baby lettuces (radicchio, mâche, curly cress, or watercress recommended for their bite), dressed in our Fresh Ginger Vinaigrette (page 24). Other good additions to this salad plate would be a contrasting pickle or two, like Ginger-Pickled Daikon (page 53), Orange-Pickled Carrot Coins (page 58), or Turmeric Tomatoes (page 59). Or, for a noodle salad, serve the wedges of fish alongside a hill of Dragon Noodles (page 391), or Cold Tomato Noodles (page 394).

BAKED SNAPPER
WITH
RED CURRY SAUCE

SERVES 3 TO 4 AS A MAIN COURSE

This is a very simple and delicious way to bake fish: seasoned with a Chinese marinade, baked on a bed of seared Napa cabbage, and dotted with tasty bits of Thai red curry paste. Most any fresh fish fillet can be cooked to this formula; however, halve the marinating and cooking times if the fillets are thin.

The red curry sauce is a delicious topping when you have the requisite sweet-smelling, full-flavored tomatoes and the time to put it together. Otherwise, the fish may be baked and served "in the nude," without a sauce. Simply add some lime wedges to the plate.

MARINADE:

1 cup Chinese rice wine or dry sherry

½ cup dry white wine

⅓ cup soy sauce

2 tablespoons coarsely chopped Chinese black beans (do not rinse them)

2 tablespoons finely chopped coriander leaves and stems

¼ cup Five-Flavor Oil (page 13), Ma-La Oil (page 17), or 2 tablespoons Japanese sesame oil

2 tablespoons finely minced fresh ginger

1 tablespoon sugar

1 teaspoon Thai red curry paste

2 teaspoons freshly squeezed lime juice

1½ pounds trimmed and boned fresh fish fillets, such as snapper, rock cod, sea bass, or flounder, cut into 6- to 8-ounce portions

1½ to 2 tablespoons corn or peanut oil, for stir-frying

1 small yellow onion, cut into ¼-inch-thick wedges

1 small carrot, cut into julienne

4 cups ½-inch-thick Napa cabbage ribbons

Scant ¼ teaspoon Roasted Szechwan Pepper-Salt (page 5)

Red Curry Sauce (recipe follows)

GARNISHES:

Coriander sprigs

Finely chopped Chinese chives or green and white scallion rings, thinly sliced on the diagonal, or ¾ teaspoon minced Chinese black beans and lime wedges, if omitting the sauce

1. In a bowl, combine all of the marinade ingredients and whisk to blend. Set aside for 5 to 10 minutes to infuse. Place the fish in a shallow non-aluminum dish just large enough to hold it snugly, scrape the marinade on top, and marinate for 20 minutes. Turn the fish to redistribute the liquids once or twice while marinating. If the fillets are thin, marinate for only 10 minutes. Drain the fish and reserve the marinade. At this point, the fish and marinade may be sealed and refrigerated, overnight if you like.

2. Up to a day in advance of serving, heat a wok or skillet over high heat until hot enough to evaporate a bead of water on contact. Add 1 tablespoon of the corn oil and swirl to glaze the pan. When hot enough to sizzle a slice of the onion, add the onion and stir-fry briskly until wilted, about 1 minute, adjusting the heat so it sears to gold without burning. Add the carrot, toss to blend, and then add the cabbage and toss to combine and wilt, about 1 minute more, adjusting the heat to

maintain a lively crackle and drizzling a bit more oil down the side of the pan, if needed to prevent sticking. Sprinkle lightly with the pepper-salt; remove from the pan. Spread the seared vegetables on a large plate or sheet pan so they do not continue cooking. If you are working in advance, they may be left uncovered for several hours, or sealed and refrigerated overnight. Bring to room temperature before using.

3. Preheat the oven to 375°F. Move a rack to the middle position.

4. To bake the fish, spread the vegetables on several small or 1 large heatproof plate. Lay the fillets on top, whisk the marinade to recombine it, and then moisten each portion with 1 to 1½ tablespoons. Bake until the fillets are 90 percent cooked through in the thickest portion, 7 to 8 minutes. They will cook to doneness while you are plating them.

5. Serve the fillets immediately on a bed of the vegetables. Top with a broad ribbon of sauce, rimmed by a sprig or two of coriander, and garnish with chives or scallions. Or, if omitting the sauce, garnish with a light sprinkling of chopped black beans and a lime wedge.

Menu Suggestions: Rice, pasta, or toasted garlic bread would complete this dish with ease. For an extra vegetable, you might stir-fry some ribbons of green and golden zucchini (page 437). Fresh corn-on-the-cob, sprinkled with a bit of Roasted Szechwan Pepper-Salt (page 5), or Gold Coin Corn Cakes (page 439) would also be wonderful.

RED CURRY SAUCE

MAKES 1 ¼ CUPS

Thai red curry paste, an ingredient in this sauce, is an "exotic" ingredient that occasionally sneaks its way into our mostly Chinese kitchen. Its bold shot of spicy, citrusy heat mates particularly well with fish. We buy it in tiny cans, with a beaming mama on the red, all-Thai label.

1 tablespoon corn or peanut oil

3 to 4 ripe but firm plum
   tomatoes, stem ends cut off,
   quartered lengthwise into
   wedges

1 medium red bell pepper,
   roasted (page 197), peeled,
   and chopped

¾ teaspoon Thai red curry paste

2 tablespoons Five-Flavor Oil
   (page 13)

2 tablespoons juice from China
   Moon Pickled Ginger
   (page 8)

1 tablespoon sugar

1 teaspoon kosher salt

1 tablespoon unseasoned
   Japanese rice vinegar

½ teaspoon finely minced garlic

¼ cup lightly packed coriander
   leaves and stems

Heat a wok or non-aluminum large, heavy skillet over high heat until hot. Add the corn oil and swirl to glaze the pan. Heat until nearly smoking, turn down the heat to moderately high, and add the tomatoes. Stand back as the tomatoes will spit and sizzle. Toss to sear all sides until the tomatoes are lightly scorched, about 1 minute. Scrape the tomatoes and any juices from the pan into a food processor. Add the roasted bell peppers and pulse to combine. Add all of the remaining ingredients except the coriander, and process to blend. Add the coriander and pulse until minced.

At this point, the sauce may be sealed and refrigerated for up to a day. Press a piece of plastic wrap directly on the surface to preserve the color. If working more than several hours in advance, buzz the coriander in at the last minute, to keep it looking and tasting best. Bring the sauce to room temperature before using.

STEAMED OR SEARED MAHIMAHI WITH TOMATO SAUCE

SERVES 3 TO 4 AS A MAIN COURSE

Mahimahi is one of those sweet, meaty, Hawaiian fish whose very deliciousness seems to conjure up images of bronzed bodies, pounding surf,

FISH LAMENTS

The state of our oceans and lakes is frightening. So, too, is the fact that Americans have not demanded a quality grading system for fish and shellfish, not to mention industry-wide tests for toxicity. When buying fish, one can feel safe dealing with a trusted purveyor, but beyond that it's a bit of a crapshoot. What to do?

On an everyday front, demand quality fresh fish from your market. If you don't like what you see or smell, speak up. You may get some scowls, but you may also get better fish.

On the political front, write to the non-profit group called Public Voice, 1001 Connecticut Avenue, N.W., Suite 522, Washington, D.C. 20036. We shouldn't need to fear our food, but an untested product born and bred in an increasingly contaminated environment is scary. We can do something about it.

and ukuleles. Not bad for a piece of fish! Mated with a fresh tomato sauce, it sends me over the edge.

The effects of steaming and pan-searing are quite different. Steamed, the flavor is very pure and light. Pan-seared, it becomes more gutsy and complex. Either way, I always pair it with daikon for its sweet radishy taste.

If mahimahi is not available, use fresh salmon or red snapper, but hold the ukuleles.

MARINADE AND FISH:
1 cup soy sauce
½ cup Chinese rice wine or dry sherry
2 tablespoons ginger juice (squeezed from finely minced fresh ginger)
2 teaspoons sugar
1½ tablespoons Five-Flavor Oil (page 13), Ma-La Oil (page 17), or Japanese sesame oil
1 teaspoon Cayenne Pepper Oil (page 11) or 1 tablespoon China Moon Hot Chili Oil (page 10)
4 scallions, cut into 1-inch nuggets and smashed
1½ to 2 pounds trimmed and boned fresh mahimahi fillets, cut into 6- to 8-ounce portions

TOMATO SAUCE:
4 to 5 slices sun-dried tomato
1 tablespoon corn or peanut oil
3 to 4 ripe but firm plum tomatoes, stem ends cut off, quartered lengthwise into wedges

1 tablespoon sugar
1½ to 2 teaspoons kosher salt
1 tablespoon Serrano-Lemongrass Vinegar (page 19) or unseasoned Japanese rice vinegar
1 tablespoon Ma-La Oil or Five-Flavor Oil
Freshly ground black pepper, to taste

¼ pound thin daikon (about 3 inches), cut into paper-thin rounds
1 tablespoon Ma-La Oil or Five-Flavor Oil, if pan-searing the fish
1½ tablespoons corn or peanut oil, for searing

GARNISHES:
2 tablespoons finely chopped Chinese chives
1½ tablespoons finely chopped coriander, or 2 to 3 tablespoons thinly sliced green and white scallion rings
2 tablespoons green or purple basil julienne

1. Combine the marinade ingredients through the scallions in a bowl and let stand for 5 to 10 minutes to infuse.

2. Put the fish fillets in a non-aluminum shallow dish just large enough to hold them snugly. Scrape the marinade over the fish and marinate for 10 minutes, turning the fish occasionally to redistribute the liquids. Drain and reserve the marinade. The fish may be marinated up to a day in advance. Seal and refrigerate.

3. To make the tomato sauce, cover the sun-dried tomatoes with boiling water and set aside until soft, about 10 minutes. Drain and coarsely chop. (If using oil-steeped tomatoes, soaking is unnecessary; just drain the oil and then coarsely chop.)

4. Heat a wok or large heavy skillet over high heat until hot enough to evaporate a bead of water on contact. Add the corn oil, swirl to glaze the pan, and heat until smoking. Add the tomato wedges and toss until soft, juicy, and slightly charred, about 1 minute. Don't worry about the smoke. Remove the tomato wedges from the pan along with any juices.

5. In a food processor, combine the sun-dried tomatoes along with the sugar, salt, vinegar, and ma-la oil. Process to combine. Add the seared tomatoes and their juices, and process until smooth. Season with black pepper to taste and a dash more sugar and/or salt, if needed to bring out the flavor of the tomatoes. At this point, the sauce may be refrigerated overnight, if you like. Press a piece of plastic wrap directly on the surface to preserve the color. Bring to room temperature before using.

6. To steam the fish: About 15 minutes before serving, bring ample water for steaming to a boil over high heat. Overlap the daikon slices on 1 or 2 heatproof plates at least 1 inch smaller in diameter than your steamer and large enough to hold the fish in a single layer; put the mahimahi on top. Drizzle each portion with 1 tablespoon of the marinade. Steam, tightly covered, over the highest heat until the thickest portion of the fillets looks 95 percent cooked through when pierced with the tip of a small knife, 9 to 10 minutes. Drain off the juices. Serve the fish immediately on its daikon bed, with a broad band of the tomato sauce spooned on top and a sprinkling of the chopped Chinese chives, coriander or scallion, and fine basil julienne to garnish.

7. To pan-sear: Preheat the oven to 400°F. Brush a baking sheet or ovenproof dish with a thin film of the ma-la oil. Lay a bed of overlapping daikon slices on top. Heat 1 or 2 heavy skillets over high heat until hot enough to evaporate a bead of water on contact. Add the corn oil, swirl to glaze the pan(s), and heat until smoking. Add the fish fillets in a single layer with plenty of room between them. (Crowding the fish means

SAUCE TIP

///

In making the tomato sauce, it is imperative that the oil-glazed pan be literally smoking hot. The flavor that the smoke imparts to the sauce, captured in the tomatoes as they're tossed in the pan, is inimitable.

lowering the heat of the pan, which inhibits the sear.) Sear on the first side until nicely browned, about 30 seconds. Turn and brown the other side for 20 to 30 seconds more. Place the fillets on top of the daikon and drizzle a bit of the marinade on top. Bake until the thickest part of the fish looks cooked through when pierced with the tip of a small knife, about 5 minutes. Serve the fish on its daikon bed on heated plates of contrasting color. Spoon a ribbon of the tomato sauce on top and garnish with the basil julienne and a scattering of the chives and coriander or scallion.

MENU SUGGESTIONS: For the steamed fish, I'd like steamed or stir-fried rice and sautéed greens and maybe an ear of fresh corn alongside. If the fish were pan-seared, I'd like an accompanying pile of sautéed daikon rounds or zucchini ribbons (page 437) and a mound of steamed rice.

SPICY FISH TOASTS

MAKES 15 TO 20 TOASTS
SERVES 6 TO 10 AS AN APPETIZER

This is party food—a pass-around hors d'oeuvre of deep-fried fish toasts spiked with the crunch of fresh water chestnuts and the sweetness of a good French baguette. It is a happy bit of extravagance at the beginning of a meal and a delightful companion to a flute of cool dry Champagne.

The fish mixture can be made in advance, but the toasts are best formed and fried just before serving. Do not bother with them if you need to be a guest at the beginning of your own party; to be truly delicious, this dish requires some fuss.

Fresh shrimp, deveined and ground to a paste, may be used in place of all or some of the fish paste. Some fresh crabmeat, stirred in to retain its texture, is another great addition.

1 to 2 densely textured French
   baguettes, cut into diagonal
   slices ½ inch thick and about
   3 inches long
1 tablespoon finely minced fresh
   ginger
¼ cup thinly sliced green and
   white scallion rings
¼ cup finely chopped coriander
   leaves and stems
1 teaspoon kosher salt
1 tablespoon Chinese rice wine
   or dry sherry
1 to 1½ teaspoons Chinese chili
   sauce
Several twists freshly ground
   black pepper

1 pound fish paste, ground from
   fresh fatty fish (see Fish
   Paste on page 360)
8 fresh water chestnuts, cut to a
   peppercorn-size dice
2 large egg whites
4 to 6 cups corn or peanut oil,
   for deep-frying

GARNISHES:
20 to 30 small feathery
   coriander leaves
1½ tablespoons finely minced
   smoked ham or carrot
2 teaspoons black sesame seeds
Whole coriander sprigs
   (optional)

1. Arrange the baguette slices side by side on a wire rack and let stand until the cut sides are dry (though not hard) to the touch, 1 to 2 hours. Alternatively, dry the bread by putting the slices on a baking sheet in a 200°F oven until the tops feel dry, about 15 minutes. Turn the slices to dry the underside. The somewhat dry bread will not absorb oil when fried. At this point, the toasts may be sealed airtight against further drying and left overnight.

2. Combine the ginger, scallion rings, coriander, salt, wine, chili sauce, and pepper in a food processor. Add the fish paste and blend to a purée. Transfer to a bowl and stir in the water chestnuts. At this point, the purée may be sealed and refrigerated overnight. Press a piece of plastic wrap directly on the surface of the purée.

3. Up to several hours in advance of serving, complete the fish mixture and ready the toasts for frying: Whisk the egg whites until stiff; fold into the purée. Using a small sandwich spatula glazed with a bit of oil to keep the fish paste from sticking, mound about 2 tablespoons of the purée on top of each bread toast. Smooth and mold the purée evenly to form a plateau ½ inch thick, with sloping sides to meet the toast. Make sure there are no holes for oil to enter when frying. Put the mounded toasts on a baking sheet. If working in advance, cover the toasts loosely and refrigerate.

4. About 20 minutes before serving, pour 2 to 2½ inches of oil into a wok or large, deep, heavy skillet. Rest a deep-fry

LEARNING HOW TO COOK

Many people would love to know how to cook, and don't know where to start. Sure, the man on TV is amusing and the stuff in the pan does sizzle, but that's mostly entertainment, not cooking.

If you really want to learn how to cook, take a class. Local cookware shops, Y's, and adult education centers offer affordable classes by a wide spectrum of teachers—anyone from your Aunt Tilly who makes great pies to the handsome French guy who used to cook in the White House.

If you can't find a class by simply asking around or

calling your local Chamber of Commerce, write to the International Association of Culinary Professionals, 304 West Liberty Street, Louisville, Kentucky 40202. They have a roster of cooking schools that includes the small and large, and plain and fancy. They're friendly folks, and their business is to promote cooking.

Good cookbooks are the best teachers of all, if you're someone who loves books. There are so many, it's hard to choose, but I'm a big believer in beginning with the classics: Julia Child's early books, if you're interested in French cooking and like meticulous instruction; anything by Elizabeth David, if you crave culture with your food and are comfortable with free-form recipes; books by impeccable modern teachers such as Paula Wolfert and Diana Kennedy if your romance is ethnic cuisine; or most any of the extraordinary cookbooks from the now out-of-print Time-Life series, Foods of the World.

I taught myself how to cook, mostly from books. It was a journey that inspired my life, and I like to cheer others on the path. Be brave and set forth! Cooking is a happy, fun-filled rainbow, with a big pot of dinner at the end.

thermometer on the rim and bring the oil to the medium-haze stage, 375°F, hot enough to foam a dab of fish paste. Adjust the heat so that the temperature does not climb. Put a baking sheet lined with a triple layer of paper towels alongside your stovetop.

5. Garnish each mounded toast by gently pressing a single coriander leaf on the top of each toast and then offsetting it with a sprinkle of the minced ham and black sesame seeds. Carefully drop the toasts, one by one, fish side down, into the oil, adding only as many as can float freely. Adjust the heat to maintain a steady temperature. Fry until the toasts float high on the surface of the oil, indicating the fish is cooked, about 4 minutes. When nearly done, ladle a bit of the oil over the bread side of the toasts to turn them golden. Let the oil return to 375°F between batches.

6. With a large Chinese mesh spoon, promptly remove the toasts and place, bread side down, on paper towels to drain. Let stand for several minutes before serving in order to cool; the fish will be blazing hot. Serve on a colorful platter or in a steamer basket for a bit of whimsy, with sprigs of fresh coriander.

CRISPY SESAME FISH SLICES WITH PERSIMMON DIPPING SAUCE

SERVES 3 TO 5 AS PART OF A MULTICOURSE MEAL, 6 TO 8 AS AN HORS D'OEUVRE

This is an ideal party appetizer. It is very pretty to look at with its combination of black and white sesame seeds and bright orange sauce, and the contrast of hot fish and cool fruit is wonderful. Look for a firm-fleshed, non-oily white fish. Fresh bass, sole, flounder, and ling cod all work well.

½ pound trimmed and boned fresh fish fillet with a neutral, sweet taste, such as sea bass, ling cod, sole, or flounder

VELVET MARINADE:
1 large egg white
1 tablespoon Chinese rice wine or dry sherry
1 teaspoon kosher salt

1 tablespoon cornstarch

1 cup untoasted white sesame seeds
⅓ cup untoasted black sesame seeds
4 to 6 cups corn or peanut oil, for deep-frying
Persimmon Dipping Sauce (recipe follows)

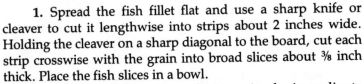

1. Spread the fish fillet flat and use a sharp knife or cleaver to cut it lengthwise into strips about 2 inches wide. Holding the cleaver on a sharp diagonal to the board, cut each strip crosswise with the grain into broad slices about ⅜ inch thick. Place the fish slices in a bowl.

2. Whisk together the velvet marinade ingredients through the cornstarch until smooth and thick. Pour over the fish slices and toss well to coat each slice. Seal airtight and marinate in the refrigerator for 2 to 24 hours to set the marinade and flavor the fish. Let come to room temperature before frying; retoss to separate the slices.

3. Toss the sesame seeds to combine, then spread half of them in a large baking pan or pie plate. Arrange the fish slices next to one another in a single layer on top. Sprinkle evenly with the remaining sesame seeds, then press with dry fingers to make the seeds adhere. Arrange the coated fish slices in a single layer on a parchment or waxed paper–lined platter or baking sheet. Seal airtight and refrigerate for 1 to 4 hours prior to deep-frying. Refrigeration will help the seeds to adhere.

4. About 20 minutes before serving, pour about 2 inches of oil into a wok or large and deep, heavy skillet. Rest a deep-fry thermometer on the rim and bring the oil to the light-haze stage, 350°F, when a fish slice will float in seconds to the surface. Adjust the heat so the temperature does not climb. Put a baking sheet lined with a triple layer of paper towels alongside your stovetop.

5. Gently slide the fish, slice by slice, into the oil, adding only as many as can float freely. Adjust the heat to maintain a steady temperature. Fry the slices until they float high on the surface of the oil and the white seeds turn pale gold, about 2 minutes. With a Chinese mesh spoon, quickly transfer the fish onto the paper towels to drain. Fry the remaining fish, but first

bring the oil to 350°F if it has dropped between batches.

6. Place the dipping sauce in a sauce bowl and center it on a platter of contrasting color. Fan the fish slices around it, and invite your guests to help themselves with their fingers.

PERSIMMON DIPPING SAUCE

MAKES 1½ CUPS

½ cup dried persimmon slices
1¼ cups boiling water
1 small yellow wax chili or red Fresno chili, tipped, halved lengthwise, and seeded
2 tablespoons China Moon Pickled Ginger (page 8)
3 tablespoons juice from China Moon Pickled Ginger

1½ teaspoons sugar
1½ teaspoons freshly squeezed lemon juice
Dash of fine sea salt
2 to 3 tablespoons coarsely chopped coriander leaves and stems

1. In a small bowl, combine the persimmon slices and the boiling water. Cover and let soak until the water cools; the fruit will be very soft.

2. In a food processor, process the persimmons, the soaking liquid, and all of the remaining ingredients through the salt until smooth. Taste the sauce and adjust with a dash more salt, lemon juice, and/or sugar, if necessary. If working less than several hours in advance, add the coriander until minced. At this point the sauce may be refrigerated overnight. Press a piece of plastic directly on the surface to preserve the color. If working more than several hours in advance, buzz in the coriander at the last minute. Bring to room temperature before using.

MENU SUGGESTIONS: If you are looking for another appetizer to keep the fish company, try Grilled Chinese Chicken Wings with Orange Zest and Garlic (page 128). Otherwise, as part of a meal, be sure to include a salad of watercress or baby greens dressed with a ginger or citrus vinaigrette to balance the richness of the fish.

PERSIMMON POSSIBILITIES

Although dried persimmon slices, which can be found in natural food stores, have an inimitable depth of flavor, a good sauce can also be made with an equivalent amount of fresh persimmon pulp or crispy Fuyu persimmon chunks. Even if you are an avowed persimmon hater, withhold judgment until you try it in combination with pickled ginger and chili. The trio is delicious!

COLD SALAD OF WOK-SEARED PRAWNS IN THEIR SHELLS

SERVES 3 TO 4 AS A LIGHT ENTREE, 6 TO 8 AS PART OF A MULTICOURSE MEAL

This is a great way to cook truly fresh prawns, the increasingly uncommon sort that have never suffered the indignities of freezing or preservative-bleaching and are consequently hard to get and pricey. We get them only sporadically, primarily from Santa Barbara and the Texas gulf, and the sweet firm flesh is heavenly.

While this recipe details a room-temperature composed salad presented with China Moon pickles, the prawns can also be served freshly seared and hot as an entrée, along with rice, simply dressed pasta, or a stir-fry of seasonal vegetables.

1 pound fresh, sweet-smelling prawns in their shells (Don't worry about size. Worry only about freshness.)

MARINADE:
⅓ cup soy sauce
1 tablespoon Chinese rice wine or dry sherry
1 tablespoon Ma-La Oil (page 17) or Five-Flavor Oil (page 13)
½ teaspoon sugar
4 quarter-size coins fresh ginger, smashed

2 scallions, cut into 1-inch nuggets and smashed
1 to 2 tablespoons corn or peanut oil
2 tablespoons diagonally sliced green and white scallion rings, to garnish the prawns
Ginger-Pickled Daikon (page 53) or Lemon-Pickled Lotus Rounds (page 55)
Orange-Pickled Carrot Coins (page 58)
An assortment of baby lettuces dressed with Fresh Ginger Vinaigrette (page 24)

1. To prepare the prawns, remove the stinger at the tail end and pull off the legs. Remove the shell down to the last digit. Butterfly the prawns with a sharp paring knife, laying them on their side on a workboard. Start at the head and cut along the back two-thirds of the way to the tail. Remove the dark vein.

2. In a large bowl, whisk together all of the marinade ingredients through the scallions until combined. Add the prawns and marinate for 10 minutes. Drain and discard the marinade; refrigerate the prawns until ready to cook, overnight if you like.

3. Heat a wok or a small heavy skillet over high heat until hot enough to evaporate a bead of water on contact. Add 1 scant tablespoon of the oil and swirl to glaze the pan. When nearly smoking, spread 4 or 5 of the prawns, tails up and flesh sides down, in the pan. Sear until golden, only 15 to 20 seconds. Turn and brown the other side for 5 to 10 seconds more. The timing will differ depending on the size of the prawns; they are done when they feel firm at the thickest spot. Remove the prawns to a large plate in a single layer, then repeat with the remaining prawns, swirling a teaspoon or so of oil into the pan with each new batch.

4. Serve the prawns immediately or at room temperature on plates of contrasting color. Arrange the shrimp jauntily to one side to get a bit of height, garnish with a sprinkling of scallion, and then complete the plate with pinched hills of the pickled vegetables and a tumble of ginger-dressed greens.

MENU SUGGESTIONS: As a room-temperature dish, you could also serve the prawns alongside a hill of cold noodles—Dragon Noodles (page 391) or Cold Tomato Noodles (page 394)—both being delicious choices. Served hot, their flavor would complement most all of our hot and sour soups.

A PRAWN IS A SHRIMP IS A PRAWN

Prawn, as far as I'm concerned, is simply a sexy word for shrimp, and occasionally a better come-on in a recipe title. Here, size of beast is irrelevant, freshness is all.

SKEWERED BAKED SHRIMP

SERVES 2 TO 4 AS A MAIN COURSE,
6 TO 8 AS PART OF A MULTICOURSE MEAL

One night when the steamer was crowded with something else, we popped these shrimp into the oven—a very un-Chinese thing to do—and were delighted with how good they were! The fragrant marinade and shrimp juices dripped down into the vegetables during the baking and made them every bit as delicious as the shrimp. Of course, if you have the steamer space, this dish is also fine steamed.

Threading the prawns on skewers is a nice bit of theater. The skewers are unnecessary but fun, and make turning the shrimp easier.

From start to finish, this dish takes an easy 30 minutes to prepare.

1 pound large fresh shrimp in
    their shells

MARINADE:
⅓ cup soy sauce
⅓ cup Chinese rice wine or dry
    sherry
2 teaspoons sugar
¼ cup Ma-La Oil (page 17) or
    Five-Flavor Oil (page 13)
½ teaspoon dried red chili flakes
2 stalks lemongrass, cut into
    finger-lengths and smashed
2 scallions, cut into 1-inch
    nuggets and smashed
5 quarter-size coins fresh ginger,
    smashed
5 cloves garlic, smashed

VEGETABLES:
1 small, thin daikon, cut into
    paper-thin rounds, or 2½
    cups lightly packed spinach
    leaves
2 to 3 teaspoons Ma-La Oil or
    Five-Flavor Oil
1 small carrot, cut into julienne
2½ cups Napa cabbage, cut into
    ½-inch ribbons, for the
    vegetable bed
¼ teaspoon Roasted Szechwan
    Pepper-Salt (page 5)
2 tablespoons finely chopped
    Chinese chives or thinly
    sliced green and white
    scallion rings, for garnish
2 tablespoons finely diced red
    bell pepper, for garnish

BUYING SHRIMP

Truly fresh shrimp are an endangered species. Typically frozen on the trawlers when they're caught and all too often dunked in a bleach solution to preserve them, 90 percent of the shrimp that are sold in our markets do not taste fresh and are without the wonderful texture that is the hallmark of the beast. It is a very sad thing. The politics of the fishing industry and the state of our oceans are such that fishermen will rarely make the commitment to *rush a fresh product to the shore and to the market.*

Shrimp that has never been frozen or bleached will have no odor. The shell will be attached stubbornly to the flesh and the legs will cling tenaciously to the belly. The shell will have body. If you are purchasing fresh shrimp that are already shelled, the intestinal vein will be elastic and hard to remove. If the head is left on, the eyes will generally be bright and beady.

Should you see shrimp that meet these requirements, buy them and settle in for a great supper.

1. Submerge 10 to 12 6-inch wooden skewers or 6 to 8 8-inch wooden skewers in hot water to cover.

2. Shell the shrimp, leaving the tails on; devein.

3. In a non-aluminum bowl, combine all of the marinade ingredients. Let stand for 5 to 10 minutes to infuse. Add the shrimp and marinate for 10 minutes, tossing occasionally to redistribute the liquids. Drain the marinade from the shrimp; strain and reserve the marinade. Drain the skewers and thread the shrimp, facing them in 1 direction, not jamming them tight, and leaving at least 1 inch free at each end of the skewer. At this point, the shrimp may be sealed and refrigerated, overnight if desired.

4. Blanch the daikon in rapidly boiling water for 10 seconds. Drain and refresh under cold water to stop the cooking, then drain thoroughly. Or blanch the spinach by the same method but for 5 seconds. Drain, refresh, and then press the leaves between your palms to extract the excess water. Fluff the leaves to loosen.

5. Heat a wok or skillet over high heat until hot enough to foam a bead of water. Add 2 teaspoons of the oil, swirl to glaze the pan, and heat until hot enough to sizzle a thread of carrot. Add the carrots and toss until hot, about 45 seconds, adjusting the heat so they crackle without burning. Don't worry if they brown a bit; they will be flavorful. Add the cabbage ribbons and toss until slightly wilted, about 1 minute, drizzling a bit more oil down the side of the pan, if needed to prevent sticking. Promptly remove the vegetables from the pan, spread on a large plate, and season lightly with the pepper-salt.

Once cool, the vegetables may be sealed and refrigerated overnight. Bring to room temperature before using and drain any water from the spinach or daikon.

6. About 20 minutes before serving, preheat the oven to 375°F. Position a rack in the lower third of the oven.

7. Arrange the vegetables on as many ovenproof serving plates as there are guests or on 1 or 2 large platters. Place the daikon in overlapping rings to cover the plates or spread out the spinach to do the same. Scatter the cabbage and carrot on top, leaving a rim of the daikon or spinach showing. Brush the skewered shrimp on both sides with the reserved marinade and arrange the shrimp over the vegetables. Drizzle 1 tablespoon more marinade over the vegetables. Do not crowd the plates with vegetables or all the vegetables will not heat through in the time it takes to cook the shrimp.

8. Bake the shrimp until glazed and golden on top, 3 to 4 minutes. Turn them over and bake the other side until golden as well, another 3 to 4 minutes. Turn the shrimp quickly or remove the plates to your stovetop while you work to prevent the oven from cooling.

9. Serve the shrimp on their vegetables beds immediately, garnished with the chives or scallions and a colorful sprinkling of the red bell pepper.

MENU SUGGESTIONS: As an entrée, the shrimp go well with simply cooked rice or noodles and Stir-fried Zucchini Ribbons (page 437). As the prelude to a meal, I can think of nothing nicer to follow with than a wild mushroom risotto.

STIR-FRIED SHRIMP WITH FRESH FENNEL AND NOODLES

SERVES 2 TO 3 AS A MAIN COURSE, 4 TO 6 AS PART OF A MULTICOURSE MEAL

This, to my tongue, is a perfectly delectable combination of flavors and textures! (When a large color picture of it appeared in *The New York Times Magazine,* it brought throngs of new customers to the restaurant.)

I particularly love using very thin noodles—they are a beautiful tangle when interwoven with the slivers of lemon zest and bright-colored vegetables—but you might easily substitute most any other size of noodle.

If truly fresh shrimp are unavailable, fresh scallops are a fine alternative. Also, if you are spice-shy, feel free to omit the chili-based ingredients. The dish still will be delicious.

Ma's grin grew wide. Next, she popped the beheaded whole shrimp into her mouth, shell and all. Wiggling her jaw and smiling all the while, she managed to eat all of the meat and a few seconds later spit a perfectly clean and intact shrimp shell into the bowl.

This was a hard act to follow, but I tried. The head number was tough, but I conquered aversion and managed a wan grin—and was actually happily surprised by how tasty the stuff actually was. The shell act was a total failure. I wiggled and smiled just like my mentor, but my American tongue didn't yet know the Chinese trick of separating the flesh from the shell. Also, I'd been raised in a home where spitting wasn't encouraged. What plopped out of my lips and stuck ignominiously to my chin was a mangled half of a shrimp. I simply swallowed the other half, shell and all. I was mortified.

I ate a lot of shrimp shells in the months that followed. But in time I became a spitter of some accomplishment. It was a matter of cultural pride, in this adopted culture that I loved. My American parents would have gasped had they seen me, but my Chinese parents applauded.

VELVET MARINADE AND SHRIMP:
1 large egg white
1 tablespoon Chinese rice wine or dry sherry
1 teaspoon kosher salt
1 tablespoon cornstarch
1 pound fresh shrimp, shelled, deveined, and cut lengthwise in half

AROMATICS:
1 tablespoon plus 1 teaspoon finely minced fresh ginger
1 tablespoon plus 1 teaspoon finely minced garlic
2½ tablespoons thinly sliced green and white scallion rings
½ teaspoon dried red chili flakes
Grated or finely minced zest of ½ scrubbed lemon

SAUCE:
1½ cups China Moon Double Stock (page 72) or unsalted chicken stock
2 tablespoons Chinese rice wine or dry sherry
2 tablespoons freshly squeezed lemon juice
2 tablespoons soy sauce

1 tablespoon sugar
1½ teaspoons kosher salt
½ teaspoon Chinese chili sauce

⅓ pound very thin (¹/₁₆ inch) fresh Chinese egg noodles
1½ tablespoons China Moon Hot Chili Oil (page 10) or China Moon Chili-Lemon Oil (page 12)
3 to 4 tablespoons corn or peanut oil
1 small yellow onion, cut into ¼-inch half-moons
1 medium red bell pepper, cut into ¼-inch strips
1 small bulb fennel, cut in half, cored, and cut crosswise into ⅛-inch half-moons
¼ pound Napa cabbage, cut into ½-inch ribbons
Zest of ½ large, scrubbed lemon, cut into very fine julienne
1 small red Fresno chili, cut into paper-thin rings
1½ teaspoons cornstarch dissolved in 1 tablespoon cold unsalted chicken stock or water
Fennel sprigs and/or thinly sliced green and white scallion rings, for garnish

1. In a bowl, briskly whisk the marinade ingredients through the cornstarch until thick. Add the shrimp and toss well. Seal airtight and marinate in the refrigerator for several hours or overnight. Let come to room temperature and re-toss before cooking.

2. Combine the aromatics in a small bowl and cover until ready to use.

3. Combine all of the sauce ingredients through the chili sauce in a bowl. Stir to blend, leaving the spoon in the bowl.

4. Fluff the noodles in a colander to separate and untangle the strands. Bring a generous amount of water to a rolling boil over high heat. Add the noodles and swish gently with chopsticks until the noodles are al dente but cooked, about 2 minutes. Drain promptly, plunge briefly into ice water to chill, then drain thoroughly. Toss the noodles with the chili-infused oil. Cover until ready to use.

All the above steps, as well as cutting the vegetables, may be done a day in advance. Seal and refrigerate the ingredients; bring to room temperature before cooking.

5. About 15 minutes before serving, bring a small pot of water to a steaming near simmer. Add the shrimp, stir gently to separate, and cook until 60 percent opaque, about 20 seconds. Drain promptly and set aside. The shrimp will be raw in the center.

6. Heat a wok or deep, heavy skillet over high heat until hot enough to evaporate a bead of water on contact. Add 2½ tablespoons of the corn oil and swirl to glaze the pan. When the oil is hot enough to sizzle a scallion ring, reduce the heat to moderate and add the aromatics. Adjust the heat so they foam without browning and stir gently until fully fragrant, 15 to 30 seconds. Add the onion and stir-fry briskly for ½ to 2 minutes. Add the bell pepper and stir-fry until the pepper strips curl slightly at the edges, 2 to 2½ minutes. Add the fennel and toss until tender-crisp, 3 to 3½ minutes more. As you work, adjust the heat so the vegetables crackle without burning and drizzle a bit more oil down the side of the pan, if needed to prevent sticking.

7. Add the cabbage, lemon zest julienne, and chili rings, and toss together until the cabbage is slightly wilted, 30 to 60 seconds. Add the noodles and toss to blend.

8. Stir the sauce to recombine it and add it to the pan. Turn up the heat to high, cover the pan, and bring the sauce to a simmer. Stir the cornstarch mixture to recombine and add it to the pan. Stir the sauce until glossy, 10 to 20 seconds. Add the shrimp and toss gently to mix. Serve immediately on a heated platter of contrasting color. Garnish with the fennel sprigs and/or a scattering of scallions.

MENU SUGGESTIONS: A small salad of baby watercress greens dressed with our Fresh Ginger Vinaigrette (page 24) or Orange Vinaigrette (page 25) would be an inviting follow-up to this dish. Or, if you wish to follow in more of a Chinese style with multiple dishes, I would recommend a dusky casserole like Bunny Stew (page 162) or Sandpot Casserole of Seared Duck Legs and Wild Mushrooms (page 176).

STIR-FRIED SHRIMP WITH LEMON AND ALMONDS

SERVES 2 AS A MAIN COURSE, 3 TO 4 AS PART OF A MULTICOURSE MEAL

This is a classic Chinese stir-fry with its contrast of tastes and textures: a fairly irresistible mix of plush sweet shrimp, crunchy almonds, colorful vegetables, and zingy fresh lemon zest. It runs out the door whenever we put it on the menu!

Like most stir-fried dishes, the various preparations can take upwards of an hour, but they may all be done as much as a night in advance. The actual cooking takes only minutes.

Shallow-frying the almonds gives them a wonderful crunch and sheen. However, if you are oil-shy, you can bake them instead.

VELVETING SHRIMP

Marinating the shrimp in the mixture of wine, salt, egg white, and cornstarch both seasons it and protects it during cooking. The precooking in barely simmering water, a process first dubbed "velveting" by Irene Kuo in her stellar book The Key to Chinese Cooking, *poaches the shrimp partway under the gentlest of conditions so that the delicate flesh never toughens in the inferno of the wok.*

Do not overestimate the time it will take the velveted shrimp to cook through. In most cases, they will be done mere seconds after they are added to the wok. If you are using giant shrimp whose thickness is more than a fat thumb's worth, cut them lengthwise in half to ensure quick cooking.

*VELVET MARINADE
AND SHRIMP:*
1 large egg white
1 tablespoon Chinese rice wine
   or dry sherry
1 teaspoon kosher salt
1 tablespoon cornstarch
½ pound fresh shrimp, shelled,
   deveined, and cut lengthwise
   in half

AROMATICS:
1 tablespoon finely minced fresh
   ginger
1 tablespoon finely minced
   garlic
2 tablespoons thinly sliced green
   and white scallion rings
½ teaspoon dried red chili flakes

SAUCE:
2 cups China Moon Double
   Stock (page 72) or unsalted
   chicken stock
2 tablespoons Chinese rice wine
   or dry sherry
2 tablespoons soy sauce
¼ cup freshly squeezed lemon
   juice

2 tablespoons sugar
½ teaspoon kosher salt
½ teaspoon Chinese chili sauce

3 ounces sugar snap peas
3 tablespoons corn or peanut oil
1 small yellow onion, cut into
   1-inch squares
1 small red bell pepper, cut into
   1-inch squares
1 small carrot, cut diagonally
   into ⅛-inch-thick coins
2 ribs celery, cut crosswise into
   ⅛-inch-thick commas
¼ pound baby Chinese celery
   cabbage, cut in half, if large
Zest of 1 scrubbed lemon, cut
   into very fine julienne
4 to 6 fresh water chestnuts, cut
   into thin coins
1 teaspoon cornstarch dissolved
   in 1 tablespoon cold unsalted
   chicken stock or water
½ cup whole almonds, toasted
   (page 34)

TOPS AND TAILS

It's a good general rule when buying unfamiliar vegetables to inspect their tops and bottoms. Like people, the extremities of something edible reveal a lot about the health and goodness of what's in the middle.

You may not know, for example, that you're looking at a bunch of Chinese broccoli. But if the leaves are ragged and scarred, and the ends of the stalks have clearly been cut days beforehand and are dry as wood, then whatever it is won't be very tasty. Beards on scallions and green tops on radishes and carrots—more familiar items—are similarly revealing of the age and wellness of the vegetable. A market that lops them off is a market with something to hide.

Trust your eyeballs. Inspect a vegetable at the top and the tail, and you'll know if it's a fresh one, even if you don't know its name.

1. In a bowl, briskly whisk the marinade ingredients through the cornstarch until thick. Add the shrimp and toss well. Seal airtight and marinate in the refrigerator for several hours or overnight. Let come to room temperature and re-toss before cooking.

2. Combine the aromatics in a small bowl and cover until ready to use.

3. Combine all of the sauce ingredients through the chili sauce in a bowl. Stir to blend, leaving the spoon in the bowl.

4. Blanch the snap peas in rapidly boiling water until cooked but still crunchy, about 1 minute. Immerse in ice water to chill. Drain and set aside. All the above steps, along with cutting the vegetables, may be done a full day in advance. Seal and refrigerate the ingredients; be sure to bring them to room temperature before cooking.

5. About 15 minutes before serving, bring a small pot of water to a steaming near simmer. Add the shrimp, stir gently to separate, and cook until 60 percent opaque, about 20 seconds. Drain promptly and set aside. The shrimp will be raw in the center.

6. Heat a wok or deep heavy skillet over high heat until hot enough to evaporate a bead of water on contact. Add 2 tablespoons of the oil and swirl to glaze the pan. When the oil is hot enough to sizzle a scallion ring, reduce the heat to moderate and add the aromatics. Adjust the heat so they foam without browning and stir gently until fully fragrant, 15 to 30 seconds. Add the onion and stir-fry briskly until slightly translucent, 2½ to 3 minutes, adjusting the heat so they crackle without burning. Don't worry if they pick up a bit of brown; they will be flavorful. Add the bell pepper and stir-fry until the pepper squares are slightly softened, 2 to 3 minutes.

7. Add the carrots and celery and toss until hot, another 1 to 2 minutes. Drizzle a bit more oil down the side of the pan, if needed to prevent sticking. Add the celery cabbage and toss until just slightly wilted. Add the lemon zest, snap peas, and water chestnuts, and toss together briefly to blend.

8. Stir the sauce to recombine it and add it to the pan. Turn up the heat to high, cover the pan, and bring the sauce to a simmer. Stir the cornstarch mixture and add it to the pan. Stir the sauce until glossy, 10 to 20 seconds. Add the shrimp and toss gently to mix. Serve immediately on a heated platter of contrasting color. Garnish with the almonds scattered on top.

MENU SUGGESTIONS: For me, this is a sublime one-dish meal—a good way to feel about a labor-intensive stir-fry—and I look only for a starch to complete it. Steamed or fried rice, or boiled or pan-fried pasta, would all be fine. So, too, would a hot and crusty loaf of bread.

CRISPY PRAWNS WITH STRANGE-FLAVOR SAUCE

SERVES 5 TO 6 AS AN APPETIZER, 3 TO 4 AS A LIGHT MAIN COURSE

This is an invariably popular dish at China Moon, whether we present it as an appetizer or an entrée. The combination of lightly fried seafood with the tart-tangy-sweet sauce is seemingly irresistible. Twenty years after I learned to make this sauce in the eccentric kitchen of my Chinese adopted family in Taipei, its flavors continue to beguile me.

The preparations are exceedingly simple, and the cooking is speedy and neat. Organization is everything when deep-frying, so be sure to read the entire recipe before you start.

VELVET MARINADE
AND PRAWNS:
1 large egg white
1 tablespoon Chinese rice wine
    or dry sherry
1 teaspoon kosher salt
1 tablespoon cornstarch
1 pound fresh prawns, shelled,
    deveined, and butterflied
    partially or fully if large

AROMATICS:
1 tablespoon finely minced fresh
    ginger
1 tablespoon finely minced
    garlic
2 tablespoons thinly sliced green
    and white scallion rings
1½ teaspoons dried red chili
    flakes

SAUCE:
1½ cups China Moon Double
    Stock (page 72) or unsalted
    chicken stock
2 tablespoons plus ½ teaspoon
    sugar
1 tablespoon cider vinegar
2 tablespoons balsamic vinegar
¼ cup soy sauce

4 to 6 cups corn or peanut
    oil, for deep-frying
1 tablespoon cornstarch
    dissolved in 2 tablespoons
    cold chicken stock or water
1 cup water chestnut starch
Finely julienned or diced red
    and/or yellow bell pepper, for
    garnish
Green and white scallion
    julienne, for garnish

SEAFOOD
SUBSTITUTIONS

*Scallops, squid cut into
rings, and fresh fish chunks
all work equally well in this
dish. With larger pieces of
fish, you will need to use a
bit more water chestnut
starch. You will also need
to adjust the frying time
accordingly.*

WATER CHESTNUT STARCH

Chinese fry cooks traditionally use this intriguing coating in place of starch. Some brands are lumpy and require whirling in a food processor to turn them properly powdery. Water chestnut starch (also called water chestnut flour) remains mostly white in quick-frying. Do not wait for the accustomed deep gold, or you will overcook whatever you are frying.

1. In a bowl, briskly whisk the marinade ingredients through the cornstarch until thick. Add the prawns and toss well to coat. Seal airtight and refrigerate for 3 to 24 hours. Let come to room temperature and re-toss before using.

2. Combine the aromatics in a small dish; cover until ready to use.

3. Combine all of the sauce ingredients in a small bowl. Stir to blend, leaving a spoon in the bowl. All of the above may be done a full day ahead. Seal and refrigerate the ingredients; bring to room temperature before cooking.

4. About 30 minutes before serving, heat a small, heavy saucepan over high heat until hot enough to evaporate a bead of water on contact. Add 1 tablespoon of the frying oil, swirl to glaze the pan, and reduce the heat to low. Add the aromatics and stir gently until fully fragrant and cooked, 1 to 1½ minutes, adjusting the heat so they foam gently without browning. Drizzle in a bit more oil if needed to prevent sticking, but "cheat" the pan so that you don't wind up with an oily sauce. Stir the sauce mixture, add it to the pan, and then raise the heat to bring it to a simmer. Stir the cornstarch mixture to recombine, add it to the sauce, and stir until the sauce turns glossy, about 20 seconds. Turn off the heat. Taste the sauce; add a dash more sugar if needed to round out the spiciness. Cover the pot. Proceed immediately to fry the prawns.

5. Choose a wok or deep heavy skillet for frying and add oil to a depth of 2 inches. Rest a deep-fry thermometer on the rim. Bring the oil to the light-haze stage, 350°F, hot enough to foam a pinch of starch. Adjust the heat so the temperature does not climb. Put the water chestnut starch in a large bowl. Ready a large Chinese mesh spoon or a fry basket and a baking sheet lined with a triple layer of paper towels alongside your stovetop. Drain the prawns of excess marinade.

6. Coat and fry the prawns in 3 or 4 batches: Toss the prawns in the water chestnut starch to coat, then put them in the spoon or basket and shake off any excess starch. Lower them into the oil and fry, turning occasionally, until they float high on the surface of the oil and are 90 percent cooked, 1 to 2 minutes depending on size. If the oil is fresh, the coating will remain mostly white. Do not fry until golden, or you will overcook the prawns. Transfer the prawns to the paper towels to drain. Fry the remaining prawns.

7. Quickly arrange the prawns on a heated serving platter or individual plates of contrasting color. Drizzle the sauce on top, garnish with the bell pepper and scallion julienne, and serve at once. (When the oil has cooled, strain, bottle, and refrigerate it for future use.)

MENU SUGGESTIONS: Although light, this dish is rich and should be paired with simple things—a steamed poultry dish or a light vegetable pasta if you are using it as an appetizer, or a sauté of seasonal greens and rice if you are presenting it as an entrée.

PRAWN SANDPOT CASSEROLE WITH RED CURRY AND BABY CORN

SERVES 2 TO 3 AS A MAIN COURSE, 4 TO 5 AS PART OF A MULTICOURSE MEAL

Shrimp and corn is one of my favorite combinations, so I am always in a rush to get this dish on the menu in those fleeting few months when fresh corn is sweet and wonderful. Fresh ears of baby corn are a visual delight in this dish, but fresh corn kernels—just-shucked and thrown raw into the casserole—are equally terrific. If fresh lotus root is unavailable, do not use the canned sort (it is ghastly!); instead, just go with another handful of corn or with fresh water chestnuts cut into coins.

Like almost all of our sandpot dishes, the cooking is a breeze. Just be sure to do the preparations in advance.

CURRY PASTE SUBSTITUTES

///

The Thai red curry paste adds a great range of flavor as well as heat to the dish. If you don't have it, you might instead add ¾ teaspoon Chinese chili sauce to the sauce, or ½ teaspoon dried red chili flakes, or 1 small red Fresno chili, sliced into paper-thin rings, to the aromatics.

VELVET MARINADE AND PRAWNS:

1 large egg white
1 tablespoon Chinese rice wine or dry sherry
1 teaspoon kosher salt
1 tablespoon cornstarch
1 pound fresh prawns in their shells, shelled (save the shells and heads) and deveined

SAUCE:

Reserved shrimp shells and heads
1 teaspoon Five-Flavor Oil (page 13), corn, or peanut oil
1⅓ cups China Moon Double Stock (page 72) or unsalted chicken stock
1½ teaspoons Thai red curry paste
3 tablespoons soy sauce
1 tablespoon sugar
1 tablespoon unseasoned Japanese rice vinegar
1 tablespoon Chinese rice wine or dry sherry

AROMATICS:

2 teaspoons finely minced fresh ginger
2 teaspoons finely minced garlic

6 to 10 ears fresh baby corn, halved lengthwise if large, or 1 cup corn kernels
1 small segment fresh lotus root, cut into paper-thin rounds
1 to 1½ tablespoons corn or peanut oil, for stir-frying
1 small yellow onion, cut into ¼-inch half-moons
1 red bell pepper, cut into ¼-inch strips
2 scallions, cut into 1-inch nuggets
½ pound Napa cabbage, cut into 1-inch squares
⅛ teaspoon Roasted Szechwan Pepper-Salt (page 5)
Thinly sliced green and white scallion rings, for garnish

1. In a bowl, whisk the marinade ingredients through the cornstarch until thick. Add the prawns and toss well to coat. Cover and refrigerate for several hours or overnight. Bring to room temperature and re-toss before cooking.

2. To make the sauce, lightly rinse the reserved prawn shells (and heads, if available) with cool water. Pound them well in a mortar, crushing to release their liquids. Heat a wok or large heavy skillet over high heat until hot enough to evaporate a bead of water on contact. Add the oil and crushed prawn shells and toss briskly until the shells turn pink, 1½ to 2 minutes. Reduce the heat to moderate and add the chicken stock. Bring the liquid to a boil, then simmer gently for 15 minutes.

3. Strain the stock, pressing down on the shells to re-

lease their liquids. Discard the shells. Stir the curry paste, soy sauce, sugar, rice vinegar, and rice wine to combine and stir into the stock. Set the sauce aside to cool. Once cool, it may be sealed and refrigerated overnight. Bring to room temperature before use.

4. Combine the aromatics in a small dish and cover until ready to use.

5. In a generous amount of boiling water, blanch the baby corn for 1 minute. Transfer to ice water to chill. Drain and set aside. Using the same water, blanch the lotus root slices for 5 minutes to rid them of their starchiness. Plunge the slices into ice water to stop the cooking, then drain.

6. Heat a wok or large heavy skillet over high heat until hot enough to evaporate a bead of water on contact. Add 1 tablespoon of the oil and swirl to glaze the pan. When hot enough to sizzle a pinch of ginger, add the aromatics. Reduce the heat to moderate so the aromatics foam without browning and stir until fully fragrant, about 30 seconds. Add the onion and toss until slightly softened, 1½ to 2 minutes. Add the bell pepper and toss for 1 minute, glazing the strips with the oil. Add the scallions and toss for 2 minutes more, adjusting the heat to maintain a merry sizzle and drizzling a bit more oil down the side of the pan, if needed to prevent sticking. Add the cabbage and toss just to wilt, about 1 minute. Spread the vegetables on a plate to cool and sprinkle with the pepper-salt.

The above steps may all be done up to a day in advance. Seal the perishables, refrigerate, and bring to room temperature before using.

7. About 20 minutes before serving, bring a small pot of water to a steaming near simmer. Add the prawns, stir gently to separate, and cook until 60 percent opaque, about 20 seconds. Drain promptly and set aside. The prawns will be raw in the center.

8. In a 2- to 3-quart Chinese sandpot or other heavy casserole, arrange the stir-fried vegetables over the bottom. Scatter the corn and lotus root on top. Stir the sauce to recombine it and add it to the pot. Bring slowly to a simmer over moderate heat. Cover and simmer until the vegetables are tender-crisp, 3 to 4 minutes.

9. Turn off the heat. Quickly lift the lid and add the prawns to the pot. Quickly stir once or twice, replace the lid,

SHRIMP SHELLS

*The heads and shells of
shrimp hold a tremendous
amount of flavor, and most
good cooks use them as a base
for stock. Here, they add an
inimitable depth of flavor to
the sauce. If you are buying
shelled shrimp, ask your
merchant for a bag of shells.
Use them promptly. Their
flavor fades to near-zero
when frozen.*

and let sit for several minutes to cook the prawns through.
Serve at once in heated bowls of contrasting color, each
garnished with a sprinkling of the scallions.

MENU SUGGESTIONS: This is a one-dish meal, requiring
only a starch to complete it. Depending on mood, I would
choose rice, Mandarin Breadtwists (page 66), or a toasty
baguette with which to soak up the sauce.

WOK-SEARED SCALLOPS WITH CARROT AND DAIKON NOODLES

SERVES 2 TO 3 AS A LIGHT ENTRÉE, 4 AS PART OF A MULTICOURSE MEAL

This is an intriguing appetizer by virtue of contrasts:
A heap of spicy seared scallops is served alongside
hills of cold carrot and daikon "noodles" that have
been tossed with a lime and ginger vinaigrette. It wakes
up many areas of the tongue all at once! Should you
wish to turn it into a light entrée, add a salad of watercress and other greens, and hot wedges of Pan-Fried
Scallion-Chive Bread (page 382) or a bundle of Mandarin
Breadtwists (page 66).

If you do not own the nifty Japanese gizmo that cuts
the vegetables into improbably long noodle-like strands,
you can simply julienne the carrot and daikon finely and
toss them with some baby greens to garner a bit of
height.

As long as you have the seasoned oil and pickled
ginger on hand, this is a dish that can be prepared and
served in under one hour.

*MARINADE AND
SCALLOPS:*
⅓ cup Five-Flavor Oil (page 13)
3½ tablespoons soy sauce
1½ teaspoons ginger juice
    (squeezed from finely minced
    fresh ginger)
¼ cup thinly sliced green and
    white scallion rings
1 teaspoon Thai red curry paste
2 tablespoons finely chopped
    coriander leaves and stems
¾ pound fresh scallops

VINAIGRETTE:
¼ cup rice bran, corn, or
    peanut oil
2 tablespoons freshly squeezed
    lime juice

1½ tablespoons juice from
    China Moon Pickled Ginger
    (page 8)
¾ teaspoon fine sea salt
¼ teaspoon China Moon Hot
    Chili Oil (page 10), optional

1 to 2 tablespoons corn or
    peanut oil
2 cups carrot "noodles"
2 cups daikon "noodles"
2 tablespoons finely chopped
    Chinese or Western chives
1 teaspoon black sesame seeds,
    toasted
Whole chives, for garnish

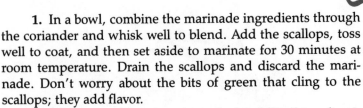

1. In a bowl, combine the marinade ingredients through the coriander and whisk well to blend. Add the scallops, toss well to coat, and then set aside to marinate for 30 minutes at room temperature. Drain the scallops and discard the marinade. Don't worry about the bits of green that cling to the scallops; they add flavor.

2. Whisk the vinaigrette through the chili oil in a bowl. Set aside for the flavors to meld, leaving the whisk in the bowl.

3. Heat a wok or small heavy skillet over high heat until hot enough to evaporate a bead of water on contact. Add 1 scant tablespoon of the oil and swirl to glaze the pan. When nearly smoking, add half of the scallops and sear until golden, only 10 to 15 seconds for large sea scallops, less for tiny bay scallops. Quickly turn the scallops with tongs or chopsticks and brown the other side, about 10 seconds more. Remove the scallops and spread in a single layer on a platter. Repeat the searing with the remaining scallops, swirling an additional 2 to 3 teaspoons of oil into the pan to sear the second batch. The timing will differ depending on the size of the scallops; they are done when they feel firm but not rubbery to the touch. Don't overcook them. Slice one open to be sure; re-toss in the pan if you've removed them too soon.

4. Mound the scallops prettily to one side of serving plates of contrasting color. Whisk the vinaigrette and combine half with the carrot noodles and half with the daikon noodles. Sprinkle half of the chopped chives over the scallops. Toss the remaining chopped chives and the sesame seeds with the noodles. Twirl a hill each of the carrot and daikon noodles alongside the scallops. Position a whole chive or 2 jauntily on each plate to give it a bit of height, and serve while the scallops are still warm.

MENU SUGGESTIONS: This is a happy partner to Dragon Noodles (page 391) or a wonderful Chinese-accented appetizer to a Western dinner of grilled meats.

SPICY ORANGE SCALLOPS WITH FRESH RICE NOODLES

SERVES 2 TO 3 AS A MAIN COURSE, 4 TO 5 AS PART OF A MULTICOURSE MEAL

The combination of scallops, fresh citrus, and Chinese greens is fabulous, and when you add the slither of fresh rice noodles, it's unbeatable. Add fresh water chestnuts and you're over the edge!

This is a simple stir-fry that shouldn't be discounted if fresh rice noodles are not available. Although their strange, plush texture is inimitable (do not substitute dry rice noodles), fettuccine can be used in their place with different but still pleasing results.

*VELVET MARINADE
AND SCALLOPS:*
1 large egg white
1 tablespoon Chinese rice wine
 or dry sherry
1 teaspoon kosher salt
1 tablespoon cornstarch
½ pound fresh scallops

AROMATICS:
2 tablespoons finely minced
 fresh ginger
¼ cup thinly sliced green and
 white scallion rings
1 teaspoon China Moon Chili-
 Orange Oil (page 15)
1 teaspoon "goop" from China
 Moon Chili-Orange Oil
Finely minced zest of 1 small
 scrubbed orange (about 2
 teaspoons)

SAUCE:
1 cup China Moon Double
 Stock (page 72) or unsalted
 chicken stock
2 tablespoons soy sauce
3 tablespoons freshly squeezed
 orange juice
2 teaspoons sugar
1 tablespoon unseasoned
 Japanese rice vinegar

1 teaspoon distilled white
 vinegar
½ teaspoon Chinese chili sauce
1 teaspoon kosher salt

1 to 2 tablespoons corn or
 peanut oil, for stir-frying
1 small red onion, cut into ¼-
 inch-thick half-moons
1 small red bell pepper, cut into
 ¼-inch-wide strips
¼ pound Napa cabbage, cut
 into ½-inch-wide ribbons
¼ pound ½-inch-wide fresh
 rice noodles
¼ pound Chinese celery
 cabbage, stems and leaves cut
 diagonally into ½-inch bands
 and flower clusters left whole
1 teaspoon cornstarch dissolved
 in 1 tablespoon cold chicken
 stock or water
6 to 8 fresh water chestnuts, cut
 into coins
Thin, diagonally sliced green
 and white scallion rings, for
 garnish

1. In a bowl, briskly whisk the marinade ingredients through the cornstarch until thick. Add the scallops and toss well. Cover and marinate in the refrigerator for several hours or overnight. Let come to room temperature and re-toss before cooking.

2. Combine the aromatics in a small dish and cover until ready to use.

3. Combine all of the sauce ingredients through the salt in a bowl. Stir to blend, leaving the spoon in the bowl. The

BUYING SCALLOPS

We buy only dry-packed scallops in the restaurant, forgoing the more typical and less expensive variety that is packed (and falsely plumped) in water. Scallops come in as many wonderful colors as they do sizes, ranging from very white to pearly pink. Their shells are spectacular. If you find freshly caught scallops sold on the half shell, looking juicy and pearlescent on their thrones, take them home and steam them in their shells for supper.

When buying scallops in the everyday market, look for a good gloss and a moist sheen. If the scallops are sitting in water, they will taste mostly like water. If they smell other than of a lovely sweetness, do not buy them.

above steps, along with cutting the vegetables, may be done a full day in advance. Seal and refrigerate the ingredients; bring to room temperature before cooking.

4. About 15 minutes before serving, bring a small pot of water to a steaming near simmer. Add the scallops, stirring to separate, and cook for 20 to 40 seconds, depending on size. Drain promptly and set aside. The scallops should be cooked on the outside but a bit raw within.

5. Heat a wok or large heavy skillet over high heat until hot enough to evaporate a bead of water on contact. Add 1½ tablespoons of the oil and swirl to glaze the pan. When the oil is hot enough to sizzle a scallion ring, reduce the heat to moderate and add the aromatics. Stir gently until fully fragrant, 30 to 45 seconds. Add the onion and toss until slightly translucent, 1½ to 2 minutes. Add the red bell pepper and toss until the ends curl, about 2 minutes more.

6. Add the Napa cabbage and toss briefly to wilt. Add the noodles and toss to blend. Stir the sauce and add it to the pan. Raise the heat, add the celery cabbage, and toss gently until the sauce comes to a simmer. Stir the cornstarch mixture to recombine, add to the pan, and stir until the sauce turns glossy, 10 to 20 seconds. Add the water chestnuts and scallops, and toss gently to heat through. Serve immediately on heated plates of contrasting color, garnished with a sprinkling of scallion rings.

MENU SUGGESTIONS: Complete with vegetables, scallops, and noodles, this dish stands easily on its own as a one-dish dinner. As a palate cleanser to follow, a salad of slightly bitter greens dressed with our Fresh Ginger Vinaigrette (page 24) would be excellent.

STIR-FRIED SPICY SCALLOPS AND BROAD NOODLES WITH FRESH PEAS

SERVES 2 TO 3 AS A MAIN COURSE,
4 TO 6 AS PART OF A MULTICOURSE MEAL

When summer hits, I go wild for fresh peas! As fast as we can shell them in the kitchen, we use them for soups and stir-fries, tossing them in at the last minute to preserve their snap.

Here, they are mated with scallops, water chestnuts, and fettuccine in a zesty stir-fry heightened with slivers of fresh basil and sun-dried tomatoes. The concentration of flavor in sun-dried tomatoes is desirable, but don't hesitate to use Oven-Dried Plum Tomatoes (page 36) or whole or halved Sweet 100's (our favorite variety of cherry tomato), if they are fresh from the garden and sweet.

All the preparations may be done a full day ahead. The final cooking takes only minutes.

VELVET MARINADE AND SCALLOPS:
1 large egg white
1 tablespoon Chinese rice wine or dry sherry
1 teaspoon kosher salt
1 tablespoon cornstarch
1 pound fresh scallops, cut in half if very large

AROMATICS:
1 tablespoon finely minced fresh ginger
1 tablespoon finely minced garlic
¼ cup thinly sliced green and white scallion rings

SAUCE:
1 cup China Moon Infusion (page 72), China Moon Double Stock (page 72), or unsalted chicken stock
2 teaspoons balsamic vinegar
2 teaspoons cider vinegar
2 teaspoons soy sauce
1 teaspoon Thai red curry paste
1 teaspoon sugar

½ *pound fresh fettuccine noodles*

1½ *teaspoons Five-Flavor Oil (page 13), China Moon Chili-Lemon Oil (page 12), or corn or peanut oil*

¾ *cup shelled fresh peas*

2 *to 3 tablespoons corn or peanut oil, for stir-frying*

1 *small red onion, cut into ¼-inch-thick half-moons*

1 *small red bell pepper, cut into ¼-inch-wide strips*

2 *scallions, cut into 1-inch nuggets*

2 *tablespoons sun-dried tomato julienne*

2 *tablespoons fresh basil julienne (optional)*

1½ *teaspoons cornstarch dissolved in 2 tablespoons cold water or unsalted chicken stock*

6 *fresh water chestnuts, cut into coins*

Thin, diagonally sliced green and white scallion rings or scallion threads, for garnish

1. In a bowl, briskly whisk the marinade ingredients through the cornstarch until thick. Add the scallops and toss well. Cover and marinate in the refrigerator for several hours or overnight. Let come to room temperature and re-toss before cooking.

2. Combine the aromatics in a small dish and cover until ready to use.

3. Combine all of the sauce ingredients in a bowl. Stir to blend, leaving the spoon in the bowl.

4. Fluff the noodles in a colander to separate and untangle the strands. Bring a generous amount of water to a rolling boil over high heat. Add the noodles and stir gently with chopsticks until al dente but cooked, 1½ to 2 minutes. Drain promptly, plunge briefly into ice water to chill, then drain thoroughly. Toss the noodles with the five-flavor oil to lightly glaze them.

5. Blanch the peas in boiling water until tender-crisp, about 30 seconds. Immerse in ice water to chill. Drain and set aside. The above steps, along with cutting the vegetables, may be done a full day ahead. Seal and refrigerate the ingredients; bring to room temperature before cooking.

6. About 15 minutes before serving, bring a small pot of water to a steaming near simmer. Add the scallops, stirring to separate, and cook for 20 to 40 seconds, depending on size. Drain immediately and set aside. The scallops should be cooked on the outside and a bit raw within.

7. Heat a wok or large heavy skillet over high heat until hot enough to evaporate a bead of water on contact. Add 2 tablespoons of the corn oil and swirl to glaze the pan. When the oil is hot enough to sizzle a scallion ring, reduce the heat to moderate and add the aromatics. Stir gently until fully fragrant, 30 to 45 seconds, adjusting the heat so they foam without browning. Add the onion and toss until a bit soft, 1½ to 2 minutes. Add the bell pepper and toss briskly for 2 minutes. Add the scallions and toss until the green parts are wilted, about 2 minutes more.

8. Add the noodles and toss to mix. Add the tomatoes and basil, and toss briefly to blend. Stir the sauce and add it to the pan. Cover the pan and raise the heat to bring the sauce to a simmer. As soon as the sauce simmers, stir the cornstarch mixture to recombine it and add it to the pan. Stir until the sauce turns glossy, 10 to 20 seconds. Add the peas, water chestnuts, and scallops, and toss gently to heat through. Serve immediately on heated plates of contrasting color, garnished with a scattering of scallion rings.

MENU SUGGESTIONS: This is a great one-dish summertime supper. You might want to follow with a salad of finely sliced cucumbers and young greens, such as slightly bitter watercress or endive, to complement the sweetness of the scallops.

STIR-FRIED SCALLOPS WITH SUMMER SQUASHES AND THAI BASIL

SERVES 3 TO 4 AS A MAIN COURSE,
5 TO 6 AS PART OF A MULTICOURSE MEAL

This dish is a summer celebration, a trumpet note of glee when the markets are full of baby zucchini, pattypan and crookneck squashes, baby corn, fresh peas, and bouquets of green-leaved Thai basil. Summer bounty of other sorts may be happily tossed in or substituted—corn off the cob, sugar snap peas, snow peas, or plum tomatoes oven-dried as instructed on page 36, for example.

This classic Chinese stir-fry is easily prepared in advance and should not daunt even a beginner.

VELVET MARINADE
AND SCALLOPS:
1 large egg white
1 tablespoon Chinese rice wine
  or dry sherry
1 teaspoon kosher salt
1 tablespoon cornstarch
¾ pound fresh scallops, cut in
  half if very large

AROMATICS:
2 tablespoons finely minced
  fresh ginger
1 tablespoon finely minced
  garlic
2 tablespoons thinly sliced green
  and white scallion rings
1 small red Fresno chili, cut
  into paper-thin rings, or ½
  teaspoon dried red chili flakes

SAUCE:
1½ cups China Moon Infusion
  (page 72), China Moon
  Double Stock (page 72), or
  unsalted chicken stock
2 tablespoons soy sauce
1 tablespoon Chinese rice wine
  or dry sherry

1 tablespoon unseasoned
  Japanese rice vinegar
1 teaspoon sugar

¼ pound green and/or yellow
  baby squash, halved if large
8 to 10 ears fresh baby corn,
  halved if large (if baby corn is
  not available, double the
  amount of baby squash or use
  1 cup corn kernels)
½ cup shelled fresh peas
2 to 3 tablespoons corn or
  peanut oil, for stir-frying
1 small red onion, cut into ¼-
  inch half-moons
1 small red bell pepper, cut into
  ¼-inch strips
5 large or 10 small whole Thai
  basil leaves
1 tablespoon cornstarch
  dissolved in 1½ tablespoons
  cold unsalted chicken stock or
  water
Thin, diagonally sliced green
  and white scallion rings, for
  garnish

A CONSERVATIVE APPROACH TO BASIL

Basil is a member of the mint family and can be overpowering if used to excess. Nibble on a leaf to know its potency, and then start out with a conservative amount. Taste the sauce just when the dish is done—the heat of the liquid will draw out the flavor of the leaves— and if the flavor needs under-lining, simply stir in a bit more basil or garnish the dish with a fine basil chiffonnade.

1. In a bowl, briskly whisk the marinade ingredients through the cornstarch until thick. Add the scallops and toss well. Cover and marinate in the refrigerator for several hours or overnight. Let come to room temperature and re-toss before cooking.

2. Combine the aromatics in a small dish and cover until ready to use.

3. Combine all of the sauce ingredients through the

sugar in a bowl. Stir to blend, leaving the spoon in the bowl.

4. Bring a generous amount of water to a boil in a large pot. Blanch the baby squash, baby corn, and peas separately until the vegetables are tender-crisp; the squash and corn will take 1 to 2 minutes, the peas about 30 seconds, all depending on size; test frequently so as not to overcook. The above steps may be done a full day ahead. Seal and refrigerate the ingredients; bring to room temperature before cooking.

5. About 15 minutes before serving, bring a small pot of water to a steaming near simmer. Add the scallops, stirring to separate, and cook for 20 to 40 seconds, depending on size. Drain immediately and set aside. The scallops should be cooked on the outside but a bit raw within.

6. Heat a wok or large, heavy skillet over high heat until hot enough to evaporate a bead of water on contact. Add 2 tablespoons of the oil and swirl to glaze the pan. When the oil is hot enough to sizzle a scallion ring, reduce the heat to moderate and add the aromatics. Stir gently until fully fragrant, 1½ to 2 minutes, adjusting the heat so they foam without browning. Add the onion and toss until wilted, 2 to 3 minutes. Add the bell pepper strips and toss until they start to curl at the edges, about 3 minutes more. Adjust the heat to maintain a merry sizzle and drizzle a bit more oil down the side of the pan, if needed to prevent sticking.

7. Add the blanched squash and baby corn, and toss to combine. Add the basil and toss to blend. As soon as the leaves begin to wilt, stir the sauce to recombine and add it to the pan. Cover the pan and bring the sauce to a simmer over high heat. Stir the cornstarch mixture and add it to the pan. Stir until the sauce turns glossy, 10 to 20 seconds. Turn off the heat. Add the scallops and the peas, and toss gently to heat through.

8. Serve immediately on heated plates of contrasting color, garnished with a scattering of the scallion rings.

MENU SUGGESTIONS: Rice, noodles, or a great loaf of bread to soak up the sauce is the only mate—other than a glass of cool, dry white wine—this dish requires. A citrus-dressed salad of slightly bitter greens would be a pleasant follow-up, if you're wanting a palate cleanser.

GOLD COIN CRAB CAKES

SERVES 2 TO 3 AS A MAIN COURSE, 4 TO 5 AS PART OF A MULTICOURSE MEAL

FRESH CRABMEAT PAR AVION

In season, we have our crabmeat flown in daily from Maine, where a family picks it while they sit around the dining room table watching TV. It is never salted, frozen, or vacuum-packed, and the taste is superb! Go out of your way to find a source for truly fresh, sweet crabmeat. Its flavor is unsurpassed.

rab cakes in most any form are irresistible, and I find these especially so. Sweet from the fresh crabmeat and coconut milk, and spicy from the blending of ginger, coriander, and chili, they are truly memorable.

To make shaping easier, prepare the mixture in advance and chill it. The cakes themselves—looking like gold coins to the lyric Chinese eye—can also be shaped ahead. The last-minute pan-frying is quick and neat.

1 large bunch fresh coriander, leaves and stems finely chopped
2 tablespoons finely minced fresh ginger
½ cup thinly sliced green and white scallion rings
2 tablespoons Chinese chili sauce
½ teaspoon kosher salt

⅔ cup unsweetened coconut milk
½ cup fresh white bread crumbs
2 large eggs, beaten
1 pound fresh crabmeat, carefully picked over and drained of any liquid
Corn or peanut oil, for pan-frying
Serrano-Lemongrass Vinegar (page 19) or unseasoned Japanese rice vinegar
Sprigs of watercress or coriander, for garnish

1. In a large bowl, combine the chopped coriander, ginger, scallions, chili sauce, salt, coconut milk, bread crumbs, and eggs. Add the crabmeat and toss well to combine. Seal airtight with plastic wrap pressed directly on the surface and refrigerate for at least 1 hour, or preferably overnight.

2. To shape the crab cakes, ready a ⅓-cup measuring cup, a bowl of ice water, and a baking sheet lined with parchment or waxed paper. Dip the measuring cup in the water and shake off the excess. Pack the crab mixture into the cup, using your fingers or the back of a spoon dipped in the water to even the top of the mixture. Turn the crab cake onto the parchment and smooth with your fingers if it needs a bit more shaping. Repeat until all of the cakes are made. Loosely covered, the cakes may be refrigerated for 1 to 3 hours; if you hold them any longer, they may begin to "weep" (give off liquid).

3. About 20 minutes before serving, heat a large heavy skillet over high heat until hot enough to evaporate a bead of water on contact. Add ⅛ inch oil and lower the heat to moderate. When the oil is hot enough to gently foam a dab of the crab mixture, add the crab cakes to the pan one by one, adjusting the heat so they sizzle without scorching. Fill the pan from the outside, working toward the center and leaving about 1 inch between the cakes. Cook the cakes until golden on both sides, then lower the heat to cook them through, 6 to 7 minutes total. Remove the cakes to a baking sheet lined with a triple layer of paper towels to drain. If making a second batch, wipe the pan clean with dry paper towels, add more oil, and repeat as above.

4. Serve the crab cakes immediately on heated plates of contrasting color, sprinkled with a dash of the vinegar and garnished with the sprigs of watercress or coriander.

MENU SUGGESTIONS: As an appetizer, we love these crab cakes topped with Minted Cucumber Sauce (page 23) and served with a salad of baby greens and a tumble of Turmeric Tomatoes (page 59). As an entrée, I would pair them with stir-fried or steamed rice garnished with pine nuts or a sauté of seasonal greens, including something with a pleasantly bitter edge like Chinese broccoli.

STIR-FRIED DANCING CRAB WITH FRESNO CHILI RINGS

SERVES 2 AS A MAIN COURSE, 3 TO 4 AS PART OF A MULTICOURSE MEAL

A lmost every day during fresh crab season, we have delivered to the restaurant kitchen an open box of spitting, clawing, bubbling, "dancing" crabs. Of-

ten to the chagrin of the cook in charge, orders are to kill, clean, and chop them, and serve them forth in short order.

Stir-Fried Dancing Crab, redolent of ginger, scallions, and black beans, is a great favorite with our customers, who lick every sliver of shell and extract every morsel of meat. I've cooked crab this way for years, adding or subtracting an element here or there as the spirit moves me. So while this recipe calls for the bright heat of Fresno chilis, you may indeed omit them.

Do not be daunted by the task of killing and cleaning a crab! The glory is their fresh, firm sweetness, and the work is quickly and easily done.

AROMATICS:
1 tablespoon coarsely chopped Chinese black beans (do not rinse them)
3 tablespoons Chinese rice wine or dry sherry
1½ tablespoons finely minced fresh ginger
2 tablespoons finely minced garlic
¼ cup thinly sliced green and white scallion rings

SAUCE:
¾ cup China Moon Double Stock (page 72) or unsalted chicken stock

1 tablespoon soy sauce
½ teaspoon sugar

2 pounds large, emphatically alive crabs (will be 2 crabs)
2 tablespoons corn or peanut oil
2 ounces coarsely ground pork butt
½ to 1 teaspoon paper-thin red Fresno chili rings
1½ teaspoons cornstarch dissolved in 1 tablespoon cold chicken stock or water
Green and white scallion julienne, for garnish

1. To prepare the aromatics, combine the black beans with the rice wine and set aside to infuse the wine for 20 minutes. Drain the beans and reserve the wine. Combine the black beans and all of the remaining aromatics in a bowl. Cover until ready to use.

2. Combine all of the sauce ingredients through the sugar in a small bowl. Stir to blend, leaving the spoon in the bowl.

3. To kill the crabs, bring a large pot of water to a gushing boil. Drop the crabs into the pot and when they stop moving, in about 1 minute, retrieve the crabs with a mesh spoon or tongs and set them aside to drain. To clean each crab,

KEEP THOSE CRABS CRAWLING

On the West Coast, we revel in Dungeness crabs, delicious monsters that weigh in at a pound or so apiece. On the East Coast, blue crabs are what you're probably after. On any coast and with any species, however, they must be kept alive up until the moment they're thrown into the pot to be splendid.

turn it belly side up. Tear off the "key" or "apron," which is recessed in the belly. (In a female, it is shaped like a wide inverted *V*. In the male, it is a narrow inverted *T*.) Then firmly grasp the top shell at the rear end and lift it off; expect to need to tug. Discard the top shell. Discard the sets of feathery gills in the body of the crab, then rinse it with cool water.

4. To portion each crab into pieces, first snap off the legs and claws. Crack them lightly with a mallet or the handle end of a cleaver to allow the seasonings to penetrate. Then, with a cleaver or heavy knife, chop the body into 2 or 4 pieces, depending upon the size of the crabs. All the above steps may be done a full night in advance. Seal and refrigerate the ingredients; bring to room temperature before cooking.

5. About 15 minutes before serving, heat a wok or large heavy skillet until hot enough to evaporate a bead of water on contact. Add the oil and swirl to glaze the pan. When the oil is hot enough to sizzle a single scallion ring, add the aromatics. Stir until fully fragrant, 20 to 30 seconds, adjusting the heat so they foam without browning. Add the pork and toss and chop until 90 percent gray, about 1 minute, raising the heat if needed to maintain a merry sizzle. Add the chili rings and crab, and toss to combine. Splash the reserved wine in the pan, toss several times to evaporate the alcohol, and then stir the sauce and add it to the pan. Even out the crab and raise the heat to bring the liquids to a boil. Cover the pan and cook until the liquids are reduced by three-fourths and the crab is cooked through, about 3 minutes.

6. Reduce the heat to moderate, stir the cornstarch mixture to recombine it, then add it to the pan. Toss until the remaining sauce turns glossy, about 15 seconds, and clings to the crab along with a dress of meaty and aromatic bits.

7. Serve the crab immediately, piled in a dramatic manner on a large platter or heated plates of contrasting color, with a claw sticking out here and there. Garnish with a flurry of scallion julienne. Arm your guests with a crab cracker, a pick, an empty bowl for the shells, and an injunction to eat with noisy gusto.

MENU SUGGESTIONS: There might well be other possibilities, but we always pair the crab with a mound of simply fried rice and Wok-Seared Spinach Relish (page 438), and everyone thinks they're in heaven!

CRAB-EATING ETIQUETTE

Being a deeply enlightened people, the Chinese encourage what seems to us a chaos of noise in the interest of good eating. Slurping, sucking, and licking are the appropriate modes of attacking stir-fried crab! Do not let mistaken politeness deter you from this route.

CURRIED SEAFOOD SANDPOT

SERVES 2 TO 3 AS A MAIN COURSE, 4 TO 5 AS PART OF A MULTICOURSE MEAL

At that rare time of year when nature blesses us with fresh crab, shrimp, and scallops all at once, we love combining them in this sweet and spicy curried sandpot. Adding slivers of fresh fennel, lotus root, and water chestnuts makes it even more special, but a wonderful dish can be created without them.

SEAFOOD:
¼ pound fresh scallops
⅓ pound fresh shrimp in their shells
¼ pound fresh crabmeat

VELVET MARINADE:
1 large egg white
1 tablespoon plus 1 teaspoon Chinese rice wine or dry sherry
1 teaspoon kosher salt
2 tablespoons cornstarch

SAUCE:
1 cup China Moon Infusion (page 72), China Moon Double Stock (page 72), or unsalted chicken stock
1 cup unsweetened coconut milk
2 tablespoons soy sauce
2 tablespoons unseasoned Japanese rice vinegar
1 tablespoon plus 1 teaspoon packed brown sugar
1 teaspoon Chinese chili sauce
1 tablespoon China Moon Curry Powder (page 7)

½ teaspoon China Moon Ten-Spice (page 6)

1 small segment fresh lotus root (about 2½ inches long), cut into paper-thin rounds
2 to 3 tablespoons corn or peanut oil, for stir-frying
1 small yellow onion, cut into ¼-inch half-moons
1 small red bell pepper, cut into ¼-inch-wide strips
1 small carrot, cut diagonally into ⅛-inch rippled or plain coins
1 small bulb fennel, halved, cored, and cut crosswise into thin arcs
2 small ribs celery, cut diagonally into thin commas
1 small red Fresno chili, cut into paper-thin rings
Infused Glass Noodles (page 30)
4 to 6 fresh water chestnuts, cut into coins
Thinly sliced green and white scallion rings, or coriander sprigs, for garnish

1. Cut the scallops in half if large. Shell and devein the shrimp, then butterfly them, cutting from head to tail along the back. Pick through the crabmeat and discard any bits of shell or cartilage; seal the crab and refrigerate until needed.

2. In a bowl, whisk the marinade ingredients until thick. Divide the velvet marinade evenly between the scallops and shrimp and toss well to coat. Cover and refrigerate for at least 1 hour or overnight.

3. Combine the sauce ingredients through the ten-spice in a bowl. Stir to blend, leaving the spoon in the bowl.

4. Blanch the lotus root in boiling water for 5 minutes to rid it of some of its starch; drain. Plunge into ice water to stop the cooking, then drain again. All of the above steps as well as the vegetable cutting may be done a full night in advance. Seal and refrigerate the ingredients. Bring to room temperature before cooking.

5. Heat a wok or large heavy skillet over high heat until hot enough to evaporate a bead of water on contact. Add 1 tablespoon of the oil and swirl to glaze the pan. When hot enough to sizzle a piece of onion, add the onion and toss until slightly soft, 2 to 3 minutes. Add the bell pepper and toss for 2 minutes more. Add the carrots, fennel, and celery, and toss until hot, 2 to 3 minutes more, adjusting the heat to maintain a merry sizzle. Drizzle a bit more oil down the side of the pan, if needed to prevent sticking. Add the chili and toss for 1 minute more. Spread the vegetables on a large platter to cool.

6. About 20 minutes before serving, bring a large saucepan of water to a steaming near simmer. In separate batches, blanch the scallops for 30 to 40 seconds and the shrimp for 20 to 30 seconds, until 90 percent opaque, lowering them into the water with a wire basket or Chinese mesh spoon and spreading them on a plate once blanched. The blanched seafood will be cooked on the outside but a bit raw within.

7. In a 2- to 3-quart Chinese sandpot or other heavy casserole, layer first the glass noodles, then the lotus root and water chestnuts, and then the vegetables. Stir the sauce to recombine it, then add it to the pot. Cover and bring to a simmer over moderate heat. Simmer until the vegetables are tender-crisp, 4 to 6 minutes.

8. Quickly lift the lid and add the scallops, shrimp, and crabmeat to the pot. Stir quickly once or twice, replace the lid, and let sit for several minutes to let the seafood cook through.

9. Serve at once, ladled into heated bowls of contrasting color and garnished with the scallion rings or coriander sprigs.

MENU SUGGESTIONS: Simply steamed or stir-fried rice is the best accompaniment to the sandpot. Corn or Wok-Seared Spinach Relish (page 438) would also partner it well.

COLD CALAMARI SALAD WITH GINGER–BLACK BEAN VINAIGRETTE

SERVES 2 TO 3 AS A LUNCHEON MAIN COURSE, 4 TO 6 AS PART OF A MULTICOURSE MEAL

I f you think of calamari as a pile of rubbery curlicues, looming sea creature–like on a plate ready to attack, think again! Here is a perfectly delectable salad of tender calamari rings laced with a spicy vinaigrette. The choice of small squid will change forever your calamari nightmares.

NO MORE RUBBERY SQUID

Blanching squid for only seconds and then plunging it into an ice water bath turns it silky with a near-crispy edge. The timing must be just right—just long enough for the rings to turn opaque (indicating that they're cooked), yet not so long that the edges curl (putting them on the road to rubberiness).

1½ pounds small squid (4 to 5 inches long and 1 inch wide), cleaned, tentacles reserved, and bodies cut crosswise into ½-inch rings (see How to Clean Squid, page 242)

2 serrano chilis, tipped and halved lengthwise

1½ teaspoons finely minced garlic

1 tablespoon finely minced fresh ginger

½ cup China Moon Pickled Ginger (page 8)

1½ teaspoons "goop" from China Moon Hot Chili Oil (page 10)

⅔ cup packed coriander leaves and stems

3 tablespoons juice from China Moon Pickled Ginger

2 tablespoons distilled white vinegar

2½ teaspoons sugar

1 teaspoon fine sea salt

¾ cup corn or peanut oil

2 cups loosely packed baby mizuna, baby red mustard, and/or tender sprigs of watercress or curly cress

1 tablespoon freshly squeezed lemon juice

1 small red bell pepper, finely diced

½ small red onion, finely diced

¾ teaspoon finely minced Chinese black beans (do not rinse them)

1. To cook the squid, separate the tentacles, if larger than the rings, and cook them separately. Bring a medium-sized pot of water to a rolling boil. Using a Chinese mesh spoon or a wire basket that fits the pot, lower the squid into the water. Blanch just until opaque, about 6 seconds at most, and then drain and plunge immediately into ice water to stop the cooking. Drain and set aside. Repeat the process with any large tentacles, blanching until they curl, 8 to 10 seconds. Refrigerate the squid until ready to use, overnight if desired. Drain off any juice that might be released during storage.

2. To make the vinaigrette, in a food processor, combine the chilis, garlic, ginger, pickled ginger, "goop," and coriander (only if using the vinaigrette right away), and blend until smooth. Scrape down the sides of the bowl with a rubber spatula. With the machine running, add the ginger juice, vinegar, sugar, and ¾ teaspoon of the salt. Add the oil in a slow stream and process until emulsified. The vinaigrette may be made a full day ahead. Seal with a piece of plastic wrap pressed directly on the surface and refrigerate. To retain its color, buzz in the coriander shortly before using.

3. Just before serving, dress the greens lightly with a bit of the vinaigrette. Arrange the greens around the outer edge of small individual plates or a large platter.

4. Toss the squid in a bowl with the lemon juice and the remaining ¼ teaspoon salt. Let stand for 2 minutes. Add the bell pepper and onion, and toss to combine. Add enough of the vinaigrette to thoroughly coat the ingredients and toss well to mix. Taste and adjust, if needed, with a shot more lemon juice and/or salt. The flavors should be zingy.

5. Mound the squid in the middle of the greens and sprinkle with the minced black beans.

MENU SUGGESTIONS: This is a lively luncheon salad all on its own. If served as an appetizer, it might be followed by something earthy and gutsy like Hot and Sour Chicken Sandpot (page 148).

HOW TO CLEAN SQUID

Cleaning squid is grotesque. If you can't give the job to someone you hate, here's the easiest way to do it yourself. For right-handers: Put the squid in a bowl on a plastic cutting board to the left of your sink. Put a bowl to catch the in-nards in the sink. Place a colander to hold the gutted squid to the right of the sink. (Lefties reverse directions.) Spread your first squid vic-tim on the board, chop off the tentacles ("the crown") just above the eyes and toss in the colander. Next, chop off the head just below the eyes and let it fall in the slop bowl. Last (and this is the worst), turn your knife over and use the dull edge to scrape the squid from the tail toward the head hole, expelling all the googly innards. Do this two or three times for good measure, then reach inside

and pull out the rather pretty, translucent quill. Pull loose any skin that may still cling to the squid, then cut the body crosswise into even thin rings a scant ½ inch wide. Toss the rings in the colander, breathe deeply, and continue. When you are done, you will have a bowl of ghastly goop worthy of bagging and putting on an enemy's doorstep, and a pristine colander of rings and crowns awaiting a good rinse with cold water. (The cold water rinse may apply to the squid handler as well.)

All such cleaning may be done a full day in advance of dealing further with the beast. Place the colander in a bowl to allow the squid to "weep," cover the whole, and stash it in the refrigerator until you are ready to cook.

In spite of any reluctance you might have about cleaning squid, beware of precleaned squid! It is typically salted or otherwise treated, and not at all worthy of eating.

HOT AND SOUR SQUID

SERVES 2 AS A MAIN COURSE, 3 TO 4 AS PART OF A MULTICOURSE MEAL

∫quid—or calamari, as it is more lyrically called—can be a ghastly affair. First comes the cleaning, which is like an episode out of a Stephen King novel. Then comes the cooking, which often yields tasteless rubber tires. I've no answer for the first problem, but this dish is a fine remedy for the second! The squid is blanched, which leaves it velvety and fine, and is then tossed into a Hunanese mélange of spicy vegetables.

1 pound small squid (4 to 5 inches long and 1 inch wide), cleaned, tentacles reserved, and bodies cut crosswise into ½-inch rings (see How to Clean Squid, page 242)

AROMATICS:
1 tablespoon finely minced fresh ginger
1 tablespoon finely minced garlic
1½ tablespoons coarsely chopped Chinese black beans (do not rinse them)
2 tablespoons thinly sliced green and white scallion rings
¼ to ½ teaspoon dried red chili flakes or 1 to 1½ teaspoons "goop" from China Moon Chili-Lemon Oil (page 12)

SAUCE:
½ cup China Moon Double Stock (page 72) or unsalted chicken stock

2½ tablespoons soy sauce
2 tablespoons Chinese rice wine or dry sherry
2½ tablespoons distilled white vinegar
¼ teaspoon sugar

2 to 3 tablespoons corn or peanut oil
2 small carrots, cut diagonally into ⅛-inch rippled or plain coins
1 large red bell pepper, or 1 small red bell pepper and 1 small yellow bell pepper, cut into ½-inch squares
3 slender zucchini, cut into ¼-inch rounds
1 tablespoon cornstarch dissolved in 2 tablespoons cold chicken stock or water
Diagonally cut green and white scallion rings, for garnish

1. To cook the squid, separate the tentacles, if larger than the rings, and cook them separately. Bring a medium-sized pot of boiling water to a rolling boil. Using a Chinese mesh spoon or a wire basket that fits the pot, lower the squid into the water. Blanch just until opaque, about 6 seconds at most, then drain and plunge immediately into ice water to stop the cooking. Drain and set aside. Repeat the process with any large tentacles, blanching until they curl, 8 to 10 seconds. Refrigerate the squid until ready to use, overnight if desired. Drain off any juice that might be released during storage.

2. Combine the aromatics in a small dish and cover until ready to use.

3. Combine all of the sauce ingredients in a bowl, stirring to dissolve the sugar. Leave a spoon in the bowl. All of the above steps, along with cutting the vegetables, may be done a full day in advance. Seal and refrigerate the ingredients. Bring to room temperature before cooking.

4. About 15 minutes before serving, heat a wok or large heavy skillet over high heat until hot enough to evaporate a bead of water on contact. Add 2 tablespoons of the oil and swirl to glaze the pan. When the oil is hot enough to sizzle a bit of ginger, reduce the heat to moderate and add the aromatics, adjusting the heat so they foam without browning. Stir until fragrant, 10 to 15 seconds. Add the carrots and toss for 1 minute, then add the bell pepper and toss for 2 minutes more. Adjust the heat to maintain a merry sizzle and drizzle a bit more oil down the side of the pan, if needed to prevent sticking. Add the zucchini and toss to combine.

5. Stir the sauce, add it to the pan, and bring it to a simmer. Cover the pan and cook until the vegetables are tender-crisp, 1 to 2 minutes. Stir the cornstarch mixture to recombine, add it to the pan, and stir until the sauce turns glossy, 10 to 15 seconds.

6. Turn off the heat and fold in the drained squid. Serve immediately on heated plates of contrasting color, garnished with a flourish of the scallion rings.

MENU SUGGESTIONS: Steamed rice, cooked pasta, or toasted or grilled garlic bread are all that is wanting here.

STIR-FRIED CLAMS AND SHANGHAI NOODLES IN BLACK BEAN SAUCE

SERVES 2 AS A MAIN COURSE, 3 TO 4 AS PART OF A MULTICOURSE MEAL

This is a yummy stir-fry of tender, small clams and the fat noodles marketed in many Chinatown stores as "Shanghai noodles." Any good fresh pasta will do, however. The succulence comes from impeccably fresh shellfish and aromatics.

1¼ pounds fresh small clams

AROMATICS:
1 tablespoon Chinese black beans, coarsely chopped (do not rinse them)
1½ tablespoons Chinese rice wine or dry sherry
1 tablespoon finely minced garlic
2 teaspoons finely minced fresh ginger
½ teaspoon dried red chili flakes, or ½ to 1 teaspoon "goop" from China Moon Hot Chili Oil (page 10) or China Moon Chili-Lemon Oil (page 12)
2 tablespoons thinly sliced green and white scallion rings

SAUCE:
½ cup China Moon Double Stock (page 72) or unsalted chicken stock
1 tablespoon soy sauce
½ teaspoon sugar

½ pound fresh Chinese noodles (the fat "Shanghai" variety is recommended)
1½ teaspoons Ma-La Oil (page 17), Five-Flavor Oil (page 13), or Japanese sesame oil
1½ to 2 tablespoons corn or peanut oil, for stir-frying
1 small red onion, cut into ½-inch squares
1 red or yellow bell pepper, cut into ½-inch squares
1 large or 2 small Anaheim chilis, tipped, seeded, and cut into ⅛-inch rings, or 1 small green bell pepper, cut into ½-inch squares
4 scallions, cut into 1-inch nuggets
¾ pound fresh spinach leaves
Thin, diagonally sliced green and white scallion rings, for garnish

DON'T WASH 'EM!

Black bean sauces are usually flat and murky affairs. A practice followed religiously by most all Chinese cooks is to wash off the salt and mash the beans. I leave the salt on, happily, and find that I then need little or no salt and only a small amount of soy. As for mashing, I love the texture of the beans and the look they give a dish. This is retained when they are just coarsely chopped.

1. In a large bowl filled with cool running water, scrub the clams to dislodge any grit. Discard any clams with open or broken shells. Refrigerate the clams in a shallow pan covered loosely with a wet towel until ready to use.

2. Soak the chopped beans in the rice wine for 10 minutes. Drain, reserving the wine. Combine the beans with the remaining aromatics. Cover until ready to use.

3. In a small bowl, combine all of the sauce ingredients and the reserved wine. Leave a spoon in the bowl.

4. Fluff the noodles in a colander to separate and untangle the strands. Bring a generous amount of water to a rolling boil over high heat. Add the noodles and swish gently with chopsticks until the noodles are al dente but cooked, 2 to 3 minutes. Drain promptly, plunge into ice water to chill, then drain thoroughly. Toss the noodles with the seasoned oil. Cover until ready to use. All the above steps, along with cutting the vegetables, may be done a full day in advance. Seal and refrigerate the ingredients; bring to room temperature before cooking.

5. About 15 minutes before serving, heat a wok or large heavy skillet over high heat until hot enough to evaporate a bead of water on contact. Add 1½ tablespoons corn oil, swirl to glaze the pan, and reduce the heat to moderate. When the oil is hot enough to sizzle a pinch of the aromatics, add them to the pan and stir gently until fully fragrant, 30 to 40 seconds, adjusting the heat so they foam without scorching. (Black bean aromatics inevitably stick to the pan. Don't be concerned.) Add the onion and toss briskly until slightly soft, 2 minutes. Add the bell pepper and stir-fry until curly-looking at the edges, 2 to 2½ minutes more. Adjust the heat to maintain a merry sizzle and drizzle a bit more oil down the side of the pan, if needed to prevent sticking. Add the chili rings and stir-fry for 1 minute. Add the scallions and toss to blend. Add the noodles and toss briskly to combine. Don't worry if the noodles pick up some color from the pan; they will be tasty.

6. Stir the sauce and add it to the pan. Toss quickly to blend, then push the noodles and vegetables to one side and

LIVE(LY) BIVALVES

Ideally, you should clean and cook clams or mussels the day you buy them. If you want a headstart, however, store the bivalves in a shallow uncovered container with a wet light towel on top so they can "breathe." Rush them under cold water shortly before cooking and discard any that don't shut tight. (When the shell of a clam or mussel is tightly shut, it means that the creature inside is fresh, i.e., alive.)

Always choose a capacious pot for cooking clams or mussels. When their shells open, it's the geometric equivalent of a couch full of people stretching every which way.

distribute the clams over the bottom of the pan. Push the
vegetables over the clams; scatter the spinach leaves on top.
Tightly cover the pan and bring the sauce to a lively simmer
over high heat. Simmer just until the clams open, 2 to 3
minutes, shaking the pan once or twice to encourage some
action. Turn off the heat, uncover the pan, and toss the
contents once or twice to wilt and distribute the spinach.
Discard any clams that do not open with a tug. There should
be only a bit of sauce left clinging to the noodles and shellfish.

7. Serve immediately, scooped into heated bowls of contrasting color and garnished liberally with a flourish of the
scallion rings. Place an extra bowl on the table for the empty
shells.

MENU SUGGESTIONS: This is a one-dish dinner. In the
summertime, a plate heaped with steamed or grilled ears of
corn and cold slices of beefsteak tomato makes a delicious,
complementary aside.

SANDPOT CASSEROLE OF CLAMS AND MUSSELS IN SPICY BLACK BEAN SAUCE

SERVES 2 TO 3 AS A MAIN COURSE, 4 TO 5 AS PART OF A MULTICOURSE MEAL

There is something about a cozy sandpot filled with
clams and mussels, each snug in its shell, that I
find wonderful. Add the dusky note of Chinese
fermented black beans and the green zip of fresh asparagus or peas, and I would order (or cook it) straightaway!

The smoky note of diced bacon adds a marvelous
tone of richness in the casserole, but it may be omitted.
What is most important is the freshness and size of the
shellfish: Look for the smallest and sweetest clams and
mussels available. This dish is easy to put together in
advance.

1 pound fresh clams
1 pound fresh mussels

AROMATICS:
1 tablespoon Chinese black
   beans, coarsely chopped (do
   not rinse them)
¼ cup Chinese rice wine or dry
   sherry
1½ tablespoons finely minced
   fresh ginger
3 tablespoons thinly sliced green
   and white scallion rings

SAUCE:
1 cup China Moon Double
   Stock (page 72) or unsalted
   chicken stock
½ teaspoon Chinese chili
   sauce
2 tablespoons soy sauce
1 teaspoon sherry vinegar
1 teaspoon sugar

2 cups lightly packed spinach
   leaves
½ cup fresh peas, fresh corn
   kernels, or fresh asparagus
   cut into nuggets
½ basket (3 to 4 ounces) red
   pearl onions, left whole, or 1
   small red onion, cut into ½-
   inch squares
2 tablespoons diced bacon
   (optional)
1 to 2 tablespoons corn or
   peanut oil, for stir-frying
   (optional)
1 red bell pepper, cut into ½-
   inch squares
2 fat scallions, cut into 1-inch
   nuggets
3 to 4 cloves garlic, slivered
Green and white scallion, sliced
   on the diagonal or julienned,
   for garnish

1. Scrub the clam shells under cold running water with a stiff brush. Beard the mussels and scrub the shells under cold running water. Discard any shellfish that do not shut quickly when rinsed or any with broken shells. Cover with a wet towel in a shallow pan and refrigerate until ready to use.

2. Combine the chopped black beans with the wine; set aside for 10 minutes to plump the beans.

3. Drain the beans, reserving the wine. In a small dish, combine the beans, ginger, and scallion rings; cover until ready to use.

4. In a small bowl, combine the reserved wine with the sauce ingredients, leaving the spoon in the bowl.

5. Blanch the spinach leaves in a generous amount of boiling water for 10 seconds to wilt. Immerse in ice water to chill. Drain well, pressing down lightly to extract any excess water. Fluff the leaves to loosen, then set aside. In the same pot, blanch the peas until tender-crisp, about 30 seconds; plunge into ice water to chill. (Blanch asparagus nuggets using the same method until tender-crisp, 30 to 60 seconds.) Blanch the pearl onions until the skins loosen, 1½ to 2 minutes. Chill

BEARDS AND BONES

Yanking beards from mussels and pulling bones from fish can be one of the better or worse jobs in a restaurant kitchen, depending upon your perspective and your tools. If you're one of our prep cooks and are faced with a giant sink of fresh mussels clinging ferociously to their ropey beards, then it can be a low day. Or, if dinner is due up in an hour and you're dealing with a king salmon so fresh that the bones are still wedded to the meat and the one needle-nose pliers that typically floats around the kitchen has disappeared, then it will be a difficult hour. Otherwise, it's fun.

In the privacy and sanity of a home kitchen, a little muscle and a needle-nose pliers are all you need to do either job easily. The pliers will grip and tug well without slipping. Don't fuss around with strawberry pickers or tweezers; they're designed for little stuff. Give the hardware store salesclerk a thrill and say you're buying pliers to yank off a stiff bunch of beards.

BEARDING MUSSELS

///

The very fibers mussels use to attach themselves to piers and pilings (often outlasting the ropes or mortar used to hold the structure together) are what you need to yank out before eating them. A pair of needle-nose pliers does the job perfectly. Mussel connoisseurs insist that the beards be yanked just before cooking, leaving the mussels alive and with all their faculties intact until the last minute. At the restaurant, however, we often beard the mussels and refrigerate them overnight, and we do not detect any difference in taste.

in ice water and drain. Cut off the root ends; peel off the skin. Cut in half if large.

6. Heat a wok or large, heavy skillet over high heat until hot enough to evaporate a bead of water on contact. Add the bacon, if using, and stir briskly until some of the fat is rendered and the cubes are golden, about 1 minute. Reduce the heat to moderate; remove the bacon to a paper towel to drain. Empty the pan of all but 1 tablespoon bacon fat, reserving any extra. If you are not using bacon, glaze the pan with 1 tablespoon corn oil and heat until a pinch of the aromatics foams upon contact.

7. Add the aromatics to the pan and stir gently until fully fragrant, about 1 minute, adjusting the heat so the mixture foams gently without browning. Add the onions and toss until translucent, 2 to 3 minutes. Add the bell pepper and toss briskly until slightly soft, about 2 minutes. Add the scallions and garlic, and toss until the garlic is fragrant and very lightly browned, about 2 minutes more. Adjust the heat to maintain a merry sizzle and drizzle a bit more fat or oil down the side of the pan, if needed to prevent sticking. Add the bacon and toss to combine. Spread the vegetables on a large platter to cool. All of the above steps may be done a full day in advance. Seal and refrigerate the ingredients; bring to room temperature before cooking.

8. About 15 minutes before serving, put the clams in a 2- to 3-quart Chinese sandpot or other large heavy casserole. Arrange the cooked vegetables on top. Stir the sauce to recombine and add it to the pot. Add the mussels in an even layer on top. Tightly cover the pot and bring the mixture to a lively simmer over moderate heat. Simmer just until the clams and mussels open, 4 to 5 minutes, shaking the pan several times to hasten them on their way. Turn off the heat, remove the lid, and quickly fold in the spinach and peas, corn, or asparagus. Replace the lid and allow them to heat through for 30 seconds. Discard any shellfish that do not open with a tug.

9. Serve at once in heated bowls of contrasting color, garnished with a sprinkling of scallion. Put an extra bowl on the table for the empty shells.

MENU SUGGESTIONS: I like to ladle the shellfish, vegetables, and sauce into a bowl lined with rounds of toasted garlic bread—totally heretical, but totally delicious. Purists might like rice. Iconoclasts might follow with a green salad.

HOMEY SANDPOTS • LUSH STIR-FRIES

BEEFY STEWS

CHILLED BEEF SALADS

CHINESE COLDCUTS

BEEF
AND
LAMB

CHINESE COLDCUTS • CHILLED BEEF SALADS • BEEFY STEWS

LUSH STIR-FRIES • HOMEY SANDPOTS

CONTENTS

eef and lamb are minor notes on the Chinese cooking scale, and that was fine by me when I arrived in Taiwan in the early 1970s. Primed by a childhood of steaks and lamb chops (the gifts of beneficent Uncle Bernie, the butcher) and impelled to a state of moral superiority by the strict vegetarianism of my college years, I was thrilled at the thought of an existence without hamburgers.

However, what little beef or lamb made its way onto my plate—in my second year of Chinese life when I threw vegetarianism to the winds—was terrifically tasty. Treated in the Chinese way with grand amounts of ginger, scallion, garlic, wine, and citrus zest to cut the richness, beef and lamb was a new experience. It was light and delicious, surprising to no one more than me.

If I were running a traditional Chinese restaurant, the beef and lamb dishes on the menu would run the small gamut from Mongolian Lamb to Szechwan Beef. At China Moon, however, we're less regionally bound and more exuberantly market-centered. Thus, when we are gifted with wild mushrooms and asparagus, we think of dusky beef flavors and accent them with a dash of oyster sauce. Or, when lamb is young and tender, we pepper it for an antipasto, slice it thinly for a cold plate, and put a dollop of smoked green chili sauce on top. Some of this is not authentic, but the Chinese flavors and balances ring true.

For those of you who have grown tired of red meats or are seeking to eat less of them, this chapter is good news. There are ideas to spark your appetite with fresh new flavors, and recipes to feed you grandly, using far less meat than you might expect.

■ ■ ■

WOK-SEARED BEEF TENDERLOIN

SERVES 6 TO 8 AS A MAIN COURSE, 10 TO 12 AS PART OF A MULTICOURSE MEAL

BUYING BEEF AND LAMB

Running a restaurant, one gets accustomed to buying large, uncut pieces of beef and lamb, judging its freshness from the state of the fat and doing the butchering one's self. On my rare forays into civilian life (otherwise known as days off), I accordingly patronize butchers where I can see most, if not all, of the beast I am buying. That generally means going to ethnic butcher shops.

Even in our more antiseptic supermarkets, however, there are simple ways to judge freshly cut and properly stored beef and lamb. The piece of whatever you're eyeballing should look moist and red. It shouldn't be sitting in its own blood. The fat that rims it should look moist. If anything is dry, gray, or bloody, the meat has been too long from the hoof. Most emphatically, it should have a good, clean smell. Smelly meat is bad meat, at least in my opinion.

This recipe is a fine example of how a restaurant takes what seems like an ordinary ingredient, like beef, and turns it into something truly extraordinary. This preparation is not at all difficult, but it does mean starting with a whole beef tenderloin. If that frightens rather than inspires, you might simply use the marinade on your next steak dinner: A well-marbled steak marinated for 10 to 20 minutes (depending on thickness) and then seared and roasted (or grilled) in this way is truly delicious.

1 fresh beef tenderloin, aged (see Aging Beef, page 255)

MARINADE:
1 cup water
½ cup soy sauce
¼ cup mushroom soy sauce
½ cup Chinese rice wine or dry sherry
3 fat scallions, cut into 1-inch nuggets and smashed
3 whole star anise, broken into their 24 points
Several pieces cassia bark or 1 short cinnamon stick, crumbled
Finely pared zest of 1 small scrubbed orange
¼ teaspoon dried red chili flakes

3 ounces Chinese golden rock sugar, smashed (rounded ½ cup bits)
3 large cloves garlic, smashed
6 to 7 quarter-size coins fresh ginger, smashed
2 teaspoons Szechwan peppercorns
1 teaspoon black peppercorns

4 teaspoons corn or peanut oil, for searing
Freshly ground black pepper
Diagonally sliced green and white scallion rings, for garnish

1. Lay the aged tenderloin flat on your cutting board. Separate the small, slender tenderloin fillet from the side of the larger loin; the membrane hugging the 2 together is easily slit. With a sharp knife, carefully trim both pieces of all fat, tendon, and tough silvery skin. Leave the exterior as smooth as possible. Next, cut off the knobby end of the loin where it starts narrowing into a tail. Cut the large loin piece crosswise in half. You will have four pieces of beef.

2. To make the marinade, combine all of the marinade ingredients through the peppercorns in a small non-aluminum saucepan and bring to a simmer over moderate heat. Reduce the heat to maintain a weak simmer and cook, stirring occasionally to dissolve the rock sugar, 10 minutes. Let the marinade cool to room temperature.

3. Put the beef into 1 or 2 deep containers that will hold it snugly. Pour the marinade on top and turn the beef to coat it evenly. Extract the thin tenderloin after 10 minutes. Let the 3 larger pieces of beef marinate for 35 minutes longer; turn them once or twice while marinating. Drain off the marinade. (It may be strained and reused to marinate beef or glaze hamburgers while they cook. Refrigerate it for up to a week, or freeze.)

4. Preheat the oven to 375°F. Move a rack to the top third of the oven.

5. Heat a wok or a large heavy skillet over high heat until hot enough to evaporate a bead of water on contact. Add 1 teaspoon of the oil and swirl to glaze the pan. Heat until nearly smoking. Add the skinny tenderloin first. Use tongs to turn the beef, searing each side until it turns a rich mahogany, about 30 seconds in all. Remove and place on a flat rack fitted in a jelly roll or roasting pan. Sear the other pieces of beef, one by one, cleaning and heating the pan each time and adding oil as above. The larger pieces will each take a minute or so to sear. Make sure the pan and the oil are blazing hot so that you get a dark, flavorful sear. Do not worry if the beef blackens a bit; it will be tasty. Place the pieces on the rack with room between them.

6. Roast the beef until rare to medium-rare, 4 to 5 minutes for the slender tenderloin fillet, 10 to 12 minutes for the end section, and 16 to 18 minutes for the 2 main loin pieces. (The timing will differ depending on the depth of the sear.) To test for doneness, roast until an instant-read meat thermometer inserted into the thickest portion of each piece registers 110°F. The meat will be very rare, optimal for great taste and texture.

7. Let the beef cool on the roasting rack for at least 10 to 15 minutes so the juices gel. Serve freshly roasted, warm, or at

AGING BEEF

*We age our own beef in the
restaurant, and the result is
a richer-tasting meat with an
inimitable texture. Doing it
at home is easy. There are
two ways:*

*For the first, you will
need to pull out the lower
shelves in your refrigerator
and suspend the untrimmed
tenderloin on a stainless-steel
S-hook from the top shelf.
Place a dish lined with a
clean towel underneath the
meat to catch the juices as
the outside of the tenderloin
dries. Leave the beef
hanging—it should dangle
more or less freely—for two
full days, changing the
towel once.*

*For the second method,
simply wrap the beef in a
clean, lint-free towel and lay
it flat in a dish in the refrigerator, turning it twice daily
for two to three days and
changing the towel once or
twice. Either way, the flavor
of the beef gains greatly in
depth and richness!*

room temperature. Slice thinly on the diagonal, embellishing the meat with some freshly ground pepper and a sprinkling of scallion.

MENU SUGGESTIONS: We feature the beef as the center-piece of a Peking antipasto plate, accompanied by a dip dish of our house or sweet mustard (page 21). To round out the plate, Wild Rice Salad with Ginger-Balsamic Dressing (page 423) or Wok-Seared New Potatoes (page 424) and a salad of baby greens tossed with either of our vinaigrettes would be great. Or, for a taste of cross-cultural delicatessen, stuff the beef and some Ginger-Pickled Red Cabbage Slaw (page 61) inside a hot Sesame-Encrusted Flatbread (page 379) and embellish it with a good schmear of mustard.

SPICY TANGERINE BEEF (OR LAMB) WITH GLASS NOODLES

SERVES 2 AS A MAIN COURSE, 4 AS PART OF A MULTICOURSE MEAL

A very simple stir-fry with appealing nubbly and slithery textures, this is a light and tangy dish. It is also one of those great examples of Chinese cook-ing magic, whereby a half pound of minced meat be-comes a quick and delectable meal for several people.

When blood oranges are in season, use them for their provocative taste and color. Pomegranate seeds are also wonderful, some tossed in during the last minute of cooking and a few more sprinkled on top.

MARINADE AND MEAT:

2 tablespoons soy sauce

2 tablespoons Chinese rice wine
or dry sherry

1 teaspoon cornstarch

1 teaspoon "goop" from China
Moon Chili-Orange Oil
(page 15)

½ pound ground beef round or
lamb shoulder

AROMATICS:

1 tablespoon finely minced garlic

1½ teaspoons finely minced
fresh ginger

½ cup thinly sliced green and
white scallion rings

2 teaspoons Chinese chili sauce

2 to 3 teaspoons finely minced
fresh tangerine or
orange
zest

SAUCE:

¼ cup China Moon Infusion
(page 72), China Moon
Double Stock (page 72), or
unsalted chicken stock

2 tablespoons freshly squeezed
tangerine or orange juice

1 tablespoon plus 1 teaspoon soy
sauce

1 teaspoon sugar

1 tablespoon Serrano-
Lemongrass Vinegar (page
19) or unseasoned Japanese
rice vinegar

1 small package (1.75 to 2
ounces) PRC glass noodles

2 tablespoons corn or peanut
oil, for stir-frying

2 tablespoons coarsely chopped
coriander leaves and stems

Sprigs of coriander or
watercress, for garnish

1. Whisk together the marinade ingredients through the "goop" in a large bowl. Add the meat and stir in one direction until well blended. Seal with plastic wrap and set aside to marinate for 1 to 2 hours at cool room temperature, or refrigerate overnight. Bring to room temperature before cooking.

2. Combine the aromatics in a small dish and seal airtight until ready to use.

3. Combine the sauce ingredients through the vinegar in a small bowl. Stir to blend, leaving the spoon in the bowl.

4. Without cutting the strings that bind the skein, soak the glass noodles in hot water to cover. Soak until translucent and pliable, 3 to 4 minutes. Cut and discard the strings; cut the noodles into 4-inch lengths. Rinse with cool water, then drain thoroughly. To this point, all may be done a day ahead. Seal and refrigerate the ingredients; let come to room temperature before cooking.

5. Heat a wok or large heavy skillet over high heat until hot enough to evaporate a bead of water on contact. Add the oil and swirl to glaze the pan. When the oil is hot enough to sizzle a single scallion ring, reduce the heat to moderate and

STORING BEEF AND LAMB

I do not freeze beef or lamb, having found from experimentation that the flavor and texture diminish steadily with the length of the freezing. I do, however, sometimes need to refrigerate beef or lamb overnight before using it, and this is how it should be done:

Keep ground beef or lamb in a perforated pan or a stainless steel strainer. Put a drip pan underneath to catch the blood and press a piece of plastic wrap directly on the surface of the meat to make it airtight. The perforated pan allows the blood to drain; if

the meat were to stand in it, it would grow stinky. The plastic wrap seals out the air, retaining the color of the meat.

Whole pieces of beef or lamb, if too bulky to refrigerate at home in a drainer pan, should be wrapped in a clean tea towel and then bagged in plastic. The towel will sop up the blood and keep the meat from decaying.

With even a night of storage, these precautions can make a significant difference in both the smell and taste of the meat, especially if what you purchased was not freshly killed.

add the aromatics. Stir gently until fully fragrant, 20 to 30 seconds, adjusting the heat so they foam without browning. Add the meat, toss to break it into bits, and stir-fry until it turns 90 percent gray, about 2 minutes. Stir the sauce to recombine it and add it to the pan. Bring the liquids to a simmer. Stir in the noodles, cover the pan, and simmer gently until the liquids are absorbed, 2 to 3 minutes.

6. Remove the cover, turn off the heat, and stir to recombine. Fold in the chopped coriander. Taste and adjust with a dash more sugar or vinegar, if desired. Remove the dish to a heated serving bowl or platter of contrasting color. Garnish with the sprigs of coriander or watercress.

MENU SUGGESTIONS: You can build a pretty salad of tossed baby greens dressed with our Orange (page 25) or Fresh Ginger Vinaigrette (page 24) to serve alongside the noodles. Wok-Seared Spinach Relish (page 438), Stir-Fried Zucchini Ribbons (page 437), or fresh corn would also be good.

STIR-FRIED SPICY BEEF WITH SUMMER TOMATOES AND PURPLE BASIL

SERVES 3 TO 4 AS A MAIN COURSE, 5 TO 6 AS PART OF A MULTICOURSE MEAL

Here is a classic Chinese stir-fry featuring summer's best produce in a colorful mélange. It's easy and the recipe can be doubled to serve the larger groups often found around a summertime table. The preparations can be done ahead and the dish cooked off in just minutes.

Given summer's bounty, feel free to play with the vegetables. Baby zucchini, young snow peas, and tender string beans would all be delicious. Green basil can substitute for purple, though you might use a bit less. Corn can be tossed in as well—just go up and down the garden.

¾ pound trimmed flank steak, all fat and tough sinew removed

MARINADE:
1 tablespoon soy sauce
1 tablespoon mushroom soy sauce
1 tablespoon cornstarch
1 tablespoon packed brown sugar
1 tablespoon China Moon Hot Chili Oil (page 10)
1 tablespoon "goop" from China Moon Hot Chili Oil

AROMATICS:
1 tablespoon finely minced fresh ginger
2 tablespoons finely minced garlic
¾ to 1 teaspoon dried red chili flakes
3 tablespoons thinly sliced green and white scallion rings

SAUCE:
1½ cups China Moon Infusion (page 72), China Moon Double Stock (page 72), or unsalted chicken stock
2 tablespoons mushroom soy sauce

2 tablespoons balsamic vinegar
1 tablespoon Chinese rice wine or dry sherry
1 tablespoon sugar

½ cup fresh peas
2 to 3 cups corn or peanut oil, for velveting and stir-frying
1 yellow onion, cut into ½-inch moons
1 red or yellow bell pepper, cut into ¾-inch squares
8 pieces Oven-Dried Plum Tomatoes (page 36), 1 rounded cup halved red and yellow cherry tomatoes, or 1 large, ripe but firm red or yellow tomato, cut into thick wedges
2 teaspoons cornstarch dissolved in 1½ tablespoons cold stock or water
3 tablespoons purple basil julienne
Diagonally sliced green and white scallion rings, for garnish

VELVETING RED MEAT

The traditional Chinese cooking technique of velveting, or bathing in warm oil, gives beef, lamb, and pork a wonderfully lush texture. Were you to simply stir-fry the meat instead, the greater heat of the wok would turn it chewy. The cornstarch in the marinade contributes to the velveting process; it binds the other flavors to the meat and seals in the juices during cooking.

To make the velveting step easy, invest a few dollars in a big Chinese mesh spoon with a diameter of 5 to 6 inches. One swoop into the pan and it scoops up the meat, then, rested on top of a bowl, it allows the meat to drain.

1. Cut the beef lengthwise into several long strips about 2 inches wide. Holding your knife at a sharp angle to the board, cut each strip crosswise into ribbons ⅛ inch thick.

2. Blend the marinade ingredients in a bowl big enough to hold the beef. Add the beef and toss to coat each slice. Seal airtight and marinate at cool room temperature for 3 to 4 hours, or refrigerate overnight. Let come to room temperature before cooking; re-toss to separate the ribbons.

3. Combine the aromatics in a small bowl; cover until ready to use.

BROWN SUGAR AND BEEF

I almost always use brown sugar with beef. It has a richness and a depth that matches the lustiness of beef, and it seems even to tenderize it in a special way. Light or dark brown sugar work the same in this application; I choose indiscriminately between the two.

4. Combine all of the sauce ingredients through the sugar in a small bowl. Stir to blend, leaving the spoon in the bowl.

5. In a small saucepan filled with rapidly boiling water, blanch the peas until tender-crisp, 10 to 30 seconds. Immerse in ice water to chill; drain well. To this point, all the above, as well as the vegetable cutting, may be done a day ahead. Seal and refrigerate the ingredients; let come to room temperature before cooking.

6. About 20 minutes before serving, velvet the beef: Heat a wok or deep heavy skillet over high heat until hot enough to evaporate a bead of water on contact. Add oil to a depth of 1 inch. Rest a deep-fry thermometer on the rim. Reduce the heat to medium and bring the oil to 350°F, hot enough to bubble a beef ribbon. Gently slide the beef into the oil and swish with chopsticks to separate the shreds. Cook until the meat is 90 percent gray on the outside, about 15 seconds. Immediately scoop the meat from the oil with a large Chinese mesh spoon; rest the spoon on a bowl to drain. The meat will be only half-cooked. Alternatively, you can work with 2 mesh spoons: Hold one above the pot to receive the meat while scooping it in small batches with the other spoon.) Carefully drain all but 2 tablespoons of the oil from the pan.

Once cool, the oil can be filtered through a fine sieve lined with several layers of dry cheesecloth. Bottle and refrigerate for future frying and stir-frying.

7. Return the pan to high heat. When the oil is hot enough to sizzle a scallion ring, reduce the heat to moderate and add the aromatics. Stir until fully fragrant, 20 to 30 seconds, adjusting the heat so they foam without browning. Add the onion and toss until slightly softened, 2 minutes. Add the bell pepper and toss for 2 minutes, adjusting the heat to maintain a merry sizzle. Add the tomatoes and toss to mix.

8. Stir the sauce and add it to the pan. Raise the heat to high, cover the pan, and bring the sauce to a simmer. When the sauce simmers, stir the cornstarch mixture to recombine, add it to the pan, and stir until the sauce turns glossy and thickens slightly, 10 to 20 seconds. Add the beef, the peas, and half the basil; toss gently to heat through, about 10 seconds.

9. Serve immediately on heated plates of contrasting

color. Garnish with the scallion rings and a shower of the remaining basil julienne.

MENU SUGGESTIONS: This stir-fry is an ideal topping for a Pot-Browned Noodle Pillow (page 401). It would also be tasty with a bowl of steamed rice. Ears of steamed corn and/or a sauté of the intriguingly bitter Chinese broccoli would make excellent additions, if you desire extra vegetables.

STIR-FRIED SPICY BEEF WITH CHARD, MUSHROOMS, AND ASPARAGUS

SERVES 3 TO 4 AS A MAIN COURSE, 5 TO 6 AS PART OF A MULTICOURSE MEAL

When winter is still upon you but asparagus have just come into the market, here is a great dish to encourage thoughts of spring. The mushrooms can be as varied as the market permits.

This is a simple, classic stir-fry that can be prepared in advance and then cooked within minutes. The beef will be tastiest if left to marinate overnight.

¾ pound trimmed flank steak, all fat and tough sinew removed

MARINADE:
1 tablespoon soy sauce
1 tablespoon mushroom soy sauce

1 tablespoon cornstarch
1 tablespoon packed brown sugar
1 tablespoon China Moon Hot Chili-Oil (page 10), China Moon Chili-Orange Oil (page 15), or China Moon Chili-Lemon Oil (page 12)
1 tablespoon "goop" from China Moon Chili-Orange Oil or China Moon Chili-Lemon Oil

ROLL-CUTTING

Pretty and practical, roll-cutting is a Chinese method of slicing long cylindrical vegetables like asparagus into lively looking nuggets. Hold your knife at a 45-degree angle to the vegetable, cut it at the end, then roll the vegetable a third of a turn away from (or towards) you; then cut it again on the same angle an inch above the first cut. The result is a 1-inch nugget with appealingly asymmetrical splayed ends. The diagonally exposed ends allow for quick cooking and great penetration of seasonings, and are fun for your tongue. Kids love roll-cutting if you want to put them to work!

AROMATICS:
1 tablespoon finely minced fresh
    ginger
2 tablespoons finely minced
    garlic
2 tablespoons thinly sliced green
    and white scallion rings
1 small red Fresno chili, minced

SAUCE:
1½ cups China Moon Infusion
    (page 72), China Moon
    Double Stock (page 72), or
    unsalted chicken stock
1 tablespoon soy sauce
1 teaspoon sugar
2 tablespoons Chinese rice wine
    or dry sherry
2 tablespoons Serrano-
    Lemongrass Vinegar (page
    19) or unseasoned Japanese
    rice vinegar

1½ cups roll-cut asparagus
    (1-inch nuggets)
2 to 3 cups corn or peanut oil,
    for velveting and stir-frying
1 yellow onion, cut into ¾-inch
    squares
1 carrot, cut into julienne
¼ pound mixed wild and
    domestic mushrooms,
    trimmed and cut, if large
2 cups red chard squares
    (1 inch)
2 teaspoons cornstarch dissolved
    in 1½ tablespoons cold stock
    or water
Diagonally sliced green and
    white scallion rings
Enoki mushrooms, spongy base
    removed, for garnish

1. Cut the beef lengthwise (with the grain) into several long strips about 2 inches wide. Holding your knife on an angle to the board, cut the strips crosswise against the grain into broad ribbons ⅛ inch thick.

2. Blend the marinade ingredients until smooth in a bowl big enough to hold the beef. Add the beef and toss well. Seal airtight and marinate at cool room temperature for 3 to 4 hours, or refrigerate overnight. Let the beef come to room temperature before cooking; re-toss to separate the shreds.

3. Combine the aromatics in a small bowl and cover until ready to use.

4. Combine the sauce ingredients through the vinegar in a bowl. Stir to blend, leaving the spoon in the bowl.

5. In rapidly boiling water, blanch the asparagus until tender-crisp, 30 to 40 seconds if pencil-thin, 50 to 60 seconds for thicker stalks. Plunge into ice water to chill; drain well.

6. About 20 minutes before serving, velvet the beef following step 6 on page 259.

7. Return the pan to high heat. When the oil is hot enough to sizzle a scallion ring, reduce the heat to moderate and add the aromatics. Stir gently until fully fragrant, 20 to 30 seconds, adjusting the heat so they foam without browning. Add the onion and toss briskly until slightly softened, about 2 minutes. Add the carrot and toss for 1 minute. Add the mushrooms and toss until very hot, about 2 minutes more. Adjust the heat to maintain a merry sizzle and drizzle a bit more oil down the side of the pan, if needed to prevent sticking. Don't worry if the vegetables brown; they will be tasty. Add the chard and toss gently until wilted, 15 to 20 seconds.

8. Stir the sauce and add it to the pan. Raise the heat, cover the pan, and bring the sauce to a simmer. When the sauce simmers, stir the cornstarch mixture to recombine and add it to the pan. Stir until the liquid turns glossy and slightly thick, 10 to 20 seconds. Add the asparagus and the beef. Stir gently to combine and cook through, about 10 seconds.

9. Serve immediately on heated plates of contrasting color. Garnish with the scallion rings and enoki mushrooms.

MENU SUGGESTIONS: This is a very satisfying meal when served with a Pot-Browned Noodle Pillow (page 401), a Broad Noodle Pillow (page 403), or simply cooked rice. If it is cold outside and you need a hearty meal, team the stir-fry with one of our hot and sour soups.

STIR-FRIED ORANGE BEEF WITH CHILIS AND WILD MUSHROOMS

SERVES 3 TO 4 AS A MAIN COURSE, 5 TO 6 AS PART OF A MULTICOURSE MEAL

Drop all thoughts of the saccharin-sweet, deep-fried orange beef that is a fixture in Hunanese-American restaurants! This is a light-style, gustily seasoned stir-fry embellished with fresh orange zest and just enough sugar to bring forth the heat.

EQUAL TIME FOR HAN-BOWS

I was lucky enough to be in the hands of a culinary adventurer when I was first learning how to eat in China. This was the old Yangchow man whom I called Po-fu ("uncle") and with whom I lived in Taiwan as a student. His first question to me at the dinner table was on the subject of Russian dressing, about which he'd heard from a Shanghai friend. (If Yangchow people were epicures, Shanghai people were indefatigable experimenters in international cuisine.) As a response, I snuck down to the U.S. Army PX the next day after school, bought some ketchup and mayonnaise, and whipped up a batch of the stuff. A friendship was born, though the mess went uneaten.

After a year of extraordinary tutelage in the hands of Po-fu, it lamentably came time for me to leave the island. Po-fu had heard of the recent opening of a Japanese nightclub featuring something called a "han-bow" (the Mandarin approximation of hamburger) and insisted we try one as a salute to my departure. Everyone got dressed up. This kind of culinary excursion was Serious Business. We hired a spiffy cab, rolled up in front of the jazzily dressed doorman, and went in like the Imperial family on parade. Po-fu strutted jauntily in the lead, his eyes shining brightly at the prospect of something new to eat. The han-bow was tasted, eyed quizzically, and pushed aside with a single disdaining finger. We left with all the pomp with which we'd arrived, Po-fu rapping the doorman with his cane. Once home, he cooked up a big bowl of noodles and insisted we all eat.

We both cried bitterly at the airport when I left. Surely the old man imagined he was sending me off to starve in a strange world of Russian dressing and han-bows, never again to know the redemption of wholesome Chinese food. Is it any wonder I adored him?

The beef will be tastiest if marinated overnight, but if you are in a hurry, the time can be cut short and the dish made in under an hour.

¾ pound trimmed flank steak, all fat and tough sinew removed

MARINADE:
1 tablespoon soy sauce
1 tablespoon mushroom soy sauce
1 tablespoon cornstarch
1 tablespoon packed brown sugar
1 tablespoon China Moon Chili-Orange Oil (page 15)
1 tablespoon "goop" from China Moon Chili-Orange Oil

AROMATICS:
2 tablespoons finely minced fresh ginger
1 tablespoon finely minced garlic
2 tablespoons thinly sliced green and white scallion rings
1 red Fresno chili, finely minced
Finely minced zest of 1 scrubbed orange

SAUCE:
1½ cups China Moon Infusion (page 72), China Moon Double Stock (page 72), or unsalted chicken stock

2 tablespoons mushroom soy sauce
¼ cup freshly squeezed orange juice
2 tablespoons balsamic vinegar
¾ to 1½ teaspoons sugar

½ cup fresh peas, or 1 cup tipped and strung sugar snap peas or roll-cut (page 260) asparagus nuggets
2 to 3 cups corn or peanut oil, for velveting and stir-frying
1 small red onion, cut into ¾-inch squares
1 small red bell pepper, cut into ¾-inch squares
½ small bulb fennel, cut crosswise into ⅛-inch arcs
4 to 6 Italian field or other wild mushrooms, cut into thick slices
2 fat scallions, cut into 1-inch nuggets
1 cup small clusters of oyster mushrooms
1 tablespoon cornstarch dissolved in 1½ tablespoons cold stock or water
1 cup loosely packed baby spinach leaves or thick ribbons of ruby chard
Green and white scallion julienne, for garnish

1. Cut the meat lengthwise (with the grain) into several strips about 2 inches wide. Holding your knife at an angle to the board, cut each strip crosswise into ribbons ⅛ inch thick.

2. Blend the marinade ingredients until smooth in a bowl big enough to hold the beef. Add the beef and toss to coat each slice. Seal and set aside to marinate at cool room temperature for 3 to 4 hours, or refrigerate overnight. Let the beef come to room temperature before cooking; re-toss to separate the shreds.

3. Combine the aromatics in a small dish and cover until ready to use.

4. Combine all of the sauce ingredients through the sugar in a small bowl. Stir to blend, leaving the spoon in the bowl.

5. In a small saucepan filled with rapidly boiling water, blanch the peas until tender-crisp, 10 to 30 seconds. Immerse in ice water to chill; drain well. If using sugar snap peas or asparagus, blanch them until tender-crisp, 20 to 60 seconds depending on thickness; refresh in ice water and drain. To this point, all the above, including the vegetable cutting, may be done a day ahead. Seal and refrigerate the ingredients; bring to room temperature before cooking.

6. About 20 minutes before serving, velvet the beef following step 6 on page 259.

7. Return the pan to high heat. When the oil is hot enough to sizzle a scallion ring, reduce the heat to moderate and add the aromatics. Stir gently until fully fragrant, 20 to 30 seconds, adjusting the heat so they foam without browning. Add the onion and bell pepper, and toss briskly until slightly softened, 2 to 3 minutes. Add the fennel and toss until the fennel is half-cooked, another 2 to 3 minutes. Add the field mushrooms and scallions, and toss for 1 minute. Add the oyster mushrooms and toss for 1 minute more. Adjust the heat to maintain a merry sizzle and drizzle a bit more oil down the side of the pan, if needed to prevent sticking. Don't worry if the vegetables brown a bit; they will be tasty. If you are using chard, add it now and toss to combine.

8. Stir the sauce and add it to the pan. Raise the heat, cover the pan, and bring the sauce to a simmer. When the sauce simmers, stir to recombine the cornstarch mixture, add it to the pan, and stir the sauce until it turns glossy and slightly thick, 10 to 20 seconds. Add the spinach, peas, and beef, and toss gently until the spinach wilts and the beef is cooked through, 10 to 15 seconds.

THE FAT QUESTION

In cooking classes around the country, I regularly "treat" my students to a taste-test of three skillet-melted fresh fats: pork, lamb, and beef. It is astounding to them to discover that while the taste of pork fat is pleasant, neutral, and light, the flavors of beef and lamb fat are comparatively overwhelming and heavy. Unlike the pork fat, both beef and lamb fat coat the tongue and leave a strong aftertaste. This is amazing news for those *who have grown up to think of pork as a "heavy" meat, and lamb or beef as the lighter choice.*

One would think that this would inspire a Chinese cook to buy leaner cuts of beef and lamb, but not so! A Chinese cook will not buy a leaner cut of meat when internal fat in the muscle means better flavor and better texture. A Chinese cook will instead alter the character of beef and lamb fat by pairing the meat with the astringent flavors of ginger, scallion, wine, and citrus zest. I am not a health expert, but my suspicion is that these acids succeed in breaking down the fats and making the meats more digestible, in addition to rendering them more tasty.

9. Serve immediately on heated plates of contrasting color. Garnish with a sprinkling of the scallion julienne on top.

MENU SUGGESTIONS: We usually serve the beef as a topping for a Pot-Browned Noodle Pillow (page 401). If you are a pasta fan, you could also use a Broad Noodle Pillow (page 403) or simply cooked fettuccine. Rice would be equally good, as would Wok-Seared New Potatoes (page 424) or a dish of great mashed potatoes. A watercress salad or ears of freshly cooked corn would partner the beef perfectly if you would like to serve another dish.

SANDPOT CASSEROLE OF HOT AND SOUR BEEF

SERVES 3 TO 4 AS A MAIN COURSE, 5 TO 6 AS PART OF A MULTICOURSE MEAL

This is a fine meal-in-a-bowl for an evening's supper. It is warming and satisfying and also quite light. If you have made beef stew but never ventured down a Chinese path, this will be an enjoyable first step.

Like any good stew, you'll want to start this one in advance. It can be marinated and cooked over the weekend, then finished on a weeknight just by adding the vegetables.

This is a zippy bowlful. For extra spice and color, include the optional fresh chilis.

MARINADE AND BEEF:

1 tablespoon mushroom soy sauce

1 tablespoon soy sauce

1 tablespoon cornstarch

1 tablespoon packed brown sugar

1 tablespoon China Moon Hot Chili Oil (page 10) or China Moon Chili-Lemon Oil (page 12)

1 tablespoon "goop" from China Moon Hot Chili Oil or China Moon Chili-Lemon Oil

1 pound beef chuck, cut into 1-inch cubes

AROMATICS:

1 tablespoon finely minced garlic

1 tablespoon finely minced fresh ginger

3 tablespoons thinly sliced green and white scallion rings

½ to ¾ teaspoon dried red chili flakes

SAUCE:

1½ cups China Moon Infusion (page 72), China Moon Double Stock (page 72), or unsalted chicken stock

2 tablespoons mushroom soy sauce

1½ tablespoons soy sauce

¼ cup Chinese rice wine or dry sherry

¼ cup Serrano-Lemongrass Vinegar (page 19) or unseasoned Japanese rice vinegar

2 tablespoons cider vinegar

1 teaspoon sugar

1 teaspoon Chinese chili sauce

3 to 4 tablespoons corn or peanut oil, for searing and stir-frying

½ pound tiny red potatoes, scrubbed and halved

1 small carrot, diagonally cut into rippled or plain coins ⅛ inch thick

¼ pound slender green and/or yellow zucchini, cut into ¼-inch rounds

1 small yellow onion, cut into ¾-inch squares

1 small red bell pepper, cut into ¾-inch squares

¼ pound domestic mushrooms, halved or quartered, if large

1 small yellow wax chili, cut into paper-thin rings (optional)

1 small red serrano or red Fresno chili, cut into paper-thin rings (optional)

2 packed cups Napa cabbage ribbons, cut ½ inch thick

Diagonally cut green and white scallion rings, for garnish

**WANTED: A
FATTY CUT**

///

*Leaner cuts of beef are so
popular these days that it's
difficult to get a properly
fatty cut for stewing. Speak
with your butcher when
seeking an appropriately
marbled cut of meat. If you
use one that is too lean, the
meat will be dry and without
flavor.*

1. Blend the marinade ingredients through the "goop" in a bowl big enough to hold the beef. Add the beef and toss to coat each chunk. Seal airtight and marinate for 3 to 4 hours at cool room temperature or refrigerate for up to 48 hours. Let come to room temperature before searing. Re-toss to separate the cubes.

2. Combine the aromatics in a small dish and seal until ready to use.

3. Combine all of the sauce ingredients through the chili sauce in a small bowl. Stir to blend, leaving the spoon in the bowl.

4. Heat a wok or large heavy skillet over high heat until hot enough to evaporate a bead of water on contact. Add 1 tablespoon of the oil and swirl to glaze the pan. Heat the oil until nearly smoking. Add the beef and sear on all sides until golden brown. Adjust the heat so the beef sizzles heartily without scorching. Stir the sauce, add it to the pan, cover the pan, and bring the sauce to a simmer over moderate heat. Adjust the heat to maintain a weak simmer, cover tightly, and cook until the meat is very tender, about 1 hour. Remove the meat to a large plate to cool. Reserve the sauce.

5. In a small saucepan, combine the potatoes and enough cold water to cover. Bring the water to a simmer over moderate heat and simmer until the potatoes are 90 percent tender when pierced with a knife, 4 to 10 minutes, depending on size. Drain the potatoes and spread them on a plate to cool.

6. Blanch the carrots in boiling water to cover until half-cooked, 10 to 15 seconds. Drain, immerse in ice water to chill, drain again. Blanch the zucchini in the boiling water for 5 seconds. Drain, immerse in ice water, drain again.

7. Heat a wok or large heavy skillet over high heat until hot enough to evaporate a bead of water on contact. Add 2 tablespoons of the oil and swirl to glaze the pan. When the oil is hot enough to sizzle a scallion ring, reduce the heat to moderate. Add the aromatics and stir gently until fully fragrant, 20 to 30 seconds, adjusting the heat so they foam without browning. Add the onion and bell pepper, and toss until slightly softened, 3 minutes. Add the carrots and toss for 1 minute. Add the mushrooms and chili rings, if using, and toss for 2 minutes more. Adjust the heat to maintain a merry sizzle and drizzle a bit more oil down the side of the pan, if needed to prevent sticking. Don't worry if the vegetables brown a bit; they will be tasty. Fold in the cabbage and toss just until wilted. Add the zucchini and toss to combine. Spread the vegetables on a platter to cool.

At this point, all the stew components may be refrigerated overnight. Bring to room temperature before the final cooking.

8. About 20 minutes before serving, spread all the vegetables except the potatoes in the bottom of a 2- to 3-quart Chinese sandpot or other heavy casserole. Scatter the beef on top. Stir the sauce and add it to the pot. Cover and bring to a simmer over moderate heat. Simmer gently until the meat is heated through, 8 to 10 minutes. Fold the potatoes into the pot during the last 2 minutes of cooking.

9. Serve in warm bowls of contrasting color. Garnish with a thick sprinkling of the scallion rings.

MENU SUGGESTIONS: Some real trenchermen will enjoy thick wedges of hot garlic bread with their sandpot. A delicate baguette brought to the table toasty from the oven will also find its fans. Steamed rice, the traditional Chinese accompaniment, is good as well.

SANDPOT CASSEROLE OF BEEF AND WILD MUSHROOMS

SERVES 3 TO 4 AS A MAIN COURSE, 5 TO 6 AS PART OF A MULTICOURSE MEAL

This is a very straightforward winter-style stew of cubed beef and mushrooms. Porcini, shiitake, and oyster mushrooms would all be good here, as would a mixture of the three.

Like most stews, this one is best begun a day or more in advance and will gain in flavor upon reheating.

FRENCH MARKET CARROTS

Small, stubby, and nearly round, French market carrots are especially good cooked into a stew as they are thick enough to hold their texture. Like all baby vegetables, however, beware! A cute face won't make up for a lack of flavor; buy them only if you're assured they're tasty.

MARINADE AND BEEF:

1 tablespoon soy sauce
1 tablespoon mushroom soy sauce
1 tablespoon cornstarch
1 tablespoon packed brown sugar
1 tablespoon China Moon Hot Chili-Oil (page 10) or Chili-Orange Oil (page 15)
1 tablespoon "goop" from China Moon Hot Chili-Oil, Chili-Orange Oil, or Chili Lemon Oil
1 pound beef chuck, cut into 1-inch cubes

AROMATICS:

1 tablespoon finely minced garlic
2 tablespoons finely minced fresh ginger
3 tablespoons thinly sliced green and white scallion rings
½ teaspoon dried red chili flakes
Finely minced zest of 1 small orange

SAUCE:

2 cups China Moon Infusion (page 72), China Moon Double Stock (page 72), or unsalted chicken stock
2 tablespoons mushroom soy sauce
1 tablespoon balsamic vinegar
1 teaspoon sugar
½ teaspoon Chinese chili sauce
1 tablespoon oyster sauce

3 to 4 tablespoons corn or peanut oil, for searing and stir-frying
6 to 8 round French market carrots or 10 to 12 baby carrots, halved or quartered lengthwise, if fat
¼ pound roll-cut (page 260) asparagus nuggets or finger-lengths of Chinese broccoli, or 2 cups lightly packed wide ribbons of ruby chard
1 small red onion, cut into ½-inch moons
2 small leeks, white part only, split lengthwise and cut crosswise into ¼-inch moons
¾ pound wild mushrooms, trimmed and cut, if large
1 package enoki mushrooms, spongy base removed
Diagonally cut green and white scallion rings, for garnish

1. Blend the marinade ingredients through the "goop" in a bowl big enough to hold the beef. Add the beef and toss well. Marinate at cool room temperature for 3 to 4 hours or refrigerate for up to 48 hours. Let come to room temperature before searing.

2. Combine the aromatics in a small dish and seal until ready to use.

3. Combine all of the sauce ingredients through the oyster sauce in a small bowl. Stir to blend, leaving the spoon in the bowl.

4. Heat a wok or large heavy skillet over high heat until hot enough to evaporate a bead of water on contact. Add 1 tablespoon of the oil and swirl to glaze the pan. Heat the oil until nearly smoking. Add the beef and sear on all sides until golden brown, adjusting the heat so the beef sizzles heartily without scorching. Stir the sauce, add it to the pan, cover the pan, and bring the sauce to a simmer over moderate heat. Adjust the heat to maintain a weak simmer, cover tightly, and cook until the meat is very tender, about 1 hour. Remove the meat to a large plate to cool. Reserve the sauce.

5. While the beef simmers, bring a generous amount of water to a rapid boil. Add the carrots and blanch until half-cooked, 30 seconds to 1 minute. Immediately plunge the carrots into ice water to chill; drain. If using asparagus or broccoli, blanch in boiling water until tender-crisp, 20 to 30 seconds. Immerse into ice water to chill; drain well.

6. Heat a wok or large heavy skillet over high heat until hot enough to evaporate a bead of water on contact. Add 2 tablespoons of the oil and swirl to glaze the pan. When the oil is hot enough to foam a scallion ring, reduce the heat to moderate. Add the aromatics and stir gently until fully fragrant, 20 to 30 seconds, adjusting the heat so they foam without browning. Add the onion and toss until slightly softened, 2 minutes. Add the leeks and toss until wilted, 1 to 2 minutes. Add the carrots and toss until hot, about 1 minute. Add the mushrooms in quick succession, thickest pieces first, and toss until hot, about 1 minute more. Adjust the heat to maintain a merry sizzle and drizzle a bit more oil down the side of the pan, if needed to prevent sticking. Don't worry if the vegetables brown a bit; they will be tasty. If using chard, add it now and toss to wilt, about 30 seconds. Spread the vegetables on a platter to cool.

At this point, all the stew ingredients may be sealed and refrigerated overnight. Let come to room temperature before you begin the final cooking.

7. About 20 minutes before serving, spread the stir-fried vegetables in the bottom of a 2- to 3-quart Chinese sandpot or other heavy casserole. Scatter the beef on top. Stir the sauce and add it to the pot. Cover and bring to a simmer over moderate heat. Simmer gently until the meat is heated through, 8 to 10 minutes. Fold in the asparagus or broccoli and half the package of enoki mushrooms during the final minute of cooking.

8. Serve in warm bowls of contrasting color. Garnish each with a straight-standing cluster of enoki and a thick flurry of scallion rings.

MENU SUGGESTIONS: Wok-Seared New Potatoes (page 424) would be excellent with the stew, as would simply boiled new potatoes in their jackets or steamed rice.

SPICY BEEF SALAD WITH CRISPY RICE STICKS AND FRIED PEANUTS

SERVES 4 AS A GENEROUS MAIN COURSE, 6 TO 8 AS AN APPETIZER

Every once in a while I eat a dish that delights me in a Thai or Vietnamese restaurant and return to the China Moon kitchen to make a Chinese variation on the theme. Here is one such amalgam, a very light and delicious beef salad, full of compelling textures and pretty colors.

There is a lot of fuss to this dish, but most of the preparation can be done a day ahead. The beef should be cooked only an hour or so before serving for the plushest texture, but its taste will not fade if you want to hold it longer.

1 pound trimmed flank steak,
    all fat and tough sinew
    removed

MARINADE:
2 tablespoons soy sauce
2 tablespoons mushroom soy
    sauce
1½ tablespoons cornstarch
2 tablespoons packed brown
    sugar
2 tablespoons China Moon
    Chili-Orange Oil (page 15)
1 tablespoon plus 2 teaspoons
    "goop" from China Moon
    Chili-Orange Oil

VINAIGRETTE:
2 tablespoons China Moon
    Chili-Orange Oil (page 15)
    or China Moon Chili-Lemon
    Oil (page 12)
3 tablespoons rice bran, corn, or
    peanut oil
⅓ cup Five-Flavor Oil (page 13)
½ teaspoon Cayenne Pepper Oil
    (page 11)
1 tablespoon sugar
¼ teaspoon Roasted Szechwan
    Pepper-Salt (page 5)
¼ cup juice from China Moon
    Pickled Ginger (page 8)
¼ cup balsamic vinegar

2 to 3 cups corn or peanut oil,
    for velveting the beef

SALAD INGREDIENTS:
4 cups lightly packed ¼-inch-
    wide spinach ribbons
4 cups lightly packed ¼-inch-
    wide radicchio ribbons
½ cup lightly packed purple or
    green basil leaves, julienned
½ cup lightly packed fresh mint
    leaves, julienned
2 cups very thinly sliced
    shiitake mushroom caps
1 package enoki mushrooms,
    spongy base removed
½ cup thinly sliced green and
    white scallion rings
½ cup 1-inch-long Chinese or
    Western chives
½ cup fried or roasted Peanuts
    (page 34)
Crispy Rice Sticks (page 31)

1. Cut the beef lengthwise (with the grain) into several long strips about 2 inches wide. Holding your knife at a sharp angle to the board, cut each strip crosswise into broad ribbons ⅛ inch thick.

2. Blend the marinade ingredients in a bowl big enough to hold the beef. Add the beef and toss to coat each slice. Seal airtight and marinate at cool room temperature for 3 to 4 hours, or refrigerate overnight. Let come to room temperature before cooking; re-toss to separate the slices.

THE ORGANIC QUESTION

Politics aside, the question of organic versus commercial beef and pork is an interesting one. I think the only way it can be answered is to do taste tests of the sort we frequently do in the restaurant, purchasing similar cuts of meat from different purveyors and cooking them in exactly the same manner in order to judge their flavors and texture.

With beef and lamb, as with most everything else, we've found that the issue of freshness is paramount. If you're faced with a piece of organic meat that has been frozen or stored improperly for too long, it is likely that it will be less tasty than a freshly slaughtered piece of commercial meat.

Given equal freshness, at the restaurant we favor organic meat in simple preparations such as a wok-seared beef tenderloin. However, once the meat is sliced and marinated Chinese-style, in soy sauce, rice wine, and aromatics, any difference in flavor and texture is indiscernible.

3. Combine all of the vinaigrette ingredients through the balsamic vinegar and whisk until emulsified. To this point, everything including the vegetable cutting may be done a day ahead. Seal and refrigerate the ingredients; bring to room temperature before using.

4. Shortly before serving (or up to several hours in advance, if more convenient), velvet the beef: In a wok or deep heavy skillet, add oil to a depth of 1 inch. Rest a deep-fry thermometer on the rim. Heat over moderate heat to 350°F, when a ribbon of beef will bubble gently. Slide the beef into the oil and stir with chopsticks or a wok shovel to separate the shreds, until the meat is 90 percent gray on the outside, 15 to 20 seconds. Remove immediately and drain in a heatproof colander or in a large Chinese mesh or slotted spoon set on top of a heatproof bowl. Spread the drained beef on a tray to cool until warm. Let the oil stand until cool, then strain it through several layers of cheesecloth; bottle and refrigerate it for future stir-frying or frying.

5. Just before serving, in a large bowl, toss together the beef, spinach, radicchio, basil, mint, mushrooms, scallions, chives, peanuts, and three-quarters of the rice sticks. Whisk the vinaigrette to recombine. Drizzle it over the salad and toss gently to combine.

6. Loosely mound the salad on individual plates or a platter that will set off the red radicchio and deep greens. Add a note of whimsy with a crown of the remaining rice sticks.

MENU SUGGESTIONS: This is an ideal one-dish lunch or light dinner. If you want another dish to accompany it, Buddha Buns (page 372), Cold Poached Salmon Tiles with Ginger–Black Bean Vinaigrette (page 183), or a bowl of chicken dumplings (page 352) would all be great.

PEPPERED LOIN OF LAMB

SERVES 4 TO 6 AS A MAIN COURSE,
8 TO 12 AS PART OF A MULTICOURSE MEAL

If you love pepper, you'll love this loin! It has the sweetness of hoisin and orange to offset the heat, but the pepper is definitely the star.

If you are somewhat shy about pepper, you can scrape it off after searing, leaving only the flavor-print behind. It will still be quite tasty, but perhaps a bit more refined.

2 small boneless lamb loins in 1
    piece, about 2½ pounds
    trimmed

MARINADE:
¾ cup hoisin sauce
1 tablespoon Chinese rice wine
    or dry sherry
1 tablespoon China Moon Hot
    Chili Oil (page 10) or China
    Moon Chili-Orange Oil
    (page 15)
¼ to ½ teaspoon China Moon
    Ten-Spice (page 6)
1 tablespoon juice squeezed from
    finely minced fresh ginger
3 tablespoons coarsely chopped
    coriander leaves and stems
Finely minced or grated zest of
    ½ small scrubbed orange
¼ cup thinly sliced green and
    white scallion rings
3 large cloves garlic,
    smashed

LAMB COATING:
¼ cup plus 2 tablespoons
    Szechwan peppercorns
½ cup fragrant black
    peppercorns, such as
    Tellicherry or Malabar
2 tablespoons white peppercorns
2 tablespoons fennel seeds

1 to 2 tablespoons corn or
    peanut oil, for searing

PEPPERCORNS
WITH PIZZAZZ!

Like coffee beans, black peppercorns differ greatly in taste and aroma from type to type. Again like coffee beans, cheap usually means bitter and acrid. In recipes like this one where peppercorns play such a major role, I like a mix of "floral" black peppercorns, such as Malabar and Telli-cherry. Shop for them in any reputable spice store or order from my San Francisco source, Freed, Teller & Freed (415) 673-0922.

1. With a sharp boning knife or other sharp, slender blade, separate the 2 thin tenderloins from the sides of the 2 larger loin pieces. Separate the two main loin halves, if the butcher has not done this for you. You will have 4 pieces of meat. Carefully trim away all fat, tendon, and tough, silvery skin.

2. Combine the marinade ingredients in a shallow dish just large enough to hold the lamb snugly. Add the lamb and massage the marinade into the meat. Seal airtight and marinate in the refrigerator for 24 to 48 hours, turning occasionally. The longer the meat marinates, the fuller its flavor will be. Let the lamb come to room temperature before proceeding.

3. Prepare the lamb coating: Heat a small heavy skillet over moderate heat until hot enough to foam a bead of water. Add the coating ingredients and stir gently until the Szechwan peppercorns crackle and become fully fragrant, 4 to 5 minutes, adjusting the heat so they toast without scorching. Expect the Szechwan peppercorns to smoke; do not let them burn. Crush the hot spices in a mortar and pestle until the black and white peppercorns are coarse. Or, grind the spices coarsely in a spice grinder. Seal the mixture until ready to use.

4. Preheat the oven to 400°F. Position a rack in the center of the oven.

5. Remove the lamb from the marinade, wiping off excess marinade with your fingers. Spread the pepper coating on a plate or baking sheet. Press the lamb pieces into the spices, coating thoroughly on all sides.

6. Heat a large heavy skillet over high heat until hot enough to evaporate a bead of water on contact. Add 1 tablespoon of the oil and swirl to glaze the pan. Heat until nearly smoking. Add the lamb in a single layer with room between the pieces. Sear the lamb to golden brown on all sides, 1 to 2 minutes per side. If the pan is not large enough to brown all of the lamb at once, clean the pan midway and drizzle in more oil. Remove the lamb to a rack set over a roasting pan.

7. Roast until an instant-read meat thermometer registers 115°F in the thickest part of each piece, 6 to 7 minutes for larger pieces, 3 to 4 minutes for the smaller pieces. Promptly remove the lamb to a cooling rack.

8. Serve the lamb freshly roasted, tepid, or at room temperature, thinly sliced against the grain. If you are serving it hot from the oven, allow the lamb to sit undisturbed for about 10 minutes so the juices gel a bit before slicing. For broad and pretty slices, use a very sharp, thin blade and slice it at an angle to the board.

TENDER LAMB LOIN

The tastiest lamb loins come from small spring lambs, ideally ones raised locally and shipped fresh. The big guys are tougher and less sweet.

Ask your butcher to know what you're buying.

MENU SUGGESTIONS: The hot lamb is excellent served with stir-fried Chinese broccoli or a mélange of seasonal vegetables, and either Wok-Seared New Potatoes (page 424) or potatoes mashed or boiled in their jackets. It could also be tossed into a dish of pasta with greens and fresh herbs.

At room temperature, we typically stuff the lamb into a Sesame-Encrusted Flatbread (page 379) that's been brushed generously with Hoisin Garlic Sauce (page 355) and sprinkled with scallions, or serve it as part of an antipasto plate with a green salad and Dragon Noodles (page 391) and a dip dish of one of our mustard sauces (page 21). A warm potato salad would also set it off well.

STIR-FRIED LAMB WITH EGGPLANT, MUSHROOMS, AND LEEKS

SERVES 3 TO 4 AS A MAIN COURSE, 5 TO 6 AS PART OF A MULTICOURSE MEAL

Lamb plays a feature role in only Northern Chinese cooking, where from ancient times it has been cooked with generous amounts of garlic, leeks, ginger, vinegar, and wine—all of these the medicinally and culinarily correct high *yang* notes to balance the cool, low *yin* note of the lamb. Pairing the meat with sweet Chinese eggplant is a part of China Moon (as opposed to Chinese) tradition; I find the match to be quite seductive.

This is a wintry dish that makes for a warming supper. Preparations can be done up to a day in advance. The last-minute stir-frying is fast.

MARINADE AND
LAMB:
2 tablespoons soy sauce
2 tablespoons Chinese rice wine
or dry sherry
1 tablespoon cornstarch
1 tablespoon packed brown
sugar
½ teaspoon finely minced fresh
ginger
1 teaspoon finely minced garlic
1 tablespoon China Moon Hot
Chili Oil (page 10) or China
Moon Chili-Orange Oil
(page 15)
1 tablespoon "goop" from China
Moon Hot Chili Oil or Chili-
Orange Oil
¾ pound trimmed loin of lamb,
cut against the grain into
slender ribbons ⅛ inch thick

AROMATICS:
1 tablespoon finely minced fresh
ginger
1 tablespoon finely minced
garlic
2 tablespoons thinly sliced green
and white scallion rings

SAUCE:
1½ cups China Moon Infusion
(page 72), China Moon
Double Stock (page 72), or
unsalted chicken stock
2½ tablespoons Chinese rice
wine or dry sherry
2½ tablespoons mushroom soy
sauce
1½ teaspoons sugar
1 tablespoon balsamic vinegar
1 tablespoon cider vinegar
¼ teaspoon Chinese chili
sauce

⅔ cup baby turnips, halved or
quartered if large, a bit of
their green stem left on
1 cup red pearl onions
2 to 3 cups corn or peanut oil,
for velveting and stir-frying
1 small red bell pepper, cut into
¾-inch squares
1 leek, white part only, split
lengthwise and cut crosswise
into ¼-inch moons
1 Chinese or Japanese eggplant,
cut into ¼-inch coins
6 ounces wild mushrooms,
trimmed and cut, if large
2 packed cups wide ribbons of
ruby chard
2 teaspoons cornstarch dissolved
in 1½ tablespoons cold stock
or water
Diagonally sliced green and
white scallion rings, for
garnish

1. Blend the marinade ingredients through the "goop"
in a bowl big enough to hold the lamb. Add the lamb and toss
to coat each slice. Seal and marinate at cool room temperature
for 3 to 4 hours, or refrigerate overnight. Let come to room
temperature before cooking; re-toss to separate the shreds.

2. Combine the aromatics in a small dish and seal until ready to use.

3. Combine all of the sauce ingredients in a small bowl. Stir to blend, leaving the spoon in the bowl.

4. In a small saucepan filled with rapidly boiling un-salted water, blanch the turnips until tender, 1 to 2 minutes. Immerse the turnips in ice water to chill; drain. Return the water to a boil and blanch the onions for 1 minute to loosen the skins. Drain, immerse in ice water, drain again. Trim, skin, and cut in half through the stem end. To this point, everything including the vegetable cutting can be done a night ahead. Seal and refrigerate the ingredi-ents; bring to room temperature before cooking.

5. About 20 minutes before serving, velvet the lamb: Heat a wok or deep heavy skillet over high heat until hot enough to evaporate a bead of water on contact. Add oil to a depth of 1 inch. Rest a deep-fry thermometer on the rim. Reduce the heat to medium and bring the oil to 350°F, hot enough to bubble a ribbon of lamb. Gently slide the lamb into the oil and swish with chopsticks to separate the shreds. Cook until the meat is 90 percent gray on the outside, about 15 seconds. Immediately scoop the meat from the oil with a large Chinese mesh spoon; rest the spoon on a bowl to drain. The meat will be only half-cooked. (Alternatively, you can work with 2 mesh spoons: Hold 1 above the pot to receive the meat while you scoop in small batches with the other spoon.) Carefully drain all but 2 tablespoons of the oil from the pan.

Once cool, the oil can be filtered through a fine sieve lined with several layers of dry cheesecloth. Bottle and refrig-erate for future frying and stir-frying.

6. Return the wok or skillet to high heat until the oil is hot enough to foam a scallion ring. Reduce the heat to moder-ate and add the aromatics. Stir gently until fully fragrant, 20 to 30 seconds, adjusting the heat so they foam without brown-ing. Add the onions and bell pepper, and toss until slightly softened, 2 minutes. Add the leek and eggplant, and toss 2 minutes more. Add the mushrooms and toss until hot, about 1 minute. Adjust the heat to maintain a merry sizzle and drizzle a bit more oil down the side of the pan, if needed to prevent sticking. Don't worry if the vegetables brown a bit; they will be tasty. Add the chard and toss to combine.

7. Stir the sauce and add it to the pan. Raise the heat to high, cover the pan, and bring the sauce to a simmer. When the sauce simmers, stir the cornstarch mixture to recombine and add it to the pan. Stir until the sauce turns glossy and slightly thick, 10 to 20 seconds. Add the lamb and turnips, and stir gently to cook the meat through, about 10 seconds.

8. Serve immediately on heated plates of contrasting color. Garnish with a thick sprinkling of the scallion rings.

MENU SUGGESTIONS: I love this stir-fry as a topping for a Pot-Browned Noodle Pillow (page 401) or a Broad Noodle Pillow (page 403), though you might also pair it with rice or Wok-Seared New Potatoes (page 424). If you would like a soup course to precede, I'd choose something light and pretty like Eggroll-Cartwheel Soup (page 87).

STIR-FRIED SPICY LAMB WITH HOISIN AND SPRING BEANS

SERVES 3 TO 4 AS A MAIN COURSE, 5 TO 6 AS PART OF A MULTICOURSE MEAL

There is a moment in spring when the marketplace bursts open and there is a sudden plethora of beans and peas. This is a dish we put on the menu to celebrate. A pretty mix of lamb ribbons and slender beans, it mates hoisin's sweet duskiness with the pow of fresh chilis.

All the preparation can be done in advance and the final dish cooked within minutes. If you're hungry and ready to go, and willing to sacrifice the extra flavor depth to be gained in marinating the meat ahead, the whole dish can be turned out in less than an hour.

NO CHINESE LONG BEANS?

It seems a travesty not to include Chinese long beans in a bean-filled recipe in a mostly Chinese cookbook! The reason they have been excluded is that we almost never find tender ones in our market; regrettably, most of our farmers grow the Chinese equivalent of the Kentucky Wonder bean—wondrous for only its toughness. If your luck is better than mine, by all means include tender Chinese long beans here and everywhere! Cut them into finger lengths and enjoy for me.

*MARINADE AND
LAMB:*
2 tablespoons soy sauce
2 tablespoons Chinese rice wine
  or dry sherry
1 tablespoon cornstarch
1 tablespoon packed brown
  sugar
1½ teaspoons finely minced
  garlic
1 tablespoon China Moon Hot
  Chili Oil (page 10) or China
  Moon Chili-Orange Oil
  (page 15)
1 tablespoon "goop" from China
  Moon Hot Chili Oil or Chili-
  Orange Oil
¾ pound loin of lamb, cut
  against the grain into slender
  ribbons ⅛ inch thick

AROMATICS:
2 tablespoons finely minced
  fresh ginger
1 tablespoon finely minced
  garlic
¼ cup thinly sliced green and
  white scallion rings
1 red Fresno chili, finely minced
Finely minced zest of 1 small
  scrubbed orange

SAUCE:
1½ cups China Moon Infusion
  (page 72), China Moon
  Double Stock (page 72), or
  unsalted chicken stock

2 tablespoons soy sauce
2 tablespoons Chinese rice wine
  or dry sherry
¼ cup hoisin sauce
2 tablespoons unseasoned
  Japanese rice vinegar
2 tablespoons freshly squeezed
  orange juice

6 to 8 round French market
  carrots or 10 to 12 baby
  carrots, halved or quartered
  lengthwise, if fat
¼ pound mixed tender string
  beans, such as yellow wax or
  Blue Lake green beans,
  tipped and halved, if long
3 ounces sugar snap peas,
  tipped and strung, or ½ cup
  fresh peas
2 to 3 cups corn or peanut oil,
  for velveting and stir-frying
1 small red onion, cut into
  ½-inch squares
1 small red bell pepper,
  julienned
1 small leek, white part only,
  slit lengthwise and cut
  crosswise into ¼-inch moons
2 teaspoons cornstarch dissolved
  in 1½ tablespoons cold stock
  or water
Diagonally sliced green and
  white scallion rings, for
  garnish

CLEAN LEEKS

*Leeks love grit and people
love work, so a lot of us
cleans leeks before cutting
them. Try this easier way:
Cut the leeks first, then rinse
them. You'll add 5 minutes of
leisure to your life.*

1. Blend the marinade ingredients through the "goop" in a bowl big enough to hold the lamb. Add the lamb and toss to coat each slice. Seal airtight and marinate at cool room temperature for 3 to 4 hours, or refrigerate overnight. Let come to room temperature before cooking; re-toss to separate the shreds.

2. Combine the aromatics in a small dish and seal until ready to use.

3. Combine all of the sauce ingredients through the orange juice in a small bowl. Stir to blend, leaving the spoon in the bowl.

4. In a large saucepan filled with rapidly boiling water, blanch the carrots until half-cooked, 30 seconds to 1 minute. Immerse the carrots in ice water to chill; drain well. Return the water to a boil and blanch the beans until tender-crisp, about 30 seconds. Immerse the beans in ice water to chill; drain well. Blanch the snap peas or peas until tender-crisp, 10 to 30 seconds for peas, up to 1 minute for snap peas. Refresh in ice water; drain. Up to this point, all the preparation, including the vegetable cutting, can be done a night ahead. Seal and refrigerate the ingredients; let come to room temperature before cooking.

5. About 20 minutes before serving, velvet the lamb following step 5 on page 278.

6. Return the wok or skillet to high heat until the oil is hot enough to foam a scallion ring. Reduce the heat to moderate and add the aromatics. Stir gently until fully fragrant, 20 to 30 seconds, adjusting the heat so they foam without browning. Add the onion and toss until slightly softened, 2 minutes. Add the bell pepper and leeks, and toss for 2 minutes. Add the carrots and toss until hot, about 1 minute.

7. Stir the sauce and add it to the pan. Raise the heat to high, cover the pan, and bring the sauce to a simmer. When the sauce simmers, stir the cornstarch mixture to recombine, add it to the pan, and stir until the sauce turns glossy and slightly thick, 10 to 20 seconds. Add the beans and peas, and toss gently to mix. Add the lamb and stir to cook through, about 10 seconds.

8. Serve immediately on heated plates of contrasting color. Garnish with a scattering of the scallion diags.

MENU SUGGESTIONS: You could plop this dish nicely atop a Pot-Browned Noodle Pillow (page 401) or alongside a mound of steamed or stir-fried rice. Boiled new potatoes in their jackets would also be a wonderful accompaniment, as would a salad of baby greens dressed with our Orange Vinaigrette (page 25).

PEPPERY LAMB SAUSAGE

MAKES 10 TO 12 SMALL SAUSAGES, A SIMILAR NUMBER OF
SMALL PATTIES, OR ABOUT 2 DOZEN TINY MEATBALLS,
ENOUGH TO SERVE 4 TO 6 AS PART OF AN ANTIPASTO

*S*ausage mixtures like this very tasty lamb version
are exceedingly simple to make. Stuffing them
takes a bit of skill, but it is really a wonderful thing
to try if you have never done it and are feeling gutsy.
Otherwise, the mixture can be shaped into small patties
or tiny meatballs and pan-fried.

The mixture gains nicely in flavor if prepared in
advance. Sausages are best left to cure overnight before
cooking, but patties may be fried up at once.

3 to 4 yards sheep casings, for
   filling sausages
1½ teaspoons finely minced
   fresh ginger
1½ teaspoons finely minced
   garlic
2 tablespoons finely chopped
   coriander leaves and stems
2 tablespoons finely chopped
   Chinese chives
2 tablespoons thinly sliced green
   and white scallion rings
½ teaspoon kosher salt
⅛ teaspoon freshly ground black
   pepper
¼ teaspoon Szechwan
   peppercorn powder

1 tablespoon soy sauce
2 teaspoons Chinese rice wine
   or dry sherry
1 teaspoon Chinese chili sauce
1 pound coarsely ground lamb

1 tablespoon corn or peanut oil
   for sausages, or 2 to 4
   tablespoons for patties or
   meatballs
Diagonally sliced green and
   white scallion rings, for
   garnish
Tiny red bell pepper dice, for
   garnish

CASINGS WORTH HUNTING FOR

*I vastly prefer the slender,
thin sheep casings to hog
casings. Go out of your way
to find them; call a specialty
meat distributor if your
butcher looks at you
cross-eyed.*

To make sausage links:

1. Soak the casings in cool water for 30 to 60 minutes.
Rinse by slipping the end over the faucet and running cool
water through the casings. Cut into manageable 2- or 3-foot
lengths. Cut off and discard any portions with holes.

2. Combine all of the ingredients through the chili sauce
in a large bowl. Add the lamb and stir in one direction until

SZECHWAN PEPPERCORN POWDER

To make this potent ingredient at home, simply stir a tablespoon or so of Szechwan peppercorns in a dry skillet over moderate heat, until they are fragrant and smoking, about 5 minutes; do not let them scorch. Pulverize the peppercorns to a powder with a mortar and pestle or in a spice grinder, then pass the mixture through a fine-mesh sieve to remove the husks.

Any leftovers can be kept and used judiciously in future dishes, though our habit is to make only as much as we need at any one time.

well blended. For easier stuffing and to develop the flavors, chill the mixture, preferably overnight.

3. To stuff the sausages, attach the stuffing horn to a meat grinder. Slip all but 2 to 3 inches of the casing over the horn. Make a knot at the end. Feed the mixture into the casings, pausing occasionally to mold the sausages; underfill the casings to prevent bursting. Knot the end, then knot, tie, or reverse-twist into 4-inch links. Repeat until all of the sausage mixture is used. Ripen the links, uncovered, in the refrigerator overnight. Suspend them from the racks for a bit of drama, or spread them in a single layer on a baking sheet.

4. Prick the sausages at several points along each link. Poach gently in a large shallow pan filled with simmering water for 5 minutes. Drain, then cool in a single layer on a baking sheet. (If you are working in advance, the sausages can be refrigerated at this point for 1 to 2 days.) Let the sausages come to room temperature before searing. Separate them into individual links.

5. Shortly before serving, heat a wok or large heavy skillet over high heat until hot enough to evaporate a bead of water on contact. Add 1½ teaspoons of the oil, swirl to glaze the pan, and heat until nearly smoking. Reduce the heat to moderate. Add half of the sausages and sear, turning, until golden brown, about 4 minutes. Remove the sausages to a paper towel–lined baking sheet to drain. Repeat with the remaining sausages, cleaning the pan, if necessary, and drizzling in more oil.

6. Serve immediately. Cut the sausages diagonally into thick slices, and garnish with the scallion and bell dice.

To make patties or meatballs:

1. Combine all the ingredients following step 2 of the instructions for sausage links. Shape small oval patties, using ¼ to ⅓ cup of the lamb mixture for each one. Or, shape into tiny meatballs 1 inch in diameter.

2. To cook, heat a large heavy skillet over high heat until hot enough to evaporate a bead of water on contact. Add 1 tablespoon oil and swirl to glaze the pan. When the oil is hot enough to sizzle a bit of meat, add the patties or meatballs. Leave room in between each and work from the outside of the pan to the center (where it is hottest).

3. Cook on each side until nicely browned, adjusting the heat so the meat sizzles merrily without scorching and drizzling a bit more oil down the side of the pan, if needed to prevent sticking. Do not overcook. Patties will take 3 to 4 minutes to cook, meatballs a touch longer. Remove to paper towels to drain. Wipe the pan, reheat, and re-oil between batches.

4. Serve the patties or meatballs promptly. Garnish with the scallion rings and bell pepper confetti.

MENU SUGGESTIONS: The sausage goes beautifully with either of our mustard sauces (page 21). As part of an antipasto plate, we like it with either Pan-Fried Scallion-Chive Breads (page 382), Wok-Seared New Potatoes (page 424), or one of our citrus-inclined cold noodle dishes. Ginger-Pickled Red Cabbage Slaw (page 61) would complete the plate prettily.

LAMB STEW SANDPOT WITH WILD MUSHROOMS AND PEARL ONIONS

SERVES 4 AS A MAIN COURSE, 6 AS PART OF A MULTICOURSE MEAL

I especially like meat dishes that are richly flavored yet light, so I especially like this dish! Drawing on the textures of wild mushrooms and pearl onions to make its statement, it is a good choice at any time of year.

The lamb needs a full hour or so to come to tenderness in the sauce, so you might like to cook it, without the vegetables, a day in advance. The final stewing with the vegetables takes only minutes.

ABOUT ORANGE ZEST

The addition of fresh orange zest to the aromatics truly enhances Chinese stir-fries and stews, but only if you first wash the fruit. Even homegrown citrus comes with a coating of pollution-born residue, so it will make a huge flavor difference if the outside of the fruit is cleaned with care. We use a mildly abrasive scrubber and a weak solution of liquid detergent. It sounds a bit nutty, but the difference is pronounced!

When pairing off the zest, take only the orange part; the white pith is very bitter.

Mincing the zest is always preferable to grating it when adding to aromatics in a stir-fry. The drier, coarser mince infuses better in the oil, with less risk of burning or clumping.

MARINADE AND LAMB:

1 tablespoon mushroom soy sauce
1 tablespoon soy sauce
1 tablespoon cornstarch
1 tablespoon packed brown sugar
1 tablespoon China Moon Chili-Orange Oil (page 15)
1 tablespoon "goop" from China Moon Chili-Orange Oil
1 pound lamb shoulder, cut into 1-inch cubes

AROMATICS:

1 tablespoon finely minced fresh ginger
1 tablespoon finely minced garlic
2 tablespoons thinly sliced green and white scallion rings
½ to ¾ teaspoon dried red chili flakes
Finely minced zest of ½ small scrubbed orange

SAUCE:

2 cups China Moon Infusion (page 72), China Moon Double Stock (page 72), or unsalted chicken stock
2 tablespoons mushroom soy sauce
⅓ cup Chinese rice wine or dry sherry
1 teaspoon packed brown sugar
1 tablespoon balsamic vinegar
1 tablespoon cider vinegar

3 to 4 tablespoons corn or peanut oil, for searing and stir-frying
1 rounded cup red pearl onions
8 to 10 French market carrots, halved or quartered, if fat, or 1 carrot, thickly julienned
1 large or 2 small Chinese or Japanese eggplants, cut into ½-inch cubes, skin left on
½ pound wild mushrooms, trimmed and cut, if large
3 fat scallions, cut into 1-inch nuggets
Fried Ginger Threads (page 29), for garnish
Fine green and white scallion julienne, for garnish

1. Combine the marinade ingredients through the "goop" in a bowl. Add the lamb and toss well to coat. Seal and set aside to marinate for 3 to 4 hours at cool room temperature, or refrigerate overnight. Bring to room temperature before searing. Re-toss to separate the cubes.

2. Combine the aromatics in a small dish, and seal until ready to use.

3. Combine the sauce ingredients through the cider vinegar in a small bowl. Stir to blend, leaving the spoon in the bowl.

4. Heat a wok or large heavy skillet over high heat until hot enough to evaporate a bead of water on contact. Add 1 tablespoon of the oil and swirl to glaze the pan. When the oil is nearly smoking, add the lamb in a single layer with room between the cubes, working from the outside of the pan to the center (where it's hottest). Brown the cubes well on all sides, 2 to 3 minutes, lowering the heat if needed to prevent scorching. Remove the lamb to paper towels to drain. If you are searing the meat in batches, wipe the pan clean, reheat, and re-oil it.

5. Return the lamb to a clean wok or a heavy saucepan to hold it snugly. Stir the sauce and add it to the pan. Cover the pan tightly and bring the sauce to a gentle simmer over moderate heat. Simmer until the meat is very tender, about 45 minutes. Lift the lid occasionally to stir the cubes and check that the liquid does not boil. Remove the meat in a single layer to a plate. Reserve the sauce; repeatedly skim the surface of grease as it cools.

6. Blanch the pearl onions in boiling water to cover for 1 minute. Refresh in ice water; drain. Trim, skin, and cut lengthwise through the root end, if large. Return the water to a boil and blanch the carrots until half-cooked, 30 seconds to 1 minute. Immerse in ice water to chill; drain.

7. Heat a wok or large heavy skillet over high heat until hot. Add 2 tablespoons of the oil and swirl to glaze the pan. When the oil is hot enough to foam a scallion ring, reduce the heat to moderate and add the aromatics. Stir gently until fully fragrant, 20 to 30 seconds, adjusting the heat so they foam without scorching. Add the onions, toss briskly 1 minute to sear, then add the carrots and toss for 1 minute more. Add the eggplant and toss for 2 minutes. Add the mushrooms and scallions, and toss until very hot, about 2 minutes more. Adjust the heat to maintain a merry sizzle and drizzle a bit more oil down the side of the pan, if needed to prevent sticking. Don't worry if the vegetables brown a bit; they will be flavorful. Spread the vegetables on a platter to cool.

To this point, all the above may be done a day in advance. Seal and refrigerate the ingredients; let come to room temperature before continuing.

8. About 20 minutes before serving, spread the vegetables in the bottom of a 2- to 3-quart

Chinese sandpot or other heavy casserole. Scatter the lamb on top. Stir the sauce and add it to the pot. Cover tightly and bring to a simmer over moderate heat. Simmer until the meat heats through, 8 to 10 minutes.

9. Serve in warm bowls of contrasting color. Garnish with a sprinkling of the ginger threads and the scallion julienne.

MENU SUGGESTIONS: I love potatoes with this dish— boiled little new potatoes in their jackets or Wok-Seared New Potatoes (page 424). Steamed or fried rice would also be good, as would thick slices of garlic bread or fettuccine dressed lightly with oil and a sprinkling of fresh herbs. A plate of sautéed greens or a green salad with some sprigs of cress or radicchio would be a nice counterpoint to the brownness of the casserole.

LAMB SAUSAGE SANDPOT

SERVES 4 AS A MAIN COURSE,
6 AS PART OF A MULTICOURSE MEAL

Peppery Lamb Sausage—in casings or in the form of patties or meatballs—can be tucked quite neatly into a savory sandpot casserole. This one is keyed to winter with its array of hearty vegetables, but you might make it in other seasons with whatever the market provides.

Once the sausage is made, this casserole can be assembled and cooked in under an hour.

Peppery Lamb Sausage, shaped
into links or meatballs and
cooked but not garnished
(page 282)

AROMATICS:

1 tablespoon finely minced fresh
ginger
1½ tablespoons finely minced
garlic
3 tablespoons thinly sliced green
and white scallion rings
Finely minced zest of ½ small
scrubbed orange

SAUCE:

1½ cups China Moon Infusion
(page 72), China Moon
Double Stock (page 72), or
unsalted chicken stock
3 tablespoons mushroom soy
sauce
½ teaspoon Chinese chili sauce
1 tablespoon unseasoned
Japanese rice vinegar
1 tablespoon sherry vinegar

1 carrot, cut into a thick
julienne
2 cups packed wide ribbons of
Napa cabbage or 2½ cups
finger lengths of Chinese
broccoli
2 to 3 tablespoons corn or
peanut oil, for stir-frying
1 yellow onion, cut into ¼-inch
moons
1 leek, white part only, cut
lengthwise then crosswise
into ¼-inch moons
4 to 6 large shiitake mushrooms
caps, cut into thick wedges
1 cup domestic mushrooms,
halved or quartered, if large
2 cups packed wide ribbons of
ruby chard
1 package enoki mushrooms,
spongy base removed
Green and white scallion
julienne, for garnish

WHAT'S YOUR PROVINCE?

People interested in Chinese cooking often ask me what style of Chinese cooking it is that we do at the restaurant—Cantonese, Hunanese, Szechwanese, whatever.

Our food is an amalgam. Mostly, the flavors belong to the culinary wheel of northern and central China—the big tastes of ginger, garlic, chili, and pepper—with a good dose of Shanghai vinegar and sweetness thrown in. However, the style is a lighter one that eschews a lot of oil, and in this way maybe our food is tipped a bit to the south.

When I'm really pressed for an answer, I reply very seriously. I say that China Moon food is eclectic northern and central Chinese home-style cooking from the province of San Francisco. This seems to set everyone straight.

1. Cut the lamb sausage into thick diagonal slices. Leave the meatballs whole.

2. Combine the aromatics in a small dish, and seal until ready to use.

3. Combine all of the sauce ingredients through the sherry vinegar in a small bowl. Stir to blend, leaving the spoon in the bowl.

4. In a large saucepan of boiling water, blanch the carrots for 10 seconds. Immerse in ice water to chill; drain. If using Chinese broccoli, blanch until tender-crisp, about 1 minute. Refresh in ice water; drain.

5. Heat a wok or large heavy skillet over high heat until hot enough to evaporate a bead of water on contact. Add 2 tablespoons of the oil and swirl to glaze the pan. When the oil is hot enough to foam a scallion ring, reduce the heat to moderate. Add the aromatics and stir gently until fully fragrant, 20 to 30 seconds, adjusting the heat so they foam

without browning. Add the onion and toss briskly for 1 minute. Add the leek and toss for 2 minutes more. Add the carrots and toss for 30 seconds, then add the shiitake and domestic mushrooms and toss until very hot, about 2 minutes. Adjust the heat to maintain a merry sizzle and drizzle a bit more oil down the side of the pan, if needed to prevent sticking. Don't worry if the vegetables brown a bit; they will be tasty. Add the chard and Napa cabbage (if using); toss briefly, just to wilt. Spread the mixture on a platter to cool.

To this point, all the above may be done a day in advance. Seal and refrigerate the ingredients; let come to room temperature before serving.

6. About 20 minutes before serving, spread the vegetables in the bottom of a 2- to 3-quart Chinese sandpot or other heavy casserole. Scatter the sausage slices or meatballs on top. Stir the sauce and add it to the pot. Cover and bring to a simmer over moderate heat. Simmer gently until the meat is heated through, 8 to 10 minutes. Scatter half the enoki in the pot during the last minute of cooking.

7. Serve in heated bowls of contrasting color. Garnish with a jaunty sprig of the remaining enoki, standing upright and ringed by a curlicue of scallion julienne.

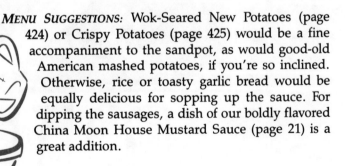

MENU SUGGESTIONS: Wok-Seared New Potatoes (page 424) or Crispy Potatoes (page 425) would be a fine accompaniment to the sandpot, as would good-old American mashed potatoes, if you're so inclined. Otherwise, rice or toasty garlic bread would be equally delicious for sopping up the sauce. For dipping the sausages, a dish of our boldly flavored China Moon House Mustard Sauce (page 21) is a great addition.

OVEN-BAKED SPARERIBS • SWEET AND SOUR MEATBALLS

SWEET AND SOUR MEATBALLS • OVEN-BAKED SPARERIBS

PORK

CONTENTS

Pork is not only the featured red meat in the traditional Chinese kitchen, it is symbolically central to the entire culture. The skin of a beautiful woman was likened to cool pork fat by Chinese poets, ritually slaughtered pigs figured historically in the propitiation of heavenly deities, and on into modern times whole roasted pigs are a fixture at almost every Chinese celebration. Indeed, the pig is so much at the heart of the Chinese scene that the character for "home" (carrying with it the additional meaning of "family") shows a pig and a woman under a roof. How's that for a model on which to build a household?

Having been raised in a Jewish home, not only without a pig but with a prohibition against them, eating pork came to me rather slowly. Alternately fearful that a thunderbolt would come through the window to strike me and attracted to what was forbidden, as a child I took a few tentative nibbles on bacon and cold ham from the deli; that was the extent of my experience with pork. Occasional pecks at Chinese-American fried rice and gnawings on sweet spareribs rounded out my knowledge as a young adult.

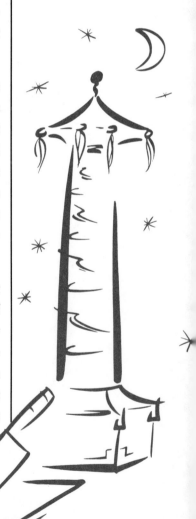

I was in for a shock upon arriving in Taiwan to discover pork on every table in its many superb forms, hardly any of them sweet and sour or lacquered with red food dye. My first year—still in the grip of a fashionably emotional vegetarianism cultivated in college—I feasted on "vegetarian ham" and various Buddhist-style gluten concoctions that mimicked the taste and texture of pork. This was excellent stuff, a feature of traditional Chinese eating that had been immortalized in vernacular novels (in which noble characters were revealed by the ordering of such a dish). Lured, however, from my lofty perch that summer by the scent of shrimp in a

Kyoto tempura bar, I returned to Taipei a fallen vegetarian with a hunger for real pork. I wasn't disappointed. Pork, as cooked in China, is a scrumptious affair.

In our China Moon kitchen, we continue the grand tradition of loving pork. While the demands of a constantly changing menu dictate that we rotate the different types of meat, pork is my unabashed favorite; pork fat is supremely clean and light-tasting, and the meat is wonderfully versatile.

Were I to have only one roof over my head and only one animal under it, the beast I would choose would be a pig. In that, I am very Chinese.

■ ■ ■

BLAH BLOSSOMS

⑥ The blossom tops of baby zucchini and pattypan squash turn limp and brown very quickly on account of their fragility. If they look unappealing, simply snap them off and discard them. There is no poetry to a soggy hat, be it on a human or a vegetable.

STIR-FRIED SPICY PORK RIBBONS WITH SUMMER BEANS AND BABY SQUASH

SERVES 2 TO 3 AS A MAIN COURSE,
4 TO 5 AS PART OF A MULTICOURSE MEAL

This is a celebratory summertime stir-fry, an ode to that orgiastic moment when tiny string beans, little squash with their blossoms intact, and baby corn hit the market in stunning array. Later in the season, you could fake it with corn niblets and bigger veggies, but if you can get the baby varieties, you can capture the moment with a great splash.

The pork will be most flavorful if marinated beforehand. The remaining preparations can also be done in advance, which leaves only the brief stir-frying for the last minute.

MARINADE AND
PORK:
1 tablespoon soy sauce
1 tablespoon mushroom soy
sauce
1 tablespoon Chinese rice wine
or dry sherry
1 tablespoon cornstarch
1 tablespoon packed brown
sugar
1 teaspoon finely minced garlic
1 tablespoon China Moon Chili-
Lemon Oil (page 12) or
China Moon Hot Chili Oil
(page 10)
¾ pound boneless pork loin, cut
against the grain into 2-inch
ribbons ⅛ inch thick

AROMATICS:
1 tablespoon finely minced
garlic
2 tablespoons finely minced
fresh ginger
2 tablespoons thinly sliced green
and white scallion rings
1 small red Fresno chili, finely
minced

SAUCE:
1½ cups China Moon Infusion
(page 72), China Moon
Double Stock (page 72), or
unsalted chicken stock

2 tablespoons soy sauce
1 tablespoon unseasoned
Japanese rice vinegar
1 tablespoon balsamic vinegar
1 teaspoon sugar
½ teaspoon Chinese chili sauce

6 to 10 ears fresh baby corn,
halved lengthwise if large, or
½ cup corn kernels
¼ pound tender string beans,
tipped and cut in half
crosswise if long
¼ pound baby green and/or
yellow squash with
blossoms, cut lengthwise in
half if fat
2 to 3 cups corn or peanut oil,
for velveting and stir-frying
1 small yellow onion, cut into
¼-inch moons
1 tablespoon whole tiny purple
or green basil leaves
8 pieces Oven-Dried Plum
Tomatoes (page 36)
1 tablespoon cornstarch
dissolved in 2 tablespoons
cold stock or water
Chiffonnade of purple or green
basil leaves, for garnish

1. In a bowl big enough to hold the pork, blend together all of the marinade ingredients through the chili oil. Add the pork and toss well. Seal and marinate 3 to 4 hours at cool room temperature or refrigerate overnight. Let the pork come to room temperature before cooking; re-toss to separate the slices.

2. Combine the aromatics in a small bowl and cover until ready to use.

3. Combine all of the sauce ingredients through the chili

if it is in a foam tray wrapped airtight in plastic. The packaging may be hygienic, but you're buying an older piece of meat.

Most important, fresh pork smells sweet. If the meat smells funny or rank, don't use it. If you bought it from a nearby store, return it promptly and raise a hullabaloo for the cause of fresh pork.

sauce in a small bowl. Stir to blend, leaving the spoon in the bowl.

4. In a generous amount of rapidly boiling water, separately blanch the baby corn, string beans, and squashes until half-cooked, 10 to 60 seconds depending on thickness. Plunge each vegetable upon blanching into ice water to chill, then drain well. All the above, including the vegetable cutting, can be done a full day ahead. Seal and refrigerate the ingredients; let come to room temperature before cooking.

5. About 20 minutes before serving, velvet the pork: Heat a wok or deep heavy skillet over high heat until a bead of water evaporates on contact. Add oil to a depth of 1 inch. Rest a deep-fry thermometer on the rim. Reduce the heat to medium and bring the oil to 350°F, hot enough to bubble a pork ribbon. Gently slide the pork into the oil and swish with chopsticks to separate the shreds. Cook until the meat is 90 percent gray on the outside, about 15 seconds. Immediately scoop the pork from the oil with a large Chinese mesh spoon; rest the spoon on a bowl to drain. The meat will be only half-cooked. (Alternatively, you can work with 2 mesh spoons: Hold one above the pot to receive the meat while you scoop in small batches using the other spoon.) Carefully drain all but 2 tablespoons of the oil from the pan.

Once cool, the oil can be filtered through a sieve lined with several layers of dry cheesecloth. Bottle and refrigerate for future frying and stir-frying.

6. Return the pan to high heat until hot enough to sizzle a scallion ring. Reduce the heat to moderate and add the aromatics. Stir until fully fragrant, 20 to 30 seconds, adjusting the heat so the aromatics foam without browning. Add the onion and toss briskly until golden, about 3 to 4 minutes, adjusting the heat to maintain a merry sizzle. Do not worry if the onions brown a bit; they will be tasty. Add the whole basil leaves and toss to mix. Add all of the blanched vegetables and toss until hot. Add the plum tomatoes and toss to combine.

7. Stir the sauce and add it to the pan. Raise the heat to high, cover the pan, and bring the sauce to a simmer. When the sauce simmers, stir the cornstarch mixture to recombine it and add it to the pan. Stir until the sauce turns glossy and slightly thick, 10 to 20 seconds. Add the pork and toss to combine and cook through, about 10 seconds.

8. Serve immediately. Garnish with a sprinkling of the basil chiffonnade.

MENU SUGGESTIONS: This is a splendid one-dish meal when served atop a Pot-Browned Noodle Pillow (page 401) or with rice. However, if the time is summer and you are wanting a grander spread, a dish of Turmeric Tomatoes (page 59) or a bowl of one of our hot and sour soups would be delicious alongside.

STIR-FRIED HOISIN PORK WITH TREE EARS, LEMON, AND TOMATOES

SERVES 2 TO 3 AS A MAIN COURSE
4 TO 5 AS PART OF A MULTICOURSE MEAL

This is a pretty, lemony dish for summer, with its tumble of red and yellow cherry or pear tomatoes and jade green cucumber.

Look for cucumbers that are seedless and unwaxed. Lemon cucumbers, Japanese cucumbers, Kirbys, or Armenians all have wonderful flavor in the warm months; in the cold months, the slimmer so-called English hydroponics will do.

All of the preparations can be done in advance, leaving only the brief cooking for the last minute.

TREE EAR BASICS

Tree ears are one of the most intriguing oddities of the Chinese kitchen. An ear-shaped fungus harvested from the forest, they range from coal-black to silver-white, from dime-size to Frisbee-size, and from beautifully thin and translucent to the texture of an old rubber tire. They are virtually tasteless but for a light smokiness, but the Chinese adore them and believe them to have a host of medicinal qualities, including the ability to quell high blood pressure. My idea of a grand retirement would be to write a thesis on tree ears!

I use the kind of small black tree ears found in plastic pouches in most all Chinese groceries. They always look puny and dusty in the bag, but will swell to about four times their size when soaked. For best flavor and texture, soak them in cold water. Use 2 cups water for every 2 tablespoons tree ears and soak until supple, about 20 minutes for the thin variety. After soaking, wash the tree ears in several changes of cold water to dislodge any grit and bits of the forest. Pluck off any woody knobs or weirdly gelatinous lumps. Tear larger tree ears into quarter-size pieces.

MARINADE AND PORK:

1 tablespoon soy sauce
1 tablespoon mushroom soy sauce
1 tablespoon Chinese rice wine or dry sherry
1 tablespoon cornstarch
1 tablespoon packed brown sugar
½ teaspoon finely minced garlic
1 tablespoon China Moon Chili-Lemon Oil (page 12)
¾ pound boneless pork loin, cut against the grain into 2-inch ribbons ⅛ inch thick

AROMATICS:

2 tablespoons finely minced fresh ginger
1 tablespoon finely minced garlic
3 tablespoons thinly sliced green and white scallion rings
2 teaspoons "goop" from China Moon Chili-Lemon Oil

SAUCE:

1½ cups China Moon Infusion (page 72), China Moon Double Stock (page 72), or unsalted chicken stock
1 tablespoon soy sauce
1 tablespoon mushroom soy sauce
1 tablespoon Serrano-Lemongrass Vinegar (page 19) or unseasoned Japanese rice vinegar
1 tablespoon freshly squeezed lemon juice
1 tablespoon Chinese rice wine or dry sherry
¼ cup hoisin sauce
1½ teaspoons sugar

2 tablespoons dried tree ears
¼ pound seedless cucumbers
2 to 3 cups corn or peanut oil, for velveting and stir-frying
1 small red onion, cut into ¼-inch moons
¼ pound shiitake mushroom caps, cut into wedges
½ pound spinach leaves
1 tablespoon cornstarch dissolved in 2 tablespoons cold stock or water
1 rounded cup cherry or pear tomatoes, halved if large, or 8 pieces Oven-Dried Plum Tomatoes (page 36)
Finely julienned peel of ½ small scrubbed lemon
Diagonally cut green and white scallion rings, for garnish

1. In a bowl big enough to hold the pork, blend together all of the marinade ingredients through the chili oil until smooth. Add the pork and toss well. Seal and marinate for 3 to 4 hours at cool room temperature or refrigerate overnight. Let come to room temperature before cooking; toss to separate the ribbons.

2. Combine the aromatics in a small bowl and seal until ready to use.

3. Combine all of the sauce ingredients through the sugar in a small bowl. Stir to blend, leaving the spoon in the bowl. All the preparation to this point, including the vegetable cutting, may be done a day ahead. Seal and refrigerate the ingredients; bring to room temperature before cooking.

4. Soak the tree ears as directed in Tree Ear Basics (page 296). Cover with cold water until use; drain before cooking.

5. Cut lemon cucumbers into wedges. Cut Japanese cucumbers or other seedless varieties into diagonal coins ⅛-inch thick. Halve and seed English cucumbers; cut each half crosswise into moons. Do not peel the cucumbers unless they are waxed.

6. About 20 minutes before serving, velvet the pork following step 5 on page 295.

7. Return the wok or skillet to high heat until hot enough to sizzle a scallion ring. Reduce the heat to moderate and add the aromatics. Stir gently until fully fragrant, 20 to 30 seconds, adjusting the heat so they foam without browning. Add the onion and toss briskly until slightly softened, about 2 minutes. Add the shiitake and the drained tree ears, and toss until hot, 1 to 2 minutes. Adjust the heat to maintain a merry sizzle and drizzle a bit more oil down the side of the pan, if needed to prevent sticking. Add the spinach and the oven-dried plum tomatoes if using them; toss gently to mix.

8. Stir the sauce and add it to the pan. Raise the heat to high, cover the pan, and bring the sauce to a simmer. When the sauce simmers, stir the cornstarch mixture to recombine and add it to the pan. Stir until the sauce turns glossy and slightly thick, 10 to 20 seconds. Fold in the cherry tomatoes, lemon julienne, and pork ribbons, and toss gently until the pork is cooked through, about 10 seconds.

9. Serve immediately on heated plates or a platter of contrasting color. Garnish with a flurry of scallion rings.

MENU SUGGESTIONS: Served on top of a Pot-Browned Noodle Pillow (page 401) or alongside rice or a Pan-Fried

JAPANESE CUKES

Japanese cucumbers are a very slender and thin-skinned cucumber varietal with a discernibly sweet, fresh taste and no seeds. They are heads and shoulders above the comparatively vapid English, or hydroponic, cucumber. Look for them in a Japanese or farmer's market. If you cannot find them, use Armenian cucumbers, lemon cucumbers, or other sweet farm varieties. Or, sigh deeply and use the ubiquitous English in their place.

*While on the hunt for
fresh pork in San
Francisco Chinatown, I was
attracted to a huge truck that
pulled up in front of one
butcher store every morning.
Out would climb a beefy
(pardon the expression) man,
who would then haul a
succession of whole pigs, on
his shoulder, into the shop. It
was clear that the meat was
fresh from the slaughter-
house, and that the driver's
mission made him happy.
What wasn't clear was how
so many pigs fit into such a
little shop.*

*It turned out that be-
hind the shop was a scene
from Dante's "Inferno."
While some of the pigs were
cut up and sold out front to
customers like me, an even
larger number were hung
whole by the butt in a trio of
vertical ovens out back and
were roasted slowly over
many hours to a crispy, deep
gold. The fat dripped in pools
beneath the ovens while the
fires in their bellies blazed.
Orchestrating the scene and
turning the pigs with great
concentration was a pair of
intensely thin young Chinese
men, garbed merely in loin
cloths and rubber sandals.
With Cantonese opera seep-
ing from a radio, it was truly
a scene out of a movie.*

Scallion-Chive Bread (page 382), this is a light, one-dish meal.
Ears of steamed corn would be great accompaniments in
summer; in winter, a dish of springrolls would be delicious.

HOT AND SOUR
PORK RIBBONS WITH
SHANGHAI NOODLES AND
WINTER CHARD

SERVES 3 TO 4 AS A MAIN COURSE,
5 TO 6 AS PART OF A MULTICOURSE MEAL

This is a terrific tumble of spicy pork, fat noodles,
smoky tree ears, and flavorful winter chard, all
laced with a sauce that is pungent and tangy. It is a
real cold weather tummy-warmer, perfect for those days
when you need to feel well fed.

In the restaurant, we use a thick style of egg noodle
that is turned out by a local noodle factory and has an
appealing, stubby toothiness. I know of nothing else like
it (except for the northern Chinese homemade noodles,
on which they were undoubtedly modeled) but any good
pasta will do, including dry shells, rigatoni or fusilli.

The marinating, chopping, and noodle blanching

can all be done ahead, leaving only 5 to 10 minutes of last-minute cooking.

MARINADE AND PORK:

1 tablespoon soy sauce

1 tablespoon mushroom soy sauce

1 tablespoon Chinese rice wine or dry sherry

1 tablespoon cornstarch

1 tablespoon packed brown sugar

1 teaspoon finely minced garlic

2½ teaspoons China Moon Hot Chili Oil (page 10)

2½ teaspoons "goop" from China Moon Hot Chili Oil

¾ pound boneless pork loin, cut against the grain into 2-inch ribbons ⅛ inch thick

AROMATICS:

1 tablespoon finely minced fresh ginger

1 tablespoon finely minced garlic

¼ cup thinly sliced green and white scallion rings

2 teaspoons Chinese black beans, coarsely chopped (do not rinse them)

¾ to 1 teaspoon dried red chili flakes

SAUCE:

1½ cups China Moon Infusion (page 72), China Moon Double Stock (page 72), or unsalted chicken stock

2 tablespoons mushroom soy sauce

1 tablespoon Chinese rice wine or dry sherry

2 tablespoons distilled white vinegar

2 tablespoons unseasoned Japanese rice vinegar

1 tablespoon sugar

¾ teaspoon kosher salt

1 teaspoon Chinese chili sauce

2 tablespoons dried tree ears

1 carrot, cut diagonally into rippled or plain coins, ⅛ inch thick

½ pound fat Shanghai noodles or other appealing pasta

1½ teaspoons China Moon Hot Chili Oil

2 to 3 cups corn or peanut oil, for velveting and stir-frying

1 small red onion, cut into ¾-inch squares

1 small red bell pepper, cut into ¾-inch squares

3 ounces mushrooms, halved or quartered if large

¼ pound red chard, cut crosswise into wide ribbons

1 tablespoon cornstarch dissolved in 2 tablespoons cold stock or water

Diagonally sliced green and white scallion rings, for garnish

STORING FRESH PORK

I refrigerate raw pork as soon as I buy it, but I never freeze pork. Although the fattier cuts of pork lose less in freezing than, say, leaner cuts of beef or poultry, the loss of any flavor or texture still dissuades me.

In my kitchen, ground pork goes immediately into the refrigerator in a stainless steel perforated pan set into a deeper drip pan. If you don't own such a nesting pan set (these are common in restaurant supply shops, where they go by the name of "perforated hotel pans"), then simply improvise by putting the pork in a colander set on top of a plate. Even very fresh pork will drip blood in the course of a day in the refrigerator, and the portion of the meat left sitting in the blood would otherwise begin to decay. To seal the color and further protect its freshness, press a piece of plastic wrap directly on top of the meat.

I also refrigerate whole pieces of raw pork, including spareribs, in a drainer pan. If your refrigerator isn't big enough to allow the larger cuts of meat to drip in this fashion, you can accomplish the same job by wrapping the meat in a dry tea towel and then bagging it in plastic. The cloth will absorb any excess blood and will keep the meat tasting and smelling fresh. Be sure that the cloth is clean and not perfumed.

Truly fresh pork will keep nicely for 1 to 2 days in this manner, assuming your refrigerator is very cold. For best flavor, however, one is always advised to marinate or cook raw pork as soon after purchase as possible.

1. In a bowl big enough to hold the pork, blend together all of the marinade ingredients through the "goop" until smooth. Add the pork and toss well. Seal and marinate for 3 to 4 hours at cool room temperature or refrigerate overnight. Let come to room temperature before cooking; toss to separate the ribbons.

2. Combine the aromatics in a small bowl and cover until ready to use.

3. Combine all of the sauce ingredients in a small bowl. Stir to blend, leaving the spoon in the bowl.

4. Cover the tree ears with 3 cups cold water. Soak until supple, 20 to 30 minutes. Drain and swish in several changes of cold water to dislodge any grit. Pinch off any tough or gelatinous bits. Tear, if necessary, into quarter-size pieces. Cover with cold water until ready to use; drain before cooking.

5. Bring a large pot of water to a boil. Blanch the carrots until half-cooked, 30 seconds. Scoop from the water and plunge into ice water to chill. Drain. Leave the blanching water on the stove.

6. Fluff the noodles in a colander to separate and untangle the strands. Bring the blanching water to a rolling boil over high heat. Add the noodles, swish with chopsticks, and cook until al dente. Plunge into ice water to chill; drain well. Toss the noodles with the chili oil. Set aside. All the above, including the vegetable cutting, can be done a full day ahead. Seal and refrigerate the ingredients; bring to room temperature before cooking.

7. About 20 minutes before serving, velvet the pork following step 5 on page 295.

8. Return the wok or skillet to high heat until hot enough to sizzle a scallion ring. Reduce the heat to moderate and add the aromatics. Stir gently until fully fragrant, 20 to 30 seconds, adjusting the heat so they foam without browning. If the aromatics are sticking, drizzle a bit more oil down the side of the pan. Add the onion and bell pepper, and toss briskly until somewhat softened, 2 to 3 minutes. Add the carrots and toss for 1 minute. Add the fresh mushrooms and toss until hot, about 2 minutes more. Adjust the heat to maintain a merry sizzle and drizzle a bit more oil down the side of the pan, if needed to prevent sticking. Don't worry if the vegetables brown a little; they will be tasty.

9. Add the drained tree ears and the noodles, and toss for 1 minute. Add the chard and toss until it wilts. Stir the sauce and add it to the pan. Raise the heat to high, cover the pan, and bring the sauce to a simmer. When the sauce simmers, stir the cornstarch mixture to recombine and add it to the pan. Stir until the liquid turns glossy and slightly thick, 15 to 20 seconds. Add the pork and toss to heat through, about 10 seconds.

10. Serve immediately on heated plates or a platter of contrasting color. Garnish generously with the scallion rings.

MENU SUGGESTIONS: This is a fine one-dish dinner, and there is nothing I can think of to follow except a generous second portion!

STIR-FRIED SPICY PORK SHREDS WITH CHINESE CABBAGE AND PEANUTS

SERVES 2 TO 3 AS A MAIN COURSE, 4 TO 5 AS PART OF A MULTICOURSE MEAL

When I was in graduate school, I was treated to dinner one night in the kitchen of one of the wilder, shadowy guys in the department, who aside from a droll sense of humor had the added distinction of being a cook. His name was Robert Delfs; he later wrote a nifty book called *The Good Taste of Szechwan*. This is more or less what we had for dinner that night, embellished by my years of California living.

A variety of string beans (tiny Blue Lakes, yellow wax beans, Chinese long beans) adds great color to this dish, but you may use one type if the flavor is a standout.

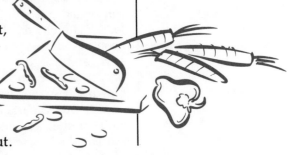

MY TAIWAN KITCHENS

I lived in two Chinese homes during my two years of student life in Taipei, and both kitchens were built on the same plan. They were offset from the living quarters so that the smoke and grease of daily cooking would always be a long way from the nostrils and eyeballs of the family. One was tiled while one was constructed of plaster and mud, but both were designed to be hosed down.

A wide, thigh-high, heatproof enclosed shelf ran along the longest wall. Buried within was a double-ring gas burner hooked up to a propane tank. Sunk into the top was a single wok that fit nearly up to its ears in a hole cut into the shelf. Alongside was plenty of work space on which to line up all one's cooking needs—the multitu-

dinous bowls and dishes holding the cut and combined raw foods, a container of oil, and a wok shovel, wok spatula, and mesh spoon or two, and the big communal platters on which to put the finished dishes.

Alongside was also a giant rice cooker and an electric burner with a giant tea kettle. Neither kitchen had a functioning refrigerator, an electric dishwasher, or a garbage disposal. The 1970s in Taiwan was a gloriously pre-modern time, when the rhythms of twice-daily shopping and cooking provided for the spirit and belly both.

Spiritual provisions were also cared for by the resident Kitchen God. A color picture of this folklore deity was hung ritually above the woks. On the occasion of each Chinese New Year, the picture would be taken down, set amidst an offering table of sticky sweets, and burned by the family patriarch, who would first smear the lips of the god with honey. The smoke and the Kitchen God would rise to the heavens, where the Lord of Heaven would ask for a report on the family's benevolence in the year past. Cheeks stuffed with sweets and lips sealed with honey, the Kitchen God could murmur only wonderful things.

From start to finish, this is an easy, quick dish. The pork will profit in flavor and texture the longer it marinates, but you can shorten the time if you're hungry.

MARINADE AND PORK:

1 tablespoon soy sauce
1 tablespoon mushroom soy sauce
1 tablespoon Chinese rice wine or dry sherry
1 tablespoon cornstarch
1 tablespoon packed brown sugar
1 teaspoon finely minced garlic
1 tablespoon China Moon Chili-Orange Oil (page 15)
¾ pound boneless pork loin, cut against the grain into 2-inch shreds ¼ inch thick

AROMATICS:

1 tablespoon finely minced fresh ginger
1 tablespoon finely minced garlic
2 tablespoons thinly sliced green and white scallion rings
1½ teaspoons "goop" from China Moon Chili-Orange Oil

SAUCE:

1½ cups China Moon Infusion (page 72), China Moon Double Stock (page 72), or unsalted chicken stock
1 tablespoon Chinese rice wine or dry sherry
2 tablespoons soy sauce
1 tablespoon cider vinegar
½ teaspoon balsamic vinegar
½ teaspoon sugar
1 tablespoon hot bean paste
1 tablespoon plus 1 teaspoon sweet bean paste

2 tablespoons dried tree ears
¾ pound tender string beans, tipped and cut into finger-lengths
2 to 3 cups corn or peanut oil, for velveting and stir-frying
1 small red onion, cut into ⅜-inch wedges
1 small red bell pepper, cut into ¾-inch squares
1 small carrot, cut diagonally into ⅛-inch rippled or plain coins
¼ pound Napa cabbage leaves, cut crosswise into 1-inch ribbons
1 tablespoon cornstarch dissolved in 2 tablespoons cold stock or water
½ cup fried or roasted peanuts (page 35)
Thinly cut green and white scallion rings, for garnish

1. In a bowl big enough to hold the pork, blend together all of the marinade ingredients through the chili oil until smooth. Add the pork and toss well. Seal and marinate for 3 to

4 hours at cool room temperature or refrigerate for up to 24 hours. Let the pork come to room temperature before cooking; toss to separate the shreds.

2. Combine the aromatics in a small bowl and cover until ready to use.

3. Combine all of the sauce ingredients through the sweet bean paste in a small bowl. Stir to blend, leaving the spoon in the bowl.

4. Cover the tree ears with 3 cups cold water. Soak until supple, 20 to 30 minutes. Drain, then swish in several changes of water to dislodge any grit. Pinch off any tough or gelatinous bits. Tear, if needed, into quarter-size pieces. Cover with cold water; drain before cooking.

5. In a generous amount of rapidly boiling water, separately blanch each type of bean until half-cooked, 10 to 60 seconds, depending on thickness. Plunge into ice water to chill, then drain. All the above, as well as the vegetable cutting, may be done a day ahead. Seal and refrigerate the ingredients; bring to room temperature before cooking.

6. About 20 minutes before serving, velvet the pork following step 5 on page 295.

7. Return the wok or skillet to high heat until hot enough to sizzle a scallion ring. Reduce the heat to moderate and add the aromatics. Stir gently until fully fragrant, 20 to 30 seconds, adjusting the heat so the aromatics foam without browning. Add the onion and toss briskly until somewhat softened, about 2 minutes. Add the bell pepper and toss for 2 minutes more. Add the carrot and toss for another 2 minutes. Adjust the heat to maintain a merry sizzle and drizzle a bit more oil down the side of the pan, if needed to prevent sticking. Don't worry if the vegetables brown a bit; they will be yummy. Add the drained tree ears, cabbage, and blanched beans, and toss until the cabbage is wilted.

8. Stir the sauce and add it to the pan. Raise the heat to high, cover the pan, and bring the sauce to a simmer. When the sauce simmers, stir the cornstarch mixture to recombine it and add it to the pan. Stir until the sauce turns glossy and slightly thick, 10 to 20 seconds. Add the pork and toss to mix.

9. Serve immediately on heated plates or a platter of

FRESH PORK TALE 2

The butcher shop with the movie scene out back (page 299) became my daily butcher shop out front. On one side of the shop, the deli counter featured the whole roasted pigs. Two were hung by their tails for ordering by the slice. Others were ensconced in open boxes with cherries in their eye sockets, to be ceremoniously picked up by those en route to weddings and funerals. On the other side of the shop was the raw pig display. For the cognoscenti, among whom my butcher proudly included me, the whole raw animals would be cut up promptly upon their arrival from the truck and would then be layered in the window in a moist, haphazard pile. They would be gone by midday. For the less discerning clientele, there was a refrigerated case, where one could buy pork pre-cut in the factory, laid out in neat rows amidst plastic parsley sprigs. This, the cognoscenti knew to be older, inferior stuff.

As the years passed, I would regularly, on shopping tours of Chinatown, take my students to the window of the pork store and give them a discourse on fresh meat. While I gestured from the outside at the pork, the butcher would gesture from the inside at me. "There is perfectly fresh meat!" I would tell the students, pointing out the deeply red pork butt, the paler rosy lean, and the thin sheen of moist fat on the spareribs. "There is the tofu-head (the white person) who knows her pork!" the butcher would shout happily to his clients. A mutual admiration society of the very first rank.

contrasting color. Garnish with a flurry of peanuts and a sprinkling of scallion rings.

MENU SUGGESTIONS: This is a delicious one-dish supper, needing only a Pot-Browned Noodle Pillow (page 401), a Broad Noodle Pillow (page 403), or rice to cushion the stir-fry.

STIR-FRIED CHINESE SAUSAGE WITH WILD MUSHROOMS AND SUN-DRIED TOMATOES

SERVES 2 TO 3 AS A MAIN COURSE, 4 TO 5 AS PART OF A MULTICOURSE MEAL

If you love Chinese sausage, then this is a particularly good way to eat it—set off by the earthiness of wild mushrooms and the tang of sun-dried tomatoes. You could, of course, use fresh tomatoes or Oven-Dried Plum Tomatoes (page 36), but this is mostly a dish about concentrated tastes.

The brown, very rich-tasting duck liver sausage found in many Chinese markets makes the dish more interesting still. If you cannot find it, use double the amount of Chinese pork sausage. You can also use andouille sausage instead of Chinese links; its flavor is terrific in Chinese dishes.

AROMATICS:

1 tablespoon finely minced fresh ginger

1 tablespoon finely minced garlic

3 tablespoons green and white scallion rings

¼ to ½ teaspoon dried red chili flakes

Finely minced zest of ½ small scrubbed orange

SAUCE:

1½ cups China Moon Infusion (page 72), China Moon Double Stock (page 72), or unsalted chicken stock

1 tablespoon mushroom soy sauce

2 teaspoons Chinese rice wine or dry sherry

2 tablespoons balsamic vinegar

1 tablespoon sugar

¼ pound each of Chinese pork and duck liver sausage, diagonally sliced into coins ¼ inch thick

2 to 3 tablespoons corn or peanut oil, for stir-frying

1 small yellow onion, cut into ¾-inch squares

1 red bell pepper, cut into ¾-inch squares

2 fat scallions, cut into 1-inch nuggets

1 small carrot, cut into julienne

6 ounces wild and domestic mushrooms, trimmed and cut, if large

3 to 4 pieces sun-dried tomatoes, cut into fine julienne

¼ pound baby bok choy or baby Chinese celery cabbage, separated into individual ribs

¼ pound Napa cabbage, cut into 1-inch squares

1 tablespoon cornstarch dissolved in 2 tablespoons cold stock or water

Diagonally cut green and white scallion rings, for garnish

THE HUNT FOR GOOD CHINESE SAUSAGE

Good Chinese sausages are hard to find; they are typically made in this country with an overdose of sugar and chemicals. The best brand I have been able to locate is Venus, made in Los Angeles.

There is no ready substitute for Chinese sausage. However, you can make a fabulous, spicy version of this dish and many others using andouille sausage!

1. Combine the aromatics in a small dish; cover until ready to use.

2. Combine all of the sauce ingredients in a small bowl. Stir to blend, leaving the spoon in the bowl.

3. Steam the Chinese sausage slices over high heat until the fat is translucent, 5 to 6 minutes. Drain well; reserve 1 tablespoon of the fat. (If you are using andouille sausage, it doesn't require pre-cooking.)

All of the above, including cutting the vegetables, may be done a day ahead. Seal and refrigerate the ingredients; let come to room temperature before cooking.

4. About 15 minutes before serving, heat a wok or large heavy skillet over high heat until hot enough to evaporate a bead of water on contact. Add the reserved sausage fat plus 1 tablespoon of the oil and swirl to glaze the pan. (If you are

I have historically been an apartment-dweller and a family of one, so I have joyfully made the kitchen the center of my life. Each of the places in which I have lived has had a kitchen big enough to hold a huge butcher block table for chopping and eating, as well as a space large enough to install a propane-fueled wok.

My wok burner is nothing fancy. It was made by an old buddy named Rex from the burner of a discarded hot water tank and a piece of metal tubing that anchors the burner in its middle. This is hooked up to a propane tank. The propane provides a fabulously high heat, and the jerry-rigged burner unit provides an appropriately deep nesting place for my wok.

I wish I could say that I have a kitchen hung with copper pots, a professional wok burner, a garbage disposal, and a dishwasher, and a covey of admiring cook's helpers to do my chopping and washing. But that's not me. My kitchen is a simple place built around one big fire and one big table, and I suppose I need nothing fancier.

using andouille, add 2 tablespoons oil.) When the oil is hot enough to sizzle a scallion ring, reduce the heat to moderate. Add the aromatics and stir gently until fully fragrant, 20 to 30 seconds, adjusting the heat so they foam without browning. Add the onion and bell pepper, and toss briskly until slightly softened, 2 to 3 minutes. Add the scallions, carrot, and sausage, and toss until seared, 2 minutes. Add the mushrooms and toss until hot, about 2 minutes more. Adjust the heat to maintain a merry sizzle and drizzle a bit more oil down the side of the pan, if needed to prevent sticking. Don't worry if the vegetables and sausage brown a bit; they will be yummy. Add the sun-dried tomatoes, baby cabbage, and Napa cabbage, and toss until the Napa is slightly wilted.

5. Stir the sauce and add it to the pan. Raise the heat to high, cover the pan, and bring the sauce to a simmer. When the sauce simmers, stir the cornstarch mixture to recombine and add it to the pan. Stir until the sauce turns glossy and slightly thick, 10 to 20 seconds.

6. Serve immediately on heated plates or a platter of contrasting color. Garnish with a sprinkling of the scallion rings.

MENU SUGGESTIONS: This is a fine dish to ladle over a simple bowl of hot rice or noodles. A platter of Wok-Seared Spinach Relish (page 438) and steamed corn would be terrific complements to the sausage.

STIR-FRIED PORK RIBBONS
WITH ASPARAGUS, ORANGE,
AND HOT BEAN PASTE

SERVES 2 TO 3 AS A MAIN COURSE,
4 TO 5 AS PART OF A MULTICOURSE MEAL

This is a zesty, one-dish supper with which to celebrate the arrival of asparagus season. It is colorful and simple to do.

All of the preparations may be done a day ahead. The last-minute stir-frying is speedy.

MARINADE AND PORK:

1 tablespoon soy sauce
1 tablespoon mushroom soy sauce
1 tablespoon Chinese rice wine or dry sherry
1 tablespoon cornstarch
1 tablespoon packed brown sugar
½ teaspoon finely minced garlic
1 tablespoon China Moon Chili-Orange Oil (page 15)
1 tablespoon "goop" from China Moon Chili-Orange Oil
¾ pound boneless pork loin, cut against the grain into 2-inch ribbons ⅛ inch thick

AROMATICS:

1 tablespoon finely minced fresh ginger
1 tablespoon finely minced garlic
2 tablespoons thinly sliced green and white scallion rings
½ teaspoon dried red chili flakes
Finely minced zest of 1 small scrubbed orange

SAUCE:

1½ cups China Moon Infusion (page 72), China Moon Double Stock (page 72), or unsalted chicken stock

2 tablespoons hot bean paste
1 tablespoon sweet bean paste
1 tablespoon hoisin sauce
2 tablespoons soy sauce
2 tablespoons Chinese rice wine or dry sherry
2 tablespoons unseasoned Japanese rice vinegar
2 tablespoons freshly squeezed orange juice

¼ pound mixed wild and domestic mushrooms, trimmed and cut, if large
1 carrot, cut into a thick julienne
½ pound trimmed asparagus, roll-cut (page 260) into 1½-inch nuggets
2 to 3 cups corn or peanut oil, for velveting and stir-frying
1 small yellow onion, cut into ¼-inch moons
1 small leek, white part only, split lengthwise, then cut crosswise into ¼-inch half-moons
¼ pound baby bok choy, larger leaves cut in half, or spinach leaves or thick ribbons of red chard
1 tablespoon cornstarch dissolved in 2 tablespoons cold stock or water
Green and white scallion julienne, for garnish

ALL IN THE FAMILY

Hot bean paste, sweet bean paste, and hoisin sauce are close culinary cousins. Soy bean- and wheat-based concoctions all, they might easily have been one in ancient times. Regional distinctions and the march of modernity have given us three separate products with flavors that work beautifully in combination.

All three are easily found in Chinese groceries. Koon Chun hoisin sauce and Szechwan brand hot and sweet bean pastes are good; both are made in Taiwan and widely distributed.

1. In a bowl big enough to hold the pork, blend together all of the marinade ingredients through the "goop" until smooth. Add the pork and toss well to coat. Seal and marinate for 3 to 4 hours at cool room temperature or refrigerate overnight. Let come to room temperature before cooking; toss to separate the ribbons.

2. Combine the aromatics in a small dish. Seal until ready to use.

3. Combine all of the sauce ingredients through the orange juice in a small bowl. Stir to blend, leaving the spoon in the bowl.

4. In a generous amount of boiling water, blanch the carrots until half-cooked, 10 to 15 seconds. Plunge into ice water to chill, then drain. Return the water to a boil and blanch the asparagus until half-cooked, 10 to 20 seconds for thin stalks, or 30 to 40 seconds if thick. Immerse in ice water to chill; drain well.

All the above, including any extra vegetable cutting, may be done a full day ahead. Seal and refrigerate the ingredients; let come to room temperature before cooking.

5. About 20 minutes before serving, velvet the pork, following step 5 on page 295.

6. Return the pan to high heat. When the oil is hot enough to sizzle a scallion ring, reduce the heat to moderate and add the aromatics. Stir gently until fully fragrant, 20 to 30 seconds, adjusting the heat so the aromatics foam without browning. Add the onion and toss briskly for 2 minutes until somewhat softened. Add the leeks and carrots and toss for 2 minutes more. Add the mushrooms and toss until hot, 1 to 2 minutes. Adjust the heat to maintain a merry sizzle and drizzle a bit more oil down the side of the pan, if needed to prevent sticking. Don't be concerned if the vegetables color a bit; they will be flavorful. Add the baby bok choy, spinach, or chard; toss just until wilted.

7. Stir the sauce and add it to the pan. Raise the heat to high, cover the pan, and bring the sauce to a simmer. When the sauce regains a simmer, stir the cornstarch mixture to recombine it and add it to the pan. Stir until the sauce turns glossy and slightly thick, 10 to 20 seconds. Add the pork and the asparagus. Toss to cook the pork through, about 10 seconds.

8. Serve immediately on heated plates or a platter of contrasting color. Garnish with a sprinkling of the scallion julienne.

MENU SUGGESTIONS: This is a one-dish meal when served in tandem with a Pot-Browned Noodle Pillow (page 401), a Broad Noodle Pillow (page 403), or rice. The flavors would also go well with Wok-Seared New Potatoes (page 424) or a bowl of boiled new potatoes. If you want a soup to start, one of our hot and sour soups would be delicious.

BRINED LOIN OF PORK WITH PASILLA PEPPER SAUCE

LOIN SERVES 6 TO 8 AS A MAIN COURSE, 10 TO 12 AS PART OF A MULTICOURSE MEAL; CHOPS SERVE 6 AS A MAIN COURSE

This is one of the world's great cold cuts—a savory, moist loin of pork imbued with the flavors of soy sauce and serrano chilis and topped with the tart and dusky flavors of roasted pasilla pepper sauce. It is cross-cultural at its core, leaning equidistant between Beijing and Santa Fe!

Brining, marinating, and then roasting the meat is a simple business that needs, ideally, three days. The sauce should be blended shortly before serving, though the peppers can be roasted ahead. For a weekend party, it would be hard to find a better dish.

1 untrimmed boneless pork loin
   (2½ to 3 pounds) or 3½ to 4
   pounds extra-thick pork
   chops with fat left on

BRINE:
¼ cup sugar
2 tablespoons kosher salt
Finely pared zest of ½ scrubbed
   orange
2 quarter-size pieces cassia bark
   or 1 (2-inch) cinnamon stick,
   crumbled

½ teaspoon black peppercorns
½ teaspoon white peppercorns
1½ teaspoons Szechwan
   peppercorns
2 whole star anise, broken into
   their 16 points
5 quarter-size coins fresh ginger,
   smashed
1½ teaspoons dried red chili
   flakes

PORK BRINING

Brining meat by submerging it in a seasoned liquid and letting it cure for several days in the refrigerator is a spectacular (and simple!) method used by many chefs to tenderize and season meat. It is easily replicated at home, either with a whole untrimmed pork loin (the ideal) or extra-thick pork chops with the fat left on (good, but second best). If you truly love the flavor range pork offers and are fascinated, as I am, by the alchemy of cooking, then brining is a technique you must try.

Pork brined in this manner likes a thin, protective layer of fat. Warn your butcher in advance so he or she doesn't denude your meat before you pick it up.

MARINADE:

2 large cloves garlic, smashed
2 large green serrano chilis,
    finely minced
⅔ cup soy sauce
⅔ cup Chinese rice wine or dry
    sherry
¼ cup corn or peanut oil
2 teaspoons China Moon Hot
    Chili Oil (page 10) or China
    Moon Chili-Orange Oil
    (page 15)
2 teaspoons Chinese chili sauce
1 tablespoon plus 1 teaspoon
    finely minced fresh ginger

2 to 3 teaspoons corn or peanut
    oil, for searing

PASILLA PEPPER
SAUCE:

2½ cups packed spinach leaves
4 large pasilla chilis, roasted
    (page 197)
¼ cup packed coriander sprigs
½ teaspoon finely minced fresh
    ginger
½ teaspoon finely minced garlic
1 tablespoon plus 1 teaspoon
    Serrano-Lemongrass Vinegar
    (page 19)
1 tablespoon freshly squeezed
    lemon juice
2 teaspoons freshly squeezed
    orange juice
¼ cup rice bran, corn, or
    peanut oil
1 teaspoon kosher salt

IF A HUNK IS
TOO MUCH

*If a whole pork loin seems
overwhelming, you can use
pork chops instead. Buy
thick chops, ideally with a
hem of fat left on. Brine them
for 1 day. Trim off the fat and
remove the bone. Marinate,
refrigerated, for 8 to 12
hours. Sear and roast as for
the loin; however, adjust the
timing to the thickness of the
chops.*

1. For a whole loin of pork, trim away excess fat, leaving
a ¼-inch-thick protective layer. With the sharp tip of a boning
knife or other small thin blade, carefully separate the slim
tenderloin muscle from the side of the larger loin. Cut the loin
crosswise in half. For pork chops, see note above left.

2. To brine the pork, combine all of the brine ingredients
through the chili flakes with 2 cups water in a non-aluminum
saucepan. Heat until the salt and sugar dissolve, stirring
occasionally. Set aside to let the mixture cool.

3. Place the pork in a stainless-steel, plastic, or glass
container deep enough to hold the pork and still have at least a
few inches of room above it. Pour the brine mixture over the
pork and add enough cool water to cover. Swish the mixture
gently to evenly distribute the seasonings. Cover and refrigerate the narrow tenderloin for 1 day, then remove it from the
brine, cover, and refrigerate separately. The 2 large loin pieces
are tastiest if left in the brine for 2 days.

4. At the end of the brining time, remove the pork;
discard the brine. Pick off any spices that cling to the meat.
Trim all 3 pieces of the pork of any extraneous fat and all tough
silvery sinew. Trim with care so that the clean muscle is
smooth, not ragged.

5. In a bowl, blend all of the marinade ingredients.
Scrape the mixture over the pork and massage well into the

meat. Seal and refrigerate for 12 to 24 hours. Turn the meat once or twice to redistribute the marinade. Let come to room temperature before cooking. Drain and discard the marinade.

6. Preheat the oven to 375°F. Move an oven rack to the top third of the oven.

7. To sear the pork, heat a wok or large heavy skillet over high heat until hot enough to evaporate a bead of water on contact. Add 1 teaspoon of the oil and swirl to glaze the pan. When nearly smoking, add the slender pork tenderloin and sear until golden brown on all sides, 1 minute or less. Remove the tenderloin to a flat rack set in a shallow roasting pan. Wipe the pan clean and repeat the searing process one by one with the 2 hefty loin pieces. Be sure the oil is nearly smoking before adding the meat. Also, turn it with tongs (not a fork) so that you don't pierce it and lose the juices. Each of the larger loin pieces require about 2 minutes to sear. Put the seared loin pieces on the roasting rack without crowding.

8. Roast the pork until an instant-read thermometer registers 140°F when thrust into the center of the thickest portion of each piece, 5 to 10 minutes for the tenderloin, 15 to 20 minutes for the heftier loin pieces. (Timing will differ depending on the depth of the sear.) Check the temperature often so you do not overcook the pork. As each piece is done, transfer it to a rack to cool.

9. Meanwhile, blanch the spinach for the sauce for 5 seconds in rapidly boiling water. Plunge into ice water to chill. Drain well, then squeeze out all excess water.

10. Shortly before serving, complete the sauce: In a food processor, process the roasted peppers and spinach until chunky. Add all of the other pepper sauce ingredients and process until smooth, 3 to 4 minutes. Seal until ready to use with a piece of plastic wrap pressed directly on the surface of the sauce to preserve its color.

11. Serve the pork tepid or at room temperature, thinly sliced against the grain. Fan the slices prettily and spoon generous amounts of the sauce on top.

MENU SUGGESTIONS: The sliced, room-temperature pork loin with its piquant green sauce appears on many of our Peking Antipasto plates. One favorite combo includes Pan-Fried Scallion-Chive Breads (page 382), Dragon Noodles (page 391), and Turmeric Tomatoes (page 59). Other happy partners to the pork are Wok-Seared New Potatoes (page 424) and a salad of baby greens dressed with either of our vinaigrettes.

TOOLS FOR ROASTING MEAT

Whether you are roasting pork, beef, or lamb in China Moon style, there are several tools that will help you to do it both safely and well:

An instant-read thermometer is the most important tool for this job. It takes the guesswork out of roasting. A nifty gadget with a delicate spoke and a tiny dial, it is often clipped to a chef's jacket, ready to be pulled out and poked into a slab of this or that. The spoke should be thrust well into the center of the thickest part of the muscle that is being roasted. The dial will record within several seconds the internal temperature of the meat. Particularly in the case of pork, a correct reading of the temperature is crucial to the final flavor, moistness, and healthfulness of the meat.

Larger, old-fashioned meat thermometers are not a

good substitute for the *instant-read variety. Not only are they slower and perhaps less accurate, but their thick spokes (as opposed to the very thin ones on the instant read thermometer) rob the meat of juice.*

For clearest, easiest reading, pull the meat from the oven (and close the oven door behind you), in order to take its temperature. Especially for home cooks who do it rarely, this allows an extra minute to do the job well.

A flat rack for roasting the meat, with a baking sheet or jelly roll pan set underneath it to catch the juices, is also important. This setup allows the heat to circulate evenly around the meat and keeps the meat from stewing in its own juice.

Finally, a pair of kitchen tongs is very helpful for moving the meat about. They won't pierce the muscle and rob it of moisture, and they make grabbing a big hunk of hot meat a whole lot easier.

BRINED LOIN OF PORK WITH HOISIN-MALTOSE GLAZE

SERVES 6 TO 8 AS A MAIN COURSE,
10 TO 12 AS PART OF A MULTICOURSE MEAL

In this second, more traditional variation on the theme of brined pork, the meat is marinated in a hoisin-based sauce before roasting, and is then finished with a glaze of sweet maltose. It is the gourmet's answer to sweet spareribs, a dish that shows off the splendor of great pork. Thinly sliced as part of a cold plate or stuffed inside the savory folds of a Sesame-Encrusted Flatbread (page 379), it is a memorable dish, worth every minute of preparation.

The steps of brining, marinating, and roasting need to be stretched out over several days, but there is nothing complex or scary, even if you are a brand new cook.

Brine (see ingredients on page 310)
1 untrimmed boneless pork loin (2½ to 3 pounds)

MARINADE:
1 tablespoon finely minced garlic
1 tablespoon China Moon Ten-Spice (page 6)
¼ cup packed brown sugar
¼ cup plus 2 tablespoons soy sauce
¼ cup hoisin sauce
2 tablespoons sweet bean paste
⅔ cup Chinese rice wine or dry sherry

2 teaspoons Ma-La Oil (page 17), Five-Flavor Oil (page 13), or Japanese sesame oil
⅓ cup thinly sliced green and white scallion rings

2 to 3 teaspoons corn or peanut oil, for searing
½ cup China Moon Infusion (page 72), China Moon Double Stock (page 72), or unsalted chicken or pork stock
2½ tablespoons maltose, or 2 tablespoons honey plus 2 teaspoons sugar
Diagonally sliced green and white scallion rings, for garnish

1. To prepare the brine and pork, follow steps 1 through 4 on page 311.

2. In a bowl, blend all of the marinade ingredients through the scallion rings. Scrape the mixture over the pork and massage well into the meat. Seal and marinate in the refrigerator for 24 hours. Turn the meat once or twice to redistribute the marinade.

3. Remove the pork from the marinade, wiping off any excess. Reserve ¼ cup of the marinade for the glaze. Let the pork come to room temperature before searing.

4. Preheat the oven to 375°F. Move an oven rack to the top third of the oven.

5. To sear and roast the pork, follow steps 7 and 8 on page 312.

6. To make the glaze: Combine the stock and maltose with the reserved marinade in a small saucepan. Bring to a boil over moderate heat, stirring to dissolve the sugars. Reduce the heat so the glaze barely simmers and cook until the mixture is a syrupy consistency and very flavorful, 3 to 4 minutes. The glaze should be sweet but not cloying or too salty. (If the glaze becomes too intense, add more stock, teaspoon by teaspoon, as required to balance the flavors.) Set the glaze aside to cool.

The glaze may be made in advance. Refrigerate once cool, then reheat slowly until warm.

7. Serve the pork hot, tepid, or at room temperature. Holding your knife at an angle, thinly slice the pork against the grain into broad slices. Overlap them prettily on a platter and drizzle generously with the warm glaze. Scatter the scallions on top for a confetti of color.

MENU SUGGESTIONS: As part of a cold antipasto, the sliced meat drizzled with the sweet glaze would go beautifully with any number of our cold noodle dishes and a salad of baby greens. Or, for the world's best thin sandwich, stuff it inside a warm Sesame-Encrusted Flatbread (page 379) slathered with the glaze. A green salad dressed with Fresh Ginger Vinaigrette (page 24) and Orange-Pickled Carrot Coins (page 58) or Peking Spicy Cabbage Pickle (page 52) would offer the right complementary notes.

WHAT IS MALTOSE?

In spite of its somewhat medicinal-sounding name, maltose is a softly sweet, intriguingly flavored sugar product that has been used by Chinese cooks since ancient times. An extract of grains, primarily barley, it has a nutty taste that finds a distant cousin in Italy's chestnut honey. Maltose is easily found in most Chinese shops that supply Chinatown delicatessens; it is the featured ingredient in the glazed ducks and stewed chickens that are on the top of everyone's deli shopping list.

MALTOSE-GLAZED BAKED SPARERIBS

SERVES 3 TO 4 AS A MAIN COURSE

For those who love sweet and spicy spareribs of the
Flintstone's variety, this is a dish to adore. Made
from the meatiest pork spareribs available, they are
first poached to cook the meat and then roasted with
several coats of a tangy, sweet glaze.

Maltose is an impossibly sticky Chinese sweetener
that is available in small plastic tubs or crocks and must
be attacked with a sturdy spoon dipped in boiling water.
There is no substitute for the experience or the taste,
although a slightly lesser amount of mild honey is work-
able in this dish.

The ribs can be poached a day or two in advance.
The two-step glazing can be done in quick succession or
spread out over two days. Given the easily stretched
timetable, this is fabulous party food.

1 large rack (2 to 2½ pounds)
  fresh, meaty pork spareribs
1 cup Chinese rice wine or dry
  sherry
2 teaspoons Szechwan
  peppercorns
4 quarter-size coins fresh ginger
6 to 8 cups unsalted chicken
  stock

SAUCE:
1 teaspoon corn or peanut oil
3 fragrant, firm plum tomatoes,
  tipped and quartered
  lengthwise
3 sun-dried tomatoes, soaked
  until softened, then chopped
  coarsely
¼ cup plus 2 tablespoons hoisin
  sauce

¼ cup Chinese rice wine or dry
  sherry
2 tablespoons packed brown
  sugar
1 to 1½ teaspoons Chinese chili
  sauce
¼ cup maltose
⅓ cup thinly sliced green and
  white scallion rings
1 tablespoon finely minced
  garlic
1 tablespoon finely minced fresh
  ginger

Diagonally sliced green and
  white scallion rings, for
  garnish

1. Divide the sparerib rack between the ribs into 2 or 3 pieces to snugly fit a large wok or a large heavy casserole. Stack the rib sections in the pot and add the rice wine, peppercorns, ginger, and enough of the stock to cover by 1 to 2 inches. Bring to a gentle simmer over moderate heat and cook the ribs until very tender, 1 hour or more. Remove the spareribs to a baking sheet and allow to cool in a single layer. Once cool, the uncut ribs may be refrigerated for 1 to 2 days. Bring to room temperature before baking. Discard the cooking liquid; or, if you're inclined to use it as a soup base, strain and discard the solids and refrigerate the liquid until the fat congeals on the surface and can be lifted off.

2. To make the sauce, heat a wok or heavy skillet over high heat until a bead of water evaporates on contact. Add the oil and swirl to glaze the pan. When the oil is smoking, add the plum tomatoes and toss briskly until seared and browned in spots, 1 to 2 minutes. Scrape the tomatoes and any juices into a food processor. Add the drained sun-dried tomatoes and process until smooth.

3. In a non-aluminum saucepan, combine the tomato mixture with all of the remaining sauce ingredients through the ginger. Bring to a slow simmer, stirring occasionally, until the maltose dissolves, about 2 minutes. Let the sauce cool to room temperature. Use immediately or seal and refrigerate for a day or more.

4. Preheat the oven to 375°F. Move the oven rack to the middle position.

5. Place the uncut spareribs, curved side up, on a rack in a roasting pan. Brush two-thirds of the sauce over the spareribs. Bake until glazed, about 15 minutes. (The spareribs can be cooled and refrigerated at this point. Let come to room temperature before finishing.)

6. About 30 minutes before serving, if necessary, preheat the oven to 375°F.

7. Cut the sparerib racks lengthwise into individual ribs. Glaze the top and sides of each rib with the remaining sauce and put the ribs, curved side up and not touching, on a baking sheet. Bake until glazed and hot, 10 to 12 minutes.

8. Serve the ribs hot from the oven. Heap in a playful tangle and garnish with a thick sprinkle of the scallion rings.

THE QUESTION OF UNDERCOOKED PORK

My generation, born in the late 1940s, was raised to think of pigs as the carriers of ghastly disease. Trichinosis and tapeworms were the stuff of my kiddie nightmares, fueled by my Grandma Millie's proclamation that if I ever ate pork, God would send a thunderbolt through my window.

Well, the thunderbolt never came and, in spite of years of eating juicy pork in Asia, I never got sick. What to make of this? At least on the subject of the health question, there is some science to lean on.

Trichinosis, a disease caused by a parasite, is largely a thing of decades long past, at least in America. An outgrowth of American habits of feeding pigs garbage, the disease has been eliminated with the commercial feeding of hogs. Therefore, if you are buying meat from a trusted commercial source, you have little if nothing to fear. (If you are cooking, however, with pork from a pig raised by your scruffy Uncle Willie in the garbage heap of his backyard, you have reason for concern.)

The parasite that causes trichinosis is killed at 137°F. Regardless, to this day the

most reliable American cookbooks recommend that pork
be roasted to an internal
temperature of 155°F. Given
that the internal temperature
of a piece of meat will usually
climb another 5 to 10°F after
it emerges from the oven
(literally cooking along on its
own steam), the extra 18°
margin for error seems exces-
sive, certainly to a person like
me who loves juicy pork. At
worst, in insisting on the
higher temperature, we are
protecting ourselves from a
shadow of the past. At best,
we are telling cooks that we
don't trust them to correctly
check the temperature of
a piece of meat, so in the
interest of safety you'd
better overcook it! Let's
compromise.

If you are cooking com-
mercially raised pork bought
from a reputable dealer, if
you have a working instant-
read thermometer and a pair
of clear eyeballs, and if you
carefully check the temperature in the center of the
thickest part of the pork you
are roasting, then you should
feel comfortable roasting pork
to an internal temperature of
140°F. If any one of those
factors is an issue, then by all
means roast it longer and
higher. For best flavor and
moisture, however, a reliable
140°F is ideal.

MENU SUGGESTIONS: A side dish of Turmeric Tomatoes (page 59) or a salad of fresh tomatoes would be welcome with the ribs. Or, if you want to make the ribs the star of a Peking Antipasto, set out hills of Ginger-Pickled Daikon (page 53) and Orange-Pickled Carrot Coins (page 58), plus a salad of baby greens dressed with Fresh Ginger Vinaigrette (page 24). Dragon Noodles (page 391) would also be excellent accompaniments, as would a simple bowl of new potato salad dressed with a tangy vinaigrette.

SANDPOT CASSEROLE OF SPICY SPARERIB NUGGETS WITH GARLIC

SERVES 3 TO 4 AS A MAIN COURSE,
5 TO 6 AS PART OF A MULTICOURSE MEAL

This is a simple, savory stew, an elaboration on a dish I cooked on a hot plate when, during graduate school, I needed a large-pot-of-something to get me through the week.

If you are in a hurry, the stew can be put together within a couple of hours, but you will need to hassle with skimming the sauce. It is easiest cooked in advance and refrigerated, so the congealed fat can be discarded in one motion. Like any stew, the flavors will only intensify with reheating.

1 large rack (2 to 2½ pounds) fresh, meaty pork spareribs, cut crosswise through the bone into 1½-inch wide strips

AROMATICS:

1½ tablespoons finely minced fresh ginger

2 tablespoons finely minced garlic

¼ cup thinly sliced green and white scallion rings

2 tablespoons Chinese black beans, coarsely chopped (do not rinse them)

1 to 1½ teaspoons dried red chili flakes, or 1 red Fresno chili, finely minced

SAUCE:

2 cups China Moon Infusion (page 72), China Moon Double Stock (page 72), or unsalted chicken stock

3 tablespoons mushroom soy sauce

¼ cup Chinese rice wine or dry sherry

2 teaspoons cider vinegar

1 tablespoon sugar

4 to 5 tablespoons corn or peanut oil, for searing and stir-frying

1 carrot, diagonally cut into rippled or plain coins ⅛ inch thick

3 cups lightly packed spinach leaves or wide ribbons of ruby chard

1 red onion, cut into ¾-inch squares

1 red bell pepper, cut into ¾-inch squares

1 leek, white part only, split lengthwise, then cut crosswise into ¼-inch half-moons

2 fat scallions, cut into 1-inch nuggets

4 to 6 ounces domestic or wild mushrooms, trimmed and cut, if large

1 package enoki mushrooms, spongy base removed

Green and white scallion rings, for garnish

SAWS FOR SPARERIBS

Look for very fresh and meaty spareribs that are rosy red and odor-free. Have the butcher cut them crosswise through the bone with an electric saw into 1½-inch-wide ribbon-like strips. If you forget to ask, you can do the chopping yourself with a thick-bladed cleaver, but it is an ear-shattering business and your neighbors will hate you. Best to turn around and go back to the butcher!

1. Trim the sparerib strips of any extra fat. Divide each strip into individual riblets.

2. Combine the aromatics in a small dish and seal until ready to use.

3. Combine all of the sauce ingredients through the sugar in a small bowl. Stir to blend, leaving the spoon in the bowl.

4. Heat a wok or large heavy skillet over high heat until hot enough to evaporate a bead of water on contact. Add 1 teaspoon of the oil and swirl to glaze the pan. Heat until nearly smoking. In 2 or 3 batches so as not to crowd them, add the sparerib nuggets to the pan and sear on all sides until deeply browned, 3 to 4 minutes. Adjust the heat so the spareribs sizzle heartily without scorching. Remove the nuggets from the pan and drain on paper towels. Wipe the pan clean and repeat with the remaining ribs.

5. Wipe the pan clean and return it to high heat until hot. Add 2 tablespoons of the oil and swirl to glaze the pan. When the oil is hot enough to sizzle a scallion ring, reduce the heat to moderate and add the aromatics. Stir gently until fully fragrant, 20 to 30 seconds, adjusting the heat so they foam without browning. Return the spareribs to the pan and toss to combine. Stir the sauce, add it to the pan, cover, and bring the sauce to a gentle simmer over moderate heat. Cook the spareribs until the thickest piece of meat is very tender, about 1¼ hours, lifting the lid occasionally to check the simmer and stir the ribs.

6. Scoop the sparerib nuggets from the sauce and set them aside on a large platter. Let the sauce sit undisturbed for 10 to 15 minutes, then skim the grease from the surface. If you are working in advance, seal and refrigerate the ribs once cool. Put the sauce, uncovered, in the refrigerator. Before finishing, let the ribs come to room temperature and discard the congealed fat from the surface of the sauce.

7. Bring a large saucepan of water to a rolling boil. Blanch the carrots for 10 seconds. Scoop into ice water to chill; drain. Blanch the spinach for 5 seconds. Chill in ice water, drain, then press to extract excess water. Fluff the leaves to loosen them.

8. To stir-fry the vegetables, heat a wok or large heavy skillet over high heat until hot enough to evaporate a bead of water on contact. Add 1 tablespoon of the oil and swirl to glaze the pan. When hot enough to sizzle an onion square, add the onion and toss briskly until slightly softened, 2 minutes. Add the bell pepper, leeks, and carrots, and toss for 3 minutes.  Adjust the heat to maintain a merry sizzle and drizzle a bit more oil down the side of the pan, if needed to prevent sticking. Don't worry if the vegetables brown a bit; they will be yummy.

9. Add the scallions and domestic or wild mushrooms, and toss until hot. Add the chard, if using, and toss just to wilt. Spread the vegetables on a large platter to cool. If you are working ahead, seal and refrigerate the vegetables once cool. Let come to room temperature before warming.

10. About 20 minutes before serving, put the spareribs in a 2- to 3-quart Chinese sandpot or heavy casserole. Layer the vegetables on top. Stir the sauce and add it to the pot. Cover and bring to a simmer over moderate heat. Simmer the ribs until hot, about 8 minutes. During the last 30 seconds of cooking, stir the spinach and half of the enoki into the pot.

11. Serve immediately in warm bowls of contrasting color. Garnish with a flurry of scallion rings and an upright sprig of the remaining enoki. Set the table with an empty bone bowl or two and encourage your guests to enjoy the ribs with their fingers.

MENU SUGGESTIONS: Rice, potatoes, a toasted loaf of garlic bread, or wedges of Broad Noodle Pillow (page 403) are all worthy companions for this stew. Add a glass of full-bodied red wine and you have a splendid meal.

SANDPOT CASSEROLE OF HOT AND SOUR SPARERIBS

SERVES 3 TO 4 AS A MAIN COURSE, 5 TO 6 AS PART OF A MULTICOURSE MEAL

This is a fine variation on the theme of stewed spareribs, one that features the hot and sour flavors of central China. It is a simple dish that can be done with most any colorful variety of market vegetables, so feel free to improvise.

Sparerib stews need long, slow cooking to turn the meat truly tender and succulent. For that reason, you might want to cook the ribs well in advance. In doing so you will also gain the advantage of being able to lift the congealed fat in a single slab from the sauce. If you are starting late, however, the ribs can be finished and the sandpot completed within two hours.

1 large rack (2 to 2½ pounds)
fresh, meaty pork spareribs,
cut crosswise through the
bone into 1½-inch wide
strips

AROMATICS:
2 tablespoons finely minced
fresh ginger
2 tablespoons finely minced
garlic
1½ teaspoons dried red chili
flakes
2 tablespoons whole Chinese
black beans (do not rinse
them)
2 tablespoons thinly sliced green
and white scallion rings

SAUCE:
2 cups China Moon Infusion
(page 72), China Moon
Double Stock (page 72), or
unsalted chicken stock
3 tablespoons distilled white
vinegar
1 tablespoon Serrano-
Lemongrass Vinegar (page
19) or unseasoned Japanese
rice vinegar
2 tablespoons mushroom soy
sauce

1 tablespoon Chinese rice wine
or dry sherry
1 tablespoon sugar
¼ teaspoon Chinese chili sauce

1 rounded cup red pearl onions
8 to 10 round French market
carrots or 12 baby carrots,
halved lengthwise if fat
8 to 12 ears fresh baby corn,
halved lengthwise if thick, or
1 cup fresh corn kernels
3 to 4 ounces sugar snap peas,
roll-cut (page 260) asparagus
nuggets, or baby zucchini,
zucchini halved lengthwise if
fat
4 to 5 tablespoons corn or
peanut oil, for searing and
stir-frying
1 red bell pepper, cut into ¾-
inch squares
¼ pound wild mushrooms,
trimmed and cut, if large
¼ pound Napa cabbage, cut
crosswise into broad ribbons
8 pieces Oven-Dried Plum
Tomatoes (page 36)
Green and white scallion
julienne, for garnish

1. Trim the sparerib strips of any excess fat. Divide each strip into individual riblets.

2. Combine the aromatics in a small dish; seal until ready to use.

3. Combine the sauce ingredients through the chili sauce in a small bowl. Stir to blend, leaving the spoon in the bowl.

4. Ready a skimmer or a Chinese mesh spoon, a large pot of boiling water, and a large bowl of ice water for blanching the vegetables. Blanch the red pearl onions for 1 minute to loosen the skins. Scoop into the ice water to chill; drain. Peel, trim, and cut the onions lengthwise in half through the root end. Return the water to a boil. Blanch the carrots for 10 seconds. Scoop into ice water to chill; drain. Blanch the baby corn for 30 seconds. Scoop into ice water to chill; drain. Blanch the sugar snap peas, asparagus, or zucchini for 10 seconds. Refresh in ice water; drain.

5. Sear the spareribs in 2 or 3 batches: Heat a wok or large heavy skillet over high heat until a bead of water evaporates on contact. Add 1 tablespoon of the oil and swirl to glaze the pan. When the oil is nearly smoking, add a single layer of spareribs to the pan and sear until deeply browned on all sides, about 3 to 4 minutes. Adjust the heat so the riblets sizzle heartily without scorching. Remove them from the pan to drain on paper towels. Wipe the pan clean and repeat with the remaining riblets.

6. Clean the pan and return it to high heat. Add 2 tablespoons of the oil, swirl to glaze the pan, and reduce the heat to moderate. When the oil is hot enough to sizzle a scallion ring, add the aromatics. Stir gently until fully fragrant, 20 to 30 seconds, adjusting the heat so they foam without browning. Add the seared spareribs and toss to combine. Stir the sauce and add it to the pan. Cover and bring to a simmer over moderate heat. Adjust the heat to maintain a weak simmer and cook the ribs until the thickest piece of meat is very tender, 1 to 1¼ hours. Uncover the pot several times to check the simmer and stir the ribs. Do not hesitate to cook them longer if needed. There is no virtue whatsoever in a tough nugget of sparerib!

7. Scoop the spareribs from the sauce and spread them on a platter. Let the sauce stand for about 15 minutes, then skim the fat from the surface. If you are working in advance, allow the riblets to cool, then seal and refrigerate them. Refrigerate the sauce uncovered; when the fat congeals on the top, discard it in one piece. Let both the spareribs and the sauce come to room temperature before finishing.

8. To stir-fry the vegetables, heat a wok or large heavy skillet over high heat until a bead of water evaporates on contact. Add 1 tablespoon of the oil and swirl to glaze the pan. When the oil is hot enough to sizzle an onion half, add the onions and bell pepper, and toss briskly until slightly softened, 2 minutes. Add the carrots and baby corn, and toss for 2 minutes more. Adjust the heat to maintain a merry sizzle and drizzle a bit more oil down the side of the pan, if needed to prevent sticking. Don't worry if the vegetables brown a bit;

they will be tasty. Add the mushrooms and toss until hot. Add the Napa cabbage and toss just until wilted. Spread the vegetables on a platter to cool. If you are working in advance, seal the cooled vegetables and refrigerate overnight. Let come to room temperature before finishing.

9. About 20 minutes before serving, put the spareribs in the bottom of a 3- to 4-quart Chinese sandpot or other heavy casserole. Layer the vegetables on top. Tuck the tomatoes amidst the vegetables. Stir the sauce and add it to the pot. Cover and bring to a simmer over moderate heat. Simmer for 8 to 9 minutes to warm the stew through. In the final minute or two of cooking, fold the corn kernels, if using, and the sugar snap peas, asparagus, or zucchini into the pot.

10. Serve immediately in heated bowls of contrasting color. Garnish with a tangle of scallion julienne. Put an extra bowl on the table for bones and encourage your company to enjoy the ribs with their fingers.

MENU SUGGESTIONS: For a one-pot dinner, I like adding parboiled new potatoes in their jackets to the sandpot during the last moments of cooking. Rice or noodles could be used instead, as could thick wedges of good bread. If you're in the mood, a salad of watercress and endive with our Orange Vinaigrette (page 25) would provide a fine note of refreshment after the stew.

PEPPERED SAUSAGE SANDPOT

SERVES 3 TO 4 AS A MAIN COURSE, 5 TO 6 AS PART OF A MULTICOURSE MEAL

*S*ausage-making is its own fascinating process, not at all hard to do at home if you have an electric mixer with the appropriate attachment. If you don't, or if links are not your thing, you could make the wonderful sausage mixture and pan-fry it in meatball form. It would be equally delicious and far less work.

As with all our dishes, feel free to alter the vegetables to what looks tastiest in the market. Asparagus tips, corn, spinach, and Oven-Dried Plum Tomatoes (page 36) would each or all be fabulous with the sausage.

3 to 4 yards sheep casings

SAUSAGE MIXTURE:
1½ teaspoons finely minced fresh ginger
1½ teaspoons finely minced garlic
1 tablespoon coarsely chopped coriander leaves and stems

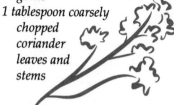

1 teaspoon freshly ground black pepper
⅛ teaspoon Roasted Szechwan Pepper-Salt (page 5)
2 teaspoons finely chopped Chinese chives
1 tablespoon plus 2 teaspoons soy sauce
1½ teaspoons Chinese rice wine or dry sherry
2 teaspoons Chinese chili sauce
1 pound coarsely ground pork butt

AROMATICS:
1½ teaspoons finely minced fresh ginger
1½ teaspoons finely minced garlic
½ teaspoon dried red chili flakes

SAUCE:
1½ cups China Moon Infusion (page 72), China Moon Double Stock (page 72), or unsalted chicken stock
3 tablespoons mushroom soy sauce
1 tablespoon balsamic vinegar
1 tablespoon Chinese rice wine or dry sherry

2 to 3 tablespoons corn or peanut oil, for searing and stir-frying
1 red onion, cut into ½-inch moons
2 to 3 large shallots, halved lengthwise
1 red bell pepper, cut into ¼-inch strips
1 small green Anaheim chili, seeded and cut into ¼-inch rings
2 fat scallions, cut into 1-inch nuggets
4 to 6 large shiitake or Italian field mushrooms, thinly sliced
¼ pound Napa cabbage, cut into 1-inch squares
1 package enoki mushrooms, spongy base removed
Thinly sliced green and white scallion rings, for garnish

BETTER BAA THAN OINK

Sheep casings are far better, in my opinion, than hog casings, the more common choice in sausage-making. Sheep casings are much thinner and more delicate, yet still quite easy to work with.

1. Soak the casings in cool water for 30 to 60 minutes. Rinse by slipping each casing over the end of the faucet and running cool water through it. Cut into manageable 2- or 3-foot lengths. Cut off and discard any portions with holes.

2. Combine all of the sausage mixture ingredients through the chili sauce in a large bowl. Add the pork and stir in one direction until well blended. Press plastic wrap directly on top and chill the mixture for easier stuffing, preferably overnight, which will also develop the flavors.

3. To stuff the sausages, attach a stuffing horn to a meat grinder. Slip a length of casing over the horn and make a knot at the end. Feed the sausage mixture into the casings, pausing occasionally to mold the meat. Underfill the casings to prevent them from bursting. Knot the end, then knot, tie, or reverse-twist into 4-inch links. Repeat until all of the sausage mixture is used. Ripen the links, uncovered, in the refrigerator overnight. You can do this by suspending them dramatically from the shelves or arranging them in a single layer, not touching, on one or more baking sheets.

4. Prick the sausages at several points along each link. Bring a large shallow pan filled with water to a weak simmer. Add the sausages and poach gently for 5 minutes. Drain, then allow to cool in a single layer. (If you are working in advance, the sausages can be refrigerated at this point for 1 to 2 days.) Let come to room temperature before searing. Separate into individual links.

5. Combine the aromatics in a small dish and seal until ready to use.

6. Combine all of the sauce ingredients in a small bowl. Stir to blend, leaving the spoon in the bowl.

7. Heat a large heavy skillet over high heat until hot enough to evaporate a bead of water on contact. Add 1½ teaspoons of the oil and heat until nearly smoking. Reduce the heat to moderate. Add half of the sausages and sear, turning, until golden brown, about 4 minutes. Remove sausages to drain on a paper towel–lined baking sheet. Repeat with the remaining sausages, cleaning the pan, if necessary, and drizzling in more oil.

8. Heat a wok or large, heavy skillet over high heat until hot enough to evaporate a bead of water on contact. Add 2 tablespoons of the oil and swirl to glaze the pan. When hot enough to sizzle a bit of minced ginger, reduce the heat to moderate and add the aromatics. Stir gently until fully fragrant, 20 to 30 seconds, adjusting the heat so they foam without browning. Add the onion and toss until softened slightly, 2 minutes. Add the shallots and toss for 1 minute. Add the bell pepper and toss for 1 minute more. Add the chili rings and scallions, and toss for 1 minute more. Adjust the heat to maintain a merry sizzle and drizzle a bit more oil down the side of the pan, if needed to prevent sticking. Don't worry if the vegetables color a bit; they will be tasty.

9. Add the shiitake and toss until hot, then add the cabbage and toss just until wilted. Spread the vegetables on a large platter to cool. All the above may be done a full day ahead. Seal and refrigerate the ingredients; bring to room temperature before finishing.

10. About 20 minutes before serving, spread the vegetables in the bottom of a 2- to 3-quart Chinese sandpot or other heavy casserole. Layer the sausages on top. Stir the sauce and add it to the pot. Slowly bring to a simmer over moderate heat. Cover the pot and simmer gently until the sausages are heated through, about 8 minutes. In the last minute or so of cooking, scatter half of the enoki into the pot.

11. Serve immediately in warm bowls of contrasting color. Garnish with a sprinkling of scallion rings and a spire of the remaining enoki.

MENU SUGGESTIONS: Sausage suggests potatoes or noodles more than rice, but any of these are great with the sandpot. A Broad Noodle Pillow (page 403) is another delicious idea.

SANDPOT CASSEROLE OF SWEET, SOUR, AND SPICY MEATBALLS

SERVES 3 TO 4 AS A MAIN COURSE, 5 TO 6 AS PART OF A MULTICOURSE MEAL

A homey stew of pork meatballs, glass noodles, and simple vegetables in a piquant sauce, this is a very appealing supper at any time of year. The selection of vegetables can include virtually anything in season— fava beans, freshly shucked corn, Oven-Dried Plum Tomatoes (page 36), and ruby chard or asparagus nuggets would all be yummy.

To make life easy, you can poach the meatballs and prepare the other ingredients a full day ahead and then simmer the casserole to doneness just before serving.

MEATBALL
MIXTURE:
2 tablespoons thinly sliced
   green and white scallion
   rings
1½ tablespoons finely chopped
   Chinese chives
2 teaspoons finely minced fresh
   ginger
1 tablespoon finely minced
   garlic
1 tablespoon plus 1 teaspoon soy
   sauce
1½ teaspoons Chinese rice wine
   or dry sherry
½ teaspoon kosher salt
Several twists of black pepper
1 teaspoon Cayenne Pepper Oil
   (page 11)
1 tablespoon cornstarch
   dissolved in 2 tablespoons
   cold stock or water
½ cup finely diced fresh water
   chestnuts
1 pound coarsely ground pork
   butt

AROMATICS:
2 teaspoons finely minced fresh
   ginger
2 teaspoons finely minced garlic
2 tablespoons thinly sliced green
   and white scallion rings
Scant 1 tablespoon Chinese
   black beans, coarsely chopped
   (do not rinse them)
¼ teaspoon dried red chili-
   flakes

SAUCE:
2 cups China Moon Infusion
   (page 72), China Moon
   Double Stock (page 72), or
   unsalted chicken stock
2½ tablespoons mushroom soy
   sauce
3 tablespoons distilled white
   vinegar
1 tablespoon Serrano-
   Lemongrass Vinegar (page
   19) or unseasoned Japanese
   rice vinegar
2 teaspoons Chinese rice wine
   or dry sherry
2 tablespoons sugar
¾ teaspoon kosher salt
1 teaspoon Chinese chili sauce

1 carrot, diagonally cut into
   rippled or plain coins ⅛ inch
   thick
¼ pound spinach leaves
2 to 3 tablespoons corn or
   peanut oil, for stir-frying
1 small yellow onion, cut into
   ¾-inch squares
1 red bell pepper, cut into ¾-
   inch squares
¼ pound wild or domestic
   mushrooms, trimmed and
   cut, if large
¼ pound Napa cabbage, cut
   into 1-inch squares
Infused Glass Noodles (page 30)
1 package enoki mushrooms,
   spongy base removed
Thinly sliced green and white
   scallion threads, for garnish

1. To make the meatballs, combine all of the meatball ingredients through the water chestnuts in a large mixing bowl. Add the pork and blend briskly in one direction. Press a piece of plastic wrap directly on the meat and chill the mixture for an hour or overnight.

2. Combine the aromatics in a small dish. Cover until ready to use.

3. Combine all of the sauce ingredients in a small bowl. Stir to blend, leaving the spoon in the bowl.

4. Fill a wide saucepan with water and bring to a rapid boil. Blanch the carrots for 10 seconds; scoop into ice water to chill; drain. Return the water to a boil and blanch the spinach for 5 seconds. Plunge into ice water, drain, then press to extract excess water. Fluff to loosen the leaves. Retain the blanching water.

5. Wet your palms and a 1-tablespoon measure with ice water. Scoop up 1 rounded tablespoon of the pork mixture and roll it lightly between your palms to form a small ball. Place the balls in a single layer on a wet plate.

6. Return the blanching water to a simmer. Add the meatballs and cook for 2 minutes after they have come to the surface, about 5 minutes in all. The water should never reach a simmer. Remove the meatballs in a single layer to a large platter. They should be 90 percent done.

7. Heat a wok or large heavy skillet over high heat until hot enough to evaporate a bead of water on contact. Add 2 tablespoons of the oil and swirl to glaze the pan. When the oil is hot enough to sizzle a scallion ring, reduce the heat to moderate and add the aromatics. Stir gently until fully fragrant, 20 to 30 seconds, adjusting the heat so they foam without browning. Add the onion and bell pepper and toss briskly until softened slightly, about 3 minutes. Add the carrot coins and toss for 2 minutes. Add the mushrooms and toss until hot, about 2 minutes more. Adjust the heat to maintain a merry sizzle and drizzle a bit more oil down the side of the pan, if needed to prevent sticking. Don't worry if the vegetables brown a bit; they will be tasty. Add the cabbage and toss briefly until wilted. Spread the vegetables on a platter to cool.

All the above can be done a full day ahead. Seal and refrigerate the ingredients; let come to room temperature before finishing.

8. About 20 minutes before serving, spread the glass noodles in a

HOLD THE HEAT!

One of the finer features of a sandpot is that it requires minimal heat underneath it. The conductivity is so fine that you can simmer over a lower heat than you'd ever imagine.

However, the converse is also true, so beware. If you jack up the heat, the sandpot will boil, which means a tough end to many a stew striving to become tender.

2- to 3-quart Chinese sandpot or other heavy casserole. Layer the vegetables on top, then nestle the pork balls among the vegetables so they are half-submerged. Stir the sauce and add it to the pot. Bring slowly to a simmer over moderate heat. Cover the pot and simmer gently for 6 to 7 minutes to heat the mixture through. In the last half-minute of cooking, fold in the spinach and half of the enoki.

9. Serve at once in heated bowls. Garnish with the scallion threads and a cluster of straight-standing enoki.

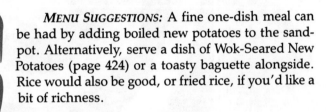

MENU SUGGESTIONS: A fine one-dish meal can be had by adding boiled new potatoes to the sandpot. Alternatively, serve a dish of Wok-Seared New Potatoes (page 424) or a toasty baguette alongside. Rice would also be good, or fried rice, if you'd like a bit of richness.

BAKED AND STEAMED BUNS • COLD NOODLES •

WON-TONS • MANDARIN DUMPLINGS • CRISPY SPRINGROLLS •

NOODLE PILLOWS • CRISPY SPRINGROLLS • MANDARIN DUMPLINGS •

DIM-SUM
AND
THEN SOME

COLD NOODLES • WON-TONS • NOODLE PILLOWS •

C O N T E N T S

The first thing to understand about dim-sum—that genre of Chinese eating typified in the great pre-World War II tea houses of south China, but found in snack places in most every region—is that it is a phenomenon of a culture that was both fixated on the eccentricities of food and had a vast population at its disposal to pleat dumplings. In terms of kitchen labor, it is the culinary equivalent of making an eleven-course meal of dainty petit fours, each a studied contrast in color, texture, and flavor. Hence, the "and then some" of this chapter. For to keep sanity amidst the dumpling pleating, we threw in some larger foods—breads, turnovers, and noodle dishes!

An early attempt at China Moon to make a full luncheon menu of dim-sum and then some, nonetheless drove us batty. The customers were very enthusiastic, as long as they had a two-hour lunch, but the cooks and waiters went wild. Tiny dishes of this and that were the stuff of waking nightmares, and we all wished for immensely large plates of a single unwrapped food.

As things balanced themselves out over the years, the China Moon lunch and dinner menus came to feature several dim-sum items each. Won-ton were balanced out by comfortably large pieces of steamed fish, and the madness of bun-making was forgotten in the relief of a sparerib stew. This is a good thing to remember when planning a meal at home. Obsessive types will adore prostrating themselves before a menu plan of a dozen dim-sum. But most of us, myself included, would best plan a salad with their springrolls.

Here, then is a chapter full of very delicious little items. They are truly among the most

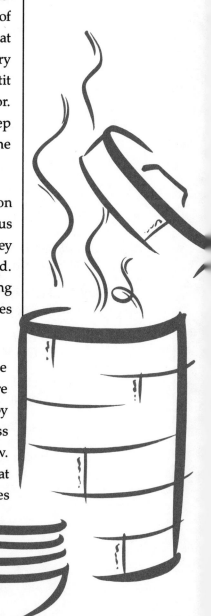

memorable of dishes to emerge from the China Moon kitchen. I dedicate them to the millions of hands that have pleated, rolled, and wrapped such savory tidbits throughout China's long and luscious history, inspiring all of us who follow blissfully and blindly in their wake.

■ ■ ■

CURRIED CHICKEN SPRINGROLLS WITH GLASS NOODLES AND FRESH CHILIS

MAKES 25 TO 30 SPRINGROLLS

Of the many springroll varieties we make at China Moon, this one is a runaway favorite. Who can quibble with lightly curried chicken, slithery glass noodles, and a fragrant mélange of chopped vegetables all housed in a golden wrapper?

If you have everything but the fresh chilis on hand, you might want to substitute about 1 to 1½ teaspoons dried chili flakes or 1 tablespoon "goop" from any of our chili-infused oils. The taste will not be quite as bright, but the zip will be there.

Like any springroll filling worth its stuff, this one is delicious eaten cold on Garlic Croutons (page 37) if you poop out before the rolling begins. For do-aheaders, the filling can be prepped on day one, cooked on day two, rolled on day three, and fried for serving on day four.

SLOW-COOKING

The whole rhythm of cooking springroll fillings—and most all of our dim-sum fillings—is low and slow! By keeping the heat relatively low and the stir-frying relatively slow, you eke out all the wonderful flavors from the aromatics and the vegetables. The longer the cooking process, the better the final flavor.

MARINADE
AND
CHICKEN:
2 tablespoons soy sauce
2 tablespoons unsweetened
    coconut milk
2 tablespoons strong tamarind
    liquid (page 336)
1½ teaspoons China Moon
    Curry Powder (page 7)
1 pound coarsely ground fresh
    chicken breast

AROMATICS:
1½ tablespoons finely minced
    fresh ginger
1 tablespoon finely minced
    garlic
2½ teaspoons China Moon
    Curry Powder
3 small green serrano chilis,
    finely minced
1 to 2 small red Fresno chilis,
    finely minced

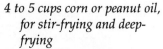

SEASONINGS:
1½ teaspoons kosher salt
1½ teaspoons sugar
1½ tablespoons soy sauce
2½ tablespoons cider vinegar

4 to 5 cups corn or peanut oil,
    for stir-frying and deep-
    frying
2 cups diced celery
1½ cups finely shredded carrots
4 cups diced Napa cabbage
2 ounces (1 small skein) glass
    noodles, soaked in hot water
    until translucent and cut
    into 2-inch lengths
2 tablespoons cornstarch
3 tablespoons cold chicken stock
    or water
About 30 very thin 7- to 8-inch-
    square springroll wrappers
¾ cup coarsely chopped fresh
    coriander leaves and stems
1 egg yolk, beaten
Green Chili Dipping Sauce
    (page 26), Pickled Ginger
    Dipping Sauce (page 28),
    Peanut-Lime Dipping Sauce
    (page 28), or Ten-Spice
    Honey Dip (page 27)
Coriander sprigs and/or scallion
    brushes, for garnish

1. To make the filling: Blend all of the marinade ingredients through the curry powder in a large bowl. Add the chicken and stir well in one direction with your fingers to coat it thoroughly. Seal airtight with a piece of plastic wrap pressed directly on the meat and refrigerate for 24 to 48 hours. The longer the marination, the fuller the flavor. Let come to room temperature before cooking.

2. Combine the aromatics in a small dish and seal until ready to use.

3. Combine the seasonings through the vinegar in a small bowl. Stir to blend, leaving the spoon in the bowl.

HOW TO FILL AND FOLD SPRINGROLLS

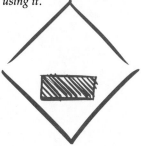

1. Put a lozenge of filling in the bottom third of the wrapper. Scatter chopped coriander on top, if you are using it.

2. Bring the bottom point of the wrapper over the filling, then tuck the point underneath it.

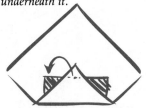

3. Enfold the filling with a roll turn of the wrapper. Do not roll too loosely, or the springroll will fall apart in frying.

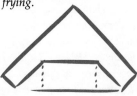

4. Bring the right side of the wrapper over the lozenge to form a neat and snug right angle.

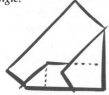

5. Bring the left side of the wrapper over the lozenge in the same manner. Dab the top point of the wrapper with egg yolk.

6. Complete the spring-roll by rolling it snugly shut. The egg yolk will seal the wrapper to itself.

4. Heat a wok or large heavy skillet over high heat until a bead of water evaporates on contact. Add 3 tablespoons of the oil, swirl to glaze the pan, and reduce the heat to moderately high. Add the chicken and toss and poke, breaking up the meat with a spatula, until the chicken is 95 percent white. Put the meat in a colander to drain. Clean the pan and return it to high heat.

5. When the pan is hot enough to evaporate a bead of water, add another 3 tablespoons of the oil. Swirl to glaze the pan and reduce the heat to moderate. When the oil is hot enough to foam a pinch of ginger, add the aromatics. Stir gently until the oil is well infused, about 2 minutes, adjusting the heat so the aromatics foam slowly without browning. Add the celery, toss to mix, then let stew until softened, about 3 minutes. Add the carrots, toss, and let stew for 4 minutes. Add the cabbage, toss, and let stew until translucent and juicy, 4 to 5 minutes more. Adjust the heat so the vegetables sizzle slowly and cook down. You want them to give up their juices (they'll be more or less willing depending on the season and their own water content), so don't rush the process.

6. Add the drained noodles and toss to mix. Stir the seasonings and add them to the pan. Toss well to combine. Return the chicken to the pan and toss until it is cooked through and very hot to the touch. Quickly stir the cornstarch with the stock or water to dissolve it, then scrape it into the pan, looped over the hot filling, in a thin, even stream. Stir until the filling turns very thick, heavy, and glossy, a full 4 to 5 minutes. Nibble a bit to be sure it leaves no floury aftertaste on the roof of your mouth, indicating that the cornstarch is cooked through.

7. Spread the filling in a thin layer on 1 or 2 large platters or a jelly roll pan. Refrigerate, uncovered, until thoroughly cool. Once cool, stir; taste and adjust the seasonings, if needed. The flavor should be keen, spicy, and a bit on the tart side. If you haven't used tamarind, adjust with an extra shot of vinegar. At this point, the filling can be sealed and refrigerated for up to 2 days before rolling. Stir before using; roll while still cold.

8. To wrap the springrolls: If you are using springroll wrappers that have brittle or badly torn edges, trim a thin, even border from each side. Following the illustrations, station 3 tablespoons of the cold filling in a lozenge-shape on each wrapper, add a sprinkle of chopped coriander, and roll as illustrated. Use a thin film of the egg yolk to seal the tube shut.

As you make the springrolls, put them side by side in a single layer on a jelly roll pan or baking sheet.

Once wrapped, the springrolls can be sealed airtight in a single layer and refrigerated overnight. They may also be frozen for up to 1 week. Fry refrigerated springrolls directly from the refrigerator. Fry frozen springrolls after only partially thawing in the refrigerator (to prevent the wrappers from getting soggy). For both refrigerated and half-frozen springrolls, plan to keep the oil over a consistently high heat while frying.

9. About 20 minutes before serving, fry the springrolls: Heat a wok or large, deep, and heavy skillet over high heat until a bead of water evaporates on contact. Add oil to a depth of 1½ to 2 inches. Reduce the heat to moderate and rest a deep-fry thermometer on the rim of the pot. Heat the oil to 350°F, until the end of a springroll bubbles immediately when dipped into the oil. One by one, slip 7 to 8 springrolls into the oil, adjusting the heat to maintain the temperature at a steady 350°F, so that the springrolls come to the surface within seconds wearing a crown of white bubbles. Add only as many springrolls as can float comfortably in a single layer.

Fry until golden, 3 to 4 minutes, turning the springrolls carefully once or twice to ensure even coloring, or bathing them with a ladle of the frying oil as they cook. Using chopsticks or tongs and/or Chinese mesh spoons, rapidly remove the springrolls to a triple layer of paper towels to drain. Before frying the next batch, wait for the oil to reach 350°F again. Don't worry about keeping the first batch warm while you fry the rest; uncut, the springrolls will hold their heat nicely for a full 6 to 8 minutes.

10. Cut each springroll on a sharp diagonal into 2 halves. Arrange them jauntily on a plate of contrasting color. Slip a dip dish of sauce alongside, and scatter the coriander and/or scallion frills decoratively between the springrolls. Serve immediately, encouraging your guests to eat with their fingers.

MENU SUGGESTIONS: Springrolls make a wonderful appetizer in most any setting, but because they require last-minute frying to be truly terrific, make it easy on yourself and follow with a simply cooked or cold entrée. My favorite way of eating springrolls is alongside a bowl of soup, particularly one of our hot-and-sour varieties. The contrast of textures is captivating.

TAMARIND LIQUID

///

Tamarind liquid—the thick, reddish liquid obtained from semisoft tamarind pulp—is a wonderful thing to have in your kitchen palette if you enjoy working with tart flavors. It is easily made once you have purchased a block of the concentrated pulp (see Glossary) and have stowed it in a corner of your kitchen shelf, where it will keep indefinitely, ready for a piece to be carved off and used. You can always use Serrano-Lemongrass Vinegar (page 19), unseasoned rice vinegar, or cider vinegar in place of tamarind in recipes such as these, but it is a bit like substituting cotton for velvet; the lushness is not there.

To make tamarind liquid, finely chop a square inch of solid tamarind pulp with a knife dipped repeatedly in hot water. Put the chopped pulp in a small heatproof bowl, pour 2 tablespoons boiling water on top, then cover the bowl and wait 10 minutes. With the back of a spoon, mash the mixture to a purée, then press it through a sieve, scraping off all the deliciously thick pulp and mixing it with the liquid.

SKINS AND WRAPPERS

When you are new to making dim-sum, the assortment of dumpling, won-ton, and springroll wrappers can seem bewildering. Here's how to choose:

For won-ton, the ideal is paper-thin wrappers 3¼ inches square. The super-thin wrappers are easy to shape, show off the filling once cooked to translucency, and are deliciously silky on the tongue. Won-ton wrappers are typically sold in 1-pound packages. If truly paper-thin, there will be about 90 wrappers to a pound. Don't count on it, however. Buy more than you need; the remainder will freeze nicely for a month or more. Look for white or nearly white wrappers. Any darker a color means food coloring instead of egg.

For steamed shao-mai dumplings, look for nearly paper-thin round wrappers 3½ inches in diameter. If you stack three of these skins on top of one another, they will nudge the ruler at ¹⁄₁₆ inch! That's thin enough to see your finger through a wrapper when you hold it up to the light, though a bit thicker than won-ton wrappers. I buy "shao-mai" wrappers in 14-ounce packages; each package is supposed to contain 90 wrappers. Buy extra

(they freeze well) rather than risk finding that you have too few. They should be white or nearly white, not gray (indicating they're old) or yellow (a sign of food dye).

If you can't find regulation shao-mai wrappers, simply cut round wrappers from paper-thin won-ton skins. The thinner won-ton skins will get soggy quickly, so be sure to steam the dumplings shortly after shaping them.

For boiled dumplings, look for 3½ inch round wrappers that are about ¹⁄₃₂-inch thin—far thicker than the ideal won-ton or shao-mai wrappers, though pretty darn thin! These are usually labeled "sue-gow" or "jyiao-tzu" skins, or some similar romanized variation of the Chinese characters for water dumpling. A 1-pound package is supposed to yield about 60 wrappers. Again, don't count on it. The untrained wrapper-shopper's eye may not be so sharp in computing thinness, and you don't want to get stuck midway through

dumpling-making with a dearth of skins! Buy extra; they freeze well. Dumpling wrappers should be white.

For springrolls, you will need paper-thin large wrappers, 7 to 8 inches square. They should be wheat (not egg) wrappers, with a papery rather than a noodle-like texture. Buy several brands, if you have a choice, then take them home and experiment to see which is best. Springroll wrappers freeze only marginally well; the best ones get brittle once frozen. If you are using frozen springroll wrappers, defrost them slowly in the refrigerator, then keep them under a towel and peel them off one-by-one to use them. A 1-pound bag of the brand we use contains 30 to 35 springroll wrappers. Buy extra; they frequently tear with even the gentlest of handling.

CURRIED PORK SPRINGROLLS WITH LIME

MAKES 25 TO 30 SPRINGROLLS

Although I can't state with scholarly assurance that lime and curry are authentic in springrolls, who cares? These are deliciously true to China's spirit, if not to her tradition.

MARINADE AND PORK:
2 tablespoons soy sauce
2 tablespoons unsweetened coconut milk
1½ teaspoons China Moon Curry Powder (page 7)
2 tablespoons strong tamarind liquid (page 336)
1 pound coarsely ground pork butt

AROMATICS:
1½ tablespoons finely minced fresh ginger
1 tablespoon finely minced garlic
2 to 3 teaspoons China Moon Curry Powder
3 small green serrano chilis, finely minced
1 to 2 small red Fresno chilis, finely minced
Finely minced or grated zest of 1 scrubbed large lime

SEASONINGS:
1½ tablespoons soy sauce
3 tablespoons unseasoned Japanese rice vinegar
1½ teaspoons sugar
1½ teaspoons kosher salt
2 tablespoons freshly squeezed lime juice

4 to 5 cups corn or peanut oil, for stir-frying and deep-frying
2 cups diced celery
1½ cups finely shredded carrots
4 cups diced Napa cabbage
2 ounces (1 small skein) glass noodles, soaked in hot water until translucent and cut into 2-inch lengths
2 tablespoons cornstarch
3 tablespoons cold chicken stock or water
About 30 very thin 7- to 8-inch-square springroll wrappers
¾ cup coarsely chopped fresh coriander leaves and stems
1 egg yolk, beaten
Peanut-Lime Dipping Sauce (page 28)
Coriander sprigs and/or scallion brushes, for garnish

SCHLEPPING SPRINGROLLS

One phenomenon of the 80s that is alive and well in the 90s is what I call the Gang Chef Event. In the interest of some worthy cause, and the less worthy stroking of some assorted overblown egos, a gang of chefs is herded into a showplace to put on a circus of food.

These events take many turns. Some are as huge and distressing as one immense party in Washington, D.C., where about a thousand overfed people were fed again from the encrusted under-ground kitchens of a huge hotel. (Superstar chef Jere-miah Tower and I bonded mightily at that one. Each of us bought our own cutting boards and chipped in on a gallon of bleach just to clean out the hotel refrigerator!) Others of these events can be charming and simple, as in the immaculate kitchens of Charlie Trotter's restaurant in Chicago, where a group of chefs conspire annually to make merry in the memory of James Beard.

Large or small, Gang Chef Events always bring out the springroll in me. This is one food that we make at China Moon that freezes, schlepps, and serves beautifully. With Styrofoam boxes and a few hunks of dry ice, you too can be winging across the country on the wings of a springroll.

Keep that in mind when you cater for a hundred in Bombay. Or when you schlepp across town to pleasure a happy gang of friends.

1. To make the filling: Blend all of the marinade ingredients through the tamarind liquid in a large bowl. Add the pork and stir well in one direction with your fingers to coat it thoroughly. Seal airtight with a piece of plastic wrap pressed directly on the meat and refrigerate for 24 to 48 hours. The longer the marination, the fuller the flavor. Let come to room temperature before cooking.

2. Combine the aromatics in a small dish and seal until ready to use.

3. Combine the seasonings through the lime juice in a small bowl. Stir to blend, leaving the spoon in the bowl.

4. Heat a wok or large heavy skillet over high heat until a bead of water evaporates on contact. Add 3 tablespoons of the oil, swirl to glaze the pan, and reduce the heat to moderately high. Add the pork and toss and poke, breaking up the meat with a spatula, until the pork is 95 percent gray. Put the pork in a colander to drain. Clean the pan and return it to high heat.

5. When the pan is hot enough to evaporate a bead of water, add another 3 tablespoons of the oil. Swirl to glaze the pan and reduce the heat to moderate. When the oil is hot enough to foam a pinch of ginger, add the aromatics. Stir gently until the oil is well infused, about 2 minutes, adjusting the heat so the aromatics foam slowly without browning. Add the celery, toss to mix, then let stew until softened, about 3 minutes. Add the carrots, toss, and let stew for 4 minutes. Add the cabbage, toss, and let stew until translucent and juicy, 4 to 5 minutes more. Adjust the heat so the vegetables sizzle slowly and cook down. You want them to give up their juices (they'll be more or less willing depending on the season and their own water content), so don't rush the process.

6. Add the drained noodles and toss to mix. Stir the seasonings and add them to the pan. Toss well to combine. Return the pork to the pan and toss until it is cooked through and very hot to the touch. Quickly stir the cornstarch with the cold water or stock to dissolve it, then scrape it into the pan, looped over the hot filling, in a thin, even stream. Stir until the filling turns very thick, heavy, and glossy, a full 4 to 5 minutes. Nibble a bit to be sure it leaves no floury aftertaste on the roof of your mouth, indicating that the cornstarch is cooked through.

7. Spread the filling in a thin layer on 1 or 2 large platters or a jelly roll pan. Refrigerate, uncovered, until thoroughly cool. Once cool, stir; taste and adjust the seasonings, if needed. The flavor should be keen, spicy, and a bit on the tart side. If you haven't used tamarind, adjust with an extra shot of lime juice. At this point, the filling can be sealed and refrigerated for up to 2 days before rolling. Stir before using; roll while still cold.

8. To wrap, fry, and serve the springrolls, follow steps 8 through 10 on pages 335 and 336.

MENU SUGGESTIONS: Fish would be wonderful with these springrolls—either a meaty fish or fresh prawns plucked straight from the grill or oven, or any of our steamed salmon dishes. Another thought, if it is summer, is our Cold Tomato Noodles (page 394).

CRISPY TEN-SPICE SPRINGROLLS WITH CRUSHED PEANUTS

MAKES 25 TO 30 SPRINGROLLS

Menu buzzwords are a favorite restaurant sport, and when one can combine "crispy" and "crushed" on the same line, it's a guaranteed best-seller. These springrolls certainly are, and not merely for the poetic value of the name; the flavors and textures are exhilarating.

Should you wish to use half chicken and half pork, go ahead. Likewise, beef, lamb, or a combination of the two would be good here, if you want to be playful.

Preparations can be stretched out over three or four days, or if you are hungry and have a freezer to quick-chill the filling, you might dash off the whole thing in a mere several hours.

SPRINGROLLS VS. EGGROLLS

An eggroll in Chinese cooking is a relatively simple thing: A thin egg crêpe is rolled around a seasoned pork mixture, steamed (then sometimes fried), and sliced into either nuggets or thinner rounds. We serve these thin, pinwheel-like eggrolls in soup (page 87).

The thicker fried eggrolls we all know from Chinese-American restaurants are expeditious variations on this old Cantonese theme. Lacking the ingredients or the economy to fashion the wrappers from freshly beaten eggs or the stuffing from freshly minced pork, the restaurateurs of my suburban childhood used thick egg and wheat wrappers and stuffed them full of mostly beansprouts. Thick and blistered on the outside and soggy within, I adored them! With duck sauce and mustard, what better way to an eight year old's heart?

The springroll of Northern Chinese eating is a totally different beast: Here is a slender roll of stir-fried stuff encased in a crispy deep-fried, paper-thin wheat wrapper. These are finger foods in the world of Chinese street-stall eating, party foods at home.

The name "springroll" harkens back to its role as a symbolic food at Chinese New Year, a lunar festival in celebration of the spring harvest to come. The food symbolized money, since it looked to the ancient (and modern) Chinese eye like a gold bar. Hence its importance on the celebratory table. Proper frying notwithstanding, a springroll is one weighty object!

MARINADE AND MEAT:

2 tablespoons soy sauce
2 tablespoons unsweetened coconut milk
1 teaspoon China Moon Ten-Spice (page 6)
2 tablespoons strong tamarind liquid (page 336)
1 pound coarsely ground pork butt or fresh chicken breast

AROMATICS:

1½ tablespoons finely minced fresh ginger
1 tablespoon finely minced garlic
1½ teaspoons China Moon Ten-Spice
3 green serrano chilis, finely minced
1 to 2 small red Fresno chilis, finely minced

SEASONINGS:

1½ tablespoons soy sauce
3 tablespoons unseasoned Japanese rice vinegar
1½ teaspoons sugar
1½ teaspoons kosher salt

4 to 5 cups corn or peanut oil, for stir-frying and deep-frying
2 cups diced celery
1½ cups finely shredded carrots
4 cups diced Napa cabbage
⅔ cup raw skinless peanuts, roasted (see page 35) and coarsely chopped
2 tablespoons cornstarch
3 tablespoons cold chicken stock or water
About 30 very thin 7- to 8-inch-square springroll wrappers
¾ cup coarsely chopped fresh coriander leaves and stems
1 egg yolk, beaten
Pickled Ginger Dipping Sauce (page 28), Peanut-Lime Dipping Sauce (page 28), or Ten-Spice Honey Dip (page 27)
Coriander sprigs and/or scallion brushes, for garnish

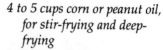

1. To make the filling: Blend all of the marinade ingredients through the tamarind liquid in a large bowl. Add the meat and stir well in one direction with your fingers to coat it thoroughly. Seal airtight with a piece of plastic wrap pressed directly on the meat, and refrigerate for 24 to 48 hours. The longer the marination, the fuller the flavor. Let come to room temperature before cooking.

2. Combine the aromatics in a small dish and seal until ready to use.

3. Combine the seasonings in a small bowl. Stir to blend, leaving the spoon in the bowl.

4. Heat a wok or large, heavy skillet over high heat until a bead of water evaporates on contact. Add 3 tablespoons of the oil, swirl to glaze the pan, and reduce the heat to moderately high. Add the meat and toss and poke, breaking up the meat with a spatula, until the chicken is 95 percent white or the pork is 95 percent gray. Put the meat in a colander to drain. Clean the pan and return it to high heat.

5. When the pan is hot enough to evaporate a bead of water, add another 3 tablespoons of the oil. Swirl to glaze the pan and reduce the heat to moderate. When the oil is hot enough to foam a pinch of ginger, add the aromatics. Stir gently until the oil is well infused, about 2 minutes, adjusting the heat so the aromatics foam slowly without browning. Add the celery, toss to mix, then let stew until softened, about 3 minutes. Add the carrots, toss, and let stew for 4 minutes. Add the cabbage, toss, and let stew until translucent and juicy, 4 to 5 minutes more. Adjust the heat so the vegetables sizzle slowly and cook down. You want them to give up their juices (they'll be more or less willing depending on the season and their own water content), so don't rush the process.

6. Add the peanuts and toss to mix. Stir the seasonings and add them to the pan. Toss well to combine. Return the meat to the pan and toss until it is cooked through and very hot to the touch. Quickly stir the cornstarch with the cold stock or water to dissolve it, then scrape it into the pan, looped over the hot filling, in a thin, even stream. Stir until the filling turns very thick, heavy, and glossy, a full 4 to 5 minutes. Nibble a bit to be sure it leaves no floury aftertaste on the roof of your mouth, indicating that the cornstarch is cooked through.

7. Spread the filling in a thin layer on 1 or 2 large platters or a jelly roll pan. Refrigerate, uncovered, until thoroughly cool. Once cool, stir; taste and adjust the seasonings, if needed. The flavor should be keen, spicy, and a bit on the tart side. If you haven't used tamarind, adjust with an extra shot of vinegar. At this point, the filling can be sealed and refrigerated for up to 2 days before rolling. Stir before using; roll while still cold.

8. To wrap, fry, and serve the springrolls, follow steps 8 through 10 on pages 335 and 336.

MENU SUGGESTIONS: Ten-spice is a pronounced flavor, so you might aim for a citrus or a "green" taste in making a match: Chili-Orange Cold Noodles (page 398) or Dragon Noodles (page 391) would go well, as would a simple green salad dressed with our Orange or Fresh Ginger Vinaigrette (page 24 or 25).

CRISPY BEEF SPRINGROLLS WITH BASIL

MAKES 25 TO 30 SPRINGROLLS

This is a very light, delicious springroll, blending the tastes of beef and roasted peanuts with the perfume of fresh basil and mint. It is tart, tangy, and spicy like most all of our China Moon springrolls, but it has a special lushness.

Preparations are easy, although best done in advance. If springroll-making is beyond your schedule, try rolling the filling in lettuce leaves.

*MARINADE AND
BEEF:*
1 tablespoon soy sauce
2 teaspoons mushroom soy
    sauce
1 teaspoon "goop" from China
    Moon Chili-Orange Oil
    (page 15) or China Moon
    Chili-Lemon Oil (page 12)
Finely minced or grated zest of 1
    small scrubbed orange or 1
    large scrubbed lemon
1 teaspoon finely minced garlic
1 tablespoon packed brown
    sugar
2 teaspoons cornstarch
2 tablespoons Serrano-
    Lemongrass Vinegar (page
    19) or unseasoned Japanese
    rice vinegar
1 pound coarsely ground top
    round beef

AROMATICS:
2 tablespoons finely minced
    fresh ginger
2 tablespoons finely minced
    garlic
3 small green serrano chilis,
    finely minced
1 to 2 small red Fresno chilis,
    finely minced

SEASONINGS:
2 tablespoons mushroom soy
    sauce
2 tablespoons Serrano-
    Lemongrass Vinegar or
    unseasoned Japanese rice
    vinegar

1 tablespoon packed brown
    sugar
1½ teaspoons kosher salt

4 to 5 cups corn or peanut oil,
    for stir-frying and deep-
    frying
2 cups diced celery
1½ cups finely shredded carrots
4 cups diced Napa cabbage
2 tablespoons julienned purple
    or green basil
2 tablespoons julienned fresh
    mint
2 ounces (1 small skein) glass
    noodles, soaked in hot water
    until translucent and cut
    into 2-inch lengths
½ cup raw skinless peanuts,
    roasted (see page 35) and
    coarsely chopped
2 tablespoons cornstarch
3 tablespoons cold chicken stock
    or water
About 30 very thin 7- to 8-inch-
    square springroll wrappers
¾ cup coarsely chopped fresh
    coriander leaves and stems
1 egg yolk, beaten
Pickled Ginger Dipping Sauce
    (page 28), Peanut-Lime
    Dipping Sauce (page 28), or
    Ten-Spice Honey Dip
    (page 27)
Coriander sprigs and/or scallion
    brushes, for garnish

WHAT'S ALL THIS MIXING THINGS WITH MY HANDS?

Psychologists would say (and
did) that I love to use my
hands in cooking—to make a
happy mess—in reaction to
my upbringing in a home
headed by two very hygienic
doctors. Other cooks (and I)
would say that the best way
to stir, mix, and otherwise
blend a lot of things is to do
it literally by hand.

    Your hand is a terrific
paddle. There is nothing like
it for stirring things around
and knowing how well a
mixture has been blended.
Likewise, there is little better
than one's own five or ten to
blend a marinade to smooth-
ness, to mix cornstarch with
a surety that it has dissolved,
and to deftly toss strips of
meat or poultry and evenly
coat each one.

    I remember a TV show
years ago in which a pastry

1. To make the filling: Blend all of the marinade ingredients through the vinegar in a large bowl. Add the beef and stir
well in one direction with your fingers to coat it thoroughly.

*chef stirred some creamy
concoction with her whole
forearm, and everyone watching nearly plotzed. I also
remember the early Julia
years, when Julia would taste
a dab of something with her
finger, go yum-yum to the
viewers, and then hold her
finger out to stage right,
where some disembodied
helper would wipe it with a
towel. Somewhere between
the forearm and the fingertip
is the hand I always use.*

Seal airtight with a piece of plastic wrap pressed directly on the meat and refrigerate for 24 to 48 hours. The longer the marination, the fuller the flavor. Let come to room temperature before cooking.

2. Combine the aromatics in a small dish, and seal until ready to use.

3. Combine the seasonings through the salt in a small bowl. Stir to blend, leaving the spoon in the bowl.

4. Heat a wok or large heavy skillet over high heat until a bead of water evaporates on contact. Add 3 tablespoons of the oil, swirl to glaze the pan, and reduce the heat to moderately high. Add the beef and toss, breaking up the meat with a spatula, until it is 90 percent gray. Put the beef in a colander to drain. Clean the pan and return it to high heat.

5. When the pan is hot enough to evaporate a bead of water, add another 3 tablespoons of the oil. Swirl to glaze the pan and reduce the heat to moderate. When the oil is hot enough to foam a pinch of ginger, add the aromatics. Stir gently until the oil is well infused, about 2 minutes, adjusting the heat so the aromatics foam slowly without browning. Add the celery, toss to mix, then let stew until softened, about 3 minutes. Add the carrots, toss, and let stew for 4 minutes. Add the cabbage, toss, and let stew until translucent and juicy, 4 to 5 minutes more. Adjust the heat so the vegetables sizzle slowly and cook down. You want them to give up their juices (they'll be more or less willing depending on the season and their own water content), so don't rush the process.

6. Add the basil, mint, and drained noodles; toss to mix. Stir the seasonings and add them to the pan. Toss well to combine. Return the beef to the pan and toss until it is cooked through and very hot to the touch. Add the peanuts and toss to combine. Quickly stir the cornstarch together with the cold stock or water to dissolve it, then scrape it into the pan, looped over the hot filling, in a thin, even stream. Stir until the filling turns very thick, heavy, and glossy, a full 4 to 5 minutes. Nibble a bit to be sure it leaves no floury aftertaste on the roof of your mouth, indicating that the cornstarch is cooked through.

7. Spread the filling in a thin layer on 1 or 2 large platters or a jelly roll pan. Refrigerate, uncovered, until thoroughly cool. Once cool, stir; taste and adjust the seasonings, if needed. The flavor should be keen, spicy, and a bit on the tart side. You may need an extra shot of vinegar. At this point, the filling can be sealed and refrigerated for up to 2 days before rolling. Stir before using; roll while still cold.

8. To wrap, fry, and serve the springrolls, follow steps 8 through 10 on pages 335 and 336.

MENU SUGGESTIONS: Especially in the winter, I love these springrolls served along with Sweet Mama Squash Soup (page 108). In a warmer month, a clear soup or an entée featuring grilled or pan-fried fish with a roasted vegetable sauce would be appealing.

WEDDING SPRINGROLLS

MAKES 25 TO 30 SPRINGROLLS

This very special springroll was the brainchild of one of my favorite sous-chefs, Mindy Schreil (aka Arminda Raymundo Asprer Schreil), who remembered something like them from her Philippine childhood. Mindy served them at her wedding, and you might do the same at yours. They are a big deal and a bit of a hassle, as befits a wedding, but the result is worth the effort. The hint of honey is appropriate to any sweet occasion.

Preparations may be completed well in advance, but to be perfect the springrolls should be fried last-minute.

CREATIVE CONFIT

Thick shreds of our Chinese-style duck confit (page 170) would be great in these springrolls, if you have some on hand and want to save yourself the first 2 steps.

WHY STIR IN ONE DIRECTION?

I am well known for a certain daffy precision, but instructing people to stir things in one direction seems like an infringement on human liberty. All true, but I did my initial culinary reading in Chinese, and there the briefly delineated steps for stirring meat mixes, fish purées, and the like always specified to stir in one direction. In the bowl, it has a happy logic: Minced meat mixtures, for example, compact less and blend more evenly when the hand stirs one way instead of back and forth.

Virgo madness knows few bounds, but this bit of madness comes with a Chinese cultural seal of approval.

3 pounds fresh duck legs

BRAISING INGREDIENTS:
1 small yellow onion, diced
1 small carrot, diced
2 ribs celery, diced
5 quarter-size coins fresh ginger, smashed
1 whole star anise, broken into its 8 points
1 thumbnail-size piece cassia or cinnamon bark
1 teaspoon black peppercorns
1 teaspoon Szechwan peppercorns
1 cup honey
8 cups unsalted duck or chicken stock

AROMATICS:
2 tablespoons finely minced fresh ginger
1 tablespoon finely minced garlic
¼ teaspoon China Moon Ten-Spice (page 6)
3 small green serrano chilis, finely minced
1 small red Fresno chili, finely minced

SEASONINGS:
1 tablespoon honey
2 tablespoons soy sauce
2 tablespoons Serrano-Lemongrass Vinegar (page 19) or unseasoned Japanese rice vinegar
2 tablespoons cider vinegar

4 to 5 cups corn or peanut oil, for stir-frying and deep-frying
1 cup thinly sliced celery
1½ cups finely julienned carrots
3 packed cups finely julienned Napa cabbage
5 to 6 large Chinese dried black mushrooms, soaked until soft, stemmed, and slivered
2 ounces (1 small skein) glass noodles, soaked in hot water until translucent and cut into 2-inch lengths
8 to 10 fresh water chestnuts, julienned
2 tablespoons cornstarch
3 tablespoons cold duck or chicken stock or water
About 30 very thin 7- to 8-inch-square springroll wrappers
¾ cup coarsely chopped fresh coriander leaves and stems
1 egg yolk, beaten
Ten-Spice Honey Dip (page 27)
Coriander sprigs and/or scallion brushes, for garnish

1. To braise the duck and make the filling: Heat a large wok or heavy casserole over high heat until hot enough to evaporate a bead of water on contact. Add the duck legs in a single layer and reduce the heat to moderate. Sear the legs, turning them once or twice, until most of the fat is rendered and the skin is crispy and a deep, golden brown, 3 to 5 minutes in all. Remove the duck to drain on paper towels. Pour off all but 1 tablespoon of the fat from the pan.

2. Return the pan to moderate heat and add the onion, carrot, and celery. Toss the vegetables until the edges start to brown, about 3 minutes. Add the rest of the braising ingredients and bring to a simmer over moderate heat, stirring. Add the duck legs and cook at a weak simmer until the meat in the thickest part of the leg is very tender, about 1 hour. Remove the duck legs to a large platter to cool. Strain and defat the stock, if you like, for use in future cooking. Once the legs are cool, pull the meat from the bones in thick shreds, then chop coarsely. If you wish to pause before making the springroll filling, seal and refrigerate the duck meat for up to 2 days.

3. Combine the aromatics in a small dish and seal until ready to use.

4. Combine the seasonings through the cider vinegar in a small bowl. Stir to blend, leaving the spoon in the bowl.

5. Heat a wok or large heavy skillet over high heat until a bead of water evaporates on contact. Add 3 tablespoons of the oil, swirl to glaze the pan, and reduce the heat to moderate. When the oil is hot enough to foam a pinch of ginger, add the aromatics. Stir gently until the oil is well infused, about 2 minutes, adjusting the heat so the aromatics foam slowly without browning. Add the celery, toss to mix, then let stew until softened, about 3 minutes. Add the carrots, toss, and let stew for 4 minutes. Add the cabbage and mushrooms. Toss and let stew until translucent and juicy, 4 to 5 minutes more. Adjust the heat so the vegetables sizzle slowly and cook down. You want them to give up their juices (they'll be more or less willing depending on the season and their own water content), so don't rush the process.

6. Add the drained noodles and water chestnuts, and toss to mix. Stir the seasonings and add them to the pan. Toss well to combine. Add the duck to the pan and toss until it is very hot to the touch. Quickly combine the corn-

OF FILLINGS IN BONDAGE

Cooked dim-sum fillings that are bound for wrappers—buns, springrolls, and moons—require a rather hideous amount of thickening and binding with cornstarch. Hideous, only meaning that a properly bound filling that will not leak from its wrapper upon reheating will range from the merely very gloppy to the consistency of library paste.

Working with this much cornstarch requires special treatment: Rather than dissolving it in advance in cold stock or water (the typical routine when stir-frying), wait to combine and stir the mixture just before adding it to the pan. If you don't wait, it will turn to near-stone in a minute and be a rugged chore to recombine. Equally important, loop the cornstarch mixture in a thin stream over the top of the hot filling so that it can be incorporated relatively quickly. Don't pour it into the pan in one splash, as can be done in a typical stir-fry, or you'll wind up with a hunk of plaster. Most important of all, expect to hang out and stir the filling for upwards of a full 5 minutes after adding the cornstarch. This seems like an eternity for a cook who's used to the sports car speed of everyday stir-frying, but truly that much time is needed for the concentrated cornstarch mixture to cook through. The way to test it for doneness is to blow on a dab of the filling (it will be very hot) and plant it on your tongue. Then close your mouth and slowly swallow it. If there's no floury taste left on the roof of your mouth, the cornstarch is cooked through.

Abandon any nouvelle notions of flourless cooking when making dim-sum! Michel Guérard is not Chinese! If you cut down on the cornstarch in the interest of chic, the filling will leak out of its wrapper, which is thoroughly depressing.

starch with the cold stock or water to dissolve it, then scrape it into the pan, looped over the hot filling, in a thin, even stream. Stir until the filling turns very thick, heavy, and glossy, a full 4 to 5 minutes. Nibble a bit to be sure it leaves no floury aftertaste on the roof of your mouth, indicating that the cornstarch is cooked through.

7. Spread the filling in a thin layer on 1 or 2 large platters or in a jelly roll pan. Refrigerate, uncovered, until thoroughly cool. Once cool, stir; taste and adjust the seasonings, if needed. The flavor should be keen and spicy with a nice edge of tartness. If needed, adjust with an extra dash of vinegar. At this point, the filling can be sealed and refrigerated for up to 2 days before rolling. Stir before using; roll while still cold.

8. To wrap, fry, and serve the springrolls, follow steps 8 through 10 on pages 335 and 336.

MENU SUGGESTIONS: Something simple and citrusy should offset the springrolls—a China Moon House Salad (page 442), Dragon Noodles (page 391), or a little dish of Orange-Pickled Carrot Coins (page 58).

VEGETARIAN SPRINGROLLS

MAKES ABOUT 40 SPRINGROLLS

In our search for an ever-expansive array of springrolls to offer our customers, a "veggie" springroll was worked on and worked on and worked on. Some were too blah, some were too mushy, but these are just right. Beefed up (forgive the expression) with peanut butter and roasted peanuts, they have a richness that delights even the carnivores among us.

Sophisticated veggie types might like to stir a cup or more of minced curried gluten, tempeh, or some such protein-laden ingredient into the filling mix. Beans or ancient grains might also be tasty, though these are ideas I have chewed on only thoughtfully.

AROMATICS:
2 tablespoons finely minced
    fresh ginger
1 tablespoon finely minced
    garlic
½ cup thinly sliced green and
    white scallion rings
3 small green serrano chilis,
    finely minced
1 to 2 small red Fresno chilis,
    finely minced

SEASONINGS:
2½ tablespoons kosher salt
2½ tablespoons sugar
⅔ cup unseasoned Japanese rice
    vinegar
⅓ cup soy sauce
3 tablespoons unsweetened
    coconut milk
1 teaspoon "goop" from China
    Moon Chili-Orange Oil
    (page 15)
3 tablespoons unseasoned
    peanut butter (page 32)
2 tablespoons strong tamarind
    liquid (page 336)

4 to 5 cups corn or peanut oil,
    for stir-frying and deep-
    frying

2 cups diced yellow onions
1½ cups diced celery
1½ cups finely shredded carrots
6 cups diced Napa cabbage
¼ cup dried tree ears, soaked in
    2 cups water until softened,
    rinsed well, and chopped
8 to 10 large Chinese dried black
    mushrooms, soaked until
    soft, stemmed, and minced
1 cup raw skinless peanuts,
    roasted (page 35) and
    coarsely chopped
¼ pound (2 small skeins) glass
    noodles, soaked in hot water
    until translucent and cut
    into 2-inch lengths (see
    Smush Note)
2 tablespoons cornstarch
3 tablespoons cold vegetable
    stock or water
About 40 very thin 7- to 8-inch-
    square springroll wrappers
1 cup coarsely chopped fresh
    coriander leaves and stems
1 egg yolk, beaten
Green Chili Dipping Sauce
    (page 26), Pickled Ginger
    Dipping Sauce (page 28),
    Peanut-Lime Dipping Sauce
    (page 28), or Ten-Spice
    Honey Dip (page 27)
Coriander sprigs and/or scallion
    brushes, for garnish

SMUSH PROBLEM SOLVED!

The veggie springroll code was finally cracked when someone (who? give that person a raise!) came up with the notion of using fat glass noodles. These are 3 to 4 times the thickness of the typical, delicate glass noodles, and they solved the smush problem straightaway. The brand we use is NICE. They are sold in skeins packaged in cellophane alongside their other dry noodle cousins.

If you can't find them, simply use skinny glass noodles, and settle in for a softer texture.

1. To make the filling: Combine the aromatics in a small dish and seal until ready to use.

2. Combine the seasonings in a small bowl. Stir to blend, leaving the spoon in the bowl.

3. Heat a wok or large heavy skillet over high heat until a bead of water evaporates on contact. Add 3 tablespoons of the oil, swirl to glaze the pan, and reduce the heat to moderate. When the oil is hot enough to foam a pinch of ginger, add the

*For fullest flavor and
plushest texture, soak
Chinese dried black mush-
rooms overnight in cold
water to cover. The hot water
soak is fast, but the mushrooms never taste as fine.*

aromatics. Stir gently until the oil is well infused, about 2
minutes, adjusting the heat so the aromatics foam slowly
without browning. Add the onions and toss until transparent
and golden, 3 to 4 minutes. Add the celery and carrots, toss,
and let stew for 4 minutes. Add the cabbage, tree ears, and
mushrooms. Toss and let stew until the cabbage is translucent
and juicy, 4 to 5 minutes more. Adjust the heat so the vegetables sizzle slowly and cook down. You want them to give up
their juices (they'll be more or less willing depending on the
season and their own water content), so don't rush them.

4. Add the peanuts and drained noodles, and toss to
mix. Stir the seasonings and add them to the pan. Toss well to
combine. When the contents of the pan are very hot to the
touch, quickly combine the cornstarch and the cold stock or
water to dissolve it. Scrape it into the pan, looped over the hot
filling, in a thin, even stream. Stir until the filling turns very
thick, heavy, and glossy, a full 4 to 5 minutes. Nibble a bit to be
sure it leaves no floury aftertaste on the roof of your mouth,
indicating that the cornstarch is cooked through.

5. Spread the filling in a thin layer on 1 or 2 large platters
or a jelly roll pan. Refrigerate, uncovered, until thoroughly
cool. Once cool, stir; taste and adjust the seasonings, if
needed. The flavor should be keen and spicy with a nice edge
of tartness. If needed, adjust with an extra shot of vinegar. At
this point, the filling can be sealed and refrigerated for up to 2
days before rolling. Stir before using; roll while still cold.

6. To wrap, fry, and serve the springrolls, follow steps 8
through 10 on pages 335 and 336.

MENU SUGGESTIONS: Perverse as it is, I
think of pairing these springrolls with something nice and *meaty*, like one of our cold
lamb, pork, or beef antipasti, or a fine piece of
fish taken hot from the steamer or grill. For a
suggestion truer to the spirit of vegetarian eating, a warm or cold salad of boiled new potatoes
and interesting greens, or a light pasta trimmed with
seasonal vegetables and herbs, would be a good match.

BOILED CHICKEN DUMPLINGS WITH PICKLED GINGER DRESSING

MAKES 30 TO 35 DUMPLINGS

This dish wins the China Moon "Cozy Award!" If there's anything cozier than a shallow bowlful of steaming chicken dumplings drizzled with a gingery light sauce, we have yet to discover it.

FILLING AND WRAPPERS:

½ pound Napa cabbage, diced

1½ teaspoons kosher salt

1 teaspoon finely minced fresh ginger

1 small green serrano chili, finely minced

1 small red Fresno chili, finely minced

2 tablespoons thinly sliced green and white scallion rings

1½ tablespoons finely slivered coriander leaves and stems

1 teaspoon Chinese rice wine or dry sherry

1 tablespoon soy sauce

½ teaspoon China Moon Hot Chili Oil (page 10)

2 tablespoons Five-Flavor Oil (page 13)

¾ pound coarsely ground fresh chicken breast

About 35 "sue-gow skins" (boiled dumpling wrappers), each about 3½ inches in diameter and ¹/₁₆ inch thin

SAUCE:

1 cup juice from China Moon Pickled Ginger (page 8)

¼ cup plus 2 tablespoons unseasoned Japanese rice vinegar

1½ tablespoons sugar

1 tablespoon soy sauce

Sprigs of tender watercress or mizuna

Cherry tomatoes or diced red bell pepper, for garnish

Green and white scallion rings, for garnish

1. To make the filling, spread the cabbage in a shallow container. Sprinkle with 1 teaspoon of the salt; toss well to mix. Set aside for 30 minutes at room temperature, then drain. Firmly squeeze in small handfuls to extract all the excess liquid.

2. In a large bowl, combine the cabbage, the remaining

HOW TO FILL AND FOLD DUMPLINGS

1. Put the filling off center in the wrapper.

2. Fold the wrapper in half over the filling and pinch it shut just at the midpoint. The sides should be open.

3. Pleat the top, open, right side of the wrapper toward the midpoint, using a series of three tiny pleats. Then, press the pleated edge to the bottom, smooth edge. The right half of the dump-ling will now be sealed shut.

4. Pleat the top, left half of the dumpling shut in the same manner, again aiming the pleats towards the mid-point. Press the newly pleated left edge to join the smooth bottom. When fully shut the dumpling will have one smooth side and one pleated side. The direction of the pleats will have formed the dumpling into a crescent.

½ teaspoon salt, and all the remaining filling ingredients through the oil. Stir to mix, add the chicken, then stir in one direction until thoroughly blended. The filling can be made a night ahead; press a piece of plastic wrap directly on the surface of the meat and refrigerate.

3. To make the dumplings, put 2 teaspoons of the filling in the center of the first wrapper. Keep the remaining wrappers covered to prevent them from drying out. Brush a thin film of cold water around the edge of the wrapper and pleat shut as shown here. Put the finished dumpling, pleated side up, on a baking sheet lined with parchment or waxed paper. Cover with a light cloth to prevent drying. Repeat with the remaining dumplings, leaving a bit of room between them, so they do not stick.

Once pleated, the dumplings can be sealed airtight and refrigerated for up to several hours before cooking. Poach directly from the refrigerator, to prevent the wrappers from becoming soggy.

4. Shortly before serving, make the sauce: Whisk to-gether all of the ingredients for the sauce; leave the whisk in the bowl.

5. To cook the dumplings, bring 4 quarts of water to a near-boil in a large wok or wide, heavy casserole. Adjust the heat so the water barely simmers. Add the dumplings one by one in quick succession; stir gently with chopsticks to sepa-rate. Poach the dumplings for a full 2 minutes after they come to the surface of the water, adjusting the heat so the water never boils. The wrappers should be nearly translucent and the filling should be cooked through; cut one dumpling open to be sure. Using a large Chinese mesh spoon, scoop the dumplings from the water and hold them aloft for a minute to drain.

If you are working in advance, let the dumplings cool, in a single layer, without touching one another, on baking sheets lined with parchment or waxed paper. Seal and refrigerate the cooled dumplings on the baking sheets; bring to room temper-ature before reheating. To reheat, poach in barely simmering water until thoroughly heated through, about 3 minutes.

6. To serve, portion the hot dumplings among heated serving bowls. Whisk the sauce to recombine, then spoon a tablespoon or two over each portion. To garnish, dress the greens lightly in the sauce and tuck them jauntily amidst the dumplings along with the little tomatoes or a sprinkling of bell pepper dice or scallion rings.

MENU SUGGESTIONS: This is a great meal-in-a-bowl for a simple dinner. A hot and sour soup, a cold vegetable salad, or some ears of steamed corn accompany it nicely, if you're wanting a larger spread. If you would like the dumplings as an appetizer, most any steamed fish dishes would follow well.

MANDARIN PORK DUMPLINGS WITH HOISIN-GARLIC SAUCE

MAKES ABOUT 40 DUMPLINGS

Boiled dumplings filled with coarsely chopped fresh pork are a favorite food in northern Chinese homes. Perfumed with Chinese chives and scallions and a bit of fresh ginger, they are plump, juicy, and thoroughly addictive. When I am down in the tooth and needing comfort, a bowl of these dumplings never fails to revive me.

FILLING AND WRAPPERS:
¾ *pound Napa cabbage, diced*
3 *teaspoons kosher salt*
3 *tablespoons thinly sliced green and white scallion rings*
2 *tablespoons finely chopped Chinese chives*
2 *teaspoons finely minced fresh ginger*
1 *tablespoon finely minced garlic*
2 *tablespoons soy sauce*
1½ *teaspoons Chinese rice wine or dry sherry*
¼ *teaspoon freshly ground pepper*

1 *teaspoon China Moon Hot Chili Oil (page 10) or China Moon Chili-Orange Oil (page 15)*
1 *tablespoon cold unsalted chicken or pork stock*
1½ *cups diced fresh water chestnuts*
1 *pound coarsely ground pork butt*
About 40 "sue-gow skins" (boiled dumpling wrappers), each about 3½ inches in diameter and ¹/₁₆ *inch thin*

POUNDING GARLIC

Pounding or mincing garlic to a paste— sprinkling it with a bit of salt to help the process along— gives it a remarkable silken texture and an inimitable smooth and mellow taste. The result is completely different than food processor– minced garlic. Try a side-by-side experiment to taste for yourself. Particularly in a rich sauce such as this one, the "pounded" garlic contributes a wonderful warmth.

SAUCE:
5 large cloves garlic, smashed
¾ teaspoon kosher salt
1 tablespoon China Moon Hot
*   Chili Oil or China Moon*
*   Chili-Orange Oil*
2 tablespoons "goop" from
*   China Moon Hot Chili Oil*
*   or China Moon Chili-Orange*
*   Oil*

1 tablespoon Ma-La Oil (page
*   17) or Five-Flavor Oil*
*   (page 13)*
2 tablespoons soy sauce
2 tablespoons plus 2 teaspoons
*   unseasoned Japanese rice*
*   vinegar*
¼ cup hoisin sauce
¼ teaspoon sugar

Thinly sliced green and white
*   scallion rings, for garnish*

1. To make the filling, spread the cabbage in a shallow container. Sprinkle with 2 teaspoons of the salt; toss well to mix. Set aside for 30 minutes at room temperature, then drain. Firmly squeeze in small handfuls to extract all the excess liquid.

2. In a large bowl, combine the cabbage, the remaining 1 teaspoon salt, and all the remaining filling ingredients through the water chestnuts. Stir to mix, add the pork, then stir in one direction until thoroughly blended. The filling can be made a night ahead; press a piece of plastic wrap directly on the surface of the meat and refrigerate.

3. To make the dumplings, follow step 3, page 353.

4. Shortly before serving, make the sauce: Pound the garlic and the salt to a paste with a mortar and pestle. Or, mince the garlic finely with a knife, then alternately sprinkle it with the salt and mash it with the side of the blade to form a smooth paste. Scrape the paste into a bowl, add the remaining sauce ingredients, and whisk thoroughly to blend. Taste; if the mixture is overly rich and thick, drizzle in up to 1 tablespoon of hot water to thin it.

5. To cook the dumplings, follow step 5, page 353.

6. To serve, portion the hot dumplings among heated serving bowls. Top the dumplings with a spoonful of the sauce. Sprinkle with the scallion rings to garnish.

MENU SUGGESTIONS: This is a hearty dish with a rich dressing. I frequently pair it with a China Moon House Salad (page 442) and a side dish of Pickled Red Cherry Peppers (page

DUMPLING PROTOCOL

Boiled dumplings are slippery critters. Go at them with chopsticks and they'll fly across the room.

Better to set your table Chinese-style with small porcelain spoons or with deep Western spoons that can cradle a slippery dumpling. This is the accident-free, traditional way to enjoy dumplings—guiding them from the spoon to your mouth with chopsticks, taking half the dumpling at a bite, and then letting the remainder slither back neatly into the spoon.

56) or Orange-Pickled Carrot Coins (page 58). Hearty eaters might enjoy these dumplings as a prelude to a platter of grilled or stir-fried vegetables and a crispy-skinned roasted chicken.

BOILED BEEF AND CHIVE DUMPLINGS WITH ORANGE-SPICE DRESSING

MAKES ABOUT 40 DUMPLINGS

The Mongols, who ruled China for several centuries, left a lasting culinary impression with their pairing of beef and lamb with orange. It's something worth pondering—visions of Genghis Khan over a bowl of dumplings—while you go about this dish.

The dumplings can be filled and poached up to a day in advance, leaving only a last-minute dunk in simmering water to heat them through. If you wish to hit a truer Mongolian note, lamb may be substituted for the beef in this recipe.

FILLING AND WRAPPERS:
½ pound Napa cabbage, diced
2 teaspoons kosher salt
¼ cup plus 2 tablespoons dried tree ears, soaked until softened, rinsed well, and chopped
1 tablespoon finely minced fresh ginger
¼ cup thinly sliced green and white scallion rings
3 tablespoons finely chopped Chinese chives
2 tablespoons finely slivered coriander leaves and stems

1 tablespoon soy sauce
1 tablespoon Chinese rice wine or dry sherry
1 tablespoon China Moon Chili-Orange Oil (page 15)
¼ teaspoon freshly ground pepper
1 pound coarsely ground beef top round
About 40 "sue-gow skins" (boiled dumpling wrappers), each about 3½ inches in diameter and ¹/₁₆ inch thin

SALTING CABBAGE

Salting chopped cabbage for dumpling fillings is an old Chinese trick. The salt simultaneously seasons the cabbage, extracts its water, and stiffens the cellular structure of the leaf, thereby giving it extra crunch. To really squeeze the cabbage free of excess moisture, keep the mixture at a comfortably warm room temperature and be sure to give the process ample time to work. This is one place where only kosher salt does a good job. Table salt leaves a lousy taste and sea salt an overly strong one.

SAUCE:
½ cup soy sauce
*¼ cup unseasoned Japanese rice
    vinegar*
¼ cup distilled white vinegar
*2 tablespoons China Moon
    Chili-Orange Oil*

*1 tablespoon "goop" from China
    Moon Chili-Orange Oil*

*Coriander sprigs and/or scallion
    rings, for garnish*

POACHING DUMPLINGS

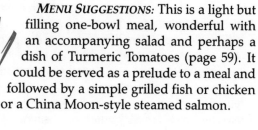

*Waiting for the dumplings
(or won-ton) to come to the
surface of the poaching
water—signaling that they
are nearly cooked—is a phenomenon known to all Chi-
nese kids and cooks who have
ever waited by a wok with
hunger in their bellies. When
a dumpling floats to the
surface, it is partially cooked.
When it floats high on the
surface of the liquid, typically
2 minutes later, it is cooked
through. The same float rule
applies to deep-frying.*

1. To make the filling, spread the cabbage in shallow container. Sprinkle with 1 teaspoon of the salt; toss well to mix. Set aside for 30 minutes at room temperature, then drain. Firmly squeeze in small handfuls to extract all the excess liquid.

2. In a large bowl, combine the cabbage, the remaining 1 teaspoon salt, and all the remaining filling ingredients through the black pepper. Stir to mix, add the beef, then stir in one direction until thoroughly blended. The filling can be made a night ahead; press a piece of plastic wrap directly on the surface of the meat and refrigerate.

3. To make the dumplings, follow step 3 on page 353.

4. Shortly before serving, make the sauce: Whisk together the ingredients for the sauce through the chili-orange oil "goop"; leave the whisk in the bowl.

5. To cook the dumplings, follow step 5 on page 353.

6. To serve, divide the hot dumplings among heated serving bowls. Whisk the sauce to recombine, then spoon a tablespoon or so over each portion. Add the sprigs of coriander and/or a sprinkle of scallion rings to garnish.

MENU SUGGESTIONS: This is a light but filling one-bowl meal, wonderful with an accompanying salad and perhaps a dish of Turmeric Tomatoes (page 59). It could be served as a prelude to a meal and followed by a simple grilled fish or chicken or a China Moon-style steamed salmon.

DEEP-FRIED CHICKEN AND CHILI WON-TON WITH PICKLED GINGER DIP

MAKES ABOUT 45 WON-TON

This is a truly untraditional, California-style won-ton. It should be fried within several hours of shaping or the wrappers will get sticky. Or you might freeze the won-ton once they're wrapped. It was a tradition in north China to freeze trayfuls of dumplings in the cold of a winter courtyard, so you might even claim authenticity in justifying convenience.

FILLING AND WRAPPERS:
8 to 10 fresh water chestnuts, finely diced
⅓ cup finely slivered coriander stems and leaves
¼ cup thinly sliced green and white scallion rings
1 small green serrano chili, finely minced
1 small red Fresno chili, finely minced
1 tablespoon China Moon Hot Chili Oil (page 10) or China Moon Chili-Orange Oil (page 15)
1 tablespoon finely minced fresh ginger
2 teaspoons finely minced garlic
1 tablespoon Chinese rice wine or dry sherry
2 teaspoons kosher salt
½ teaspoon Roasted Szechwan Pepper-Salt (page 5)
1 pound coarsely ground fresh chicken breast

About 45 thinnest possible, 3-inch-square won-ton skins
2 egg yolks, beaten (optional)

SAUCE:
1 cup juice from China Moon Pickled Ginger (page 8)
¼ cup plus 2 tablespoons unseasoned Japanese rice vinegar
1½ tablespoons sugar
1 tablespoon soy sauce

3 to 4 cups corn or peanut oil, for deep-frying
Green and white scallion rings and paper-thin rings of Fresno chili, to garnish the sauce
Fresh coriander sprigs or scallion brushes, to garnish the won-ton

THE VERSATILE WON-TON

A won-ton can be eaten in at least three ways: floating in a bowl of soup; poached and splashed with a spoonful of dressing; or deep-fried and served alongside a dip dish of sauce. All of our won-ton are interchangeable in all of these ways!

Poached won-ton are the most pristine and, to my tongue, the best. They are best poached just-wrapped, and best eaten freshly poached. Won-ton in soup are a good variation on the same theme. The same rule of excellence applies.

Fried won-ton are in a realm of their own. They are sexy, and people lust for them, at least at China Moon! My head thinks they are a distant second best, but I scarf them up just as quickly as anyone, and because I am the boss, I am often first in line and can get the most.

One way to poach your won-ton and deep-fry them, too, is to make a full batch to serve at two different meals. Wrap, poach, and eat half the won-ton straightaway, in a Proustian mood with elevated thoughts. Let the second half cool, then stow them in the fridge. Then, several days later, turn on Madonna, drag out Colette, and deep-fry the rest.

1. To make the filling, combine all of the ingredients through the pepper-salt in a large mixing bowl. Add the chicken and stir briskly in one direction until thoroughly blended. Poach a dab of the filling in simmering water until cooked. Taste, then adjust the filling with a dash more of this or that if your tongue desires. If you are working in advance, press a piece of plastic wrap directly on top of the filling and refrigerate for several hours or overnight.

2. Shape the won-ton following the directions in step 2 on page 95. If you are refrigerating the won-ton before frying, fry them directly from the refrigerator to prevent the wrappers from becoming soggy. If you are freezing the won-ton, fry them only partially defrosted for the same reason.

3. To make the sauce, combine the pickled ginger juice, vinegar, and sugar in a small, non-aluminum saucepan. Heat over low heat, stirring, until the sugar dissolves. Remove from the heat, let cool to room temperature, then stir in the soy sauce.

4. About 20 minutes before serving, preheat the oven to 250°F and move a rack to the lower third.

5. Heat a wok or wide, heavy, and deep skillet over high heat until hot enough to evaporate a bead of water on contact. Add oil to a depth of 1½ to 2 inches, reduce the heat to moderately high, and rest a deep-fry thermometer on the rim of the pot. When the oil wears a heavy haze and is hot enough to sizzle a won-ton, 375°F, add as many won-ton in quick succession as can float freely on the surface of the oil. Adjust the heat to maintain a steady temperature. Fry the won-ton, occasionally dunking or turning them to ensure even coloring, until they are a medium gold, 1½ to 2 minutes. Using a large Chinese mesh spoon, scoop them from the oil, hold them briefly above the pot to drip, then spread them apart on a baking sheet lined with a triple layer of paper towels. Do not over-fry the won-ton. They will continue to cook and darken a bit even after pulled from the oil. Pop the baking sheet in the oven while you fry the remaining won-ton. Before frying each batch, wait for the oil to regain 375°F.

6. Serve the won-ton immediately, on a platter of contrasting color, nestled around a dip dish or two of the sauce. Garnish the sauce with the scallion and chili rings; garnish the won-ton with a few sprigs of green.

MENU SUGGESTIONS: Fried won-ton are as at home at a Western barbecue as at a Chinese buffet. For the latter, you might team the won-ton with any of our cold fish, beef, lamb, or pork dishes and a platter of China Moon-style cold noodles. A steamed salmon would be particularly good if you'd prefer to follow with something hot.

DEEP-FRIED CRAB AND CORN WON-TON WITH GREEN CHILI SAUCE

MAKES ABOUT 36 WON-TONS

Corn and crab are frequent partners in Chinese cooking, hence their easy pairing in this otherwise untraditional won-ton. Studded with bright yellow corn kernels, they are as appealing texture-wise as they are to the taste buds.

Purer palates might like to poach these won-ton or stir them in soup (see directions on page 95). However, my staff and customers inhale them deep-fried, so there's no arguing with success.

*FILLING AND
WRAPPERS:*
*2 teaspoons finely minced fresh
    ginger*
1 teaspoon finely minced garlic
*1 green serrano chili, finely
    minced*
*3 tablespoons coarsely chopped
    coriander leaves and stems*
*¼ cup thinly sliced green and
    white scallion rings*
½ cup fresh corn kernels
1 teaspoon sugar
*2 teaspoons Chinese rice wine
    or dry sherry*

*2 teaspoons unseasoned
    Japanese rice vinegar*
1 teaspoon fine sea salt
Several twists of pepper
1 pound fresh crabmeat
½ pound fish paste
*About 36 thinnest possible, 3-
    inch-square won-ton skins*
2 egg yolks, beaten (optional)

MAKING YOUR OWN FISH PASTE

If the gelatinous fish paste found in many Chinatown fish markets is not easily or freshly gotten, you can experiment with many seafoods. I've used fresh salmon, crab, and scallops with success, always adding some fresh shrimp to give the paste its "glue." Blend the mixture to a purée in a food processor.

SAUCE:

*3 Anaheim chilis, seeded,
deribbed, and coarsely
chopped*

*2 yellow wax chilis, seeded,
deribbed, and coarsely
chopped*

1 large clove garlic, peeled

*¾ cup juice from China Moon
Pickled Ginger (page 8)*

*2 tablespoons distilled white
vinegar*

2 tablespoons corn or peanut oil

*1½ cups coarsely chopped
coriander leaves and stems*

*3 to 4 cups corn or peanut oil,
for deep-frying*

*Paper-thin rings of Fresno chili
or diced red bell pepper, to
garnish the sauce*

*Coriander sprigs, to garnish the
won-ton*

1. To make the filling, combine all of the ingredients through the crabmeat in a large mixing bowl. Add the fish paste and stir briskly in one direction until thoroughly blended. Poach a dab of the filling in simmering water until cooked. Taste, then adjust the filling with a dash more of this or that if your tongue desires. If you are working in advance, press a piece of plastic wrap directly on top of the filling and refrigerate for several hours or overnight.

2. Shape the won-ton following the directions in step 2 on page 95. If you are refrigerating the won-ton before frying, fry them directly from the refrigerator to prevent the wrappers from becoming soggy. If you are freezing the won-ton, fry them only partially defrosted for the same reason.

3. To make the sauce, combine the chilis, garlic, pickled ginger juice, and vinegar in a food processor. Blend until fine, scraping down the bowl once or twice. With the machine running, add the oil in a thin stream. Add the coriander and process until finely minced. If you are working in advance, wait until the last minute to buzz in the coriander.

4. About 20 minutes before serving, preheat the oven to 250°F and move a rack to the lower third.

5. To fry the won-ton, follow step 5, page 359.

6. Serve the won-ton immediately, on a platter of contrasting color, nestled around a dip dish or two of the sauce. Garnish the sauce with the chili rings or bell pepper dice; garnish the won-ton with a few sprigs of coriander.

MENU SUGGESTIONS: For a summertime supper, I'd partner the won-ton with a platter of thickly sliced garden tomatoes in a fresh basil vinaigrette. Or, a side dish of Cold-Tossed Corn Relish (page 441) and a bowl of fresh vegetable soup would be equally fine.

WORTH THE WAIT

///

Fresh corn, like freshly shelled peas and summer tomatoes, does for me what a slab of chocolate cake does for most folks. Growing up in a New Jersey suburb built on farm and nursery land, my palate was spoiled at an early age for these naturally and intensely sweet foods. We recently tried frozen corn in testing these recipes and the results were ho-hum blah. If you adore frozen corn, certainly use it. But if you want those won-ton to knock your socks off, then save the recipe for summer and gild it with an ear of freshly picked corn.

POACHED SHRIMP WON-TON WITH CORIANDER VINAIGRETTE

MAKES ABOUT 40 WON-TON

O wing to their paper-thin wrappers and tiny, hat-like shape, won-ton as we make them at China Moon are very delicate. In this recipe they are poached and dressed simply with an herbal vinaigrette.

Work with only the freshest shrimp. Or, substitute scallops or crab if you like. The won-ton can be wrapped and poached up to a day in advance and then plunged into simmering water for a last-minute reheating.

FILLING AND WRAPPERS:

6 fresh water chestnuts, finely diced

2 tablespoons finely minced fresh ginger

½ cup thinly sliced green and white scallion rings

1 tablespoon finely minced smoked ham

2 teaspoons kosher salt

2 teaspoons Chinese rice wine or dry sherry

1 tablespoon China Moon Hot Chili Oil (page 10) or China Moon Chili-Lemon Oil (page 12)

¼ teaspoon freshly ground pepper

1 egg white, beaten to a froth

1 pound fresh shrimp, peeled, deveined, and minced

About 40 thinnest possible, 3-inch-square won-ton skins

2 egg yolks, beaten (optional)

SAUCE:

½ cup Five-Flavor Oil (page 13)

2 tablespoons juice from China Moon Pickled Ginger (page 8)

3 tablespoons minced coriander leaves and stems

¼ teaspoon Roasted Szechwan Pepper-Salt (page 5)

Diced red bell pepper and coriander sprigs, for garnish

WON-TON HELPER

Helpful hosts provide their guests with Chinese spoons (or some other deep-bowled spoons) along with poached won-ton. Spearing a boiled won-ton with a chopstick is akin to landing a live fish with a fork.

Dumpling wrappers are sold in many thicknesses in a traditional Chinese market, all depending upon whether the dumplings are to be poached, fried, or steamed. Wrappers for boiled dumplings are of medium thickness—nearly 1/32 inch thick—a great contrast to paper-thin "shao-mai" steamed dumpling wrappers, for instance. Boiled dumpling wrappers, called something on the order of "sue-gow skins" in English translation, are available in many Chinese groceries with a large fresh noodle shelf. If you cannot find them, try using the somewhat thicker pot-sticker skins, or make a super-supple wrapper yourself, following the recipe in my first cookbook, "The Modern Art of Chinese Cooking." Medium-thick won-ton wrappers can also be used; just use a 3½-inch cookie cutter to cut circles from the squares. (For more on wrappers, see page 337.)

1. To make the filling, combine all of the ingredients through the egg white in a large mixing bowl. Add the shrimp and stir briskly in one direction until thoroughly blended. Poach a dab of the filling in simmering water until cooked. Taste, then adjust the filling with a dash more of this or that if your tongue desires. If you are working in advance, press a piece of plastic wrap directly on top of the filling and refrigerate for several hours or overnight.

2. Shape and poach the won-ton following steps 2 and 3 on pages 95 and 96. If you are poaching the won-ton in advance, rewarm them in a large pot of barely simmering water until thoroughly heated through, about 3 minutes.

3. Just before serving, whisk the sauce ingredients to emulsify.

4. Portion the drained won-ton among heated serving bowls of contrasting color. Ziggle a spoonful of sauce on top, garnish with a scattering of the bell pepper dice and a coriander sprig or two, then serve at once.

MENU SUGGESTIONS: For a light and elegant one-dish summer dinner, accompany the won-ton with a salad of baby greens and a dish of Cold-Tossed Corn Relish (page 441) or a platter of steamed corn or asparagus. Or, in a different mood, you might garnish them with Turmeric Tomatoes (page 59) and serve them as an appetizer, to be followed by a light poultry dish, such as Ma-La Steamed Poussin with Roasted Szechwan Pepper-Salt (page 153).

BASIC BUN DOUGH

MAKES 24 STEAMED OR BAKED BUNS

This is Amy's master recipe for both our steamed and baked bun doughs. It is a bit sweet on its own but balances perfectly with the full character of our well-spiced bun fillings.

Amy uses a KitchenAid–type mixer fitted with a flat paddle for her dough work. If you do not have one, you can mix the dough in a food processor or by hand.

Great buns of any kind take time, as all of us gym-enthusiasts can attest! Count on at least 12 hours for the first rising of the dough, and then another hour or more for the finished buns to rise.

FOR THE SPONGE:
1½ teaspoons active dry yeast
½ teaspoon sugar
⅓ cup warm (110°F) water
¾ cup all-purpose flour

DOUGH:
3¼ cups all-purpose flour
½ cup sugar
3 tablespoons solid vegetable shortening

2 tablespoons finely chopped Chinese chives
½ cup cold water
2 tablespoons milk
1 egg, beaten

Extra flour, for dusting the board
1 egg yolk beaten with 1 egg, for the egg wash
Black and/or white sesame seeds, for garnish

1. To make the sponge: Combine the yeast, sugar, and warm water in a medium bowl. Stir to dissolve. Add the ¾ cup flour and stir to mix. Seal airtight with plastic wrap and set aside in a warm (70 to 85°F) spot for about 10 minutes, until the mixture starts to rise.

2. To complete the dough: Combine the 3¼ cups flour, the sugar, shortening, and chives in the bowl of a mixer fitted with the flat paddle. Separately combine the cold water, milk, and egg, and stir them into the risen sponge. Scrape the sponge mixture into the flour mixture, then blend on slow speed to bring the dough together in a soft, ragged mass. If the dough is too wet and sticks badly to the paddle, sprinkle in a bit more flour to make it behave.

3. Turn the dough and any unincorporated bits from the bowl out onto a lightly floured board. Knead gently several times into a soft, lopsided ball. Do not overwork the dough. Put it in a large mixing bowl nearly double its size, then press a large piece of plastic wrap directly on the dough. Refrigerate the dough until it is 1½ to 2 times its original size, at least 12 to 15 hours, or a full day if more convenient. The refrigeration

---

HOW TO SHAPE AND FILL BUNS

1. Roll the pin towards the center of the dough round, leaving a plump "bellybutton" unrolled in the middle.

2. Put the filling on top of the bellybutton, then begin pleating the edge.

3. Continue making tiny pleats, enclosing the filling as you go.

4. When the last pleat is made, twist the closure shut in the same direction.

5. The finished bun is gathered in a tight closure. Turn it upside down (pleated side down) to bake or steam.

will ensure that the dough rises slowly, resulting in a fine crumb and high loft for the buns.

While the dough rests and rises, make and cool the filling for the buns.

4. To shape and fill the buns: Turn the risen dough out onto a lightly floured board and divide the dough into 2 pieces. While you work with one piece, cover the other with a dry towel. On a lightly floured board, roll the first piece into a 1-foot-long even log, then slice it crosswise into twelve 1-inch pieces (each weighing about 1½ ounces). Put the pieces on one side of the board, cut side down and not touching; cover with a dry cloth. Roll out and slice the remaining dough; cover the second batch of dough pieces.

5. Working with one piece at a time and leaving the rest covered, roll out the first piece of dough, as illustrated here, into a 4-inch circle with evenly thin edges and a puffy 1-inch belly button in the middle. Try not to use any additional flour, as the bun can then become difficult to pleat together. Put 1 heaping, compressed tablespoon of filling on top of the belly button, then pleat and twist the bun shut as illustrated.

If you are baking the buns, put the finished bun, pleated side down, on a baking sheet lined with parchment paper. Shape and fill the remaining buns, one at a time, placing them on the baking sheet with 1½ inches between them.

If you are steaming the buns, put each one, pleated side down, on its own 2-inch square of parchment, then position them 1½ inches apart on the baking sheet. For a full batch of dough and filling, you will need 2 baking sheets to allow for the spread.

6. Lightly brush the tops and upper sides of the buns with the egg wash. To decorate, sprinkle a dusting of sesame seeds on top. Let the buns rise, uncovered, in a warm (70 to 85°F) spot until they are half again their original size, 1 to 1½ hours. If your kitchen is very cold, settle yourself in for a longer rise.

7. To bake the buns: Preheat the oven to 350°F. Move the racks to divide the oven evenly into thirds. (If you are doing a half-recipe on one baking sheet, arrange a single rack in the middle of the oven.) Bake the buns until golden, 10 to 12 minutes. Midway through baking, to ensure even coloring, quickly rotate the trays from front to back and from the upper rack to the lower.

If you are baking the buns in advance for reheating later, bake them only to a light gold; they will pick up a bit more color when rewarmed. Let the buns cool to room temperature, then wrap and refrigerate them if you are holding them more than 6 to 8 hours. Let come to room temperature before rewarming. Reheat in a preheated 250°F oven until thoroughly hot, about 5 to 6 minutes.

8. To steam the buns: Bring ample water for steaming to a boil over moderately high heat. Arrange the buns on their parchment squares and 1 inch apart on steaming racks. Steam the buns for 10 minutes, adjusting the heat so the steam gushes heartily around the buns. Rotate the tiers carefully midway through steaming. Steam them for 2 to 3 minutes longer if you are steaming several tiers at a time.

If you are steaming the buns in advance, put them aside to cool to room temperature. Seal and refrigerate if you wish to hold them for more than 6 to 8 hours; let come to room temperature before resteaming. Reheat over gentle steam, each bun still on its parchment square, until thoroughly hot, about 8 minutes.

9. Serve the buns hot, either on a platter of contrasting color or nested prettily in a woven bamboo tray.

BUNS OF STEEL

Kneading dough, whether by hand or machine, develops the gluten, which the Chinese call "flour muscle." Gluten needs time to relax. Cut the resting or rising time short and you'll wind up with tough (not fluffy) buns!

HOISIN PORK BUNS WITH GINGER AND GARLIC

MAKES ABOUT 24 BUNS

*S*teamed or baked, these savory and spicy pork buns are several provinces (and maybe light-years) north of the classic Cantonese pork buns with their heavy though compelling sweetness. I adore them and think them worth the trouble.

The beauty of buns is that they can be prepared well in advance—days ahead, if you wish—and then popped into the steamer or oven to reheat at any given hungry moment.

BROOM HANDLE BOOGIE

My favorite tool for rolling out dough disks to shape them for buns is a 6-inch length cut from a broom handle. Amy uses a classier French rolling stick that is a big longer and tapered at the ends but is about the same 1 inch in diameter. Both are very easy to control. You roll with the seat of one palm while the fingers of the other hand are busy turning the dough. You can perform the same feat with a larger rolling pin, but be a bit more demure, lest the weightier pin steamroller the dough and crush the belly button.

Basic Bun Dough (page 363)

MARINADE AND PORK:
1 tablespoon hoisin sauce
2 teaspoons soy sauce
1½ teaspoons China Moon Chili-Orange Oil (page 15)
1 teaspoon "goop" from China Moon Chili-Orange Oil
2 teaspoons cornstarch
2 teaspoons Chinese rice wine or dry sherry
1 pound coarsely ground pork butt

AROMATICS:
2 tablespoons finely minced fresh ginger
2 tablespoons finely minced garlic
½ cup thinly sliced green and white scallion rings
1 small red Fresno chili, finely minced
1 small green serrano chili, finely minced

SEASONINGS:
2 tablespoons mushroom soy sauce
1 tablespoon Serrano-Lemongrass Vinegar (page 19) or unseasoned Japanese rice vinegar
1½ tablespoons cider vinegar
½ teaspoon Chinese chili sauce

4 to 5 tablespoons corn or peanut oil, for stir-frying
1 large yellow onion, finely diced
1 cup finely diced celery
2 cups diced Napa cabbage
2 tablespoons cornstarch
3 tablespoons cold pork or chicken stock or water

1. Make the bun dough as detailed in steps 1 through 3 on page 364.

2. Combine all of the marinade ingredients through the rice wine in a bowl; stir until the cornstarch is smooth. Add the pork and stir with your hand in one direction until thoroughly blended. Press a piece of plastic wrap directly on top of the meat and set aside to marinate at cool room temperature for several hours, or refrigerate overnight. Bring to room temperature before cooking.

3. Combine the aromatics through the serrano chili in a small dish; cover until ready to use.

4. Combine the seasonings in a small bowl. Stir to blend, leaving the spoon in the bowl.

5. Heat a wok or large heavy skillet over high heat until hot enough to evaporate a bead of water on contact. Add 1 tablespoon of the oil, swirl to glaze the pan, and reduce the heat to moderately high. When the oil is hot enough to sizzle a bit of pork, add the pork to the pan. Toss and poke briskly with a spatula to break up the meat, adjusting the heat so it sizzles heartily. As soon as the pork is 95 percent gray, remove it from the pan and drain it in a colander. Clean the pan and return it to the stove.

6. Heat the pan over high heat until a bead of water evaporates on contact. Add 1 tablespoon of the oil, swirl to glaze the pan, and reduce the heat to moderately high. When the oil is hot enough to sizzle a bit of onion, add the onion and toss until translucent and golden, about 4 minutes. Adjust the heat to maintain a merry sizzle and drizzle a bit more oil down the side of the pan, if needed to prevent sticking. Spread the onions on a platter, wipe the pan clean, and return it to the stove.

7. Heat the pan over high heat until a bead of water evaporates on contact. Add 2 tablespoons of the oil, swirl to glaze the pan, and reduce the heat to moderate. When the oil is hot enough to sizzle a scallion ring, add the aromatics. Stir gently until fully fragrant, 20 to 30 seconds, adjusting the heat so they foam without browning. Add the celery, toss to combine, then lower the heat and let stew until softened. Add the cabbage, toss to combine, and let stew until juicy, 5 to 6 minutes in all. Return the pork to the pan. Slide the onion along with any of its liquids into the pan as well. Toss to combine. Stir the seasonings and add them to the pan. Toss until the mixture is very hot and the liquids come to a simmer.

8. Quickly blend the cornstarch and the stock or water until smooth, then add it to the pan in a thin stream looped over the filling. Stir until the mixture is thick, heavy, and glossy, and a dab cooled briefly and then chewed leaves no floury taste on the roof of your mouth, about 5 minutes. Spread the filling in a thin layer on 2 large platters or a jelly roll pan. Refrigerate, uncovered, until thoroughly cold. Once cool, taste; add a dash more of this or that if needed. The cold filling may be sealed and refrigerated for a day or two before using.

9. Shape, cook, and serve the buns as detailed in steps 4 through 9 on pages 365 and 366.

MENU SUGGESTIONS: A China Moon House Salad (page 442) would be one approach here, or a pairing of the buns with most any salad you enjoy. For heartier times, a hot and sour soup would fit my own personal bill. If you are serving

SMOOTH BUNS TAKE TIME

For the best crumb and loft in the final baking, as well as the easiest handling during shaping, be sure to let the dough relax in the refrigerator for a full 12 to 15 hours—or up to 24 hours, if you like—before shaping and filling.

If you are in the grip of bun desperation, you can let the dough rise to nearly double its bulk at room temperature, which should take 1 to 2 hours if the rising spot is 70 to 80°F. But, your buns (nothing personal) may look slightly wrinkled. Never mind, an imperfect bun can still be quite appealing.

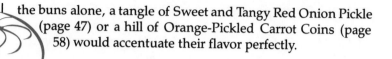

the buns alone, a tangle of Sweet and Tangy Red Onion Pickle (page 47) or a hill of Orange-Pickled Carrot Coins (page 58) would accentuate their flavor perfectly.

STEAMED OR BAKED BUNS STUFFED WITH CHICKEN AND OYSTER SAUCE

MAKES ABOUT 24 BUNS

The warm, wonderful taste of these buns reminds me of one of my favorite cartoons, depicting a happy, bread-kneading character who is so seduced by the smell and feel of the rising dough that she is gradually consumed by her creation. If one could jump into a bun, this one would be it!

Steamed buns are tricky in that the activity of the yeast and the humidity of the steamer often leave them looking shipwrecked. It is definitely worth a try, however, and even a new cook can produce a beautiful batch. Faint hearts can bake the buns instead of steaming them, and lesser souls can settle for simply munching the filling right out of the bowl or rolling it in lettuce leaves instead.

The filling and dough-making are both best done a full day in advance. The buns can be filled and steamed on day two, and then reheated before serving a day or two later, so there's lots of flexibility en route. Or, if you're famished for buns, make the filling and dough very early in the morning, and then fill them and cook them for a late-night supper.

Basic Bun Dough (page 363)

MARINADE AND CHICKEN:

2 teaspoons oyster sauce
1 tablespoon soy sauce
2 teaspoons China Moon Chili-Orange Oil (page 15) or China Moon Hot Chili Oil (page 10)
1 teaspoon sugar
2 teaspoons cornstarch
⅛ teaspoon freshly ground pepper
1¼ pounds coarsely ground fresh chicken breast

AROMATICS:

1 tablespoon finely minced fresh ginger
1 tablespoon finely minced garlic
½ cup thinly sliced green and white scallion rings
¼ teaspoon dried red chili flakes

SEASONINGS:

⅓ cup oyster sauce
1½ tablespoons mushroom soy sauce
2 teaspoons cider vinegar
2 teaspoons Serrano-Lemongrass Vinegar (page 19) or unseasoned Japanese rice vinegar
1 teaspoon sugar
¼ teaspoon freshly ground pepper

4½ to 5½ tablespoons corn or peanut oil, for stir-frying
1 small yellow onion, finely diced
1 cup very thinly sliced domestic mushrooms
2 teaspoons Chinese rice wine or dry sherry
1½ cups diced Napa cabbage
2½ tablespoons cornstarch
¼ cup cold chicken stock or water

BAKING SHEETS

Heavy-duty baking sheets are a great helpmate in baking buns, in addition to cookies. They hold the heat and distribute it evenly, allowing the bottom to cook and color slowly in tune with the top.

1. Make the bun dough as detailed in steps 1 through 3 on page 364.

2. Combine all of the marinade ingredients through the pepper in a bowl. Add the chicken and stir with your hand in one direction until thoroughly blended. Press a piece of plastic wrap directly on top of the mixture and set aside to marinate at cool room temperature for several hours or refrigerate overnight. Bring to room temperature before cooking.

3. Combine the aromatics in a small dish and cover until ready to use.

4. Combine the seasonings in a small bowl. Stir to blend, leaving the spoon in the bowl.

5. Heat a wok or large heavy skillet over high heat until hot enough to evaporate a bead of water on contact. Add 1½ tablespoons of the oil, swirl to glaze the pan, and reduce the heat to moderately high. When the oil is

BELLY BUTTONS

The trick to forming a perfect dough round to enclose a bun filling is to leave an inch-wide belly button (an "outie") in the center of the dough disc. That means that you roll toward but not fully into the center of the dough, turning the dough after every roll of the pin and totally avoiding the puffy middle of the round. The thinner edges are perfect for pinch-pleating, and the thicker belly can then stretch and puff happily over the filling. If all this seems oblique, catch the illustrations on pages 364 and 365.

hot enough to sizzle a dab of chicken, add the chicken to the pan. Toss and poke briskly with a spatula to break up the meat, adjusting the heat so it sizzles heartily, until the outside of the chicken is 95 percent white. Put the chicken in a colander to drain. Thoroughly wipe the pan clean and return it to the stove.

6. Heat the pan over high heat until a bead of water evaporates on contact. Add 1 tablespoon of the oil, swirl to glaze the pan, and reduce the heat to moderately high. When the oil is hot enough to sizzle a bit of onion, add the onion and toss until golden and translucent, about 2 to 3 minutes. Add the mushrooms and toss until they soften and begin to give up their juices, about 1½ minutes more. Adjust the heat to maintain a merry sizzle and drizzle a bit more oil down the side of the pan, if needed to prevent sticking. Drizzle the wine around the edge of the pan, toss several times to deglaze it, then spread the mixture on a platter. Wipe the pan clean and return it to the stove.

7. Heat the pan over high heat until a bead of water evaporates on contact. Add 2 tablespoons of the oil, swirl to glaze the pan, and reduce the heat to moderate. When the oil is hot enough to sizzle a scallion ring, add the aromatics. Stir gently until fully fragrant, 20 to 30 seconds, adjusting the heat so they foam without browning. Add the cabbage and toss until wilted, then lower the heat and let stew until juicy, about 4 minutes in all. Return the chicken to the pan. Slide the mushroom mixture along with any of its liquids into the pan as well. Toss to combine. Stir the seasonings and add them to the pan. Toss until the mixture is very hot and the liquids come to a simmer.

8. Quickly blend the cornstarch and the stock or water until smooth, then add it to the pan in a thin stream looped over the filling. Stir until the mixture is thick, heavy, and glossy, and a dab cooled briefly and then chewed leaves no floury taste on the roof of your mouth, about 5 minutes. Spread the filling in a thin layer on 2 large platters or a jelly roll pan. Refrigerate, uncovered, until thoroughly cold. Once cool, taste; add a dash more of this or that if needed. The cold filling may be sealed and refrigerated for a day or two before using.

9. Shape, cook, and serve the buns as detailed in steps 4 through 9 on pages 365 and 366.

MENU SUGGESTIONS: A small bowl of Peking Spicy Cabbage Pickle (page 52) and a large bowl of any of our hot and sour soups (pages 102 through 107) are favorite partners to the buns. Otherwise, a China Moon House Salad (page 442) or a fresh vegetable soup would be good.

BUDDHA BUNS

MAKES ABOUT 24 BUNS

*S*picy and tangy with a slight edge of sweetness, these golden baked buns stuffed with curried vegetables are the kind of buns I always yearned for and never found during my year of vegetarian eating in Taiwan. They are a lunchtime restaurant favorite among vegetarians and carnivores alike.

The filling can be done in advance and is delicious, by itself, on Garlic Croutons (page 37). The buns can also be shaped and baked ahead, then re-warmed just prior to serving.

Basic Bun Dough (page 363)

AROMATICS:
1 tablespoon finely minced fresh ginger
1½ tablespoons finely minced garlic
1 small green serrano chili, finely minced
1 to 2 small red Fresno chilis, finely minced
¼ cup thinly sliced green and white scallion rings

SEASONINGS:
1½ tablespoons mushroom soy sauce

2½ tablespoons cider vinegar
1½ teaspoons kosher salt
1½ teaspoons sugar

GREAT BUNS

When I arrived in Taipei in 1971 in the midst of monsoon season, it was only to land on my butt emotionally. I was a vegetarian in those days and expected Taiwan to be a Chinese Happy Land of meatless eating. As the weeks rained on, my spirits dampened with the streets. It seemed that the Chinese adored putting a dash of meat, poultry, or fish in everything, and that the only vegetarian dish to be had in the average non-vegetarian restaurant was a grim plate of stewed green cabbage with black mushrooms. I remember going to bed, hungry and in tears, and watching a giant Asian cockroach whiz across my room. ("So big they can fly," as one expatriate student had warned me.) In these perilous first weeks on the island that was later to become a beloved home, I would have traded my kingdom for a falafel.

Rescue came in the unexpected form of Harvey Stupler, now one of America's great Chinese art historians and teachers, then merely a hated classmate. I'd known him at Princeton, thought him a snob, and took him as one more note of injury to add to the rain and the cabbage and mushrooms. But dislike bloomed to platonic love, steered wisely by a full stomach. Harvey, who was very mobile in the world of Chinese restaurants (thanks to a childhood in New York's Chinatown surrounded by the Chinese workers in his father's barrel factory), took me literally by the hand. We went to a Buddhist vegetarian restaurant he'd heard about, a rickety closet-size joint behind the train station where they made only one thing: steamed vegetarian buns. Maybe they made other things, but that is what I remember. The dough was vaguely sweet and pleasantly squishy; the inside was a savory mix of mushrooms and Chinese mushroom greens. In memory, they combined the textures of our duck buns with the excitement of our Buddha buns. I can taste those buns still, more than twenty years later.

FILLING:
2 to 3 tablespoons corn or peanut oil, for stir-frying
1 cup diced celery
1 cup finely shredded carrots
3 cups diced Napa cabbage
6 large dried Chinese black mushrooms, soaked until softened, stemmed, sliced paper-thin
1 can (10 ounces) curried gluten, drained and minced (see page 374)

2 ounces (1 small skein) glass noodles, soaked in hot water until translucent, cut into 2-inch lengths
2 tablespoons cornstarch
3 tablespoons cold vegetable or chicken stock or water
¼ cup coarsely chopped coriander leaves and stems

1. Make the bun dough as detailed in steps 1 through 3 on page 364.

2. Combine the aromatics in a small dish and seal until ready to use.

3. Combine the seasonings in a small bowl. Stir to blend, leaving the spoon in the bowl.

4. Heat a wok or large heavy skillet over high heat until hot enough to evaporate a bead of water on contact. Add 2 tablespoons of the oil, swirl to glaze the pan, and reduce the heat to moderate. When the oil is hot enough to sizzle a bit of minced ginger, add the aromatics. Stir gently until fully fragrant, 20 to 30 seconds, adjusting the heat so they foam without browning. Add the celery and toss until softened, about 2 minutes. Add the carrots, toss to combine, then lower the heat and let stew until juicy. Add the cabbage, toss to wilt, and let stew for 1 minute more. Adjust the heat to maintain a steamy sizzle and drizzle a bit more oil down the side of the pan, if needed to prevent sticking. Add the mushrooms and gluten, and toss to mix. Add the glass noodles and toss to combine. Stir the seasonings and add them to the pan. Toss until the mixture is very hot and the liquids come to a simmer.

5. Quickly blend the cornstarch and the stock or water until smooth, then add it to the pan in a thin stream looped over the filling. Stir until the mixture is thick, heavy, and glossy, and a dab cooled briefly and then chewed leaves no floury taste on the roof of your mouth, about 5 minutes. Fold in the coriander. Spread the filling in a thin layer on 2 large platters or a jelly roll pan. Refrigerate, uncovered, until thoroughly cold. Once cool, taste; season if needed. The cold filling may be sealed and refrigerated for a day or two before using.

6. Shape and bake the buns as detailed in steps 4 through 7 on page 365. Serve them hot.

MENU SUGGESTIONS: Buddha Buns are great all by themselves or alongside a homey bowl of soup. They are also wonderful as part of a Chinese-style buffet, served along with most any of our cold noodles and/or cold poultry or fish dishes.

MANY MUSHROOM BUNS

MAKES ABOUT 24 BUNS

Onions, mushrooms, and oyster sauce are made for each other; the marriage is happily consummated in these yummy baked buns. It is a very simple, flexible filling, one that can be dressed down with humble button mushrooms or made exotic with the addition of wild mushrooms.

Both the filling and dough can be made a day or more in advance; the buns can be baked in advance as well. They rewarm nicely, making them a good choice for a party or for fueling a busy week.

Basic Bun Dough (page 363)

AROMATICS:
1 tablespoon finely minced fresh ginger
2 tablespoons finely minced garlic

SEASONINGS:
¼ cup Vegetable Infusion (page 82), China Moon Infusion (page 72), or unsalted vegetable or chicken stock

⅓ cup oyster sauce
3 tablespoons mushroom soy sauce
2 tablespoons Serrano-Lemongrass Vinegar (page 19) or unseasoned Japanese rice vinegar
2½ tablespoons Chinese rice wine or dry sherry
½ teaspoon kosher salt
1 teaspoon sugar
⅛ teaspoon freshly ground pepper

FILLING:
3 to 4 tablespoons corn or
  peanut oil, for stir-frying
1 yellow onion, finely diced
2 shallots, minced
2 pounds domestic or wild
  mushrooms, very thinly
  sliced
½ cup finely chopped Chinese
chives

1½ cups thinly sliced green and
  white scallion rings
3 tablespoons cornstarch
5 tablespoons cold vegetable or
  chicken stock or water

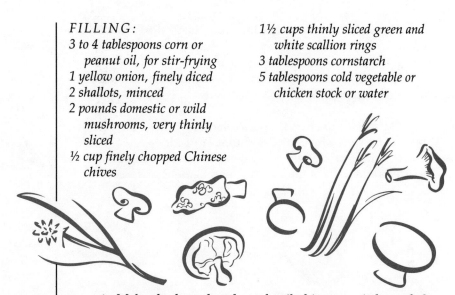

1. Make the bun dough as detailed in steps 1 through 3 on page 364.

2. Combine the aromatics in a small dish. Cover until ready to use.

3. Combine the seasonings in a small bowl. Stir to blend, leaving the spoon in the bowl.

4. Heat a wok or large heavy skillet over high heat until hot enough to evaporate a bead of water on contact. Add 2½ tablespoons of the oil, swirl to glaze the pan, and reduce the heat to moderate. When the oil is hot enough to sizzle a bit of minced ginger, add the aromatics. Stir gently until fully fragrant, 20 to 30 seconds, adjusting the heat so they foam without browning. Add the onion and shallots, and toss until translucent, about 2 minutes. Add the mushrooms and toss until they begin to give up their liquid, about 2 minutes more. Adjust the heat to maintain a merry sizzle and drizzle a bit more oil down the side of the pan, if needed to prevent sticking. Add the chives and half of the scallion rings, and toss to mix. Stir the seasonings and add them to the pan. Toss until the mixture is very hot and the liquids come to a simmer.

5. Quickly blend the cornstarch and the stock or water until smooth, then add it to the pan in a thin stream looped over the filling. Stir until the mixture is thick, heavy, and glossy, and a dab cooled briefly and then chewed leaves no floury taste on the roof of your mouth, about 5 minutes. Fold in the remaining scallion rings. Spread the filling in a thin layer on 2 large platters or a jelly roll pan. Refrigerate, uncov-

LIBRARY GLUE

The texture of this mushroom filling when properly cooked should be, in the words of my great friend and former sous-chef Barbara Haimes, "a near approximation to library glue." Any filling to be put inside a bun or springroll needs to be sufficiently thick so as not to leak. A fresh mushroom filling, which grows extra juicy upon reheating, is especially in need of binding—or, should I say, straight-jacketing.

ered, until thoroughly cold. Once cool, taste; add a dash more of this or that if needed. The cold filling may be sealed and refrigerated for a day or two before using.

6. Shape and bake the buns as detailed in steps 4 through 7 on page 365. Serve them hot.

MENU SUGGESTIONS: I particularly like these buns with a tangle of Sweet and Tangy Red Onion Pickle (page 47) and a bowl of most any of our soups. For a Western companion, a roasted or braised poultry dish would be delicious.

BRAISED DUCK BUNS WITH MUSHROOMS AND MUSTARD GREENS

MAKES ABOUT 24 BUNS

Baked or steamed, this is one exotic bun! The flavors of Chinese black mushrooms and duck are wonderful together, and their richness is offset perfectly by the piquant mustard greens.

If you have our duck confit (page 170) on hand, you can eliminate the braising and simply hop down to step 4.

The filling and dough can be done in advance, as can the shaping and cooking of the buns. They rewarm beautifully, making this a good choice for one big dinner, or several small dinners stretched over a busy week.

TOO POOPED TO PLEAT

If after making the bun dough, your computer takes a nosedive, your parents call to hassle you, or your kids turn the kitchen upside-down, you can cash in on the notion of making buns and simply bake off the dough in other ways. Over the years, little round rolls, small loaves, and giant braided challahs have all made appearances at staff meals when Amy had either too much dough or too much other stuff going on to cope with buns.

Simply roll the dough into whatever shape you like, egg-wash it, and decorate as you would the buns, then bake it in the middle of a preheated 350°F oven until golden on top and baked through—when the bottom sounds hollow when you thump it. If you made the filling before you gave up the ghost, smooth it on top of the hot bread and enjoy!

Basic Bun Dough (page 363)

DUCK AND BRAISING MIXTURE:

2 to 3 tablespoons corn or peanut oil, for searing and stir-frying
2 pounds fresh duck legs
1 small yellow onion, diced
1 small carrot, diced
1 rib celery, diced
10 quarter-size coins fresh ginger, smashed
6 cloves garlic, peeled and smashed
1 stalk fresh lemongrass, smashed and cut into 1-inch lengths
2 teaspoons Szechwan peppercorns
2 teaspoons black peppercorns
8 cups unsalted duck or chicken stock

AROMATICS:

2 teaspoons finely minced fresh ginger
2 teaspoons finely minced garlic

SEASONINGS:

1½ tablespoons soy sauce
¼ teaspoon Roasted Szechwan Pepper-Salt (page 5)
½ teaspoon kosher salt
1 teaspoon Ma-La Oil (page 17), Five-Flavor Oil (page 13), or Japanese sesame oil
1 tablespoon Dijon mustard

1 tablespoon corn or peanut oil, for stir-frying
½ cup finely diced celery
4 to 6 large dried Chinese black mushrooms, soaked until soft, stemmed, and minced
1 packed cup diced Chinese mustard greens
1 cup diced Napa cabbage
2 tablespoons cornstarch
3 tablespoons cold unsalted duck or chicken stock or water

1. Make the bun dough as detailed in steps 1 through 3 on page 364.

2. To sear the duck: Heat a large wok or large heavy skillet over high heat until hot enough to evaporate a bead of water on contact. Add 1 tablespoon of the oil and swirl to glaze the pan. Reduce the heat to moderate and add the duck legs in a single layer. Sear, turning once or twice, until the fat is rendered and the skin is crispy and golden, about 4 minutes. Adjust the heat so that the skin crisps nicely without the fat smoking too much. Remove the duck legs to paper towels to drain. Wipe the pan and return it to the stove.

3. To braise the duck: Heat the pan over high heat until a bead of water evaporates on contact. Add 1 tablespoon of the oil, swirl to glaze the pan, and reduce the heat to moderately high. When the oil is hot enough to sizzle a bit of onion, add the onion, carrot, celery, ginger, and garlic to the pan. Toss until softened and browned at the edges, about 3 minutes, adjusting the heat to maintain a merry sizzle and drizzling a bit more oil down the side of the pan, if needed to prevent sticking. Add the lemongrass, peppercorns, and stock, and stir to combine. Bring the mixture to a boil over high heat. Add the duck legs, adjust the heat to maintain a weak simmer, then braise the duck until the meat in the thickest part of the leg is very tender, about 1 hour. Remove the duck to a platter to cool. Once cool, strip the meat in large shreds from the bones and chop it coarsely. Strain the liquid; skim any fat from the surface. Reserve ⅔ cup for the seasonings. The rest can be seasoned and served alongside the buns as a light soup, or can be refrigerated or frozen for other cooking needs.

4. Combine the aromatics in a small dish and cover until ready to use.

5. Combine the seasonings with the ⅔ cup reserved braising liquid in a bowl. Stir to blend, leaving the spoon in the bowl.

6. Heat a wok or large heavy skillet over high heat until hot enough to evaporate a bead of water on contact. Add the oil, swirl to glaze the pan, and reduce the heat to moderate. When the oil is hot enough to sizzle a bit of minced ginger, add the aromatics. Stir gently until fully fragrant, 20 to 30 seconds, adjusting the heat so they foam without browning. Add the celery, toss to combine, then lower the heat and let stew until softened, about 2 minutes. Add the mushrooms and toss until hot, then add the mustard greens and Napa cabbage and toss 2 minutes more. Add the chopped duck meat and toss to mix. Stir the seasonings and add them to the pan. Toss until the mixture is very hot and the liquids come to a simmer.

7. Quickly blend the cornstarch and the stock or water until smooth, then add it to the pan in a thin stream looped over the filling. Stir until the mixture is thick, heavy, and glossy, and a dab cooled briefly and then chewed leaves no floury taste on the roof of your mouth, about 5 minutes. Spread the filling in a thin layer on 2 large platters or a jelly roll pan. Refrigerate, uncovered, until thoroughly cold. Once cool, taste; add a dash more of this or that if needed. The cold filling may be sealed and refrigerated for a day or two before using.

8. Shape, cook, and serve the buns as detailed in steps 4 through 9 on pages 365 and 366.

MENU SUGGESTIONS: The rich taste of the buns is nicely offset by a salad of greens and baby beets with our Orange

CHINESE VS. WESTERN MUSTARD GREENS

///

Chinese mustard greens have a softer flavor when cooked than Western mustard greens. If you are unable to find the Chinese variety, substitute twice the amount of Napa cabbage or ruby chard for a different but good flavor. Or, if you like the sharpness of Western mustard greens, use 1 part Western mustard greens to 2 parts Napa or chard.

Vinaigrette (page 25), or a bowl of China Moon Infusion (page 72) seasoned simply with Roasted Szechwan Pepper-Salt (page 5) and decorated with glass noodles and chopped chives. If you are looking for a more robust companion, a corn chowder would be delicious.

SESAME-ENCRUSTED FLATBREADS

MAKES 18 FLATBREADS

This is one of the great treats of northern Chinese eating—a rectangular, flaky flatbread that is cooked in a skillet with a blanket of sesame seeds. It is classically a breakfast food, split and stuffed with a deep-fried dough wand and then dunked cheerfully into a bowl of hot soybean milk. At China Moon, however, we love it as a crispy sandwich bread. Stuffed with thin slices of any of our roasted meats and cut into diagonal lozenges for finger eating, it is a great lunchtime favorite.

The flatbreads can be made in an hour. If you wish to prepare them in advance, be sure to leave them at room temperature. Refrigerated, they turn a bit leathery.

ROUX:
¼ cup Japanese sesame oil,
  Ma-La Oil (page 17), or
  Five-Flavor Oil (page 13)
¼ cup plus 2 tablespoons
  corn or peanut oil
1 cup all-purpose flour

DOUGH:
4½ cups plus 2 tablespoons all-
  purpose flour

1¾ teaspoons Roasted Szechwan
  Pepper-Salt (page 5)
1 tablespoon baking powder
¾ cup very hot tap water
1 cup very cold tap water

*Extra flour, for rolling out the
  dough*
*About 2 cups untoasted white
  sesame seeds*
*½ to 1 cup corn or peanut oil,
  for pan-frying*

1. Make the roux: Combine the sesame and corn oils in a heavy 1-quart saucepan and set over moderate heat until the oil is hot enough to foam a pinch of flour, 4 to 5 minutes. Add the 1 cup flour and stir constantly for 2 minutes while the mixture bubbles and turns a pale gold. Watch the heat so the temperature does not rise and scorch the oil. Remove from the heat and let cool to room temperature, stirring occasionally.

2. Make the dough: Combine the flour for the dough, the pepper-salt, and baking powder in the bowl of a mixer fitted with the flat paddle. With the machine running on low speed, add first the hot and then the cold water in quick succession, and mix until the mixture masses in a soft ball. If the dough is very wet and sticks badly to the paddle, sprinkle in a bit more flour to make it behave.

3. Turn the dough out onto a lightly floured board. Cover with plastic wrap and let rest for 10 minutes. (If you have mixed the dough in a food processor, it will need to rest upwards of 30 minutes.)

4. Divide the dough into 2 equal portions and gently roll each portion into an even 9-inch log. Slice each log into 1-inch nuggets (each weighing 2¼ ounces), for a total of 18 nuggets. Put the nuggets, cut side down, on a lightly floured portion of the board, cover with plastic wrap, and let rest 5 minutes more. While the dough is resting, put the roux, a pastry brush, a shallow dish holding the sesame seeds, and 2 parchment or waxed paper–lined baking sheets alongside your work table.

5. One at a time, shape the flatbreads: Roll the first dough nugget into a rectangle 6 inches long and 3 inches wide. Flour the board only very lightly, if needed; if too much flour is used and the dough gets dry, the sesame seeds won't stick. Brush 1 teaspoon of the roux over the top two-thirds of the rectangle, as illustrated on this page, brushing all the way out to the edge. Then, as you would fold a letter into even thirds, bring the bottom third up over the middle and fold down the top. (The roux will squish out a bit; simply wipe it up as you go to keep the board clean for rolling.) Pick up the dough packet, press the bottom side down into the sesame seeds, then turn it sesame side up and roll it out lengthwise into the original rectangular shape. Put the rolled-out flatbread, sesame side up, on the baking sheet. Proceed to roll out the remaining dough nuggets. Keep the board clean as you work. There will be extra roux when you finish; discard it.

ROLLING
FLATBREADS

1. Brush the top two-thirds of the dough rectangle with the roux.

2. Fold the bottom third over the middle third. Then, fold the top third down over the middle. You will have a neat 2- × 3-inch packet.

3. Press the dough packet into the sesame seeds, encrusting the bottom.

4. Turn the packet sesame seed side up, turn it 90 degrees, then roll it out into a 6- × 3-inch rectangle.

5. The finished flatbread will be the size of the dough rectangle you began with. Only the top will be wearing a blanket of sesame seeds.

6. Proceed immediately to fry the flatbreads: Heat a large heavy skillet over high heat until a bead of water evaporates on contact. Add enough oil to lightly glaze the bottom of the pan, then swirl to coat the sides. Reduce the heat to moderately high. When the oil is hot enough to sizzle a sesame seed slowly, add as many flatbreads as can fit in a single layer, sesame side down, in the pan. Fry until lightly golden and crusty, 1½ to 2 minutes, adjusting the heat so the seeds sizzle gently without scorching. Turn and fry the second side until lightly golden, about 1 to 1½ minutes more. Remove the flatbreads to a paper towel to drain. Wipe the pan clean, reheat it, and add oil as above, then fry the next batch of flatbreads.

7. The finished flatbreads can be kept side by side on a baking sheet at room temperature for up to 8 hours. If not serving immediately, reheat in a low (200°F) oven until thoroughly hot but not dry, about 4 minutes. Munch the hot flatbreads on their own, cut crosswise on the diagonal into halves or thirds. Or, split them along their natural fold, stuff with thinly sliced meats and a generous swath of dressing, and slice on the diagonal into easily managed fourths.

MENU SUGGESTIONS: For plain eating, the flatbreads are wonderful with soup. If you wish to stuff them, choose from among any of our roasted meats: Brined Loin of Pork with Hoisin-Maltose Glaze (page 313) or Pasilla Pepper Sauce (page 310), Wok-Seared Beef Tenderloin (page 253), or Peppered Loin of Lamb (page 274). You can also stuff the flatbreads with most any cold meat or poultry, and then spread on some Sweet Mustard Sauce (page 21) and maybe a layer of Ginger-Pickled Red Cabbage Slaw (page 61) for a crazy East-West Sloppy Joe.

PAN-FRIED SCALLION-CHIVE BREADS

MAKES FOUR 6-INCH BREADS

This is a gussied-up version of the elementary scallion bread I made years ago and wrote up in my first cookbook, *The Modern Art of Chinese Cooking*. The classic version is delicious, but this untraditional model is just grand.

Scallion-chive breads are best made in the hour before a meal. They can be made in advance and reheated, but there is a definite flavor loss—making them merely terrific as opposed to heavenly.

1 tablespoon Ma-La Oil
  (page 17)
1 tablespoon China Moon Hot
  Chili Oil (page 10)
1½ cups thinly sliced green and
  white scallion rings
½ cup coarsely chopped
  coriander leaves and stems
½ cup finely chopped Chinese
  chives

2 cups all-purpose
  flour
2 teaspoons baking
  powder
⅓ cup very hot tap water
⅓ cup cold water
1½ teaspoons kosher salt
⅓ to ½ cup corn or peanut
  oil, for pan-frying

1. Combine the ma-la and chili oils in a small dish.

2. Combine the scallions, coriander, and chives in a small bowl.

3. Combine the flour and baking powder in the bowl of a mixer fitted with the flat paddle. With the machine running on low speed, add the hot and cold water in quick succession. Stop the machine as soon as the dough comes together in a soft ball. If it is very tacky and sticks badly, add a bit more flour to make it behave.

4. Turn the dough out onto a lightly floured board. Cover with plastic wrap and let rest for 15 minutes. (If you have made the dough in a food processor, let it rest upwards of 40 minutes.) Roll the dough gently into a smooth log. Cut the log evenly into 4 pieces, then put each piece, cut side down, on the lightly floured board. Cover the dough rounds with plastic wrap and work with 1 piece at a time.

5. To shape the dough: Roll the first piece into an evenly thin circle 7½ inches in diameter. Brush the top of the dough with a generous film of the oil, then sprinkle evenly with a rounded ¼ teaspoon of the salt. Heap the dough with ⅔ cup of the greens, then spread them evenly over the top with your fingers. (It will look like a lot!) Roll up the dough into a fat carpet, neither too tight nor too loose. Grasp one end of the dough and wind the other end around it in a flat spiral. Tuck the tail end underneath and press lightly with your hand to flatten the bread. Gently roll out the spiral into a 6-inch circle. Expect the greens to pop out here and there, but take care to use a light touch so that the dough does not tear badly. Put the rolled-out bread aside on a freshly floured spot on the board, then shape the remaining pieces one by one.

As soon as the breads are filled and rolled out, proceed directly to cook them to prevent the salt from leaching the scallions, which would cause the dough to become soggy.

6. To pan-fry the breads: Heat an 8- to 10-inch heavy skillet over high heat until a bead of water evaporates on contact. Add enough oil to glaze the bottom by ⅛ inch. Swirl to glaze the sides of the pan and reduce the heat to moderate. When the oil is hot enough to foam a pinch of flour, add the first rolled-out bread to the pan. Cook until the bottom is golden and a bit crusty, 3 to 4 minutes, adjusting the heat so the bread sizzles gently without scorching. Flip and fry the other side until it, too, turns golden, about 3 minutes more. Remove the bread to a paper towel to drain. Add more oil to regain a depth of ⅛ inch. Heat and test the oil with a pinch of flour, then fry the second bread. Repeat the process with all the remaining pieces.

7. Serve the breads fresh from the skillet, cut into fourths. Or, let cool and hold at room temperature for up to 8 hours. Reheat in a 350°F oven until thoroughly hot, about 5 minutes.

MENU SUGGESTIONS: Delicious on their own, I adore these breads with just about everything—soup, stir-fries, sandpots, and salami.

THE CHIVE LADY

When I first moved to San Francisco, I became enamored of the Chinese granny contingent that sold home-grown greens on the corners of Chinatown. The most vociferous of the pack—out-shouting her competitors by a loud mouthful—was a fat lady who sold skinny Chinese chives.

This is China Moon's Chive Lady, the irascible Mrs. Wu. Her chives are the best—tender, never longer than a hand, each little bunch bound with a twist of colored string. We buy dozens of bundles every week. How does she grow them all, we've wondered? A sweatshop of chive growers out in the suburbs . . . an unseen Mr. Wu who owns a farm in Sacramento . . . a home that is turned over to planter boxes of baby chives and watering cans and tiny balls of pink string? The Chive Lady is a mystery, though her wares are delicious.

CRESCENT MOON TURNOVERS FILLED WITH LEMONY LAMB

MAKES ABOUT 30 SMALL TURNOVERS

With a name like China Moon, it was inevitable that we have something moon-shaped on the menu. This is it: a short-crust pastry crescent stuffed with a spicy mixture of minced lamb and fresh lemon zest. They are a distant cousin of the traditional Cantonese pork curry crescents, but the flavors fall somewhere between Mongolia and Morocco.

The good news for a home cook is that "moons," as we call them, freeze perfectly in their unbaked form. That gives plenty of leeway for a party, when you want to do everything short of reheating in advance.

The filling is also yummy (hot or cold) on Garlic Croutons (page 37), or rolled into crispy leaves of lettuce, should the pastry-making seem too much.

PASTRY:

6 ounces (1½ sticks) cold
   unsalted butter, cut into ½-
   inch cubes
¼ cup solid vegetable
   shortening
3 cups all-purpose flour
2 tablespoons sugar
Pinch of salt
⅔ to ¾ cup ice water

MARINADE AND
LAMB:

2½ teaspoons soy sauce
2½ teaspoons China Moon
   Chili-Lemon Oil (page 12)
½ teaspoon sugar
½ teaspoon dried red chili flakes
1¼ teaspoons cornstarch

4 to 5 twists of freshly ground
   pepper
¾ pound finely ground lamb
   shoulder

AROMATICS:

1½ tablespoons finely minced
   garlic
1 tablespoon finely minced fresh
   ginger
1½ teaspoons dried red chili
   flakes
1 to 2 small green serrano
   chilis, finely minced

MOONS OVER MANHATTAN

As I write this, 1,200 crescent moon turnovers are sitting in the sub-zero depths of one of San Francisco's nearby hotel kitchens. About two months ago, Amy rolled and stamped out what seemed like a million pastry circles and nested them in our own freezer (our restaurant freezer will hold them longer than a home freezer; 2 weeks should be your limit). For the last four weeks, our cooks and prep team have been madly making moon filling and wearily crimping it shut in the pastry wrappers. About two weeks from now, I'll layer the little rocks in bubble paper, box them in Styrofoam with dry ice, and fly them to New York City. Upon arrival, we'll all defrost. I'll then bake the moons in the kitchen of the 21 Club, courtesy of my buddy and its consulting chef, Anne Rosenzweig. Anne is charged not only with the moons, but with the assorted goodies of some dozen female chefs who are being flown to New York in large part to prove that our species exists. From mid-Manhattan, the moons and I will travel uptown— hopefully with few potholes en route—to Lincoln Center. Somewhere in that glorious constellation of theaters, we'll reheat the moons and serve them up to a thousand-plus guests at an event to celebrate the hugeness of James Beard. With luck, we'll all survive and be thought delicious.

I chronicle this to inspire anyone who needs to cater for a mob! Also, to show that behind the à la minute glamour of every Gang Chef Event is the thankful power of modern refrigeration.

SEASONINGS:

1½ tablespoons soy sauce

1 tablespoon Chinese rice wine or dry sherry

1 tablespoon unsalted chicken stock

1 tablespoon Serrano-Lemongrass Vinegar (page 19) or unseasoned Japanese rice vinegar

¼ teaspoon kosher salt

1 teaspoon freshly squeezed lemon juice

About ¼ cup corn or peanut oil, for stir-frying

1 large yellow onion, finely diced

1½ teaspoons finely minced lemon zest

1 tablespoon plus 1 teaspoon cornstarch

2½ tablespoons cold chicken stock or water

2 tablespoons finely slivered coriander leaves and stems

1 egg yolk beaten with 1 whole egg

Finely chopped Chinese chives or lacy, whole coriander leaves, for garnish

1. To make the pastry: Combine the butter, shortening, flour, sugar, and salt in a food processor. Pulse until the mixture resembles coarse meal. With the machine running, add the ice water in a thin, steady stream. Stop the machine as soon as the dough clumps together in a near ball. (The dough can also be made in a KitchenAid mixer fitted with the flat paddle. Combine the solids on low speed until mealy, add the water all at once, and stop the machine when the dough clumps together.) Turn the dough out onto a board, divide it into 2 even pieces, and press each piece into a 1-inch-thick disk. Wrap separately in plastic wrap and refrigerate or freeze until firm. Frozen, the disks will keep for up to 2 weeks; defrost just until malleable before rolling.

2. To roll out the pastry: Work with 1 disk at a time. Roll the cold dough on a lightly floured board to an even thickness of ⅛ inch. Run your fingertips over the dough to check for bumps. Use a 4-inch cutter to cut rounds from the dough, cutting them directly next to one another to minimize scraps. Dip the cutter in flour, if needed to prevent sticking. Remove the circles in a single layer to a baking sheet lined with parchment or waxed paper. Build layers of circles with sheets of paper between them. Stack the scraps, roll them out, and cut out more circles; if the scraps have warmed too much, then refrigerate them before rolling. Proceed to cut more circles from the second disk of dough. Seal the baking sheet and refrigerate the pastry circles for up to 2 days, or freeze for up to 2 weeks. Defrost until malleable before using.

3. To make the filling: Combine all the marinade ingredients through the pepper in a bowl and blend until smooth. Add the lamb and stir with your hand in 1 direction to blend thoroughly. Seal and set aside at cool room temperature for 3 to 4 hours, or refrigerate overnight. Bring to room temperature before cooking.

4. Combine the aromatics in a small dish; seal until ready to use.

5. Combine the seasonings in a small bowl. Stir to blend, leaving the spoon in the bowl.

6. Heat a wok or large heavy skillet over high heat until a bead of water evaporates on contact. Add 1 tablespoon of the oil and swirl to coat the pan. Reduce the heat to moderately high. When the oil is hot enough to sizzle a dab of lamb, add the meat and toss briskly, poking with a spatula to break it into bits, until 95 percent gray, about 1½ minutes. Adjust the heat so it sizzles without scorching and drizzle a bit more oil down the side of the pan, if needed to prevent sticking. Remove the lamb to a colander to drain. Clean the pan and return it to the stove.

7. Heat the pan over high heat until a bead of water evaporates on contact. Add 1 tablespoon of the oil, swirl to glaze the pan, and reduce the heat to moderately high. When the oil is hot enough to sizzle a bit of onion, add the onions and toss until golden, 2 to 3 minutes, adjusting the heat so they sizzle without scorching. Drizzle a bit more oil down the side of the pan, if needed to prevent sticking. Spread the onions on a plate. Wipe the pan clean and return it to the stove.

8. Heat the pan over high heat until a bead of water evaporates on contact. Add 1 tablespoon of the oil, swirl to glaze the pan, and reduce the heat to moderate. When the oil is hot enough to foam a pinch of ginger, add the aromatics. Stir gently until fully fragrant, 20 to 30 seconds, adjusting the heat so they foam without browning. Drizzle in a bit more oil if needed to prevent sticking. Return the lamb, onions, and any onion juices to the pan, and toss to combine. Add the lemon zest and toss to mix. Stir the seasonings and add them to the pan. Toss until the mixture is very hot and steaming.

9. Quickly combine the cornstarch with the stock or water to dissolve it, then loop it in a thin stream over the filling. Stir until the filling is thick, heavy, and glossy, and a dab of the mixture leaves no floury taste on the roof of your mouth, 4 to 5 minutes. Fold in the chopped coriander. Spread

ORCHESTRATING MOONS

The best time to approach moon-making is a good one to two weeks ahead of baking. Make the pastry first. Cut it out into circles and freeze on layers of parchment or on a baking sheet. That done, make the filling—a simple job. Step three, a day or two later, is filling the moons. From there you can bake them directly or pop them back in the freezer for another nice rest.

the filling on a platter or jelly roll pan and refrigerate, uncovered, until cold. Once cold, the mixture can be sealed and
refrigerated for up to 2 days. Use directly from the refrigerator.

10. To fill the moons: Put 2 level teaspoons of the filling
off center on the first dough round. Run a finger dipped in
cold water around the edge of the pastry, then bring the dough
over the filling to form a half-moon. Secure the edge by
crimping it firmly with a fork. Set the filled crescent on a
parchment-lined baking sheet. Continue to make the remaining moons. If you are baking them directly, leave 1½ inches
between them. Or, if you are working in advance, put them
closer together but not touching on the baking sheet, and
refrigerate overnight or freeze until firm. To save space, the
moons can be bagged once frozen. They can be frozen for up
to 2 weeks. Defrost on baking sheets until malleable but still
firm.

11. Preheat the oven to 350°F. Move the racks to divide
the oven evenly into thirds.

12. Lightly brush the top and exposed side of the first
crescent with an even film of the egg wash. Be sure to brush
the wash thinly at the crimped edge so it doesn't pool.
Sprinkle the top sparingly with chives, or lightly apply a small
coriander leaf or two decoratively on top. Arrange the decorated crescents 1½ inches apart on a parchment-lined baking
sheet. Bake until lightly golden, 14 to 15 minutes. Rotate the
pans from front to back and top to bottom midway through
baking to ensure even coloring.

13. Serve immediately. Or let cool and hold at room
temperature for up to 8 hours, or refrigerate overnight. Reheat
in a low (200°F) oven until thoroughly hot, about 5 minutes.

MENU SUGGESTIONS: The turnovers are perfect with a
bowl of soup—either one of ours or your own favorite. As part
of a buffet, they are a very tasty foil to cold dishes of noodles,
poultry, and fish. Peking Spicy Cabbage Pickle (page 52) is
wonderful alongside.

CRESCENT MOON TURNOVERS FILLED WITH SPICY PORK

MAKES ABOUT 30 SMALL TURNOVERS

A more classically inclined filling for "moons," but still a far cry from its traditional, bland, Cantonese cousin, this minced pork concoction is zippy with the flavors of ginger and chili. An example of one of those many times when intriguing taste wins the gold and authenticity places a distant second!

Pastry (see ingredients on page 384)

MARINADE AND PORK:
1 tablespoon soy sauce
1 tablespoon China Moon Chili-Orange Oil (page 15)
1½ teaspoons "goop" from China Moon Chili-Orange Oil
¼ teaspoon sugar
1½ teaspoons cornstarch
¾ pound finely ground pork butt

AROMATICS:
2 tablespoons finely minced fresh ginger
1½ tablespoons finely minced garlic
⅓ cup thinly sliced green and white scallion rings
1 small green serrano chili, finely minced
1 red Fresno chili, finely minced

SEASONINGS:
1½ tablespoons unsalted chicken stock
1½ tablespoons soy sauce
1 tablespoon unseasoned Japanese rice vinegar
⅛ teaspoon kosher salt
1 tablespoon Chinese rice wine or dry sherry

About ¼ cup corn or peanut oil, for stir-frying
1 large yellow onion, finely diced
1 tablespoon plus 1 teaspoon cornstarch
2½ tablespoons cold chicken stock or water
1 egg yolk beaten with 1 whole egg
Finely chopped Chinese chives or lacy, whole coriander leaves, for garnish

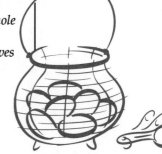

1. Make the pastry dough and roll it out as detailed in steps 1 and 2 on page 385.

2. To make the filling: Combine all the marinade ingredients through the cornstarch in a bowl and stir to dissolve the cornstarch. Add the pork and stir with your hand in 1 direction to blend thoroughly. Seal and set aside at cool room temperature for 3 to 4 hours or refrigerate overnight. Bring to room temperature before cooking.

3. Combine the aromatics in a small dish; seal until ready to use.

4. Combine the seasonings in a small bowl. Stir to blend, leaving the spoon in the bowl.

5. Heat a wok or large heavy skillet over high heat until a bead of water evaporates on contact. Add 1 tablespoon of the oil and swirl to coat the pan. Reduce the heat to moderately high. When the oil is hot enough to sizzle a dab of pork, add the meat and toss briskly, poking with a spatula to break it into bits, until 95 percent gray, about 1½ minutes. Adjust the heat so it sizzles without scorching and drizzle a bit more oil down the side of the pan, if needed to prevent sticking. Remove the pork to a colander to drain. Clean the pan and return it to the stove.

6. Heat the pan over high heat until a bead of water evaporates on contact. Add 1 tablespoon of the oil, swirl to glaze the pan, and reduce the heat to moderately high. When the oil is hot enough to sizzle a bit of onion, add the onions and toss until golden, 2 to 3 minutes, adjusting the heat so they sizzle without scorching. Drizzle a bit more oil down the side of the pan, if needed to prevent sticking. Spread the onions on a plate. Wipe the pan clean and return it to the stove.

7. Heat the pan over high heat until a bead of water evaporates on contact. Add 1½ tablespoons of the oil, swirl to glaze the pan, and reduce the heat to moderate. When the oil is hot enough to foam a scallion ring, add the aromatics. Stir gently until fully fragrant, 20 to 30 seconds, adjusting the heat so they foam without browning. Drizzle in a bit more oil if needed to prevent sticking. Return the pork, the onions, and any onion juices to the pan, and toss to combine. Stir the seasonings and add them to the pan. Toss until the mixture is very hot and steaming.

8. Quickly combine the cornstarch with the stock to dissolve it, then loop it in a thin stream over the filling. Stir until the filling is thick, heavy, and glossy, and a dab of the mixture leaves no floury taste on the roof of your mouth, 4 to 5 minutes. Spread the filling on a platter or jelly roll pan and refrigerate, uncovered, until cold. Once cold, the mixture can be sealed and refrigerated for up to 2 days. Use the filling directly from the refrigerator.

9. To fill, bake, and serve the moons: Follow steps 10 through 13 on page 387.

MENU SUGGESTIONS: A moon is a moon is a moon. See page 387 for suggestions on pairings.

■ ■ ■

NOODLES

Noodles are fabulous food the world around, but especially in China, where one has both wheat-based egg noodles in the north and rice noodles in the south. The diversity is stunning. Noodles are eaten cold and hot, stir-fried, deep-fried, boiled, and pan-fried in what I love to call a pillow. They are fun for the spirit, as well as food for the belly.

Being a mostly northern- and centrally-inclined Chinese cook, I probably devise two or three noodle dishes for every one based on rice. We go through hundreds of pounds of noodles every week at China Moon! The cooks and the customers never tire of them.

DRAGON NOODLES

SERVES 2 TO 3 AS A MAIN COURSE,
4 TO 6 AS PART OF A MULTICOURSE MEAL

TOASTING BLACK SESAME SEEDS

To toast black sesame seeds, heat a dry heavy skillet over moderately-low heat. Add the sesame seeds and toast, tossing occasionally, until fragrant, about 5 minutes. Use your nose as a guide; the color of the seeds won't change.

For our Chinese New Year's feast in 1988 (the lunar year symbolized by the dragon in Chinese cosmology), our talented bartender-artist, Larry Yung, suspended a writhing, 60-foot paper dragon from our 20-foot ceiling, and I put together a new noodle dish for the menu. It is this one—a tangle of cold thin egg noodles dressed in a light, zippy dressing redolent of chili, lemon, and ginger.

Given the requisite ingredients, this is a dish that can be made in minutes. It will multiply to feed a mob or, if you are celebrating the new year romantically, will feed just you and a friend.

DRESSING:
¼ cup Ma-La Oil (page 17)
1 tablespoon China Moon Chili-Lemon Oil (page 12)
1 teaspoon Chinese chili sauce
2½ tablespoons black soy sauce
2 tablespoons juice from China Moon Pickled Ginger (page 8)
1½ tablespoons freshly squeezed lemon juice
2½ tablespoons unseasoned Japanese rice vinegar
2½ tablespoons sugar
½ teaspoon kosher salt

½ pound very thin (¹⁄₁₆ inch) fresh Chinese egg noodles
Grated zest of 1 scrubbed lemon, or more, if needed
2 tablespoons black sesame seeds, toasted
¾ cup thinly sliced green and white scallion rings
Grated red radish, for garnish
Green and white scallion julienne, for garnish
Toasted black sesame seeds, for garnish

1. Combine all of the dressing ingredients, whisking to blend. Set aside, leaving the whisk in the bowl.

2. Fluff the noodles in a colander to separate and untangle the strands. Bring a generous amount of water to a rolling boil over high heat. Add the noodles and swish gently with chopsticks until the noodles are al dente but cooked, about 2 minutes. Drain promptly, plunge briefly into a generous amount of ice water to chill, then drain thoroughly.

3. Re-whisk the dressing to combine. Toss the noodles with just enough of the dressing to moisten them well, using your fingers to coat and separate the strands. Let sit for 10 minutes.

4. Taste the noodles. If they have absorbed the dressing and seem dry, add a bit more dressing and toss again. Add the lemon zest, black sesame seeds, and scallion rings. Toss well to mix. Taste and adjust with more dressing and/or lemon zest if needed. The taste should be bright and sparkly. At this point, the noodles may be sealed and refrigerated for up to a day. (If you are working in advance, you might like to wait until serving to add the scallions so the rings look bright and fresh.) For best flavor, bring to room temperature or serve only slightly chilled.

5. To serve, mound the noodles in a bowl or twirl into individual bowls of contrasting color, garnishing each with a pinch of the grated red radish, a tuft of scallion julienne, and a sprinkling of black sesame seeds.

✳ *MENU SUGGESTIONS:* These noodles go well with most all of our cold fish, meat, and poultry dishes. On an antipasto plate, I love them with Brined Loin of Pork with Pasilla Pepper Sauce (page 310) and a green salad. Given their light and lemony flavor, they also go well with grilled or roasted chicken.

I BEG TO DIFFER, MR. POLO

On a few points of noodle-making and eating, the Chinese and the Italians differ greatly.

Chinese like their noodles slithery, not rough. A meaty sauce, if plopped on top of a well-behaved Chinese noodle, should slip from the noodle, not cling to it. A silken noodle is perfect to a Chinese tongue.

The water for boiling noodles in China is not salted. In the yin-yang world of Chinese eating, noodles remain unseasoned, while the sauces or other foods eaten with them carry the fuller flavors. The noodles themselves, to a Chinese palate, should be deliberately unseasoned to be tasty— tasting of the wheat and the water, and not the salt.

The water used for poaching fresh noodles is not necessarily tossed. It is often drunk in a little bowl along-side the noodles, with a bit of chopped scallion and a drizzle of seasoned oil swirled in.

Finally, al dente is not a high desirable in China. The Chinese love their noodles either soft (boiled) or crisp (fried), with little variation in between.

COLD TOMATO NOODLES

SERVES 4 TO 6 AS A MAIN COURSE,
8 TO 10 AS PART OF A MULTICOURSE MEAL

I am a sucker for the flavor of tomato and ginger in combination, so as soon as we have truly summer-ripe tomatoes, I rush to put this dish on the menu. It has become a warm-weather favorite, and I emphatically recommend it.

The sauce is also a yummy topping for fish, meat, pasta, or poultry. It will hold in the refrigerator for up to a week.

SMOKE ALLOWED

Wok-searing or pan-searing the tomatoes over the highest possible heat will imbue the sauce with an inimitable smokiness. Do not fear allowing the oil to smoke, for that is exactly the flavor edge you want.

SAUCE:
2 tablespoons coarsely chopped sun-dried tomatoes
1½ teaspoons corn or peanut oil
¾ pound fragrant, ripe plum tomatoes, tipped and cut lengthwise into fourths
⅓ cup juice from China Moon Pickled Ginger (page 8)
1½ teaspoons China Moon Hot Chili Oil (page 10)
1½ teaspoons "goop" from China Moon Hot Chili Oil

2½ tablespoons sugar
1½ teaspoons kosher salt

½ pound fresh bean sprouts
1 pound very thin (¹/₁₆ inch) fresh Chinese egg noodles
¼ cup minced China Moon Pickled Ginger
¾ cup thinly sliced green and white scallion rings
¼ cup coarsely chopped coriander stems and leaves
Coriander sprigs, for garnish

1. To make the sauce, combine the sun-dried tomatoes with ¼ cup boiling water. Cover and set aside for about 10 minutes, or until the tomatoes are soft. Drain, reserving the soaking water. (If using oil-steeped tomatoes, simply drain the oil; do not soak.)

2. Heat a wok or large, heavy non-aluminum skillet over high heat until hot enough to evaporate a bead of water on contact. Add the corn oil, swirl to glaze the pan, and heat until smoking. Add the tomato wedges and toss until soft and hot, about 1 minute. Do not worry if they brown in spots; the searing gives the flavor.

3. In a food processor, combine the seared tomatoes and any juices, the sun-dried tomatoes, the reserved soaking water, and all of the remaining sauce ingredients through the salt. Process until nearly smooth. Don't worry if chunks or skins remain; this looks great on the finished dish. Taste; if you desire a spicier sauce, add a dash more chili oil or "goop."

4. Blanch the bean sprouts in boiling water to cover for 15 seconds. Plunge into ice water until chilled. Cover with cold water and refrigerate until ready to use. Drain well just before using.

5. Fluff the noodles in a colander to separate and untangle the strands. Bring a generous amount of unsalted water to a rolling boil over high heat. Add the noodles and swish gently with chopsticks until the noodles are al dente but cooked, about 2 minutes. Drain promptly, plunge into ample ice water to chill, then drain thoroughly. Put the noodles in a large tub or bowl.

6. Sauce the noodles with 1½ cups of the sauce. Toss well with your fingers. Let sit for 10 minutes. Taste and add more sauce if you like; the noodles should be flavorful but not soupy. At this point, the noodles may be sealed and refrigerated for up to a day. Bring nearly to room temperature before serving, and check if the noodles have absorbed the sauce and a touch more is needed.

7. Just before serving, add the bean sprouts, ginger, scallions, and coriander, tossing lightly to mix.

8. To serve, mound on a platter or twirl into individual bowls of contrasting color. Garnish with the coriander sprigs and serve at once.

MENU SUGGESTIONS: As part of an antipasto plate, these noodles team beautifully with any of our wok-seared meats—Wok-Seared Beef Tenderloin (page 253), Peppered Loin of Lamb (page 274), or Brined Loin of Pork with Pasilla Pepper Sauce (page 310)—and a green salad. They would also be a wonderful companion to a platter of Skewered Baked Shrimp (page 212) or Gold Coin Salmon Cakes (page 188).

NOODLE TOSSING TIPS

To keep the sauce from overwhelming the bright colors and tastes of the vegetables in cold noodle dishes, first dress the noodles, then let them sit a bit to absorb the dressing. Only after that is done should you toss the noodles with the vegetables.

When tossing cold noodles with a thin sauce, use a shallow tub instead of a bowl, so that the noodles can be spread out. Especially if you are multiplying the recipe, it is important to give the noodles a lot of room so they don't sit in a dry heap on top, pressing out a puddle of sauce below.

The tubs I use are plastic rectangles that measure about 12 inches by 24 inches and are about 6 inches deep. Called "bus tubs" because they are commonly used to bus dirty dishes and glassware from the dining room to the dishwashing station, they are fixtures in most restaurant kitchens. We use them for noodle-tossing and a thousand and one other things, and I cannot recommend them more if you are someone who likes to cook for a crowd and is always needing the requisite big tub for marinating, storing, or tossing! They most often come in grim colors like gray and black, but a restaurant supply shop in Chinatown will almost always have them in red, symbolizing good fortune for you and your noodles.

PARIS NOODLES

SERVES 4 AS A MAIN COURSE, 8 AS PART OF A MULTICOURSE MEAL

This is the sprightly noodle cousin to our Paris Salad (page 444). Light, spicy, and alive with crunchy textures, it's a fine example of a dish of pseudo-Chinese cool noodles.

The various slicings and dicings may be done in advance.

¼ cup dried tree ears
¼ pound fresh white bean
    sprouts
½ pound very thin (¹/₁₆ inch)
    fresh Chinese egg noodles

DRESSING:
¾ cup juice from China Moon
    Pickled Ginger (page 8)
¼ cup Five-Flavor Oil (page 13)
¼ cup soy sauce
2 tablespoons plus 2 teaspoons
    sugar
¾ teaspoon Roasted Szechwan
    Pepper-Salt (page 5)
1 teaspoon kosher salt
1 teaspoon Chinese chili sauce

1 cup julienned daikon

1 cup julienned Japanese or
    English cucumber
¾ cup shredded carrots
¾ cup finely shredded strands
    of red cabbage
1 small red bell pepper, diced
4 to 6 fresh water chestnuts, cut
    into thin half-moons
2 tablespoons black sesame
    seeds, toasted

Thinly sliced green and white
    scallion rings, for garnish
Finely chopped Chinese chives,
    for garnish

1. Soak the tree ears in 3 cups cold water until supple, about 30 minutes. Rinse well to dislodge any grit. Pinch off any tough or woody bits; tear into nickel-size pieces.

2. Blanch the bean sprouts in boiling water for 15 seconds. Refresh in ice water. Cover with water and refrigerate until ready to use. Drain just before using.

3. Fluff the noodles in a colander to separate and untangle the strands. Bring a generous amount of water to a rolling boil over high heat. Add the noodles and swish gently with chopsticks until the noodles are al dente but cooked, about 2 minutes. Drain promptly, plunge briefly into ample ice water to chill, then drain thoroughly.

4. Combine all of the dressing ingredients, whisking to blend. Pour two-thirds of the dressing over the noodles and toss well with your fingers to coat and separate each strand. Set aside for 10 minutes. Toss, taste, and add a bit more dressing if needed. The noodles should be moist but not soupy. At this point, the noodles may be sealed and refrigerated overnight. Bring nearly to room temperature before serving.

5. Just before serving, scatter the bean sprouts, tree ears, daikon, cucumber, carrots, cabbage, bell pepper, water chestnuts, and half the black sesame seeds over the noodles. Toss lightly to mix.

6. To serve, heap the noodles in bowls of contrasting color and garnish with the scallions, chopped chives, and a sprinkling of the reserved black sesame seeds.

MENU SUGGESTIONS: Gold Coin Salmon Cakes (page 188) or Gold Coin Crab Cakes (page 235) would make lovely partners for the noodles. So, too, would most any of our cold fish and shellfish dishes. A roast chicken is another great choice.

CHILI-ORANGE COLD NOODLES

SERVES 3 TO 4 AS A MAIN COURSE, 6 TO 8 AS PART OF A MULTICOURSE MEAL

This is one of the most popular cold noodle dishes in the China Moon repertoire. The combination of chili spice and fresh orange zing with slithery noodles and crunchy peanuts spells heaven for most of our customers and staff.

With the seasoned oil and the fabulous "goop" on hand, this dish can be whipped up within minutes. The dressing may be made well in advance, but for finest flavor the noodles and other ingredients should be tossed together just prior to serving.

as possible in unsalted boiling water for 15 seconds. (This rids them of their grassy taste and seals the color.) Then, chill in ice water. They can be refrigerated in water to cover for 2 or 3 days without losing their crispness; drain the sprouts just before using.

In fanatic Chinese homes (equipped with many hands for menial labor), plucking the heads and tails of bean sprouts was a mark of refinement in the food. If you have someone you hate, give them this job. Otherwise, enjoy your bean sprouts heads, tails, and crispy middles!

DRESSING:
2½ tablespoons China Moon Chili-Orange Oil (page 15)
1 tablespoon "goop" from China Moon Chili-Orange Oil
2 tablespoons black soy sauce
2 tablespoons distilled white vinegar
1 teaspoon kosher salt
1 tablespoon sugar

½ pound very thin (¹/₁₆ inch) fresh Chinese egg noodles

½ pound fresh bean sprouts
¾ cup finely shredded carrots
½ cup thinly sliced green and white scallion rings
¾ cup slivered coriander leaves and stems
½ cup chopped roasted peanuts
Coriander sprigs for garnish

1. Combine all of the dressing ingredients, whisking to blend. Set aside, leaving the whisk in the bowl.

2. Fluff the noodles in a colander to separate and untangle the strands. Bring a generous amount of water to a rolling boil over high heat. Add the noodles and swish gently with chopsticks until the noodles are al dente but cooked, about 2 minutes. Drain promptly, plunge briefly into ample ice water to chill, then drain thoroughly.

3. Blanch the bean sprouts in boiling water for 15 seconds. Refresh in ice water. Cover with cold water and refrigerate until ready to use. Drain well just before using.

4. Re-whisk the dressing. Scrape the dressing over the noodles and toss well with your fingers to coat and separate each strand. Scatter the bean sprouts, carrots, scallions, coriander, and two thirds of the chopped peanuts on top; then, toss lightly to mix. Taste and adjust, if needed, with a dash more sugar to bring forth the heat.

5. To serve, heap the noodles in bowls of contrasting color and garnish with sprigs of coriander and a sprinkling of the peanuts.

MENU SUGGESTIONS: On the Chinese end of things, these noodles mate perfectly with any of our smoked foods, such as Tea and Spice Smoked Quail (page 160). We'll often use the noodles and a green salad on an antipasto plate along with Wok-Seared Beef Tenderloin (page 253). If your mood is more Western, the noodles go well with burgers or most anything from the grill.

NOODLE TALES AND TYPES

I grew up, culinarily speaking, in northern and central Chinese homes where noodles were a Big Deal. They were bought freshly made, ideally in the hours immediately preceding the meal, from a vendor in the local market who kneaded and cut them on the spot. Once home, they were cooked in unsalted water to differing degrees of doneness, depending on both the style of the dish and also the condition of the head of the household's teeth. (Some of my adopted Chinese parents were quite old.) The merits of the different noodles were debated fiercely. It

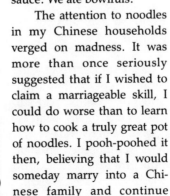

was a matter of familial pride.

In both of my Chinese families, we went on regular outings to eat noodles around town. This was serious business, and everyone got dressed up. In my second family, the noodle scouting went on literally around the clock: By day we would comb the city markets and alleyways to ferret out the elusive Best Noodle, and by night the quest would continue into the wee hours to discover the Best Noodle Stall, streetside eating being a nighttime scene. There was one downtown favorite that opened at noon for spicy cold Szechwan noodles, and another adjacent to the botanical gardens that got going only at midnight for steaming noodles topped with a gingery meat sauce. We ate bowlfuls.

The attention to noodles in my Chinese households verged on madness. It was more than once seriously suggested that if I wished to claim a marriageable skill, I could do worse than to learn how to cook a truly great pot of noodles. I pooh-poohed it then, believing that I would someday marry into a Chinese family and continue

pounding the streets in search of great noodles, with never a downslide in the quest. However, I returned to America and married a Caucasian, and indeed Pasta à la Maison (a mélange of macaroni with fresh veggies) is perhaps my greatest culinary contribution to our household.

At China Moon, the vast majority of noodles that we use are wheat-based egg noodles, as befits my mostly northern Chinese palate. We buy them in several shapes:

Very thin fresh egg noodles, about $^1/_{16}$ inch thick uncooked, are what we use in all of our cold noodle dishes and in our everyday pot-browned noodle pillows. They have maximum surface area on which to hang a tangy dressing and a great ability to tangle perfectly in a skillet. Once poached—a matter of only several minutes—they swell to a thickness of ⅛ inch. We occasionally use these very thin egg noodles in a stir-fry, but the wok must be very fast and hot, or they go gloppy in the sauce.

This style of thin egg noodle is widely available both fresh and frozen in 1-pound bags in Asian markets. They should be white or only a very pale yellow. Gray indicates old noodles; sunburst yellow means the manufacturer dumped in food dye instead of egg. The fresh noodles freeze nicely. Defrost slowly in the refrigerator for best texture.

This thin type of egg noodle is often called "angelhair" and is available fresh in many of the Italian-style pasta stores.

If I am unable to find fresh egg noodles, I use a good brand of dried Italian noodles in their place. I avoid dried Chinese noodles, which I find flavorless.

Broad Chinese egg noodles of a ribbony, fettuccine-like character and shape are our favorite for stir-frying. Poached until al dente, they then can be stir-fried to a perfect doneness with little fear of a mushy ending. Broad noodles make pretty beds for shapely ingredients like prawns and sausage coins that can nestle in the loops without getting lost in the tangle.

Broad egg noodles also make a terrific, textural noodle pillow. They are a bit rakish because they won't compact as well in the skillet as their obedient thinner cousins, but in noodles as in life, a little wildness has its charm.

These broad Chinese egg noodles can be purchased fresh or frozen in 1-pound bags. The noodles should be white or only the very palest yellow.

If Chinese fresh or frozen noodles are unavailable, I substitute fresh or dried Italian fettuccine. I do not use dried Chinese noodles; they have no character.

Shanghai noodles is the name our San Francisco manufacturer gives to a style of fat and lopsided noodles that really hold their sauce. A close relative to the appealingly lumpy noodles made in many northern Chinese homes, this factory-made noodle may be a California-Chinese regional specialty. The strange shape is wonderful in stir-fries. Fresh Shanghai noodles are ⅛-inch thick uncooked. Boiled, they swell to nearly twice their thickness.

If your Asian market does not carry them, look for a similarly thick fresh or frozen Chinese noodle. Typically packaged in 1-pound plastic pouches, they freeze reasonably well. Defrost in the refrigerator for best texture. Any thick fresh or dried Italian spaghetti will do, if the Chinese item is nowhere to be found. Avoid the dried Chinese species; it is virtually flavorless.

LIGHT-STYLE PEANUT-LIME NOODLES

SERVES 3 TO 4 AS A MAIN COURSE,
6 TO 8 AS PART OF A MULTICOURSE MEAL

One of the great seductions of Thai cooking is its frequent combining of peanuts, lime, and chilis. That is definitely the founding influence here, although the flavor of soy and the sharpness of daikon and radish do pull it a bit toward China. The important thing is that this is a *great* bowl of cold noodles!

DRESSING:
¼ cup plus 2 tablespoons unseasoned peanut butter, preferably homemade (page 32)
2 tablespoons soy sauce
2 tablespoons Serrano-Lemongrass Vinegar (page 19)
1½ tablespoons freshly squeezed lime juice
2 tablespoons juice from China Moon Pickled Ginger (page 8)
2 tablespoons sugar
¼ teaspoon kosher salt
¼ teaspoon Roasted Szechwan Pepper-Salt (page 5)
¼ cup Five-Flavor Oil (page 13)
1½ teaspoons China Moon Hot Chili Oil (page 10)

1 teaspoon "goop" from China Moon Hot Chili Oil

1 pound very thin (¹/₁₆ inch) fresh Chinese egg noodles
1 cup julienned carrot
1 cup julienned Japanese or English cucumber
1 cup julienned daikon
¼ cup thinly sliced green and white scallion rings
2 tablespoons black sesame seeds, toasted (page 391)
Grated zest of 1 scrubbed lime

GARNISHES:
Ginger-Pickled Radish Rounds (page 57)
½ cup chopped roasted peanuts
Green and white scallion julienne

1. Combine all of the dressing ingredients, whisking to blend. The dressing may be sealed and left at room temperature for several hours or in the refrigerator overnight. (If it thickens in the refrigerator, whisk to a pourable consistency over a hot water bath.)

insert to the sink and plunge the whole rig into ice water to chill.

The minimal weight of the pot is fabulous. For us small cooks, it's enough to lug a gallon and a half of water plus pasta to the sink for draining, without adding another 10 pounds to the load in the interest of fancy metal.

I also love the inserts. They are riddled from top to bottom with big holes, which is just what you want for a quick plunge and then a speedy drain.

2. Fluff the noodles in a colander to separate and untangle the strands. Bring a generous amount of water to a rolling boil over high heat. Add the noodles and swish gently with chopsticks until the noodles are al dente but cooked, about 2 minutes. Drain promptly, plunge briefly into ample ice water to chill, then drain thoroughly.

3. Just before serving, combine the noodles and three fourths of the dressing in a large tub or bowl, using your fingers to coat and separate each strand. Taste and add more dressing if needed. The noodles should be moist but not soupy. Toss the carrot, cucumber, and daikon with the noodles, then scatter the scallions, black sesame seeds, and zest evenly on top. Toss again lightly to mix.

4. To serve, mound the noodles onto a platter or twirl into individual bowls of contrasting color. Garnish with pinched tufts of the pickled radish rounds alongside and top with the chopped peanuts and scallion julienne.

MENU SUGGESTIONS: As part of a cold buffet, the noodles would go well with Brined Loin of Pork with Pasilla Pepper Sauce (page 310), Cold Salad of Wok-Seared Prawns in Their Shells (page 210), or Grilled Chinese Chicken Wings with Orange Zest and Garlic (page 128). They would also be lovely with Tea and Spice Smoked Poussin (page 155).

POT-BROWNED NOODLE PILLOW

SERVES 3 TO 6

Every restaurant has at least one dish that customers adore and the chef (who used to adore it) now hates. Familiarity breeds both addiction and contempt in the case of this favorite, such that when the chef even flirts with the idea of taking it off the menu, the customers don't complain, they cry!

This is our love/hate child, a thick disk of subtly seasoned, thin egg noodles that is pressed into a hot skillet and browned on both sides. Called "two yellow faces" in Chinese, we turn them out by the score in our downstairs kitchen and use them in our upstairs finishing kitchen to pillow zesty stir-fries. Eaten plain (by our morning cooks, who consider them great breakfast fare) or topped with a lush stir-fry (by our customers, who are passionate about them), they are our house favorite and may well become yours.

You can make either one large pillow, as instructed in the recipe, or two small pillows using two 7-inch skillets.

½ pound very thin (¹/₁₆ inch) fresh Chinese egg noodles	1½ tablespoons finely chopped Chinese chives
Scant 2 teaspoons Five-Flavor Oil (page 13), Ma-La Oil (page 17), or Japanese sesame oil	1½ tablespoons thinly sliced green and white scallion rings
1 teaspoon kosher salt	4 to 5 tablespoons corn or peanut oil, for pan-frying

1. Fluff the noodles in a colander to separate and untangle the strands. Bring a generous amount of water to a rolling boil over high heat. Add the noodles and swish gently with chopsticks until the noodles are al dente but cooked, about 2 minutes. Drain promptly, plunge briefly into ample ice water to chill, then drain thoroughly.

2. Toss the noodles with the sesame-infused oil, salt, chives, and scallions, using your fingers to distribute the seasonings and separate the strands. At this point, the noodles may be sealed and refrigerated overnight.

3. Swirl 2½ tablespoons of the corn oil into an 11- to 12-inch nonstick skillet set over moderately high heat. When hot enough to sizzle a noodle, coil the noodles in the skillet and press to even them with a spatula. Cook the noodles until golden on the bottom, 5 to 7 minutes, adjusting the heat so they sizzle without scorching. Flip the pillow over (or invert it onto a plate and slip it back into the skillet browned side up) and drizzle the remaining 1½ to 2 tablespoons oil down the side of the pan. Swirl the pan to distribute the oil under the noodles and brown the second side, 5 to 7 minutes more. Slip the pillow onto a baking sheet lined with 4 to 5 layers of paper towels; let drain.

NONSTICK PILLOWS

After years of making noodle pillows in cast-iron skillets—the way I'd learned from the pot-sticker man who lived near our Taiwan alleyway and cooked on a streetside brazier—I discovered nonstick cooking and gave up kitchen aerobics. You still will need to use an ample amount of oil to achieve proper browning, but the light skillet makes it a cinch to flip the pillow, and it's thus easy to check the pillow bottom to see if it's golden.

If working in advance, let the pillow cool on a rack to room temperature after draining. Place it on a bed of dry paper towels, seal, and refrigerate for 1 or 2 days. (There is a slight flavor loss, but pillow-lovers are undeterred.) Rewarm on a baking sheet set on the middle rack of a preheated 400°F oven until the pillow is crisp and hot, about 5 minutes.

4. To serve, cut the noodle pillow into appealing thick wedges and place alongside (or underneath) a saucy stir-fry.

MENU SUGGESTIONS: Any saucy stir-fry mates perfectly with a noodle pillow. You can also serve the golden wedges alongside a big bowl of soup or a main-course salad. Children are known to like them as much as Big Macs, and everyone loves to eat them with their fingers.

BROAD NOODLE PILLOW

SERVES 3 to 6

When looking for an appropriate companion for one of our sandpot casseroles, someone in the kitchen hit on the idea of making a noodle pillow with broad egg noodles and slivered vegetables. The experiment was a grand success.

You can be creative with this recipe and add slivers or bits of your own devising: Smoked ham, slivered sweet or spicy peppers, yellow and gold zucchini julienne, or julienned basil would all be good.

Everything short of the actual pan-frying may be done ahead. Or, you can sacrifice a bit of the flavor and do the browning in advance and then reheat the pillow in the oven.

FLIP-FLOPS

If you're inclined to theatrics but shy about flipping food, practice with a wet sponge. One large, wet (not sopping) sponge is just about the right heft to stand in for a noodle pillow, and if you flip it onto the floor, there will be much less of a mess. Two to three sessions of sponge-flipping should put you in good shape to try a pillow. Especially if your dining area adjoins the kitchen, this little bit of drama will raise applause as well as appetites.

½ pound fresh broad Chinese
egg noodles or fresh
fettuccine
½ cup finely shredded carrots
¼ cup finely slivered leeks
2 tablespoons finely chopped
Chinese chives
2 tablespoons thinly sliced green
and white scallion rings

2 teaspoons Five-Flavor Oil
(page 13), Ma-La Oil (page
17), or Japanese sesame oil
Scant teaspoon kosher salt
Several pinches of Roasted
Szechwan Pepper-Salt (page
5)
4 to 5 tablespoons corn or
peanut oil, for pan-frying

1. Fluff the noodles in a colander to separate and untangle the strands. Bring a generous amount of unsalted water to a rolling boil over high heat. Add the noodles and swish with chopsticks until the noodles are al dente but cooked, about 3 minutes. Drain promptly, plunge briefly into ample ice water to chill, then drain thoroughly.

2. Toss the noodles with the carrots, leeks, chives, scallions, oil, salt, and pepper-salt, using your fingers to distribute the seasonings and separate the strands. At this point, the noodles may be sealed and refrigerated overnight.

3. Swirl 3 tablespoons of the corn oil in an 11- to 12-inch nonstick skillet set over moderate heat. When hot enough to sizzle a noodle, coil the noodles in the skillet and press to even them with a spatula. Cook the noodles until golden on one side, 7 to 8 minutes, adjusting the heat so they sizzle without scorching. Flip the pillow over (or invert it onto a plate and slip it back into the skillet browned side up) and drizzle the remaining 1½ to 2 tablespoons oil down the side of the pan. Swirl the pan to distribute the oil under the noodles and brown the second side, 8 to 9 minutes more. Slide the pillow (it may be a bit fragile) onto a baking sheet lined with a thick mat of paper towels to drain.

If working in advance, let the pillow cool on a rack to room temperature after draining. Place it on a bed of fresh paper towels, seal, and refrigerate for 1 or 2 days. Re-warm on a baking sheet set on the middle rack of a preheated 400°F oven until the pillow is crisp and hot, about 5 minutes.

SKINNY NOODLE
NOTE
///

If this recipe appeals to you on a day when only thin noodles are on hand, go ahead and use them! The result will be equally fine and tasty.

4. To serve, cut the noodle pillow into thick wedges and place alongside (or underneath) a saucy stir-fry.

MENU SUGGESTIONS: Delicately flavored casseroles that can use the extra vegetable lift are excellent served with this pillow. Bunny Stew (page 162), any of the duck sandpots, or Lamb Stew Sandpot with Wild Mushrooms and Pearl Onions (page 284) come to mind. You could also serve pillow wedges alongside most any soup and encourage your guests to enjoy them with their fingers.

PETITE PILLOWS

For smaller, individual pillows, divide the noodles into halves or thirds and use a tiny skillet. Nonstick surfaces are easiest to use, but a heavy cast-iron skillet or most any skillet will brown a noodle pillow well.

RICE SALADS • VEGETABLE STIR-FRIES

WHITE RICE AND WILD RICE

CHINESE-STYLE POTATOES

RICE AND VEGETABLES

VEGETABLE STIR-FRIES • RICE SALADS

CONTENTS

Rice is the basic foodstuff of most modern Chinese the world over. Whether sitting in the midst of south China's verdant rice fields or working in the basement kitchen of a San Francisco Chinese bistro run by an eccentric girl from New Jersey—every *bona fide* Chinese craves and eats rice. Vast amounts of it! An average, active Chinese person eating a traditional Chinese diet will consume about 8 cups of cooked rice daily. Most of the Chinese people with whom I lived in Taiwan ate even more.

Rice is the staple of the archetypal Chinese diet. Even northern Chinese, whose basic starch is noodles and breadstuffs, eat rice. Those who grow up in regionally schizophrenic north-south households, like myself, are hooked on both—often in the same bowl and at the same meal.

Vegetables occupy the second-most important tier in the Chinese diet. They are what perches gloriously on top of the rice in the everyday Chinese bowl.

Yet, in spite of the Chinese love for vegetables and the primacy of vegetables in the diet, it is difficult to be strictly vegetarian in a traditional Chinese setting. If you proclaim yourself a Buddhist, there is a nook of vegetarian eating imported centuries ago from India. However, if you proclaim guilt in killing a chicken or concern for your health, the average Chinese will think you are silly or perhaps sick. For, to the Chinese way of thinking, a vegetarian life is one-sided and out of balance. The culture is tipped always to inclusion: For every 3 cups of rice and 2 cups of vegetables in the typical Chinese bowl, there is a crowning dollop of meaty sauce or perhaps a few slices of fish. Without them, the meal is considered nutritionally incomplete and culturally un-Chinese.

That, as much as anything, is the reason for the sparseness of strictly vegetable dishes in this book. The Chinese know perhaps better than anyone how to cook vegetables and how to show them off, but the yin-yang scheme of Chinese eating demands that a bit of animal protein enter the picture and the bowl. Poultry stocks are happily splashed into vegetable stir-fries, and bits of dried shrimp are insistently strewn amidst the beans. It's all the tradition, which may be very wise.

■ ■ ■

HOW TO GREET SOMEONE IN CHINESE

If you live in China or Chinese society, regardless of the province or time of day, your greeting to others is always the same. Never mind if you're hailing your buddy across the way, meeting the Great Leader in the Great Hall of the People, or simply saying hello to your granny, the words are identical: literally, "Have you eaten rice yet?"

The phrase establishes and echoes the primacy of grains in the Chinese diet since ancient times. It is a resounding punctuation mark on the role of rice in the life of every Chinese. The question says "How are you doing?" and "Is everything okay?," all in the form of a focus on one's belly.

BASIC STEAMED RICE

MAKES 4 OR 8 CUPS

A generous bowl of freshly steamed white rice is the foundation of a classic Chinese meal. If you've previously thought rice a dull bit of whiteness, you've probably not had good rice or have not been very hungry. There is little that is more satisfying, at least to my tongue, when the palate is sharp and the rice is properly steamed.

A single recipe makes about 4 cups of steamed rice. The double recipe makes 8 cups. If this is more than you need, simply stir-fry the remainder a day or two later.

If you have only long-grain rice in the house and are hungering to steam it, add an extra ¼ cup water to the measurements that follow.

Exact water measurements for rice are always something of a crapshoot. Depending on the size and dryness of the grain, and at least a half-dozen other factors, the resulting rice may be a bit dry or a bit too moist. Read the advice on page 423 for the "cure."

SINGLE RECIPE
(ABOUT 4 CUPS):
1¼ cups short- or medium-
   grain white rice
1¾ cups plus 2 tablespoons cold
   water

DOUBLE RECIPE
(ABOUT 8 CUPS):
2½ cups short- or medium-
   grain white rice
2¾ cups cold water

1. Put the rice in a large bowl. Cover generously with cold water. Let stand a minute or two, then stir gently in one direction with your hand 6 or 7 times. Drain the water, refill the basin, and repeat the process until the water runs clear, upwards of 5 or 6 rinsings. The repeated rinsing freshens the flavor enormously.

2. Put the drained rice in a heavy pot with a tight-fitting lid. Use a 2- to 3-quart pot for a single recipe or a 4- to 6-quart pot for a double recipe. Add cold water as specified and bring it to a rapid boil over high heat. When the big starchy bubbles climb nearly to the rim, in about 30 seconds, reduce the heat to low and cover the pot. Simmer the rice undisturbed for 15 minutes. Check the simmer with your ear near the pot to hear bubbling and your eye near the lid to detect tiny wisps of steam; do not uncover the pot.

3. Remove the pot from the stove and let it sit undisturbed for 20 minutes. Do not lift the lid.

4. At the end of the resting time, uncover the pot. Fluff the rice gently with a wooden rice paddle or a fork. Serve immediately.

TRADITIONAL FRIED RICE

SERVES 3 TO 4 AS A ONE-BOWL MEAL

Fried rice in China is a meal-in-a-bowl—typically a dish of cold cooked rice that is stir-fried with a mélange of colorful diced meats and vegetables. It can be as simple as last night's leftover rice tossed

A RICE COOKER

A typical modern Chinese kitchen has an electric rice cooker, and these are very versatile objects. My Chinese family in Taiwan had a giant rice cooker that measured more than a foot in diameter. It occupied the star spot in the kitchen and turned out enough rice to feed the old gentleman patriarch, his two wives, a fat servant, any number of his dozen children, and the big family dog, Harry, in addition to myself. The old man's artist son, whom I visited in Paris several years after I left Taiwan, was living the life of a European bohemian, but he, too, had a tiny rice cooker, which he kept alongside his easel. For both father and son, it was the centerpiece of each meal.

A rice cooker does more than cook rice. It also steams. It can steam cakes and puddings and last night's leftovers. The pail can serve as a basin and also as a pot. If I had only one plug-in tool, this might well be it.

together with last night's chicken, or as glamorous as a Chinese banquet featuring pricey bits of minced cured ham, tiny shrimp, matchsticks of honeyed pork, and so on into colorful lushness. Real fried rice is always white! Unlike the Chinese-American version that is stained with soy sauce, the authentic bowlful is left pristinely white and pure, seasoned only with salt.

The cooked rice for stir-frying behaves best in the pan when it has been left uncovered overnight to dry. If you are hungering for the dish and working with freshly cooked rice, a nonstick skillet will help.

STICKY RICE ALERT!

There are no recipes in this book that use the profoundly sticky rice called no-mi in Chinese (pronounced naw-mee, in Mandarin). This type of rice is 100 percent amylopectin, the stuff that makes rice stick. In English, it is called glutinous or sweet rice. In China, it is a specialty rice used mainly for sweets and stuffings.

The short- and medium-grain white rice I use daily is sticky only when compared to long-grain white rice, which in its profoundly antisocial way falls apart in individual grains—murder, if you're using chopsticks. The rice I like is sticky enough to hang together and cling politely to your utensils but is still a texturally recognizable cousin of everyday white rice.

2 to 3 tablespoons corn or peanut oil
1 small yellow or red onion, diced
1 small red bell pepper, diced
1 small carrot, diced
3½ cups cold cooked white rice, short- or medium-grain preferred, broken into separate grains
Stock or water, if needed (see Note, page 412)

1 cup blanched fresh greens, such as asparagus nuggets, peas, broccoli florets, or zucchini coins
¼ pound cooked cold meat, poultry, or fish, such as slivered or cubed chicken, beef, or pork, or chunks of cold salmon, shrimp, or scallops
1 to 1½ teaspoons kosher salt
¼ cup thinly sliced green and white scallion rings

1. Heat a wok or large heavy skillet over high heat until hot enough to evaporate a bead of water on contact. Add 1½ teaspoons of the oil and swirl to glaze the pan. Reduce the heat to moderately high, add the onion, and toss until half-cooked, about 1½ minutes. Add the bell pepper and carrots, and toss until tender-crisp, about 2 minutes more. Drizzle a bit more oil down the side of the pan, if needed to prevent sticking; adjust the heat, as needed, to maintain a lusty sizzle without scorching the vegetables.

2. Add the rice and toss to blend and heat through, 2 to 3 minutes. Add a bit more oil, if needed to prevent sticking. (If the rice is overly dry, now is the moment to reduce the heat to low and swirl in the stock. Toss to combine, cover the pan, and cook until the liquid is absorbed, about 4 minutes.)

3. When the rice is very hot to the touch, add the greens and toss to heat through, about 1 minute. Add the meat, poultry, or fish, and toss to combine. Season with salt to taste. Fold in the scallion rings.

4. Serve at once in heated bowls of contrasting color.

MENU SUGGESTIONS: Fried rice in this simple, traditional form is a nutritionally balanced one-bowl meal. If you were eliminating the meat, however, it would be a colorful accompaniment to any of our steamed fish or poultry dishes.

NOTE: Overly dry rice requires a bit of stock or water to turn it pleasantly moist. This can be added to the pan just after the rice is tossed with the first vegetables: Cover and steam the rice and stock mixture over low heat until the rice steams through and absorbs the stock. For 3½ cups of overly dry rice, you would need about 1 cup of unsalted stock.

CURRIED LAMB (OR PORK) FRIED RICE

SERVES 3 TO 4 AS A ONE-BOWL MEAL

At China Moon, we have two untraditional ways of making fried rice, and the method we use depends on the time of day. At lunchtime, it is tossed to order and seasoned to the whims of the daytime wok cook. Rarely content with a mere sprinkle of seasoning, our cooks concoct flavor-laden sauces that they personalize with labels like "Formula 2001," making for a spicier or richer fried rice than one might normally find in a Chinese home.

Here is one zippy lunchtime original dotted with curried meat.

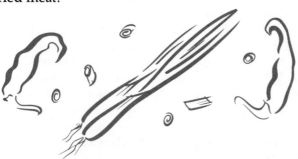

DRYING RICE FOR STIR-FRYING

Ideally 12 to 24 hours in advance of stir-frying, spread the freshly steamed rice in a thin layer on a large platter or baking sheet. Leave uncovered at room temperature to cool, then refrigerate, still uncovered, for up to one day. To stir-fry most easily with minimal oil, the grains should be dry enough to break apart in your hand, but not so dry that they rattle on the plate: dry on the outside but moist within.

To dry rice quickly, spread it very thinly and put it in a slow (200°F) oven and turn occasionally, until the outside is a bit dry. Or, following the method I adopted once in Taiwan where there were no ovens, get the blow dryer out and do the job!

RICE IS RICE AND SOUP IS SOUP

The fact that we add chicken stock to our dinnertime fried rice would appall my adopted Chinese ancestors. Traditionally, Chinese cook rice with only water. It is a mating of two purities. Old Chinese texts go on lyrically for pages about the correct aging and storing of mountain or rain water for the cooking of rice, with much the same seamless combination of Fannie Farmer–style wisdom and mystical revelation as is used in writings about the proper brewing of tea.

On the occasion that I suggested to the elderly patriarch of my second Chinese family that we jazz things up by steaming the rice with stock, he looked at me like I was an ignorant barbarian, bellowed, "Soup is soup and rice is rice!" and stomped from the room, his red silk bathrobe flapping in injured disapproval. I felt as if Confucius had just spoken, and was left stewing in my Western juices for days while he ignored me.

MARINADE AND MEAT:
2 teaspoons China Moon Curry Powder (page 7)
¼ teaspoon freshly ground pepper
1 teaspoon China Moon Ten-Spice (page 6)
1 tablespoon soy sauce
1 tablespoon sugar
1 tablespoon Serrano-Lemongrass Vinegar (page 19) or unseasoned Japanese rice vinegar
2 teaspoons cornstarch
½ pound coarsely ground lamb shoulder or pork butt

AROMATICS:
1 tablespoon finely minced fresh ginger
1 tablespoon finely minced garlic
½ cup thinly sliced green and white scallion rings

1 small red Fresno chili, finely minced

SAUCE:
½ cup unsalted chicken stock
1 tablespoon Serrano-Lemongrass Vinegar or unseasoned Japanese rice vinegar
1 tablespoon cider vinegar
1 tablespoon plus 1 teaspoon soy sauce
1 tablespoon plus 2 teaspoons Chinese rice wine or dry sherry

4 to 5 tablespoons corn or peanut oil
1 red bell pepper, finely diced
3 fat scallions, cut into ½-inch nuggets
3½ to 4 cups cold cooked white rice, short- or medium-grain preferred

1. Blend the marinade ingredients through the cornstarch until smooth in a bowl big enough to hold the lamb. Add the lamb and stir with your hand to blend thoroughly. Seal and set aside to marinate at cool room temperature for 2 to 4 hours, or refrigerate overnight. Let come to room temperature before cooking.

2. Combine the aromatics through the chili in a small dish; seal until ready to use.

3. Combine all of the sauce ingredients in a small bowl. Stir to blend, leaving the spoon in the bowl.

4. About 15 minutes before serving, heat a wok or large heavy skillet over high heat until a bead of water evaporates on contact. Add 2 tablespoons of the oil, swirl to glaze the pan, and reduce the heat to moderately high. When the oil is hot enough to sizzle a dab of lamb, add the lamb and toss briskly to break up the meat, until it is 95 percent gray, 1 to 1½ minutes. Remove the meat to a colander to drain. Wash the pan and return it to the stove.

5. Reheat the pan over high heat until hot enough to evaporate a bead of water. Add 2 tablespoons of the oil, swirl to glaze the pan, and reduce the heat to moderate. When the oil is hot enough to sizzle a scallion ring, add the aromatics and stir gently until fully fragrant, 15 to 20 seconds. Adjust the heat so they foam gently without browning. Add the bell pepper and toss until slightly softened, 30 seconds to 1 minute. Add the scallions and toss for 1 minute more.

6. Add the rice and toss until hot to the touch. Adjust the heat so it crackles happily and drizzle a bit more oil down the side of the pan, if needed to prevent sticking. Reduce the heat to moderately low. Stir the sauce and add it to the pan. Return the lamb to the pan and toss gently until the liquids are almost absorbed. Taste; adjust with a dash more salt and/or pepper, if desired.

7. Serve at once in heated bowls of contrasting color.

CHICKEN AND BACON FRIED RICE

SERVES 3 TO 4 AS A ONE-BOWL MEAL

Another noontime favorite, this version of fried rice features large cubes of plush chicken and tiny bits of fragrant bacon. Purchase a strip of good slab bacon from your butcher. It lends magic to many dishes.

VELVET MARINADE
AND CHICKEN:
1 large egg white
1 tablespoon Chinese rice wine
or dry sherry

1 teaspoon kosher salt
1 tablespoon cornstarch
½ pound boneless, skinless
chicken breast, cut into ¼-
inch cubes

RICE RINSING

Of greatest import to the taste of rice is the rinsing of the grain. For a clarity of flavor (with no concern for vitamins), rice must be washed by gentle, methodical rinsing and swishing in six or more ample changes of cold water, until any talc or mill stuff— bits of rice bran and the occasional, odd pebble—are removed and the water runs clear. This is an old and hallowed ritual in Chinese and Japanese kitchens, where one cook often specializes (for years!) in the sole task of rinsing and cooking rice. It is nice to do it in this spirit— cleansing the mind as one rinses the rice.

Our most accomplished rice-rinser at China Moon was a stubby lady named Hao. Built like a rock and standing 4 feet 5 inches, her morning rice rinsing was a silent meditation done with enormous rhythm and concentration. No bit of chaff, no battered grain escaped her eye. Her rice was incomparable; never once would she stoop to rinsing it less than her self-prescribed eight times.

Too bad she was a hellion away from rice! She badgered our meat and vegetable cutters so badly, we were forced to bid her a tearful adieu. Our rice has never been the same since.

AROMATICS:
1 tablespoon finely minced garlic
1 tablespoon finely minced fresh ginger

SAUCE:
½ cup China Moon Double Stock (page 72) or unsalted chicken stock
3 tablespoons soy sauce
2 tablespoons unseasoned Japanese rice vinegar

1 cup diced carrot
1 cup fresh peas or corn kernels
½ cup diced smoked bacon
2 to 3 teaspoons corn or peanut oil
3 fat scallions, cut into ½-inch nuggets
3½ to 4 cups cold cooked white rice, short- or medium-grain preferred
2 tablespoons finely chopped Chinese chives or fresh coriander
2 large eggs, beaten
Kosher salt and freshly ground pepper

1. Briskly whisk the marinade ingredients through the cornstarch until thick. Add the chicken and toss well. Seal and refrigerate for several hours or overnight. Let come to room temperature; re-toss before cooking.

2. Combine the aromatics in a small dish; seal until ready to use.

3. Combine all of the sauce ingredients through the vinegar in a small bowl. Stir to blend, leaving the spoon in the bowl.

4. In a saucepan filled with rapidly boiling water, blanch the carrots for 15 seconds. Scoop into ice water to chill; drain. Blanch the peas until tender-crisp, 15 to 30 seconds, or the corn for 5 seconds. Plunge into ice water; drain.

5. About 15 to 20 minutes before serving, bring a small pot of water to a steaming near simmer. Add the chicken, stir gently to separate the cubes, and cook until the outside turns 95 percent white, less than 1 minute. Drain promptly; set aside. The chicken will be pinkish in the center.

6. Heat a wok or large heavy skillet over high heat until hot enough to evaporate a bead of water on contact. Add the bacon and reduce the heat to moderate. Toss the bacon until it turns golden and renders most of its fat, 1½ to 2 minutes. Remove the crisped bacon to a dish, leaving the fat in the pan.

7. Return the pan to moderately high heat. Add 2 teaspoons of the corn oil and swirl to glaze the pan. Add the aromatics and stir gently until fully fragrant, 10 to 15 seconds, adjusting the heat so they foam gently without browning. Add the scallions and toss for 1 minute. Add the carrot and toss to mix. Add the bacon and rice, and toss until the rice is very hot to the touch, 2 to 3 minutes. Adjust the heat to maintain a gentle sizzle and drizzle a bit more oil down the side of the pan, if needed to prevent sticking.

8. Whisk the chives with the beaten eggs and add them in a thin stream over the rice; toss to blend. Stir the sauce and add it to the pan. Toss until the rice has absorbed almost all of the liquid, adjusting the heat so that it does not scorch.

9. Add the peas or corn and chicken, and toss until the chicken is cooked through, 20 to 30 seconds. Season to taste with kosher salt and pepper.

10. Serve in heated bowls of contrasting color.

DINNER FRIED RICE

SERVES 2 TO 4

This second method of pseudo fried rice is our evening standard, when our upstairs woks are always occupied, and the rice is bumped to the downstairs prep kitchen to be cooked in a fashion that is a bit like the one used to make risotto. While totally untraditional as far as I know, it is nonetheless delicious!

Home-rendered chicken fat is the secret to the lushness. For the how-to on rendering, see page 420. You can use corn or peanut oil, but it is no replacement for the schmaltz.

3½ to 4 cups cold cooked white
    rice, short- or medium-grain
    preferred
3 tablespoons rendered chicken
    fat (page 420)
2 teaspoons kosher salt
About ½ cup China Moon
    Double Stock (page 72) or
    unsalted chicken stock

½ teaspoon Roasted Szechwan
    Pepper-Salt (page 5)
Green and white scallion rings
    and/or toasted sliced
    almonds, or toasted pine
    nuts, for garnish

BROWN RICE AND OTHER ANCIENT GRAINS

Every once in a while, we'll receive a request from a guest for brown rice with supper. Or, I'll get a letter from a brown rice–lover who wants cultural approval for his or her favorite grain. The problem in the restaurant is one of space and demand. The problem in Chinese culture is a strong and insistent favoring of white rice.

The cultural prejudice stems at least partly from issues of storage. The outer layer of rice bran, which contains many vitamins, is the first part of the grain to go rancid. Consequently, the Chinese discovered early on that milled rice held better and that the bran, meanwhile, could be pressed for oil. Nutritionally enlightened Chinese and very poor Chinese (both of whom might be expected to tilt in the unmilled direction) still favor white rice to this day. It is a cultural standard of purity that goes centuries deep.

Brown rice, of course, tastes delicious with Chinese foods, so if one loves it, one should eat it!

Ditto millet, barley, and buckwheat (aka kasha). These are, in fact, the ancient grains of China. Excellent on their own, they also offer a great change from rice. If they were good enough for Confucius, they should be good enough for us!

1. With your hands, crumble the rice until no hard lumps remain.

2. Heat a wok or large heavy skillet over moderate heat until hot enough to evaporate a bead of water on contact. Add the chicken fat, swirl to glaze the pan, and reduce the heat to moderately high. When the fat is hot enough to sizzle a grain of rice, add the rice and toss briskly until it starts sticking together, 2 to 3 minutes. Adjust the heat so it crackles happily without scorching. Sprinkle the salt over the rice and toss to combine.

3. Turn off the heat. Add ½ cup of the chicken stock in a thin necklace around the rim of the rice, and toss to mix. The rice will look a bit soupy. Spread the rice in an even layer over the bottom of the pan; use a wok shovel or the back of a spoon or spatula to compress and smooth the rice so it holds the heat in like a cap. Let the mixture sit for 10 to 15 minutes.

4. Toss the rice and taste. If it is wet (meaning the rice was too wet to begin with and/or the pan didn't hold the heat), toss the rice over moderately low heat until hot and pat it smooth a second time. Turn off the heat and sit back for another 10 minutes. If it's too hard (indicating the rice was overly dry to begin with), then toss the rice over moderate heat until it crackles. Kill the heat and add another thin necklace of stock (as much as you think is needed) around the rim of the rice. Toss to blend, smooth to compress, then wait another 10 minutes or so for the rice to steam through to doneness.

5. When the rice is just right—pleasantly moist but firm—sprinkle it with the roasted pepper-salt and toss to combine.

6. Serve the rice immediately (just warm, as I like it) or hold it in a water bath (for convenience or further heating) for up to 1 hour. Sprinkle the rice with some color or crunch to garnish.

MENU SUGGESTIONS: Most everything likes this simple fried rice cozied up next to it, even a dish of rewarmed meat loaf or that famous chicken starring 40 cloves of garlic.

SHANGHAI RICE WITH SMOKED BACON

SERVES 4 TO 6

This is an invention in the ineffable spirit of old Shanghai, an elaboration of a favorite dish from my first cookbook. It is an almost creamy, savory dish studded with bits of color.

2 cups uncooked short- or
   medium-grain white rice
⅓ cup diced smoked bacon
2 tablespoons thinly sliced
   shallots
2 tablespoons Chinese rice wine
   or dry sherry
3 cups water
1½ teaspoons kosher salt
1¼ cups cubed butternut
   squash

½ to 1 teaspoon Roasted
   Szechwan Pepper-Salt
   (page 5)
3 tablespoons thinly sliced green
   and white scallion rings
1 small red bell pepper, finely
   diced
1 small red pasilla pepper or red
   Anaheim chili, finely diced
   (optional)
Diagonally cut green and white
   scallion rings, for garnish

1. Rinse the rice, following step 1 on page 410.

2. Heat a small heavy casserole over high heat until a bead of water evaporates on contact. Reduce the heat to moderate and add the bacon. Stir until most of the fat renders and the bacon turns golden and crispy, 2 to 2½ minutes. Adjust the heat so it renders without scorching. Add the shallots and stir until softened and translucent, 1 to 1½ minutes. Add the rice wine in a necklace around the edge of the pan; stir briskly to mix. Add the rice and stir to combine. Add the water, sprinkle in the salt, and stir to blend. Raise the heat and bring the mixture to a lively simmer. Cover the pan tightly, reduce the heat to low, and cook the rice for 30 minutes. (If you are working on an electric stove, transfer the pot to a burner set to low heat.) After 5 minutes, put your ear near the pot and check for fine wisps of steam escaping from the lid to know that all is simmering gently within; do not lift the lid.

SMOKED BACON

It is unfashionable these days to dwell on the flavor of fat, but the bacon fat used here gives the rice an inimitable richness. Fat, in China, was a nutritionally important feature on the mostly rice and vegetable landscape; this dish is a great example of its traditional use.

Buy smoked bacon cut from the slab at a quality butcher shop. It should smell clean and fresh, not overwhelmingly smoked. Slab bacon stores beautifully in the freezer. I like to keep a small amount on hand, to give a fine bit of lushness to an otherwise Spartan meal.

RICE HARMONY

The success of Dinner Fried Rice in the first 10 to 15 minutes cooking is mostly a matter of luck. Rice dried to a perfect degree, a perfectly heavy pan, and a perfectly strong pilot light or gradually cooling electric coil are all that is needed! To have each of these elements in ideal harmony is comparatively easy when you've made it two or three times, but don't be discouraged the first time around. A second or even a third reheating will usually repair the rice, if not your ego.

3. Remove the pot from the heat, still without disturbing the lid. Let the rice stand for 30 minutes.

4. While the rice is cooking and resting, blanch the squash in rapidly boiling water for 1 minute. Plunge into ice water to chill; drain.

5. At the end of the resting time, uncover the pot and gently stir the rice to loosen it. Add pepper-salt to taste; the amount needed will differ, depending on the bacon. Stir the squash, scallion rings, and the chili and bell peppers into the rice.

6. Serve the rice in heated bowls of contrasting color, garnished with the scallion diags.

MENU SUGGESTIONS: I love this dish on its own for a simple brunch. In that mood, you might pair it with a fluffy asparagus omelette. It also mates nicely with other light Chinese dishes, like Ma-La Steamed Poussin with Roasted Szechwan Pepper-Salt (page 153) or a simply steamed fish scattered with ginger threads.

STIR-FRIED WILD RICE WITH WILD MUSHROOMS

SERVES 4 TO 6

This is a very wild bowlful, at least from the Chinese point of view. Not even a distant cousin of classic fried rice, this is a Western-style mélange of wild rice and wild mushrooms seasoned in a Chinese manner with roasted Szechwan pepper-salt.

The rice is best cooked and left to cool overnight before stir-frying. If you are in a rush, however, a light touch and a nonstick skillet will help get the dish on the table in an hour.

1 cup uncooked wild rice

2 cups China Moon Infusion
(page 72), Duck Infusion
with Szechwan Peppercorns
(page 74), Vegetable Infusion
(page 82), or unsalted
chicken, duck, or vegetable
stock

2 to 3 tablespoons home-
rendered chicken or duck fat
(pages 420 or 170) or corn or
peanut oil

⅔ cup thinly sliced leeks

½ cup thinly sliced celery

½ cup diced red bell pepper

1½ cups thinly sliced wild
mushrooms

½ cup thinly sliced green and
white scallion rings

2½ cups hearts of baby bok choy
or baby Chinese celery
cabbage, halved lengthwise
if fat

2 tablespoons Chinese rice wine
or dry sherry

1½ teaspoons kosher salt

Roasted Szechwan Pepper-Salt
(page 5)

1. Rinse the wild rice, following step 1 on page 410.

2. Combine the wild rice and 2 cups infusion in a heavy
2- to 2½-quart pot. Bring to a boil, reduce the heat to a weak
simmer, cover tightly, and cook for 20 minutes. Remove to a
cool burner and let sit undisturbed for 20 minutes. Half of the
grains should be split, and the stock should be absorbed. (If
the rice is overly firm and dry, sprinkle with additional stock
or water and cook, covered, over low heat until the liquid is
absorbed and the rice is pleasantly soft.) Spread the cooked
rice thinly on a baking sheet and refrigerate uncovered until
thoroughly cold.

3. About 15 minutes before serving, heat a wok or large
heavy skillet over moderate heat until a bead of water evaporates on contact. Add the chicken or duck fat, swirl to glaze the
pan, and reduce the heat to moderate. When the fat is hot
enough to sizzle a slice of leek, add the leeks and toss until
supple, about 2 minutes. Add the celery and bell pepper dice,
and toss for 1 minute. Add the mushrooms and half of the
scallions, and toss for 1½ minutes more. Adjust the heat to
maintain a merry sizzle and drizzle a bit more fat down the
side of the pan, if needed to prevent sticking.

4. Add the cabbage hearts and toss until they are very
hot and the mushrooms begin to render their juices, about 2
minutes more. Add the wine in a necklace around the rim of
the pan and toss to blend. Add the wild rice and toss gently to
mix. Sprinkle with the salt and toss to heat through. If the rice
sticks to the pan, drizzle in a bit more fat. Sprinkle with the
pepper-salt to taste and toss to combine.

SCHMALTZ (AKA CHICKEN FAT)

For adding a bit of dash
to a bowl of stir-fried
something, there's nothing
better than a dab of fresh
chicken fat!

Rendering your own is
easy. Start with fresh, odor-
free chicken skins and the
little blobs of fat clinging to
them. Accumulate them in
your freezer as you skin a
breast here and there or trim
a whole chicken for dinner.

For a golden fat with a
toasty flavor, follow the
Western way and put the
skins in a heavy, wide pot
with enough cold water to
cover. Bring to a simmer,
then let the mixture bubble
along, stirring occasionally,
until the water evaporates,
the fat turns golden and the
skins turn crispy. Don't let
the fat brown; it will taste
burnt. Strain the fat through
dry cheesecloth or a very fine
sieve.

The Chinese method is
to simply steam the skins,
uncovered, in a bowl. As the
fat melts, pour it off into a
heatproof container. It's an
undramatic, foolproof
method. The fat produced by
steaming is pale yellow and
very light in flavor.

Home-rendered chicken
fat can be kept in the refrigerator or freezer.

HEARTS OF VEGETABLES

///

Back in my Mickey Mouse years, hearts of palm struck me as a romantic vegetable. I'd never seen one (nor have I yet), but I imagined they were eaten by elegant ladies who wore fishnet stockings and elbow-length gloves.

Hearts of baby Chinese cabbages hold something of the same literary lure. These are the 2-inch or so miniature cabbages that reside at the core of the baby vegetable. Chinese artisans traditionally crafted them out of jade, they are so pretty, and they are beautiful in stir-fries. If you can't find them, use any tiny, fresh green; if substituting something solid, like baby zucchini, blanch them first before adding to the stir-fry.

5. Serve the rice immediately or hold in a covered pot in a low oven for up to 30 minutes. Garnish with the reserved scallion rings.

MENU SUGGESTIONS: A simple roast chicken, duck, or a festive Christmas goose are all set off to advantage by this rice. Ma-La Steamed Poussin with Roasted Szechwan Pepper-Salt (page 153) or Wok-Seared Duck Breasts (page 164) also work well with it.

WILD RICE CONGEE

SERVES 2 TO 4

ongee is the anglicized term for what in Cantonese is called *jook*—the steaming bowlful of last night's leftover rice that is turned into this morning's porridge, with the help of some nutritious slivers of preserved fish, meat, poultry, or egg. It is a jump-start breakfast not only throughout southern China but also in outposts of Chinese eating worldwide. Indeed, Chinese far away from home think of *jook* with the fondness that ex-New Yorkers reserve for bagels.

This is a wild version of the classic. It heretically mixes wild and white rices, and untraditionally opts for the lushness of stock as opposed to water. It is something I love to eat when I am dog-tired. Never one for morning porridge, I like it best at dusk or midnight.

½ cup uncooked short- or
  medium-grain white rice
⅓ cup uncooked wild rice
5 cups China Moon Infusion
  (page 72), Duck Infusion
  with Szechwan Peppercorns
  (page 74), or Vegetable
  Infusion (page 82), or
  unsalted chicken, duck, or
  vegetable stock
1 tablespoon Chinese rice wine
  or dry sherry
Kosher salt and Roasted
  Szechwan Pepper-Salt
  (page 5), to taste

1 cup finely shredded Chinese-
  Style Duck Confit (page
  170), or other tasty shredded
  meat
Thinly sliced green and white
  scallions and/or coarsely
  chopped coriander leaves and
  stems, for garnish
Fried Ginger Threads (page 29),
  for garnish

1. Rinse the white rice in several changes of cold water, stirring gently with your hand, until the water runs clear; drain. Rinse the wild rice in several changes of cold water; drain.

2. In a heavy 2½- to 3-quart pot, combine the white rice, wild rice, infusion, and wine. Bring to a slow boil over moderate heat, stirring occasionally; let bubble for 5 minutes.

3. Reduce the heat to maintain a weak simmer, cover tightly, and cook for 1 hour. At the end of the hour, the mixture will be soupy and the wild rice will be splayed at the ends.

4. Taste the rice. Season as needed with kosher salt, then add a dash or more of the pepper-salt to tingle your tongue.

5. To serve, portion the congee among heated bowls of contrasting color. Top with the duck confit, scallions and/or coriander, and ginger. Set the table with deep-bowled Chinese spoons.

MENU SUGGESTIONS: Congee is the quintessential one-bowl meal. A glass of cool white wine is the only desirable accompaniment.

WINDOW DRESSINGS

///

The bits of this and that used to dress up rice salads and the like are frills that can change easily with mood and weather. The rice and the seasonings are the real nuts and bolts of the dish. All the rest is yummy frou-frou— dots of color and dashes of flavor and texture that invite improvisation.

THE IMPONDERABLES OF RICE-MAKING

It is impossible to specify exact amounts of water and the exact amount of time needed to cook rice, regardless of type. The size of the grain and the condition and length of the storage—among other factors—make hard-and-fast rules impossible. If you buy the exact same box of commercial rice time after time, you'll hit easily on a formula. But, if you experiment with different sources (which you should, to experience the fabulously broad range of flavors and textures rice has to offer), then you'll be left with a bit of guesswork.

What to do? Relax! Follow the remedies given here. Too wet: Put it uncovered in the oven or over low heat on your stovetop, stirring, until the excess liquid evaporates. Too dry: Sprinkle in some additional liquid, toss to glaze the grains, then cover and put the pot over low heat or in the oven to let the moisture be absorbed. The guests are waiting? Well, then pour them (and yourself) another glass of wine.

WILD RICE SALAD WITH GINGER-BALSAMIC DRESSING

SERVES 4 TO 6

We have great-tasting wild rice on the northern California Coast near Mendocino and we show it off to best advantage in this very delicious salad. It is nutty and spirited and also very pretty.

The rice can be made a night ahead, if you like. Tossing the salad is a very simple business.

1½ cups uncooked wild rice
½ teaspoon Roasted Szechwan Pepper-Salt (page 5)
1 red bell pepper, finely diced
½ cup thinly sliced green and white scallion rings

DRESSING:
¼ cup rice bran, corn, or peanut oil

¼ cup Szechwan Peppercorn Oil (page 18)
2 tablespoons fresh ginger juice (squeezed from finely minced fresh ginger)
2 tablespoons balsamic vinegar
1½ to 2 tablespoons freshly squeezed lemon juice
1½ teaspoons kosher salt

1. Rinse the wild rice in several changes of cold water, stirring gently with your hand, until the water runs clear; drain.

2. In a 3- to 4-quart heavy saucepan, combine the wild rice, pepper-salt, and 4 cups water. Bring to a slow boil over moderate heat. Adjust the heat so the liquid simmers gently and cook, uncovered, for 20 minutes. Turn off the heat, tightly cover, and let sit for 10 minutes. The rice should be cooked but a bit al dente; about half the grains should be split. If underdone, return the liquid to a simmer and cook until done. Drain off any excess liquid. The rice can be dressed immediately or refrigerated overnight. Bring to room temperature before dressing.

3. Shortly before serving, toss the rice with the red bell pepper and most of the scallions. Whisk all of the dressing ingredients to emulsify, then toss well with the rice. Let stand for 5 to 10 minutes, toss, and taste. Adjust with a dash more salt and/or lemon juice, if needed. The flavor should be very lively.

4. Serve in large spoonfuls on plates to show off its color. Garnish with a sprinkling of the reserved scallion.

MENU SUGGESTIONS: We use this salad as a regular feature on our Peking antipasto plates. It mates perfectly with all of our smoked poultry, as well as with our sliced beef and lamb tenderloins. Add a green salad and you have a wonderful, light meal.

WOK-SEARED NEW POTATOES

SERVES 4 TO 6

I adore potatoes! And perhaps none more than these. Tinged by the smoke of the wok and piquant with a dusting of roasted szechwan pepper-salt, they are mouth-watering.

For spicy potatoes, use our China Moon Hot Chili Oil, Chili-Orange Oil, or Chili-Lemon Oil in place of the sesame-infused oil. For lusher potatoes, use the schmaltz.

1½ pounds very small (new) potatoes, halved or quartered if large
2 to 3 tablespoons home-rendered chicken fat (page 420) or corn or peanut oil
2 to 3 tablespoons Ma-La Oil (page 17) or Five-Flavor Oil (page 13)

½ teaspoon Roasted Szechwan Pepper-Salt (page 5)
1 tablespoon finely slivered coriander leaves and stems
1 tablespoon finely chopped Chinese chives or thinly cut green and white scallion rings

1. Place the potatoes in a single layer in a large wok or a wide heavy pot. Add enough cold water to cover generously.

POTATO VARIETIES

I like tiny round potatoes with red skins, as well as several odd, finger-shaped varieties with red or yellow skins. These are marketed under very colorful names, including yellow finn, rose fir, and bintje. I avoid blue potatoes and would have to be paid to eat one.

New potato, as far as I know, refers to a tiny potato that is plucked from the ground when it is less than the size of a Ping-Pong ball. Why they're not called baby potatoes beats me. It may be a question for the too-cute department of the ad agency that handles the Potato Board account.

Bring to a gentle simmer over moderate heat and cook until the potatoes are tender but firm, 3 to 4 minutes. A knife inserted into the center of each potato should meet little resistance. Drain. If working in advance, plunge into ice water to chill, then drain. At this point the potatoes can be sealed and refrigerated. Bring to room temperature before proceeding.

2. Combine the oils.

3. Divide the potatoes into 2 batches. Heat a wok or large heavy skillet over high heat until a bead of water evaporates on contact. Add 2 tablespoons of the oil, swirl to glaze the pan, and reduce the heat to moderately high. When the oil is hot enough to sizzle a piece of potato on contact, add the first batch of potatoes. Toss until crispy and golden brown, 2 to 3 minutes, adjusting the heat so they brown without scorching and drizzling a bit more oil down the side of the pan, if needed to prevent sticking. Sprinkle the potatoes with half of the pepper-salt; toss to blend. Sprinkle with half of the coriander and chives, and toss to mix.

Wipe the pan clean and repeat with the remaining batch.

4. Serve the potatoes hot from the pan. Or, spread on a baking sheet and let cool to room temperature. When ready, rewarm in a 350°F oven until hot, about 5 minutes.

MENU SUGGESTIONS: Many of our sandpots, especially those featuring chicken and lamb, are happily partnered by these potatoes. Ditto for many of our cured and smoked meats, especially when served as part of an antipasto.

CRISPY POTATOES

SERVES 4 TO 6

A deep-fried variation on the preceding recipe, this is just one more way to a potato-lover's heart. Different potatoes will yield different results. We have excellent luck with a large range of varieties, as long as the potatoes themselves are very small.

The potatoes can be parboiled a day in advance. Fry them just before eating.

1½ pounds very small (new) potatoes, halved or quartered if large
4 to 6 cups corn or peanut oil, for frying

½ teaspoon Roasted Szechwan Pepper-Salt (page 5)
¼ cup thinly sliced green and white scallion rings

1. Place the potatoes in a large wok or a wide heavy pot and add enough cold water to cover generously. Bring to a gentle simmer over moderate heat and cook until the potatoes are tender but firm, 3 to 4 minutes. A knife inserted into the center should meet little resistance. Drain. If working in advance, plunge in ice water to chill, then drain. At this point, the potatoes can be sealed and refrigerated. Bring to room temperature before proceeding.

2. About 20 minutes before serving, heat a wok or large, deep, and heavy skillet over high heat until hot enough to evaporate a bead of water on contact. Add oil to a depth of 2 inches, rest a deep-fry thermometer on the rim of the pot, and reduce the heat to moderately high. When the oil is hot enough to foam a piece of potato, 375°F, add half of the potatoes and fry until golden, 1½ to 2 minutes. Scoop the potatoes from the oil with a large Chinese mesh spoon and drain on paper towels. Reheat the oil to 375°F over high heat and fry and drain the second batch.

3. Toss the newly fried potatoes in a large bowl with the pepper-salt and most of the scallion rings.

4. Serve immediately. Portion among heated plates and garnish with the reserved scallion.

MENU SUGGESTIONS: Maybe it's a variation on the fish and chips theme, but I adore these potatoes with fish! Baked Snapper with Red Curry Sauce (page 199) comes immediately to mind.

POTATO TALES

I first learned the Chinese word for potato when my adopted younger Chinese brother called me one. "Dirt bean" was the direct translation, and he was telling me that I was a bumpkin!

The second time I heard the word was a year later, while sitting in my lyric scholar's studio. In the spirit of every traditional Chinese urban household of note, the compound was separated from the street by a high wall, over which would waft scents and sounds of the city.

"Poooo-taaaaay-tooooes!" crooned an old man's voice, in a near-wail. "Pooooo-taaaaay-tooooes, too good to ignore!" I was so curious to see what he was about, after two years of living in Taiwan with nary a potato in sight but me, that I put aside my books and peered out the gate. There he was, a real country bumpkin. He was thrilled to see me. Gesturing to his cart, which was a simple brazier on wheels with glowing coals in its belly, he pulled out a long stick with a potato on the end! I bought it. It was yummy! Neither white nor orange, something in between a potato and a yam, it was the best roasted potato I ever ate.

DRY-FRIED CHINESE EGGPLANT NUGGETS

SERVES 3 TO 4 AS PART OF A MULTICOURSE MEAL

This is my favorite Chinese eggplant dish, bar none. Meaty in texture and sweet from both the natural flavor of the slender eggplant and the veil of brown sugar, it is deeply satisfying. If Chinese eggplant are within reach and you have never before cooked them, this is the recipe to try.

Preparations are simple and can be done ahead. The dish is also excellent at room temperature.

DRY-FRYING

"Dry-frying" refers to a style of stir-fried dish in which the sauce liquids are purposely reduced while the components are tossed over moderately high heat. It is a way of enriching a dish with concentrated flavors, and is a favored treatment with meaty vegetables.

AROMATICS:
1 tablespoon plus 1 teaspoon finely minced fresh ginger
1 tablespoon plus 1 teaspoon finely minced garlic
⅓ cup thinly sliced green and white scallion rings
1 teaspoon Chinese chili sauce
1 tablespoon dried shrimp, soaked in hot water for 15 minutes, drained, and minced (optional)

SAUCE:
2 tablespoons soy sauce
2 tablespoons packed brown sugar
1 tablespoon balsamic vinegar
2½ tablespoons hot water

4 to 5 tablespoons corn or peanut oil, for stir-frying
1½ pounds long, slender Chinese eggplant, tipped and roll-cut (see page 260) into chunky nuggets about 1 inch long
Thinly sliced green and white scallion rings, for garnish

1. Combine the aromatics in a small dish; seal until ready to use.

2. Combine the sauce ingredients through the water in a small bowl. Stir to blend, leaving the spoon in the bowl.

3. Heat a wok or large heavy skillet over high heat until hot enough to evaporate a bead of water on contact. Add 3 tablespoons of the oil and swirl to glaze the pan. Reduce the heat to moderate. When the oil is hot enough to sizzle a scallion ring, add the aromatics. Stir gently until fully fragrant, 20 to 30 seconds, adjusting the heat so they foam without browning. Add the eggplant and toss well to combine. Toss until the eggplant is very hot and the skin is mostly brown, about 4 minutes. Adjust the heat so the eggplant cooks without scorching, and drizzle a bit more oil down the side of the pan, if needed to prevent sticking. Be stingy with the oil; eggplant will soak up all you give it.

4. Stir the sauce, add it to the pan, and toss well to combine. Bring the liquid to a simmer, cover the pan, and simmer until the liquid is 90 percent absorbed, 2 to 3 minutes.

5. Serve the eggplant hot, tepid, or at room temperature on a plate of contrasting color. Garnish with the scallion rings.

Menu Suggestions: For a vegetarian array, try pairing the eggplant with Dragon Noodles (page 391) and add a zesty condiment, such as Ginger-Pickled Daikon (page 53) or Ma-La Cucumber Fans (page 48). The eggplant is also a wonderful partner to roasted or grilled fish or chicken.

Grilled Chinese Eggplant with Spicy Peanut Sauce

SERVES 3 TO 4 AS A LIGHT MAIN COURSE, 6 TO 8 AS PART OF A MULTICOURSE MEAL

Eggplant and spicy peanut sauce are made for one another, so well do their flavors marry. It seems to be the solid, taste-truth—whether you start in northern China with its classic dish of cold shredded eggplant topped with a soy and peanut sauce, or wind up at

DRIED SHRIMP

One of the weirder food flavorings on the Chinese scene, dried shrimp range from the size of a melon seed to ¾ inch in length. Sometimes they wear shells, heads, tails, and/or a fringe of tiny feet. They are strange, salty, and smell funky to boot. In polite culinary terms, their flavor could be described as tang. Many people adore dried shrimp, some abhor them; it is a matter of choice. In dry-fried preparations, they are wonderful.

Dried shrimp should be soaked in hot water for 15 minutes or so. They will grow somewhat softer but not soft. Drain the briny liquid and pick off any large bits of shell.

Keep dried shrimp sealed airtight in the refrigerator. If kept at room temperature in warm weather, they can grow moldy.

China Moon with this left-of-center version done on a Western grill.

Japanese eggplant, which has thicker skin and less sweet flesh than Chinese eggplant, is also good in this preparation. You also have a choice of peanut sauces. This one is a personal favorite, but equally good would be the sauce used in our Light-Style Peanut-Lime Cold Noodles (page 400). If you don't want to use a grill, you can cook the eggplant in an oven: Roast the oiled eggplant, scored side up, on a baking sheet in a preheated 350°F oven until the flesh is tender, 10 to 20 minutes, depending on the thickness of the eggplant.

The sauce and the scoring of the eggplant can be done in advance.

CHINESE EGGPLANT

One of the sexier entries in the exotic culinary sweepstakes, Chinese eggplant are long, leggy, often curvy, and a beautiful amethyst in color. They have an edible skin and a sweet flesh, and there are no seed pockets per se, only a scattering of tiny, freckle-like seeds at some times of the year.

Japanese eggplant, which are stubbier and a deep purple, are not nearly as sweet. They can be substituted, but they are only a distant second best.

SAUCE:
2 tablespoons finely minced garlic
⅓ packed cup coriander leaves and stems
½ cup unseasoned peanut butter, preferably homemade (page 32)
½ cup soy sauce
¼ cup sugar
1 teaspoon Serrano-Lemongrass Vinegar (page 19) or unseasoned Japanese rice vinegar

1 to 1½ tablespoons China Moon Hot Chili Oil (page 10) or China Moon Chili-Orange Oil (page 15)

4 to 6 long Chinese eggplants
About ½ cup Five-Flavor Oil (page 13)
Coriander sprigs, for garnish

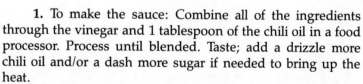

1. To make the sauce: Combine all of the ingredients through the vinegar and 1 tablespoon of the chili oil in a food processor. Process until blended. Taste; add a drizzle more chili oil and/or a dash more sugar if needed to bring up the heat.

If working in advance, seal the sauce and set it aside. To refrigerate overnight, leave out the coriander and buzz it in at the last minute.

2. Without removing the leaves (which will serve as a decorative note), evenly cut the eggplants in half lengthwise. Score the flesh lightly with crisscross hatch marks. Brush the cut sides liberally with the flavored oil. Place the eggplants, cut sides down, on a baking sheet. If you are working in advance, the eggplant can be left at room temperature for up to several hours; brush them only lightly at first, then more liberally just before grilling.

3. About 30 minutes before serving, prepare the grill. Let the coals burn until they are gray and only moderately hot. Place the eggplant halves, cut sides down, on the grill and cook until the cut surface is golden and striped with score marks and the thickest portion of the skin side is tender to the touch, about 5 minutes.

4. Serve hot or tepid. Cut the eggplant halves into wedges on the diagonal and arrange, scored sides up, on a plate. Spoon a thin ribbon of sauce on top and garnish with a leggy sprig of coriander alongside.

MENU SUGGESTIONS: This is great summer fare, served up alongside a cold tomato salad, fresh corn-on-the-cob, a platter of simply grilled or stir-fried shrimp, and a lemon-tinged pasta like Dragon Noodles (page 391). Because the eggplant are grilled over only moderately hot coals, you might plan a high heat item like fish or shellfish to occupy the grill first.

HOT AND SOUR HUNAN VEGETABLES

SERVES 4 TO 6

When the wear and tear of being a carnivore is weighing on me—or when I simply have the lust for a zesty, great plate of stir-fried vegetables— this is the dish I make. It is simple, deeply satisfying, and delicious eaten straight out of the pan.

You can gussy it up, if you like, with the addition of baby squash, boutique sweet peppers, wild or domestic mushrooms, or even the Martian-looking green cauliflower I sometimes spy in stores. It will be good in any fashion.

CHOOSING FRESH CHINESE VEGETABLES

A vegetable, like a person, generally wilts and wrinkles as it ages. So if you're looking for fresh, young vegetables, you'll want them "full of juice"— plump, firm, and generally smooth to the touch.

The ends tell a lot. Even if you've never seen a bunch of Chinese broccoli, moist stems and straight-standing leaves will tell you it's in good shape. Similarly, a head of Chinese celery may be a new sight, but a cluster of moist roots at the base and a flag-waving of perfect leaves at the mast should reassure you that it's fresh.

There are exceptions to the rule: A Chinese bitter melon will look rightfully warty, and a hank of tender Chinese longbeans will seem limp. But even the bumpy bitter melon should have smooth and juicy (not pitted) bumps, and a properly limp longbean should be smooth and uniformly green (not brown or scaly).

If your eye gauges that a vegetable is worthy of buying, but you don't know the taste or name, here are two approaches to finding out whether you want to eat it with your supper: One is to nibble on a bit of the leaf right there in the market. (If you do this with appropriate gravity, while clutching a fat bunch of stuff to purchase, even a sour-stomached grocer will not look at you too askance.) Or, a second route is to take the vegetable home, untasted, and submit it to a taste test: Slice off three pieces of the case study. Nibble on the first one raw; blanch the second piece; sauté or stir-fry the third. You'll learn not only what the vegetable tastes like but also the way you like it best.

AROMATICS:
1 tablespoon finely minced fresh ginger
1 tablespoon finely minced garlic
2 tablespoons Chinese black beans, coarsely chopped (do not rinse them)
¾ teaspoon dried red chili flakes

SAUCE:
½ cup China Moon Double Stock (page 72), Vegetable Infusion (page 82), or unsalted chicken or vegetable stock
2½ tablespoons soy sauce
2 tablespoons distilled white vinegar

¼ teaspoon sugar

¾ pound trimmed cauliflower florets, cut into walnut-size pieces
½ pound trimmed and peeled carrots, cut diagonally into rippled or plain coins ⅛ inch thick
1 pound slender green and golden zucchini, cut into ¼-inch rounds
2 to 3 tablespoons corn or peanut oil, for stir-frying
1 tablespoon cornstarch dissolved in 1½ tablespoons cold stock or water
Diagonally cut green and white scallion rings, for garnish

1. Combine the aromatics in a small dish and seal until ready to use.

2. Combine all the sauce ingredients through the sugar in a small bowl. Stir to blend, leaving the spoon in the bowl.

3. Bring a large pot of water to a rolling boil. Blanch the cauliflower for 1 minute. Scoop into ice water to chill; drain. Return the water to a boil and blanch the carrots for 15 seconds. Scoop into ice water to chill; drain. Return the water to a boil and blanch the zucchini for 5 seconds. Scoop into ice water to chill; drain. Once blanched, the vegetables may be held at room temperature for several hours or refrigerated overnight. Bring to room temperature and drain off any excess liquid before stir-frying.

4. About 15 minutes before serving, heat a wok or large heavy skillet over high heat until hot enough to evaporate a bead of water on contact. Add 2 tablespoons of the oil and swirl to glaze the pan. Reduce the heat to moderately high. When the oil is hot enough to sizzle a bit of ginger, add the aromatics and stir gently until fully fragrant, 20 to 30 seconds, adjusting the heat so they foam without scorching. Don't worry if the black beans stick to the pan; they will loosen when the sauce is added. Add the cauliflower and toss for 2 minutes. Add the carrots and toss for 1½ minutes more. Add the zucchini and toss for 30 seconds. Adjust the heat to

maintain a merry sizzle and drizzle a bit more oil down the side of the pan, if needed to prevent the vegetables from sticking.

5. Stir the sauce, add it to the pan, and stir to combine. Bring to a simmer. Cover and cook until the vegetables are tender-crisp, 30 seconds to 1 minute. Quickly stir the cornstarch mixture to recombine it and add it to the pan. Stir until the sauce turns glossy and slightly thick, 10 to 20 seconds.

6. Serve the vegetables immediately on a heated platter or plates of contrasting color. Garnish with a sprinkling of scallion rings.

MENU SUGGESTIONS: A Pot-Browned Noodle Pillow (page 401) is the ideal landing pad for this stir-fry. It is also comfortable alongside a bowl of rice and/or a wedge of roasted chicken or even a good burger.

STIR-FRIED CURRIED VEGETABLES

SERVES 2 TO 3 AS A MAIN DISH, 4 TO 6 AS PART OF A MULTICOURSE MEAL

When a vegetarian appears at the gate and there is nothing suitably uncarnivorous on that day's tiny menu, we stir-fry whatever vegetables have been gleaned from the morning marketing and serve them forth in this spicy bath of coconut-curry sauce, typically on top of a noodle pillow (pages 401 to 403).

The vegetable selection is highly improvisational; choose what is freshest and best in the market, with an eye to color and shape. If you are a tofu-lover, also add some fresh white tofu to your shopping list. Sliced into rectangular tiles, deep-fried, and slipped into the sauce at the last minute, it gives a wonderful meatiness to the plate.

Preparations are easy and can be done a day ahead. The last-minute stir-frying takes only minutes.

BLANCHING VEGGIES FOR STIR-FRYING

I first learned about blanching vegetables in advance of sautéing or stir-frying them when we opened China Moon. It is a classic Western restaurant technique whereby cut vegetables are partially cooked in rapidly boiling water and then finished on the stovetop as many as 8 hours later. The vegetables retain their color and moisture, and the time required for cooking is cut in half. Though I wrinkled my naive brow and worried about lost vitamins and injured traditions, it seemed an imperative in our kitchen—which is the size of a closet—and also important for our guests, who are often dashing off to a show after dinner.

I now almost always blanch vegetables for stir-frying, even at home. Vitamin loss may be a storm cloud for the nutritionally concerned cook, however, blanching cuts down on that modern villain OIL!. A vegetable destined for the wok that has first been dunked in boiling water requires only half the amount of oil it would otherwise need.

If the idea of blanching is appealing to you, here is what you will need to blanch veggies with panache:

▲ *A capacious, light pot. I typically blanch all the vegetables for a dish one at a time in one pot of water. A big pot means that I don't run out of water midway. I'm no Trojan, so I like a light pot. Mine is an inexpensive aluminum pasta-cooking pot that comes with a handy, deep insert. I take it everywhere.*

▲ *If you don't have a practical perforated insert for the pot then you will need a strainer to scoop the veggies from the water. A large Chinese mesh spoon works nicely here, except when you are blanching bitty things like peas and corn, in which cases a fine-mesh strainer works best.*

▲ *A tub of ice water is also very handy. I've lived in apartments where the freezers never worked, so I know that one can get by with a good rush of cold water from the tap. However, for the speedy chilling of freshly blanched vegetables, nothing beats a basin of very icy water.*

▲ *Here's what you don't need: SALT! My Western chef friends look at me cross-eyed when I say that salt is unnecessary for blanching, but it is. The Chinese never use it, and neither do I.*

AROMATICS:

1½ tablespoons finely minced fresh ginger
1½ tablespoons finely minced garlic
3 tablespoons thinly sliced green and white scallion rings
¼ to ½ teaspoon dried red chili flakes

SAUCE:

¾ cup unsweetened coconut milk
2 tablespoons mushroom soy sauce
2 tablespoons unseasoned Japanese rice vinegar
1 tablespoon juice from China Moon Pickled Ginger (page 8)
1 tablespoon packed brown sugar
¾ teaspoon Chinese chili sauce
1 teaspoon China Moon Curry Powder (page 7)
¼ teaspoon China Moon Ten-Spice (page 6)
1 cup Vegetable Infusion (page 82) or unsalted vegetable stock

1 carrot, cut diagonally into rippled or plain coins ⅛ inch thick

⅓ cup fresh peas, ½ cup sugar snap peas, or 6 to 8 fresh baby corn, halved or quartered lengthwise if thick
3 to 4 tablespoons corn or peanut oil, for stir-frying
1 yellow onion, cut into ¼-inch moons
1 red or yellow bell pepper, cut into ¾-inch squares
1 leek, white part only, split lengthwise, then cut crosswise into ¼-inch half-moons
2 to 3 Chinese eggplants, cut diagonally into rounds ¼ inch thick
½ pound assorted domestic and/or wild mushrooms, trimmed and cut, if large
2 packed cups wide ribbons of Napa cabbage or ruby chard
2 packed cups spinach
2½ teaspoons cornstarch dissolved in 2 tablespoons cold stock or water
1 package fresh enoki mushrooms, spongy base removed
Diagonally cut green and white scallion rings, for garnish

1. Combine the aromatics in a small dish and seal until ready to use.

2. Combine all of the sauce ingredients in a bowl. Stir to blend, leaving the spoon in the bowl.

3. Bring a saucepan of water to a rolling boil. Blanch the carrots for 15 seconds. Submerge in ice water to chill; drain. If you are using them, blanch the peas or snap peas for 10 seconds, or the baby corn for 30 to 60 seconds, until tender-crisp. Chill the vegetable in ice water; drain.

4. About 15 minutes before serving, heat a wok or large heavy skillet over high heat until a bead of water evaporates on contact. Add 2½ tablespoons of the oil and swirl to glaze the pan. Reduce the heat to moderately high. When the oil is hot enough to foam a dab of ginger, add the aromatics to the pan. Stir gently until fully fragrant, 20 to 30 seconds, adjusting the heat so they foam without browning.

5. Add the onions and toss briskly until wilted, about 2 minutes. Add the bell peppers and leeks, and toss until somewhat softened, 2 minutes more. Adjust the heat to maintain a merry sizzle and drizzle a bit more oil down the side of the pan, if needed to prevent sticking. Add the carrots and toss to combine. Add the eggplant and mushrooms, and toss until hot, about 2 minutes more. Drizzle in a bit more oil only if the vegetables are sticking. Don't rush to feed the eggplant; it will drink up all you give it.

6. Add the cabbage or chard and toss just until wilted. Add the spinach and toss to combine. Stir the sauce and add it to the pan. Bring it to a simmer, stirring once or twice. Quickly stir the cornstarch mixture to recombine and add it to the pan. Stir until the sauce turns glossy and slightly thick, 15 to 20 seconds. Add half of the enoki and toss to mix.

7. Serve immediately. Garnish each portion with a straight-standing cluster of the reserved enoki and a scattering of scallion rings.

MENU SUGGESTIONS: This is a great one-dish supper when served on top of a Pot-Browned Noodle Pillow (page 401) or a Broad Noodle Pillow (page 403). A less sexy but equally good choice would be a bowl of steamed rice. The vegetables can also be served as an accompaniment to fish, meat, or poultry. The sauce is rich so the main course needs to be very simple.

VEGETABLES IN SEASON

I often call Chinese cooking "the original California cooking." Shopping at a daily market and buying vegetables in season and fish and meat from beasts raised close to home are the truisms of traditional Chinese cooking, as well as good cooking the world over.

Sure, you may yearn for asparagus before or after the season is in full swing. But the first stuff is typically undeveloped in flavor, while the late stuff is often dull. When something has been shipped "fresh" from another continent, it often means that it was picked too young for its flavors to ripen.

Seasonality and locality are the great bywords in choosing vegetables. Find what's local; it will be best. Farm stands are better sources than supermarkets. Local markets with farm connections and daily shipments are better than giant chains with warehouses. Even in big cities, look for weekend farmer's markets or the modest shops in ethnic neighborhoods that buy directly from the source. Patronize them so that they will flourish along with your stock of delicious vegetables.

STIR-FRIED CHINESE GREENS

SERVES 4 TO 6

Chinese greens are the glory of Chinatown markets. Crisp longbeans, flavorfully bitter Chinese broccoli, buttery rape, baby bok choy in several white to dark green varieties, the long, white icicle radishes known commonly by their Japanese name of *daikon*, and the hairy, short squashes called "fuzzy melons"—each has its own taste and texture, not quite like anything on our Western shelves.

While intimidating if you have never cooked them, these greens are quickly cut and easily stir-fried. They are especially nice in combination with something familiar like a handful of skinny carrot sticks.

1½ pounds Chinese greens, such as Chinese broccoli, rape, baby bok choy, baby celery cabbage, Chinese longbeans, or a combination
1 carrot, cut into matchstick strips
¼ pound fuzzy melon or daikon, peeled
1½ to 2 tablespoons Ma-La Oil (page 17), Five-Flavor Oil (page 13), or corn or peanut oil

¼ cup Chinese rice wine or dry sherry
¼ cup plus 2 tablespoons China Moon Double Stock (page 72), Vegetable Infusion (page 82), or unsalted chicken or vegetable stock
Roasted Szechwan Pepper-Salt (page 5)

1. Prepare the Chinese greens as follows: Trim the base of Chinese broccoli only if woody; the stems are prized more than the leaves! Cut the stalks on the diagonal into finger-lengths; leave the leaf and flower clusters attached to the stem, or separate if large. Cut Chinese rape in the same manner. Cut off the base of the baby cabbages; trim and reserve them, if pretty. Leave smaller leaves whole; cut larger leaves on the diagonal in half; leave intact the miniature cabbages at the core. Trim Chinese longbeans and cut them into finger-lengths.

CHINESE HALF-AND-HALF

We sauté all of our Chinese greens with a mixture of 1 part Chinese rice wine and 1-plus parts unsalted chicken stock. This concoction is poured into an empty wine bottle, boldly labeled half-and-half, and propped in our streetside kitchen window within reach of the stove. It draws many quizzical stares from the spectators who cluster on the street to ogle the cooks.

2. If thick, blanch the broccoli and longbeans in rapidly boiling water for 5 to 10 seconds. Submerge in ice water to chill; drain. Blanch the carrots for 5 seconds. Plunge into ice water; drain.

3. Cut the fuzzy melon into rounds ⅛ inch thick or the daikons into rounds 1/16 inch thick.

4. Just before serving, heat a wok or large heavy skillet over high heat until a bead of water evaporates on contact. Add 1½ tablespoons of the oil and swirl to glaze the pan. Reduce the heat to moderately high. When the oil is hot enough to sizzle a carrot stick, add the carrots and toss for 30 seconds. Add the fuzzy melon or daikon and toss for 30 seconds more. Add the greens and toss for 30 seconds if raw, or just to combine if blanched. Adjust the heat to maintain a merry sizzle and drizzle a bit more oil down the side of the pan, if needed to prevent sticking.

5. Add the wine and stock to the pan and bring to a boil. Cover the pan and reduce the heat to low. Steam-simmer the greens until they are tender-crisp, 30 seconds to 1½ minutes, depending on the greens. Sprinkle with the pepper-salt to taste and toss to combine. Again dependent on the vegetables, they will have absorbed more or less of the liquid.

6. Serve immediately on heated plates of contrasting color. Pull some carrots to the top for a colorful note of contrast, and drizzle any pan juices over the greens.

Menu Suggestions: Depending on their character, the greens invite different mates. Stronger-tasting Chinese broccoli will be lovely with steamed chicken, milder Chinese rape happily partners spicy pork, and neutral daikon is fabulous with fish, and so on.

STORING VEGETABLES (HOLD THE BATH WATER!)

Some vegetables, like carrots, will hold well for a relatively long time, but the general good-cooking rule is to use vegetables soon after buying them. Storing vegetables for more than several days robs them of the freshness and sweetness that were there on the farm.

For storing many vegetables at home, a cook's great friend is a high-density polyurethane bag. These are the opaque plastic bags that are now a feature in many markets; unlike the slippery, clear plastic bags, they are exasperatingly difficult to open. This particular sort of bag has a semipermeable membrane whereby a vegetable can sweat (and most do) and not grow moldy or bad in its own juice.

Mushrooms—we use lots of them!—should not be kept in plastic. Leave them uncovered on the shelf so they can feast on the air.

Also, as much as it may rub against the puritanical grain, don't wash or trim vegetables until ready to use them! The premature bath may salve your soul, but it starts the vegetable en route to rotting. Leave the water chestnuts muddy and let the bits of soil clinging to the leeks sit just where they are. They won't pollute your refrigerator, and the vegetable will last longer and taste better than if you bathed it prematurely.

STIR-FRIED ZUCCHINI RIBBONS

SERVES 4 TO 6

*S*licing a zucchini lengthwise into thin ribbons (instead of crosswise into coins) is a revelation, or at least it was to me. The resulting tangle is a smashing addition to a plate, especially if you can mix green and gold zucchini.

A mandoline or a Benriner (page 58) is the best tool for the task. Some cheese slicers are up to the chore, as well as some surgeons.

2 to 3 tablespoons Ma-La Oil (page 17), Five-Flavor Oil (page 13), or corn or peanut oil
1 red bell pepper, cut into thin julienne
2 pounds slender green and/or gold zucchini, tipped and cut lengthwise into ribbons 1/16 inch thin

3 tablespoons Chinese rice wine or dry sherry
1/4 cup China Moon Double Stock (page 72), Vegetable Infusion (page 82), or unsalted chicken or vegetable stock
Roasted Szechwan Pepper-Salt (page 5)

1. Heat a wok or large heavy skillet over high heat until hot enough to evaporate a bead of water on contact. Add 2 tablespoons of the oil and swirl to glaze the pan. Reduce the heat to moderately high. When the oil is hot enough to sizzle a sliver of the bell pepper, add the bell pepper julienne and toss briskly for 1 minute. Add the zucchini and toss for 1 minute more. Adjust the heat to maintain a merry sizzle and drizzle a bit more oil down the side of the pan, if needed to prevent sticking.

2. Add the wine and stock mixture and bring the liquid to a boil. Cover the pan, reduce the heat to low, and steam-simmer the zucchini ribbons until they are tender, 1 to 1½ minutes. Turn off the heat. Season to taste with the pepper-salt. Depending upon the zucchini, there may be some liquid left in the pan.

3. Serve immediately. Arrange the vegetable ribbons in a pretty tangle and drizzle any pan juices evenly on top.

MENU SUGGESTIONS: This is an all-purpose vegetable accompaniment, as at home next to Yankee pot roast as it is alongside many of our simpler fish, poultry, and meat dishes.

WOK-SEARED SPINACH RELISH

SERVES 4 TO 6

Equally good hot, tepid, or at room temperature, this is a "relish" as much as a vegetable. The texture is silken and vibrant, and the flavor is very clean.

Blanching the spinach can be done well in advance of stir-frying; simply leave it in a strainer to siphon off the extra water.

8 packed cups spinach leaves
2 to 3 teaspoons corn or peanut oil, for stir-frying
½ small red onion, cut into moons ¹/₁₆ inch thin
2 to 3 cloves garlic, sliced paper-thin

½ small red bell pepper, finely diced
½ teaspoon kosher salt
¼ teaspoon sugar
¼ teaspoon Ma-La Oil (page 17), Five-Flavor Oil (page 13), or Japanese sesame oil

1. Bring a generous amount of water to a rolling boil. Add the spinach, push under the water, and blanch for 5 seconds. Submerge in ice water to chill; drain. Squeeze in small handfuls to extract excess water. Fluff to loosen the leaves.

2. Heat a wok or large heavy skillet over high heat until a bead of water evaporates on contact. Add 2 teaspoons of the corn oil and swirl to glaze the pan. Reduce the heat to moderately high. When

the oil is hot enough to sizzle an onion slice, add the onion and toss briskly until tender-crisp, about 2 minutes. Add the garlic and toss until translucent, 30 to 60 seconds. Adjust the heat to maintain a merry sizzle and drizzle a bit more oil down the side of the pan, if needed to prevent sticking. Don't worry if the vegetables color a bit; they will be tasty.

3. Add the bell pepper dice and spinach, and toss briskly to mix. Turn off the heat. Sprinkle the salt and the sugar into the pan and quickly toss to combine. Drizzle in the seasoned oil and toss to blend. Move quickly so that the spinach does not have time to release its juices.

4. Serve immediately. Or, spread the spinach relish on a platter to cool and serve tepid or at room temperature on a platter that shows off its deep green color.

MENU SUGGESTIONS: For its simplicity of flavor, the spinach is an excellent accompaniment to many steamed, stir-fried, and deep-fried fish dishes. I particularly love it alongside Stir-Fried Dancing Crab with Fresno Chili Rings (page 236). The tang of the spinach cuts the voluptuously rich messiness of the crab.

FRESH CORN KERNELS

Cutting corn kernels off the cob can be a sweet but messy business. The kernels fly and the milk drips from the cob, and there you are covered with the stuff. What to do?

Stand the cob in a wide, shallow container, then angle it to the right (or to the left, if you're a lefty), which will allow the kernels to fall rather then fly. It's a bit harder to see what you're doing, but your blade will "feel" the cob if you keep your grip on the knife light.

A final penny's worth of advice is to cut straight down on the cob, rather than sawing back and forth. The sawing helps the flying, and the straight shot helps the fall.

GOLD COIN CORN CAKES

MAKES 1 DOZEN 2½-INCH FRITTERS

One of our sous-chefs, Nance Tourigny, devised these terrific corn fritters during her first month on the job. The staff thought them absolutely delicious and they and our customers could not get enough of them.

Frozen corn will not work here; we tried it. The taste is flat and uninspired. Wait for the real thing to make them.

The batter can be made up to an hour in advance. Frying the fritters takes only minutes.

½ cup all-purpose flour
½ teaspoon baking powder
½ teaspoon kosher salt
½ teaspoon Roasted Szechwan
  Pepper-Salt (page 5)
1 egg, beaten
2 tablespoons unsweetened
  coconut milk
1 teaspoon finely minced fresh
  ginger

½ teaspoon fresh ginger juice
  (squeezed from finely minced
  fresh ginger)
¾ teaspoon Chinese chili sauce
1⅓ cups fresh corn kernels
¼ cup finely chopped coriander
  leaves and stems
¼ cup thinly sliced green and
  white scallion rings
2 to 3 tablespoons corn or
  peanut oil, for pan-frying

1. Combine the flour, baking powder, salt, and pepper-salt in a bowl.

2. In a second, larger bowl, combine the egg, coconut milk, minced ginger, ginger juice, and chili sauce.

3. Add the flour mixture to the liquid mixture and stir gently just until combined.

4. Add the corn, coriander, and scallions, and stir gently just until mixed. Do not overmix or the fritters will be tough. At this point, the mixture may be sealed and refrigerated for an hour. Let it come to room temperature before making the fritters.

5. About 15 minutes before serving, heat a large heavy skillet over high heat until a bead of water evaporates on contact. Add enough oil to thinly glaze the pan, then reduce the heat to moderate. When the oil is hot enough to foam a dab of the fritter mixture, drop it by heaping tablespoons into the pan, about 4 fritters at a time with at least 1 inch between them. Gently smooth the top of each fritter a bit to flatten. Fry until plump and golden, about 1½ minutes on each side, adjusting the heat so the fritters foam without scorching. Cut open the first fritter to be sure it is cooked through. Remove the first batch to paper towels to drain, then fry the second batch; add oil between batches as needed.

6. Serve promptly, overlapping one fritter with its plate-mate to garner a bit of height.

MENU SUGGESTIONS: I particularly like these corn cakes with our steamed and baked fish dishes, such as Baked Snapper with Red Curry Sauce (page 199). Or, for a summer buffet, team them with your favorites among our cold fish, poultry, and noodle dishes.

COLD-TOSSED CORN RELISH

SERVES 6 TO 8

During a recent corn season, I made this corn and water chestnut relish to go with a plate of fried wonton stuffed with crabmeat and corn (page 360). It was so good that we all spooned it onto lettuce leaves and wolfed it down for our staff dinner.

Fresh corn and fresh water chestnuts are de rigeuer. If you don't have them, don't bother making this.

3 cups fresh corn kernels
1 small red bell pepper, finely diced
6 to 8 fresh water chestnuts, finely diced
¼ cup thinly sliced green and white scallion rings

1 teaspoon sugar
¼ teaspoon kosher salt
¼ teaspoon Roasted Szechwan Pepper-Salt (page 5)

DRESSING:
⅓ cup Five-Flavor Oil (page 13)
2 tablespoons Serrano-Lemongrass Vinegar (page 19)

Finely slivered coriander leaves and stems and/or chive blossoms, for garnish

1. Blanch the corn in rapidly boiling water for 5 seconds. Drain immediately and plunge into ice water to chill. Drain thoroughly.

2. Combine the corn, bell pepper dice, water chestnut dice, and scallions in a large bowl. Toss well to mix. Seal and refrigerate, if working in advance.

3. In a small bowl, whisk all of the dressing ingredients through the pepper-salt to emulsify. If you are working in advance, leave the whisk alongside the bowl.

4. Just before serving, whisk the dressing to re-emulsify. Add it to the corn mixture and toss to combine. Add the coriander and/or chive blossoms and toss to mix. Taste and add a dash more pepper-salt if needed to bring out the sweetness of the corn.

SPIRIT OVER FORM

My love of Chinese cooking is a wedding to a tradition rather than a caring for authenticity. Yin and yang—the spirit of contrast and opposition that is the energy of the Chinese diet—is my culinary imperative. Eyes on this, it doesn't much matter that I introduce non-Chinese ingredients in a dish (baby lettuces, red bell peppers, corn, ruby chard, and the like), as long as the yin-yang reading is delightful on the tongue. I wouldn't be interested in butter and cream because they mask a vividness of flavor that Chinese insist upon in their food. But I would be enthusiastic about tossing into a stir-fry a vegetable that, while very American in origin, had great color and crunch.

It's hard to define, this odd land where the spirit of a cuisine has eccentricity and integrity both. But that's our country, here at China Moon.

5. Serve promptly in dishes that show off the color of the corn.

MENU SUGGESTIONS: True to its origin, this relish is a great accompaniment to fried and poached won-ton and to steamed and boiled dumplings. It is also delicious in lettuce leaf boats and alongside burgers, ham, or steamed or grilled fish—anywhere that sweet crispness is welcome.

CHINA MOON HOUSE SALAD WITH FRESH GINGER VINAIGRETTE

SERVES 3 AS A LUNCHEON SALAD, 4 TO 6 AS AN ACCOMPANIMENT

The Chinese almost never eat raw salad greens. It is the legacy of a history of fertilizing fields with human excrement (aka "night soil"), and a consequent habit of eating only cooked foods. At most, Chinese in modern times will cradle a spoonful of minced squab in an iceberg lettuce cup or down some shreds of lettuce as the icing on a Big Mac.

Tradition notwithstanding, it was a natural that we devise a House Salad at China Moon. The daily California market holds an abundance of beautiful baby greens, some sweet, some bitter, and the mix makes great sense on my mostly-Chinese tongue. Topped with a zippy vinaigrette and sparked with the crunchy textures of croutons, red cabbage, fresh water chestnuts, and fried ginger threads, it is wonderfully refreshing with our oil-based foods.

When shopping for lettuces, look for a good mix of colors, textures, and tastes. Frilled, spiky, and smooth

COLD-TOSSED DISHES

///

"Cold-tossed" is a literal translation from the Chinese. It refers technically to a cold food that is tossed in a dressing and served either chilled or at room temperature. It implies that the dish is refreshing. I use the technique often, and love the implication.

CORN STORIES

I don't have many stories to tell of "fabulous foods when I was a girl." (The tastes I best remember are of deli food and Danish.) But I did grow up on a New Jersey street only several blocks away from a corn stand, and I did grow up on the taste of just-picked corn. There is nothing like it! The sweetness of the flavor and crispness of the kernels are lost within hours after picking. My mother knew this and sent my father off to get the corn literally after she put the water on to boil.

There's not a farm stand on Post Street in San Francisco, but what comes through our door in the height of the season is great. The moistness of the husk and the silk is one index of just-pickedness. The other is the sweetness of the raw niblets. As the corn ages and the season fades, the corn goes from sweet to starchy.

Shop for corn where you know it's brought in daily. Look for supple husks, swishy silk, and plump kernels. If they're selling the corn husked, they're not doing you a favor! It could be a cover-up for weeks-old, starchy corn.

leaves make for a pretty plate, and a blend of sweet and bitter greens is best. If buying pre-cut greens, look at the stems. If brown, they are not freshly cut.

VINAIGRETTE:
¼ cup juice from China Moon Pickled Ginger (page 8)
2 tablespoons Five-Flavor Oil (page 13)
3 tablespoons rice bran, corn, or peanut oil
⅛ teaspoon Roasted Szechwan Pepper-Salt (page 5)

6 cups loosely packed, mixed baby lettuces
1 cup finely shredded red cabbage
½ cup thinly sliced green and white scallion rings
5 to 6 fresh water chestnuts, cut into thin coins
12 to 15 Garlic Croutons (page 37)
Fried Ginger Threads (page 29), for garnish

1. Combine all of the vinaigrette ingredients in a small bowl. Whisk until emulsified, leaving the whisk alongside the bowl.

2. In a large bowl, toss together the lettuces, cabbage, and scallion rings.

3. Just before serving, whisk the vinaigrette to re-emulsify. Drizzle it over the greens and toss gently to combine.

4. Mound the greens on individual plates, placing a few of the larger leaves on the bottom to anchor the smaller ones on top. Quickly rearrange the lettuces so that the prettiest edges face out and the vein sides of the show-off leaves face down. Tuck the water chestnut slices and the croutons amidst the greens. Scatter the ginger threads on top and serve.

MENU SUGGESTIONS: Many of our salad-loving guests enjoy this salad alongside a dish of springrolls, buns, or cold noodles for a simple lunch. I love it most with our smoked poultry and seared meats, where the brightness of the salad is a great counterpoint to their richness.

PARIS SALAD

SERVES 3 AS A LUNCHEON SALAD, 4 TO 6 AS AN
ACCOMPANIMENT

I adore Paris and love to spend leisurely weeks there—gathering goodies on long daytime walks, spreading them out on a little table in a rented apartment, and sitting down for a dinnertime feast like a fat, happy cat. In addition to all the wonders that are very French, the street-eating scene has been much enlivened in recent years by a bloom of Asian take-out shops.

It was in one such shop, located near the hubbub of the Bastille and run by a Chinese couple newly emigrated from northern China, that I found the salad that was the inspiration for this dish. It was refreshingly light and colorful, and I was wedded to it for days.

The China Moon version is filled with interesting textures. It was later metamorphosed into Paris Noodles (page 395), but the original is still my favorite.

2 tablespoons dried tree ears
1 cup fresh corn kernels
2 cups fresh white bean sprouts
1 cup seedless cucumber
   julienne

VINAIGRETTE:
¼ cup plus 2 tablespoons juice
   from China Moon Pickled
   Ginger (page 8)
¼ cup Five-Flavor Oil (page 13)
¼ cup rice bran, corn, or
   peanut oil
¼ teaspoon Roasted Szechwan
   Pepper-Salt (page 5)
Several drops Cayenne Pepper
   Oil (page 11), or ½ to 1
   teaspoon China Moon Hot
   Chili Oil (page 10) or China
   Moon Chili-Orange Oil
   (page 15)

1 cup carrot julienne
1 cup daikon julienne
1 cup finely shredded red
   cabbage
1 small red bell pepper, finely
   diced
4 fresh water chestnuts, cut
   into thin half-moons
1 small green serrano chili, cut
   crosswise into paper-thin
   rings
Crispy Rice Sticks (page 31)

SALAD TOPOGRAPHY

A salad can look terrible or terrific, all depending on the geometry of the leaves. Choose good ones to begin with; loops, frills, dips, and feathery edges all make for a great-looking plate. Once you've tossed the lettuces with the vinaigrette, take a second to study the leaves and "build" the salad. A bigger, flatter leaf can anchor a plate; a little or frilly one can enliven the edge or flag the top. If you spy a pretty leaf, arrange it so it can be seen. Tuck the stem ends in if they're sticking out. Plant some leaves vertically to add some height. Make sure your show-off leaves are face side up and vein side down. All of this takes a bit of fiddling (and maybe some lip biting if you're clumsy), but the minute spent will make a difference. In salads as in life, it's best to show off what you've got.

BABY LETTUCE PRIMER

The most important factors in choosing baby lettuces is texture (tender or crisp) and taste (interesting, whether it be on the sweet or bitter end of the scale). Nibble on a leaf to know.

Green leaf and red leaf lettuces, including the finger-like oak leaf and the frilly-edged varieties, lend sweetness to a salad and a great look to the plate.

Baby red mustard, baby mizuna, and arugula (also called roquette or rocket) give bright and pleasant notes of bitterness. I don't use baby green mustard, usually finding it too one-sidedly bitter.

Mâche, or lamb's lettuce, is a good counterpoint to the tarter greens. Ditto for baby limestone and baby butter lettuce.

Curly cress, if tender, gives a peppery note and a lacy bit of height. Tender young watercress, used judiciously, is also good.

Radicchio is nice sliced in ribbons.

Just about the only greens I avoid are the sorrel, endive, chicory, escarole, dandelion, and kale varieties. Their bites clash very oddly with the ginger in our vinaigrettes.

1. Cover the tree ears with 2 cups cold water. (They will swell a lot in soaking!) Let stand until supple, 15 to 20 minutes; drain. Swish in several changes of cold water to dislodge any grit, then pinch off any woody or weirdly gelatinous bits. Tear, if large, into nickel-size pieces.

2. Bring a saucepan of water to a rolling boil. Blanch the corn for 5 seconds. Scoop into ice water to chill; drain. Return the water to a boil. Blanch the bean sprouts for 10 seconds. Scoop into ice water to chill; drain just before serving.

3. Combine all of the vinaigrette ingredients through the oil in a bowl. Whisk to emulsify, leaving the whisk in the bowl.

4. Just before serving, toss together the tree ears, corn, and bean sprouts with all the remaining salad ingredients except for the rice sticks in a large bowl. Whisk the vinaigrette to re-emulsify, drizzle over the salad and toss to combine. Add the rice sticks and toss once or twice to mix.

5. Serve immediately. Mound the salad on plates of contrasting color and start dreaming of your next trip to Paris.

MENU SUGGESTIONS: This salad invites partnering with poultry. Shreds of Chinese-Style Duck Confit (page 170) or nopoach or smoked chicken breast (pages 115 and 119) are terrific tossed in with the salad. So, too, are thin ribbons of Wok-Seared Duck Breast (page 164). Or, simply set a platter of the salad alongside grilled chicken wings (page 128) or any of our poussin dishes and watch it disappear.

LIGHT ICE CREAMS • HAPPY ENDINGS

COOKIES OF GOOD FORTUNE

TARTS AND TARTLETS

COOKIES OF GOOD FORTUNE • TARTS AND TARTLETS

TARTS AND TARTLETS

HAPPY ENDINGS • LIGHT ICE CREAMS

DESSERTS

CONTENTS

hinese cuisine is not known for its desserts. Bowls of sweet peanut soup and milky slabs of almond-flavored jelly (the endnotes of many Chinese banquets) cause few non-Chinese hearts to throb. Ditto the platters of orange wedges that are the classic palate-refresher at the end of a Chinese home meal. In a world without cream or butter, Chinese were stuck for better ideas.

Fortunately for me (and for you, if you're of like mind and tongue), I have a Westerner's love for baked desserts and ice cream coupled with an Oriental leaning toward combinations of tart and sweet. In the China Moon kitchen, that means that we have fabulous, Western-style desserts that are light, refreshing, vibrant with flavor, and never too sweet or rich. While untraditional, they blend seamlessly with our food, a happy crescendo to a meal of many flavors.

FABULOUS COOKIES OF GOOD FORTUNE

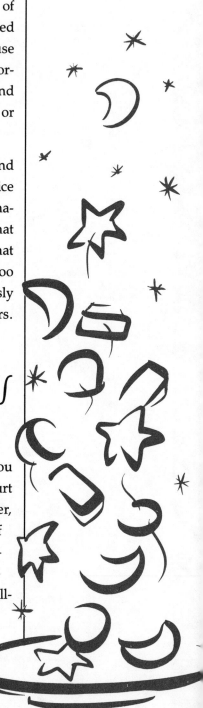

f you were truly lucky in the late 1970s and early 1980s, you were invited to Forneau's Ovens in the Stanford Court Hotel to dine with its extraordinary owner/manager, Jim Nassikas. Likely to be at the table was one or more of Jim's buddies—Danny Kaye, Jim Beard, Craig Claiborne—and an assortment of similarly smart, wicked, down-to-earth people for whom food, wine, and friends were all-important. For a novice Chinese cook, it was heady stuff.

The food was fabulous—little potato shells stuffed with American golden caviar, toasted hazelnut soup, tiny oysters flown in daily from Washington, and local birds and game roasted to perfection. This was California-American cooking before either came into vogue. But the thing that always touched my heart was the tray of miniature cookies brought to the table at the end of the meal. Filled as I was with conversation, food, and fine wine, they were irresistible. The flavors were so intense and the care in crafting each one so exact that they ended the evening on a spectacularly effervescent note—like a shower of exquisite fireworks.

The creator of the cookies was the hotel's now-famous pastry chef, Jim Dodge. It was Jim who discovered the art deco Chinese coffee shop that would become China Moon Cafe, and it was Jim who gave China Moon a unique opening present: his assistant pastry chef, Amy Ho. "Can she make cookies?" was all I could ask, in shock at the vision of an endless, sweet orgy.

For sure, Amy can make cookies, and here they are! Each is a little gem, to be savored at the end of a meal with the finest tea, rich espresso, or a glass of nectar-like wine, or to be given as a freshly baked gift bound with a pretty ribbon. At China Moon, we present a different selection of seven cookies each night, on a silver tray that commands center stage in Amy's daily-changing dessert display. Our customers adore them, and the staff lusts after them! Long after the Stanford Court sold its soul to the corporate world and Jim Dodge moved on to his own ventures, I like to think that a little bit of that fabulous wonder is still alive at China Moon.

∎ ∎ ∎

COOKIE CONCERNS

Could it be possible, in this time of eroding family values (oh, please), that we are raising our kids to be ignorant of cookies? Fresh from an interview with a nine-year-old close to me, I've discovered she doesn't like cookies. What could be the source of this dilemma, with its potential perils for the national economy (if not the national security)? Lousy store-bought cookies, a lack of cookie consciousness on the part of her parents, the loss of cookie values in the younger generation? It's all too terrible to contemplate.

CAPPUCCINO COINS

MAKES 10 DOZEN COOKIES

Here are the cookies that fueled my first year of 16-hour days at the restaurant, those little coins of caffeine bliss that cried out, "Eat me and you'll be able to cook off that next batch of chickens!" They remain my very favorite, blending the flavors of chocolate and coffee for which I have a particular weakness.

These are easy to make. If you wish to gild the lily, you can pipe the cooled coins with fine crisscrossed lines of white chocolate. Amy used to do this trick of dazzlement in our early show-off years, but then we discovered that our guests adored these cookies even without the extra finery.

*4 ounces (1 stick) cold unsalted
    butter, cut into 8 pieces
¼ cup packed dark brown sugar
¼ cup granulated sugar
1 extra-large egg
1 cup plus 2 tablespoons all-
    purpose flour
1½ teaspoons instant coffee
    powder or granules*

*1½ teaspoons unsweetened
    cocoa powder
½ teaspoon ground cinnamon
¼ teaspoon fine sea salt
½ cup (2 ounces) finely chopped
    semisweet chocolate (⅛-inch
    bits)*

1. In the bowl of an electric mixer, cream the butter and both sugars on medium speed until smooth, 3 to 4 minutes. Add the egg and mix until smooth. Scrape down the sides of the bowl with a rubber spatula. Add the flour, instant coffee, cocoa, cinnamon, salt, and chocolate bits; mix thoroughly for 2 to 3 minutes.

2. Gather the dough together and turn onto a lightly floured board. Using lightly floured hands, roll the dough into 2 or 3 even 1-inch-thick logs. Wrap the logs separately in plastic wrap. Refrigerate until firm, about 1 hour.

3. Preheat the oven to 350°F. Move an oven rack to the middle position. Line large baking sheets with parchment paper.

4. Slice the logs into ¼-inch-thick coins;

place ½ inch apart on the prepared baking sheets.

5. One sheet at a time, bake until the cookies are lightly golden and are firm enough at the edges to slide off the parchment without sticking, 15 to 17 minutes. Cool on the baking sheets set on wire racks.

WALNUT CRISPS

MAKES 9 DOZEN COOKIES

A very pretty, buttery cookie coin, this is only as good as the walnuts you use. Last year's package of walnuts from the supermarket will not get you where you want to go! Shop for newly harvested nuts, perhaps best gotten at a natural food store, and keep them chilled airtight in the refrigerator until you are ready to use them. The difference is really very striking!

4 ounces (1 stick) cold unsalted butter, cut into 8 pieces
½ cup sugar
¾ cup all-purpose flour

1 cup (3½ ounces) walnut halves and pieces
Pinch of fine sea salt

1. In the bowl of an electric mixer, cream the butter and sugar on medium speed until smooth, 3 to 4 minutes. Add the flour, walnuts, and salt, and mix the dough until well blended, about 2 minutes.

2. Turn out the dough onto a lightly floured board. Roll out the dough into 2 or 3 even 1-inch-thick logs. Wrap the logs separately in plastic wrap. Refrigerate until firm, about 1 hour.

3. Preheat the oven to 350°F. Move an oven rack to middle position. Line large baking sheets with parchment paper.

4. Slice the logs into ¼-inch-thick disks; place ½ inch apart on the prepared baking sheets.

5. One sheet at a time, bake the cookies until the edges are lightly golden, 12 to 15 minutes. Cool the cookies on the baking sheets set on wire racks.

CHOCOLATE STARS

MAKES 4 DOZEN COOKIES

Who can resist a star-shaped cookie? Hardly anyone! Add chocolate to the equation and you've seduced the few soul-less people who said they didn't like stars.

Go out of your way to find truly excellent cocoa powder and chocolate bits for these little stars. Specialty coffee shops will often sell exceptional chocolate products, so don't overlook them in your search.

4 ounces (1 stick) cold unsalted butter, cut into 8 pieces
½ cup sugar
½ teaspoon vanilla extract
1 cup all-purpose flour
¼ cup unsweetened cocoa powder

⅛ teaspoon fine sea salt
⅛ teaspoon baking soda
½ cup (2 ounces) finely chopped semisweet chocolate (⅛-inch bits)

1. In the bowl of an electric mixer, cream the butter and sugar on medium speed until smooth and light, 3 to 4 minutes. Add the vanilla, flour, cocoa, salt, baking soda, and chocolate bits, and mix until well blended, about 2 minutes. Gather the dough into a ball and flatten slightly.

2. Dust a large piece of parchment paper with flour. Place the dough in the center. With a lightly floured rolling pin, roll out the dough to an even ¼-inch thickness. Cover with plastic wrap and refrigerate the rolled-out dough until firm, about 1 hour.

3. Preheat the oven to 350°F. Move an oven rack to the middle position. Line large baking sheets with parchment paper.

4. Using a 2-inch star-shaped cookie cutter, cut out the cookies. Place ½ inch apart on the prepared baking sheets. The scraps can be re-rolled and cut.

5. One sheet at a time, bake until the cookies are firm enough at the edges to slide easily off the parchment, 12 to 15 minutes. The cookies will be soft but will crisp as they cool. Cool on the baking sheets set on wire racks.

COCOA POWDER NEWS

Amy uses a "full-Dutch" process cocoa called "Jersey cocoa" that has 22- to 24-percent fat and is available through the San Francisco–based cookware chain Williams-Sonoma. (Yes, there really is a Chuck Williams, and he really is devoted to scouting out the best!)

If you are shopping for cocoa near to home, look for the darkest unsweetened sort available. As with coffee beans, darkness should not equate with bitterness; the flavor, while not sweet, should be smooth.

COOKIE TIPS

 Use the best ingredients. Great unsalted butter, newly harvested nuts, rich vanilla extract, and excellent chocolate can add immeasurably to a cookie. More than any baking technique, your ingredients will make you a star.

▲ Wrap the cookie dough airtight for chilling or freezing so that it doesn't dry out or discolor. Plastic wrap is best, especially the super-clingy kind that might otherwise drive you wild.

▲ Chill the dough thoroughly and cut it with a very sharp knife with a thin, large blade. Both steps make for the perfect slices that result in evenly baked, pretty cookies. Amy uses a Chinese cleaver for cutting her cookies and stares down the cooks if they even think of borrowing it for vegetables. The heft of the knife makes cutting the dough easy, and the sharp blade cuts it cleanly.

▲ Invest in a couple of heavy-duty baking sheets, if you don't already have them. They distribute heat with consummate evenness and they won't warp—both important assets when baking miniature cookies.

▲ Invest, too, in a roll of parchment paper or, better yet, if you have access to a restaurant or baking supply store, a box of large parchment sheets. These save fabulously in the dish-washing department.

▲ Use the center rack position of the oven for baking and rotate the baking sheet midway through the allotted baking time. If you are baking on two racks, rotate the sheets top to bottom as well as back to front. Do the rotation(s) quickly to minimize the amount of heat that escapes from the oven.

▲ Get into the habit of pulling the cookies from the oven several seconds earlier than you might otherwise and letting them cool undisturbed on the baking sheet. The benefit is that the cookies won't need handling before they turn crisp and won't suffer the damage usually inflicted (at least by me) when moving them with a spatula to a cooling rack. The cookies will finish their final bit of baking on the hot baking sheet, which you should balance on a trivet or rack to speed the cooling.

▲ Store thoroughly cooled cookies at room temperature in an airtight container; their flavor will hold better than if they were frozen. If the cookies soften, re-bake them in a preheated 350°F oven for 3 to 5 minutes, or until heated through. Then remove the tray to a cooling rack where the cookies will recrisp as they cool.

GINGER MOONS

MAKES 7 DOZEN COOKIES

With a name like China Moon Cafe, it was a delicious bit of inevitability that we would have moon-shaped cookies. These little crescent moons, flavored with a mixture of powdered and fresh ginger, have a rich brown color. Add a little dot of crystallized ginger close to the top of the crescent and you will have a "Lady in the Moon" cookie (see note at right), certain to steal a heart.

If you are selecting cookies for a cookie tray, do include these. Their unique shape and taste offer a wonderful contrast to most all of our other cookies.

4 ounces (1 stick) cold unsalted
    butter, cut into 8 pieces
½ cup packed dark brown sugar
1 tablespoon finely minced fresh
    ginger
1 tablespoon powdered ginger
½ teaspoon vanilla extract

1 cup plus 2 tablespoons all-
    purpose flour
¼ teaspoon baking soda
Pinch of fine sea salt
¼ cup finely diced crystallized
    ginger (⅛-inch bits)

1. In the bowl of an electric mixer, cream the butter and sugar on medium speed until smooth, about 3 minutes. Add the fresh ginger, powdered ginger, vanilla, flour, baking soda, and salt; mix just until the dough comes together. Turn out the dough onto a lightly floured board, gather into a ball, and flatten slightly.

2. Lightly dust a large piece of parchment paper with flour. Place the dough in the center and roll out to an even ⅛-inch thickness. Lightly flour the rolling pin as needed to prevent sticking. Cover and refrigerate the dough until firm, about 1 hour.

3. Preheat the oven to 350°F. Move an oven rack to the middle position. Line large baking sheets with parchment paper.

4. Using only half of the edge of a round 1½-inch cookie or biscuit cutter, cut out ¾-inch-wide (at widest point) crescent moons. Place ½ inch apart on the prepared baking sheets.

Press a tiny cube of the crystallized ginger near one tapered end.

5. One sheet at a time, bake the cookies until the edges are lightly golden, 10 to 12 minutes. Cool on the baking sheets set on wire racks.

Currant-Ginger Shortbreads

MAKES 7 DOZEN COOKIES

These pretty rectangular cookies are to my adult tongue what Sunshine Raisin Bars (remember them?) were to my kiddie tongue—a delicious bit of buttery sweetness studded with the flavor of concentrated grapes.

Look for plump, "fresh" currants brimming with flavor. If the ones on hand are shriveled and hard, steam them, uncovered, in a small dish for about 10 minutes and watch them fatten up.

The trick to chopping crystallized ginger is to use a wet, sharp knife. Cold water works best.

4 ounces (1 stick) cold unsalted
   butter, cut into 8 pieces
¼ cup sugar
1 cup all-purpose flour
   Pinch of fine sea salt

½ cup currants
1 packed tablespoon finely diced
   crystallized ginger (⅛-inch
   bits)

1. In the bowl of an electric mixer, cream the butter and sugar on medium speed until smooth and light, 3 to 4 minutes. Add the flour, salt, currants, and ginger; mix the dough until well blended, about 3 minutes. Gather the dough into a ball and flatten slightly.

2. Lightly flour a 12-inch-square piece of parchment paper. Place the dough on top and roll out, using a flour-dusted rolling pin, into a 10-inch square that is an even ¼ inch thick. Cover and refrigerate the dough until firm, about 1 hour.

3. Preheat the oven to 350°F. Move an oven rack to the middle position. Line large baking sheets with parchment paper.

4. Using a sharp knife, divide the dough into ten 1-inch-wide strips. Cut each strip into 1½-inch-long shortbreads; place them ½ inch apart on the prepared baking sheets. Gather and roll out the scraps and cut out more short-breads.

5. One sheet at a time, bake the cookies until the edges are lightly golden, 12 to 15 minutes. Cool the cookies on the baking sheets set on wire racks.

SESAME-BROWN SUGAR SHORTBREADS

MAKES 5 DOZEN COOKIES

This lovely cookie is as simple and appealing as its name. Be sure to get untoasted sesame seeds that are blonde, fat, and fresh-tasting. The best place to buy them is usually a natural food store.

For a happy trick, sprinkle some black sesame seeds in addition to the white over a portion of the dough. This will give you two different cookie looks for the labor of just one.

4 ounces (1 stick) cold unsalted butter, cut into 8 pieces
¼ cup packed dark brown sugar

1 cup all-purpose flour
¼ cup plus 1 tablespoon sesame seeds

1. In the bowl of an electric mixer, cream the butter and sugar on medium speed until smooth, 3 to 4 minutes. Add the flour and mix until well blended, about 2 minutes. Gather the dough into a ball and flatten slightly.

2. Dust a large piece of parchment paper with flour. Place the dough on top and roll out to an 11- by 9-inch rectangle, ¼ inch thick.

3. Dip a large pastry brush in water and brush over the cookie dough. Sprinkle on the sesame seeds, evenly covering the entire surface of the dough. Cover and refrigerate until firm, about 1 hour.

4. Preheat the oven to 350°F. Move an oven rack to the middle position. Line large baking sheets with parchment paper.

5. Using a sharp knife, cut the dough lengthwise into nine 1-inch strips. Cut each strip into 1½-inch-long pieces; place them ½ inch apart on the prepared baking sheets.

6. One sheet at a time, bake the cookies until the edges are lightly golden, 15 to 17 minutes. Cool on the baking sheets set on wire racks.

CHOCOLATE CHIP-PEANUT BLOCKS

MAKES 9 DOZEN COOKIES

These are miniature cookie "bricks," featuring chopped peanuts and chocolate bits against a peanut butter background. Great for kids and also great for adults who still appreciate the seduction of such flavors.

4 ounces (1 stick) cold unsalted
    butter, cut into 8 pieces
½ cup unseasoned peanut
    butter (page 32)
½ cup sugar
1 extra-large egg
1½ cups all-purpose flour

1 teaspoon baking soda
¼ teaspoon fine sea salt
½ cup raw skinless peanuts,
    chopped (¼-inch bits)
½ cup chopped semisweet
    chocolate (¼-inch pieces)

1. In the bowl of an electric mixer, combine the butter, peanut butter, and sugar, and beat on medium speed until smooth and well blended. Add the egg and mix to combine; stop the machine once or twice to scrape down the sides of the bowl with a rubber spatula. Add the flour, baking soda, salt, peanuts, and chocolate pieces; mix until combined, about 2 minutes longer.

2. Scrape the dough onto a large piece of plastic wrap. Shape into a 6-inch square, about 1 inch thick. Use the plastic wrap to help shape the sticky dough. Seal well in plastic and refrigerate until firm, about 2 hours.

3. Preheat the oven to 350°F. Move an oven rack to the middle position. Line large baking sheets with parchment paper.

4. Cut the square of dough into 4 equal strips 1½ inches wide. Slice each strip crosswise into ¼-inch-wide blocks. Place the blocks ½ inch apart on the prepared baking sheets.

5. One sheet at at time, bake the cookies until the edges are lightly golden, 15 to 18 minutes. Cool on the baking sheets set on wire racks.

CHOOSING CHOCOLATE

Semisweet chocolates differ as greatly in flavor as, say, Italian-roast coffee beans. If you're shopping for semisweet chocolate, experiment by nibbling on a few brands to see which you like. A specialty chocolate shop, a local fine pastry shop, or even a good kitchenware store should be able to give you recommendations.

PECAN-CHOCOLATE NUGGETS

MAKES 10 DOZEN COOKIES

A refined little cookie nugget that blends unsweetened and semisweet chocolate with the richness of pecans. The ingredients are everything here; go out of your way to find plump and fresh pecans and excellent chocolate.

1 ounce unsweetened chocolate, cut into ½-inch chunks
2 ounces semisweet chocolate, cut into ½-inch chunks
2 ounces (½ stick) cold unsalted butter, cut into 8 pieces

½ cup plus 2 tablespoons sugar
1 extra-large egg
1½ cups (5½ ounces) pecan halves
¾ cup all-purpose flour
Pinch of fine sea salt

1. In the top of a double boiler, melt the unsweetened and semisweet chocolates over hot, not simmering, water, stirring until smooth. Set aside.

2. In the bowl of an electric mixer, cream the butter and sugar on medium speed until smooth, 3 to 4 minutes. Add the egg and mix until incorporated; stop the machine once or twice to scrape down the sides of the bowl with a rubber spatula. Add the melted chocolate and mix until well blended. Add the pecans, flour, and salt and mix again, about 2 minutes.

3. Scrape the dough onto a large piece of plastic wrap; the dough will be sticky. Loosely wrap the dough in plastic. Mold and shape the dough into an 8- by 4-inch rectangular block, about 1 inch thick. Refrigerate the dough until firm, about 2 hours.

4. Preheat the oven to 350°F. Move an oven rack to the top third of the oven. Line large baking sheets with parchment paper.

5. Using a sharp knife, cut the dough lengthwise into 8 strips ½ inch wide. Turn the strips on their wider side, then cut each strip crosswise into ½-inch nuggets. Place the nuggets ½ inch apart on the prepared baking sheets.

6. One sheet at a time, bake the cookies until the edges are firm, 10 to 12 minutes. The cookies will be a bit chewy in the center. Cool on the baking sheets set on wire racks.

GOOD CHEWS

Most people have Oreo memories. Mine are of Mallomars. Not that I was (or am) a marshmallow fan. Simply, it was irresistible for a Virgo-in-training not to tap a Mallomar upside down on a counter, break its chocolate shell into a hundred smithereens, then fastidiously pick them off with her tongue while leaving the naked mallow to shiver all alone. I don't remember actually eating those cookies, but I recall the pleasure of that eroding chocolate mosaic.

HAZELNUT MOUNDS

MAKES 6 DOZEN COOKIES

Here is a cookie for those among us (young and old) who love to roll dough into little balls! For that's all there is to these rich, hazelnutty cookies dusted with powdered sugar.

Use only plump, fresh hazelnuts with a clear sweet taste. Roasting and rubbing them to remove the skins is a bit of a bother, but the results are worth it.

1 cup (4½ ounces) whole raw
   hazelnuts
4 ounces (1 stick) cold unsalted
   butter, cut into 8 pieces
¼ cup plus 2 tablespoons sugar
1 cup all-purpose flour
Pinch of fine sea salt

½ teaspoon vanilla extract
¼ teaspoon almond extract
Finely grated zest of 1 scrubbed
   lemon
Confectioners' sugar

1. Preheat the oven to 350°F. Move an oven rack to the middle position.

2. Spread the hazelnuts out on a baking sheet and toast until the skins blister and the nuts turn pale brown beneath the skin, 10 to 12 minutes. Stir the nuts midway to ensure even toasting. Wrap the hot nuts in a clean, dry kitchen towel and rub vigorously to remove as much of the skins as possible. Coarsely chop.

3. In the bowl of an electric mixer, cream the butter and sugar on medium speed until smooth and light, 3 to 4 minutes. Add the flour, salt, vanilla, almond extract, lemon zest, and chopped hazelnuts. Mix until well blended, 2 to 3 minutes.

4. Gather the dough together into a ball. Pinch off pieces of the dough and form into ¾-inch balls. Place the balls on a baking sheet. Cover and refrigerate until firm, about 1 hour.

5. Preheat the oven to 350°F. Move the oven rack to the middle position. Line large baking sheets with parchment paper.

6. Arrange the balls of dough 1 inch apart on the prepared baking sheets. One sheet at a time, bake the cookies until the mounds flatten out slightly and the edges are lightly golden, 15 to 17 minutes. Cool on the baking sheets set on wire racks.

7. Once cool, lightly dust the cookies with a pretty veil of confectioners' sugar.

COOKIE TRAYS (AND OTHER PRESENTATIONAL GAMBITS)

Cookies, like people, sometimes need a bit of sexy oomph in the presentation in order to be appreciated for their flavor! What cookbook lover among us would ever forget the fabulous cookie array on the cover of Maida Heatter's "Book of Great Cookies"? Or, what restaurant-goer hasn't been moved to oohs and aahs by a crisp cookie tuile perched atop an ice cream sundae? Delicious is delicious, as we all know, but attractive allure can mean a lot.

So if you are considering cookies for dessert, consider their presentation. At China Moon, Amy takes great pride in arranging the seven varieties of cookies she bakes daily in contrasting vertical rows on a large rectangular tray. Each cookie overlaps the one above it to give some height, and the rows are purposely arranged so that there's a wonderful juxtaposition of shapes and colors. It's a literal feast for the eye, one worth replicating at home. Even if you're baking only two or three varieties of cookies, you can arrange them in alternating rows to terrific effect.

A cookie tray of this show-off sort needs to be flat and prettily bordered, but not much else. I've picked up many cheap ones in flea markets and thrift shops— covering a hunting scene with a doily or painting a chipped border with nail polish. (Cooks rarely get to polish their nails, but a fantasy life inspires many of us to buy polish regardless.) The final look can really be quite splendid and can turn an otherwise simple cookie dessert into a memorable finale for a meal.

Even cookie accents for other desserts, like ice creams, can be imaginatively placed to give a little thrill. Consider placing a cookie on top of a peak of ice cream like a happy flag, or overlapping a trio of cookies on the rim of a plate featuring another dessert, or spiraling them on a silver coaster alongside a cup of espresso. Especially with miniature cookies, a little bit of easy drama goes a surprisingly long way.

BABY SESAME BISCOTTI

MAKES 4 DOZEN COOKIES

I am a biscotti maven. Gnawing on a cookie that resists with a sweet dryness has a particular appeal that must go back to my high chair. These cookies have that allure.

4 ounces (1 stick) cold unsalted butter, cut into 8 pieces
¾ cup sugar
3 extra-large eggs, beaten
2½ cups all-purpose flour
1½ teaspoons baking powder

¾ cup sesame seeds, toasted
¼ cup chopped candied orange peel
½ cup golden or dark raisins
About ½ cup untoasted sesame seeds

1. In the bowl of an electric mixer, cream the butter and sugar until light. Add the eggs and continue to beat until well blended. Add the flour, baking powder, toasted sesame seeds, orange peel, and raisins; blend until combined.

2. Seal the dough airtight in plastic wrap. Refrigerate until firm, overnight, if desired. (The longer chilling allows the fruit peel flavor to permeate the dough.)

3. Divide the dough into 4 equal pieces. Roll each piece into a smooth even log 1 inch thick. Roll each log in the untoasted sesame seeds until coated.

4. Preheat the oven to 350°F. Move an oven rack to the middle position. Line 2 large baking sheets with parchment paper.

5. Place 2 of the logs, spaced 5 inches apart, lengthwise on each baking sheet.

6. One sheet at a time, bake the logs until golden, about 20 minutes, turning the sheet midway.

7. Remove the first sheet from the oven and set aside on a wire rack to cool for 10 minutes. Then, while the logs are still warm, slice them crosswise into cookies a scant ¼ inch thick. Place the cookies on their sides, ¼ inch apart. (While you are slicing the first logs, you can bake the remaining 2 logs.)

8. Return the sliced cookies to the oven and bake until lightly golden, 7 to 10 minutes. Cool on the baking sheets set on wire racks.

Crystallized Ginger Butter Squares

MAKES 6 DOZEN COOKIES

Avery elegant and simple cookie, this is a perfect choice to accompany that cup of fragrant tea. Spiced with ginger and orange zest, it is also a happy match for most all of our other cookies.

Be sure to give the orange a good soapy scrub and an equally good rinse before grating. It will taste zestier and brighter for the bath.

4 ounces (1 stick) cold unsalted butter, cut into 8 pieces	⅓ cup (2 ounces) chopped crystallized ginger (¼-inch bits)
⅓ cup sugar	
1 extra-large egg yolk	1 teaspoon finely grated orange zest
1 cup plus 1 tablespoon all-purpose flour	

1. In the bowl of an electric mixer, cream the butter and sugar on medium speed until smooth, 3 to 4 minutes. Add the egg yolk and mix until blended. Add the flour, ginger, and orange zest, and mix until combined, about 2 minutes.

2. Gather the dough together and place on a large piece of plastic wrap. Shape and mold into a 4- by 4½-inch block, 1 inch thick. Use the plastic wrap to help shape the sticky dough. Wrap tightly in plastic wrap. Refrigerate until firm, about 2 hours.

3. Preheat the oven to 350°F. Move a rack to the top third of the oven. Line large baking sheets with parchment paper.

4. Using a sharp knife, cut the block of dough into four 1-inch-wide strips. Cut each strip into ¼-inch-wide slices. Place the cookies ½ inch apart on the prepared baking sheets.

5. One sheet at a time, bake until the cookies are firm and the edges are lightly golden, 10 to 12 minutes. Cool on the baking sheets set on wire racks.

GRATING FRUIT ZEST

I long ago learned the trick of grating lemon or other fruit zest directly into wherever it was going. That way, there's no loss of the flavorful oils that are the beauty of the zest. Rather than wasting them on your cutting board or measuring spoon, grate the zest directly into the pot or workbowl (right on top of the sugar or other ingredients) to trap its taste.

For the same reason, I prefer a grater with tiny, flat holes that lets the zest fall in comparatively dry flakes. The puckered sort hugs the zest in a juicy blob, which wastes the zest on the grater and requires some banging to free it.

TARTƧ AnD TARTLETƧ

I n the realm of baking as viewed by a timid outsider, a tart seems a rather friendly thing. Not too large, not too small, not too high, it represents an approachable world where fruit or nuts meet crust. For the would-be baker intimidated by cakes, a tart beckons cheerily, "Come make me!"

A tart for dessert presents an enticing range of options. If you are wanting something pretty and easy, you can make a single large tart. Or, with a bit more work, you can achieve a lot more formality and drama by making individual tartlets (the culinary equivalent of a fabulous string of pearls). For a homey touch, you can make a lattice-weave tart or one topped with streusel. Or, for a more streamlined bit of dazzlement, you can crown a tart with a berry bonnet or a swirl of sliced fruit. Wintertime suggests nut tarts, summertime means berry tarts. For sheer versatility, this is an unbeatable dessert.

■ ■ ■

PREBAKED TART SHELL

MAKES ONE 9-INCH TART SHELL

T his is Amy's basic recipe for a single 9-inch tart shell. If you are making two shells, make the recipe twice as opposed to doubling it.

The dough is exceptionally easy to work with, neither too stiff nor too crumbly. For tips on rolling it out and transferring it to the pan, see page 471.

3 ounces (¾ stick) unsalted
　butter, cut into 6 pieces
¼ cup sugar

2 extra-large egg yolks
1 cup all-purpose flour

BAKER'S BONUS

 *Never toss the odd bits of tart shell dough that are leftover after the rolling and shaping. Instead, dip them in sugar and bake them as cookies—a great prize for the baker!*

1. In a bowl, cream the butter and sugar with an electric mixer on medium speed until smooth, 3 to 4 minutes.

2. Add the egg yolks and mix until smooth and well blended. Add the flour and mix until blended.

3. Gather together the dough and press it out into a thick disk. Wrap in plastic and refrigerate until firm but malleable, at least 1 hour.

4. To roll out the dough, sprinkle the work surface and the top of the disk with 1½ tablespoons flour. Roll the dough into an even ⅛-inch-thick circle with a 12-inch diameter. Periodically rotate the dough on the board and dust the top as needed to prevent sticking.

5. Fold the dough in half, center it in a 9-inch tart pan, and unfold. Or, reverse-roll the dough over the pin and unroll over the tart pan, leaving about a 2-inch hem all around. Using your fingers, gently fit the dough into the sides of pan. Fold the hem into the shell so that the trimmed edge meets the bottom where it joins the wall. (This forms a wall that is twice as thick as the bottom.) Press the folded edge gently into the sides of the pan, then go around the inside of the pan again with the side of the first finger, pressing the lower wall to the pan. With the corner of a pastry scraper or knife, trim the excess dough even with the top of the pan, cutting away from the center of the tart in brisk movements to form a clean edge.

6. Cover the shell with plastic and refrigerate for at least 30 minutes before filling and baking. (The shell can be refrigerated overnight or frozen for up to 2 weeks.)

7. To prebake the tart shell: Preheat the oven to 350°F. Move a rack to the middle position of the oven.

8. Line the bottom of the tart shell with a double thickness of aluminum foil. Weigh down with pie weights or dried beans. Fold the foil over the beans to expose the rim of the shell. Bake the shell for 20 minutes. Remove the foil and weights. If the recipe calls for a **partially baked** tart shell, return the shell to the oven for 5 to 10 minutes, until the bottom is dry; if the recipe calls for a **fully baked** shell, return the shell to the oven and bake until the bottom and the edges are golden, 10 to 15 minutes.

TART TOOLS

///

Only a few tools are required to make professional-quality tarts and tartlets:

▲ For large tarts, use a 9-inch tart pan that is 1 inch deep and has a removable bottom. For tartlets, you'll need a total of 8 removable-bottom tartlet pans 4 inches in diameter and ¾ inch deep. Both should be made of stainless steel.

▲ To weigh down the tart shell for the initial prebaking, use a large double layer of lightweight aluminum foil that overhangs the shell by about 1 inch. You'll also need several cups of dried beans or metal or ceramic pie weights to keep the shell from buckling while it bakes.

▲ A slender, so-called French rolling pin that is about 20 inches long and tapered at the ends will speed and ease the job of rolling the dough. It is a lightweight tool that is particularly appropriate for rolling a thin crust. A larger pin on ball bearings will do the job, but it is a bit like using a steamroller to squash a bug.

▲ A good-size cooling rack is important. The bottom of the tart pan is independent of the sides, so if you perch it on a small cookie rack the outer ring can pull away prematurely and tear the crust. If you don't own a large rack, simply use your second oven rack; pull it out before turning on the oven.

▲ A cardboard cake circle on which to slide the tart and a flexible metal baker's spatula to release the tart from the bottom of the pan are both extremely useful. The cardboard circles are 9 inches in diameter, ⅛ inch thick, and can be bought at a good kitchenware shop (or from a friendly restaurant or bake shop). The flexible spatula has a blade 9- to 10-inches long and about 1 inch wide. It is a relatively inexpensive cook shop purchase. You can (and I have) cut the tart directly in the pan, but you dull your knife and scratch the pan in the process. Likewise, you can jimmy around with a pancake-flipper to release the tart from the base, but it's a clumsy, inefficient tool. So if you think you have a career in tarts, invest in these two items.

▲ For slicing even freshly baked tarts quickly and neatly, nothing beats a long, serrated slicing knife. It's best if the blade is a full 12 inches long; then you can cut across the diameter with a single easy stroke.

LEMON BUTTER TART

MAKES ONE 9-INCH TART

Aperennial China Moon favorite, this tart has a smooth texture, a lustrous look, and a zingy taste. It is also exceedingly easy to make. For do-ahead occasions, the lemon butter may be made a week in advance and refrigerated. Simply reheat it in a double boiler, stirring until the mixture falls in ribbons from a spoon, before pouring it into the shell.

LEMON BUTTER:
Finely grated zest of 7 scrubbed
  lemons
1 cup granulated sugar
6 extra-large eggs
1 cup freshly squeezed lemon
  juice

3 ounces (¾ stick) unsalted
  butter, at room temperature,
  cut into 6 pieces

Prebaked Tart Shell (page 463),
  fully baked
Confectioners' sugar, for garnish

1. In a food processor or blender, combine the lemon zest with ¼ cup of the sugar and process until fine and moist, several minutes.

2. In a medium-size bowl, combine the eggs, the remaining ¾ cup sugar, and the zest mixture. Whisk briskly until well blended. Stir in the lemon juice. Place the bowl over a saucepan half-filled with slowly simmering water and stir until the mixture thickens enough to lightly coat the back of a wooden spoon, 6 to 8 minutes.

3. Stir in the butter, a piece at a time, mixing until melted and smooth. Strain through a fine-mesh sieve. Immediately pour the lemon butter into the tart shell and set aside. The filling will set as it cools. Let cool completely before serving.

4. Just before serving, lightly dust the edges of the tart with confectioners' sugar.

NEAT SLICES

We cut eight slices from a 9-inch tart. That's a nice portion. If you're wanting to stretch a tart to serve ten, you can, especially if you're adding a dollop of cream or a scoop of ice cream alongside.

Slicing a tart is easiest when it's cool. If you're serving it warm, wait until the last minute to cut it.

CRYSTALLIZED LEMON TART

MAKES ONE 9-INCH TART

CLEAN ZEST WITH ZEST

A nice way to accent a tart dough is with a generous grating of orange and/or lemon zest. Scrub the fruit peel well to clean it, then grate it directly on top of the sugar before you cream it with the butter. The flavorful oil-rich peel will perfume the dough; be careful not to grate any of the bitter white pith.

This tart is to lemon lovers what crystallized ginger is to ginger aficionados—a sweet whammy of sharp flavor. It is also irresistible for its ease. Aside from some fine slicing of fruit, there is nothing off-putting for even a beginning baker.

Be sure to scout your markets for pretty lemons with thin, unblemished skin. Meyer lemons would be lovely here. So would Ranjipur limes or kumquats, or even a mixture of these puckery fruits.

This is a nice tart to serve while still a bit warm from the oven. A dollop of crème chantilly would be a fine adornment.

2 large lemons with thin, unblemished skin	*2 extra-large eggs*
Finely grated zest of 1 scrubbed lemon	*Prebaked Tart Shell (page 463), partially baked*
1½ cups sugar	

1. Scrub the lemons under warm water with an abrasive scrubber and a light liquid soap. Rinse well. Cut off both ends of the lemons to expose the fruit, then cut into paper-thin slices. Remove any seeds. Layer the lemon slices, zest, and sugar in a large bowl. Toss gently with a flexible spatula; set aside for 30 to 60 minutes. Toss again. Seal and set aside at room temperature for 8 hours or overnight, stirring once or twice, if convenient.

2. Preheat the oven to 350°F. Move a rack to the upper third of the oven.

3. Stir the lemon mixture and carefully remove any lingering seeds with a teaspoon. Whisk the eggs until light. Pour into the lemon mixture and mix well. Pour into the prebaked shell, distributing the lemons evenly and unfolding them, if necessary, with your fingers.

4. Bake the tart until the filling is set and lightly golden, 25 to 30 minutes. Rotate the tart midway through baking to ensure even coloring. Remove to cool on a wire rack.

5. Serve the tart warm or cool. It keeps beautifully overnight. Seal when completely cool, refrigerate, and let come to room temperature before serving.

WALNUT CHOCOLATE TART

MAKES ONE 9-INCH TART

Another delicious variation on a decadent theme, this is a rich but simple dessert. I especially like it late at night with a cup of Lapsang tea.

The web of fine chocolate lines that Amy pipes over the top is very easy to make, but if you feel at all shy, just drizzle the chocolate from the edge of a spoon. The result will look a bit like a Jackson Pollock painting, just fine to a modern eye.

If you are looking for a cool accompaniment, try a scoop of ginger, lemon, or mango ice cream (pages 487, 490, and 491, respectively).

2 ounces semisweet chocolate, coarsely chopped
1 ounce unsweetened chocolate, coarsely chopped
Prebaked Tart Shell (page 463), partially baked
2 cups (7 ounces) walnut halves and pieces, toasted
2 tablespoons dark molasses

¾ cup light corn syrup
¼ cup packed dark brown sugar
3 extra-large eggs
1 teaspoon finely grated lemon zest
2 tablespoons unsalted butter, melted
Confectioners' sugar, for garnish

1. Preheat the oven to 350°F. Move a rack to the middle position.

2. In the top of a double boiler over hot, not simmering, water, melt the semisweet and unsweetened chocolates until

smooth. Spread ¼ cup of the melted chocolate evenly over the bottom of the tart shell. Reserve the remaining chocolate for decorating the tart. Scatter the walnuts over the chocolate in the bottom of the tart shell.

3. In a large mixing bowl, whisk together the molasses, corn syrup, brown sugar, eggs, lemon zest, and melted butter until smooth and well blended. Pour the mixture into the tart shell, filling it almost to the rim and taking care not to let the syrup overflow.

4. Bake the tart until the filling is set yet still soft to the touch, 35 to 40 minutes. Remove to a rack to cool.

5. Remelt the reserved chocolate, if necessary. Pour the chocolate into a small parchment paper cone. Cut off the tip to make a tiny opening and hold the parchment cone about 1 inch above the tart. Using quick motions, pipe a succession of broken lines of chocolate over the tart. Or, drizzle the liquid chocolate from the edge of a spoon.

6. Serve the tart warm or cool. Just before serving, dust the edge of the tart with confectioners' sugar.

HOT TARTS

Serving a tart freshly baked and still warm from the oven is the ultimate seduction. Most tarts hold their heat remarkably well, meaning that a tart finished an hour or more before dinner can still be warm when it's served. Rewarming tarts is a tricky business; some will get doughy (if they're topped with streusel) while others can get inappropriately runny or soft. So if your passion is for hot, you'd best experiment in private!

CHOCOLATE-PECAN RUM TART

MAKES ONE 9-INCH TART

If buzzwords will sell a dessert, then here is a runaway hit! Given the requisite fine chocolate, plump nuts, and a bit of quality booze, you'll have a fabulous ending to a meal.

With a prebaked shell on hand, this tart can be made in an hour. Letting it rest an hour and serving it slightly warm would be fabulous. So, too, would a scoop of Fresh Ginger Ice Cream or Lemon Ice Cream (pages 487 and 490) plopped on top.

1 ounce unsweetened chocolate,
     coarsely chopped
1 ounce semisweet chocolate,
     coarsely chopped
Prebaked Tart Shell (page 463),
     partially baked

3 ounces (¾ stick) unsalted
     butter, cut into 6 pieces
⅔ cup granulated sugar
½ teaspoon finely grated lemon
     zest

2 extra-large eggs
1 tablespoon all-purpose flour
2 cups (7 ounces) pecan halves,
     toasted and coarsely chopped
3 ounces semisweet chocolate,
     finely chopped
1½ tablespoons dark rum
16 to 20 untoasted pecan halves
Confectioners' sugar, for
     garnish

1. In the top of a double boiler over hot, not simmering, water, melt the coarsely chopped, unsweetened and semisweet chocolates until smooth. Spread the chocolate in an even layer over the bottom of the tart shell.

2. Preheat the oven to 350°F. Move a rack to the middle position.

3. In a bowl, cream the butter, sugar, and lemon zest with an electric mixer on medium speed until light and smooth, 2 to 3 minutes. Add the eggs and mix until well blended. Add the flour, toasted pecans, finely chopped chocolate, and rum. Mix until combined. Pour the mixture into the tart shell and level the surface with a spatula.

4. Arrange 2 pecan halves at the outer edge of the tart, pressing them lightly into the tart in a *V* shape. (The point of the *V* should face the center of the tart.) Space 8 to 10 *V*s evenly around the tart, depending on how many portions are needed.

5. Bake the tart until the filling is set and lightly golden, 20 to 25 minutes. Remove the tart to a rack to cool.

6. Serve warm or cool. Just before serving, lightly dust the edge of the tart with confectioners' sugar.

DRESSING UP A TART

A slice of tart on a plate can look a little simple and severe, so a light dusting of powdered sugar or fine cocoa can lend a nice bit of pizazz. You can dust the edge of the tart, or you can dust the entire top. Or, you can dust the center of the plate, or (if you're very chichi) you can instead dust the rim. In any case, do your dusting just before serving (for more on dusting, see page 472).

TART TIPS

Rolling out tart dough and fitting it into a fluted frame can seem a bit treacherous for a beginner. Here are some helpful tips:

▲ Weigh out the dough after you make it. For a 9-inch tart shell, you'll need 10 ounces of dough. For every 4-inch tartlet shell, you'll need 2½ ounces of dough. Most professional bakers would sooner give up their spatula than their scale, so sure-proof does it make their work.

▲ To prevent the dough from cracking when you roll it, work the freshly made soft dough into an inch-thick disk, first by kneading it gently into a ball and then flattening and shaping it with your palms. Refrigerate the dough until firm to relax the gluten, 1 to 24 hours. However, roll it when it is malleable enough so that a gentle finger press leaves a mark. If the dough is hard it will crack.

▲ To speed the rolling, lightly dust the board and the top of the dough with flour. Roll with even pressure in quick strokes from the center of the dough out to the edge. Periodically rotate the dough a quarter-turn and re-dust the board and dough with flour, as often as is needed to prevent sticking.

▲ Use a ruler to check your roll: For a large 9-inch tart, you'll want a 12-inch round; for a 4-inch tartlet shell, you'll need a 6-inch round. Both shells should be an even ⅛ inch thick; a hand run over the dough is the best check for evenness.

▲ To center the dough in the tart pan, fold the circle in half, lift it with two hands into the center of the pan, and then unfold it. Or, if you're handy with a rolling pin or feeling gutsy, reverse-roll the dough over the pin and then unroll it into the tart pan. With the dough centered correctly, you'll have a skirt about 2 inches wide all around the shell.

▲ For a sturdy, no-crumble crust, fold the hem back into the shell so the dough forms a double wall. To stabilize and even the wall, gently press it into the sides of the pan by going around it two or three times, using the thumb of one hand to press and smooth the wall while the other hand turns the shell. Make the wall ¼ inch thick, pinching off the excess dough that rises above the edge of the pan in the too-thick spots and using it to patch any too-thin spots.

▲ To prevent shrinkage, refrigerate or freeze the rolled-out tart shell before baking so the dough is very firm. Loosely covered shells can be refrigerated for 1 to 2 days or frozen for up to 2 weeks. Bake them directly from the refrigerator or freezer.

▲ Bake filled tarts on the middle rack of the oven for even cooking. Too high, and the top colors before the filling cooks. Too low, and the bottom cooks through while the top stays underdone.

▲ For evenly colored tarts, rotate the tart a full half-turn in the oven midway through baking. Set a timer so you don't forget.

▲ For a properly cooked tart, trust your eye before your timer! Look for the visual standards cited in each recipe, and make a knife test or a skewer test when called for. Don't be afraid to bake longer if your eye suggests it's needed.

BLACK FRIAR PLUM-FRANGIPANE TART

MAKES ONE 9-INCH TART

I adore the nubbly texture and almondy fragrance of frangipane, and nowhere better than in this tart. With the purple-black plums showing through here and there, it is an absolutely regal dessert.

The frangipane can be made a week or more ahead. Then with the fruit and a prebaked tart shell on hand, this dessert can be assembled in an hour.

Black Friar is a fragrant plum we especially like, but any sweet plum—be it red, purple, green, or yellow—will be good. If you are looking to adorn the tart, try a dollop of unsweetened crème chantilly or, for a different effect, a scoop of Lime-Rum Ice Cream (page 493).

1¼ pounds ripe but firm,
fragrant Black Friar plums
Prebaked Tart Shell (page 463),
partially baked

Frangipane (recipe follows)
Confectioners' sugar, for
garnish

1. Preheat the oven to 350°F. Move an oven rack to the middle position.

2. Halve the plums lengthwise and remove the pits, then cut each half lengthwise into 3 wedges. Arrange the plum wedges on their sides, in a spiral pattern, completely covering the bottom of the tart shell.

3. In a bowl, beat the frangipane with an electric mixer on medium speed until light. Spread the frangipane evenly over the plums. It's okay if the plums show through in a few places.

4. Bake the tart until lightly golden, 40 to 45 minutes. Remove to a rack to cool.

5. Serve warm or cool. Just before serving, lightly dust the edge of the tart with confectioners' sugar.

FRANGIPANE

MAKES 1 ¾ CUPS, ENOUGH FOR ONE 9-INCH TART

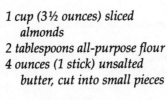

1 cup (3½ ounces) sliced
   almonds
2 tablespoons all-purpose flour
4 ounces (1 stick) unsalted
   butter, cut into small pieces

⅓ cup sugar
1 extra-large egg
1 teaspoon finely grated lemon
   zest
¼ teaspoon almond extract

1. Combine the almonds and flour in a food processor and process until finely ground but not oily.

2. In a bowl, cream the butter and sugar with an electric mixer on medium speed until smooth and fluffy, about 3 minutes. Beat in the egg and lemon zest. Add the almonds and almond extract, and beat, scraping down the sides of the bowl occasionally, until smooth and light.

3. Use the frangipane immediately or seal airtight and store in the refrigerator for up to 2 weeks.

RASPBERRY FRANGIPANE TART

MAKES ONE 9-INCH TART

This is a princess variation on the frangipane theme, featuring delicate berries and a topping of sliced almonds. Wait until summer to do this. The berries need to be fabulous in order for the result to be celestial.

Serving this tart warm, only an hour out of the oven, is very special. Accompany it with a scoop of Pear Ice Cream (page 495) for another special effect.

1 cup raspberries
Prebaked Tart Shell (page 463),
    partially baked

Frangipane (page 473), at
    room temperature
¼ cup sliced almonds
Confectioners' sugar, for
    garnish

1. Preheat the oven to 350°F. Move an oven rack to the middle position.

2. Scatter the raspberries in an even layer in the tart shell.

3. In a bowl, beat the frangipane with an electric mixer on medium speed until light. Spread the frangipane evenly over the raspberries. Sprinkle the almonds on top.

4. Bake the tart until lightly golden, 40 to 45 minutes. Remove to a rack to cool.

5. Serve the tart warm or cool. Just before serving, lightly dust the entire surface of the tart, including the rim, with confectioners' sugar.

BLACK FIG STREUSEL TART

MAKES ONE 9-INCH TART

Move over fruitcake! This is a dessert I associate with winter holidays and crackling fires and good cheer among fellows! Strange it should be the concoction of a Chinese pastry chef, but such is the inscrutability of China Moon Cafe.

Nothing is complicated here—just a short bubbling of fruit that will fill your house with fragrance. The filling and the streusel can be made in advance, leaving only the baking for the last minute.

If you are feeling cozy and wintry, serve the tart still warm an hour or so after baking. For further grandeur, add a scoop of ginger, hazelnut, or lemon ice cream (pages 487, 498, and 490, respectively).

1 large crisp, tart green apple
1¾ to 2 pounds fresh black figs
¼ cup currants
2 teaspoons grated orange zest
1½ teaspoons grated lemon zest
¼ cup packed dark brown sugar
1 teaspoon ground cinnamon
¼ teaspoon ground cloves

1 tablespoon freshly squeezed
   orange juice
2 tablespoons freshly squeezed
   lemon juice

Prebaked Tart Shell (page 463),
   partially baked
Streusel Topping (recipe follows)

ROPE 'EM IN

You can decorate the rim of a tart with an appealing rope pattern by crimping the chilled dough with chopsticks dipped in flour. This was the trick of Clay Wollard, a beloved friend who was Amy's co-pastry chef during China Moon's opening months. Leave it to a creative "tofu head" (my Chinese little brother's gleeful name for Caucasians) to think up another use for chopsticks!

1. Peel and core the apple and cut it into ½-inch cubes; you should have 1½ cups. Quarter the figs. Combine the apple, figs, currants, citrus zests, sugar, spices, and citrus juices in a heavy, non-aluminum saucepan. Cook over moderate heat, stirring gently to avoid scorching, until the fruit is soft and the juices are bubbly and slightly thickened, about 10 minutes. Set aside to cool to room temperature. If working in advance, the filling can be refrigerated for several days.

2. Preheat the oven to 350°F. Move a rack to the top third of the oven.

3. Pour the cool filling into the tart shell and spread out in an even layer. Evenly sprinkle the streusel topping over the filling, keeping the streusel about ½ inch from the rim. (It will expand when baked.)

4. Bake the tart until the filling is bubbly and the streusel is lightly golden, 40 to 50 minutes. Remove to a rack to cool.

5. Serve the tart warm or cool.

STREUSEL TOPPING

MAKES 1¼ CUPS, ENOUGH FOR ONE 9-INCH TART

½ cup all-purpose flour
2 ounces (½ stick) cold unsalted
   butter, cut into 4 pieces

¼ cup plus 2 tablespoons packed
   dark brown sugar
½ teaspoon ground cinnamon

Combine all of the ingredients in the bowl of an electric mixer. Blend on medium speed until the mixture resembles coarse meal. Use promptly or seal airtight and store for up to 2 weeks in the refrigerator.

SUMMER PEACH-HAZELNUT STREUSEL TART

MAKES ONE 9-INCH TART

With a name like this, who can resist? If you have fantasized about your (or someone else's) mother's peach pie, then this is a dessert to make as soon as peaches hit their prime. It is homey yet sophisticated, which is what we would all like to be.

Don't waste your time using peaches that have no aroma. To taste terrific, peaches must be fabulously fragrant, right then and there in the market when you are lifting them to your nose.

This dessert, still wearing the warmth of the oven, is more than enough for the stuff of dreams, but if you want to gild the lily, add a scoop of ginger, lemon, or mango ice cream (pages 487, 490, and 491, respectively).

8 firm but ripe, fragrant peaches
   (about 3 pounds)
Finely grated zest of 1 scrubbed
   lemon
1 tablespoon freshly squeezed
   lemon juice
⅓ cup sugar
3 tablespoons cornstarch

Prebaked Tart Shell
   (page 463), partially
   baked
Hazelnut Streusel
   Topping (recipe follows)

1. Preheat the oven to 350°F. Move an oven rack to the top position.

2. Cut each peach lengthwise in half, pit, and quarter each half into wedges. Combine the fruit with the lemon zest and lemon juice in a heavy non-aluminum saucepan. Cook over medium heat, stirring occasionally, until the peaches are wilted and soft, 5 to 8 minutes.

3. Drain the peaches, reserving ¼ cup of the cooking juice. Return the juice to the saucepan and stir in the sugar and cornstarch. Cook over medium heat, stirring until the mixture turns glossy and slightly thick, 3 to 4 minutes. Pour the mixture over the peaches and toss gently to blend.

*Ice cream served with a
tart is pleasure times
two! Who can resist the
thought of something à la
mode, especially if the something is a freshly baked tart?
Our spicy ginger ice cream is
the perfect yin-yang partner
to many of our tarts, but our
other light ice creams may
tempt you even more.*

*Whipping some cold
cream into the soft, sexy
peaks that the French call
crème chantilly is another
great accompaniment, either
plopped alongside or on top of
a slice of tart. If you use great
fresh cream, don't add sugar,
vanilla, or booze. This is
typically done, but in my
opinion it's a distraction if
the cream you're using tastes
terrific.*

4. Spoon the peaches into the tart shell. Sprinkle the
streusel evenly over the fruit, keeping the streusel about ½
inch from the rim. (It will expand when baked.)

5. Bake until the streusel is golden, 45 to 55 minutes.
Remove to a rack to cool.

6. Serve the tart warm or cool.

HAZELNUT STREUSEL TOPPING

MAKES 1 ¾ CUPS, ENOUGH FOR ONE 9-INCH TART

Heaping ½ cup (2 ounces)   Streusel Topping (page 475)
   hazelnuts

1. Preheat the oven to 350°F. Move an oven rack to the
middle position.

2. Spread the hazelnuts on a baking sheet and toast until
the skins blister and the nuts turn golden beneath their skins,
10 to 12 minutes.

Promptly fold the hot nuts into a clean, dry kitchen towel
and rub together to remove most of the skins.

3. Coarsely chop the nuts. Add to the streusel topping
and toss to combine.

APRICOT-RASPBERRY
LATTICE TART

MAKES ONE 9-INCH TART

Just as gold and red go together, so do apricots and
raspberries. Plant them in a tart shell and top them
with a lattice, and you have the equivalent of a
Chanel suit—an understated bit of irrefutable pizazz.

With the prebaked shell and the ingredients on
hand, the tart can be assembled shortly before dinner
and served warm.

*5 cups pitted fresh apricot
   halves (about 2 pounds)*
1 tablespoon unsalted butter
*Finely grated zest of 1 scrubbed
   lemon*
½ cup sugar

2 tablespoons cornstarch
1 cup raspberries

*Prebaked Tart Shell (page 463),
   partially baked*
*Dough for Lattice Top (recipe
   follows)*

**THE HEARTBREAK
OF TARTBREAK**

*To prevent a broken tart
shell, let the tart cool
until lukewarm before removing the sides of the pan.
Then, balance the tart with
one hand on the bottom and
let the ring slip down your
arm. Or, stand the tart on a
wide can and guide the ring
gently downward to release
it. If a bit of sugar is gluing
the ring to the crust, return
the tart to a flat surface and
break the seal with the tip of
a knife.*

1. Preheat the oven to 350°F. Move rack to the top third of the oven.

2. In a heavy, non-aluminum saucepan, combine the apricot halves, butter, lemon zest, and ¼ cup of the sugar. Cook over medium heat, stirring occasionally, until the fruit is wilted and soft, 6 to 7 minutes. Strain the apricots, discarding the juices.

3. Transfer the cooked apricots to a mixing bowl. Combine the cornstarch and the remaining ¼ cup sugar, stirring to blend. Sprinkle over the apricots, add the raspberries, and toss gently to mix. Pour the filling into the tart shell and spread the fruit in an even layer. Lay the lattice strips on top of the fruit as directed in Step 2 of lattice recipe below.

4. Bake the tart until the lattice strips are lightly golden and the fruit filling is bubbling, 45 to 50 minutes. Remove to a rack to cool, pressing up gently on the tart base to break the sugar seal before it sets.

5. Serve warm or cool.

LATTICE TOP FOR TART SHELLS

*½ recipe Prebaked Tart Shell
   dough (page 463),
   made through Step 3*

1. To roll out the dough, sprinkle the work surface and the top of the disk with flour. Roll out the dough into a 7- by 12-inch rectangle that is ⅛ inch thick. Dust the rolling pin with flour as needed to prevent the dough from sticking. Cover and chill the sheet of dough until firm, at least 15 to 20 minutes.

2. With a long, sharp knife, cut the dough lengthwise into 14 strips ½ inch wide. Arrange 7 of the strips 1 inch apart across the filled tart shell. Pinch off the excess dough at the edges. Lay the remaining dough strips diagonally over the first 7 strips. Pinch off the excess dough at the edges.

3. Bake the tart as directed in the individual recipe.

4. If you like, roll the excess dough into balls, roll the balls in sugar, and bake them as cookies.

STRAWBERRY-RHUBARB LATTICE TART

MAKES ONE 9-INCH TART

If you are trying to seduce someone (or simply yourself) with memories of Mom and rhubarb pie, then this is a dessert to try. Serve it warm and à la mode, and the seduction will be foolproof.

Wait until fragrant summer strawberries are in the market to make this tart. Don't be taken in by the tasteless fakes that appear in winter.

1 pint (2 cups) strawberries,
   stemmed and halved
½ cup sugar
1½ pounds rhubarb, cut into
   1-inch pieces

2 tablespoons plus 1 teaspoon
   cornstarch
Finely grated zest of 1 scrubbed
   lemon

Prebaked Tart Shell (page 463),
   partially baked
Lattice Top for Tart Shells
   (page 478)

1. Preheat the oven to 350°F. Move rack to the top third of the oven.

2. Heat a non-aluminum small saucepan over high heat until hot. Add the strawberries and stir or shake the pan until the berries start to exude their juices, 2 to 3 minutes. Depending on the berries, they'll give up 2 to 3 tablespoons of juice. Drain the fruit and set aside. Drink or discard the juice.

3. Combine ¼ cup of the sugar and the rhubarb in the same saucepan. Stir over high heat until the rhubarb wilts and exudes several tablespoons of juice, 2 to 3 minutes. Drain the rhubarb. Drink or discard the juice.

4. In a large mixing bowl, combine the strawberries and the rhubarb. Blend the remaining ¼ cup sugar with the cornstarch and lemon zest, then add the mixture to the bowl with the fruit and toss gently until blended. Spoon the filling into the tart shell. Lay the lattice strips on top of the fruit as directed on pages 478 and 479.

5. Bake until the pastry is golden and the fruit filling is bubbling, 40 to 45 minutes. Remove to a rack to cool, pressing up gently on the tart base to break the sugar seal before it sets.

6. Serve warm or cool.

YIN-YANG TART

MAKES ONE 9-INCH TART

The book cover trumpets a colorful way to end a China Moon meal on a deliciously symbolic note: a fresh fruit tart wearing a yin-yang face with an almond frangipane surprise beneath. It takes a happy bow to Oona Aven, a wonderful baker friend who gave me a gift of my first yin-yang tart over a decade ago, and to Clay Wollard, a dearly missed pastry chef friend.

Lots of fruit pairings will work here. Raspberries and mandarin orange sections, kiwi and banana slices, blueberries and strawberries, cherries and apricots, or peaches and plums. You can even use different-colored varieties of the same fruit, for example, yellow and red raspberries or green and purple plums.

The tart shell and frangipane can be made in advance. Bake and cool the frangipane before adding the fruit; arrange the fruit only shortly before serving.

Frangipane (page 473), at room
　temperature
Prebaked tart shell (page 463)
¼ to ⅓ cup raspberry or orange
　marmalade

About 1 pound each of 2
　contrasting fruits (You'll
　have extra, but it's good
　insurance against squashed
　slices and bashed berries.)

YIN AND YANG

Yin and yang is the underlying scheme of lively opposites in balance that pervades the whole of Chinese culture, including its cuisine. Yin and yang in cooking means classic sauces like sweet and sour, the tradition of pairing deep-fried crispy foods with soft, steamed ones, and a culinary insistence on variety in every meal.

Yin and yang is the Chinese insurance against too-muchness. Nothing is ever too sweet, salty, meaty or oily when a cook is grounded firmly in yin and yang. A meat dish requires a vegetable dish to balance it, a salt-crust chicken demands a heap of plain unseasoned rice to be eaten with it, and a meal that is mostly stir-fried begs an ending of fresh fruit.

This is totally unlike our Western way. Our culture is imagined as a box divided squarely in two. We have good and evil, God and the Devil, and divider plates that keep separate our meat, potatoes, and peas. We eat only fried foods or only sweet foods, or only puréed foods in little hills alongside a fan of rare meat. We like our worlds separate, bounded, and clear.

The Chinese mix everything up with great, unconscious joy. Theirs is a fluid world where a circle is divided into two by an elastic S-shaped river, and where a pregnant dot of the opposite color appears in the center of each half. This means that even the gods can be devilish, women can wear pants, and the veggies, meats, and rice can be jumbled in the bowl. In China, variety is not merely a spice, it is the heart of living and eating.

1. Preheat the oven to 350°F. Move a rack to the middle position.

2. In the bowl of an electric mixer, beat the frangipane on medium speed until light. Scrape the mixture into the tart shell and spread it to level and smooth out the surface.

3. Bake the frangipane until lightly golden, 40 to 45 minutes. Set aside and allow to cool before adding the fruit. The cool tart can be sealed and refrigerated overnight.

4. Up to several hours in advance, heat the marmalade over low heat until liquid. Strain and discard any seeds or solids. If you'd like an extra note of sweetness, brush a light film of the glaze over the frangipane and the rim of the tart.

5. Trim the fruit as appropriate: Skin stoned fruit with care, then cut it into wedges. Softer stoned fruit can be denuded with a sharp paring knife; firmer fruit can be dropped into boiling water and then into ice water to loosen the peel. Pit cherries; cut kiwi and banana into evenly thick coins (wait until the last minute to cut bananas to avoid discoloration); cut off the tops of strawberries so they can stand on their heads; section oranges, remove any seeds, and hold them in a colander to drain off excess juice.

6. Arrange the yin-yang pattern on top of the frangipane: Start by making an S-shaped line of one type of fruit in the center of the tart, arranging berries side by side or gently overlapping sliced fruit. Then, ring this first fruit inside its half of the rim. Repeat the process with the second fruit, bordering the S-curve and completing the outer circle. Next, put a circle of the opposite fruit in each half of the tart. (This is the "eye" of the yin-yang through which opposites penetrate and merge.) Finally, fill in each field of color with the appropriate fruit.

7. If the marmalade glaze has hardened, liquify it once more over low heat. Then gently brush or drizzle the fruit with the glaze. Fruit that might discolor like bananas will appreciate a light dress of glaze; berries or other easily toppled fruit will like a drizzle.

8. To serve, either divide your guests into a yin-yang group, half getting one fruit and half getting the other, or divide the tart into thinner slices and serve everyone a slice of each.

PREBAKED TARTLET SHELLS

MAKES EIGHT 4-INCH TARTLET SHELLS

This recipe makes enough dough for 8 tartlet shells. If you are serving a larger crowd, do the recipe twice rather than doubling it. If you are new to working with tart doughs, see Tart Tools and Tart Tips (pages 465 and 471) to help you on your way.

6 ounces (1½ sticks) unsalted
   butter, cut into 12 pieces
⅓ cup plus 3 tablespoons sugar

3 extra-large egg yolks
2 cups all-purpose flour

1. In a bowl, cream the butter and sugar with an electric mixer on medium speed until smooth, 3 to 4 minutes. Add the egg yolks and mix until blended. Add the flour and mix until combined. Gather the dough together and roll and form into a thick log. Wrap in plastic and refrigerate until firm but malleable, at least 1 hour.

2. Divide the log of dough into 8 equal portions (2½ ounces each). On a lightly floured board, roll out each portion into an even 6-inch round ⅛ inch thick. Periodically rotate the dough on the board and dust the top as needed to prevent sticking.

3. Fit each dough circle into a 4-inch tartlet pan. Gently press the dough into the sides of the pan. Fold the hem back into the shell so that the outer edge meets the bottom of the tart; this forms a wall that is twice as thick as the bottom. Press the dough gently into the sides of the pan. Go around the inside of the pan again with the side of the first finger, pressing the lower wall to the pan. With the corner of a pastry scraper or knife, trim the excess dough even with the top of the pan, cutting away from the center of the tart in brisk movements to form a clean edge. Cover the tartlet shells with plastic wrap and refrigerate until thoroughly firm, about 30 minutes, before baking. (The shells can be refrigerated overnight or frozen airtight for 1 to 2 weeks.)

4. Preheat the oven to 350°F. Move an oven rack to the middle position.

5. Bake the shells until lightly golden, 15 to 20 minutes.

FILL 'ER UP

For the best tart and tartlet fillings, use the best ingredients. Nuts with rich flavor and fruit that is ripe with taste give great results. Avoid fruit that is overly juicy; if it is too moist, you'll be stuck with a runny filling.

BLUEBERRY OR RASPBERRY LEMON CREAM TARTLETS

MAKES EIGHT 4-INCH TARTLETS

When summer comes and with it the fragrant entrance of berries into the China Moon kitchen, the staff clamors for Amy to make these tartlets. Presenting these gorgeous mountains of berries on their pastry thrones on our dessert cart is like dangling a Bulgari jewel in front of a crook. Who could say no?

If you make the shells and the lemon butter in advance, assembling the tartlets is quick and easy. Once finished, they may be held in the refrigerator for several hours. Do not, however, plan to hold them overnight. The cream will soften the crust, and the tartlets will break into sad (albeit delicious) bits.

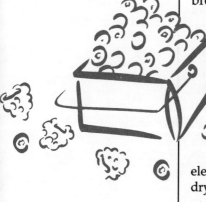

1 cup heavy cream
2 tablespoons sugar
   Lemon Butter (recipe
      follows), at room
      temperature

Prebaked Tartlet Shells (page
   482)
2 pints ripe, fragrant
   raspberries or blueberries
½ cup currant jelly

1. In a bowl, whip together the cream and sugar with an electric mixer on high speed until the cream forms stiff but not dry peaks. Fold the lemon butter into the cream until blended.

2. Fit a pastry bag with a large, plain tip. Fill the bag with the lemon cream. Starting from the center of each tartlet shell, pipe the cream in a spiral pattern to fill each shell.

3. Arrange the berries in a layer on top, completely covering the lemon cream. Pile a heaping second layer of berries on each tartlet.

4. Melt the jelly in a small non-aluminum saucepan over low heat. Set aside to cool until warm. Fill a small parchment paper cone with the jelly, cut a tiny opening at the tip, and quickly pipe fine lines and beads of jelly over the berries. Refrigerate, uncovered, until ready to serve, no more than several hours.

LEMON BUTTER

MAKES ¾ CUP

*Finely grated zest of 2 scrubbed
  lemons*
2 extra-large eggs
¼ cup sugar

*¼ cup freshly squeezed lemon
  juice*
*2 tablespoons unsalted butter, at
  room temperature*

1. In the top of a double boiler, combine the lemon zest, eggs, sugar, and lemon juice, and whisk until blended. Over very low heat, simmer, stirring occasionally, until the mixture is thick enough to coat the back of a wooden spoon, 6 to 8 minutes.

2. Stir in the butter until melted and smooth. Immediately strain through a fine-mesh sieve. Chill the lemon butter, uncovered, in the refrigerator until cool, 30 to 40 minutes.

3. Store the lemon butter airtight in an impeccably clean container in the refrigerator. It will keep for up to 1 week.

BLACKBERRY OR STRAWBERRY ORANGE CREAM TARTLETS

MAKES EIGHT 4-INCH TARTLETS

When the word got out on the street about Amy's lemon cream and berry tartlets, there was no stopping the China Moon clientele—or the waiters who adored selling them, or the linen man who loved scarfing up the broken bits. "What's a girl to do?" cried Amy, and then she came up with this equally yummy variation on her popular summer theme.

Many berries call themselves blackberries. Any will be fine here, as long as they're luscious and sweet.

1 cup heavy cream
2 tablespoons sugar
Orange Butter (recipe follows),
    at room temperature
Prebaked Tartlet Shells (page
    482)

2 pints sweet blackberries, or 3
    pints fragrant strawberries
½ cup currant jelly

1. In a bowl, whip together the cream and sugar with an electric mixer on high speed until the cream forms stiff but not dry peaks. Gently fold the orange butter into the whipped cream until blended.

2. Fit a pastry bag with a large plain tip. Fill the bag with the orange cream. Starting from the center of each shell, pipe the cream in concentric circles to cover the bottom of each shell.

3. Arrange the blackberries in a single layer, completely covering the orange cream. Place a second layer of blackberries on top of the first to form a mound. (If using strawberries, stem the berries. Place 1 whole berry in the center of each tartlet and halve the remaining strawberries. Arrange the halves, overlapping slightly, with their pointed ends up and their rounded sides toward the edge of the tartlet in a row just beneath the whole berry. Add another row beneath, overlapping the one above. The orange cream will be completely covered.)

4. Melt the jelly in a small non-aluminum saucepan over low heat. Set aside to cool until warm. Fill a small parchment paper cone with the jelly, cut a tiny opening at the tip, and quickly pipe fine lines and beads of jelly over the berries. Refrigerate, uncovered, until ready to serve, no more than several hours.

ORANGE BUTTER

MAKES A GENEROUS ½ CUP

½ cup freshly squeezed orange
    juice
¼ cup plus 1 teaspoon sugar
Finely grated zest of 2 scrubbed
    oranges

3 extra-large egg yolks
2 tablespoons unsalted butter, at
    room temperature

1. In a small non-aluminum saucepan, combine the orange juice and 1 teaspoon of the sugar. Bring to a gentle simmer over moderate heat and cook until the juice is reduced to ¼ cup, 5 to 6 minutes. Remove the saucepan from the heat and set aside to cool.

2. Combine the orange zest, the remaining ¼ cup sugar, and the egg yolks in a mixing bowl. Whisk until the yolks turn pale. Add the reduced orange juice and whisk until blended.

3. Set the bowl over a saucepan of gently simmering water and stir until the mixture thickens enough to coat the back of a wooden spoon, 6 to 8 minutes. Stir in the butter until melted. Quickly strain the cream through a fine-mesh sieve. Chill the orange cream, uncovered, in the refrigerator until cool, 30 to 40 minutes.

4. Store the orange cream airtight in an impeccably clean container in the refrigerator. It will keep for up to 1 week.

LIGHT AND LIGHTER ICE CREAMS

I ce cream, to our Western palates, seems a logical conclusion to a Chinese meal. It's refreshingly cool and sweet—a return to something that's familiar after the exotic heat of the meal.

If the customers at China Moon are any index, ice cream is the overwhelming dessert favorite among Americans of every ethnic stripe. While our spicy fresh ginger ice cream outsells all our other desserts combined, our "daily special" ice creams follow in close pursuit. Surely there must be an ice cream button in the brain of every American! One push and our tongues start wagging.

GINGER ICE CREAM FOR A THOUSAND

One of the memorable food events of the San Francisco year is a benefit for Meals-on-Wheels held in the grand foyer of the Opera House. Where divas usually tread, a dozen or so beneficent restaurants and an equal number of excellent wineries set up tables laden with fine food and wine. It is a glamorous evening—a great oppor-

tunity to put on a tux or a ball gown and eat grandly on your feet.

One recent year, the word went around that more desserts were needed so China Moon decided to serve up ginger ice cream instead of our usual crispy, spicy, hot springrolls. I figured if they loved being zapped with chili, they'd adore being zapped with ginger. My guess wasn't half bad. We scooped over 1,000 tiny cups of the stuff (a few hundred people had seconds), each cup lined with chocolate sauce and crowned with a little chocolate butterfly.

To add fun to the frolic, our vegetable purveyor donated 150 pounds of exquisitely fresh Hawaiian ginger. We covered our long serving table with a thick sea of ginger, making it look like an exotic coral reef, and perched the sundae cups between the tubers. It was a grand event. I departed both happy and sticky.

Aside from its popularity, ice cream is a terrifically practical choice for entertaining at home—especially our no-cook "light ice creams" that require little more than mixing (see page 493). Served with an assortment of little cookies and/or a spoonful of fresh fruit for garnish, ice cream is an easy and elegant way to bring a sweet ending to a meal.

▪ ▪ ▪

FRESH GINGER ICE CREAM

MAKES ABOUT 1 QUART

This is the "house special dessert" at China Moon, a refreshing spicy ice cream made from an infusion of fresh ginger. It involves making a custard base—something you may not have done before—but rest assured it is an easy process and the results are fabulous.

This is one ice cream formula I've not reduced to a "light" ice cream. The flavor is so superb, I've never wanted to toy with it.

⅓ cup water
½ cup plus 2 tablespoons sugar
¼ packed cup very finely minced, puréed, or grated ginger
1 cup whole milk

2 extra-large egg yolks
1 cup cold heavy cream
About 1 teaspoon freshly squeezed lemon juice

1. Combine the water and ¼ cup of the sugar in a small heavy saucepan. Bring to a steaming near-simmer over moderate heat, stirring to dissolve the sugar. Add the ginger, stir to blend, then bring the mixture to a boil. Reduce the heat to maintain a weak simmer and simmer for 5 minutes. Remove the pot from the heat.

2. In a larger heavy saucepan, combine 2 tablespoons of the sugar with the milk. Bring to a near-simmer over moderate heat, stirring to dissolve the sugar. Remove from the heat, then carefully scrape the sugar syrup into the milk mixture. Stir to combine, cover the pot to hold in the heat, and set the mixture aside to steep for 20 minutes.

3. Briskly beat the egg yolks with the remaining ¼ cup sugar until the mixture is thick and pale yellow and falls in wide ribbons from the whisk.

4. Place the heavy cream in a large bowl and nest in a larger bowl of ice. Place a fine-mesh sieve alongside.

5. When the steeping time is up, return the milk mixture to scalding, stirring as it heats. Slowly drizzle about ¼ cup of the hot milk into the beaten eggs, whisking as you pour. Immediately scrape the tempered egg mixture into the hot milk, whisking to combine. Cook over moderate heat, whisking slowly, until it reaches the custard stage, 180°F on an instant-read thermometer; it will be thick enough to coat and cling to the back of a wooden spoon. Don't let the milk boil or you'll wind up with scrambled eggs.

6. Immediately pour the hot custard through the sieve into the chilled cream. Press down on the trapped ginger to extract every drop of liquid, then scrape the bottom of the sieve clean. Discard the ginger.

7. Let the custard cool completely, stirring occasionally. Once cool, it may be refrigerated for a day or two before freezing. Don't worry if the mixture separates; simply stir to recombine.

8. Just before freezing, adjust the mixture with the lemon juice, adding it in drops until the flavor peaks perceptibly on the tongue.

9. Freeze the ice cream in an ice cream maker according to the manufacturer's instructions. Store the ice cream with a piece of plastic wrap pressed directly on the surface. Let soften slightly before serving.

SERVING SUGGESTIONS: I've eaten vatfuls of this ice cream in the nude (both me and the ice cream), and it needs no garnish to be delicious. However, Bittersweet Chocolate Sauce was literally made for it; the yin-yang contrast of hot and cool is stunning. Fresh strawberries and/or Cappuccino Coins (page 450) are other worthy counterpoints.

TOO SWEET IS JUST RIGHT

One of the secrets of making ice cream is to make it a touch too sweet before freezing. Then, once it is frozen, it will taste balanced. Chilling and freezing dulls flavors—whether we're talking ice cream or Champagne.

BITTERSWEET CHOCOLATE SAUCE

MAKES 1 PINT

This is a thin bittersweet chocolate sauce that is a fine mate for several of our ice creams and the perfect partner to our Fresh Ginger Ice Cream. It is easy to make and will store indefinitely in the freezer.

Ideal serving consistency is warm, not hot. Different temperatures have their defenders, but you don't want to melt the ice cream.

Extra-rich milk is just that. If unavailable in your market, simply use whole milk. The taste and consistency will be a bit lighter, but that's fine.

10 ounces semisweet chocolate,
chopped into bits (2¼ cups)
1 cup extra-rich milk

¼ cup plus 2 tablespoons
unsweetened cocoa

1. Place the chocolate bits in a heatproof bowl. Place a fine-mesh sieve alongside.

2. In a small heavy saucepan, bring the milk to a scalding near-simmer over moderate heat. Remove the pan from the heat and whisk in the cocoa.

3. Immediately pour the milk mixture through the sieve into the bowl with the chocolate bits. If there are any cocoa lumps in the sieve, press them through with a spatula, dunking the sieve into the hot liquid to help them dissolve. Scrape the sieve clean, then whisk the milk mixture to melt the chocolate bits. You should have a smooth sauce that is the consistency of a light cream soup.

4. For best flavor and texture, leave the sauce uncovered for several hours at room temperature. It will thicken and the flavor will round a bit.

5. Let the sauce cool completely, then seal and refrigerate for several days or freeze indefinitely. (Even frozen, it remains soft enough to scoop.) To reheat for serving, melt over low heat in the top of a double boiler, stirring just until warmed through and fluid.

TOOLS FOR MAKING ICE CREAM

Making ice cream at home is easy. There are several inexpensive devices on the market that make it cheap and fun.

Probably the simplest is a French machine called a Donvier that needs no ice or salt. You simply put the ice cream liquid in the bowl and stick it in your freezer. It's a snap.

I've never lived in an apartment with a freezer bigger than a shoe box, and all my freezers together could not between them make an ice cube! So I use a kind of plug-in ice cream maker that requires salt and ice cubes (from the store). I stick it in the bathtub while it's running (for sound-proofing and ease), which is a neat and amusing way to make dessert.

LEMON ICE CREAM

MAKES ABOUT 2 QUARTS

This is my unabashed favorite ice cream, a silky light ice cream alive with the taste of lemon. It is to my adult tongue what the Italian lemon ices on the Bradley Beach, New Jersey boardwalk were to my kid tongue—happy addiction, almost a reason for living.

Commercial supermarket lemons, as long as you scrub them zealously before use, are fine here. If you're living in California, also try this recipe with the indigenous Meyer lemons; they're super.

This ice cream holds its flavor for two to three days. The unfrozen mixture can be refrigerated for a day or two before freezing.

4 to 5 very large or 6 to 8 smaller lemons with smooth, unblemished skin (to yield 1⅛ cups strained juice)	About 2 cups sugar 4 cups half-and-half Pinch or 2 kosher salt

1. Scrub the lemons vigorously in a basin of warm water dotted with a bit of dishwashing liquid. Use an abrasive scrubber to clean the rind until it no longer feels waxy to the touch. Rinse the lemons thoroughly; pat dry. (Even if you're using organic lemons or lemons straight off the backyard tree, scrub them well.)

2. Put 2 cups sugar in a food processor. Using a sharp vegetable peeler or zester, remove the zest from the lemons in thin strips; take care not to remove any of the bitter white pith. Let the peel fall directly into the food processor.

Halve, juice, and strain the lemons to obtain 1⅛ cups juice; set the juice aside.

3. Run the food processor until the peel is finely ground and the sugar is liquidy, 3 to 4 minutes. Old machines with worn blades take a bit longer and require several pauses to scrape down the bowl. Add the juice and process to blend.

4. Scrape the sugar-lemon mixture into a large, non-aluminum bowl. Add the half-and-half and the salt, and stir to combine. Set aside for 15 to 30 minutes, stirring occasionally. It

ADD SALT TO MAKE IT SWEET OR SOUR

Salt is an extraordinary ingredient! Used properly, it will underscore other flavors rather than adding a perceptible flavor of its own.

In ice cream making, this point is made very clear on your tongue when you're tasting the final mixture just before freezing. A dash of salt added to a lemon or lime ice cream, for example, amplifies the sour. A dash of salt added to an otherwise sweet ice cream adds dimension to the sweetness.

I use kosher salt for these adjustments, in appreciation of its mildness. Sea salt can be used; just make those pinches tiny on account of its saltier taste. Iodized table salt I relegate to the trash can—too vile-tasting to use, even in a pinch.

STORING HOMEMADE ICE CREAM

Most homemade ice creams diminish in flavor and texture if stored for more than several days. This is the negligible down-side to creating a pure product without stabilizers and preservatives.

To store it properly, pack newly frozen ice cream into an impeccably clean con-tainer. I like deep containers; shallow ones are sometimes easier for storage and scoop-ing, but they invite a bigger surface area for unwelcome crystallization.

To minimize crystalliza-tion, do two things: First, pack the soft, just-churned ice cream into the container so that there are no air bub-bles. If you're storing it in a clear plastic container, you can see any bubbles from the side. Otherwise, occasionally plunge your spatula into the mixture at various spots to release any air while you pack it down. Second, smooth the top of the packed mixture and press a piece of plastic wrap directly on the surface of the ice cream. This inhibits crystallization by blocking out the air.

will thicken slightly. At this point, the ice cream mixture can be sealed and refrigerated for a day or two before freezing. Don't worry if it separates; simply stir to recombine.

5. Just before freezing, stir and taste the mixture. Adjust, if needed, with a dash more lemon juice, sugar, or salt to achieve a flavor that is very zippy with a nice undertone of sweetness. The mixture should taste a bit too sweet at room temperature if it is to taste balanced once frozen.

6. Freeze in an ice cream maker according to the manu-facturer's instructions. Store with a piece of plastic wrap pressed directly on the surface. Let soften slightly before serving.

SERVING SUGGESTIONS: If you like chocolate (what a ques-tion!), try this ice cream with one of Amy's chocolate cookies.

MANGO ICE CREAM

MAKES ABOUT 1 QUART

I ate my first mango with a Chinese boyfriend on the steps of a hillside Buddhist temple overlooking rice paddies in Taiwan. Not a bad introduction to one of Mother Nature's more sensual fruits!

A ripe mango of any color or persuasion exudes an overwhelming perfume. To ripen the hard green ones sold in supermarkets, seal them inside a plastic bag and leave them at room temperature for a day or more. They will turn soft, sweet, and fragrant.

This is a simple ice cream to make. Owing to the fragility of the flavor, it should be frozen as soon as it's made and eaten shortly after freezing.

6 to 8 tablespoons sugar
1 very large fragrant mango
   (about 1 pound)
2 cups half-and-half

3 to 4 teaspoons freshly
   squeezed lime juice
1 teaspoon dark rum (optional)

1. Put 6 tablespoons sugar in a food processor. Holding the mango over the workbowl, remove the peel with a sharp paring knife and discard, then cut the soft flesh from around the seed and let it plop directly into the workbowl along with all of its juices. Process the sugar and pulp to a purée.

2. Add the half-and-half and process to blend. Taste and adjust as needed with an additional tablespoon or more of sugar until the mixture tastes a bit too sweet (the mixture should taste a bit too sweet at room temperature if it is to taste perfect when frozen). Run the machine after every small spoonful to incorporate any extra sugar.

3. Add the lime juice in teaspoonfuls until the flavor rounds on the tongue. Stir in the rum if you wish to further deepen the flavor.

4. Freeze in an ice cream maker according to manufacturer's instructions. Store with a piece of plastic wrap pressed directly on the surface. Let soften slightly before serving.

SERVING SUGGESTIONS: Ginger cake or ginger cookies (page 454) make a wonderful partner to this ice cream. So do fresh cherries, peaches, and plums, as well as pies or tarts made from any of these fruits.

GRAPE ICE CREAM

MAKES ABOUT 1 QUART

When you live near a grape-growing region as I do, it's easy to become fascinated with the flavors of different grapes. They are as intriguing to the tongue as wine, which is not surprising!

This is a delicate ice cream, totally dependent on the quality of the grape. Small or large, red or green, it will not matter; what you need is a bursting-with-flavor grape with a good-tasting skin. I favor seedless organic grapes with thin skins for this recipe.

Grape ice cream is a fleeting beauty; be sure to eat it within a day.

FRESH GINGER JUICE

I'll sometimes use the juice squeezed from fresh ginger instead of lemon juice when seasoning an ice cream. It's a nice change and a good jolt of the exotic. Especially with grapes, the ginger flavor is superb.

For an easy route to fresh ginger juice, simply mince or grate fresh ginger, then squeeze it in your hand (over a small bowl) to glean the juice. There's no need to bother with cheesecloth, strainers, or the like; just make a fist and squeeze. The amount of fresh ginger you need to start with will vary with the juiciness of the ginger. A good general rule is to plan on 1 tablespoon of the minced stuff for every teaspoon of juice.

LIGHT ICE CREAMS

Becoming a Chinese cook undid my addiction to traditional American ice cream. For a tongue regularly used to the bright clarity of Chinese flavors infused in oil, the rich onslaught of egg and cream became too much. (Sorbet did not provide an answer; for me, it is too sweet.)

My solution, instead, was what a decade ago I began calling "light ice cream." Based on a simple, egg-less formula of half-and-half combined with fruit and sugar, this is a no-cook solution to producing a vividly flavored but not overly rich ice cream. The result blends some of the silkiness of traditional ice cream with a loud volume of flavor. Most of our China Moon ice creams are of this sort.

The practical beauty of light ice creams is that there is no need to cook a traditional ice cream custard, which cuts down hugely on the time and worry spent on dessert. The comparative healthfulness of these light ice creams is also striking. If sugar is one of your bugaboos, you won't be happy. But if avoiding eggs and heavy cream is a goal, here's a way to make your ice cream and enjoy it, too.

½ cup plus 1 to 2 tablespoons sugar
1 tangerine, orange, or lemon, well scrubbed
¾ pound stemmed seedless grapes with thin, tasty skins
2 cups half-and-half
1½ to 2 teaspoons freshly squeezed ginger juice (from finely minced fresh ginger)

1. Put ½ cup sugar in a food processor. Grate a bit of fruit zest directly onto the sugar, more or less as the spirit moves you. Don't grate any of the bitter white pith. Process for 30 seconds to infuse the sugar with the peel. Add the grapes and process until puréed.

2. Scrape the mixture into a large, non-aluminum bowl. Stir in the half-and-half. Taste, then add sugar if and as needed until the mixture tastes a touch too sweet. Add the ginger juice by ½ teaspoons until the flavor rounds on your tongue. If the grape skins were thick or your food processor blade dull, sieve the mixture and discard the skins.

3. Freeze in an ice cream maker according to manufacturer's instructions. Ripen the soft mixture in the freezer with a piece of plastic wrap pressed directly on the surface. Let soften slightly before serving.

SERVING SUGGESTIONS: This ice cream invites a visual play of grape on grape. I like a small cluster of another variety of grape as a garnish alongside each serving. Blood orange slices or slivers of candied kumquat offer other interesting contrasts.

LIME-RUM ICE CREAM

MAKES ABOUT 2 QUARTS

Temperance types will make an issue of this ice cream; others of us will make an addiction of it. Light, silken, and zippy, it is one of my favorites.
Scrub limes with the same vigor as lemons and use a quality rum; otherwise, omit it.

6 to 8 limes with soft,
     unblemished skin (to yield
     1 cup strained juice)
About 2 cups sugar
4 cups half-and-half

Pinch or two kosher salt
3 tablespoons dark
     rum

1. Scrub the limes vigorously in a large basin of warm water dotted with dishwashing liquid. Use an abrasive scrubber to clean the rind until it no longer feels waxy to the touch. Rinse the limes thoroughly; dry them. (Wash them carefully in this manner even if you're using organic or homegrown fruit.)

2. Put 2 cups sugar in the food processor. Using a sharp vegetable peeler or zester, remove the zest from 6 of the limes, letting the zest fall directly into the food processor. Be careful not to remove any of the bitter white pith.

Halve, juice, and strain enough limes to obtain 1 cup juice; set the juice aside.

3. Run the food processor until the zest is finely ground and the sugar is liquidy, 3 to 4 minutes. Old machines with worn blades take a bit longer and require several pauses to scrape down the bowl. Add the lime juice and process to blend.

4. Scrape the sugar-lime mixture into a large, non-aluminum bowl. Add the half-and-half and the salt, and stir to combine. Set the mixture aside for 15 to 30 minutes, stirring occasionally. It will thicken slightly.

5. Pour the ice cream mixture through a fine-mesh sieve and discard the peel. At this point, the mixture can be sealed and refrigerated for a day before freezing. Don't worry if it separates; just stir to recombine.

6. Just before freezing, add the rum and stir to blend. Taste the mixture and adjust, if needed, with a dash more sugar or lime juice. The flavor should be round, and just a touch too sweet; the mixture should taste too sweet at room temperature if it is to taste perfect when frozen.

7. Freeze in an ice cream maker according to the manufacturer's instructions. Store with plastic wrap pressed directly on the surface. Let soften slightly before serving.

SERVING SUGGESTIONS: I like Amy's Chocolate Stars (page 452) or Ginger Moons (page 454) with this ice cream. It is also a splendid partner to a toasted slab of your favorite banana bread. If you are serving ice creams in pairs, try this one alongside its lemony cousin (page 490).

GILDING THE LILY

In today's trendy restaurants, you are likely to be served ice cream in perilously tall, stemmed glasses with improbable squiggles of caramelized sugar rising threateningly from the scoop. To a food historian, this must be the 90s equivalent of the 60s paper umbrella or the 50s flurry of sprinkles (aka jimmies). To the Freudian food psychologist, it's another matter altogether!

At China Moon, we also indulge in a bit of dash, albeit a more simple, patently feminine variety. We put a double scoop in the bowl and add a chocolate butterfly to the top scoop. On the plate beneath the cup, we fan some tiny cookies for contrast.

Such simple, dramatic effects are easy to replicate at home: A stemmed martini glass on a plate will give height and glamour to ice cream and also provide a surface beneath on which to arrange some cookies or a square of cake. Wide goblets are terrific if you're wanting to add a swirl of warm chocolate sauce (page 489) or some colorful slices of fresh fruit. Taller pilsners can be used to layer sauce or fruit between the scoops of ice cream.

PEAR ICE CREAM

MAKES A GENEROUS QUART

This is a snow-white light ice cream with an astonishingly vivid pear taste. Were you to make a pear ice cream with eggs and heavy cream, you could never achieve this flavor. The perfume of the pear is your shopping guide. What you want for this ice cream is something you can smell an aisle away.

Plan to serve the ice cream on the same day you make it. Its flavor is fragile and doesn't last.

¼ cup plus 2 tablespoons
   freshly squeezed lemon juice
1¼ pounds very fragrant
   pears
About ¾ cup sugar

2 cups half-and-half
1 tablespoon Poire Williams or
   other quality pear liqueur

1. Combine ¼ cup of the lemon juice and ¼ cup water in a 2- to 2½-quart non-aluminum saucepan. One at a time, halve the pears lengthwise, remove the core, and peel; then slice the flesh thinly, dropping the slivers directly into the acidulated water to prevent discoloration.

2. Add ¾ cup sugar and stir to combine. Bring the mixture to a gentle simmer over moderate heat, stirring to dissolve the sugar. Cover and simmer for 8 minutes. Remove the pot from the heat and let the mixture steep for 15 minutes. Once cooked, the pears can be refrigerated in their juices for 1 to 2 days.

3. Purée the pear mixture, either still hot or cold, in a food processor. Scrape the purée into a non-aluminum bowl and stir in the half-and-half. Add sugar if and as needed to bring out the flavor of the pears; the mixture should taste a bit too sweet at room temperature if it is to taste perfect when frozen. Add up to 2 tablespoons more lemon juice to round out the flavor. Stir in the pear liqueur.

4. Freeze the mixture in an ice cream maker according to manufacturer's instructions. Ripen the soft mixture in a freezer with a sheet of plastic wrap pressed directly on the surface. Let soften slightly before serving.

INGREDIENTS FOR ICE CREAM

If an ice cream recipe contains little more than fruit and a milk product, the two had better be of top quality or you've shot your chances for a great dessert.

The fruit for ice cream needn't be pretty, it only need be at peak flavor. Regular ice cream makers love, for this reason, snapping up so-called "distressed fruit"—the fruit that is too ripe and soft for sale to the eat-out-of-hand public, but is actually at its true flavor peak.

As for the milk product, it should be the freshest and most flavorful you can buy. Doing a side-by-side taste test of the various brands of half-and-half available in your local markets is easy and interesting. It takes little time, and the differences between brands are often striking. Ask any truly fine pastry cook—the quality of the milk and cream they use is a paramount concern.

SERVING SUGGESTIONS: Pears poached in red wine, then thinly sliced and fanned, make an elegant base for this ice cream. It would also be lovely alongside a plate of Hazelnut Mounds (page 459).

HONEYDEW ICE CREAM

MAKES A GENEROUS QUART

This is a very delicate ice cream that can be made with many types of exotic melons, but one that I find particularly nice with honeydew.

Choose a melon that is sweet and ripe but not so ripe that the flesh is watery, translucent, or mushy. To judge a melon for sweetness, smell the round spot opposite the stem end; it will taste exactly as sweet as it smells.

You will need a literal pound of flesh (melon flesh, that is) for this recipe. For safety, start with a melon that weighs nearly twice that amount. Use only the very sweet flesh, not the less flavorful layer that hugs the rind.

This ice cream won't hold. Mix and freeze it in the morning for serving that night.

1 pound sweet honeydew flesh, cut into chunks	2 cups half-and-half
½ cup plus 2 to 3 tablespoons sugar	About 1 tablespoon freshly squeezed ginger, lemon, or lime juice

1. Purée the melon and ½ cup sugar in a food processor, scraping down the bowl, as needed, until smooth.

2. Scrape the mixture into a non-aluminum bowl and stir in the half-and-half. Taste and adjust if and as needed with the additional sugar; the mixture should taste a touch too sweet at room temperature if it is to taste perfect when frozen. Add the ginger, lemon, or lime juice by ½ teaspoons until the flavor rounds on your tongue. Don't be shy; splash in a bit more and watch the flavor grow.

3. Freeze in an ice cream maker according to the manufacturer's instructions. Store with a piece of plastic wrap pressed directly on the surface. Let soften slightly before serving.

SERVING SUGGESTIONS: I like this ice cream with cookies, particularly Crystallized Ginger Butter Squares (page 462). Another delicate butter cookie, a simple lemon cake, or a very thin caramelized apple tart would also partner it well.

ANY BERRY ICE CREAM

MAKES A GENEROUS QUART

I confess to not being wild about strawberries and raspberries (I say this quietly, fearing it indicates some character flaw), but I do adore blackberries, olallieberries, and their kin. Pick your berry; this recipe is your formula! It produces a vividly colored light ice cream that tastes powerfully of the fruit.

Judge berries by their smell. If you can't smell 'em, they won't taste good. Dinged and banged berries may be too ugly for the buffet, but they will work wonderfully in ice cream as long as they're sweet and not moldy.

Once sieved, the unfrozen ice cream mixture can be refrigerated for a day or two. Adjust it with the liqueur and lemon juice just prior to freezing. Frozen, it keeps nicely for two days.

¾ cup plus 1 to 2 tablespoons
   sugar
¾ pound fragrant sweet berries
   (weight after any trimming)

2 cups half-and-half
2 to 3 teaspoons crème de
   cassis
About 1 teaspoon freshly
   squeezed lemon juice

1. In a food processor, grind ¾ cup sugar until fine. Add the berries and blend to a rich purée, scraping down the workbowl 2 or 3 times.

2. Scrape the mixture into a non-aluminum bowl and stir in the half-and-half. Taste and adjust if and as needed with the additional sugar; the mixture should taste a touch too sweet at room temperature if it is to taste perfect when frozen.

3. Sieve the mixture through a fine-mesh sieve into a bowl to eliminate any seeds. Stir in the liqueur. Add lemon juice by ½ teaspoons until the flavor rounds on your tongue.

4. Freeze in an ice cream maker according to the manufacturer's instructions. Store with a piece of plastic wrap pressed directly on the surface. Let soften slightly before serving.

SERVING SUGGESTIONS: Pile on the berries! A spoonful of fresh berries of a similar or competing sort is a great adornment for berry ice cream.

TOASTED HAZELNUT ICE CREAM

MAKES ABOUT 3 CUPS

This is an intensely flavorful ice cream. The color is a pretty pale tan, and the texture is either nubbly or silken depending on whether or not you choose to sieve it. The final flavor will be only as good as the nuts. Taste them before buying; they should be sweet.

The ice cream mixture can be refrigerated for a day or two before freezing. Once frozen, it holds nicely for two days.

¾ cup (3 ounces) plump
  hazelnuts
2 cups half-and-half
½ cup sugar

1 teaspoon Frangelico liqueur
About ¼ teaspoon freshly
  squeezed lemon juice

PROPER SERVING CONSISTENCY

To appreciate the full flavor of our ice creams, they should be soft enough to scoop easily but not so soft that they melt upon serving. That means they're warm enough so the chill won't dull the flavor, but firm enough so as not to taste overly sweet.

*One of my childhood thrills
was the Good Humor ice
cream truck that plied its
slow, sweet way along the
main streets of our town.*

*The white truck was
memorable. On both sides
was a tantalizing painting of
a giant Brown Cow—a slab of
vanilla ice cream on a stick—
with one evocative, big bite
taken out of it. As a kid, I
used to wonder who ate all
those bites.*

*The Good Humor man
was naturally very cheerful.
He jangled a happy band of
bells and the neighborhood
came running. Some kids
would buy Brown Cows,
others would stain their lips
blue with mint Popsicles,
while neat little girls like
myself would buy Dixie cups
and lick the lids clean of ice
cream, revealing pictures of
well-known stars.*

*My lid-licking days
came one day to a sorry end.
Between the melting white
ice cream and the photo of
Mickey Mantle was a
squashed spider. I remember
it as huge (and improbably
furry). I was traumatized to
sleeplessness and swore off ice
cream for at least a day.*

1. Preheat the oven to 350°F. Move a rack to the middle position.

2. Spread the nuts on a baking sheet and toast until they turn pale brown beneath the skin, 10 to 12 minutes. Stir the nuts midway to ensure even toasting. Wrap the hot nuts in a clean, dry kitchen towel and rub vigorously to remove the skins. Don't get hyper; a bit of skin is flavorful in the final mix.

3. Immediately after toasting, process the nuts in a food processor, running the machine for a minute or more to obtain a relatively smooth, oily paste. Add the half-and-half and sugar, then process a minute more to blend.

4. Should you wish a smooth-textured ice cream, strain the mixture through a fine-mesh sieve into a bowl. (I never bother; I like the tongue-feel of the nuts.)

5. Add the liqueur, then add the lemon juice in drops until the flavor peaks on your tongue.

6. Freeze in an ice cream maker according to the manufacturer's instructions. Store with a piece of plastic wrap pressed directly on the surface. Let soften slightly before serving.

SERVING SUGGESTIONS: This is a good mate to Amy's Hazelnut Mounds (page 459) or to her Summer Peach Hazelnut Streusel Tart (page 476). It's redundant, but delicious.

CAPPUCCINO ICE CREAM

MAKES A GENEROUS PINT

I first began drinking coffee in Taipei, oddly enough. It was thanks to a Central American coffee baron who built a swank, bohemian coffee shop to house his devastatingly beautiful mistress, who played her flamenco guitar into the wee hours to the applause of me and my artist friends. It was all deliciously bizarre, and I became a coffee maven.

My coffee passion extends to ice cream, of which this is a special example. "Bracingly unsweet, absolutely refreshing, for espresso-lovers only!" read my collected tasting notes.

If you like an iced coffee effect, stick to the formula below. For a richer taste, add another ¼ cup half-and-half and a bit more sugar to compensate.

The ice cream mixture can be refrigerated for up to three days before freezing. Once frozen, it holds well for two to four days, the longer time if you add the extra cream.

¼ cup whole espresso beans
1 fat cardamom pod
A 1-inch length of crumbly cinnamon stick

1¾ to 2 cups half-and-half
About ½ cup sugar
½ cup strong brewed espresso

1. Grind the espresso beans, cardamom, and cinnamon in a coffee or spice grinder until fine.

2. Combine the ground mixture with 1¾ cups half-and-half and ½ cup sugar in a small heavy saucepan. Bring to a foaming near-boil over moderate heat, stirring to dissolve the sugar. Remove the pot from the heat, cover, and let the mixture steep for 30 minutes or until cool. (The acidity of the beans may give the mixture a curdled look; disregard it.)

3. Strain the mixture through a fine-mesh sieve, pressing to extract every drop. Discard the grounds. If you don't like the texture of the tiny grains that slip through the mesh (an opinion on which people divide quickly into warring factions), filter it a second time through a finer sieve.

4. Stir in the brewed espresso. Taste. If the mixture is too strong for you, add ¼ cup more half-and-half and sugar by teaspoonfuls until the mixture is a touch too sweet; the mixture should taste a touch too sweet at room temperature if it is to taste perfect when frozen.

5. Freeze in an ice cream maker according to the manufacturer's instructions. Store with a piece of plastic wrap pressed directly on the surface. Let soften slightly before serving.

SERVING SUGGESTIONS: I like this ice cream straight, in private and at midnight. For company, add Cappuccino Coins (page 450) or a drizzle of Bittersweet Chocolate Sauce (page 489).

ESPRESSO TO GO

If you are a true espresso aficionado, the powdered sort is repulsive. Once, on a several-week trip through mainland China, I took along a jar, thinking it would pull me through the misery of tourist banquets, but even the pallor of State dinners couldn't diminish its awfulness.

I also don't own a home espresso machine. I've blown up two of them in less years and called it quits.

So what do I do when making espresso ice cream at home? In the old days, I used to appear with my mug in hand at a friendly, nearby restaurant and purchase a double espresso to go. Now, with espresso bars on every street corner, I go without my cup. Neither ploy would work in China, but that's another trip.

GLOSSARY OF SPECIAL INGREDIENTS

This is not an exhaustive glossary of ingredients, but rather a sampling of those most likely to intrigue or confuse. Those wanting more detailed information are recommended to the glossary of my first cookbook, *The Modern Art of Chinese Cooking*.

For fresh "exotic" ingredients, I highly recommend the writings of Elizabeth Schneider, in particular her articles in *Food Arts* magazine and her landmark book, *Uncommon Fruits and Vegetables*, a treasure in the field of exotica.

BALSAMIC VINEGAR: I use this in place of Chinese black vinegar, having been disappointed with the thin acridity of the Chinese brands available in America. Balsamic is a bit sweet and smooth from aging, just what a Chinese black vinegar strives to be. You don't need a high-priced balsamic for use in a Chinese-style sauce; the standard-issue imported stuff is fine. We use two brands, one with a green label packaged by Monari Federzoni, the other with the picture of a duke in a red sash, also known as Duke's Balsamic Vinegar.

BEAN PASTE: A family of condiments made from soybeans, these change names and character as one travels throughout China. We use two varieties, both standard on Chinese grocery shelves in America.

The first is **hot bean paste.** A frankly hot, lumpy concoction with a rather revolting look, this is stirred into sauces to great spicy effect. We buy it canned by Szechwan brand in the R.O.C. (Taiwan).

Our second variety is **sweet bean paste.** A smoother sweet variation on the bean paste theme, we use this in both marinades and sauces. We again use Szechwan brand in a can.

BLACK SOY SAUCE: A concentrated soy sauce, this Chinese brew is made with molasses. It's perfect when you want a lot of soy color and flavor with less liquid, as in a cold noodle dish where the sauce should cling to the noodles, rather than float in a puddle beneath them. My favorite brand is Pearl River Bridge; the English label reads "Soy, Superior Sauce." A distant second-place best is Koon Chun brand. The Chinese name for black soy sauce is "old head soy," referring to the extra aging process that gives this soy its savor. This product is immortal; it requires no refrigeration.

BROWN SUGAR: I use brown sugar a lot; it gives a special depth of flavor when combined with soy sauce that greatly enhances eggplant, mushrooms, and meat dishes. The commercial brown sugar available to restaurants is typically a cross between light and dark brown sugar. You can choose whichever you like, or mix the two together.

CASSIA BARK: A Chinese native cinnamon, its bark is typically thicker and the fragrance stronger than its Western cousin. It is sold in Chinese groceries or pharmaceutical shops in plastic bags. Judge it by its smell; the more pungent the better. Substitute Western cinnamon sticks in slightly larger amounts.

CAYENNE PEPPER POWDER: This is high-velocity pepper, the kind that rips your hat off. I use it exclusively to create an infused oil that gives maximum heat with minimal oil. I purchase "90-firepower" imported cayenne pepper powder, just about the hottest available in the U.S. Check with a specialty merchant to be sure that you aren't buying a lesser heat. San Francisco Herb Company, 250 14th Street, San Francisco, CA 94103, is our merchant for cayenne pepper and red chili flakes. They will send a mail order catalog if you'd like to purchase from them directly.

CHILIS, FRESH: I am by no means an expert in this red-hot field, but we do use a sizable medley of fresh chilis at China Moon. Unless a recipe specifies otherwise, we remove only the green stem and use the whole chili—seeds, flesh, ribs, and all. Our favorite varieties are as follows:

Anaheim is a slightly twisted pale green chili about 6 inches long. Its flavor is quite variable, from mild to sharply hot, always with a slightly bitter, albeit tasty, end note. We use Anaheims in sauces, either raw or roasted, or cut into thin rings in seafood stir-fries.

Fresno is my favorite fresh chili on account of the sweetness that comes with the heat. We buy them red and ripe, when the flavor is fullest. The size can vary from 1½ to 2½ inches long. The top is often an inch around,

tapering to a pointy tail. We grind these for aromatics and cut them into very thin rings to infuse cold sauces.

Jalapeño is an infrequent guest in our kitchen. We use this chili, which has a great bite and a thick flesh, when we can't get Fresnos. It has perhaps more heat but not the sweetness of the Fresno, and also tends to have a necklace of black, crack-like scars.

Serrano is a slender, deep-green chili about 1½ inches long. It is almost invariably strong and hot, with a bite that is fresh and sharp. We grind these for aromatics (always pairing them with the sweeter red Fresno), infuse them in vinegar and soups, and very occasionally slice them paper-thin to add voltage to a cold salad.

Yellow wax (also called Hungarian wax) is a finger-length yellow chili with a waxy skin (hence the name) that is regularly found in Cantonese groceries. It is wildly variable in flavor, either having no taste whatsoever or a quiet, clean heat. When we find them hot, we include them in aromatics, sauces, and stir-fries, typically pairing them with one of the red and green varieties above.

CHILI FLAKES, DRIED RED: I look for bright red flakes that are so pungent that one whiff

makes me sneeze. The sort we buy come from New Mexico and have a ratio of about one part yellow seeds to three parts red flesh. Judge them by sneezability. Store chili flakes airtight in a clean glass jar. If you can't smell them, toss 'em out.

CHILI OIL, HOT: I always make my own (see page 10) and urge everyone to do the same! If I were stuck in a situation where I was forced at knife-point to purchase commercial chili oil, I'd hope there was a bottle of Kadoya brand on the shelf. This Japanese brand tastes fine, though you can still do better with your own brew.

CHINESE BROCCOLI: A seasonal, full-flavored, deep green vegetable with a terrific texture that makes the Western sort look wimpy by comparison. The stalks are individual, topped by a thick, wavy leaf; the whole plant is edible. Look to the stem to judge it; it should be moist and an even light green, with no sign of white at the center.

CHINESE CABBAGES: Any one of a dozen different sorts of cabbage-type vegetables, called by a multitude of Chinese and English names. Get hung up on the precise name of any one type, and the name is sure to change when you move to the next village. In China Moon's kitchen, we differentiate between these varieties:

Napa cabbage is a thick, rounded oblong head of uniformly wide, very pale green (almost white) leaves. It has a very light flavor and adds bulk to a dish, and is thus especially useful in a saucy stir-fry.

Baby bok choy is a diminutive cabbage about the size of a hand. It is built of individual white stalks attached to a base, with an ovalish deep green leaf atop each stalk. The stalks are crisp and the leaves are relatively thick, so they don't go wimpy when tossed into a dish. The flavor is mild but brisk and slightly sweet.

Baby Shanghai cabbage is a similarly tiny cabbage, but the stalks and leaves are uniformly pale green. It has a more delicate taste and texture than baby bok choy.

CHINESE CHILI SAUCE: This is a very spicy sauce with a jam-like consistency that features red chilis, salt, and vinegar cooked in an oil base. It is not hot bean paste (see page 501), but rather a brighter-tasting cousin. I love Koon Yick Wah Kee brand, which comes in a terrific bottle with a picture of

a Chinese junk and a big red chili on the front. Koon Yick has a lot of citron tossed in and is ground to a smooth consistency, making it very easy to incorporate into sauces. This stuff is immortal. Put it out in the blazing sun and it will still be there long after you and I are gone.

CHINESE CHIVES: Often called garlic chives in English on account of their flavor, these are flat green chives best harvested when small. They are sold in bunches in Chinese markets, sometimes in their flowering state with a white bulb on top. Chives are one of the vegetables that the Chinese traditionally grow at home. For the smallest and best chives to be found in Western Chinatowns, look for the "granny contingent" (older women street vendors) who sell their produce on street corners. Chives are best kept refrigerated, wrapped in a dry paper towel. They last for about a week.

CHINESE DRIED BLACK MUSH-ROOMS: One of the glories of the Chinese pantry, the dried mushroom is particularly pungent. Choose thinner, fawn-colored caps or thicker ones blistered with white starbursts. The smoky flavor will be similar, although the texture of the latter is strik-

ingly plush. Buy small amounts; they can grow buggy if kept too many months. To use, soak in cold water to cover for several hours or until pliable, then snip off and discard the stems. Hot water soaks are good if you're in a hurry, though the flavor is somewhat impaired.

CHINESE EGG NOODLES: Recently, the *New York Times* featured a picture of a Chinese family in Peking joyfully wolfing down bowls of steaming noodles. In the background stood a grinning noodle-maker happily looping a rope of freshly made dough. Ah, were we so lucky to have this gentleman set up his stand nearby!

Instead, for the rest of us, 1-pound bags of fresh or frozen Chinese egg noodles are available on American supermarket shelves as well as in smaller Chinese shops. The best are whiter rather than yellow (indicating a lack of food dye). I do not like dried Chinese egg noodles; they have no savor. If the fresh or frozen sort is unavailable, I'll choose a fresh or dried Italian-style pasta.

Thin egg noodles, $1/16$ inch thin when raw, are used in our cold noodle dishes and to make our standard noodle pillows. We occasionally use them in stir-fries, but prefer thicker noodles for texture.

Wide egg noodles are a fettuccine variety, a thin ribbon about ¼ inch wide. They will hold up easily in stir-frying and make a special noodle pillow.

Shanghai noodles are a fattish, irregular noodle that is addictively appealing. These are too loony to curl nicely in a noodle pillow, but lend a lot of toothy pizzazz to any stir-fried dish.

Chinese egg noodles will keep refrigerated for 3 to 5 days; if they gray, then toss them out. Frozen, they may keep for several months, although the flavor edge is dulled after a week or so.

CHINESE EGGPLANT: The *ne plus ultra* of eggplants, these are slender amethyst plants with a thin, edible skin, a strikingly sweet flesh, and at most a modest, freckle-like scattering of seeds. Why all our supermarkets don't carry them is beyond me! They are as superior to the stubbier, deep-purple Japanese eggplant as that sort is to the Western globe variety. We use Chinese eggplants regularly in stir-fries and stews. We do not use them, strangely enough, in Strange-Flavor Eggplant (page 62), where the bitterness of Western eggplant lends its own inimitable taste.

CHINESE RICE WINE: This is a brown, nutty-tasting wine that should smell and taste like a good-quality sherry. I use Pagoda brand "Shao Hsing" wine with a blue label for everyday cooking. Shao-Hsing is the city near Hangchou famous for its wine. If Pagoda isn't stocked in your nearest Chinese grocery, look for a square, clear glass bottle with a red label packaged by the Taiwan Liquor and Tobacco Monopoly. When in doubt, use any good Western sherry. Some of the lesser Chinese brands are vile; one brand packaged in America will take off nail polish. When choosing Chinese rice wine, follow the old rule: If you wouldn't drink it, don't cook with it.

COCONUT MILK: A culinary exotic limited mostly to the southern and southwest reaches of mainland China, I like to include this as a sweet, lush note in occasional hot and cold sauces. Our favorite brand is Chaokoh, imported from Thailand. Use only unsweetened coconut milk in our recipes. Whisk it well and pulverize the lumps, if needed, before use. Coconut milk, once opened, will hold in the refrigerator for several days.

CORIANDER: Also known as cilantro or Chinese parsley, this is a schizophrenic herb. Depending on the chemistry of your saliva, this flat-leafed green with its slender stems will taste either ambrosial or soap-like. To the Chinese who call it "fragrant vegetable," it is considered a delicately herbal addition to soups, dumplings and many other dishes. The Latin root refers to a stinky bedbug, which gives you an idea of how the other half thinks and tastes.

Coriander is used for its leaves and stems both. It should be highly pungent when you buy it, with the leaves in a fresh wiggle atop the stems. Store in a water-misted plastic bag for use within a day, or wash and spin it in a salad spinner if you wish to refrigerate it for several days.

DAIKON: This is the Japanese name for a common Chinese vegetable, a long white "icicle radish" that grows upwards of 2 feet long. I favor the whitest, thinnest daikon I can find, usually 2 inches around at the collar. Daikon should be rock-hard to be appealingly crisp and juicy. We slice it into thin rounds for pickling, steaming, and stir-frying. Wrapped airtight in the refrigerator, it will keep for a week or more. The smell of blanched daikon is frankly weird. Don't be put off, as it disappears quickly in cooking or pickling.

DRIED SHRIMP: One of the funky standbys of Chinese cooking, you either love them or hate them. Pungent, salty, and odd, they come in various sizes and with different degrees of shells left on. I look for pinkish shrimp about the size of a thumbnail. I refrigerate them because they can mold, then soak them to relative tenderness in warm water before use.

GINGER: This is a tuber, not a root, and a source of flavor without which my cooking would be dead and dull. We favor Hawaiian ginger for the ease of its elongated fingers, as opposed to Fijian ginger, which is a mass of knobby ends. Ginger should be rock-hard when purchased, the skin stretched taut over the bulb. To store ginger, refrigerate it unwashed and unpeeled in a high-density

polyurethane bag—one of those opaque, pesky plastic bags that are a common feature in supermarket produce sections. These bags have a semipermeable membrane that allows the ginger to breathe and sweat without molding in its own juice.

So-called "baby ginger" is the Hawaiian stuff pulled out of the ground several months early, before the skin has had a chance to thicken and turn tawny. This is fiber-free ginger, excellent for pickling. It is highly perishable and will not keep. Most cooks say the baby variety has a particular flavor. I don't find this true, but simply appreciate it for its texture.

Unlike most cooks, I rarely bother peeling ginger unless I am using it as garnish and want a uniformity of color. I buy it when the skin is so new and thin, it's inconsequential, at least to me.

GLASS NOODLES: Also known as mung bean noodles, Chinese vermicelli, and green bean threads, this is a wire-thin specialty noodle made from mung bean starch. Sold dry and in tightly looped rectangular skeins, the typical tiny package that is perfect for home use weighs just shy of 2 ounces. Giant skeins are available for restaurant use. I favor a P.R.C. brand of glass noodle called "Lungkow Vermicelli," sold in cellophane bags tied with a ribbon.

I use glass noodles in soups and casseroles for their wonderful, slithery quality. For frying, I prefer rice sticks, though glass noodles can also be fried into a puffy nest.

HOISIN SAUCE: This brown, salty-sweet sauce has a fascinating history in China; it changes in name and style from region to region, being wheat-based in some areas and soybean-based in others. No matter, in current usage it is almost always the same jam-like substance with a rich, slightly sweet flavor. I use Koon Chun brand and prefer the bottled to the canned variety.

MALTOSE: Maltose is an ancient Chinese sweetener extracted from barley. It has a very pleasant, soft sweetness—a bit like caramel—and an impossibly sticky consistency that requires attack with a sturdy spoon dipped into boiling water. I use Butterfly brand in a squat plastic jar. There are more picturesque crockery jars available under one or two competing brands; they're perhaps a bit duller in flavor, but the empty crocks are good for holding pencils.

MUSHROOM SOY SAUCE: A very tasty concoction, this is a seasoned black soy sauce flavored with dried Chinese black mushrooms. It is very meaty and round in flavor, and I truly love it for sauces and stews. This is the one soy sauce I take with me to deserted islands. The brand I use, Pearl River Bridge, is now available in my local supermarket.

OYSTER SAUCE: This stuff can be heavenly or ghastly, depending on the brand. I use top-of-the-line Hop Sing Lung brand, the best and most expensive I've tasted. I don't refrigerate oyster sauce. Neither do the Chinese who live in the tropics.

RICE STICKS: Wiry dried noodles made from rice flour, I deep-fry them when I want a crispy addition to a dish. Opaque when dried, they become snow-white when fried. My favorite brand is Sailing Boat, sold four flat wads to a 1-pound bag.

RICE VINEGAR (JAPANESE, UN-SEASONED): Made from rice wine lees, this is the clear to light golden vinegar esteemed as a daily vinegar in China. Less harsh than distilled white vinegar and less sweet than cider vinegar, it is a pleasant in-between. I find modern Chinese brands

harsh and acrid. Japanese brands such as Marukan (with a green label, indicating unseasoned) or Mitsukan are milder and better to my taste. Marukan green label is sold in supermarkets.

SALT: I use kosher salt in 98 percent of my cooking, prizing it for its mild, clean flavor and its ability to turn up the volume on bigger tastes like garlic, ginger, and chili. Sea salt has a good taste, but it is twice as strong as kosher salt and too competitive a taste for my cooking. Table salt is lousy, at least to my tongue.

In my recipes, there is no substitute for kosher salt. It's not an issue of rabbinical blessing; it's purely a matter of flavor and mildness.

SALTED BLACK BEANS: An ancient Chinese seasoning, these are black soybeans preserved in salt. The best are very tasty, often with pieces of ginger packed amidst the beans. I love Pearl River Bridge brand, packed in a yellow, round cardboard box. Mee Chun brand in a plastic pouch is second best. Don't wash them before use; there's

no need to. Store airtight so that they stay soft.

SCALLIONS: Often called green onions, these are the indigenous allium of China. (The Chinese refer to yellow onions as "foreign scallions.") Buy them with their white beards on and their green tops long and perky. If you're storing them for more than a day or two, refrigerate them in a plastic bag lined with a wet paper towel. Chinese use both the white and green parts of the scallion. When cutting rings, first slit the white part lengthwise so the rings will fall apart when you cut them crosswise.

SESAME OIL (JAPANESE): In the Chinese and Japanese world this is a dark, highly aromatic oil that is pressed from toasted sesame seeds. Chinese brands are frequently rancid or burnt; I never buy them. I favor Japanese brands, in particular Kadoya. Whatever you do, don't buy a sesame oil packaged in a plastic bottle; it will almost assuredly be rancid.

Toasted sesame oil should be stored in a cool place. I prefer a cupboard to the refrigerator for ease. If you're refrigerating oil, allow it to come to room temperature before using.

Sesame oil of this toasted sort is potent. It is a seasoning oil, not a cooking oil, on account of its low burn point as well as its strong flavor. Use only several drops or it will overwhelm a dish like a bad perfume.

SOY SAUCE: So-called regular soy sauce, as opposed to specialty soys like black soy and mushroom soy, is a mainstay of a Chinese kitchen. Like any other bit of culinary bedrock—olive oil, butter, wine, or vinegar—there's a huge variety between brands, but nothing so exotic about it that some simple tasting won't dispel. Buy several brands of soy sauce to know which you like. My favorite brand is Pearl River Bridge; its label reads "Superior Soy." The flavor is large and round and well-balanced. Kikkoman is all right; so too is Kikkoman "light soy," if you're worried about sodium. Soy sauce keeps forever. It needs no refrigeration, except if the label advises. Tamari, its Japanese cousin, is not a substitute for Chinese soy sauce.

STAR ANISE: One of the most common Chinese dried spices, people either love it or hate it. The key is to use star anise sparingly, so that it doesn't overwhelm. The individual stars have eight points (hence its Chinese name, "eight corners"). When unbroken, it is a pretty pod on a little curvy stem, each point cupping a smooth, shiny seed. Buy the whole spice. The pre-ground sort is usually wretched. Buy the most pungent star anise available and store it in an airtight jar. So long as it's fragrant, it's good.

SUGAR: The role of sugar in the Chinese kitchen is as much of a flavor-expander as a sweetener. Certainly, in my kitchen this is true. I'd guess that nine out of ten times, I use sugar to enlarge the spiciness of a dish. For example, if you season something with chili, it will often read as a sharpness on the tip of the tongue—a sear without dimension. Add sugar and the sensation of hotness spreads around the lips. I often tell students not to eliminate or lessen the sugar in my recipes, even if they're wanting to lose that extra pound! Cut back on the sugar and the flavor will suffer.

SZECHWAN PEPPERCORNS: Szechwan peppercorns are called "flower pepper" in Chinese, an allusion to the brown, flower-like open pod. They grow on a bush and often come complete with the tiny, slightly bitter black seeds in addition to an array of twigs, thorns, and tiny leaves. Look for bags that feature pods, not seeds. Szechwan peppercorns are indigenous to China and are a member of the botanical family called *fagara*. This makes them totally unrelated to our black and white peppercorns, which the Chinese naturally call "barbarian pepper."

The only imperative for a Szechwan peppercorn to taste lively is that it smell pungent. You should be able to smell them clear through the bag—a clean and almost camphor-like aroma that led Chinese in former generations to fill sachets with the spice. Poke through to eliminate any thorns, then store the pepper in an airtight jar.

TAMARIND LIQUID: This is the reddish, wonderfully sour liquid made by softening taramind pulp in boiling water. The pulp is available in Thai, Vietnamese, and most large Chinese markets, packaged in rectangular blocks weighing about 14 ounces. To use, chop the sticky pulp with a knife dipped into hot water, then place the pulp in a bowl and cover it with boiling water. Cover the bowl, let steep 10 to 15 minutes, then strain the liquids and solids through a sieve, pressing down on the solids to extract everything but the seeds. For 2 tablespoons tamarind liquid, use a square inch of pulp covered with 2 tablespoons boiling water. The pulp keeps indefinitely at room temperature.

TIENTSIN PRESERVED VEGETABLE: A shredded, salted, and preserved cabbage that is a condiment of northern and central Chinese cooking, this is the stuff that adds its particular savor to several famous Chinese vegetable dishes, such as Dry-Fried String Beans. I buy it in a squat brown crock, which is a design from antiquity and a terrific odds-and-ends jar to boot. The cabbage inside should be pungent, soft, and light brown; if it has crystallized to hard black shards, throw it out. Preserved vegetable doesn't need rinsing or refrigeration. Store airtight.

TOFU: This protein-rich white substance made from soybeans delights the Chinese and baffles Westerners. It is a great texture food as well as a sopper-upper of other flavors. We use a firm, Chinese-style tofu that is packed in water in 1-pound tubs and has the consistency of a smooth cottage cheese; it is easily cut into pieces that stay together with careful handling. Look for a date stamped on the tub, or at least check the clarity of the water, which is an indication

of freshness. Once home, refrigerate the tofu in fresh water and change the water daily. It will keep for several days before souring.

TREE EARS: Also known as wood ears because their Chinese name can be translated either way, tree ears are one of the intriguing oddities of Chinese cooking. Members of a family of dried funguses that are soaked to a supple state, these wavy, black bits of texture have a slightly smoky flavor. For our recipes, look for thumbnail-size tree ears that look dull and dusty in the bag. They will swell to three or four times their size when covered with three or four times their volume of cold water. Tree ears are the stuff of the forest so you'll need to swirl and agitate them to get rid of bits of bark.

WATER CHESTNUTS: Called horse's hoof in Chinese, on account of their mud-pie shape and dark black skin, these are incomparably sweet and juicy—as far away from their canned cousins as a fresh string bean is from one similarly imprisoned. They should be rock-hard when purchased, still wearing the dirt of the bog. Don't wash them before peeling; that will speed their rotting. To peel, simply use a sharp paring knife and cut away the black

skin. Use shortly after peeling to prevent discoloration. Truly rock-hard, unwashed water chestnuts will keep refrigerated in a plastic bag for up to a week. If they're yellow and sour-smelling once peeled, toss them out. The nearest substitute is jicama, which has a bit of the same crunch, albeit without that special sweetness. Fresh water chestnuts are available nearly year-round in larger Chinese areas, or at Chinese New Year's time (around early February) in smaller areas. Munch on a raw one to know their glory. I typically serve them raw and cut into cubes with cool Champagne.

WATER CHESTNUT STARCH: The flour-like starch of fresh water chestnuts makes a fine, super-white coating for deep-fried foods. The best brands are talc-like; we use King's. Other brands are lumpy and require pulverizing in a food processor before use. This stuff is expensive, but the results are well worth it. One caution: water chestnut starch stays relatively white when cooked in fresh oil, so don't wait for the golden tones of everyday flour or you will have over-cooked your food.

INDEX